THE BATTLE OF MANILA

THE BATTLE
OF MANILA

POISONED VICTORY IN THE PACIFIC WAR

NICHOLAS EVAN SARANTAKES

OXFORD
UNIVERSITY PRESS

OXFORD
UNIVERSITY PRESS

Oxford University Press is a department of the University of Oxford.
It furthers the University's objective of excellence in research, scholarship,
and education by publishing worldwide. Oxford is a registered trade mark of
Oxford University Press in the UK and certain other countries.

Published in the United States of America by Oxford University Press
198 Madison Avenue, New York, NY 10016, United States of America.

Library of Congress Cataloging-in-Publication Data
Names: Sarantakes, Nicholas Evan, 1966– author.
Title: The battle of Manila : poisoned victory in the Pacific war /
Nicholas Evan Sarantakes.
Description: New York, NY : Oxford University Press, [2025] |
Includes bibliographical references and index.
Identifiers: LCCN 2024031402 (print) | LCCN 2024031403 (ebook) |
ISBN 9780199948857 (hardback) | ISBN 9780199948864 |
ISBN 9780199392803 (epub)
Subjects: LCSH: Manila, Battle of, Philippines, 1945. |
World War, 1939–1945—Campaigns—Philippines—Manila. |
Manila (Philippines)—History, Military.
Classification: LCC D767.4 .S27 2025 (print) | LCC D767.4 (ebook) |
DDC 940.54/2599—dc23
LC record available at https://lccn.loc.gov/2024031402
LC ebook record available at https://lccn.loc.gov/2024031403

Printed by Sheridan Books, Inc., United States of America

This book is dedicated to professors who made a difference:

Contents

Introduction

MacArthur's Funeral

"One of America's greatest heroes is dead," declared President Lyndon Johnson on April 6, 1964, having ordered that flags at all federal facilities fly at half-staff.[1] General of the Army Douglas MacArthur had died at Walter Reed Army Medical Center. His widow had his body returned to New York, where they had lived for the last thirteen years, to lie in repose. He was eighty-four.[2]

Tributes poured in from all over the country and the world. From the floor of the United States Senate, Leverett Saltonstall of Massachusetts and Spessard Holland of Florida praised the general under whom their sons had served in the Pacific. Olin Johnston of South Carolina noted that he had served under MacArthur in France in World War I.[3]

Former presidents Herbert Hoover, Harry S. Truman, and Dwight D. Eisenhower had all dealt with MacArthur and their relations with him had been—at best—mixed. Truman had famously fired him. All three decided to take the high road. "He was one of the world's outstanding military commanders," Hoover stated. In Independence, Missouri, Truman said, "I am deeply sorry at the passing of Gen. Douglas MacArthur who has given of himself with exceptional strength and valor and will be remembered as one of the great military men in our history." Eisenhower, from his farm outside Gettysburg, Pennsylvania, noted that he had been "privileged" to serve under him. "I share with all his friends a feeling of special loss and sorrow and send deepest sympathy to his family."[4]

In Manila, President Diosdado Macapagal declared MacArthur had been a "great soldier" and a "true and loyal friend." In South Korea, President Park Chung-hee expressed "deep sorrow." The Japanese ambassador to the United States, Takeuchi Ryuji, emphasized MacArthur's role in the postwar occupation rather than his combat leadership when he said the general had been a "friend of the Japanese people." Tokyo newspapers printed page one extras. Flags flew at half-staff in all three countries. The nation prepared to give him a hero's send-off. A special seven-car funeral train carried MacArthur's body from New York to Washington, DC, where it would lay in state under the rotunda of the Capitol. Before the train departed, the caisson passed a line of gray uniformed cadets from West Point that had assembled at Pennsylvania Station. Small crowds gathered along the route, standing in the cold fog and rain, and saluted. Active-duty units stationed at nearby bases also assembled at stations along the route and presented arms. Aboard the train were old friends. General George Kenney came into the press car and told stories about World War II. Staff Sergeant Gaetano Faillace, an Army photographer on MacArthur's staff, was on the train as well: "I made the film of the General as he waded ashore to return to Luzon. I was with him at Leyte and the other landings and on the *Missouri* and the ticker tape parade up Broadway after Korea. Look at those people out there in the rain. Despite what they say, people don't always forget."[5]

As the train arrived in Washington, the gray skies continued to drizzle. The president greeted the train at Union Station and rode in the funeral procession as it passed the government buildings of Washington, including the White House, before reaching the Capitol. A crowd of one hundred thousand lined the route. "It's one of those occasions when you want to be present, when you feel you should be there," one local resident explained to a newspaper reporter. The procession was led by the Washington Metropolitan Police and included units from each of the armed services and all the service academies. A nineteen-gun salute greeted the casket when it arrived at the Capitol. As the body lay in state, the chaplains of the House and Senate delivered eulogies, which a throng of Washington notables attended, including Johnson. When the service ended, lines of people—later estimated to be sixty thousand—entered to pay their last respects. While they did, the president and the first lady received MacArthur's widow, Jean; his son, Arthur; and the general's nephew, Ambassador Douglas MacArthur II, at the White House.[6]

The next day, April 9, the military flew his body to Norfolk, Virginia, for internment at the MacArthur Memorial—the museum, library, and archive dedicated to his career. When the plane landed, an honor guard gave a nineteen-gun salute. Another 150,000 lined the streets as the motorcade drove from Norfolk Naval Air Station to the downtown area. The crowd was five deep in some areas.[7]

Three miles away from the Memorial, the formal military parade began. A ceremonial horse-drawn cortege with a riderless black horse led a company of cadets from West Point into downtown Norfolk. After the funeral detail placed the general's coffin under the dome of the building, the public entered in single file to pay their respects.[8]

* * *

The man lying in the mausoleum in Norfolk was, by almost any measure, a great soldier. He was also a controversial one.[9]

His role in Korea dominated the tributes. *The Washington Post* devoted a full page to a biographical summary of his career; thirteen paragraphs focused on Korea; nine on World War II. Manila was barely mentioned.[10] The focus on 1950 and 1951 was no accident. MacArthur himself saw to it that Korea, rather than World War II, dominated the news coverage. An interview that he had given with reporters Jim Lucas and Bob Considine about Korea in 1954 and embargoed appeared in *The New York Times* three days after his death. In it, MacArthur had argued that he had been prevented from doing his job. Disputes about whether he had been quoted accurately developed almost immediately and it was debated in the major papers.[11]

* * *

Revisiting the Korea controversy at the time of MacArthur's death was understandable. It was the middle of the Cold War, and his controversial dismissal was little more than a decade old. This issue, however, obscured more significant events in his life.

MacArthur had commanded more troops in World War II than he did in Korea, and the outcome of his battles and campaigns was, arguably, more significant. At a time when most people his age are set in their ways—he was sixty-one years old when the Japanese attacked Pearl Harbor—MacArthur showed impressive professional dexterity. He conducted conventional infantry battles, but his use of irregular forces, air power, amphibious assault, airborne troops, and naval assets gave him an edge over his Japanese opponents. For a time, Allied soldiers—Filipino, Australian, and New Zealanders—made up the majority of forces under his command. Coalition warfare always comes with diplomatic and logistical complications. MacArthur handled these well. He also used intelligence and psychological warfare in various ways.[12]

All of these were in play during the battle for Manila in February and March of 1945. The best and the worst of MacArthur were also in play.[13] The invasion of Luzon and the rapid, integrated drive into the central region of the island, in January 1945, was a military effort that danced on the edge of brilliance. This success obscures the fact that the battle that mattered—the month-long fight to liberate Manila—was a victory, but a poisoned one. Angry at the destruction of the city that he loved and eager to deflect attention away from his own failures during this battle, MacArthur blamed General Yamashita Tomoyuki, the commanding general of the Fourteenth Area Army.

Battles always come with costs and pyrrhic victory, in which the costs of achieving the victory outweigh the benefits is nothing new. In a poisoned outcome, the outcome is even more disproportionate, and actually counterproductive, to the interests of the victor. Manila was poisonous.

* * *

Two books have played a huge role in changing approaches to military history and, by extension, to our understanding of the Battle of Manila. One is Russell Weigley's *The American Way of War: A History of United States Military Strategy and Power*, published in 1973. Weigley argues that the United States adopted a distinct approach to fighting in wars, moving from attrition designed to wear out an opponent to one aimed at utter destruction of the enemy's military power. John Keegan's *The Face of Battle*, published in 1976, is the second. Adopting social history issues to a study of combat, Keegan explored individual soldiers. In war, he argued, the training and behavior of troops had a significant impact on the outcome of the fight.

These books were profoundly important and are still in print decades later for a reason, but Manila requires a different approach. The instinct for annihilation and a soldier's behavior were key elements of this battle, but the fight for the city requires looking at mobility, tactics, doctrine, and intelligence. As a result, this book will use a "whole of army" approach. This form of military history looks not only at events at the main point of contact among combat units, but the efforts of service and support units. Understanding what happened in Manila requires looking at the experiences of all combatants who were involved, be they in the infantry or the signal corps. Manila was a battle where danger extended from the main point of contact to the rear areas. The mobility that characterized MacArthur's approach to war was a service-wide effort. The speed of his campaigns required coordination among various types of units. The U.S. Army basically took the bulk of the city of Manila—other than the Walled City and the government buildings—in two weeks. This was much, much faster than other comparable urban battles in World War II, including those for control of Stalingrad or Berlin.

* * *

Poisoned victory or not, Manila is crucial to understanding the strategic contours of the entire war in the Pacific, which ended six months later. Its effects are felt to this day in international affairs and in the life of the Philippine nation.

Battles in cities are different because cities are homes to religious shrines and diverse population groups. They are transportation hubs, production centers, political capitals, major markets, concentrations of finance, and cultural centers; they are culturally significant in and of themselves. Fighting for their control has, by nature, disproportionate results compared to other battles. History is full of examples: Rome in 410, Constantinople in 1453, Vienna in 1683, Atlanta in 1864, Paris in 1871, and Stalingrad in 1943. And so it was in Manila in 1945.

I

MacArthur's War,
MacArthur's Men

Douglas MacArthur had a special relationship with the city of Manila.
Many years before, when he had decided to make a career in the U.S.
Army—like his father—and had bounced around the globe, he kept coming
back to the city. He received his first promotion in Manila and contracted malaria so severe that the Army had to send him back to the United States. The
city was a constant in a life without many others. He was by any measure an
exceptional soldier. At the U.S. Military Academy, he earned an athletic letter
in baseball, became the First Captain of the Corps of Cadets, and finished first
in a class of ninety-three.[1] Commissioned in the Corps of Engineers, he had his
first assignment in the Philippines.

In 1905, 1st Lieutenant McArthur became a general's aide, a good indicator that senior officers saw potential in the junior officer, and a year later he
returned to the United States where he became a presidential aide to President
Theodore Roosevelt. In 1914, he was part of the US intervention in Mexico. He
led a small patrol, with authorization, looking for railroad locomotives to move
cars backed up in Vera Cruz. MacArthur and his men were ambushed three
separate times, and in a series of tactical actions he regularly showed bravery
that was both daring and inspirational. He was nominated for the Medal of
Honor, which he probably deserved, but his nomination was later rejected
because he had been acting without orders.[2] In World War I, McArthur was
named the chief of staff of the 42nd Infantry Division, one of the first units to
arrive in France. When the war ended, MacArthur had the star of a brigadier
general. Using a leadership by example approach, he used gallantry on a regular
basis, often exposing himself to risk to inspire his men and had another Medal
of Honor nomination, two Distinguished Service Crosses, seven Silver Stars,

two Purple Hearts, and the Distinguished Service Medal when the war ended.[3] After the war, he became the superintendent of the U.S. Military Academy. The assignment was one of the most prestigious in the Army and allowed him to keep his general's stars while others reverted to their prewar ranks.[4]

It took him a long while to achieve success in his personal life. After his stint at West Point, he married in 1922, but both parties confused lust for love. A relationship built on that type of foundation can last only so long and the marriage ended after seven years.[56] MacArthur used another assignment in Manila to hide from the shame of this failure. In the Army of that day, things like divorces often blocked promotion, but not in MacArthur's case. He became chief of staff of the U.S. Army in 1930. He was the youngest man to hold this office.[7]

When MacArthur's term ended, President Franklin D. Roosevelt retained him for an extra year, believing he could manage the general.[8] Roosevelt then sent him to the Philippines for a retirement assignment as the military advisor to the government of the Commonwealth. During the voyage across the Pacific, he struck up an acquaintance with Jean Marie Faircloth, who, at thirty-six, was nineteen years his junior. Independently wealth, she enjoyed traveling with her siblings. Going to Shanghai, she decided to get off at Manila. Described as "vivacious" and "meticulous," a friend had once commented that the only men that stood a chance with her were those in uniform. After an eighteen-month courtship, the two married in Manila, and they moved into the penthouse at the Manila Hotel. MacArthur wrote that marrying Jean "was perhaps the smartest thing I have ever done. She has been my constant friend, sweetheart, and devoted supporter ever since." In February 1938, ten months into their marriage, Jean MacArthur delivered a little boy whom they named Arthur IV, after his uncle, grandfather, and great-grandfather.[9]

Recalled to active duty as the United States was on the verge of war, MacArthur wanted to defend the entire archipelago. "We are going to make it so very expensive for any nation to attack these islands that no one will try it," he explained. On the first day of the war, the Japanese caught the air forces under his command on the ground and destroyed them. MacArthur then attempted to defend the entire island of Luzon. While his men did well tactically—fighting the Japanese to a standstill—their supplies were in the wrong positions, which sealed their fate as they retreated into the cul-de-sac that was the Bataan Peninsula. Afraid that MacArthur's capture would be a major propaganda victory for the Japanese and needing an experienced commander, Roosevelt ordered him to leave for Australia.[10]

Many historians have noted MacArthur's ego. His actions in 1932 in breaking up the bonus army marching on Washington and his refusal to salute Harry S. Truman in 1950 at Wake Island are often used as good examples. MacArthur had, of course, not been in a position where he had to initiate a salute in a decade and a half, but more importantly these arguments ignore the fact that arrogance was and is commonplace among flag officers. It is also misleading. General George Kenney observed that while MacArthur was a "brilliant strategist and leader," he was also "sentimental, soft-hearted." His men were devoted to him. He was, according to Kenney, the "kind of a man soldiers swear by—a winner." A British officer assigned to MacArthur's staff once noted of the general that he was "shrewd, selfish, proud, remote, highly strung, and vastly vain." He also had "no humour about himself, no regard for truth and is unaware of these defects." Had MacArthur had "moral depth" he might have been a great man. However, in MacArthur's case, he was a "near-miss, which may be worse than a mile." Perhaps, though, the best assessment of the man came not from a military associate or historian, but from the actor Gregory Peck, who played the lead in the 1977 film *MacArthur*. Peck studied the general's personality, mannerisms, and record for six months and then concluded, "MacArthur's virtues were greater than his faults."[11]

* * *

In the film *MacArthur*, the general quickly turns around defeatist thinking in Australia and goes on the offensive, but the reality was much different. MacArthur was actually a complication to US strategy. The war against Japan would be a maritime contest, but MacArthur was senior to any admiral the Navy could send to the region. There was no way that Admiral Ernest J. King, the Chief of Naval Operations, was about to let the Army run a war fought at sea. After much heated debate, the Joint Chiefs of Staff agreed to a compromise, creating two theaters. MacArthur would command the Southwest Pacific Area, while Admiral Chester W. Nimitz, who had been named commander-in-chief of the U.S. Pacific Fleet shortly after Pearl Harbor, would command the Pacific Ocean Areas. MacArthur criticized the decision—and he was not alone—to split command into two, arguing that it violated the basic military principle of concentrating force.[12]

The decision, however, reflected the sheer size of the unfolding conflict. In a north–south context, the twin US drives had started in 1942 out of bases in Australia and were aimed at the Japanese home islands. Put another way geographically, if the war had started in South America, in northern Chile, then the destination would have been roughly the California–Oregon state line, 6,500 miles to the north. The men and supplies had to cross the Pacific, which, on an east–west axis, was more than three times the size of the continental United States. Almost from the beginning of the war, distance was a brutal factor. In his works on military strategy, Carl von Clausewitz believed in unity of effort, though he realized there were circumstances that would necessitate division. These included logistics, location, geography, and size, all of which easily became issues in the Pacific theater.[13]

The real strategic issue for the United States in 1942 was one of priorities. The main fight was against Germany. At the time, Europe was the center of world affairs, just as it had been for centuries. Any power that dominated the continent posed a threat to nations across the globe. Defeating Germany was the main objective. The war against Japan was of secondary importance. The United States was fighting in the Pacific as a sea power and the primary fight was between the two navies. Their battles have become legend: Midway, Philippine Sea, and Leyte Gulf. Others, although almost forgotten, were no less critical in their way: Empress Augusta Bay, Vella Lavella, and Cape St. George. U.S. Navy submarines—adopting the ideas of the German U-boat community—were devastating the Japanese merchant marine, undermining the Japanese economy.

As significant as those maritime engagements and campaigns were, people live on land, and drives led by MacArthur and Nimitz involved battles against Japanese bases and outposts. These actions facilitated the naval war—giving the United States airfields and ports with major docks, which both allowed the Americans to get closer to the Japanese home islands and forced the Japanese Navy to give battle. The Pacific War, nonetheless, was a naval conflict and MacArthur's command was ultimately a supporting effort in a contest that was already of secondary importance to the nation.

With two theater commanders, there was no central plan for the twin drives. A good deal of thinking, however, had taken place during the interwar period, and that shaped strategic ideas during the war itself. Nonetheless, the Joint Chiefs of Staff, unable to reach an agreement, would oversee the direction of the fight and develop plans on an ad hoc basis. This approach gave the United

States a great deal of flexibility, but it also made setting priorities—particularly between Europe and the Pacific, but also between MacArthur's and Nimitz's theaters—difficult. For his part, MacArthur learned how to challenge the strategic direction of the war, sometimes using the Australians to put political pressure on the Joint Chiefs.[14] Nimitz, meanwhile, navigated his way between assessing his own strategy and adhering to that set by Admiral King.[15]

By 1943, it had become clear that the war against Japan, although junior in importance to the war in Europe, was also far more than a holding action. Brigadier General George H. Decker, chief of staff of the Sixth U.S. Army, for one, could see the impact of strategic-level decisions on his supply and manpower resources: "The European Theater was the primary one so we had to take more or less what was left, and this cut us down to a shoestring substantially during the first part of our operations out there." Decker noted in an oral history, compiled in 1972, that by the time of the Philippine landing in 1944, "we were pretty well fixed."[16] Indeed, after the cross-channel invasion of France, MacArthur was unable to even make good his losses.

Although the war against Japan had become a near peer to the one against Germany, MacArthur's command was still of secondary importance. At least in terms of the Army, there were many indicators that the European fight remained the priority. The Army sent MacArthur units that were considered second tier; of the eighteen infantry divisions that were deployed to his command, ten had the origins in the National Guard and another two had Guard regiments. Regular officers tended to look down on Guard units and officers because they never had as much training as regular units and local political issues affected command assignments. The 1st Cavalry Division had clung to its horses well after the war started in Europe and when it had to dismount and fight on foot. It was weak in numbers without the mobility and strike power its name suggested.[17]

MacArthur resented his lot. "Out here I am busy doing what I can with what I have," he groused in a letter to an old Army friend, "but resources have never been made available to me for a real strike. Innumerable openings present themselves which because of the weakness of my forces I cannot seize."[18]

He knew, nonetheless, he had to adjust to the realities of his situation and began a process of rethinking doctrine, tactics, and operations. He could not cling to established methods when he did not have the resources to implement those approaches. Much of this effort required new and different instruction once units arrived in the Pacific. He adapted what troops he had to the situation at hand. That adaptability was—oddly enough—also a problem. "I think one of the negative highlights was the fact that we did so well with so little" Decker recalled.[19] Decker's comment underlined the fact that doing well with limited resources was counterproductive to the bureaucratic interests of the command and a good way of not getting more resources, as they had found ways to make do with what they had. Oddly enough, this was a point of pride. As Decker put it, "The ability to do a lot with so little was probably the highlight of the entire campaign in the Pacific."[20]

MacArthur's mission was to seize control of New Guinea, return to the Philippines, and, finally, invade the Japanese home islands. "I came through and I shall return," he pledged shortly after his arrival in Australia in 1942. The statement was more than the product of a monumental ego. Carlos P. Romulo, a prewar Manila journalist who was working on the general's staff, told his colleagues the statement would keep hope alive in the Philippines. "America has let us down and won't be trusted, but the people still have confidence in MacArthur," Romulo explained. "If *he* says he is coming back, *he* will be believed."[21]

In 1942, while Nimitz's command fought for the Solomon Islands— including Guadalcanal—MacArthur's worked to take control of New Guinea. The second largest island in the world—after Greenland—New Guinea is the size of the southeastern United States (Florida, Georgia, Tennessee, Alabama, Mississippi, Arkansas, Missouri, and Louisiana). Two other islands that MacArthur fought to take were quite large as well—New Britain is the size of Massachusetts, Connecticut, and Rhode Island combined, and New Ireland is the size of Maryland. Since he was short of Army units, MacArthur did what the ground commanders of sea powers have done in the past; he used foreign troops. The majority of soldiers under his command were Australians.[22]

The campaign at Papua started off poorly, mainly because the Americans lacked heavy equipment to defeat the well-entrenched Japanese defenders. Despite this poor start, MacArthur's command moved steadily forward with victories in the Bismarck Sea, and at Bougainville, Admiralties, Hollandia, and Biak. His ability to recognize and promote quality combat commanders was near perfect. Robert Eichelberger, George Kenney, Thomas C. Kinkaid, Walter Krueger, Robert S. Beightler, Oscar W. Griswold, Ennis Whitehead, Joseph Swing, Daniel Barbey, and Jonathan Wainwright—many of whom will figure prominently in the liberation of Manila—were officers of impressive competence.[23] Kenney, his air commander, proposed using planes as the tactical situation demanded instead of sticking to the doctrine of strategic bombing that dominated the prewar U.S. Army Air Forces and turned MacArthur into a convert.[24]

Not everyone was as enamored of MacArthur. As more U.S. Army units arrived in his theater, MacArthur pushed the Australians to the side. The Allies were a means to an end. During Operation Cartwheel, which isolated the Japanese-occupied port town of Rabul on the island of New Britain, MacArthur effectively restrained the authority of his ground commander, General Sir Thomas Blamey, to Australian troops only. He assigned them to operations of marginal importance, giving them the thankless task of mopping up Japanese forces in bypassed areas.[25]

As the twin drives launched by MacArthur and Nimitz reached a convergence point, the question became where the United States should go next. The decision came down to Taiwan or the Philippines. The Americans could move in either direction—east or west—and seal the victory. The Joint Chiefs of Staff wanted to go to Taiwan. MacArthur wanted to take Luzon, the largest and most populous island in the Philippines. Again, attributing MacArthur's choice to his ego—the desire to redeem himself for 1942, and to honor his pledge to return to the Philippines—is easy, but there were sound reasons to avoid Taiwan. The occupied Chinese island, which was quite large, was going to require a significant number of ground troops. Moreover, it was not on a direct path to Japan, and it represented a detour for both Nimitz's and MacArthur's advances.[26]

There were good reasons to go to the Philippines. The invasion of Japan on a logistical basis was going to be the hardest operation of the war. "A landing and a major invasion of a powerful country are not the same thing," the editorial board of the *New York Herald* declared in February 1945. Many observed that the United States would need bases to invade Japan, major air bases and ports. In 1945, Manila was home to the only major harbor facilities in the western Pacific, which would be crucial in launching an invasion of the Japanese home islands.[27]

MacArthur also believed the United States had a moral obligation to liberate the Philippines. While that position might have been in part subjective, he nonetheless had an objective point when it came to strategic and policy-level considerations. The Philippines would be independent after the war—the United States had already made that political commitment—and the question was how cooperative it would be toward US foreign policy in the region.

Much of that would depend on what actions Americans took during the war to liberate the islands.[28]

The Philippines had one other factor that made it a better choice than Taiwan. There was a massive guerrilla resistance in the Philippines, one that already made it an active theater of combat in many ways.[29] Some 250,000 men were involved, a number equivalent to two field armies. Sea powers usually relied on allies to conduct ground operations, underwriting the expense with their stronger economies. And so it was in Luzon in 1945. To fight the Japanese, the United States was sending supplies to the Filipinos, who were waiting for the Americans to arrive so they could fight out in the open. There were no troops waiting for MacArthur on Taiwan.

In addition to being the largest island in the Philippines, Luzon is home to Manila. José P. Laurel, the president of the Second Republic of the Philippines, the collaborating regime the Japanese put in place when they took control, admitted the city's strategic importance: "Manila represents a population equivalent to one-eighth of the entire Philippines and that the city of Manila is the repository of Filipino culture and everything Filipino."[30] Only Tokyo was a bigger strategic prize in the Pacific war.

* * *

The men MacArthur commanded were at their peak as they prepared to invade Luzon. Given the size of the Philippines—Luzon is the size of several Midwestern states combined—only the U.S. Army could liberate the island. It was too big for a naval blockade, and there were not enough U.S. Marines for such an operation. The officers and enlisted personnel assigned this task were a highly formidable force. This level of skill was the result of years of training. Unable to invest in weapons and technology in the interwar period, the Army invested in people. The U.S. Military Academy was the main entry into the service for officers, and a Congressional appointment to the school was highly desired because it offered a free education and a job to follow. The experiences of Verne D. Mudge offer a good example of the prestige associated with selection. The commanding general of the 1st Cavalry Division during the battle for Manila, Mudge had attended West Point—although he had previously graduated from the University of Florida. After cadets graduated and received a commission, they could expect a series of appointments to active-duty units alternating with assignments to the professional schools as either students or instructors. The most important school in the interwar period was the Command & General Staff College at Fort Leavenworth, Kansas. Dwight D. Eisenhower called his time at Leavenworth "a watershed in my life."[31] In his oral history, Decker recalled the importance of his Staff College education, describing the instructional matter presented at the school as "excellent in developing one's ability to analyze situations and make proper decisions."[32]

This type of education made the continued training required in the Pacific possible. Several historians have noted that prewar training emphasized firepower and mobility. That approach was not always applicable in the war against Japan. The different geographical and topographical conditions of the Southwest Pacific Theater demanded that Army officers find new ways to use equipment designed for fighting in Europe. The lack of roads and undeveloped jungle terrain made using trucks and tanks impossible. In infantry units, the Army limited the number of foot soldiers assigned to regiments, while increasing heavy guns that needed multiple men to operate. The heavy density of vegetation in places like New Guinea and New Britain forced soldiers to use fire power and a combined arms approach (some combination of different Army branches and/or munitions working together) in an attritional fight rather than one of maneuver. The leadership of junior officers in these types of engagements became exceptionally important.[33] "The real leaders were and are officers," Charles A. Henne, a major in the 37th Infantry Division, remarked in a questionnaire after the war. Frank Mathias, who served in the same division, agreed. As he wrote in his own response, "Officers were the leaders. They had the power to act. The idea that 'old sarge' was the 'real' leader is Hollywood baloney."[34]

MacArthur's men, who were about to arrive on Luzon, were a mixture of draftees and volunteers but their morale was high. When asked years after about the objectives the United States fought for in the war, Sergeant Floyd N. Birdwell of the 11th Airborne Division, who had never finished elementary school, expressed himself simply: "necessary."[35] Corporal Murphy Foret of the 37th Infantry Division had a similar view: "My reaction was not 'gung ho' but I felt that it was my duty to go."[36] In the end, a number soldiers who served under MacArthur found their military service to be a positive factor in their life. Staff Sergeant Horrace Craddock called his war years "the opportunity for a farm boy to learn."[37] Johnston S. Harrison, a physician who went from first lieutenant to colonel in six years, said he was "fortunate to have varied travel experiences."[38]

Some were looking forward to the clash of battle. "I was gung ho—and wanted to see some action," Corporal Salvatore V. DeGaetano declared.[39] Mathis was looking forward to battle as well: "I looked on it as an exciting game, a chance to leave the boring old home town, BUT, there was a sensible fear lurking underneath."[40] Others were not so eager. One of the great myths of World War II is that the American public immediately rallied to the cause after Pearl Harbor. The truth is that men had to be drafted, and they did not want to be in either the Army or the Philippines. Willard Higdon was honest about his motivations: "I was 27 yrs old, with a wife and a 5 yr. old dtr. I did not want to go."[41]

Among the vast majority of US soldiers there was also a strong hatred of the enemy—which should hardly be surprising in any war. "We hated the Japs," Henne recalled years after the war was over. "I still do."[42]

The hostility toward the Japanese—throughout the ranks of MacArthur's Army—had a racial tint to it. When asked about the Japanese, a staff sergeant in the 37th Infantry Division remarked, "As people, they weren't!"[43] Another infantryman from the 37th had similar views, stating, "They were animals." He also blamed them for forcing him to fight and kill: "They made us become animals and my opinion has never changed."[44] Officers shared this attitude as well. Frank M. Lutze, a captain in the 145th Regiment, which was part of the 37th Division, would later say that the Japanese had "no respect for life."[45]

While the quality of MacArthur's manpower conferred advantages, the American military enjoyed immense material advantage over its opponents, both in Europe and the Pacific. There were limits, however, and those were coming into play in 1945. MacArthur's theater was never impoverished, but it clearly was not getting the same resources as France or Italy, or, for that matter, Nimitz's Central Pacific Command. There were many indicators about supply priorities, but food was the one that mattered most to the average soldier. As a company commander early in the war, Henne had found that good food often worked wonders on unit morale.[46] A combat engineer in the XIV Infantry Corp concisely summarized the situation: army rations were "eatable at times."[47] Given the physical demands of combat and the poor quality of the food, American soldiers faced a real problem. "You would starve on nothing but K-rations and D-bars, and they left a funny taste [sic] in your mouth," Major Henne remembered.[48] "Rations in combat were horrible," Major Hughes Seewald added.[49]

Enterprising soldiers could improve their diets in a way that the soldiers in Europe could not. "Most of us grew up in the Great Depression," said Mathias, "we were not used to much and made do. We augmented our rations with bananas, mangoes, papayas, coconuts and wild cucumbers, camotes, and many other tropical fruits and fish."[50]

By early 1945, most of the men in MacArthur's command had spent the past two or three years living on undeveloped islands in the Pacific. The living conditions were rudimentary. "I thought of it as another case of going to summer camp except it was open-ended," Julius S. Gassner, a New York City schoolteacher turned first lieutenant in the 37th Infantry Division, recalled.[51] He was not the only soldier in his unit to make that comparison. A private first class called his service "like an extended campout."[52] A sergeant in the 11th Airborne Division agreed, noting of his sleeping facilities, "From tents, barracks to foxholes. During Luzon campaign—only foxholes." These dugouts were not nice places to sleep. "Foxhole to foxhole sometimes full of water," remembered an enlisted engineer. "Breaks were few + Far between. For 3 years I didn't know when Sunday came."[53]

Because they were serving in primitive locations, the recreational venues were restricted. "Little or no time for recreation—an occasional movie," a master sergeant in the Quartermaster Corps recalled. Options in sports were limited because of a lack of equipment. Volleyball was fairly popular because it only required a ball and a net. "We had volleyball tournaments all over the place," Colonel Bruce Palmer, Jr., the chief of staff of the 6th Infantry Division, remembered. The soldiers gambled, more as something to do rather than to garner winnings. "On the island of Bouganville, there was hardly any use for money," Gassner explained. Poker and dice were popular, but most men sent their extra money home.[54]

Reading was a regular activity, be it mail, a newspaper, a magazine, or a used book that was passed around among men in a unit. When asked what he read, a technical sergeant in the 37th Division replied, "Anything We Could our Hands on. Mail from Home (Best)."[55]

A major advantage the Americans had over the Japanese was "jointness"— the ability (and willingness) of the different military services to work together. The rivalries between the U.S. Army and Navy, between Nimitz's headquarters and MacArthur's were real, but the Americans could and did collaborate. That cooperation brought more power and options to combat operations. "There was very good coordination between the Air Force, the Navy, and the

Army," Decker recalled. "We had really fine cooperation from the other services." Even foot soldiers saw this teamwork. A private first class from the 37th Infantry Division remarked on joint operations: "Very, Very Good. All of the Services Helped One Another + if We needed to Borrow Ammunition We always got it."[56]

The battle for Manila would draw on all those advantages. Urban warfare was something in which MacArthur's men had no experience or training. It was not a skill that was required much in Europe either. The last time the U.S. Army had fought extensively in cities was during the Civil War (there was almost no urban warfare in the War with Spain or World War I). It is hardly a surprise then that the U.S. Army had no doctrine or training manuals for fighting in a settlement larger than a village. The official U.S. Army history of the Philippine campaign contends that the basic doctrine of the service had nonetheless been sound. Infantrymen accustomed to fighting in the jungle quickly adapted to the urban terrain of Manila. "The adjustment was made rapidly and completely at the sound of the first shot fired from a building within the city."[57]

That argument is a bit too simplistic. In the Battle of Manila, the lack of guidelines put the burden for adaptation on frontline soldiers and officers, not the staffs of higher commands. Some units struggled to adapt and even experienced ones made mistakes. The case of the 112th Cavalry Regiment, a Texas National Guard formation, is instructive. On Luzon, the learning process in this unit had been mixed. The regiment had fought in the thick jungles of New Britain and New Guinea, but the flat, open ground of Luzon and the concrete of Manila were different. The 112th was not part of a division, which had the resources to train men fighting in new environments, and adaptation among these guardsmen was haphazard, and often conveyed by word of mouth rather than as part of a formal process.[58] Many of MacArthur's men were not ready for what lay ahead.

* * *

As the planning started, a bitter feud developed between the headquarters of Sixth U.S. Army and that of the Southwest Pacific Theater. The dispute involved intelligence analysts, and it represented an honest difference of opinions about the reading of the data. It soon became enflamed, however, due to the personalities involved, bureaucratic infighting, and professional rivalries. Some of this dispute was petty, but not all; the stakes were too significant.

The main formation responsible for the invasion and liberation of Luzon would be the Sixth U.S. Army. One of the two field armies in MacArthur's theater, the Sixth was under the command of Walter Krueger. In a service heavy with middle-class graduates of West Point, Krueger stood out in several different ways. When he received his fourth star, in March 1945, he became the first former enlisted man in the 169-year history of the United States Army to receive that rank. He was also the first foreign-born full general in U.S. Army history—he and his family moved to the United States from Germany when he was five years old. In his student papers at the Naval War College, he cited Clausewitz from the original German.[59]

Public affairs officers and a number of reporters tried to portray Krueger as a GI general—tough and gruff, but beneath that rough veneer he had a kindness that inspired devotion among his troops. "We would follow him through hell, and I suppose the boys feel the same way today," a sergeant who served with him in the Spanish–American War recalled. His aide agreed with this view: "No man has a deeper, more sincere or whole-hearted feeling for men in the ranks than General Walter Krueger," Lieutenant Colonel H. Ben Dechard, Jr., told a journalist. "He will take a military risk—but he won't gamble with the lives of his men."[60] Those views could easily be dismissed coming, as they did, during the war, but years after the conflict had ended, and Krueger was long gone, Decker, who had earned the four-star rank himself, stated: "He was one who although having a gruff exterior, I think, had a heart as big as all outdoors."[61]

There was more than kindness to Krueger's approach. "One of the most important responsibilities of an Army Commander consists of building up the esprit, morale, and confidence of his troops," he explained after the war. "Thoughtful consideration of the needs of the troops is of paramount importance."[62] He communicated that view clearly to his subordinates. Decker observed, "This was one of the things that he always insisted on that the commander think first of his men and next of himself."[63] Many officers under his command knew Krueger's feelings. "His view of the Officer Corps was a rather low one," General Palmer recalled after his own Army career had ended. "He said, 'You know the trouble with the Army is the officers. They're a necessary evil.' He meant it too."[64]

The enduring image of Krueger is his rough edges. "Don't make me out to be a kindly old man, because I'm not," he groused to a reporter from *Time* magazine. Major General Oscar W. Griswold, commanding general of the XIV

Infantry Corps, called Krueger the "damndest man to serve with I ever saw!" Swing, commanding general of the 11th Airborne Division—another key figure among MacArthur's men—was a little more generous in his assessment. "Krueger was a dedicated man," he said. "It was very hard for him to relax and realize that there were other ways of doing things than bing, bing, bing, right down the line."[65]

MacArthur and Krueger worked well together and throughout the Philippines campaign agreed on the basic approach toward the conduct of operations. They had known each other for over forty years, but it would be wrong to call them friends. "General Krueger was not one to be a buddy with anyone," Decker commented. The Sixth Army commander had been loyal to MacArthur, and that was something that he valued and rewarded. He also respected his abilities. "MacArthur felt that when he asked Krueger to do anything, if Krueger said he could do it, MacArthur could forget it," Roger O. Egeberg, MacArthur's personal doctor, recalled.[66]

A "whole of army" analysis of the Battle of Manila—which this book will attempt—requires that Krueger get his due. He excelled at training troops. Having survived George C. Marshall's purge of older officers in 1941 (when Krueger was sixty), he expected to spend the war in the United States running training commands. The opportunity to command in combat as a flag officer was both a surprise and a major career achievement. Krueger believed the traits a general needed to be successful included strong willpower, moral courage, resolution, energy, resourcefulness, patience, tenacity, simplicity in thought, enthusiasm, and personal persuasion. Using these traits, he adjusted quickly to combat in the Pacific. MacArthur's emphasis on speed, surprise, and maneuver, he knew, would require additional training. Seeing the utility of mechanization, Krueger had begun training his units in mechanized warfare in the summer of 1941 (his men began calling themselves "blitzkruegers"). Before the war, he created additional training programs for junior officers that were informally dubbed "Krueger tech." Krueger became a believer in aggressive, combined-arms movement, both in the open and in constrained areas like jungles and urban areas. The idea was to avoid becoming a target for the enemy and to coordinate complex actions of various types of units so that the soldiers could exploit breakthroughs. This type of intricate effort would allow smaller units to have greater impact when armed with heavy weapons and delivered with focus. These efforts were the result of months of training, practice, and support from service units.[67]

With the invasion of the Philippines, the commanding general of the Sixth Army knew that victory was hardly certain. "I used to box; and if you had the other fellow wavering, that was the time to step in and hit him all the harder," Krueger explained. "My suspicion is that Japan is trying to drag this out as long as she can. Time is of the essence. We have got to hit and hit again."[68]

* * *

Planning for the assault on Luzon officially began on September 30, 1944, with a target date of December 20, 1944. The Sixth Army would invade with two infantry corps, totaling four divisions, or roughly one hundred thousand men. The paperwork required to prepare for the operation was massive—slightly smaller than the D-Day invasion of Normandy where five divisions landed—and involved various headquarter staffs around the Pacific hammering out the specifics. The Sixth Army had actually begun this effort while its infantry units were fighting on Leyte, one of the larger sized islands that make up the Philippines.[69] "Planning an operation while conducting one certainly has its drawbacks," Krueger's operations officer, Brigadier General Clyde D. Eddleman, recalled years later. "But it [sic] does have one great advantage: The realities of an operation are constantly staring you in the face."[70] The staffs at both Sixth Army and MacArthur's theater command worked seven days a week, staying at their desks until late in the evening. "Nobody ever knew when it was Sunday—never," Colonel Bonner F. Fellers recalled.[71]

It soon became apparent that meeting the December 20 deadline that MacArthur had set would be impossible. Construction of airfields on Leyte that would provide cover for the landing force was going slower than expected, and the number of amphibious assault ships that would be available was insufficient. As a result, MacArthur, on November 30, postponed the operation until January 9.[72]

During the planning for the invasion of Luzon, the Americans were facing a big question about both Japanese troop numbers and the types (combat versus support units). The Japanese were sending more units to Luzon—there was no dispute on that—but how many were actually arriving was a different story. Almost all troop convoys were suffering from air and submarine attacks.[73] To answer this question, the Americans faced two serious problems. The first was an imbalance in sources of information. Aerial reconnaissance and signal intercepts, which had worked well for MacArthur's headquarters in the past, were failing to collect the required data. While it had deciphered Imperial Japanese Navy messages, the United States had not broken the regimental codes of the Imperial Japanese Army and had little information on tactical and operational deployments. Filipino guerrillas supplied information, but they were focused on the tactical level and the reliability of their information at the operational and strategic levels was questionable.[74]

A second issue involved the analysis of that information. Major General Charles Willoughby was the chief of military intelligence in MacArthur's headquarters. One of the small group of individuals that had escaped from the Philippines with MacArthur in 1942, Willoughby was an archbishop in the one, true faith: MacArthur. His skill as an intelligence analyst was hit or miss. He also tended to personalize questions about his findings and resented inputs from others. In trying to assess the force facing the United States on Luzon, Willoughby was challenged by Colonel Horton White, the chief intelligence officer for the Sixth Army. White was best known for his role in supervising the rescue of American prisoners of war at Cabanatuan, which has since become known as the "Great Raid."[75] One asset that White had that Willoughby did not was the 6th Army Special Reconnaissance Unit, better known as the "Alamo Scouts." Krueger had created this unit to collect intelligence far behind enemy lines.

Early in the planning process for the Luzon operation, Willoughby estimated that the Japanese had 121,000 men on Luzon. Based on signals intelligence, he upped that number to 172,400 in December 1944. He also believed that General Yamashita Tomoyuki, commanding general of the Fourteenth Area Army, would defend against the landing and would fight in central Luzon using maneuver and mobility.[76] White came to different conclusions a few days later, arguing that the Japanese had 234,500 soldiers. He also believed—correctly—that the Japanese lacked training, and that most of them would not fight in central Luzon.[77]

In White's view, Willoughby had failed to account for service units and soldiers in unattached formations. As a result, he missed 230 separate units. White, on the other hand, came up with a figure of 158,000, but believed there were an additional 51,000 on the central plain of Luzon—in units that Willoughby had missed. Knowing that medical, logistic, transportation, and base units always support combat formations and having some reconnaissance reports that suggested as much, White multiplied the number of combat soldiers by 1.5, which gave him 234,500.[78]

Both men turned out to be wrong. Yamashita actually had 275,000 men. Yet in an examination of the dispute conducted years later, Captain Michael E. Bigelow, a U.S. Army intelligence officer, called White's assessment "a reasonably accurate count." Intelligence reports are rarely one hundred percent accurate, and since MacArthur's staff tended to personalize disputes, Bigelow also speculates that Willoughby reported what the general wanted to hear.[79]

These disputes came to a head in late 1944. Krueger sent Eddleman to deliver the Sixth Army's plan for assault. The briefing did not go well for anyone. Four people were in the room: Eddleman, MacArthur, Willoughby, and Eddleman's assistant. MacArthur had intentionally excluded Lieutenant General Richard Sutherland, his chief of staff. Technically, Sutherland was under house arrest for bringing his Australian mistress to the Philippines in violation of MacArthur's orders. His absence would prove significant.[80]

Eddleman began with a report on the intelligence numbers. He was only a few seconds into his delivery when MacArthur interrupted him, calling the figures, "Bunk." He tried to continue, and the general interrupted again with another "bunk." Eddleman explained that the numbers had come from MacArthur's own headquarters.[81]

Eddleman asked MacArthur if he could continue, and the general agreed. When he finished, the general's only question was about why there was no provision for getting to Manila. Eddleman explained that Krueger wanted to focus on getting a beachhead established. MacArthur agreed with that answer. Chief Warrant Officer Paul P. Rogers, who was on the staff of theater headquarters for the entire war, believed that had Sutherland been in the room, MacArthur's response would have been stronger.[82] As they left, MacArthur apologized to Eddleman. "There are only three great [intelligence officers] in history and mine is not one of them," he remarked.[83]

MacArthur did more than just apologize. In mid-December, he gave Krueger more troops. The Sixth Army would now have nine infantry divisions rather than six, two regimental combat teams, and an armored group when it landed on Luzon. Whatever problems the Americans would face, a lack of either manpower or firepower would not be one of them.[84]

Despite this gesture, the significance of the intelligence dispute explains much of what happened in Manila. The units sent to Luzon were based on Willoughby's estimates. Although MacArthur gave Krueger more troops, the force he had provided for the invasion was smaller than it should have been. Krueger, as a result, had to face risk that he would have avoided otherwise and had to manage the danger accordingly.[85]

The Americans still had time to resolve these concerns. MacArthur waited until December 26, 1944, to hold his final command conference at Price House—a large square mansion that was only a few hundred feet from the water at Tacloban—which was home to his headquarters on Leyte. The group had just assembled when a Japanese air attack briefly broke up the meeting. Officers and men gathered at one end of the building to watch the battle. A Japanese plane was getting in position to attack the building, and many began to realize their lives were on the line. The threat ended almost immediately when a US plane shot up the attacker. Rogers yelled out some obscenities in triumph. Realizing where he was, he looked around nervously and saw General Kenney smiling at him.[86]

When these officers reassembled again, they had little time to ponder this near-death experience as they had to resolve strategic issues. The invasion of Luzon had three purposes. The liberation of Manila was one. Establishing bases for the invasion of Japan was a second, which meant that seizing the port facilities intact in Manila was an important subgoal. The third was to destroy the island forts that blocked the sea lines of communication. Correspondingly, there were to be three phases to the operation. The first would be the amphibious landings in Lingayen Gulf. The second would be to destroy all Japanese forces north of the Agno River. The third was the destruction of enemy units in Central Luzon and the liberation of Manila.[87]

The planners had not worked backward from achieving a secure Luzon. They had simply addressed each phase of the operation, putting a good deal of attention into the amphibious landing, which was clearly the priority, mainly because it came first. The next phase was the second priority, and so on. The final goal, the real objective—taking Manila—received the least amount of consideration because it came at the end, nearly an afterthought. Plans to continue the attack and liberate the city were both vague and optimistic. No one in the theater headquarters, Sixth Army headquarters, or XIV Corp headquarters had a plan for operations in the metropolitan areas of Manila should the Japanese resist. Everyone hoped that they could clear the city quickly and without much damage.[88]

MacArthur did not want to waste time planning. He knew that time cut both ways. He could read the room and realized that many gathered in Price House were unhappy with the operation. The general told them that he understood their concerns. "He further stated that he realized we were not as fully prepared as we would like to be, but that the largest pot he ever lost in a poker game was when held four kings in his hand," Eddleman recalled. "He argued that while we were taking time to become stronger, the Jap would also become stronger and therefore make our problems more difficult."[89]

Strength, though, would not be the main issue facing the Americans on Luzon. Everything would depend on how the fight was fought. There was little tactical intelligence analysis done on Manila before the battle began. American soldiers, as a result, were blind to the nature of the combat facing them. Fighting in an urban environment would be far different from the jungle fighting in which they had gained experience. The troops would need good intelligence; not only street maps, but aerial reconnaissance photos, local informants, and detailed sketches that told them where the Japanese were located and with what type of weapons. "Our chief source of intelligence continued to be the Guerilla forces operation on Luzon," remembered Eddleman.[90]

The problem was that the guerrillas on Luzon were poorly organized compared to the ones on Leyte. The result was information that was—as Eddleman put—nothing more than "mere rumors."[91] Some of this lack of regulation and structure was due to Japanese counterinsurgency efforts. While they had surrendered the countryside to the Filipinos, they held the city and were good at breaking espionage efforts inside the metro area. The poor quality of information was obvious to even low-ranking officers. A captain in the 37th Infantry Division believed that interviews with civilians and guerrillas "proved to be of no valuc." He blamed the combat interrogation teams, which had inexperienced and untrained personnel who ended up making futile, unproductive efforts.[92]

While there is truth to that view, a study conducted for the U.S. Army in the 1980s on urban warfare noted that the intelligence failures of the Manila operation started at the top: "XIV Corps' greatest need, and MacArthur's greatest mistake involved gathering intelligence confirming or denying Japanese intentions." The White–Willoughby dispute ignored the significance of the presence of Imperial Japanese Navy shore units. While signals intelligence indicated that Yamashita would not defend Manila, no one told MacArthur about the Navy. "His staff also made an error of overconfidence," continues the report, "only believing intelligence that supported what MacArthur (and his G-2, Major General Willoughby) wanted to hear and disregarding anything suggesting otherwise." The Army study—still in use decades later—found that attackers normally emerge victorious, but when they were defeated, a failure in intelligence was always the cause.[93]

2

Waiting in Hate, Waiting in Hope

The Japanese and the Filipinos

While MacArthur's soldiers adjusted to the changing character of the war, the Japanese knew that the conflict had turned against them. Partly as a result, there were profound divisions among the defenders of Luzon that worked against their own cause.

The Japanese faced serious problems. The first was the terrain of Luzon. The situation had been no different in 1942 when the Japanese had invaded and been a significant reason for the US defeat. General Yamashita Tomoyuki understood this basic fact. Commanding the Fourteenth Area Army—the main Japanese formation on Luzon—Yamashita believed that he did not have enough men to hold the island. The United States had total air superiority and that gave the Americans an advantage that Yamashita could not counter. He realized the Americans were going to take Luzon. All he could do was delay and inflict as much damage on his enemy as possible. He was going to do that in the mountains of northeast Luzon, a setting that would limit some of the advantages the United States had in mobility and firepower.[1]

Manila was therefore not part of Yamashita's plan. He and his staff saw the city as both peripheral in importance and as a liability in the campaign to hold Luzon. "Manila is geologically unfit for fortification and topographically hard to defend," the general stated. Knowing that Manila was going to attract an American attack, he withdrew Army units in late 1944. "The city of Manila was to be abandoned and the main force in that area was to be stationed in the mountains to the east of the city," Colonel Shujiro Kobayashi, an officer on the staff of the Fourteenth Area Army, explained after the war.[2]

Despite these assessments, war came to the city. Three separate Japanese formations fought the Battle of Manila, a reason the battle developed as it did. The first of these was the Shimbu Group, a large Imperial Army formation to the east of the city limits and under the command of Lieutenant General Yokoyama Shizuo. (The Japanese changed the designation of the Shimbu Group to the "Forty-First Army" after the Battle of Manila ended; what the Japanese called an "army" was what Americans called a "corps.") The Manila Defense Force was another Imperial Army unit, under the command of Major General Kobayashi Takashi. His immediate military superior was Yokoyama. The troops in Kobayashi's formation were both in the city and to the north of the municipality. The Manila Naval Defense Force (MNDF) was the third Japanese formation and was the one that did most of the fighting in the metropolis. The name of this unit in Japanese is *Manira kaigun boeitai*. Written using eight characters in both katakana and kanji, the name was often reduced to a three-character abbreviation (pronounced as *makaibo* much the way the North Atlantic Treaty Organization's abbreviation of NATO is pronounced as "nay tow"). The Navy created this new unit on December 22, 1944, using the 31st Special Base Force as its foundation. Command of this group went to Rear Admiral Iwabuchi Sanji.[3]

In 1945, Iwabuchi was forty-nine years old and had enjoyed a successful career in the Navy, although he had never had any joint assignments or duty that required him to consider issues of strategy. While he had a proven track record in naval matters, his understanding of infantry tactics and ground operations was almost non-existent. The records that remain suggest an inclination on Iwabuchi's part to depend on Army officers and junior naval officers with any type of experience in ground operations.[4]

In any case, the original Japanese mission was not to defend Manila. In mid-1944 Rear Admiral Arima Kaoru, while he was in command of the 31st Special Base Force, read a report that the U.S. Army conducted on Manila as a military asset. (He took the report from MacArthur's personal library, which was still housed in the Manila Hotel, where the general had lived for six years before being evacuated.) This study convinced Arima that fighting for the city was a bad idea. He also believed that the job of his sailors would be to destroy some bridges, remove ammunition, and retreat to stronger defensive positions outside the city. Yokoyama and his staff had the same understanding. "The Shimbu Group had no intention of defending Manila to the death, but planned to make the city a forward position and, after engaging in some combat, to withdraw its forces to the main positions," Colonel Asano Kenichiro, a staff officer of the Shimbu Group, stated in a report after the war.[5]

Yokoyama and his staff wanted the MNDF to concentrate to the east of Manila, and at a favorable opportunity, counterattack by "infiltration." It was to hold Fort McKinley, a base the U.S. Army had built in the prewar era and located to the southeast of the city. Occupying a high ground a mile from the runway at Nichols Field, Japanese control of McKinley would have made it impossible for the Americans to use the airfield.[6]

Admiral Iwabuchi changed all these plans. In an inter-service conference held in Montalban on January 14, 1945, he requested that the Navy be allowed to conduct a slightly more vigorous defense of the city. "I was present at that meeting," Colonel Asano later stated. Iwabuchi made explicitly clear that while he would not fight to the last in Manila, he would use the Navy to destroy the naval facilities in the city to keep them from the Americans. Iwabuchi's command would destroy the docks and harbors to deny the US "effective use" of these facilities. General Yokoyama approved of this policy, although did not have command authority over Iwabuchi. Given the constitutional structure of Imperial Japan, both the Army and the Navy answered only to the emperor, which in practical terms made them independent of one another and the cabinet, which is why inter-service operations were so difficult. Yokoyama, however, outranked Iwabuchi and that seemed sufficient for the coordination of efforts. In fact, at the conference, the admiral told the general that the Navy had placed him under his command. This development was news to Yokoyama, but welcome nonetheless. As a result, there was no reason not to give the admiral command of Army units because indications were that Iwabuchi would comply with the direction of its operations. In retrospect, it appears that Iwabuchi's gesture was an effort on his part to get command authority over the Army units still in Manila.[7]

Proving this point, the Navy was not particularly good at communicating with the Army. "We knew nothing about the situation in Manila," Asano later insisted, "we knew nothing about the presence of the Navy."[8]

The issue of command structure poses challenges for historians, even decades later. Few Japanese would survive the Battle of Manila, and even fewer still—almost none—would discuss it in the years afterward. Compounding this silence, the defenders destroyed most of their records. That qualification is important. The U.S. Army military intelligence units took letters, diaries, and records off the dead and began translating them immediately. These documents were a major source of intelligence on the Japanese Army during the course of the Pacific war. As the conflict progressed, units got better about destroying their written records to keep them out of enemy hands. As a way of compensating, the Americans turned to prisoner of war debriefings. Guerrillas took a small but significant number of Japanese POWs, and U.S. Army military intelligence detachments conducted interviews. Put together, these sources provide at least some firsthand accounts of the defenders. One final consideration, the Manila Naval Defense Force was a Navy formation, yet it was doing the work of infantry. Ground combat is alien to what sailors are trained to do.[9] Manila, as a result, was an atypical engagement.

As noted, officers in the Army understood that they could not win the battle for Manila. On January 10, General Kobayashi told his men that the main goal was to do attritional damage to the Americans. "By firmly occupying the key points in the city, the Manila detachment, even in a hopeless situation, will vigorously and constantly carry out infiltration and diversionary action, thus doing the utmost in destroying the enemy's fighting power." The primary targets would be bridges leading into the city. Soldiers had to engage in combat at these locations to prevent the Americans from repairing the structures.[10]

General Yokoyama agreed. Two days after his conference with Iwabuchi, he issued directions concerning the Shimbu Group's role in the coming battle, one whose momentousness was clear to him. "The engagement which will shortly take place in Manila and vicinity is a great battle which will be watched by the whole world and will decide future development of the Imperial Army." The Americans held the material advantage, and to engage with the enemy, the Japanese had to rely on their intangible advantages, such as *esprit de corps*. "We must stubbornly exhaust all means of attack. We must not be disheartened though we fail once or twice. We must believe in the power of the gods until the very end." At the operational level, the Japanese defenders were to use infiltration. "The principle of surprise attack must be thoroughly inculcated. To take the enemy by surprise is the source of certain victory. Fronts where the enemy is prepared must be avoided, and sudden attack against his rear must be devised." At the tactical level, Japanese soldiers should make sure every bullet had a target, taking out three Americans before embracing death. "The officers and men who participate in it must deeply feel its importance, and, profoundly moved by the gloriousness of the struggle, must devote their whole beings to the destruction of the enemy Americans."[11]

Kobayashi also ordered improvement in infantry tactics. At the beginning of 1945, he organized training sessions in sharpshooting, infiltration, suicide attacks on tanks, and antiaircraft fire. The Naval Defense Force followed the lead of the Army on these war fighting methods. Naval personnel used these documents in preparing for ground combat, and in what little training they were able to do. American military intelligence personnel found these Army directives in MNDF files.[12]

Despite these efforts, the Defense Force was not a particularly competent organization, consisting of a motley collection of sailors from sunken ships, hospitals, and shore units. The Navy had also press-ganged a number of people into service. These included Korean, Taiwanese, and Manchurian laborers, as well as Japanese civilians living on Luzon. The civilians comprised, according to one survivor, a full third of the MNDF and were a poor military resource. They were often well past the prime age for military service, and a number were in poor health. These older men had civilian careers that had brought them to Manila, and they were not particularly interested in dying for the *bushido* code of the samurai. Although officers, they were junior in rank and often a decade and a half older than their superiors. They also usually had less experience on technical military topics than would have been normal for others holding the same rank.

The non-Japanese fighters were even less reliable. Most were not even allowed to enlist in the Navy but were expected to fight as told. The motivation of these men was low. Those who deserted or became prisoners of war tended to be from the ranks of the foreigners or the civilians. All told, there were between fourteen thousand and twenty thousand in the unit. Even Iwabuchi probably did not know, as the *makaibo* acquired most of its men in January. The fact that the Navy had a formation of this size in Manila came as a surprise to General Yokoyama.[13]

The Japanese had another problem—lack of supplies. An official Japanese study conducted after the war found that there were simply not enough weapons available for all the men in the MNDF. When the defenders did have weapons, they often had no experience in their use. As late as the day before the Americans crossed the Manila city limits, Iwabuchi was ordering his men to pull guns off Japanese ships in Manila Bay, and to use them on land. The sailors did not have time to train with these weapons before the battle started.[14]

Still another problem was the quality of the Japanese fortifications. "The arrangement of these installations followed no standard pattern and great variance was found in the materials for barricades and for mining the street," Captain John B. Lukens of the 117th Engineer Combat Battalion stated in a post-battle report. "The installations seem to have been the result of the efforts of personnel not experienced in such work." The official U.S. Army history of the battle was more succinct, stating, "Tactically, Iwabuchi's defensive preparations left much to be desired."[15]

Japanese intelligence efforts in the Philippines were also poor. The *kempei tai*—which was both a traditional military police force in the Imperial Japanese Army and a secret security service—never had personnel fluent in English, Spanish, Tagalog, or any of the other languages used in the Philippines. As a result, they depended heavily on collaborators for basic information. The Japanese also needed the cooperation of officers in the Philippine constabulary.[16]

One effect of this is that the Japanese tended to underestimate the quality of the U.S. Army, believing the Americans depended on technology to mask the poor training of their soldiers. This cultural arrogance led to a good deal of laziness in intelligence work. Knowledge of the XIV Corps was almost nonexistent. Iwabuchi learned about the US march on Manila only a week before the Americans reached the city.[17] The defenders believed that the linguistic complexity of Japanese was enough of a code to thwart their opponents. As the admiral declared: "The enemy sometimes use our passwords against us, but it can easily be detected from their pronunciation that they are not Japanese. Also when suspicion arises, it is necessary to converse in fluent Japanese to make sure." There was also a racial element to Japanese actions. In the weeks leading up to the battle, security forces arrested, interrogated, tortured, and sometimes executed Europeans—even those of Axis nations allied with Japan—failing to realize that Filipinos were a bigger threat to them.[18]

Illustrating the problems with intelligence, the Japanese knew an attack was coming but did not know from where. The defenders assumed that the Americans would come from Leyte and land in southern Luzon. As a result, most of the defense fortifications in the city faced in that direction. A secondary possibility, they thought, was an amphibious assault from Manila Bay with some form of parachute assault. A partially burned Japanese document informed the defenders: "There are strong indications that the enemy will carry out combined operations with an air-borne force joined by guerrillas and the troops that will penetrate into the city after landing in Manila Bay . . . ." The rest of the sentence is illegible.[19]

The Japanese understood this type of mobility would undermine many of their defensive efforts. "It is absolutely vital that the enemy force attacking Manila does not take us by surprise," one Japanese document declares. As a result, the defenders spent time training to defend against paratroopers. Their doctrine was basic and sound: attack quickly while the airborne soldiers were scattered and recovering from the jump, using close-quarter tactics.[20]

Despite their lack of training, however, the sailors of the MNDF were exceptionally dependable as infantrymen. They were motivated and morale was high. They were healthy and well fed, and knew they were going to be involved in a fight in which the odds were against them. "Even when the situation of the force becomes hopeless, the Northern Force will continue to fight to the last man," one set of regulations decreed. These sailors often did just that because they were in situations where their only choices were either to fight or die.[21] A study the Japanese Ministry of Defense conducted in the 1980s, when there was profound fear that the Cold War would turn into an armed conflict in urban areas, found that individuals and small groups fought "relentlessly to the end."[22]

Despite its limitations, the MNDF commanded the respect of their opponents. A military intelligence study that the XIV Corps conducted of the Japanese defenses declared: "Any deficiencies . . . in the plan adopted or tactics employed were not reflected in the combat qualities of individual soldiers and small groups. These fought tenaciously and skillfully, to the bitter end, using all available weapons and barriers, natural and artificial." Many individual US soldiers shared this view. One from the 37th Infantry Division observed, "Not too good—But Courageous to Their Cause." Others in the division agreed, "Japanese—tough—did not give up ever." Daniel J. Sears, a technical sergeant in the 37th Infantry Division, captured both the regard and contempt Americans had for their opponents: "Japs not the best trained but willing to fight to the end—at all costs—no regard for human life."[23]

There was some irony to this qualified approval. The Imperial Japanese Army was far more reluctant than the U.S. Army to give the *makaibo* its due. "We place little hope on the fighting power of the naval force since they are not used to land fighting," Kobayashi told Lieutenant Commander Kayashima Koichi. This assessment had nothing to do with Army–Navy rivalry, but instead reflected an honest evaluation of the Defense Force's limited military capabilities.[24]

The confounding thing about these contradictory assessments is that both are correct: the tactical and operational incompetence of the Japanese defenders did not undermine the hard, military logic of their actions. The Japanese hoped to do attritional damage to MacArthur's forces. Several US military intelligence officers saw this objective as the main reason to hold the city. The Japanese also wanted to ruin Manila as a port and at all costs keep it from the Americans. The sewing of the waters of the harbor and the Pasig River with hulks reflected that determination. Destroying the city would deny its use as a US base and increase logistical problems for the Americans, which might keep them from reaching Japan itself. The damage would also bring chaos to the Philippines, rendering the city useless as an administrative center. General Yokoyama explained that the sacrifice of his soldiers would "block the hated enemy's plans for a northward advance."[25]

These Japanese views and objectives reflect the changing nature of strategy during the war. Manila had always been important, but in 1943 and 1944 it had been a backwater while the war was being fought in the South Pacific. In late 1944 and early 1945, the city was in the process of changing again.[26] Manila was again becoming a major transportation hub, and its large port facilities would be vital to supporting US logistical efforts in the Philippines and for the expected invasion of Japan. In short, Manila was the key strategic prize in the Philippine campaign. "The Luzon campaign will officially end with the fall of Manila," Bonner Fellers, MacArthur's military secretary, told his wife before the battle had started.[27]

These two factors—political significance and transportation networks— were major reasons other municipalities had become battlegrounds during the war. MacArthur had wanted to declare Manila an open city to spare it destruction, but that was uncharacteristically naïve. Yamashita did not want to fight in an urban environment, but it was simply not in Japan's interest to hand Manila over to the Americans intact.[28]

On the eve of battle, when one weighs Japanese strengths and weaknesses against those of the United States, it is clear MacArthur's men were in the better position. Fellers was hardly bragging when he told a British officer a month before the landings on Luzon, "While there will be desperate fighting ahead, the fate of the Japanese in the Philippines is sealed."[29]

It had, however, become clear that the Japanese had no intention of giving up without an actual fight, and, as events would show, the combat that followed posed a serious risk to the United States at the strategic level.

All of these issues would all come into play as the United States drove into Manila and fought to liberate the city.

* * *

Caught between the Americans and the Japanese were the Filipinos. The residents of Luzon and Manila were hardly neutral. Whatever ambiguity Filipinos had toward Americans for the limitations they had put on self-rule were minor compared to the two-and-a-half years of mismanagement and brutality they suffered under the Japanese. "The educated Japs were fine," Saturnino del Villar, an elementary student during the occupation, recalled. "Unlike the ill-bred soldiers who were brutish toward the Filipinos." Villar often did menial work for the Japanese. "If they caught you goofing off, they hit you on the head with bamboo canes. Or if you didn't finish the job, they whacked you till you got it done, even though it took you the whole night."[30]

This type of cruelty alienated the bulk of the populace. "The Japanese occupation was my generation's trial by fire," Carmen Guerrero Nakpil, one of the most important Filipino writers of the twentieth century, reflected. "Bataan and Corregidor turned out to be national suicide and the Americans had abandoned us."[31]

The Philippines is rich in natural resources, but its economy at the time was closely tied to that of the United States. The Japanese conquest severed access to US markets and factory goods, which economists and planners in Tokyo were unable to make good over the course of their two-and-a-half years in control. As a result, basic staples tied to agriculture—like food, clothing, and fuel—became scarce. Inflation became rampant. Food in Manila had remained accessible in 1942, but in the second half of 1943 and in early 1944 the distribution network collapsed. "The worst of it was the moral disaster it inflicted. Good and evil, right and wrong were pragmatic decisions," Guerrero Nakpil noted. "Fathers hid tins of meat from their children, brothers informed on their brothers, everyone was some kind of prostitute." If Filipinos in Manila helped the *kempei tai*, it was at least in part because the Japanese had food. Others began leaving the city, hoping to avoid the coming battle, but also expecting that food might be easier to obtain in the countryside.[32]

For his part, MacArthur refused to believe that Filipino collaboration was widespread or voluntary. Recent scholarship supports this position. Many of the leaders of the Second Republic, the government formed in October 1943 under Japanese occupation, had no illusions about their occupiers. The modern samurai were fighting for Japan, not the Philippines. The main reason for their invasion in 1941 and 1942 was geopolitical. The Philippines had few natural resources that the Japanese economy required. What they wanted was to drive the Americans out of the western Pacific and, once that was done, they wanted to liquidate their commitment to the Philippines quickly. The Japanese had little interest in turning the archipelago into a Japanese colony.[33]

A small group of Filipino political leaders began meeting in early 1942 to discuss what they should do: resist or collaborate. These meetings were largely a waste of time because the Japanese refused to consider any other option than the creation of a new republic that would be a weak client state, which is what the Second Republic was.[34]

President José P. Laurel and most other leaders were nonetheless nationalists. Laurel's comments during the constitutional convention for the new government are worth noting. "Our problem is to remove this flag and replace it with our own," he said, pointing to the Japanese flag. Quintín Paredes, who would serve in the cabinet, was stunned at the tone: "We thought that Laurel was going to finish his speech with a declaration of war against Japan."[35] There were divisions among the collaborators, but most worked with their new colonial masters only out of necessity.

Laurel was hardly anti-American, having earned a PhD from Yale University, nor was he pro-Japanese. "This independence we have is an independence which is not independence," he confided a few months after his inaugural address. Most Filipinos agreed with him, seeing Japanese actions as a sham. Laurel later explained that he had gone along with the Japanese to make the best of a bad situation.[36]

Many, though, took Japanese statements about independence at face value and noted that Tokyo had offered and delivered independence, which is only half of what Washington had ever done. "I am not anti-American nor pro-Japanese: I am pro Filipino," Paulino Santos, a leader in the Second Republic, explained. Japan "gave us our national freedom, the freedom that America promised but lost the chance to give." This sentiment reflected thinking that was common among the Filipino public. A crowd of five hundred thousand gathered in Manila on October 14, 1943, to watch the ceremonies declaring the Philippines independent.[37]

Others responded to the moral chaos with arms. There was a strong insurgent movement on Luzon almost from the very beginning of the Japanese occupation, involving a number of different groups with different political objectives, ranging from Chinese nationalists to Filipino Communists. Some were from the upper class of Philippine society, while others were formed around the thousands of U.S. Army personnel that had never surrendered to the Japanese. "The independence Japan has promised you will be a spurious independence," Leopoldo Y. Yabes, a guerrilla leader, publicly declared in 1943. "Let us instead make ourselves worthy of the true independence that America will give us after the Philippines is retaken by the United States liberation forces." Other groups like the *Hukbong Bayan Laban sa Hapon* (the People's Army Against the Japanese)—better known simply as the *Huks*—were not eager to see the Americans return. One U.S. Army officer stated that "discussing the guerrillas as a unified 'movement' is perhaps a misnomer." What united these groups was a desire to get rid of the Japanese and, in many cases, it was their only bond.[38]

There were also Filipino guerrillas—the Makabayan Katipunan ng mga Pilipino (the Patriotic League of Filipinos), or *makapili* for short—fighting for the Japanese. The Japanese created it after the US landings on Leyte in October 1944. The ceremony formally inaugurating the *makapili* was held on December 8, 1944—the third anniversary of the attack on Pearl Harbor. Most of its members had either lived in Japan or were individuals alienated from the mainstream of Filipino society. They fought for Japan, not the Second Republic. As a consequence, the Japanese had confidence in the *makapili* in a way that they never had in any other Filipino group and saw as its essential mission to do counterinsurgency work against Filipino guerrillas. The *makapili* was never that large; estimates put its numbers between five thousand and seven thousand. While the return of the Americans raised questions about collaboration among Filipinos, there was little confusion about the *makapili*. They were nothing more than traitors.[39]

Armed groups on both sides contributed to the downward spiral of the Philippine economy during the occupation. A number of large landowners and managers of agricultural businesses fled the countryside for Manila to escape the violence. Fields went fallow, or tenant farmers converted empty fields into farms for the production of their own food. This phenomenon was particularly widespread in the sugar industry, which had sold ninety percent of its crop to the United States in the prewar years.[40]

The result was that support for Japan faded. Sergeant Major Marioka Sakae, who worked in the political and economic branch of the *kempei tai*, noted this decline. Marioka's job had been to regulate and enforce food prices. As food became scarcer, he saw Filipinos who had cooperated with the Japanese early in the war change sides and take up arms against Japan.[41]

During their three years in the archipelago, the Japanese never gained total control of any island in the Philippines. In some cases, the Filipino guerrillas and the prewar commonwealth government remained in control. Panay is a good example. On Luzon, where the Japanese had better control, the irregular threat was still a real concern. A Japanese journalist noted, "The threat of the guerrillas constantly hung over occupied Manila. It constituted the chief problem for the Japanese military administration and cropped up in almost every conversation with Japanese officials and Filipino newsmen." The East Central Luzon Guerrilla Area, an irregular unit of forty thousand under the command of 1st Lieutenant Edwin Ramsey, a U.S. Army officer who had refused to surrender to the Japanese in 1942, initiated a sabotage campaign in Manila in the summer of 1944 that blew up a ship in Manila Bay; the resulting inferno spread to several others. This guerrilla unit also burned Piers 5 and 7 in the South Port area.[42]

The destruction Manila had seen so far in the war was nothing at all compared to what was about to come. Nothing at all.

3

Returning to Luzon

At 9:30 a.m., the 1st Battalion, 129th Infantry Regiment, 37th Infantry Division reached the sands of Luzon. "Landing not opposed" is the terse description in the unit journal.[1] The final stage of Douglas MacArthur's return had started. This effort was more challenging for the United States than it appears in retrospect. While the Americans had a significant advantage over the Japanese in both material supplies and manpower numbers, they faced serious challenges. The ability of the U.S. Army to adapt and move quickly would be one of the more significant factors in this operation. The landing in Lingayen was the first key event in shaping the Battle of Manila.

The amphibious landings were by their very nature a joint Army–Navy operation and MacArthur refused to have a joint commander in his theater, not wanting another flag officer who might undercut his authority. He knew that Walter Krueger had much experience working with the other services, which gave him the ability to do joint planning. Krueger would have preferred to have command authority over all the assets in the invasion, but he knew what the moment demanded, explaining after the war to the Armed Forces Staff College that joint operations required the "close and sympathetic understanding on the part of the members of each service, whether army, navy, or air force, of the powers, limitations, and requirements of the other services." There is no doubt that attitude existed in the Sixth Army. There was also good communication between the services. Krueger and the commanding officer of the Seventh Fleet, Vice Admiral Thomas C. Kinkaid, were both on the USS *Wasatch* as the invasion force made its way to Luzon. He took little for granted. "We were blessed with a great deal of luck." Had the Japanese mounted a serious defense, he doubted the system would have held up for long.[2]

The professional climate among the Sixth Army staff allowed for an honest exchange of ideas and differences with navy and air force officers. This pattern

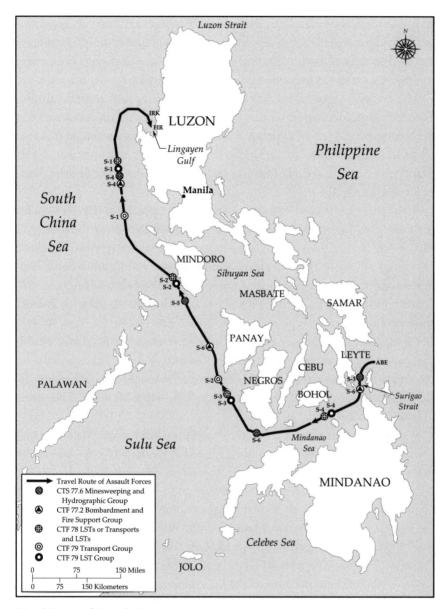

Travel Route of Assault Forces

started at the top, with the commanding general, and permeated the organization. Krueger and officers in the other services adopted what some have called a "managerial approach," which was the direct product of the creation of the professional military education system in the late nineteenth and early twentieth centuries. In essence, the staff colleges and war colleges of this system had promoted the concept that the various branches of the US military had established standards, skills, and knowledge unique to them. The best way to achieve success was to combine these skills and work together as a team.[3]

The invasion force arrived in the Lingayen Gulf in four separate groups. Even in transit, MacArthur's headquarters and Krueger's Sixth Army staff had different expectations. MacArthur thought that the Japanese would make no effort to interdict their passage, while Krueger and his men anticipated a serious Japanese naval action, similar to the one at Leyte that became the Battle of Leyte Gulf.[4]

What they got was something in between. The passage to Luzon was, for the most part, uneventful—even boring. Soldiers whiled away the time with mail from home, books, card games, regular religious services, checkers, chess, and other board games. Many found enough administrative and command routines to keep them busy. Others cleaned their weapons or exercised. Chatting and gossiping with other soldiers kept their minds off what awaited them on Luzon.

All that ended on January 4 when Japanese pilots on kamikaze missions hit the ships. One plane destroyed the carrier *Ommaney Bay*. "The action was so fast and so continuous that it is hard to sort out the images of what happened," Bill Chickering, a correspondent with Time-Life, wrote his wife. "They came in from all sides."[5]

Watching the kamikaze attacks from his command ship was Major General Oscar W. Griswold. The commanding general of the XIV Corps—one of the main subordinate units of the Sixth Army—Griswold was part of a prominent Nevada family (a cousin had been governor) and a member of the West Point Class of 1910. In 1945, he was fifty-eight years old and on his second war. He had served on the Western Front in World War I and had been wounded, receiving the Purple Heart. Nicknamed "Griz," he had taught in the Reserve Officers' Training Corps (ROTC) program at Syracuse University in the interwar period and was in command of his second corps, having been the commanding general of IV Corps during the 1941 Louisiana maneuvers. He had been in command of the XIV for two years. MacArthur considered him one of the best field commanders in his theater and would put his name forward to take command of the Tenth U.S. Army in June, when its commander was killed during the Battle of Okinawa. The Corps had a good deal of experience, having fought at Guadalcanal, Munda, and Bougainville.[6] Griswold was

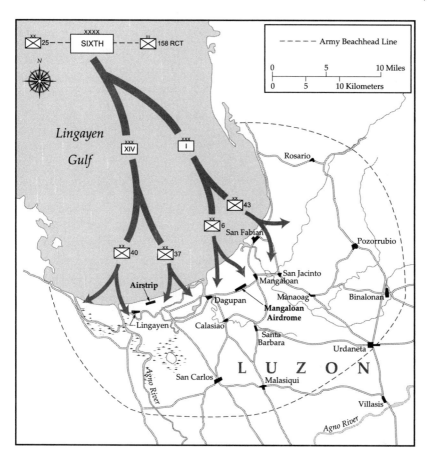

Luzon Landings

in good position to observe. The air was clear, and he had fine visibility. "It is one of the most spectacular things I have seen in this war to date," he wrote in his diary. "You've got to hand it to the Jap—he has guts!"[7]

On January 6, another plane hit the USS *New Mexico* on the port side of the bridge. The battleship's heavy armor kept it from suffering any major structural damage, but the blast killed the ship's commanding officer, Captain Robert Walton Fleming; the British Army observer on MacArthur's staff, Lieutenant-General Sir Herbert Lumsden; a Royal Navy lieutenant; and Chickering. Individuals standing fifteen feet away from the point of impact— including Admiral Sir Bruce Fraser, the new commander-in-chief of the British Pacific Fleet—were unharmed. In his report to the Admiralty, a shaken Fraser attempted to draw lessons from this experience for his new fleet, but his biographer believes that the main purpose of the trip was so that the admiral could face the danger of the kamikazes, a danger he would not face as a land-based commander. He had a sense of guilt over the needless deaths of both his lieutenant and Lumsden, and he never talked about this incident again.[8]

Chickering's death received significant attention at the time. *Life* magazine devoted a full page to it. Both MacArthur and Krueger paid him tribute. Carl Mydans, another Time-Life correspondent, told Chickering's widow that MacArthur called her husband "one of the greatest and one of the most honest correspondents he had ever known." Krueger, despite his sour nature, acknowledged his skill: "No-one out here can ever take the place of Bill Chickering."[9]

After personally explaining the circumstances of Chickering's death to Mydans, MacArthur leaned over the railing of the USS *Boise* and cast an eye toward the sea. "We land tomorrow," he remarked, "and there'll be no opposition. We'll walk in." His intentions were straightforward. He was going to move south as fast as he could before the Japanese could respond.[10]

Griswold, though, knew the human cost of what was about to happen. "Tomorrow is landing day on Luzon," he wrote in his diary. "It will be a bitter fight. As I looked at the ships bearing the XIV Corps, my heart was sad. I know some of my boys who are on these ships will, by this time tomorrow, have laid down their lives."[11] He dreaded what was about to happen yet saw it as redemptive. "War is a terrible thing—yet it is the only medium by which the U.S. can keep alive the American institutions."[12]

The landing beach awaiting Griswold and his men was in the Lingayen-Mabilao area, located at the base of the gulf. This region had a well-developed road network, which would allow the Sixth Army to expand the beachhead quickly. There was also enough space for airfields that could support the ground troops. Krueger expected a counterattack, and believed he could anchor the flanks of his command in time to hold off the Japanese.[13]

Krueger had another reason for picking this beach. He wanted to surprise the defenders. He expected the Japanese would look at the difficult terrain to the west of the beaches and dismiss this area as a probable landing area. As he explained later in a speech to cadets at West Point, "Although aware that these beaches were not the best available and were at times subject to high surf, and that wide estuaries, rivers and fish ponds obstructed the littoral, I had nevertheless chose them, because of my belief that the Japs would not expect us to land there, and I was not mistaken."[14]

Krueger was underestimating his opponent, which he normally did not do. In a postwar interview with US military intelligence officers, Yamashita explained that he and his staff had taken bets on where they thought the landing would take place. The general thought the odds were six to four, Lingayen over Batangas. Major Hori Rizo, Yamashita's chief of intelligence, agreed with him. Based on the US invasion of Mindoro, which took place in December and which seemed like a feint, the Japanese expected the full weight of the US force to arrive on Luzon. Their interception of US radio signals convinced them that the Americans considered their deception effort a success. Based on the intervals between previous US amphibious landings, Yamashita expected that the Americans would arrive in the Lingayen Gulf between January 10 and 20. He was off by a day.[15]

It made little difference. Yamashita knew his command was doomed. His objective was to engage with as many US units for as long as possible to keep the enemy away from Japan. Fighting on the beaches—with few places to shield themselves from US naval gunfire—would play to the advantages of the Americans and undercut his own goals. The Americans conducting these interviews were astonished and simply refused to believe that the Japanese had been in the know.[16] The weight of evidence supports Yamashita's explanation.[17]

As the landing craft approached the beaches, what stood out was what did not happen. The major underwater obstacles simply did not exist. Intelligence had suggested the presence of a controlled minefield in the water in front of the town of Lingayen. "If the troops have to land at Lingayen beach," Vice Admiral Theodore Wilkinson stated quietly, "we'll go in, mines or no mines." That statement says as much about Wilkinson as it does about the Army–Navy relations in the theater. The U.S. Navy had spent the previous three days clearing the path to the beaches of Lingayen. "Fortunately, the mine-field was found to exist merely on the Jap chart," Krueger remarked.[18]

As the landing craft moved forward, the U.S. Navy unleashed what Griswold called a "savage naval bombardment."[19] The ships of the Seventh Fleet found no Japanese resistance to their efforts and ran out of targets.[20] Min Hara, a U.S. Army Japanese linguist, was astonished to watch battleships move sideways from the recoil of their guns. He was further impressed with the gunfire of the U.S. Navy: "The whole Gulf was full of floating brass shells which reminded me of timberland cut down with nothing but tree stumps." John Higgins, an infantryman in the 169th Regiment, was in a landing craft that made its way ashore as shells from the USS *California* arced over them: "Most of us could not hear for a long while after."[21] Arthur Coleman of the 37th Infantry Division was a gunner on an amtrack, and was glad to see this raw naval power: "I was apprehensive as were most all the way in but I think after so many months of training and waiting they were glad to start fighting. There was no return fire. The entire beachhead was virtually unopposed."[22]

Most of the men on the beaches were grateful for the lack of opposition. Leonard Hall, a soldier in the 43rd Infantry Division, had strong recollections of the first moments on shore: "We reached the beach without opposition and gawked at the huge fragments of naval shells. Someone remarked that it seemed impossible for a puissant to have survived such barrage but some two hundred yards inland we encountered scores of Filipinos." Ray E. Hale of the 6th Infantry Division welcomed the easy landing: "There was some bloodshed, but it wasn't nearly as serious as we thought it would be because they did a heck of a job in the Navy and Air Corps."[23] Some thought the situation too good to be true. Correspondents for *Yank* magazine were at the frontlines with the infantry. These reporters found many foot soldiers uneasy at how simple it all had been.[24]

The biggest problem the US assault force faced initially was the rough water. The surf was only four feet in height during the landing, but it increased significantly the next day.[25] These issues with the tides and waves led to situations that would have been quite serious had the Japanese been contesting the landing. Corporal Robert H. Kiser was in the first landing wave, and his ship became stuck. He and the men of C Company, 1st Battalion, 148th Infantry Regiment in the 37th Infantry Division had to wade to shore in waist-deep water. The 37th Cavalry Reconnaissance Troop, Mechanized, which was attached to but not part of the 37th Infantry Division, was in one of the later landing waves and its landing ship ran aground on a sand bar two hundred yards off the coast. It would be stuck there for sixteen hours. Another Landing Craft Infantry (LCI) got stuck as well and almost capsized. Yukio Kawamoto, a Japanese linguist in the 37th Infantry Division, noted that he was "never wounded, but nearly drowned at Lingayen landing due to our LCI hitting a sand bar about 100 yards out."[26]

Father Juan Labrador, a Catholic priest from Spain and academic administrator first at the Colegio de San Juan de Letran and then the University of Santo Tomás, was watching the shelling from the receiving end on Luzon, and he had a much different reaction. The Japanese had abandoned the area. "All the liberators lamented the destruction caused by their equipment," he wrote in his diary. "They were as useless as they were unnecessary."[27] The reaction of most Filipinos was far different. Crowds were forming a parade in Lingayen, waving American and Philippine flags. The U.S. Navy had to hold its fire while planes dropped leaflets telling them to disperse. No one seemed to grasp that the crowds were a good indicator that there were no Japanese to shell.[28]

In a radio report, William J. Dunn of CBS called the invasion of Lingayen "an almost bloodless landing." He told his listeners he had seen four major amphibious operations, but "yesterday's assault was, at once, the dullest and most thrilling of my experience."[29]

There remained a real edge of danger to this operation, and the Japanese showed they still posed a threat. "What worried me most, I guess, was the threat from the air," James E. Caudle, a soldier in the 37th Infantry Division, recalled. "We controlled the skies, but we heard a lot about kamikazes, and surely enough, some of them were out that day."[30] Caudle had reason to worry. Japanese kamikazes found a number of ships. Seven hit HMAS *Australia* during the operation. The USS *Columbia* was also hit. "A dramatic sight—a terrific blast, smoke, fire, etc.," General Griswold noted in his diary. Despite the damage and casualties, the ship resumed its bombardment after a few minutes.[31]

When Stanley Frankel, a lieutenant in the 37th Infantry Division, landed, the shelling was still ongoing. "As I hit dry land I pulled out my shovel and began digging like hell. I was almost underground, frantically throwing the wet sand all around the hole." The shelling let up and he started to hear strange noises. "This was the sound of human voices yelling, 'Veectorie!' I looked up and to my astonishment I recognized the friendly faces of a dozen Filipinos, who were swarming all around us."[32]

The Japanese perspective was significantly different. "The bombardment from 600 ships was dreadful," Nagata Takeji, a Japanese soldier recalled. "Trees were uprooted. Cows and horses were blasted sky high."[33] This devastation was exactly what MacArthur wanted. He went ashore later in the day and told reporters that the situation was "better than could be expected."[34] The biggest military operation of his career looked more like a field training exercise than a combat operation. He had outsmarted Yamashita and was on his way to Manila. He decided to celebrate that evening with a quart of ice cream. (This dessert was a small privilege of rank in theater.)[35] There was a realization among MacArthur's staff that it would take a while to take full control of Luzon, particularly in remote places that worked to the advantage of the

Japanese infantry soldier. "But he won't last long in essential places," Brigadier General Bonner Fellers stated.[36] Father Juan had a similar view, "The enemy had lost the battle of Luzon when it allowed the gigantic invading equipment to land unopposed," he wrote in his diary on February 4.[37]

Dunn offered the American radio-listening public a guarded alternative view. "No one expects," he reported, "the Jap to give up this island without a fight but its becoming more and more obvious that he's waiting until he can draw us into combat on something near his own terms."[38]

The Americans returned to Luzon with many strengths. The U.S. Army had ample supplies, good weather, numerous sources of water, and a Filipino public that was willing, and even eager, to provide labor for construction projects. The railroads and paved roads on the island were in working order, requiring almost no new repair or construction efforts. While the Japanese had done no maintenance work for the previous two-and-a-half years, fuel shortages had limited wear and tear on these thoroughfares. Most Filipinos traveled about using bicycles or horse-drawn carriages. These factors, along with the Army's proven administrative structure, allowed supply and con-struction projects to operate on a twenty-four-hour basis.

Another advantage MacArthur enjoyed was a gifted Signal Corps officer on his staff. Major General Spencer B. Akin had been part of the small group that had escaped Corregidor in 1942 with MacArthur. Akin had focused on making signal units mobile since the Louisiana maneuvers in 1941, which was a series of exercises that tested training and doctrine that ultimately involved one-quarter of the U.S. Army. Signalmen landed on Lingayen beach on January 9. Within an hour, they had established a high-frequency radio relay on Luzon that put MacArthur in contact with his ground forces.[39] Communication was never going to be a problem for the U.S. Army on Luzon.

* * *

While the landings were a lopsided military operation, the Americans began facing logistical problems almost the very moment soldiers stepped on the beach. On Luzon, MacArthur's command was attempting, in the words of Colonel H. D. Vogel, an engineering officer on the Sixth Army staff, "a radical departure from earlier procedures" used in the war. Up to this point, quar-termaster units that were part of the Sixth Army had been responsible for supplying the combat units. Under the approach implemented in this cam-paign, an Army service command, which was a separate unit, was responsible for supplying the Sixth. The command was also responsible for overseeing military engineering projects.[40] Although this allowed for professional specialization, it created the potential for bureaucratic confrontation and redundancy. The strain of combat would determine the soundness of this idea.

The Americans also faced significant supply issues. The uncontested landing caught quartermaster units unprepared to begin immediate unloading operations. The men of the 37th Infantry Division's band were doing duty as dock workers, but there was nothing for them to do. Frank F. Matthis, one of the bandsmen, remembered going for a swim in the surf as he waited for the war to start.[41]

While the railroad tracks on Luzon were in fine shape, the rolling stock, and the fuel to power them, was absent. One solution was to put jeeps on the railroads with flanged wheels and have them haul freight cars. "Though this was not very effective, it helped," Krueger stated. The main problem was that the service command lacked both the trucks required to get equipment to frontline units and the cranes to unload ships rapidly. Transportation officers prioritized the unloading of ships holding trucks. Still facing shortfalls, companies, battalions, and brigades provided their own transportation assets to get supplies or reduced supply requests. The crane issue was more significant and it took much longer to solve because parts for new cranes had to be assembled and activated. The limited number of supply dumps and their often-inconvenient locations only complicated these transportation issues.[42]

Another problem was the unpredictable nature of the waves in the gulf. Unloading operations often had to stop after dark because the water was too choppy. Since it was winter, the days were short and the beachmasters had short windows of time in which to operate. On one occasion, quartermaster units had to stop unloading efforts for twenty-four hours.[43] The tides were so bad that they kept Griswold from establishing his headquarters on January 10. His ship had to turn back because of what he called "dangerously high surf."[44]

Krueger managed to reach the beach on the January 10 to see the situation for himself. The I Corps was on the east side of the beachhead, which was on the left, while the XIV Corps occupied the west side on the right. He decided to shut down unloading operations on the right side of his lines and concentrate efforts in the zone of I Corps. All these complications created additional strain. The unloading on the left would have to serve both the I and XIV Corps. This decision created traffic problems inland for Griswold's command. Krueger understood this complication but it was "unavoidable."[45]

As a result of the problems, the Sixth Army was vulnerable to counterattack. Krueger admitted after the war: "If the enemy, who had some 72,000 troops in the mountains northeast of our landing area, had promptly launched a determined large-scale attack against our eastern flank, it would have had most serious results."[46]

Things looked a bit different to the Japanese. Major General Konuma Haruo, the chief of staff of Yamashita's Fourteenth Area Army, later noted that the Japanese had intended to attack Krueger's flank in an effort to slow or stop the American march toward Manila. In fact, it never got started, because the Sixth Army moved faster than they had expected.[47]

There was also a breakdown in communications among the Japanese. In Manila, no officer had any firsthand information. As a result, their assessment was superficial, and wishful thinking often substituted for reasoned analysis. Major General Kobayashi told the men of his command that the slowness of the American advance was the product of attrition: "The enemy has with difficulty made a landing in Lingayen Gulf, but more than one third of his shipping has been sunk by our Special Attack units."[48] He did not want to admit that MacArthur had just undone weeks of work. The south-facing fortifications were doing little to stop an attack from the north.

As noted, the Americans had expected more resistance. Although they faced serious problems, they held the advantage in ways large and small over the defenders. Transportation and communication between the Japanese Fourteenth Area Army headquarters and its subordinate units was intermittent. Strong US air power required that transportation take place under the cover of darkness when it would be difficult for planes to spot military units on the roads.[49]

The start of the Luzon campaign had gone stunningly well for the Americans. There was, nonetheless, more work to do before the U.S. Army could reach Manila. Getting there meant overcoming differences within the Army. Indeed, clashes between generals seemed to present bigger obstacles than anything posed by the Japanese defenders.

4

The March South

On D-Day + 5, Douglas MacArthur established his headquarters ashore. His advanced staff took over the Lingayen provincial capitol complex that was located four blocks from the beach and 150 miles from Manila. There was a small airstrip within walking distance of these buildings. Officers and men pitched tents among the bushes and small trees. MacArthur's residence was in an old school. The air was hot and humid, and the blackout drapes installed in the capitol cut off the circulation of air, limiting the ventilation. MacArthur's staff would operate in this area for two weeks.[1]

The first major piece of business for MacArthur was responding to a cable from the War Department, inquiring whether he would support Walter Krueger's promotion to the rank of General. For MacArthur, there was no question. He had Lieutenant General Richard Sutherland, his chief of staff, write as he dictated a response. MacArthur had been a flag officer in the U.S. Army for close to thirty years. As a result, he knew most of the individuals in the service holding flag rank to one degree or another. Krueger, he stated, deserved a fourth star more than George S. Patton, Jr., or Omar Bradley. "I know both Krueger and Patton intimately and I believe not only that Krueger is an abler army commander but I believe his contribution is more outstanding than that of Patton." Later in the year when there was talk in Washington of sending Bradley to the Pacific, MacArthur was unenthusiastic. "Bradley is junior to Krueger and the latter is in my opinion is not only the more competent officer of the two but is entirely familiar with this theater."[2]

While this matter of the promotion seemed fairly straightforward, there was a subtext. Krueger and Sutherland had never gotten along well, and Sutherland, as MacArthur's chief of staff and deputy commander, had always had the upper hand. That was about to change. Krueger would outrank him. Sutherland was technically still under house arrest, and MacArthur was giving him the humiliating job of processing the paperwork to give his rival higher rank. Sutherland had once said that MacArthur needed him because he could never play the role of a "son of a bitch." He was learning in blunt fashion that he had been wrong.[3]

Sutherland was unwilling to tolerate this treatment. Two days later, he told MacArthur he was leaving Luzon to get medical and dental treatment. He had tooth decay, fungus on his feet, and an ear infection. These ailments were, in themselves, minor, even if they were causing him some real pain. He would travel first to medical facilities on the island of Tolosa, and, if that failed, he would go back to Australia. MacArthur was flabbergasted. There were many doctors and dentists in the command. There was only one reason for Sutherland to return to Australia. When Chief Warrant Officer Paul P. Rogers delivered some documents to the general office, MacArthur took a quick glance and then remarked in what Rogers called a soft growl: "A general who leaves his post in the middle of a battle . . ." He did not finish his thought. There was no need. Rogers had been on MacArthur's staff in 1941 and 1942 and had been part of the group that escaped from Corregidor with him in patrol torpedo (PT) boats. He had known danger firsthand. Rogers had worked directly for Sutherland in the years since and knew the man well. Like MacArthur, he could not understand his boss's behavior.[4]

Sutherland's departure tempest temporarily resolved his status, but MacArthur still needed to fix a problem with Krueger. While MacArthur supported Krueger's promotion, he was becoming more and more frustrated with the slowness of his subordinate's advance into the interior of Luzon. As the Sixth Army marched south from the Lingayen beachhead, gaps were opening up between units and Krueger faced three significant groups of Japanese infantry, two directly in front of him. General Yamashita Tomoyuki also had 150,000 in the mountains of northern Luzon, which put them on a left flank that was unsecured. Krueger's headquarters' concern was that the Japanese were trying to overextend the Americans. There were several spots the staff saw as vulnerable, believing that if the Japanese hit them there it would bring operations to a standstill.[5]

The response of the Sixth Army was safe and careful. As one journalist in the Philippines noted, "Krueger uses a steam-roller to crush an eggshell, but on the other hand he never dents his steam-roller."[6] MacArthur was less than pleased with this caution. Yamashita, he believed, lacked the ability to

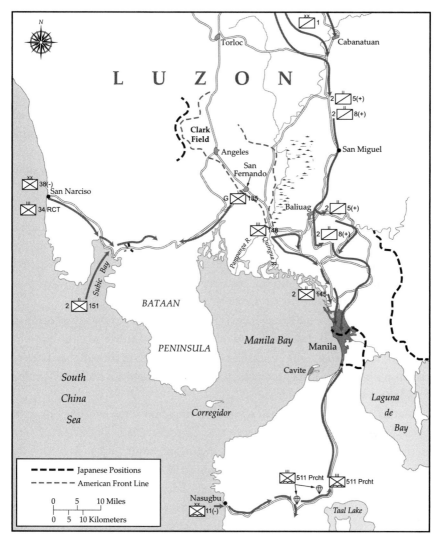

Approach to Manila

maneuver. If he tried to move into the open, the U.S. Army Air Forces, which owned the skies, could pound him without pause. "The futility of trying to conduct ground operation in the face of hostile and dominating air power was never more demonstrated," General George Kenney stated. Major General Konuma Haruo, the chief of staff of the Japanese Fourteenth Area Army, confirmed this assessment after the war. Konuma explained in a debriefing that it was exceptionally difficult to conduct mobile defense in the face of US air superiority. Despite what MacArthur thought, the Americans were moving much faster than the Japanese, at least, expected.[7]

As a result, MacArthur and others believed the gaps and unsecured flanks were not as important as Krueger feared. As Rogers notes in his memoirs, there was a general sentiment among MacArthur's staff that Krueger's indecision reflected the fact that he was out of his depth. After he returned from Australia, Sutherland announced in front of others, "If I were commanding the Sixth Army, we'd be in Manila right now." The rift was coming out into the open as William J. Dunn, a reporter for CBS Radio, notes in his memoirs.[8]

Krueger's main objective on Luzon was to find and do battle with the Fourteenth Area Army. The problem was MacArthur wanted a geographic location—Manila—to be the primary objective. The disconnect was fundamental. Krueger expected to take and liberate the city, but he simply was not going to rush the job. "I did not consider a precipitate advance for that purpose feasible with the forces initially available to me."[9]

Given his main focus, Krueger never made any real plans for urban combat. What makes this all the more confounding is that—unlike MacArthur—he expected an eventual fight for the city. His main concern, though, had been to establish a beachhead and protect his force from Yamashita's soldiers. Planning for Manila was a step too far.[10]

MacArthur and Krueger had several meetings about the strategic direction of the Luzon campaign. On January 12, Krueger and Clyde D. Eddleman went to the USS *Boise* for a conference with the theater commander. According to Krueger's account, he made it clear he needed a secure base before he could attack the south. While loyal to Krueger, Eddleman offers a dramatically different version of events. It was "the only time I ever saw the two of them when they had cross words." MacArthur peppered Krueger with questions and challenges: What kind of casualties was he taking? Why hold back the I Corps on his eastern flank? Krueger resisted. "The old man stuck to his guns, Eddleman explained, "but he didn't feel too good going back across Lingayen Gulf to our flag ship."[11]

Frustrated with Krueger's invasion pace, MacArthur took all sorts of actions to get him to move faster. "General Krueger had to withstand considerable pressure from MacArthur to prevent pulling apart and exposing the flank of XIV Corps to the Japanese concentration on the eastern side of the central plain," George H. Decker, chief of staff, Sixth Army, recalled.[12]

MacArthur went around Krueger. On January 14, he visited the XIV Corps headquarters and those of the 37th and 40th Infantry Divisions. He let Major General Oscar W. Griswold know it was time to take risks. In his diary, the corps commander recorded that MacArthur "said he expected little opposition—that the battle of the Philippines had already been won on Leyte." Griswold was less inclined to take this gamble. "I do not have his optimism."[13]

On January 21, MacArthur visited Sixth Army headquarters and discussed operations in the screened-in porch of the wooden shack that Krueger used as a command post and that contained his personal library. MacArthur again tried to prod him. Again, he failed. On the way back to his own headquarters, the general told his personal physician, "Walter is pretty stubborn. Maybe I'll have to try something else."[14]

MacArthur began using carrots and sticks. He moved his headquarters to Hacienda Luisita, a sugar plantation near the city of Tarlac. The plantation had much to offer. The officers stayed in bungalows rather than in tents. MacArthur lived in the residence of the hacienda's general manager, which had a small, but well-tended, tree-lined lawn. The offices were in a one-story building that was within walking distance. These facilities improved the living and work conditions of the staff, but what was really important about this location was that his headquarters was ten miles further south than the command post of the Sixth Army in Calasiao, putting him closer to the frontlines than Krueger.[15]

Despite his relative luxury, MacArthur regularly visited units in combat. On one inspection, MacArthur accidentally went ahead of his own troops and was therefore, for a few moments, out in the lead of the US advance on Luzon. He also reprimanded Robert S. Beightler's 37th Infantry Division for a sluggish performance.[16] Gossip, meanwhile, was swirling about the MacArthur–Krueger confrontation. Robert Eichelberger wrote in his diary, "Lee Van Atta informed me that General MacArthur had been laying down the law to Krueger about the slow advance at Lingayen and that he had given him the ultimatum to be in Manila by the 5th of February."[17]

A major point of contention between the two generals was air power. MacArthur tended to think in more three-dimensional terms than Krueger. The United States controlled the skies. "Air support, after the landings, was generally excellent," Eddleman observed. In fact, Major Isaac Hoppenstein of the 11th Airborne Division recalled that he had not seen one Japanese plane in the air. That advantage allowed the United States to take the calculated gambles MacArthur wanted. The assistant chief of staff of the Fourteenth Area Army, Major General Nishimura Toshio, admitted that MacArthur's view was basically correct. Japan had lost control of the air rapidly in late December and early January and was at a significant disadvantage as a result.[18]

Krueger understood air power as well—he had actually attended the U.S. Army flight school in an effort to earn pilot wings—but his view was more ground-centric than MacArthur's. He continued to believe that a rapid advance, which created gaps between units and ignored the large Japanese force in northern Luzon, was unwise. Air power simply lacked the permanent presence to make up the difference.[19]

Even if he were inclined to move in what he considered a reckless fashion, supply and transportation problems limited his mobility. One of the key issues he and the Sixth Army faced in Luzon was the rebuilding of bridges. As the general noted, this requirement put "inordinate demands upon my engineers, but they never failed me."[20] Griswold might not have liked his commanding officer much, but he came to much the same conclusion. In his diary, he noted: "Logistic situation is much more serious than enemy is thus far." Getting across waterways was the real problem. "The bridging problem is considerable."[21]

MacArthur wanted to move faster when Krueger only wanted fast, but, in the end, there was only so far MacArthur would go in applying pressure. He was not going to meddle with the command of the Sixth Army. He had a theater to run and there was only so much he could do. As Rogers noted, "MacArthur's aggravation was not all that deep." He knew enough to know that Krueger had a point.[22] In many ways, as he also knew, he had been unreasonable in the demands he put on Kruger.[23] Despite that fact, Krueger responded to the prodding, particularly after MacArthur had put himself closer to the enemy than Sixth Army headquarters. "It had the right effect," Roger O. Egeberg, MacArthur's doctor explained. "Krueger moved everything he could right up forward."[24]

Yamashita would soon prove that both Krueger and MacArthur had valid arguments. He saw the opportunities that the gaps between US units offered and tried to take advantage of the situation by ordering an attack. His subordinate commanders were slow, and even timid, in following through and it never posed a serious threat to the Sixth Army.[25]

* * *

By late January, Krueger had put some of his best units in a position to take Manila. The XIV Corps was the main operational force, occupying the western flank as the Americans moved south. The corps had a good deal of experience, having fought at Guadalcanal, Munda, and Bougainville. Griswold is not one of the better-known generals of World War II, but he knew how to lead in combat. Before he ended his career, he would receive the Legion of Merit, the Distinguished Service Medal, the Silver Star, and the command of a field army. After the war, he told the superintendent of the U.S. Military Academy, "To me, successful combat leadership down to and including the regiment means that the responsible commander possesses, not one, but a host of diversified qualities, including character, integrity, aggressiveness, force, knowledge, emotional stability, physical fitness, personal example, and experience."[26]

Griswold also believed that not every officer had these skills to the same degree, which is why a junior officer in command of an infantry company might not make a good regimental commander. To move into higher levels of command, an officer needed certain other skills, including "a keen appreciation of the value of discipline, and basic working knowledge of human nature."[27]

Griswold also believed military leadership required hardness, or at least the ability to "recognize mediocrity and to eliminate it promptly from all echelons of the command." At the same time, a commander had to be fair. To expect inexperienced units to perform in the same manner as veteran units was simply unrealistic. The question was whether, given the circumstances, better leadership was possible: "If at any time the answer to this question is in the affirmative, relief of the subordinate concerned must be accomplished promptly without fear, favor or affection."[28]

Griswold knew that with this approach he had ruined careers. "This is a distasteful job—one which bothers all conscientious higher echelon combat commanders." It was necessary, though, especially if commanders had to work with the less professional elements of the U.S. Army. "It is particularly applicable to cases where National Guard or Reserve Divisions are called into Federal Service for active operations under their own officers."[29]

One of the divisions under Griswold's command was the 37th Infantry Division, which was originally a National Guard unit from Ohio. Others had different views of their combat readiness. Bruce Palmer, after a long career in the U.S. Army, one that included a brief stint as the acting chief of staff, which required him to oversee all elements of the service, looked back on his wartime service in the Philippines and remarked, "There really wasn't a heck of a lot of difference between an AUS [Army of the United States] division—one that was started from scratch—or a Regular Army division or a Guard division. They were essentially the same."[30]

In fact, after three years of fighting, the 37th Division earned a reputation as one of the best units in the theater. It had been a federalized formation and had men from every state in the Union in its ranks. "The overall impression the 37th gives you is one of power and competence," Sergeant John McLeod wrote in *Yank* magazine. "It's a big, tough, skilled division for a big, tough job. It's a heavyweight." Estanislado Reyna, an enlisted man in the unit, recalled, "The training was hard." Despite his feelings toward the National Guard, Griswold appreciated the 37th, calling it "one of the outstanding combat Divisions in the Pacific Theater." One statistic points to the high level of discipline in the division. During the campaign on Luzon, which included the Battle of Manila, all but one division in the XIV Corps lost more men to disease than combat—the 37th Infantry Division.[31]

Griswold attributed much of its success to the division's commanding general, Beightler. Griswold called him "able, active and competent," a man "of force, character and integrity" who "possessed in high degree the will and force to eliminate deadwood in any and all ranks and grades." Acting along those lines, Beightler, just before the Luzon operation, reviewed all personnel in his division and removed anyone who was medically or psychologically unable to take part in combat operations.[32]

Beightler was the only Guard officer to retain command of his division throughout the war. While many might see that as an indication of the regular Army's bias against the Guard, it was a reflection of Beightler's skill and competence. Like many Guard officers, he owed some of his professional success to partisan politics. Born and raised in Ohio, he attended Ohio State University, majoring in civil engineering but dropping out after his sophomore year to take a job as the assistant engineer for Union County. Beightler joined the National Guard and went to war in 1917, serving in the 42nd Infantry Division, or the "rainbow division," during the time Colonel Douglas MacArthur was its chief of staff. After the war, he became an engineer in the state's highway department.

In 1926, Beightler took a leave of absence from the highway department to attend a short course designed for Guard and reserve officers at the U.S. Army Command & General Staff College. His classmates were Dwight D.

Eisenhower, Eichelberger, and Joseph W. Stilwell. He was elected mayor of Marble Cliff, OH, but his marriage was falling apart (he and his wife divorced in 1933) and he decided to attend another short course at the Army War College rather than serving out his term in office. He then secured an active-duty assignment to serve on the general staff in Washington, DC, where he became better acquainted with Eisenhower and Eichelberger. He also got to know the chief of staff of the U.S. Army, General Douglas MacArthur, as he put it, "fairly well."

Krueger returned to the general staff while Beightler was in Washington. Krueger had worked with Guard units several times before. Guard officers were, as far as he was concerned, an incompetent lot. Needless to say, Krueger and Beightler did not get along well with one another. After four years, Beightler returned to Ohio and, in 1939, his friend, John W. Bricker, who also happened to be the state's new Republican governor, named him the director of the Ohio Department of Highways. When Beightler remarried later that year, Bricker was his best man. A year later, Bricker made him the commander of the 37th Infantry Division.[33]

As a combat commander, Beightler liked to lead by example. He took this a bit too far during the Bougainville campaign in New Guinea, where he won a Silver Star for personally leading an infantry assault. He also relied on heavy artillery to provide fire support to maneuvering infantry units. This approach required a good deal of training, effective leadership from field grade officers, good communications, and it worked best in unpopulated areas. This method was effective and it kept US casualties down.[34] When off-duty in the isolated and undeveloped regions of MacArthur's command on Bougainville, Beightler, like his men, sat through motion pictures in the rain and read mysteries.[35]

Led by Griswold and Beightler, the XIV Corps and the 37th Division were part of the initial assault on Luzon. Beightler established division headquarters once he landed, but given the lack of opposition, the division kept moving and moving. Years later, Colonel Lawrence K. White, commanding officer of the 148th Infantry Regiment, stated, "I think it's fair to say that my regiment led the parade for about three weeks, all the way into Manila."[36] This quick progress had unintended consequences. Until he reached Manila, Beightler had to operate under tents in fields rather than in any type of permanent structure.[37]

To sustain the rapid advance, MacArthur's command needed to maintain communications between headquarters and the advanced elements. Signal Corps units were constantly establishing and reestablishing telephone networks. "I never thought I'd be climbing telephone poles at 2:00 in the morning, but I did plenty of that on the way to Manila," Delmore Evans, an artilleryman, recalled. "The Japanese were the greatest nuisances," he explained, "our tanks came to being a close second." They tended to break things: "If we strung the lines on the ground, the tracks cut them up, and if we tied them to the poles, their radio antennas broke them."[38]

Foot soldiers on the frontlines welcomed the unchallenged advance. "For the next two weeks the 37th Division, as if in payment for past hardships, probably enjoyed soldiering more than any other outfit in World War II," Frank Mathias, a member of the unit's band, later stated.[39] John Carney, a soldier in the 145th Regiment Infantry Regiment, chuckled as he recalled the advance south: "It wasn't very dangerous."[40] Griswold agreed with this assessment. The move south was not taxing his units. "Opposition light in XIV Corps sector," he noted in his diary.[41]

The Filipinos continued to welcome the Americans with enthusiasm. Individual soldiers were amazed at the warm greetings they were getting as they marched south "Landing in Luzon, Jan. '45, was like returning to civilization, rejoining society, being welcomed as liberators & victors over the Japanese," 1st Lieutenant Julius S. Gassner of the 37th Division noted in an assessment he did for the U.S. Army. "The Filipinos made us (me) feel appreciated, and that made our efforts seem worthwhile."[42] A foot soldier in the same division agreed. "I remember the excitement as people poured into the streets to greet us," James E. Caudle recalled in a questionnaire for Army historians.[43]

Contemporary accounts support the accuracy of those recollections. "There's an air of cheer we haven't seen before in the Philippines," Dunn told his radio audience. On Highway 3, he came across a huge sign made of woven bamboo that declared, "Welcome Our Liberators."[44]

Part of that welcome involved survival. Food had been in short supply during the occupation. Father Juan Labrador noted in his diary that the Americans were giving "food, medicines, clothes gratuitously." At one point during the drive south, a long, long line of men, women, and children formed at a 37th Infantry Division field kitchen, holding large leaves that they intended to use as plates. Soldiers of the division declined their hot meals, and the mess sergeants doled out helpings of chipped beef on toast on to these "plates." Labrador also observed that they were "demonetizing the Occupation bills issued by Japan and leveling all wealth to a communistic equality." The U.S.

Army was injecting both cash and assistance into the economy with a twofold purpose: defeat the Japanese and empower the recovery of the Philippines.[45]

Given the transportation issues on the beachhead, however, the Army started facing food shortages. On January 11, the 129th Infantry Regiment issued orders to its soldiers not to share rations with Filipinos or face court-martial charges. The men of the regiment ignored these instructions, and five days later, the commanding officer repeated the directive.[46] The attitude of Thomas Howard of the 754th Tank Battalion, which operated with the 129th, explains why that order had to be issued twice. Howard, who was in the rear echelon doing maintenance on the machines and guns, explained: "Little kids beg for food with an old number ten can with wire handles," he said. "You can't help but feel sorry for them, even going without part of your food yourself."[47]

Many of the Filipinos needed medical attention. Public health declined during the Japanese years due to a lack of supplies. Common issues included malnutrition, malaria, dysentery, and a number of assorted venereal diseases. Filipinos asked for help, and the Americans could hardly say no. The demands of the civilian population quickly overwhelmed U.S. Army medical resources and would continue to do so during the entire Luzon campaign.[48]

Army discipline held in areas where it mattered. As the soldiers of the XIV Corps discovered, the area around Lingayen was not particularly healthy. The terrain was littered with fishponds and rice paddies, and many troops lived in areas heavily populated with dogs, chickens, pigs, and children. "Such living conditions had surprisingly little effect upon the health of troops, and practically no cases of gastro-enterith or other communicable diseases were hospitalized," the XIV Corps after action report notes.[49]

While the general population welcomed the Americans, the guerrillas on Luzon gave them a mixed welcome. The Japanese invasion and occupation that had followed had divided an already diverse Filipino populace. Guerrilla bands were fighting for different reasons and had different objectives. Some were hostile toward one another, divided along political, cultural, or ethnic lines. Some Chinese groups were Nationalist, supporters of Chiang Kai-shek, and others were Communist. Some guerrillas were fighting only to keep their towns safe. Others were fighting for independence or social revolution.[50]

One guerrilla group, the ROTC Hunters, were pro-American, middle-class soldiers. "We kept our country's hopes alive," Rudy de Lara, who fought as a teenager, explained. "I like to believe I played a small role in the freedom our country came to enjoy."[51]

The Communist *Huks*, short for *Hukbalahops*, on the other hand, wanted real independence for the Philippines, not the sham version Tokyo had offered. This hostility toward Japan, however, did not make them pro-American. "I regard the GI's with mixed feelings," said Luis Taruc, a leader of the Huks. "When the Americans came in 1898 they crushed the people's movement that had come into being in the struggle against Spain." The Huks did not want independence on US terms. "History, we determined was not going to repeat itself," Taruc declared. "This time the Filipino people were not going to be crushed; they were going to win."[52]

Some other guerrilla groups were little better than bandits. They used the war as an opportunity to mask their criminal behavior. Their goals and motivation were plunder for economic gain, and they had no interest in issues of patriotism. They were more a threat to Filipinos than the Japanese.[53] The one thing that united these armed groups was hostility towards the occupiers.[54] "Three years they kill us," one guerrilla hissed to a US war correspondent. "Now we begin to kill."[55]

The Americans were aware of these divisions and divided themselves about the guerrilla bands. Many respected the *Huks* and their fighting ability. Others saw them as dangerous. "The Hukbalahops are very strong hereabouts," Griswold noted in his diary. "They go about armed, put in their own mayors, pillage where they will, and are quite truculent." He noted that MacArthur would not allow them to be disarmed—"a bad mistake in my opinion."[56]

Working with the guerrillas required finesse. The last thing MacArthur wanted was a Filipino civil war fought behind American lines. His intelligence officers had hoped that the guerrillas would see collecting information on the Japanese as their primary mission, but the Filipinos preferred fighting the Japanese. As things turned out, they were better at fighting than in gathering information.[57]

The public was another complication. Civilians showed up to welcome the Americans and often got in the way. As a 37th Infantry Division intelligence officer noted: "Although it would have been desirable from a security and tactical viewpoint to exclude all such individuals from the CP, it was physically impossible to do so and from a psychological point of view it might have been undesirable as we were coming to the Philippine as liberators not conquerors."[58]

Religion played a key role. "We are getting more and more surprised at the number of Catholics in the United States Army and we are edified by their religious fervor," Father Juan observed. "They are giving a very good and timely example to the toughs of Filipino Catholics who are in name only." The Catholic chaplains in the U.S. Army were simply unable to keep up with the demand of their soldiers, turning to Filipino priests to conduct services. Father Juan guessed that half the Americans were Catholic, although he noted that many Protestants attended Mass as well.[59]

* * *

While the Filipinos reveled in their gradual liberation, the Japanese waited, seething. The defenders were ready for the fight. Their training, as noted, was generally poor—even non-existent—but that did not matter to them. Even the ones who were aware that the Luzon campaign was doomed still believed in ultimate victory. First Class Private Miyakawa Takeo held onto this view even after he became a prisoner of war. "As a Japanese citizen, I cannot think otherwise," he explained.[60] Morale was good. The Japanese were supplied in adequate fashion in munitions and food rations.[61]

Many soldiers resented the Filipinos' pro-American attitude, seeing it (rightly) as dangerous. One Japanese soldier who survived an early skirmish with the 148th Infantry Regiment mixed in with the Filipinos greeting the Americans at Lingayen. He tried to surrender, but the battalion intelligence officer, thinking that he was a Filipino, told him to get lost. Knowing the fate that awaited him at the hands of the guerrillas, he refused to go. It was only when an interpreter arrived that the Americans learned he was Japanese.[62]

As the American march south continued, there were gunfire exchanges with Japanese defenders. These firefights were fairly small in the number of soldiers engaged and ended quickly. The weather was good. "I am really enjoying myself here in comparison to New Guinea," Mathias wrote his parents.[63] He was not the only one. "My first thought on seeing the open countryside after spending 17 months in the jungle was this is like going from night to day," Robert H. Kiser of the 148th Infantry Regiment recalled.[64]

The Japanese were still dangerous. Master Sergeant Mahlon Peden remembered watching the battalion surgeon Donald W. Whitehovee working in a tent at night with gasoline lanterns providing the illumination. He was amputating arms and legs, "and doing his best to save the ones that could be saved." It was a powerful moment. "I remember vividly laying the dying with the dead in a row as the moon light filtered through the trees. This picture is with me today just as if happened last night," he recalled fifty years later. A medical officer from MacArthur's headquarters later said that the surgeon had done one of the best jobs he had ever seen in the field. A few days later, Whitehovee was killed in a Japanese artillery barrage.[65]

Where the Japanese were was unclear. "Trying to follow this war on Luzon is like trying to track down the elusive will o' the wisp," Dunn told his radio listeners. There was uncertainty about the location of the frontlines. The Manila Railroad was in operation but conducting limited runs because the Filipino crews and the Army engineers did not know exactly how far they could go before they would meet Japanese defenders. One day, Dunn and a number of Signal Corps officers got lost and discovered that they were at the front of the advance. "You just passed our forward patrols coming back," an infantry officer informed them as they wandered around.[66]

The march south came to an end outside of Clark Field, the huge airbase north of Manila. To the southwest of Clark Field was Fort Stotsenburg, which overlooked the airfield. To the west were a series of ridges that ran on an east–west basis, with a number of deep, sharp valleys in between. These ridges ended abruptly in steep slopes that overlooked Clark, Stotsenburg, and Highway 3, which ran to Manila.

Clark Field was of real importance. General Kenney's air force units required the use of the paved runways and maintenance facilities, having outgrown the limited resources at Lingayen. MacArthur also had to offer bomber support to Admiral Chester W. Nimitz as the Pacific Fleet and its amphibious forces seized control of Iwo Jima and Okinawa. Clark was the only field on Luzon that could sustain heavy, long-range aircraft. The Japanese understood the importance of these runways and were not about to give up the facility without a fight. "Japs are evidently going to vigorously defend Clark Field," Griswold observed in his diary.[67]

Seventeen days into the Luzon campaign, Krueger made a push on Clark Field. He was still worried. The heaviest fighting the Sixth Army was facing remained in the north. "At this stage of the operation, our base was still considered insecure," Eddleman explained. "General Yamashita's inflexible plan for the defense of Luzon apparently caused him to overlook the golden opportunity for a strong counter-attack against the left of our beachhead." Eddleman noted that the Japanese had the resources—three divisions—and they were in the right positions to inflict serious harm on the Americans.[68]

For Clark to be a useful facility, the Americans would have to take the air-field, Fort Stotsenburg, and drive the Japanese from the hills and ridges to the west that had commanding views of both installations. Griswold gave the task of taking Clark to the 40th Infantry Division. The Japanese, he knew, had the terrain working for them. "This will be a hard fight," he observed.[69] He deter-mined to take a calculated gamble, ordering his men to turn ninety degrees to the right (west) and attack. As a result, he was leaving the left (eastern) flank exposed. If the Japanese had struck with any strength, the Americans could have been driven back.[70]

On January 24, the 160th Infantry Regiment of the 40th Infantry Division attacked up the steep slopes of two separate ridges. The Japanese had dug an extensive trench system and were ready for them. The 40th brought out its heavy artillery and blasted Japanese positions. As the 40th Division charged forward, Griswold ordered the 37th Division to swing to its right and take the fort.[71]

Japanese artillery scored some successes against the 37th. They held the high ground and had good observation of the approaching Americans. The Japanese directed counterbattery fire against the 135th and 136th Field Artillery Battalions and managed to slow the advance of the 129th Infantry Regiment. This success lasted only so long. As soon as US artillery observers found Japanese positions, their big guns silenced them. This process, though, was slow. Aerial observers circled directly above Japanese locations, but they were hampered by concealment efforts. Forward observers with a map were many times better. Japanese fire cut telephone wires, however, degrading com-munication efforts.[72]

After the first day of fighting ended on January 28, MacArthur announced that Fort Stotsenburg had been liberated: "We have secured the line of the Bamban River and have taken Clark Field and Fort Stotsenburg. Our forces are engaged in clearing enemy troops from the near-by hills." In the article car-rying MacArthur's announcement, George E. Jones of *The New York Times* added that infantry patrols were "encountering only isolated small-arms fire from enemy stragglers" at these two locations.[73] Griswold, for his part, was stunned by the announcement. "Why does he do this?" he wrote in his diary. "It is evident we are going to have to fight a battle at Stotsenburg before we can go on."[74]

The general was correct. The fight for the airfield was intense and hardly over. The Japanese had pre-plotted fire plans. The amount of munitions they threw at the 129th Infantry on January 28 was, in the words of one staff officer, on a "scale hithertofore not seen by the regiment in fighting in the Solomon Island and Central Luzon Plain."[75]

Not only were the Japanese well-armed, but they had orders to hold firm rather than engage in suicidal banzai charges. As a result, machine gun and rifle fights for control of the plane hangars lasted all of January 28. Japanese artillery hidden in the rubble of the airbase, and also in the hills to the west, held fire until individual infantry companies took the hangers and moved out into the open. Japanese snipers kept the 129th Infantry's regimental command post under fire. Medics had to use armored vehicles to remove casualties. To add insult to injury, there was friendly fire. The U.S. Army Air Forces strafed and bombed the Americans just as the Japanese fire let up.

The next day, the Japanese committed their tanks to the fight. Griswold had already sent many of the 637th Tank Destroyer Battalion's vehicles into the mountains to fight with the 40th Division, and the unit was therefore not as strong as it should have been when the Japanese tanks arrived. The fire from the Japanese was so intense that the American medics had to leave the wounded where they fell. Retrieval operations—even those using tanks as ambulances— were simply not possible. Only on the morning of the January 30, the third day of the battle, was the 129th able to recover its injured soldiers.[76]

The tide was starting to turn slowly. In 1945, one of the U.S. Army's strengths was that it could integrate its various units together and conduct combined arms operations. Griswold gave Beightler the use of the 517th Artillery Battalion and their 155-millimeter guns, which had a longer range than those in the 37th Division. These helped drive the Japanese back.[77]

The fight for Fort Stotsenburg, on the other hand, hung in the balance. Beightler sent the 129th and 145th Infantry Regiments to seize the fort. Both Krueger and Griswold thought the regiments were not making enough progress, and Beightler spent three days at the headquarters of the 129th in an effort to prod it to move faster.[78] The problem was that the Japanese were well-fortified. They had machine guns and artillery positions on both sides of the hills that overlapped with minefields. The defenders also had high powered naval binoculars. The Nippon Kogaku firm, later known as Nikkon, built these "big eyes" binoculars for long range sea duty and, with the short distances in play at Clark Field, they gave the Japanese perfect views of the approaching Americans. Their positions were, according to one American, "probably the most elaborate and extensive system of cave and tunnel defenses encountered in the Southwest Pacific." Captured Japanese documents show that the defenders began retreating, but they were unable to do so in good order.[79] "After a very hard fight the 37th Division took Fort Stotsenburg by nightfall," Griswold wrote in his diary. "Lots of casualties. Five bitter days' fight after Gen. MacArthur had announced its capture!"[80]

Even then, the fighting was hardly over. Griswold wanted the Japanese pushed back beyond the range of their artillery, so that they could not interdict traffic on Route 3. A steep, grassy hill overlooking both facilities —one that Americans dubbed "Top of the World"—needed to be taken. The 129th attacked on the morning of January 31. For a day and a half, Japanese and American soldiers fought so close that it looked like they were playing a game of catch with hand grenades. The 129th was halfway up by dark, and they took the crest at midday on February 1. Clark Field and Fort Stotsenburg were now secure.

The XIV Corps could again resume its march toward Manila. With that point made, the rear still remained dangerous. Japanese snipers hit and killed individual soldiers. The Americans often responded to these lone shooters with artillery and anti-aircraft artillery, which quickly tore apart the bodies of individual Japanese soldiers. The 40th Division also continued to push the Japanese to the west and would be engaged in combat for over a month. The unit also began to suffer from a significant number of dysentery cases, which came from a fly infestation that was feeding off the dead on the battlefield.[81]

The taking of Fort Stotsenburg was an emotional moment for many U.S. Army personnel. It was the first US fort Americans had taken back from the Japanese. It had been the prewar home of the 26th U.S. Cavalry Regiment, which had been destroyed during the defense of Luzon in 1942. On January 28, Griswold met with an Air Force lieutenant who had spent three years fighting on Luzon as a guerrilla. The lieutenant presented the general with the 26th Cavalry's national colors. After smuggling the flag off the Bataan peninsula, his guerrilla band had flown the flag regularly at their base. "The American flag has never ceased to wave over the Island of Luzon," he told Griswold. The general was touched. "I think this whole thing will go down in the future as one of the finest examples of loyalty ever known to a national color," he reflected.[82] Three days later, Krueger arrived at the fort for a short ceremony reestablishing US command. Griswold was outraged that Kruger refused to meet the Air Force lieutenant.[83]

Despite these firefights in areas behind the front, the field, the fort, and the highway were now secure but the easy march south was over. Rogers saw this firsthand. He decided to take a small vacation from the grinding work at MacArthur's headquarters. With a few associates, he drove a jeep south to Clark Field. He stopped when he came within five hundred yards of a firefight with the Japanese. "As we drove off the highway we passed a long column of infantry soldiers who were forming from columns of two into a line of advance." It was the first time in his Army career that he had personally witnessed men going into combat. "I looked into their faces and saw resigned anxiety and fatigue."[84]

The morale of the Japanese, on the other hand, was still good. They believed the enemy's slow advance was a sign of their success. "Though four weeks have lapsed since the landing, the enemy is not yet very active," Kobayashi assured his subordinates. "It seems that American supply has not been operating smoothly, and that they cannot use shipping as they wish due to the fact that their losses in shipping and killed and wounded have been enormous."[85]

Things looked different to the Americans. As the U.S. Army neared Manila, military intelligence units began making significant contributions to combat operations. They had an enormous amount of military documents, personal letters, and diaries to read and translate. Maps turned out to be the most valuable. Intelligence analysts could quickly use the information on these diagrams to direct heavy fire on Japanese locations, with results that were usually devastating.[86]

Following the seizure of Clark Field, engineers of the U.S. Army Air Forces began immediate efforts to restore its facilities, such as filling the craters in the runways. The wreckage of over six hundred Japanese airplanes dotted the area, and engineers soon found that fifty of them were still in working order. Another fifty could be repaired with reasonable amounts of effort. A few days into that effort, General Kenney inspected the airfield. Although the facility was well behind the frontlines at that point, there were still Japanese stragglers in the area and a sniper opened fire during his visit. "We got out of range in a hurry," Kenney noted. A Filipino guerrilla began stalking the Japanese sniper. Two gunshots rang out and the Filipino emerged from tall grass holding a Japanese rifle and cap.[87]

While the Air Force took hold of the base, American infantry units continued their advance to the south. As early as January 28, a task force of the 37th Division had entered the town of San Fernando, about thirteen miles south of Clark Field. The notation in the operations journal of the battalion in this task force reads: "There were no greeting crowds of civilians. The town was graveyard quiet." The next morning, however, two thousand Huks entered the town and a confrontation ensued. The Americans ordered them to retreat. They refused until six US planes began strafing them.[88]

Incidents like these occurred despite XIV Corps patrolling on both foot and in vehicles. Norman Mailer, the future novelist, was a soldier with the 112th Cavalry, a Texas National Guard unit that spent most of the Luzon campaign attached to the 1st Cavalry Division. His experiences suggest why these reconnaissance missions did not produce that much information. They would stand at a distance from their sergeants and then report that they could not see anything through their binoculars. Others on the patrol would do the same, confirming to the sergeant the negative report. "I had already read *War and Peace*—and I started thinking, Yes, it was Tolstoy who said: 'Every army moves on waves of ignorance.' I thought, 'We're sure contributing to it.'" Nobody wanted to get killed "for too little."[89]

5

The Race to Manila

As the 40th and 37th Infantry Divisions retook Clark Field and Fort Stotsenburg, Walter Krueger assigned the 1st Cavalry Division to the XIV Corps and Oscar W. Griswold's command started to grow. A few days later, Douglas MacArthur intervened, and soon he had the "horse soldiers" charging into Manila on steel ponies in a race against the foot soldiers of 37th Infantry Division. The race to Manila was on.

The 1st Cavalry was the pride of the branch, and, like equestrian soldiers in former times, considered itself an elite formation. Anyone could trudge into war on foot, but the soldiers in this division were trained to ride and shoot. The training "was as rigorous and as demanding as our division commander could contrive to make it," a senior officer in the prewar division recalled.[1]

The division itself had been formed after World War I and had no combat record until 1943, but its subordinate units were some of the oldest in the Army. Before the Civil War, Lieutenant Colonel Robert E. Lee had once commanded the 5th Cavalry. During the Indian Wars of the 1870s, George Custer had commanded the 7th Cavalry. "Having joined an old line unit with long tradition of service—discipline was very evident but never seemed forced," a chief warrant officer in the 7th Cavalry observed.[2] That type of training bore fruit in December 1941, when the 26th Cavalry stymied the Japanese advance on Luzon in what was the last combat action of a U.S. Army unit on horseback. Despite this victory, it was becoming obvious to most officers within the cavalry branch that the days of fighting on steeds were over. Many began transferring to new armor units.[3]

Despite its name, the 1st Cavalry was basically an infantry division, and it was another of the "inferior" units—or at least those perceived as such—that the general staff sent to the Pacific. As late as 1941, the division trained to advance into combat on horseback, but lost their mounts in 1942. Officially it was fighting as dismounted cavalry, and there was a bit of truth to that claim. There were still plenty of men in the division who had been trained to ride. "My horse was Sir Walter and he was a good horse," one veteran remembered. Private First Class Allan MacDonald of the 5th Cavalry recalled, "One thing about our Cavalry horses they knew every bugle call." The division was still organized and structured as a cavalry division.[4]

There was also some hope in the cavalry branch that the unit would return to using horses after the war. A biography of Major General Verne D. Mudge, commanding general of the division that the unit's public affairs officers generated, had him declaring that the troopers of the 1st Cavalry would "fight like hell so they can get their horses back." After the war, the division established private riding clubs and even held some events with soldiers on horseback. Major General John K. Herr, a former head of the cavalry branch, argued as late as 1954 that the horse could travel on broken terrain and in mountains that were simply inaccessible to tanks and other tracked vehicles.[5]

A horse soldier for his entire career, Mudge was determined to keep true to tradition. He refused to add new men to the division before they arrived on Luzon. He wanted to maintain the pride and cohesion of his veteran force. "I think unquestionably, he was the finest division commander I saw during the whole war," Clyde D. Eddleman of the Eighth Army staff observed.[6]

The 1st Cavalry had been in the Pacific since 1943 but was assigned to the XIV Corps only after it arrived on Luzon as a follow-on formation. The division was committed to combat before it had time to recuperate from the combat on Leyte, which had created a strong sense of comradery among the men. What little recovery time the division would get would come in transit to Luzon. The men were so exhausted that small luxuries, such as dry bunks, showers, fresh food, and ice cream, made a real difference in their morale.[7]

When the horsemen arrived on Luzon, the beach at Lingayen was no longer an active combat zone. Because of that, MacArthur finally had enough units to make bold moves. He had slowly and reluctantly come to realize that Krueger might be right. There were more Japanese on Luzon than he had expected, and the invasion force was not strong enough to take the island without taking some calculated risks.[8] He jumped the chain of command once the division was on Luzon, circumventing both Krueger and Griswold. He told Mudge: "Get to Manila, Go around the Nips, bounce off the Nips, but get to Manila."[9]

His instructions to Robert S. Beightler were less colorful and less direct. The two generals met on Route 3—the road leading south to Manila—and

MacArthur shared with him the instructions he had given Mudge. According to Beightler, MacArthur told him that "he would like to see his old Rainbow comrade reach Manila first but that the cards were stacked against me." MacArthur explained that the 1st Cavalry was fresher than the 37th. "He said it would be much easier for the 1st Cavalry, which was mechanized and motorized and had seen little fighting on Luzon, to slash into the center of Manila and reach civilians interned at Santo Tomás than it would be for the 37th Division which had had to foot-slog and fight all the way from Lingayen Gulf." Beightler disagreed. He was not going to lose out to the cavalry.[10]

At this stage, MacArthur had three objectives regarding Manila. First, he wanted to liberate the civilian internees being held at Santo Tomás University. The camp was full of American civilians who had been in Manila when the Japanese seized control in 1942 and were a diverse group of the city's expatriate elite, including business executives, housewives, bankers, missionaries, children, nurses, journalists, and engineers. MacArthur also wanted to take control of Malacañan Palace, the official residence of the president of the Philippines. Finally, he wanted to secure the government buildings located at the eastern end of Luneta Park.[11]

Mudge assembled a task force. Its mission was simple: move south as rapidly as possible, using only what force was necessary to break through Japanese defensive positions. The cavalrymen were to avoid large-scale battle.[12] He had little intelligence on enemy locations, but Marine Air Groups 24 and 32 would provide flank protection from above. The Marine Corps provided a seven-man liaison team that rode with the column, communicated with the pilots via radio, and were the subject of several jokes. "Despite the kidding," Robert B. Holland, one of the Marines testified, "they couldn't have treated us better. They knew we were there to protect their . . . flank."[13]

Mudge and Beightler may have had the same instructions, but they did not have the same resources. Mudge had jeeps and tanks. Beightler did not. Mudge assembled his unit commanders together and explained what was going to happen. "Gentlemen," he said, "our objective is Manila. We will move there by motorized columns, spearheaded by tanks. I want the First Cavalry Division to be there first!"[14]

There has been a great deal of speculation among veterans of the campaign as to why MacArthur assigned this "mad dash" to two divisions and yet did not provide the same resources to both. William J. Dunn, in his memoirs, argues that the general was trying to avoid provoking a strong, Japanese counter-response until it was too late.[15] This assessment was made with an understanding of how the story would end and does not make sense given concerns, at the time, in MacArthur's headquarters. The explanation is far simpler. The United States faced shortages on Luzon and it could not provide the transportation assets for two divisions. MacArthur admitted as much to Beightler during their conversation.[16]

News of the decision leaked. This development reflected the mixed relationship MacArthur had with the media, an association that is essential to how the Battle of Manila was covered. Throughout his career, MacArthur had always had a good sense of how to control and use information, be it in the realm of military intelligence or public affairs. His public affairs officer, Colonel LeGrande "Pick" Diller, was a regular Army infantry officer with no training in public relations nor a background in journalism. Diller had maintained that his limited background was an asset in dealing with journalists. "It was very fortunate that I didn't know who they were because some of them were the most prominent war correspondents really in the world," he explained years after the war. "But I didn't know who they were, their names didn't mean anything to me. I just handled everybody the same and put out the information."[17] Others had a slightly different take on him. Lewis B. Sebring, Jr., of the *New York Herald Tribune*, believed that Diller was in over his head. After watching the public affairs staff make some bad mistakes, Sebring offered some suggestions on how to improve coordination based on things he had seen at Army bases in the United States. The colonel was less than interested. "If you people would stop asking me questions, maybe we could get some work done around here," Diller snapped back. He had no interest in getting along with reporters. "Diller's job as he envisioned it," observed Russell Brines of the Associated Press, "was to build up MacArthur and to win the war. He didn't make any bones about that."[18]

Diller basically agreed with that assessment. He always believed a public affairs officer "should be an aide to the commander, rather than a newsman who is trying to find out what the military is all about." He believed that public relations officers who had journalism backgrounds got into trouble for failing to put their old careers behind them, or for playing favorites with their former colleagues. "If I was fair to all the rest of them, they couldn't criticize that I was playing favorites or that the information was incorrect."[19]

Dunn disagreed with both Brines and Diller. He had been in Manila before the war and he had covered MacArthur's headquarters since 1942. He found Diller to be competent and professional. Events suggest that Dunn's assessment has merit. Diller started the war as a lieutenant colonel, but was promoted twice, receiving the star of a brigadier general during the battle for Manila. That said, Dunn thought that Diller did play favorites, and that he was one of them. "When he arrived in Melbourne as the designated press officer, we became instant *amigos*," Dunn stated. More importantly, he believed that Diller was in a difficult position attempting to be both the public affairs officer for MacArthur's command as well as its chief censor. The two positions were at odds with one another. The public affairs officer basically should help reporters do their jobs, giving them contacts, gathering information, and providing support facilities, while a censor restricts news coverage that might "prejudice the command or the commander."[20]

During the drive on Manila, Diller and his staff decided to play the role of public affairs officers. Colonel Larry Lehrbas, an aide to MacArthur, saw Dunn visiting headquarters. The colonel had been a newspaper reporter before joining the Army and told Dunn that if he heard of a named division getting motorized assets that he should join it immediately. Dunn knew that Lehrbas knew a good story, and there was only one that mattered—Manila and the internees at Santo Tomás.[21] "I didn't really need anything else," Dunn stated.[22]

The problem was Dunn had already learned about a mission assigned to the Alamo Scouts—which became later known as "The Great Raid"—that liberated the American prisoners of war at Cabanatuan. "This was a story to rival Santo Tomás and I was faced with an immediate dilemma: how to cover two major stories breaking at the same time."[23] As it turned out, the liberated prisoners were all located close to the headquarters of the 1st Cavalry Division, and he could cover both events without having to bounce all over Luzon. Dunn provided one of the first detailed reports of the raid.[24]

Dunn was in for a bit of a surprise when he arrived at Mudge's command post in Cabanatuan and discovered he was not the only one who had heard of the mission: Carl Mydans of Time-Life, Dean Schedler of the Associated Press, and Frank Hewlett of United Press were there as well. All these correspondents had worked in Manila before the war and had learned about the drive on Manila from their own contacts at headquarters. Mydans and Hewlett had personal connections to Santo Tomás. Mydans had spent a year as an internee in the camp before he was released. Hewlett—author of the sardonic poem, "The Battling Bastards of Bataan," and who had given Brigadier

General Frank Merrill's 5307th Composite Unit (Provisional) the nickname it was better known by, "Merrill's Marauders"—had last seen his wife in Manila in early 1942 when he went to cover the US defense against the Japanese invasion. He had heard she was possibly being held at Santo Tomás—maybe.[25]

* * *

Command of the horse soldiers' drive on Manila went to Brigadier General William C. Chase, commanding general of the 1st Cavalry Brigade. Well-liked by the men in the division, Chase was a Rhode Islander who had graduated from Brown University and then enlisted in the artillery of the Rhode Island National Guard in the days just before World War I. During the war, he earned a commission, and afterward decided to make a career in the U.S. Army as a horse soldier. Like many of the best officers of the interwar era, he spent a good chunk of his career in the classroom. He taught ROTC at what later became Michigan State University, and he was an instructor at both the Cavalry School and the Command & General Staff College.[26] "General Chase was quite a character," one soldier remembered.[27]

Mudge temporarily removed Chase from command of his brigade so he could lead this special task force. Having been stationed in Luzon before the war, Chase knew that the quickest route into Manila was not necessarily the most direct. He divided his command into three detachments and had them swing toward the east as they drove south. This route minimized the number of bridges they would have to cross, bridges being natural chokepoints for defenders trying to stop an advance.[28] Given MacArthur's instructions, Chase knew an unrelenting focus on speed was the key to success. He made sure all his commanders and men understood their main mission was to keep moving. The message got through. Frank Mendez, a long-serving trooper in the 8th Cavalry who had actually trained on horseback, learned they were going to Manila at midnight. "They said, 'You're going to go all the way into Manila. You're not going to stop and fight, unless you have to. You're supposed to just go through.' Just go hell bent and high water."[29]

Mudge assigned the journalists—Dunn, Mydans, Schedler, and Hewitt—to ride with the Eighth Cavalry under the command of Lieutenant Colonel Haskett "Hack" Conner. When they arrived, the four were not impressed with the detachment. It was small and not particularly well-armed. They seriously considered staying in Cabanatuan, although after some hesitation decided to go forward.[30]

They had another chance to reconsider when they met Conner in his command post, which was nothing more than a canvas tent in a dry rice patty. Mydans noted that the flat area was surrounded with the glow of small campfires and lit cigarettes. The colonel turned to them and asked a simple, but powerful question: were they ready? "We really had no solid idea of what lay ahead," Dunn recalled, "but we were not about to admit it."

Conner knelt on the ground and laid out the maps to show them that he had a forward patrol at the Angat River. They needed to reach this unit before dawn, or it would have to fall back. Conner's command authority was apparent to the four, and that reassured Dunn about the decision to stay with the column.[31]

Dunn and his colleagues rested and got a couple of hours of sleep that evening. "An officer awakened us to a moonlight night that was almost as bright as day," he reported.[32]

The 1st Cavalry began its charge south one minute after midnight on February 1. The flying columns were traveling light with only their weapons, ammunition, water, gasoline, and four days of rations. Initial Japanese resistance was "negligible" and mainly consisted of isolated groups of soldiers.[33]

The 37th Infantry Division began its advance a few hours later. The 129th Infantry Regiment had not expected the order. After the battle for the "Top of the World," its men were sleeping in late and washing their clothes, expecting a day or two off. Instead, they were marching south before noon. Corporal Robert Kiser found the expedition exhausting. He and his comrades would march for 15 or 16 hours, get a few hours of sleep and begin all over again.[34]

The Japanese knew they could not challenge the advance directly. Yamashita instead decided to attack the flanks of the advancing columns, hoping to degrade the US force and delay their arrival in Manila. The Sixth Army used I Corps to attack the Japanese units threatening its left flank while XIV Corps began the march south into central Luzon. Yamashita's plan had failed.[35]

Because of their instructions to keep moving, the detachments of the 1st Cavalry refused to engage with the enemy any longer than the time it took to break contact and keep moving. Mudge actually led the fight at the Valdefuente Bridge over the Pampanaga River. Seeing that the bridge was rigged to explode, he ordered a group of troopers to follow him, and they ran across the bridge—despite mortar fire—and threw the explosives over into the river.[36] Mudge had risked the command authority of a two-star general so he could be a platoon sergeant.[37] It would not be the last time.

The engagement destroyed the two Japanese units holding the bridge. The squad of Private First Class Kitamura Takeshi was patrolling the banks of the river and beat a hasty retreat. Their platoon leader ordered them back to the bridge. Obedient samurai, they returned directly into the hail of US artillery shells. Kitamura was wounded during this action and captured shortly thereafter.[38]

Despite these lopsided results, there was still danger in the drive to Manila. Lieutenant Colonel Tom Ross, the commanding officer of the third column, was shot and killed as his men crossed the Pampanaga River. His command was to the south of where Mudge was located when they became entangled in a firefight. The column had both surprise and the firepower of tanks, but Ross was hit while riding in his jeep. His men, however, won the brief exchange, which opened up the road.[39]

This type of small action was common on the ride south. The flying column was basically a traveling firefight. The Japanese shot at the advancing units columns constantly. Speed often allowed them to move faster than the Japanese could aim. The detachments were strung out—often a mile from one end to the other. The troopers of the 1st Cavalry were nonetheless enjoying paved roads, which they had not seen for over a year.[40] The four reporters meanwhile moved about freely among their column—talking to soldiers and getting assessments of the situation. For journalists, the European theater had been the preferred destination and had offered many opportunities for journalists to engage in participatory journalism. Now the time had come for reporters working in the Pacific. This opportunity was unique and all four of them were determined to make the most of this chance. For a time, Mydans was, for all practical purposes, the sixth crew member of the tank "Georgia Peach."[41]

The total absence of Japanese aviation allowed the columns to advance relentlessly. "We sideslipped one or two Japanese road blocks, using air attacks on them as much as possible," Chase explained.[42] Monopoly of the skies helped aerial route reconnaissance. Knowing that there was a Japanese ambush site ahead of them made it easier to simply go around.[43] The coordination was so good that the ground observers often directed fighters to targets before the request from the cavalrymen reached them.[44]

At the major waystation for the 1st Cavalry columns a firefight greeted the unit when it arrived. George Fischer, a crewman in the "Georgia Peach," was astonished at what happened next. "Mydans left the tank and through my periscope, I observed him out in the middle of the fire fight taking pictures with no regards for his life."[45]

It had taken the horse troopers roughly seven hours to cover twenty-six miles. "We made good time on the concrete highways," Don Mercier, a tank crewman, noted. The problem was when the roads were less good. The advance continued unhindered until 11:00 a.m. on February 1, when the Americans reached San Vicente. Ambushes remained small, but they slowed the pace of the advance. "You would never know when you'd run into antitank guns. Their 37 mm armor-piercing shells could set a tank on fire," Mercier explained.[46]

Filipinos made it clear that the Americans were welcome. In town after town, the public came out to cheer them. In Baliuag, residents began running toward the highway when a church bell announced the arrival of the Americans, and the crowd was so thick it actually forced the column to a halt. "It was a very pleasant sight to see," John Hencke, a tank crewman, recalled. The town prepared a luau for the troopers, knowing it would take the Americans hours to cross the Angat River. Holland, of the U.S. Marine Corps, ate a full plate of meat with fresh vegetables and talked with several young girls. "It was wonderful." In the village of Balintwak, Fred Hampson of the Associated Press reported, "We met no Japanese once we were in the city—only cheering, weeping, and clapping civilians. The nearer we press into the center of the city the more joyous and vociferous becomes the welcome." Hampson was not alone in making that observation. Soldiers found the adulation empowering. Filipinos would present the Americans with gifts of flowers and food. "In fact the whole column seemed to be eating its way toward Manila," Chase observed.[47]

The experiences of the soldiers in the 1st Cavalry and 37th Infantry Divisions were varied. Many were simply afraid and fell back on their training. "I was in serial combat situations," Sergeant First Class Robert L. Boyd of the 145th Infantry recalled. "You use your skills, mental ability and all your faculties to overcome the enemy."[48]

The Philippines presented a different type of battlefield for most of these men because of the large number of non-combatants and their suffering. Dorsey Robbins, a medic in the 8th Cavalry Regiment, always remembered the "deprivation of living conditions + Hunger of the natives—esp. the children begging for food."[49] That was something that even high-ranking officers noticed. Brigadier General Carlos P. Romulo was pensive. The prewar publisher and editor of the *Philippines Herald*, he had won the Pulitzer Prize for essays he had written on international affairs in Asia and the Pacific. He had joined MacArthur's staff at the beginning of the war and reached flag rank. "The starvation signs on Filipino faces grew more marked as they neared Manila."[50]

Others focused on the jubilation. One of Romulo's former writers, Pacita Pestaño-Jacinto, offered a significantly different take. "It is like a carnival here," she wrote in her diary. "The soldiers are amused at our small ways of trying to show them how grateful we are. They seem to like it." There was a reason for that gratitude. Pestaño-Jacinto saw a profound difference between the Japanese and the Americans. The Japanese had plundered. "The Americans give to us knowing that we have been without many things for the last three years. The Japanese took away our homes, the Americans pitch their own tents, eat their own food, give when people ask."[51]

Whatever else they meant, the celebrations were an indicator that there were few Japanese between the flying columns and Manila. The resistance that the cavalry faced had come from small, isolated tactical units. Homer Bigart of the *New York* Herald Tribune saw this firsthand. Bigart was among the best correspondents covering the Philippine campaign and would win two Pulitzer prizes over the course of his career. The first was for his reporting from the Pacific in 1945. He showed an exceptional understanding of the military in all three domains (air, land, and sea) and all three levels (tactical, operational, and strategic). As he made his way through Luzon toward Manila, he recognized that the speed of the advance had been due to Japanese mistakes. The U.S. Army units under Mudge and Chase had advanced "on a narrow road that could have been easily blocked by a few score Japanese."[52] One of the easiest ways was to destroy bridges at river crossings. "Bridgeless rivers gave us more pause than Yamashita's entire disorganized army," Dunn wrote.[53] This danger put enormous pressure on combat-support units, like the military police, who were posted on the bridges twenty-four hours a day.[54] Until they arrived, both divisions had to leave small units behind to do guard duty while the rest of the men pushed on toward Manila.[55]

Firefights between small groups of Japanese and the Americans were often unexpected. Troopers of the 5th Cavalry were at a road junction which had a gas station on the corner when they heard vehicles coming up from behind them. "The engines didn't sound quite normal," Norman Laub, one of those cavalrymen, explained. "We were a bit mystified, for no one we knew should be on this road that close behind us, much less traveling at night." The convoy was traveling in the dark without headlights, and it was not until several passed that the troopers could see from silhouettes that they were Japanese. Their defensive positions were facing south, not north, and there were Americans on either side of the road so they could not fire without hitting their own. It was not until the last two trucks passed by that the Americans opened fire. A truck crashed into the gas station, slaming into one of the pumps, which started a fire and an explosion. The Japanese ran for cover, but "in keeping with our number one assignment, we loaded up and moved on."[56]

Other 1st Cavalry troopers followed in units that were not part of the "flying columns." The division, though, had stripped these formations of their vehicles. As a result, these horse soldiers marched south on foot just like regular infantry units. "I did not realize how hot it got in the Philippines until that first day we moved on foot," Richard J. Foss, a machine gunner in the 7th Cavalry, stated. "Many men got sick from the heat. A number passed out."[57]

Bridges were also a problem for the 37th Infantry Division because their route crossed many waterways. The Japanese had destroyed several steel truss bridges of significant lengths, including those of 150, 300, and 450 feet. These demolition jobs were not particularly well done, but were effective enough because the National Guardsmen did not have the engineering resources needed to do repair work. This shortfall had more to do with transportation issues than a lack of parts. The bridge sections were on several different ships, and it took a while for construction units to put them together. It was shortages, rather than Japanese actions, that slowed down the 37th Division's march on Manila.[58]

Despite these problems, the engineers were key in sustaining the advance of the foot soldiers. Often working under enemy fire and short of equipment, they repaired bridges or built Bailey, pontoon, or treadway spans to replace them. Some went as many as sixty hours without sleep. They dismantled the treadway bridge at Bayambang and essentially leapfrogged it ninety-eight miles to Calumpit, where they reassembled it over the Pampanga River. Parts of other bridges had to be used to finish the job. The engineers at first thought that a truck had failed to deliver the missing piece, but they later learned that the missing section had floated away as the bridge was being disassembled in blackout conditions. It was thirty-six hours before the span could carry heavy equipment.[59]

The engineers were working quickly—finishing projects in hours that otherwise would have taken weeks back in the United States—but it was not fast enough for some. The 37th Cavalry Reconnaissance Troop, Mechanized was the lead element of Beightler's advance, but spent the better part of a day in San Fernando, waiting in the old Constabulary Building. "Restlessness prevailed here," 1st Lieutenant John K. Winn, the troop's historian, noted in his report.[60] The day, though, was not a total loss. "Civilians as usual went wild with joy to see the first American Troops enter their cities, villages and barrios," Winn recorded. He observed that this enthusiasm was a powerful morale booster.[61]

Crossing rivers was less of a challenge for the 1st Cavalry, but it remained an issue nonetheless. In his radio dispatches, Dunn reported on the engineers who were trying to ford rivers and build bridges over them at the same time. On the morning of February 3—the third day of the race—the 1st Cavalry was trailing behind the 37th Infantry, trying to cross the Angat, a wide but shallow river. This effort became something of a challenge for the columns under Chase. American soldiers had destroyed the bridge across the river in 1942, and the Japanese had never done any repair work. A small span to the north was too weak to support tanks, and the width of the river along with its steep banks prevented fording. While the engineers were trying to figure out what to do, the Japanese opened fire with rifles, machine guns, and mortars, forcing the men of Battery A, 82nd Field Artillery to fire back with their 105s from the prone position.[62]

The engineers eventually found a crossable location. The problem was the water was still too high for the light vehicles in the column. The solution was to create a train, using a tank as a locomotive and lashing the trucks and then jeeps together. The jeeps were often totally submerged in the crossing and could not start again until the water had evaporated from their engines, which did not take long in the climate of Luzon. "It was an unusual operation," Dunn told his listeners, "but it worked."[63]

As a result, the race south was stop-and-go. "Once in a while we would get up to 30 miles per hour, and would think we were going to get there quickly," Holland recalled. "But that never lasted long. We would always run into an obstacle, like a strong Jap position, which forced the 1st Cavalry to dismount and fight their way through."[64] Men tried to avoid stops by eating and sleeping in their vehicles.[65]

The generals could see the impact of these actions. Beightler later figured that construction issues had cost his division two days in the march toward Manila.[66] Griswold believed the destruction of the crossings over the rivers represented a successful Japanese defensive effort. "Having much trouble with blown bridges," Griswold noted in his diary.[67]

Congestion on the roads increased the closer the Americans got to Manila, greatly annoying Krueger. He believed much of the volume was due to Filipino refugees. "These people interfered seriously with our advance and with the movement of ammunition and other supplies." He was also annoyed with Major General Spencer B. Akin's signal corpsmen. "To complicate matters still more, the premature efforts of the chief signal officer of GHQ to get equipment into Manila early clogged Highway 5 with a long column of heavy Signal Corp vehicles." The historians of the official U.S. Army history of the Signal Corps in World War II have rejected this complaint, seeing Akin's work to get equipment into Manila as a reasonable effort to keep MacArthur's communications network functioning.[68]

The traffic jams were nonetheless monumental. William A. Owens, an agent in the 306th Counter Intelligence Corps, was more than twenty miles behind the lead elements of the 37th Infantry Division. "The troops had proved that an army bent on sudden conquest can be as disorganized as an army in retreat," he noted. They made it to the town of Camiling, where they joined a huge traffic jam and waited the entire night to cross a blown bridge.[69]

* * *

The advance to the south bypassed a number of Japanese defenders. As a result, the rear was less than secure. "At night it was a lot more dangerous to travel those roads . . . not because of the Japanese but because of the damn Filipino guerillas that we had organized to help us," Bruce Palmer, chief of staff of the 6th Infantry Division, maintained. "They were down right dangerous because they shot anything that moved." The safe move for officers visiting the frontlines was to stay put until dawn. "And they were our friends!" added Palmer.[70]

The advance south was so relentless that it put pressure on the command-and-control apparatus of the invaders. Beightler had to move the headquarters of the 37th Infantry Division no fewer than eight times between the landing at Lingayen on January 9 and crossing the Manila city limits. Half of these moves came during his race with the 1st Cavalry.[71]

The 37th Cavalry Reconnaissance Troop found it had advanced so fast that Army Air Forces planes mistook them for Japanese and began strafing them. American soldiers were outraged. Lieutenant John K. Winn, the troop historian, found that most of the remarks from the soldiers in the unit could not be reprinted in his report.[72]

One incident that was widely reported at the time occurred on February 4, at 9:30 a.m. When the 37th Division arrived at the Balintawak Brewery in San Miguel, it discovered that it was in working order, and—this next point is important—it was fully stocked. Filipinos handed out bottles to units as they filed past. Some soldiers used their helmets to scoop up the beer. An engineer detachment was building a bridge over the Tulihan River, and Colonel Herbert W. Radcliffe told the men of his battalion to rest. If they wanted to do so at Balintawak, that was fine with him. "That was probably the biggest beer party that ever was," Robert F. Minch, a truck driver with the 756th Field Artillery Battalion, noted. "We captured the brewery and tested it," Ray Smith, a foot soldier in the division, admitted. "If Japs had poisoned it, much of the Buckeye Division would have gone down the drain that Sunday afternoon," Mathias observed.[73]

The beer was fairly weak, and few were truly intoxicated. Most were simply reminded of a better life outside of combat. Nonetheless, many overindulged. Technician Grade Four Joseph P. Fennelly of the 145th Infantry explained, "I filled a bucket that held about 10 quarts of beer. I drank all I could hold and the next day I thought I was dead."[74] He was not the only one. "We all got sick from it," Sergeant William Harvey stated.[75]

Beightler and Griswold arrived at the brewery in midafternoon. Seeing Beightler approach, one Filipino ran up to the general and offered him a bottle of beer.[76] "I saw no reason to stop them," he stated in his final report as commanding general. "I'll never forget the sight of the Buckeye Division invading Manila gulping beer from steel helmets as it marched!"[77]

Even Krueger accepted the situation. When he saw what was going on, he demanded an explanation from the commanding officer of the 148th Regiment, Colonel Lawrence K. White. He wanted to know what White thought of soldiers drinking beer before going into combat. "General," the colonel replied, "I don't know, but I don't think I'd like to try and stop it." Krueger replied, "I don't think I would either."[78]

While the Buckeyes drank their brew, the horse soldiers were getting closer to Manila. The reporters traveling with the 1st Cavalry were learning what it meant to be embedded with a combat unit. "The four of us in our jeep, positioned near the center of the column, had firsthand information on whatever was happening a hundred years ahead or behind us, as well as any enemy action leveled in our direction," Dunn observed. "The rest of the time we guessed at developments or listened for scuttlebutt."[79]

As the column neared the city, Hewlett's anxiety grew. He had known Dunn before the war and opened up to him about his wife. He cracked a bit under the strain. "Bill this has *got* to be it. Virginia *has* to be there." Dunn assured him she would be. "I could tell that those last few miles were to him maddeningly slow." After the war, he admitted he had no way of knowing where Virginia Hewlett was, but that was not what his friend needed to hear.[80]

As the cavalry got closer to Manila, the more Japanese resistance they encountered. "Those last twenty miles into Manila on Saturday produced a lot of enemy action," Dunn observed, "but nowhere did the Japs mass enough strength to pose a real threat."[81] Rank was no real protection. Captain John "Jack" Titcomb, one of the Marine Corps liaison officers, noted in this diary that Chase's jeep had a number of bullet holes when it reached Santo Tomás.[82]

At the town of Novaliches, the road into Manila took the troopers over a narrow but deep gorge cut by the Tuliahan River. Getting to the bridge required a sharp left turn. Part of the column made the turn, and Japanese defenders opened fire with small arms and mortars. "We stayed pinned down to that corner for what seemed like an hour," Dunn recalled. The situation was bad. Marine pilots flying overhead were reporting that the bridge looked like it was rigged to explode. They were right. Lieutenant Colonel Conner could see that the fuses were lit. Lieutenant James Sutton, U.S. Navy, was a demolition expert traveling with Conner's group. Before the war was over, Sutton would win the Silver Star, multiple Purple Hearts, and the Distinguished Service Cross, the second-highest award for bravery in the U.S. Army. Sutton showed why when he ran out on to the Novaliches Bridge and with snipers shooting at him and disarmed the mine the Japanese had used as a bomb.[83]

Major Jim Gerhart, the executive officer of the 8th Cavalry Regiment, ran out onto the bridge with Sutton. The two ran back to Gerhart's jeep. Suddenly, the major saw a Japanese solider roughly seventy-five yards away. Mydans watched as Gerhart took out his carbine "without slowing his pace" and shot the enemy soldier "John Wayne style"—meaning from the hip. Gerhart swung himself into his jeep, and his column advanced across the bridge shooting at the Japanese as they went forward. Mydans was stunned. Gerhart had not even aimed. "Hell," he later explained, "I've been teaching my boys to shoot from the waist for three years. I sure had to show them I could do it myself."[84]

The 2nd Squadron, 5th Cavalry was driving south on Route 52 near Talipapa, a neighborhood in Quezon City, when they spotted a column of four Japanese trucks to their left that was about to turn onto the highway. The troops in the front vehicles motioned to the Japanese drivers to halt, which they did for some odd reason. As the US vehicles drove past, they fired all their weapons into the Japanese trucks. The horsemen had executed the naval maneuver of crossing the "T" on land. Flames quickly engulfed all four Japanese vehicles.[85]

Incidents like that one impressed the Marines working with the cavalrymen. After the drive was over, Titcomb noted in his diary: "The 1st Cavalry Division is a real outfit—more like a Marine Division!!"[86] The respect was mutual. In official correspondence with the air groups' commanding officers, Mudge praised the pilots who had covered the troopers. "On our drive to Manila, I depended solely on the Marines to protect my left flank from the air against possible Japanese counterattack. The job they turned in speaks for itself. We are here."[87]

Now there was nothing between the cavalrymen and Manila. In XIV Corps headquarters, nonetheless, Griswold thought the 37th Infantry would be first. Based on that assumption, he drew boundaries between the two divisions that put most of the developed urban area of Manila in the 37th Division's area of responsibility. At the start of February 2, elements of Beightler's division were closer to the city than Chase's units. Bigart reported that the cavalry was losing the race to the infantry.[88]

During the day, though, the 1st Cavalry took the lead, pushing forward in the rain as blown bridges slowed the 37th to a crawl. The Ohio Guardsmen were also facing strong resistance in the northern suburbs of Manila. The battalions of the 117th Gyoro Unit had orders to stand firm and "halt" or "disrupt" the US advance. The order did not necessitate suicide. The situation would determine the level and nature of the resistance they offered.

In the end, the fighting here would last ten days, and, as Stanley Frankel argues in his history of the 37th Infantry Division, crossing the city limits became largely irrelevant because the fight for Manila actually started outside of the city.[89] Not everyone shared that perspective. Late in the day, Griswold redrew the boundary lines again to avoid having the two units accidently shoot at one another, and only then gave Mudge and the 1st Cavalry permission to enter the city.[90] There had been too many downed bridges in front of the Buckeye Division. Griswold also noted in his final report that Japanese resistance within 37th Division's sector was strong. In contrast, no one was standing in the way of the 1st Cavalry. Those three factors, in his opinion, were key in determining the final outcome of the race.[91] The official report of the 129th Regiment states that the 1st Cavalry had an unfair advantage. They "came in mechanized to nose out the 37th Division on the last lap."[92]

Covering ninety miles in three days was, given the circumstances, remarkable. The 37th Infantry Division might have been bested in the race but making thirty miles on foot a day for three days is a testament to the physical conditioning and military discipline of Beightler's command. Both the 1st Cavalry and the 37th Infantry faced Japanese defenders and destroyed bridges. The Filipinos often unintentionally hindered the effort with throngs so massive that they ground traffic to a halt. The Japanese, meanwhile, began work to destroy the city.

6

The Race North

Setting the race between the 37th Infantry and 1st Cavalry divisions was only one of the moves that Douglas MacArthur made to prod Walter Krueger into moving faster toward Manila. He had another field army and he used it to do the same thing; this time between Krueger and his rival, Lieutenant General Robert Eichelberger, commanding general of the Eighth U.S. Army. MacArthur told Eichelberger to have one of his divisions, the 11th Airborne, launch an invasion of Luzon from the south. Eichelberger quickly agreed.

The commanders of both the Eighth Army and the 11th Airborne were eager for the challenge. Like MacArthur, Eichelberger was the son of a Civil War veteran. He had attended The Ohio State University with the intention of becoming a lawyer like his father, but his plans changed when his father's law partner was elected to Congress and offered him an appointment to the U.S. Military Academy. With one year of college behind him, Eichelberger went to West Point as a member of the Class of 1909. He was not a particularly good student, finishing sixty-eighth in a class of 103. As a young infantry officer, he saw a considerable amount of combat in the 1910s, taking part in the Mexican Expedition and the Siberian Expedition of 1918–1920, where the United States intervened in the Russian Civil War. Eichelberger won the Distinguished Service Cross during this mini-combat deployment. The turning point in Eichelberger's career was his year at the Command & General Staff College in 1926. He sat next to Dwight D. Eisenhower—seating was alphabetical—and finished on the Distinguished Graduates List. "I learned more at thirty-nine, than I ever did at twenty-one," he later wrote.[1]

In October 1940, the Army promoted Eichelberger to the rank of brigadier general and assigned him to serve as the superintendent of West Point. When asked how he obtained such a high position, he replied: "I guess it's on account of my wife, Emma. Everybody's crazy about her." After less than a year at West Point, Eichelberger was promoted to major general.[2]

In 1942, General George C. Marshall sent Eichelberger to the Pacific to command an infantry corps. It was not an assignment he wanted. "I knew General MacArthur well enough to realize that he was going to be difficult to get along with," as he put it. He also had an up-and-down relationship with Krueger during this time.[3] Two years later, he became the commanding general of the Eighth U.S. Army. He learned about his new assignment accidentally when the chief of staff of the new formation asked where he should locate the headquarters. Neither MacArthur nor Krueger gave him any formal notice.[4]

Eichelberger's resentment toward MacArthur grew over time. He was particularly infuriated when the theater commander announced that the invasion of Leyte was over. Yes, there were some "minor mopping up" operations, MacArthur conceded, but these were small things. Eichelberger saw it differently: "The bullets go by just as fast."[5]

MacArthur was aware of the animosity between his two field army commanders. MacArthur used this feuding to prod Krueger to move faster. To do that, he told Eichelberger this opportunity was his chance to become the "Jeb Stuart of World War II."[6] Eichelberger was only too willing to take part in the Luzon campaign. His staff had been developing plans for an invasion since November. There was more to this effort than simply humiliating Krueger; it was a chance to take the biggest prize in the Philippines. If he humiliated Krueger in the process, all the better.

Seeking to maximize mobility, Eichelberger turned to the 11th Airborne Division. Although less legendary than the 82nd and 101st Airborne Divisions, the 11th was, in fact, the first airborne division in the U.S. Army. It was created in 1943, and its first and only commander in the war was Major General Joseph Swing. A West Point classmate of Eisenhower and Bradley, Swing was in his third war, having served in the Mexican Expedition of 1912 and World War I.

Despite this long and varied career, Swing was deeply committed to his division. He had personally designed its unit patch—the number "11" with a pair of wings. The division's nickname was the Angels.[7]

In return, his men were deeply attached to him. As one soldier put it, "He looked like Mars himself." In retirement he was flooded with so many

Christmas cards each year that he could not respond. When he died in 1984, the feeling of loss was strong. "He was everyone's idea of what a general ought to be," Chaplain Lee Walker said in his eulogy at Swing's funeral. One soldier reflected at the time: "I had an instinctive certainty that, somehow, I had lost something to me."[8]

An incident that Philip Schweitzer, an enlisted paratrooper in the division, witnessed captures Swing's approach toward leadership. Schweitzer and a number of other soldiers were playing volleyball without their shirts on, which was a violation of Army regulations. Swing and another general saw them, and then asked if they could join the game. "Well," Schweitzer mumbled, "two star general and a one star general." He mumbled again, "not going to refuse them." They played for a while until a second lieutenant came across the men and demanded to know who was in command. The soldiers looked at Swing. He winked at them. The lieutenant told the group to put their uniforms back on. The group formed around Swing as he put his shirt on and then the lieutenant realized he had been chastising the division commander. Before leaving, the general told the men to return to their game. "He was all for his men," Schweitzer remarked.[9]

Paratroopers like Schweitzer considered themselves the best infantry in the U.S. Army. "We were the elite. We were above all the other Army people," Lyman "Tex" Black said. "We wore shiny boots on a parade [ground]—you could tell the difference." The hard exercise and drill that Swing demanded from them fed that attitude. The general personally led hour-long runs that his staff called "Swing sessions." Every officer in the division had three tries to finish the race, and if they could not, they were reassigned to another unit. Swing's staff was well-led by Colonel Irvin Schimmelpfenning, a West Point graduate and a Rhodes Scholar.[10]

The 11th Airborne Division was on Leyte until January 14 recovering from combat operations. Morale was high. The main problem facing the division was that it did not have a mission that exploited what it had to offer—shock, surprise, and speed.[11]

Swing believed that the fight against the Japanese was going to get harder, and the ability to use the shock power of airborne infantry could shatter their defenses. "My proposal is to hit at one of the more difficult landing areas once the main attack has gained a foothold," he explained to his father-in-law, Peyton C. March, who had been U.S. Army chief of staff during World War I. "If I can be dropped at one of several places inland where converging roads will allow me to hold off all reinforcements, a secondary landing might turn out to be the quickest way to Manila."[12]

The original plan the Eighth Army staff developed involved a three-division amphibious assault. Swing thought that was overly ambitious, and he recommended two.[13] When MacArthur began seriously considering a southern operation, the Eighth Army staff changed its recommendation and agreed with Swing. The problem was that the Southwest Pacific Theater lacked the landing craft to put even one division in southern Luzon.[14]

During this process, a disagreement developed between Eichelberger's and MacArthur's staff that was the mirror opposite of that between Krueger and the headquarters staff. Military intelligence officers were now saying that there were too many Japanese in southern Luzon to initiate an amphibious assault. Eichelberger argued that guerrillas—from whom they were getting this information—tended to exaggerate, and the number of defenders was likely significantly lower. This dispute led to a compromise between Eighth Army and the theater headquarters staff. The landing would involve only two regimental combat teams. The plan called for the division to conduct a reconnaissance in force to test Japanese defenses. If the 11th Airborne Division paratroopers made rapid advances, Eichelberger could give them permission to advance toward Manila in strength.[15] "It's going to be a good show and a fast one," Swing predicted.[16]

As a result, the 11th Airborne would conduct an amphibious assault on an enemy-held beach, while keeping one of its battalions in reserve to conduct an airborne assault—if Eichelberger ever authorized this mission. Swing and his men were given a week and a half to prepare.[17]

* * *

The waters off the town of Nasugbu were calm on January 31 when the invasion of southern Luzon began. The operation went well for the 11th Airborne ("uneventful," as one officer put it). Air Force planes and naval escort ships raked the landing zone with ordnance. The first soldiers landed at 8:15 and reported no Japanese opposition. The historical report of the division states: "By almost any standards in the Pacific the landing was a picnic."[18] The biggest challenge turned out to be the inexperience of the crews operating the landing craft. They often stopped well short of the water line, forcing the infantry to wade forward in water that was waist deep, and on occasion, chin deep. A number of vehicles sank in water that was above their engines.[19]

Swing and his division staff arrived just behind the second wave at 8:45 a.m. A Japanese machine gunner opened up on the command group moments after they landed. One of the landing craft turned their guns on the machine gun nest and silenced it quickly. It did not seem fast, though, to the men on the beach. Lieutenant Colonel William Crawford, the chief supply officer for the division, was frustrated at the slow response from the Navy. He started to get up with the intention of manning one of the guns on the landing craft himself. Swing grabbed his boot and pulled him down, telling him to stay put.

After the Japanese machine gunners stopped firing, Swing established his command. "Operation off to a good start," Eichelberger noted. "No opposition of any major nature was noted and it was planned to continue the advance during the night." Every element of the 11th Airborne was supporting the operation. Members of the division band operated bulldozers and the anti-aircraft battalion and Filipino guerrillas unloaded supplies from landing craft.[20]

The terrain, though, was made for a defender. The paratroopers had to march through narrow defiles with steep, wooded banks. "The Japanese, had they used their forces available in coordinated counterattacks, could have greatly delayed our troops," Isaac Hoppenstein, a supply officer in the 187th Glider Infantry Regiment, stated.[21]

It was becoming evident that intelligence reports were wrong. Eichelberger had expected to see much larger numbers of Japanese, and empty, evacuated towns. He was seeing the exact reverse—few Japanese and busy towns. Swing was unhappy. "The G-2 information on the situation confronting me is absolutely 'lousy.' I'm going in blind," he told his father-in-law before the operation.[22]

What he did not know was that the Japanese were withdrawing. Toi Hannosuke, the commander of the 111th Fishing Battalion—a special forces/suicide unit—had ordered his men to retreat to Manila. A few companies were to remain to cover the withdrawal, but they were generally out of position to do much of anything. On February 1, Rear Admiral Iwabuchi Sanji issued Manila Naval Defense Force Operation Order Number 38, ordering a withdrawal from Cavite, the area south of Manila through which the Angels would have to advance. Retreating soldiers were to destroy the Cavite–Tagaytay Road, the main artery south: "As to the places to be demolished, bridges will be selected as much as possible."[23]

MacArthur and his staff had given Eichelberger the freedom to convert his reconnaissance into a full-fledged assault should enemy resistance prove weak. The general went ashore that first afternoon. He was there, he later wrote his wife, so he could authorize Swing to advance north and to conduct an airborne assault. When it was clear that there was little Japanese resistance, he did just that. Swing knew perfectly well that Eichelberger was trying to beat Krueger to Manila: "If he isn't standing at the bar in the Army and Navy Club when Krueger walks in the door, then it won't be for lack of trying."[24]

The 11th Airborne Division's operation might have been a lopsided one, but it was still combat. At the intersection of the Nasugbu road and Highway 17, Colonel Robert "Shorty" Soule, commanding officer of the 188th Gilder Infantry Regiment, was studying a map spread out on the hood of a jeep when Japanese artillery began firing on him. He dived into a ditch, but not before he took a piece of shrapnel into his buttock.[25] Even at sea, it was dangerous. While there were no kamikaze air attacks, suicide boats tried to crash into US ships. Given the calm water, the fleet had to do "twist and turn" maneuvers to create sea conditions that helped them avoid contact, which made for a bumpy stay aboard. Eichelberger spent the night on his command ship, the *Spencer*, a converted U.S. Coast Guard cutter. "It was not a restful night," he observed.[26]

At dawn on February 1, US paratroopers reached the Mount Carillao–Mount Aiming–Mount Batulao area. Highway 17, basically a two-lane road, ran between these three large hills. Mount Carillao and Mount Aiming were on the north side of the road; Mount Batulao was on the south. Japanese defenders were dug in, occupying caves and trenches that gave them a perfect line of sight on the Americans. "They could see us coming," one soldier remarked. The twelve-hundred-foot-tall Mount Aiming was the key to the Japanese line of resistance. A battle for the hill raged all day. The 11th Airborne was beginning to take casualties in noticeable numbers. The Americans took Japanese positions and withstood small counterattacks. At 8:30 a.m. on February 2, the paratroopers launched another assault. Air strikes from the Fifth Air Force were key in destroying many enemy artillery positions. The Japanese took a beating. The daily report of the division simply notes: "Enemy made hasty withdrawal." The 11th Airborne captured the enemy command post at 1:30 p.m. The Japanese were retreating so fast that they left behind large amounts of food, ammunition, weapons, equipment, and the personal packs of many soldiers with clean clothes and fresh food. Hoppenstein personally recovered several cases of liquor, documents, and an officer's sword.[27] Swing later called the seizure of Mount Aiming an action of "decisive significance."[28]

Back on Nasugbu beach, follow-on units were landing and marching through quickly to sustain the advance. Schweitzer and his unit entered City Hall and found a safe that was ajar, overflowing with currency. They used the bills to start a fire and heat some coffee. Only after the war did they realize the cash was actually Japanese Yen rather than the worthless occupation pesos. Chuckling, Schweitzer said, "We figured maybe we had about a million dollar cup of coffee that night."[29] In another incident, a company of engineers marched past a sugar mill on the edge of town and discovered that the Japanese had been using it to make sugar alcohol to run their vehicles. "We liberated a few gallons, for the possibility when we got into the mountains to 'take the chill off,'" the company commander recalled.[30]

After a long day on February 2, exhausted men simply camped on the side of the road. Many ignored important security precautions. Japanese resistance was "sporadic," to use Swing's description in his after-action report. That evening a small Japanese patrol attacked the command post of the 2nd Battalion, 187th Glider Infantry Regiment. Eli Bernheim, a lieutenant in the unit, recalled that it sounded like a thousand Japanese were yelling and screaming. They hit a truck that contained flame throwers and white phosphorous ammunition. The truck exploded. Bernheim got out of his bed roll just in time to be hit in the ribs by a bazooka round. It was not armed and did not explode, but the full force of the kinetic energy went into his chest. "It felt like Ted Williams hitting me with a bat and the wind was knocked completely out of me."[31]

With the 11th Airborne making rapid advances on the ground, Eichelberger decided to conduct a parachute assault that would put a force of US infantry in the Japanese rear. The objective was Tagaytay Ridge, which dominated the terrain in the area. Using paratroopers would maintain a rapid tempo, which Eichelberger believed would keep the Japanese from regrouping and offering a tougher defense. "All considerations were disregarded except to keep the enemy on the run," Hoppenstein stated.[32]

There was an element of bluff in this effort. Despite its claims to elite status, the 11th Airborne was essentially a light infantry division, lacking both heavy weapons and the manpower to hold positions in depth. Had the Japanese responded with force, they could have rolled back the Americans easily. The best way to keep that from happening was for the 11th Airborne to keep moving ahead. As Swing told the division's historian, "We're pulled out now like a rubber band. The tension is increasing and it will continue to increase until we get to the top of Tagaytay. Then, we hope, we'll snap downhill—all the way to Manila."[33]

The airborne assault began at 7:30 a.m. on February 3. The flight to the ridge was a somber one for many of the soldiers. Private First Class Deane Marks said he was in a blank day dream. "I cannot remember <u>any</u> conversation taking place during the trip."[34] Everyone knew that they were operating with little depth in the Philippines. The U.S. Army Air Forces had limited lift resources in the Southwest Pacific Theater, and, as a result, it would take three drops instead of one to get the entire 188th Regiment Combat Team and the 511th Parachute Regiment on the ridge.[35]

The operation basically went well. Major Henry A. Burgess, the commanding officer of the 1st Battalion, 511th Parachute Infantry Regiment, in a letter home, declared, "It was the easiest jump I've ever made."[36] Staff Sergeant Steve Hegedus agreed: "nothing spectacular, it was a routine drop."[37] A reporter with the *Los Angeles Times* added that it was a "perfect" operation."[38] In addition to dropping men, the crews on the plane ejected supply canisters with heavy machine guns, ammunition, medical supplies, and communication equipment to sustain the division while it was behind enemy lines.[39]

The jump still required skill. There was, of course, the immediate shock as they exited the plane. Private Jim Holzem was knocked unconscious. One of his harness straps had slipped and was on his neck. Holzem managed to twist and reduce the pressure the strap was putting on his neck.[40] Larry Davis, a soldier in the 511th, wrote about the operation forty years later still using the third person, present tense: "The bullets sing by with a terrible hiss. Your pack is hit, but it is still a miss." He was profoundly scared. "A terror grips you, like you've never known, Your macho has vanished, your bravado is gone. You lay there clutching your shanking gun. If you had the guts, you'd turn and run. But fear of scorn is the stronger fear."[41]

Many others, however, remembered the view. "I will always remember the beautiful sight of Lake Taal as we approached from the south, made a wide circle around the lake and dropped on an east–west pass," Second Lieutenant William Miley recalled. Some paratroopers could see Filipinos waiving at them as they came down, and many swarmed the men when they landed, offering them food.[42]

The landing was actually less than "perfect." Paratroopers often got too close to one another. "Somebody walked right across my canopy," Earl Winsor, a medic in the division, remembered. This type of "sky walking" is possible because parachutes become rigid when full of air. "I heard them up there— klonk, klonk, klonk." Supply canisters drifted away from troop concentrations. Individual soldiers found themselves isolated. Some broke bones when they landed and had to be carried from the drop zone by their buddies.[43] "Drop was entirely too dispersed and dropping grounds were missed by a considerable margin," Eichelberger noted in his diary.[44]

The general was correct. Men landed as far as six miles away. Of the 1,750 men that took place in the operation, only 425 landed in the drop zone. As a result, it was not until 2 p.m. that Swing had effective command and control of his men. After the war, the general was blunt in his assessment. He argued that the mistakes that led to a wide dispersion were the fault of the Army Air Forces. Airmen had refused to cooperate in joint training exercises. As a result, they had little experience working with his men.[45]

The operation was nonetheless an impressive achievement. "Tagaytay Ridge was by all odds the most important military position in southern Luzon," Eichelberger stated. "We were ready for the dash on Manila."[46]

The 11th Airborne had momentum on their side, and Swing kept pushing, sending a patrol out under First Lieutenant George Skau to report on conditions to the north. Hours passed but at 4 a.m. Skau reported back that the road to Manila, some twenty-five miles away, was open. The Japanese had blown the bridge over the Imus River and set up a defensive position to fire on the US advance. A dirt road bypassed that bridge. The Japanese had wired the bridge to explode but using that dirt road the reconnaissance patrol removed the demolitions.[47] Skau established a series of posts, using guerrillas and his own men, keeping the route open and avoiding the Japanese trap.[48]

The elements of the division that had landed at Nasugbu, meanwhile, were rushing forward to reach the men on the ridge. The Japanese resistance was light, but ever-present and coming from different directions. Al Ulman, a medic, recorded in his diary: "Tired of marching, slept on the ground last night. Expect trouble soon." He got it on February 2. "Jap artillery open up, everyone dived for ditches but some were not so lucky. At least ten killed and no wounded." He helped a major perform an amputation with a trench knife while they were in a trench with artillery landing around them. "A miserable day. That night was on guard, boy was I scared."[49]

At one point in the advance, a small group of Japanese soldiers in a hut fired on a patrol. Private First Class James E. Richardson and two other men approached the hut, which was made of light wood and woven grass, sitting on stilts. When he was close enough, Richardson threw a grenade in and then charged through the door and unloaded the clip of ammunition in his rifle. Expecting some type of recognition for his bravery, he was surprised when his platoon leader and platoon sergeant scolded him for reckless behavior. The hut was made of flimsy material that normally would not have stopped grenade fragments. The main reason Richardson survived was that the Japanese defenders absorbed the full explosion of the grenade.[50]

Soldiers at all levels of command were in harm's way as the 11th Airborne marched north. During the amphibious landing, Eichelberger himself had been patrolling with the forward infantry company. In the towns of Imus and Las Pinas, the general was again in the lead and was actually pinned down for a while by Japanese riflemen. While sharing the risks with the common foot soldier might seem admirable in a commander, he was allowing tactical action to dominate the responsibilities of his rank. He was, after all, the commanding general of a field army—one of only three in the Pacific.[51]

Other risks were more calculated. The 11th Airborne had Japanese on three sides. "The Japs seemed to be everywhere, in the trees, behind shrubbery and in the hills," Technician Grade Five Theolbald Kobus remembered. The division had not secured its flanks.[52] "As you can see, I am making a rapid dash with a very small force," Eichelberger told his wife in a letter. "We are taking big risks." He believed the gamble was worth taking because of the quality of the unit he was using. "I am very keen about this 11th Airborne. They are small in number but they are willing to fight." The next day, he added, "I must admit that we have been very fortunate so far."[53]

Media coverage of the Eighth Army's advance on Manila was almost nonexistent. This lack of coverage rankled Eichelberger. Despite a brief flurry of interest with the amphibious assault, and a few mentions on radio reports, Frank Smith of the *Chicago Daily Times* was the only correspondent directly covering their march toward Manila.[54]

Soldiers in the 11th Airborne Division were upset that they were getting no recognition for their dangerous and hard work. Two wounded enlisted men, Privates First Class Ralph Merisiecki and Charles Feuereisen, who were temporarily assigned to a chute-packing unit while they recovered from their wounds, were equal parts astonished and dismayed to learn while in recovery that the exploits of their division had received little recognition in the theater or back at home. They went to MacArthur's headquarters, then at Price House on Tacloban, and requested to see the theater commander. "I don't know how they got in; I know Sutherland wouldn't have let them," Swing stated. Aides were trying to turn them away when the general overheard the conversation and overruled his staff. They met with MacArthur and asked blunt questions about their division's lack of recognition. The general told them that he was keeping the 11th Airborne Division out of dispatches because he did not want the Japanese to know who they were up against. The Angels were his secret weapon. Swing was not impressed: "He had the blarney all right."[55]

The paratroopers were moving north as fast as they could, but it was not easy. They had few vehicles and most of their advance was on foot. "It was the hardest march I've ever made," Burgess told his parents in a letter. Men were passing out on the side of the road. "These men are superb," Burgess stated. "I saw one boy whose legs wouldn't work trying to crawl." Private First Class Rod Serling, a writer who became famous as the creator of the television series *The Twilight Zone*, was one of those soldiers. "The packs, the ammo belts, weaponry, all fused to us like extensions of our bodies, the weights so constant that it was all part of us," he wrote. These rapid marches brought the two elements of the division together at 1:30 p.m. on February 3.[56]

At the time, Swing was worried about a Japanese counterattack. "I kept truck trains running all night with their lights on to make the Japs think after we got in behind and ran up the road, that there more troops than there actually were."[57] At least his intelligence was getting better, mainly because of the guerrillas. They were proving to be informative and helpful in informing of the location of Japanese defenses. They were also quite good at providing security on his flanks and in rear areas.[58]

The 11th Airborne Angels were also helped in that they faced a cooperative adversary. In a study that he conducted after the war, Hoppenstein was stunned at the level of Japanese incompetence: "With the best defensive terrain, he continually allowed his position to be outflanked." Poor leadership and a lack of training seemed to be key issues. "Each time our troops hit a new defensive position it seemed to catch the Japs completely by surprise." Swing was even more damning: "We can never be sure what their next move will be, since their thought processes are so alien to ours. The best method seems to be to figure out what a logical military move would be and then prepare for the exact opposite."[59]

While this might describe an overall lack of Japanese strategy, small bands of Japanese were valiant in their efforts. The 11th Airborne Division faced strong resistance in the town of Imus, for example, where the Angels attempted to bypass a blown-out bridge. Company D of the 511th found the Japanese in a well-constructed complex of stone buildings that covered all the avenues of approach. Technical Sergeant Robert C. Steele of the 511th played a key role in breaking the defense at Imus. He ordered his platoon to provide covering fire to divert Japanese attention away from him and then advanced over an open field with a can of gas. He climbed to the roof of one building, tore a hole open, and poured the fuel in, then threw in a white prosperous grenade. "That's all she wrote," one soldier remarked. The Japanese that survived rushed out of the building only to be cut down by Steele's platoon. Steele was awarded the Distinguished Service Cross.[60]

While D Company was involved in this firefight, a detail of engineers advanced to the remaining bridge across the Imus River. They found it intact but rigged to explode. They removed the fuse from an aerial bomb in the roadway arch of the bridge and then found a route that led back to Highway 17.[61]

As the paratroopers advanced, they were often overwhelmed by well-wishers. This started almost from the moment they arrived at Nasugbu, where a crowd had gathered with a band. The official division report makes distinct mention of Filipina, European, and American women greeting them as well. These celebrations continued as they moved inland. People lined the road. In Silang, a brass band began playing as the first US patrol entered the town. A guerrilla group flying the US flag formed up along the side of the road and rendered Present Arms as the Americans passed by. In other locations, people gave the Angels bananas and alcohol. "The sheer joy on their faces is hard to forget," Private Marks recalled three decades later. One Filipino Army officer called the 11th Airborne advance a "festive motorcade."[62]

In one town, a woman handed her child to Private Holzem, a paratrooper who had landed at Tagaytay Ridge, as his unit took a break from its road march. Trying to be polite, he took the child and said nice things about it. "Then I looked up—and the woman was gone!" Quickly realizing she intended to abandon the child, he ran after her, "carrying the baby like a grocery sack in my arms." It was not easy for him to catch up with her. "She went up one street and down another. She had the edge on me because she hadn't been marching all day and wasn't loaded down with gear as I was." He caught up with her just as she was about to enter a house, thanked her, but said food was the only thanks required, and returned to his unit, which was already on the move. He had to run to catch up. "Instead of spending the

ten-minute rest period relaxing on the ground I had spent the whole damn
time running."[63]

The division had a good view of Manila from the top of Tagaytay Ridge,
as well as from the positions they held along the coast. As he drove between
Tagaytay Ridge and the forward lines of the 11th Airborne, Eichelberger could
see the city burning. "Great fires were noted in all sections of the city," he
noted in his diary.[64] Even from thirty miles away they could hear the crackling
of wood and rumble of cement collapsing.[65]

* * *

The 11th Airborne had faced logistical problems that were far more significant than those the Sixth Army was confronting. These had started right at the
beginning. The beach at Nasugbu was big enough for a landing, but shallow,
making it difficult for the landing craft to reach dry land. Unloading in the
water made stocking of supply dumps a slow process. The Angels also had few
exit lanes. Swamps, rice paddies, and coastal streams limited the avenues for
departure to two roads. The Americans had needed civilian labor and guerrilla
units to unload their supplies and while Filipinos were more than willing, they
wanted to be paid in food, and rations started to run out during their second
day on Luzon. Supplies were short even for the paratroopers themselves. The
457th Parachute Field Artillery Battalion brought two liaison aircraft onto
Luzon during the amphibious assault. The planes were disassembled for transport and intended to be used as spotters for artillery fire. Under enemy fire,
the gunners assembled them and then used them to drop supplies to forward
elements marching north. That helped with some supply difficulties. On top
of all these issues, the Filipinos wanted real food and not Army rations.[66]

The advance came to a stop in Las Piñas when, for all practical purposes,
the 11th Airborne joined the Battle of Manila. The Japanese had heavy naval
guns based at Nichols Field—Manila's main airport—that were preregistered
on key road intersections. "We were stopped cold," Private Marks declared.[67]
The Angels managed to push through Las Piñas, but they were slowed to a
crawl in the town of Parañaque. The 11th Airborne was suddenly coming up
against the artillery of the Genko Line, the southern Defensive positions of the
Manila Naval Defense Force Their advance would now be measured in yards
rather than miles.[68]

The southern invasion was dramatic, but there is the question of its significance. Eichelberger argued the march north had drawn defenders away from

Manila, assisting the drive south. Given how the Japanese had organized the defense, and the limited command and control resources Iwabuchi had, this view was more wishful thinking than anything else. The real contribution is the one Eichelberger's biographer, John F. Shortal, advances: that the general goaded Krueger into moving the Sixth Army faster. The 11th Airborne Division moved with speed and created a tempo that was difficult for the Japanese to resist. There was little damage done in the places that the Americans zoomed through. In a 2004 study conducted for the U.S. Army Command & General Staff College, the study's author, Major Matthew H. Faith, contended that speed also kept casualties low and was due to Eichelberger's ability to adapt to fast-changing circumstances.[69]

To be sure, the march north to Manila was impressive tactically. In four days, the division had advanced sixty-seven miles on foot, using what the unit's operations report called "Stonewall Jackson tactics" of avoiding a direct confrontation and advancing on the enemy's flanks. That advance required soldiers to march an average of sixteen to seventeen miles a day, which is no easy thing, particularly with the Japanese shooting back from defensive positions. As one soldier joked, "The 11th Airborne Division has established a beach-head 200 yards wide and 65 miles deep," which, as the division's history notes, was "literally true."[70]

The question remains as to what impact the advance had at the operational and strategic levels. In an operational sense, the advance was more important not for what it accomplished, but for what it prevented. While the 11th Airborne was pushing against a mostly open door, that door could easily have been closed on them had they moved slower and given the Japanese time to react. The march north also suggests what might have happened had MacArthur advanced on Manila with even greater speed. However courageous the 11th Airborne Angels had been, the Japanese were still in Manila, waiting for the Americans.

7

Santo Tomás

In the early evening of Saturday, February 3, while the 11th Airborne was confronting the Genko Line in the south, the 1st Cavalry crossed the northern Manila city limits. The race for Manila was over. For decades, the division and its alumni would proudly celebrate February 3 as "Manila Day" with the slogan: "The 1st was first."[1]

When the Japanese took control of the Philippines in 1942, they found thousands of foreign nationals living in Manila. Most were Americans, although there were other nationalities as well. The Japanese had to decide what to do with them. The citizens of neutral nations and those allied with Japan were allowed to keep living their lives uninterrupted. Enemy aliens, however, were interned instead in a large camp that the Japanese established on the grounds of the Pontifical and Royal University of Santo Tomás. In the 1940s, the campus was a large, fifty-three acre square, bounded by four streets in the Sampaloc district north of the Pasig River. Much of the campus at the time was undeveloped land that had served as sports fields and lawns before the war. During their incarceration, the internees built many shacks and shanties for individual dwellings on this open land. A wall that was about eight to ten feet tall encircled the grounds of the school. Several thousand people came to live at the university and living conditions—food rations in particular—began to decline in 1944. At the start of the new year, the internees were slowly starving to death.[2]

In early 1945, the residents of Santo Tomás knew the Americans were coming. "With all the air activity, we knew that the end was near," Terry Wadsworth, who was a child at time, observed years later. On one occasion, American pilot flew so low that the civilians could see his face. On January 6, they watched the Japanese burning records and removing equipment. The guards left for a day, making the civilians think their liberation was close at hand. News reports on radios in nearby houses—that Filipinos deliberately set to maximum volume so the internees could hear them—confirmed what many had suspected: the Americans had returned.[3]

In the three-and-a-half weeks it took for the U.S. Army to reach Manila, signs were growing that liberation was coming. The residents could hear artillery exchanges, and they watched fires and smoke reach into the air as the Japanese destroyed extra supplies. "Every day and night the audible signs of war are more with us," Frank Carry, one of the residents, wrote to his family in a letter dated February 3. "There is no doubt that the boys are nearer," Fay Cook Bailey, a prewar official of the Manila branch of the National City Bank of New York, recorded in his diary.[4]

The internees were becoming more optimistic and confident. The Japanese were becoming, on the whole, more respectful. Conversations focused on the food that U.S. Army might bring. Yet there was concern and impatience. "Those were tense days and hours," Herman E. Strong, recalled. "We felt that great events were in the making, but we did not know where, when, or how they would affect us."[5]

Nothing less than their survival was at stake. "There was a race between death from starvation for our internees, and the Americans entering Manila," Evelyn M. Witthoff and Geraldine V. Chappell wrote in a memoir of their stay at Santo Tomás. "Would the Americans arrive in time to save our lives we wondered."[6]

The horse soldiers were confident that they would reach Santo Tomás and liberate the internees. "Everybody who knows the 1st Cavalry Division of the United States Army 'just knew' that it would be the first into Manila," Lewis B. Sebring, Jr. of the *New York Herald Tribune* reported afterward.[7] Excitement and confusion were in the air. "Jap equipment was on fire on both sides of the road," George Fischer, the loader on the tank called "Georgia Peach," observed.[8] He watched through the vehicle's periscope as Filipinos gathered on the side of the road, cheering and singing.[9]

At the internment camp, anticipation, confusion, and desperation were rampant. If the Americans were going to arrive, they needed to come soon. The average caloric intake of the internees was between seven hundred and eight hundred a day. In her diary, Tressa R. Cates, a nurse, recorded that twenty-three people died of starvation between the landings at Lingayen and the liberation of the camp.[10]

Ten minutes after the 1st Cavalry crossed into Manila, US planes buzzed the compound. Rick Lawrence looked up and said, "My God, those don't look like Japanese planes." A pilot dropped a pair of goggles with a note attached: "Roll out the barrel. Santa Clause is coming Sunday or Monday." Freedom was coming in one or two days, but the noise of combat was growing louder. What did it mean? "Keyed up as we were, the suspense was unbearable," Emily Van Sickle, a resident at Santo Tomás, explained.[11]

After crossing the city limits, it took the Americans more than two hours to make their way to the university. In the dark it was difficult for the soldiers to know what street they were on. Carl Mydans and Frank Hewlett helped guide the troops.[12] During the confusion, two former members of the Philippine Scouts, a prewar U.S. Army special forces formation, made contact with the column and offered to guide the Americans to the university. Lieutenant Colonel Haskett Conner was skeptical at first, but after some questioning, he decided to trust them. Strong Japanese resistance was forcing the column to look for another path to Santo Tomás.[13]

Conner also ordered Captain Emery Hickman, a graduate of the Oklahoma Military Academy, to take Troop F of the 8th Cavalry and a tank platoon from the 44th Tank Battalion to secure Malacañan Palace, the second of the three objectives. When the Americans arrived, the presidential guard hesitated to open the gate, afraid they might be mistaken for Japanese soldiers or assumed to be collaborators. The lead US tank ended that hesitation when it plowed through the wrought-iron gate. The palace staff quickly decided the best thing to do was to make the best of the situation and was waiting to greet the Americans with mugs of hot coffee and freshly baked cookies.[14]

The rest of the flying column seemed less focused. Brigadier General William C. Chase was traveling in a jeep loaded with radio equipment, which allowed him to keep in constant contact with 1st Cavalry Division's commander, Verne D. Mudge; the Marine aviators flying above; and the various elements of his column. He knew that Santo Tomás was intact and that the prisoners were still present. He also knew that fires were starting in various parts of the city and street fighting had begun. Three Japanese trucks pulled out of an alley and began driving parallel to the general's convoy, shooting at them. The Americans returned fire. The general pulled out his pistol and emptied a clip of ammunition at the driver of one truck. The trucks were so close that when one exploded, the flames burned Chase.[15]

When the first element of the 1st Cavalry arrived at Santo Tomás, the compound was dark and quiet. The Americans stopped on the grass meridian in the middle of España Street, which put them about forty feet away from the main gate of the university. At the time, the main building and the plaza in front of it were at the end of a quarter-mile long, tree-lined road leading into the interior from España Street. (The fountains, statues, and the Arch of the Centuries, a triumphal arch with Doric columns and baroque styling, came after the war.) On either side of this road were open lawns.

The Americans were not sure what to expect. The university was dark and silent. Some speculated that the Japanese had abandoned the camp and moved the prisoners. "No," Hewlett replied. "They're in there. It's only the Japs are gone."[16]

Mydans and Hewlett volunteered to enter the compound. "What are we waiting for?" Mydans asked. The two went through the half-opened main gate. "Hello, anyone!" he shouted. "This is Carl Mydans. Are there any Americans in there?" There was no reaction. Then a bullet struck the ground between them. Mydans scrambled to the other side of the wall where William Dunn was sitting. Dunn could see his friend was terrified: "Bill, I'm afraid to go in there, afraid of what we're going to find. I don't think there's anyone still alive."[17]

Conner, who was responsible for the journalists, was trying to figure out what to do. He was holding a quick conference with his subordinates and Captain Manuel Colayco, a guerrilla leader who was briefing Conner about the camp, when a Japanese solider threw a grenade from the other side of the wall. Shrapnel tore up Colayco's torso. Conner was lightly wounded, and he acted quickly, ordering an attack. A tank—nicknamed "Battling Basic"— plowed through the front gate, and four others followed, firing. The guards on duty, who were mostly Formosans, surrendered immediately.[18]

In the university's main building, Lieutenant Colonel Hayashi Toshio, the camp commandant, was talking with the internee leaders, trying to get them to serve as go-betweens to arrange a transfer of authority. As they were talking, Hayashi was getting reports: a tank was at the gate; several tanks had entered the compound; many tanks were in front of the building. He left the room, then returned and repeated his request for an orderly transfer of power.[19]

The tanks reached the main building. Doug Luyendyck recalled, "A hush came over the whole building. It was silent as a tomb just before the tanks came."[20] Powerful lights then shot through the windows. "What looked like a gigantic moving house was a brilliantly lighted tank."[21] Some internees were blocking the doors as gunfire was exchanged. After the shooting stopped, two soldiers approached the main building and asked in loud voices if there were any Americans present.

Back on España Street, Joe Aiello heard a noise that, as he recalled, reminded him of one he had once heard before in Yankee Stadium when Joe DiMaggio hit a home run.[22] Mack Thomson was driving a jeep in part of the column that had not yet reached the university campus, "We were quite a ways behind the lead tanks, but we could hear the cheers of the Filipinos and the prisoners as they saw their liberators at the university gate."[23]

According to the official report of the Sixth Army, the column had liberated 3,521 people.[24] Dunn informed his radio audience that the crashing of the gate, the brief exchange of gunfire, and a search of the compound had taken about an hour.[25]

* * *

Inside the camp, the internees suddenly realized they were free. "The place went crazy; absolutely nuts," Lawrence recalled.[26] Children were soon swarming over the tanks, as the soldiers gave them chocolate bars and candy.[27] "The atmosphere was electric with excitement," Witthoff recalled. "Suddenly it seemed as if all hell had broken lose."[28]

The internees inside the main building who were too weak to come outside began singing "God Bless America," their voices floating out to the crowd below.[29] Soon everyone was singing "God Bless America" and "The Star-Spangled Banner." People were cheering and dancing.[30]

The soldiers looked alien to many of the children. "They looked so big and fat," Wadsworth recorded in her diary. Robin Prising, a twelve-year-old, was terrified. The men were tall, yellow, and wearing German helmets. His reactions were quite common among civilians in Manila. There were two reasons. First, many soldiers had yellow skin, which was a side-effect from their use of Atabrine pills to fight malaria. The second reason was that the U.S. Army in 1942 had gotten rid of the M1917 helmet, which had been first used in World War I and replaced it with the M1, or "steel pot" helmet, which has some resemblance to the *stahlelm* or "coal scuttle" helmet of the German Army.[31]

Despite this type of confusion, the celebrations continued through the night. "We scarcely tried to sleep that night," Van Sickle remembered. "The realization of our sudden freedom flooded away all weariness, and we all lay in the darkness talking of our wonderful soldiers."[32] In her diary, Eva Anna Nixon, writing in the present tense, wrote: "We thought you'd never come. You mean life to us. So many were dying."[33]

The strong emotional reaction affected the soldiers. "I guess that was probably the most satisfactory event of my career was getting the liberation of those civilians," Sam E. Harris, a trooper in the 1st Cavalry, asserted years later. Men and women were coming up to them hugging and kissing them. Most stood around with "big silly grins." Frank Mendez of the 8th Cavalry Regiment recalled, "You can't imagine how the prisoners reacted. It's a hard thing to describe because they were so overjoyed."[34] When the prisoners asked the soldiers how they could thank them, some requested that they write their families and let them know they were okay. Bob Cryster, for one, wrote to the family of Denny Norton, a soldier in the flying column, informing them of their son's health and expressing his gratitude for his role in bringing about his freedom. It was one of the last notes that reached them before news of his death arrived.[35]

Strong was impressed with the professionalism of the soldiers. "I have never seen such calm deliberation in all my life as these boys methodically went about their job, coddling us like we were babies with one hand, while shooting Japanese with the other."[36]

Madeline Ullom, an Army nurse among the internees, saw Conner limping in front of the main building. She took him to the hospital and dressed his wound. Only after treating him did she get his name as she filled out the required paperwork. She was a bit surprised and asked if he was related to Colonel Haskett Lynch Conner of the Army Medical Corps. Connor admitted that he was. The colonel was the lieutenant colonel's father. Ullom was a bit flabbergasted. The elder Conner had chaired the physical evaluation board that had approved her commission in the Army. They two talked for a long time, and after the war Ullom would correspond with both Conners for decades.[37]

Colayco, wounded in the same firefight as Connor, was brought to the hospital. He asked that one of his men find a Catholic priest so he could take last rites. Father John Hurley arrived. Hurley had been an instructor of Colayco's at Ateneo de Manila College and the two had a quick reunion. After confession and last rites, Colayco underwent surgery. The operation failed and he died seven days later, on February 10.[38]

Hewlett did not wait for the campus to be secured. He began looking for his wife the instant he entered the grounds of the university. He quickly recognized Charles Van Sickle. "Hello, I know you but I can't think of your name," Hewlett said from the top of a tank.

"Van Sickle."

Hewlett jumped down and gave him a hug, asking if Van Sickle knew anything about his wife. He did. She was in the camp hospital. Hewlett ran into the main building to find her.[39]

Dunn reluctantly entered the compound. He was still a little worried about the Japanese presence. As he neared the tank, a woman ran up to him and shouted, "Your're Bill Dunn." He was surprised to be recognized, but also that he remembered her: "You're Mary Roberts—and just as beautiful as ever!" He had known her and her husband in prewar Manila.[40]

As Dunn was talking with a group of internees, someone clapped him on the back. It was Hewlett. "I found her!" he yelled. "*I found her!*" he exclaimed again as he gave Dunn a huge bear hug. Dunn watched as his friend danced off to share the news with others. "We were in the midst of thousands of deliriously happy people, but not one could top the happiness of Frank Hewlett," he observed.[41]

Hewlett's wife, a nurse, had been in the hospital as a patient rather than as staff. She was coming down some stairs and he did not recognize her at first. She weighed eighty pounds and was recovering from a nervous breakdown. "I found her in excellent spirits," he wrote in a news story that he filed that day.[42]

The story of the Hewletts is well-known, although always told from Frank Hewlett's point of view. Virginia Hewlett's account is more obscure. When the cavalry arrived, she and Rita G. Palmer, a First lieutenant in the Army Nurse Corps, heard the commotion in the camp hospital. Both were weak from hunger and watched the scene from a hospital window. Hewlett told Palmer it was a shame her husband was not present to watch and record their liberation.[43]

Despite the jubilation at the arrival of American soldiers at Santo Tomás, they were not in a good tactical situation. Firefights were taking place behind them. On Highway 52, the Japanese struck back. They demolished the Novaliches Bridge over the Tuliahan River that Sutton, the Navy lieutenant, had saved the day before. Now the flying columns in the city were cut off from the rest of their division. The road was blocked with burning Japanese vehicles. From the darkness Japanese defenders were throwing grenades and snipers were targeting individual soldiers. When a convoy under the command of Colonel Charles A. Sheldon, the chief of staff of the 1st Cavalry Division, arrived at the "hot corner," he quickly understood the danger. Sheldon ordered the vehicles pushed down the bank of the steep gorge. Just as this was finished, one of the vehicles exploded, indicating it was a bomb on wheels. What little supplies they would get would have to come from the 37th Infantry Division. "It fell to the 37th Division to rescue the rescuers," Mathias noted in his memoirs.[44]

In Manila itself, the column was spread out over several different streets. The rear guard of the column got "chewed up—as First Lieutenant William H. Swan put it—in the firefights that took place after dark. "For friend and foe it was an inferno of confusion," Swan recalled. The Japanese blocked the streets with old vehicles and fired at the Americans from their flanks. Some troopers dismounted and ran for cover. The tanks tried to pick some up, but they kept going. "Our tank platoon had to get out," Swan explained. "As sitting ducks we were vulnerable to Molotov cocktails and satchel charges." These tanks were out of radio contact with the rest of the column and lost in the city. They found a park and pulled into defensive positions to wait out the night. Other Americans continued to arrive at Santo Tomás. Chase arrived an hour after the "Battling Basic" had plowed down the main gate.[45]

* * *

A Japanese attack against these isolated formations was not long in coming. Troop F of the 8th Cavalry and the tank platoon from the 44th Tank Battalion, under the command of Captain Hickman, held Malacañan Palace during the night against a Japanese counterattack. The tank group that Swan was riding with made contact via radio with one vehicle and made their way there with the assistance of a couple of young boys, who acted as guides. When they arrived at the palace, they found forty dead Japanese in front of Hickman's positions and the burning wrecks of five cars.[46]

The Americans were able to hold their positions mainly due to the weak response of the Japanese. "We were short of food and ammunition, and would have been hard pressed to hold the compound," Chase admitted. "Again—we were lucky."[47]

At Santo Tomás, the internees could hear the angry sound of battle. "But what did we care, we were all too drunk with happiness," Elizabeth "Bim" Meyer, a teenager at the time, observed.[48] The soldiers, on the other hand, aware that they were isolated, began establishing defensive position. The internees wanted to help, but their offers were declined. George Fischer was manning a heavy machine gun on the "Georgia Peach" when a young boy came over and suggested he take over, so Fischer could get some sleep. "This request, I had to refuse," the tanker stated. "I could have been court martialed."[49]

Another problem the Americans faced was that there was still a group of guards in the Education Building holding internees hostage, some 276 in all. The Japanese used the first floor as a garrison and positioned their heavy machine guns to interdict the stairwells and to keep the internees that lived on the top two floors in place. Some of the prisoners understood what the Japanese were doing and cut bed sheets into ropes that they could use to climb out of the building. Live fire exchanges took place for several hours. The hostages yelled at the Americans to stop, but the soldiers could not hear them. The tanks lined up in front of the building, and using only their machine guns, shot up the first floor. Soldiers in the main building, which was next to the Education Building, put a 50-caliber gun on the fourth floor of the main building. Peter Wygle watched the firefight from the window of his room in the main building. "It was the noisiest thing I have ever heard in my life." Irene Hecht's view was a bit more philosophical. As she lay on the ground with her mother, she pondered her fate. "I was thinking how ridiculous it would be to die now just as we were finally free!"[50]

Combat was not what any of the Americans wanted. "Everybody was dead tired," Fischer recalled. When the soldiers learned the identities of the prisoners the Japanese were holding on the third floor, they ceased their fire.[51] Hayahshi sent a small delegation, a mix of officers and civilians, to negotiate with the Americans. One of them, Hirose Toshio, was a diplomat who was part of the Japanese Foreign Service. Lieutenant Abiko Nanakazu, who was not part of the delegation, approached from behind. Abiko was a heavy-set individual and clearly was not one of the Imperial Japanese Army's finest. In the past, he had taken out his frustrations on the prisoners, bullying and humiliating them. He was not interested in negotiating now. Standing in front of the tanks, he reached for a grenade. Major James Gearheart shot him. The rest of the Americans held their fire.[52]

A group of internees began immediately taking out their anger on Akibo, kicking and stabbing him as he lay on the ground, writhing in pain. They yelled a number of obscenities at him. "It was pretty ugly," Lawrence recalled. Emily Van Sickle turned back: "To me, there was no joy in gloating over a dying man's body, however, great the satisfaction in knowing that the world will forever be rid of a foul blot that once defiled it." The soldiers intervened and took Abiko to the camp hospital. Surgery failed to save his life.[53]

General Chase arrived at the university after the confrontation had started. He realized he had no good options. The Japanese had soaked the first two floors in oil, daring the Americans to fire on them. "I have been criticized for turning these Japanese loose as I did, but they really had me in a bind, and there was little else I could do," the general explained. He gave the job of overseeing the negotiations to Colonel Charles E. Brady. Two of the internees—Ernest Stanley, a British missionary, and Carry—along with a Japanese American soldier named Ken Uyesugi—did the translation work. Uyesugi was in profound cultural shock. He was astonished at the Japanese refusal to accept defeat.[54]

There were stops and starts in the talks, exchanges of gunfire, and individual meetings between Hayashi and Brady, over the course of February 4. A few hostages escaped as the guards began to nod off. During a cease fire, the Americans provided an Irish stew for both the Japanese and the hostages, which the prisoners found difficult to consume. After several hours, the two sides reached an agreement: the Japanese would release the hostages. In return they would retain their weapons and US soldiers would escort them to a location in Manila of their choosing. Japanese civilians, though, would not be part of the group allowed to depart.[55]

While these negotiations were taking place, Colonel Noguchi Katsuzo, commanding the defense in northern Manila, sent a platoon under the command of Second Lieutenant Murakami Kyosaku to retake the internment camp. The platoon was climbing the wall of the university when Murakami was shot in the knee. With their lieutenant wounded and unable to lead them, the unit retreated, carrying him back to their base at the General Post Office.[56]

Despite this showdown, the celebration in Santo Tomás continued. On February 4, Mydans commemorated the moment by rounding up the ten men with whom he had shared a room during his eight-and-half months at Santo Tomás and took their picture.[57]

The hostage crisis ended on February 5. The Japanese left Santo Tomás at 7:00 a.m., marching out of the Education Building with Stanley, Mydans, and a detachment of about one hundred US soldiers. Mydans raced ahead, taking pictures. The internees cheered their departure. The Americans tried to stop their escort and return to Santo Tomás several times, but the Japanese objected. They continued on to Sampaloc Rotonda—the agreed destination—the Americans and Japanese exchanged salutes, and Brady and his men departed. The Japanese were on their own and in a part of Manila that was actually now in US hands. As they marched toward Malacañan Palace, they ran into a US guard post and were cut to pieces. Some escaped, but most were killed, including Lieutenant Colonel Hayashi.[58]

From the rotunda of Santo Tomás, Colonel Brady took a group to Malacañan Palace. In an example of the kind of confusion in the battle during its early stages, a Japanese vehicle became intermixed with Brady's group. When his driver informed him of the enemy presence, he had his vehicles pull over and as the Japanese truck attempted to keep going, the Americans opened fire. They arrived at the palace in time to watch a Cadillac drive onto the grounds. The defenders shot the four Japanese officers inside the car. An investigation soon determined that the car belonged to Douglas MacArthur.[59]

While the hostage situation at Santo Tomás built to its conclusion, the internees faced serious health issues. "The internees were emaciated," Dr. John R. Hall, a 1st Cavalry surgeon who was part of the column, recalled, and "had been deprived of security and liberty to the extent that many had difficulty realizing that help had arrived."[60] Starvation and malnutrition were the major problems. "The critical thing we were spared after February 3, 1945 was hunger, a change bordering on the miraculous," Hecht later stated.[61] The devastation was so bad that several people who had known Dunn before the war had to introduce themselves to him because their physical appearance had changed enormously.[62] The soldiers shared food despite instructions to the contrary.[63] "The soldiers were very generous in sharing their rations with internees— and many internees were shameless in the way they stole and/or begged stuff from the 'boys,'" Carry noted. As with the Irish stew, the problem was the proteins in the food were too complex for their weakened bodies to process. Many of the released prisoners gorged themselves only to vomit out the food a little later. "In spite of the diarrhea and illness, we could not leave the good food alone," Cates admitted.[64] Starvation is a slow process that does not pivot quickly.[65] Former prisoners continued to die from malnutrition even after the Americans had begun providing food.[66]

Bedridden patients suffered the most. Although the committee running the camp made efforts to feed them, the individuals tasked with this chore often stole food for themselves.[67]

Within two days, the Army had Red Cross packages to hand out and officials were surprised that they ran out before all the internees got one. Some individuals had gotten in a second column after they got their first package.[68]

The internees at the university were, on the whole, in much better shape than those being held at Bilibid Prison, which was about a mile away to the south. To reach it, Mudge ordered Chase to seize control of the Manuel L. Quezon Memorial Bridge, which crossed the Pasig River and was still intact. As they neared the span, a squadron of the 5th Cavalry walked into an ambush. Some two hundred Japanese opened fire from buildings on the campus of Far Eastern University. The university was on the corner of the Quezon Boulevard and Azcarraga Avenue intersection. Quezon Boulevard was a large, multi-lane paved road that led directly to the bridge. The Japanese had a staggered mine-field and two groups of obstacles blocking travel on the boulevard and access to the bridge.

The battle was now taking place across the street from Bilibid Prison, which was full of civilian internees and U.S. Army prisoners of war (POWs). "We were transfixed and utterly dumbstruck at the sight of such a powerful armed force," James V. Thompson, a civilian internee, recalled. Thompson and others watched as the firefight took place a few feet away from them. Heavy Japanese guns laced defensive positions with shell after shell. Machine-gun fire cut down a number of the dismounted troopers in the open. Tanks turned to the rear and used their flame throwers to reach into the hiding places of Japanese riflemen.

The prisoners believed they were watching an imminent US victory, but it was nothing of the kind.[69] A number of soldiers hid on the other side of their tanks until the 5th Cavalry had to retreat to Santo Tomás. "I sure don't want to get into anything like that again," a survivor told Emily Van Sickle back at the university. In Bilibid, Thompson watched what he called "the cleansing fires of vengeance" burn Japanese positions. Despite that enthusiastic analysis of the US effort, the Japanese had won and Colonel Noguchi's Northern Force blew up the bridge. The prison was on the other side of Quezon Boulevard and neither the Japanese nor the 5th Cavalry tried to enter the facility.[70]

* * *

By the time the Americans took Santo Tomás, the Japanese in Manila still outnumbered them. The arrival of the 37th Infantry Division changed the calculus quickly. The first elements crossed the city limits between Malbon and Manila at the Bonifacio Monument, a huge obelisk, in column at 1:07 p.m. on February 4. The 145th and 148th Infantry regiments were pushing through city streets abreast of one another; sometimes the soldiers of each regiment were on either side of Highway 3. They were dirty and tired, having made the march on one meal a day. "We had a tough road in," war correspondent Royal

Arch Gunnison, who had hiked in with the division, informed his readers. As the soldiers reached the monument, a Japanese machine gun opened up. Dick Hanley, a correspondent for *Yank* magazine, declared: "The fight for Manila was on."[71]

After waiting for a patrol to deal with the machine gun, the Ohio infantrymen ran low, zigzagging across the plaza in front of the obelisk one by one. As the last man made his run, the machine gun opened up again, but it was too late. "We were in the city now," Hanley stated.[72]

The stink was one of the first things the men noticed. The collection of garbage had stopped a long time ago. Combined with the smell of gunpowder, burning buildings, and dead bodies, this created a powerfully rank smell.[73]

Smoke was curling in the air from fires the Japanese had set, and artillery shells were going off as the Americans marched through Grace Park, just north of the city, and past the Chinese Cemetery on the other side of the city limits. Filipinos came up to them and warned of Japanese riflemen in the cemetery and mines planted in the road. As a precaution, the soldiers marched single file, making sure to walk in the footsteps of the man in front of him. "We looked up only once or twice to try to figure out what had been blown up nearby," Hanley explained.[74]

Combat had started but there were real divisions among the Americans. After departing Santo Tomás, Dunn stopped off at the headquarters of the 37th Infantry Division and ran into Beightler almost immediately. Thinking that the journalist was looking for a story, the general invited him to join him as he entered the city.[75] Dunn told him he was just leaving Manila. The prize of entering Manila first had been within Beightler's grasp, and he nursed a grudge. "The atmosphere changed instantly. 'You went with First Cavalry,'" the general stated. "It was more an accusation than a statement," Dunn noted. The conversation between the two ended instantly.[76]

Beightler later called the 1st Cavalry Division "feather merchants" (slang for a malingering soldier), which ended up in media accounts. Beightler apologized to Mudge for the comment.[77] He also wrote to *Newsweek* magazine, denying that he had ever made the remark.[78] (The quote appeared in many other publications.)[79] Beightler always blamed Krueger for stacking the odds against the division's getting to Manila first. He refused to believe MacArthur had anything to do with denying his men their due.[80]

It did not help that the soldiers of the 1st Cavalry Division reveled in their achievement of getting to Manila first. In hospitals, wounded cavalrymen would taunt wounded Buckeye infantrymen. The alumni newsletters would keep this rivalry alive for many more years.[81] The truth is more complicated. The 1st Cavalry had advanced so fast and was spread so thin that Japanese counterattacks along Highway 52 cut off the advanced elements of the unit from its own supply depots. For a time, the 37th Infantry had to support the cavalry.[82] The supply lines of the Buckeyes were not in particularly great shape either. The bridges along Route 3 were rickety and not strong enough to support tanks. As a result, the 637th Tank Destroyer was encamped in San Juan waiting until the engineers could make add structural support to make the bridge more secure.[83]

February 3 was a happy day. The cavalry had liberated the internees of Santo Tomás. The problem was the transformation that was taking place rapidly on February 4 and 5. Some were getting ready. At Malacañan Palace, the staff began setting up beds, and the president of the Philippine Women's University arrived with clean bed linen and medical instruments. Wounded from the street fighting were beginning to arrive.[84] Battle had come to Manila.

8

Phantom Victory

The battle for Manila had begun. Yet newspapers across the United States reported that the liberation of Manila was over. Much of this misleading news coverage was in service of MacArthur's ego and it infuriated his subordinates. It also did a disservice to the men who were fighting for control of the city, and it ignored the real damage that was taking place.

The news that the United States had taken control of the city was page one news across the country.[1] The *San Francisco Examiner* placed "EXTRA" above its banner and the headline "YANK TANKS MASS TO STORM MANILA" in bold, uppercase font that was bigger than the paper's masthead. The *Kokomo Tribune* had the headline that seemed best designed for the General's ego: "MacArthur Liberates Internees at Manila."[2] The eleven-word headline in Chicago's *Daily Times* took up the entire front page: "The Complete Story HOW YANKS WON MANILA 3,700 Prisoners Describe Rescue."[3]

These early accounts were the product of a strenuous effort on the part of reporters and the U.S. Army to get word back to the outside world. When the Japanese cut off Chase and his men with local offensives against the rear of the column, the reporters covering the liberation were cut off as well. To get word back to the public, the U.S. Army arranged for a small plane to use España Street as a runway. "Eventually we set up a regular service for the press to fly out their copy and pictures," Chase recalled. Back at headquarters, Colonel LeGrande Diller and his staff worked to expedite rather than restrict delivery of the news.[4]

Only a small number of newspapers had their own reporters on Luzon, and most US newspapers used accounts from one news service or another, with the Associated Press offering accounts that were the most authoritative—and the closest to the truth. Russell Brines of the Associated Press hinted at the actual situation in Manila in his news article. "What lies ahead nobody knows for certain," he wrote. He observed that there were thousands of mines buried in the streets and many bridges and buildings were rigged for demolition.[5]

When *Time* reported on the battle, on the other hand, the article made it sound like the war was over: "Manila was the crown and symbol of the entire Southwest Pacific campaign. The war that had begun in defeat and humiliation had yielded a great victory: clear-cut, renowned—and semi-final."[6] Most papers echoed the triumphalism.[7] With few exceptions, the vast majority of them gave credit to MacArthur personally.[8] *The Washington Post* called the seizure of Manila the culmination of an "extraordinary brilliant campaign." The *New York Herald Tribune* said the fight for the Philippines was over. In Illinois, the *Alton Evening Telegraph* declared, "The recapture of Manila not only is a military and naval achievement in itself. It is a symbol—of the power of free people fighting to keep that freedom." In that vein, the *Dayton Daily News* compared Manila to Warsaw as an indicator that the strategic direction of the war had turned against the Axis powers. The *Pittsburgh Post-Gazette* and the *Tampa Daily Times* both declared that Manila's strategic importance in the war ranked only behind the eventual seizure of Tokyo. The *Los Angeles Times* offered a page-one editorial and editorial cartoon praising MacArthur.[9]

There were some minor exceptions to the focus on MacArthur, although they had their own partisan edge. The *Akron Beacon Journal*, a Scripps-Howard paper, ran the editorial of the syndicate "Manila and After," but also published an open letter to Robert S. Beightler: "Congratulations to you and to every man in the 37th! Your entrance to Manila is the fitting climax of three years of brilliant effort!" In El Paso, the prewar home of the 1st Cavalry Division, *The El Paso Times* heaped praise on the horse soldiers, which *The Honolulu Advertiser* did as well.[10] One of the very few editorial boards that was less than pleased with this development was that of *The Arizona Daily Star*. That it had taken three years to liberate Manila, it argued, was a testament to the impoverished military policies of the United States in the 1930s and early 1940s for which it blamed the Roosevelt administration.[11]

* * *

Meanwhile, military operations were turning what had been a raid into something quite different: a street brawl of the first magnitude. From the start, Manila was two battles rolled into one. It was a fight determined by firepower and maneuver against static defense. It was easy to mark this on maps with frontlines and rear areas. All throughout the battle, Japanese holdings continued to shrink. At the same time, Manila was a series of small, isolated, tactical engagements. Americans often bypassed Japanese positions—to their own surprise and also to that of the defenders—and service and support soldiers often found themselves fighting as infantrymen rather than doing their signal or supply jobs. Buildings became islands of combat in otherwise "secure" areas. None of these small gun fights would be of any significant consequence, but they had a cumulative effect, adding up bit by bit.

The US soldiers quickly realized they had to engage in some new forms of combat if they wanted to liberate Manila. The arrival of the 37th Infantry Division was a significant factor in this shift. In a letter to a friend, Beightler summarized the situation succinctly: "This campaign, after a fantastically easy beginning, has developed into some of the bitterest and toughest street fighting I ever expect to see."[12] His division was less strung out than the 1st Cavalry, but he had to worry about attacks on his service and support units behind the main line of contact. To do this, he created a provisional organization called the Special Security Force to patrol rear areas.[13]

The Japanese were fully aware that the Filipinos had chosen the Americans over them. "When the enemy invaded Manila," Iwabuchi reported, "the citizens were welcoming the enemy well and disrupted all our fighting actions." In those first few days, the average Manileños committed various "guerrilla actions," ranging from communicating with US soldiers, shooting Japanese defenders, and reporting on Japanese locations to the Americans. "As a result, our surprise attack was infeasible, and many of our troops were unable to achieve their objectives."[14]

One of perplexing things about the Battle of Manila is MacArthur's lack of strategic guidance. His main focus had been getting to the municipality, not dealing with it once American forces were there. This preoccupation was a product of his sincere belief that the city had fallen easily—reflecting a failure on the part of his staff to report to him honestly. He tried to enter Manila on February 1, 2, 3, and 4. "Things went wrong each time," Bonner Fellers wrote to his family. MacArthur got close on February 4, but found himself stuck at the Novaliches Bridge with the rear elements of the 1st Cavalry. His presence unnerved junior officers because the bridge remained an active combat zone. "MacArthur was insisting that Mudge and Griswold join him without much protection. Dead bodies were still lying on the side of the road. He is insane on this subject!" Griswold wrote in his diary. "Finally prevented from getting in by enemy action." Griswold failed to understand the reasons for the risk. "Why we didn't all get killed I don't know! This, in my opinion, was a most foolhardy thing for a C in C to attempt."[15]

The first factor in the failure of the staff to report honestly was the fading influence of Lieutenant General Sutherland. MacArthur's chief of staff had returned to the Philippines and was trying to reassert his authority. This effort was not succeeding. "We all expected that he would go," Paul P. Rogers stated. Underlining that point, Rogers had taken advantage of Sutherland's absence, and gotten MacArthur to approve giving him a commission as a second lieutenant, which the chief of staff had opposed. Enlisted men on the staff were taking bets on how long he would last. The only reason he seemed to be holding on was that MacArthur could not find a suitable replacement.[16]

While the press celebrated the phantom victory in Manila and while head-quarters politics absorbed the time and attention of staff officers, the Americans had yet to arrive in the city in full force. Elements of Chase's column were still strung out on Highway 52. Captain John "Jack" Titcomb, the Marine Corps aviation liaison, had not even crossed the Manila city limits. After almost no sleep, he called February 4 "the most rugged day so far." He had spent twenty straight hours directing air coverage. "Lots of shooting around us," he jotted in his diary.[17]

A second factor was the uneven intelligence effort. The G-2 staff at Hacienda Luisita never had good signals or imagery intelligence. The Central Bureau, which was MacArthur's signal intelligence agency, had aimed its efforts against the Imperial Japanese Army and never managed to crack the regimental codes. Even if they had, how useful this ability would have been against the Manila Naval Defense Force is open to question.[18]

As far as aerial photography was concerned, the Americans owned the skies over Luzon and should have been able to exploit that advantage to the utmost. That dominance turned out to be of limited value. The Japanese had effectively neutralized this form of intelligence. The MNDF was using existing buildings and structures in the city for its defensive positions, so there were fewer indicators for photo analysts to detect. American intelligence officers had a hard time figuring out where defensive positions in the city were located. Information collection efforts therefore relied primarily on human intelligence—prisoner of war debriefings, translated Japanese documents, and reports from guerrillas and the Alamo Scouts. That type of information was useful primarily at the tactical level rather than the operational or strategic levels.[19]

There were other reasons why American intelligence failed to recognize what awaited them in Manila. Wishful thinking was perhaps the biggest. In 1942, MacArthur had declared Manila an open city—meaning he would make no effort to defend it if the Japanese made no effort to attack—and he expected Yamashita to do the same in 1945. Yamashita had spared Singapore in 1942, so there was some basis for this hope. The next biggest reason stemmed from the feud between MacArthur and Krueger and their intelligence efforts. Even on the eve of battle there was profound disagreement on the probability of a battle. Complicating matters more, reports from frontline units were so contradictory that they made little sense.[20]

For his part, Krueger appears to have been an exception to the anticipation of an easy victory. Intelligence was not matching the reports his soldiers were sending in from the frontlines. He realized that the city's water supplies would be a crucial factor in taking control of the city. Sanitation for nearly a million people would be next to impossible if the water stopped running. That was why Krueger directed Griswold to seize control of the Novaliches Dam. He also wanted XIV Corps to take control of the Balara Water Filters, the San Juan Reservoir, and the pipelines leading from these locations into Manila. All these facilities were located to the north and east of the city and were close to 1st Cavalry's line of march.[21]

Beyond those directions, however, Kruger offered no specific guidance to Griswold on how to conduct the fight for Manila.[22] His original plan was to assign the conquest of the city to the 37th Infantry Division and have the 1st Cavalry march into the hills to the northeast of the city. Having no detailed instructions from Krueger, Griswold decided to have both divisions take the city with two counterclockwise movements. While the Ohio unit moved inside Manila, the dismounted cavalry would encircle the city.[23]

The 37th Division progressed down Juan Luna Street, a large north–south thoroughfare in the Tondo district, which was the northwestern corner of the city that contained the ports north of the Pasig River. The Guardsmen were moving roughly parallel to the 1st Cavalry and were approximately two miles from the University of Santo Tomás. Elements of the division made contact with the horse troopers later in the day. The first major obstacle it faced was the Chinese Cemetery, four miles south of the Bonifacio Monument and heavily fortified by the MNDF.[24]

A second was that the residents of Manila were emerging to greet the Americans and to celebrate their liberation. Their numbers overwhelmed good military order and discipline, and the column lost its organizational coherence as Filipinos offered the men whisky, cigars, candy, coffee, and chewing gum. The crowds were shouting: "Victory!" and "God bless the Americans, God bless the Americans!" The celebration lasted until the Japanese opened fire and the crowd quickly dispersed.[25] "I saw no civilian injuries," 1st Lieutenant Bernard L. Patterson, a platoon leader in the 145th, recalled.[26] At this point in the battle, the Japanese were willing to make tactical withdrawals, destroying their supplies when they retreated.[27]

Despite this, Beightler's men got as far south as the Pasig, which connects Laguna de Bay to Manila Bay and effectively bisects the city, that first day.[28] Then there was a breakdown in communications. Beightler had to use whatever methods he could—telephone, radio, and runners—to stay connected with his subordinates.[29]

Despite these problems, the 37th continued its march south. At Bilibid, the prisoners eagerly awaited their liberation. "No one slept very much on the night of the 3rd," James V. Thompson remembered years later. "Yet as I recall, no one worried very much either." As February 4 started, they talked among themselves, recounting what they had seen. The Japanese guards were still on duty at the prison and that was a bad sign. "By now the terrible truth began to dawn on us: the United States Army did not know about Bilibid." Late in the morning, the Japanese left the prison, giving the prisoners an honest warning to stay in Bilibid for their own safety. "There is no explaining the Japanese," Thompson stated. Another internee watched their Japanese guards depart in what he called a "sullen way." The former prisoners began celebrating immediately—an American flag smuggled into the prison was unfurled, and the prisoners of Bilibid began singing "God Bless America."[30]

That evening at 8 p.m., the Buckeyes of the 37th Division reached Bilibid. When the soldiers arrived at the prison, they did not expect to find American prisoners and were stunned at what they had stumbled upon. "For as hard men as we were, not too many could hold their tears back," Corporal Murphy Foret recalled.[31] "If you never hated Japs," Major Charles Henne testified, "you would hate them upon seeing those men. They were walking skeletons and covered with sores. The Japs had deliberately starved them." Other infantrymen looking at men who were brothers-in-arms were angry as well.[32]

There was also genuine happiness. "It's like Christmas morning when I was a kid running downstairs to see the tree and pick up my presents," Technical Sergeant Joseph T. Hyland told Homer Bigart of the *New York Herald Tribune* when the war correspondent visited later. Private M. B. Scopa, another prisoner, recalled, "I feel like Rip van Winkle." Many prisoners were startled by their liberator's appearance. As at Santo Tomás, many of them focused on their coal pot helmet, thinking these men were German auxiliaries fighting for the Japanese.[33]

Civilian internees housed on the other side of the prison were in better physical condition than the POWs, "better" being a relative term. The strongest ones were those with the energy to walk and greet their liberators.[34]

Unlikely reunions take place in every theater of the war. One of them took place at Bilibid when Colonel Memory Cain, a prisoner who had survived Bataan and the death march, heard someone yelling: "Where's Memory Cain? Where's Memory Cain?" It was Colonel Hugh Milton, chief of staff of the XIV Corps. Cain was a graduate of New Mexico A&M University, and Milton, an officer in the New Mexico National Guard, had in civilian life been president of the university. After they found each other, the two old friends talked for half an hour. Milton also spent time looking in on other A&M grads and New Mexico Guardsmen at the prison.[35]

The numbers rescued at Bilibid were smaller than Santo Tomás, but still significant. Officially, the 37th Infantry rescued 1,024 prisoners. As at Santo Tomás, the internees still faced real dangers. The effects of malnutrition take time to reverse and improvements in their diet came too late for several.

* * *

One of the major turning points in the battle for the city was the fire that engulfed the city on February 5 and 6. It was the second major element of the battle and the only one the Japanese initiated. It was, however, due more to Japanese incompetence than brutality. Colonel Noguchi Katsuzo's Northern Force was destroying military supplies in the parts of the port under their control. The Japanese had warned residents of their intentions. Around 8:30 p.m. on February 5 the garrison lost control of the situation when the wind changed direction and sent the flames inland toward the north and west of Manila.[36]

The flames shot a thousand feet into the air. The smoke curled fifteen thousand feet up, creating a copper-colored canopy above the city that reflected the light of the fires back down to the ground. The 37th Infantry Division had its headquarters at the Ang Tibay shoe factory, five miles to the north of central

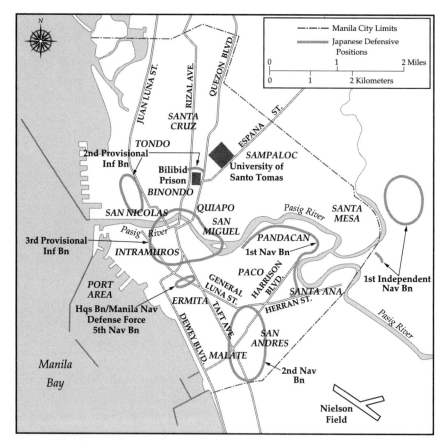

City of Manila

Manila in the suburb of Caloocan. The factory was a two-floor, art deco structure that was on slightly elevated ground. Soldiers and officers congregated
on top of the building, which gave them an unobstructed view looking south
toward Manila, which was just above sea level. The Buckeyes could also hear
the roar of the inferno and feel the ground shaking at times.[37]

Further to the north, the vats of the Balintawak Brewery were still dispensing
lager and malt. "The beer is warm and flat, but it is incredibly refreshing in the
heat and dust of the afternoon," a reporter for *Life* magazine observed. William
A. Owens of the Counter Intelligence Corps (CIC) spent the night there and
watched the city burn with many other soldiers of the 37th Infantry. (The
brewery was a five-story building and offered good views of the city.) "Soldiers
crowded at the windows and grieved," he recalled. "There was angry bitching."[38]

In Quezon City, a suburb to the northeast of Manila that escaped serious damage, Jurgen Goldhagen, a teenage refugee from Hitler's Germany, saw seven distinct fires on the horizon.[39] Jose Espino, a Filipino, roughly the same age as Goldhagen, was also in the suburbs and counted sixteen separate fires. Soon a solid curtain of flame dominated the entire horizon. Some of the more historically minded thought of the burning of Rome.[40]

The closer one was to the flames, the more intense the experience. For those in the city, the inferno cast a brightness equal to daylight. "It seemed to me at one time that the whole place was burning," General Chase observed. Arthur Feldman, a reporter for the Blue Radio Network, stood on top of the belfry at Santo Tomás, and told his listeners, "The buildings of the university, which had been a prison for thousands of Americans and allied internees for over three years, shivered and shook from twilight on Monday thru most of the night."[41] Estanislado Reyna, a soldier in the 37th Division, recalled years later in an interview, "The whole city was burning." After a moment, he added, "A lot of people died in those fires."[42]

Individual Japanese soldiers were horrified as well. "Flames are leaping up from within Manila and it is a like a bloody spectacle during a storm," one defender recorded in his diary.[43] The inferno consumed Japanese ammunition depots and food storage facilities. Several buildings they had intended to use in defense of the city were destroyed.[44]

One of the few people in a position to do anything about the unfolding disaster was Beightler: "From the roof of our headquarters, I watched, enraged at the wantonness of what I saw." He ordered his men to create a fire break to stop the spread of the blaze. Combat engineers from the 37th Division set off a series of explosions, although they failed to stop the flames. Many Buckeye soldiers tried to fight the flames until Japanese riflemen shot at them and they were forced to retire.[45]

The inferno did help the Americans in an indirect way. The flames forced many Japanese from their defensive positions. The 2nd Battalion, 148th Infantry claimed two hundred kills.[46] Perhaps more importantly, it compelled correspondents to report accurately and ignore MacArthur's spin. Brines, of the Associate Press, captured the dilemma of many journalists who were covering the Luzon campaign, "When we got to the edge of Manila, we were on the north bank of the Pasig River, the fire was too hot to even stand up there, and the communique said we had captured Manila." The fire was forcing them to deviate from the official American line.[47] William Dunn faced a moment of cognitive dissonance. "There's something unreal about watching a great city go up in flames. You know it's happening because it's right there before your eyes, but still there's a feeling that your senses must be playing you false."[48] The fire and its cause remained a subject of debate for years. Even before the battle ended, Arthur Veysey of the *Chicago Daily Tribune* returned to the United States and delivered a talk on what he had seen to the Union League. Manila would not have burned had the Americans not returned, he admitted, yet he also maintained that Filipinos did not blame them. "Their faith in America is a challenge. I only hope we can live part way up to their expectations."[49]

The fire raging in Manila soon required that the 148th evacuate Bilibid. Division headquarters rounded up as many trucks as possible. It took about three hours to remove all the residents. Thompson and his wife, Marie, packed their belongings and walked out of the back gate with other former prisoners. There were not enough vehicles to carry the entire group. So they walked and passed lines of infantry hiking into battle in "endless columns."[50] They had not walked long before a weapons carrier picked them up. As he sat in the vehicle, Thompson contemplated what he was witnessing. "Behind us was Manila, Pearl of the Orient, dying in fire, and with it the ambitions of an evil empire. Ahead was the cold dark night, and freedom. 'Then the lord rained upon Sodom and Gomorrah, brimstone and fire from the Lord out of heaven.' Genesis 19:24."[51]

The sky over Manila was blood-red that evening. The novelist John Dos Passos was in Luzon as a war correspondent for *Life* magazine and described what he saw. "For a long time now we have been watching a pillar of smoke on the southern horizon ahead of us. It's dark and towering and spreads out like a pedestal under a pile of milky white cumulus cloud." When they arrived in Manila, the single column had spread and multiplied until it filled the horizon. "They didn't lie when they said Manila was burnin'," his jeep driver mumbled.[52] He was right. The fires did more to destroy Manila than combat, eventually destroying roughly a third of the city.

* * *

Despite the inferno engulfing the city, the US presence in Manila was growing. On February 6, XIV Corps established its headquarters in the Grace Park area. "I entered the city today for the first time," Griswold noted in his diary.[53]

Others evacuated. By early February, the German community in Manila knew they would be considered enemy aliens to the United States and had good reason to leave Manila. In January, the Japanese offered to help Germans relocate to Baguio. Many were willing to accept this offer. The rapid advance of the US troops cut off this advance and forced many Germans to relocate to Holy Ghost College in the San Miguel section of the city north of the river. A contingent of physicians from the Imperial Japanese Army was using the College as a base. The major in command spoke German fluently and the Japanese soldiers and German refugees got along well. One of the soldiers gave the Kuehne family a can of Kilm Milk immediately before they left. It was an important gift. Manila was on the verge of famine and the calories and nutritional value of the milk was exceptional. "To us, this gift was as valuable as the gesture was touching," Walter Kuehne remarked. On February 3, the major informed the Germans that they were evacuating and would leave all their supplies behind.[54]

As the Japanese tried to leave, a patrol from the 1st Cavalry arrived at Malacañan Palace, cutting them off from leaving the city to the north and west. The trucks turned around and returned to the college. The German major asked if there was anyone that could guide them out of the city to the mountains to the east. An older German gentleman agreed. They hiked out on foot without any other problems. The Japanese had to leave their trucks at the college, which were well-stocked with medical supplies, food, gasoline, and ammunition.[55]

Even though the Americans had reached this part of the city, the successful evacuation of the Japanese medical detachment shows that they were not in control. In the afternoon of February 7, the 148th Regiment found itself in a firefight in the Escolta section of Manila on the northern bank of the Pasig River, populated with upscale art deco hotels and office buildings. One company came within two hundred yards of the river when the Japanese started fires—this time intentionally—in several locations. Winds spread the flames and time-fused explosions engulfed buildings, creating a wall of heat that forced the regiment to retreat. Other elements of the unit had crossed the Estero de la Reina, a small canal about ten yards wide that was a tributary of the Pasig. Under the command of Captain Labin W. Knipp, Company K went two blocks beyond the canal before the inferno forced them to retreat. After making sure that his men were in position, Knipp walked into the middle of an intersection, drawing Japanese fire from a pillbox that was blocking their withdraw, using his Browning automatic rifle. He took a bullet to the stomach. He stayed in position and was the last man to cross the intersection. The canal stopped the flames from following after them.[56]

During this extraction, Japanese machine gun positions blocked the retreat of the 3rd Battalion, 148th Infantry Regiment. Second Lieutenant Robert M. Viale led his platoon into a building that overlooked the enemy. Viale's plan was to use this position to drop grenades down on the Japanese. "He not only had a hell of a lot of nerve, he was very courageous, if not a little bit on the reckless side," Henne reflected years later. Suffering from a wound to his arm, Viale climbed up a ladder and had another soldier pull the pin on a grenade and hand it to him. He slipped and the grenade fell to the floor activated. The lieutenant jumped down, grabbed the grenade, and looked for a place to throw it. Seeing no place, he tucked the grenade into his stomach and ran into the corner of the room. The explosion tore open his abdomen. One of his men, Harold Vogel, ran over to him and turned him over. "You can't help me Vogel, I'm going to die." He was right, and his wife accepted the Medal of Honor he was awarded posthumously.[57]

That fighting like this was transpiring all across Manila was not a fact that the staff officers at General Headquarters appreciated. Hacienda Luisita, where they were located, was some sixty miles from Manila. This detachment led to a professional arrogance that permeates many of the written records in the archives—how the Japanese had been defeated and the easy advance in January was proof of that.[58]

Dos Passos visited the headquarters and interviewed MacArthur. "There's an air of breeding about him," Dos Passos observed. He noted the general had a "somewhat old-fashioned courtesy" about him. "His sentences are long with carefully balanced clauses." Like many visitors before and after, Dos Passos thought that he would be on the receiving end of a long-winded lecture. The writer soon realized he was wrong. "Only gradual[ly] you discover from the turn of his language that he is acutely aware of his listeners and of their interests and affiliations." MacArthur told his guest that he knew Manila had taken a beating. Even given that point, a close reading of Dos Passos's account suggests that the general failed to understand fully the level of destruction taking place.[59]

It was in this environment in which the victory parade in Manila became a contentious issue. Sutherland was trying to kill it as a way of reasserting his lost authority. The staff kept planning though. When Dunn returned from Manila, he immediately went to see Diller to warn him that the whole idea of a parade was absurd. Staff officers who were over sixty miles outside Manila had no idea of what was happening—the damage the flames had inflicted and the now-undeniable fact that the Japanese were still a military presence in the city. According to Dunn, Diller was not sure how to react. Had Dunn gone mad or was he being a difficult prima donna? Did he deserve sympathy or anger?

Dunn held his ground and repeated that the staff was operating under the influence of some exceptionally bad information. They would look foolish if they issued a press release about a victory parade.[60] Despite Dunn's warning, it would take time for the idea to die. What was significant about the parade was not the wasted planning effort, although there was that, but how disengaged MacArthur and his staff were from the actual events.

Even as late as February 5, MacArthur had no plan for an urban battle. "I do not believe anybody expected the Japs to make a house-to-house defense of Manila," Eichelberger told his wife. The general belief—at MacArthur's headquarters, at Krueger's headquarters, and with the press—was that the Japanese would evacuate without a fight.[61] Thirty years later, when he sat down to write his memoirs, Chase could not understand why anyone had made this assumption. "It was counter to everything the Nips had done in previous campaigns."[62]

The reasons now seem clear. Krueger and his Sixth Army staff had focused their planning efforts on the amphibious assault rather than on Manila. As a result, they ignored or never fully considered critical issues, such as force size and distribution, resources, and tactics. The vague discussions that took place were about general concepts. As a result, technical considerations drove much of the battle rather than matters of strategy or policy issues.[63]

Speed and maneuver, the driving forces behind the invasion of Luzon, would still play an important role in Manila but the tempo was clearly slowing down. The fighting would be marked not in miles covered but in city blocks taken. This type of engagement would be in the interest of Japan, but not in that of the United States or the Philippines.

9
The Battle Begins

MacArthur had declared Manila liberated, but the Japanese had a different view of the matter. Combat operations in the suburbs and the areas outside the city began immediately and would be just as important as events in Manila to determine the overall fate of the Philippine capitol.

The city of Manila sits on the east side of Manila Bay. It looks like a funnel sitting on its side with the wide mouth on the shoreline and the narrow neck pointing to the east. In 1945, there were eleven districts in the city and the Pasig River, despite some turns, dissects the city nearly evenly. The districts of Binondo, San Miguel, Santa Cruz, Sampaloc, and Tondo were to the north of the river, while Ermita, Intramuros, Malate, Paco, and Pandacan were to the south. About half of Santa Ana was on either side of the river due to the twists of the waterway. The city was an interesting mix of Spanish and American architecture styles. Most of southern Manila had been developed after the United States took the Philippines in 1898. The city had paved roads, but little upkeep had been done during the Japanese occupation. The throughfares in the north were narrow, while those in the south were wider, reflecting the fact that they had been built to accommodate automobiles. Although much of Manila was modern, with gas stations, multi-level office buildings of reinforced steel, and department stores, other areas were undeveloped, barrio slums with houses made out of flimsy, flammable material like wood and bamboo. What separated one type of area from the other was often nothing more than a two-lane road. This geography would shape much of the battle.

Fighting in a city for its control is a type of fighting that is old, with examples going back to antiquity, but it is also a form of combat that the U.S. Army had little experience with in 1945. Other than some short operations in World War I and a few in the European theater, the last time Americans had fought in cities had been in 1864 and 1865 with the battles of Atlanta and Richmond. There are seven major characteristics of urban warfare. The first is that artificial terrain features constrain and channel movement. Buildings become significant geographical objectives. Roads direct advances in certain directions. Both can be barriers. Depending on the material used in their construction, they might be quite vulnerable to military action or quite impervious. Some weapons have better utility than others in the city, and these issues often influence tactics. Another feature is that ground operations are compressed and decentralized. Engagements are between small, tactical units—squads, platoons, companies—for small, geographic objects—a room, a building, or a city block.

A third factor is that combat usually becomes three-dimensional. Soldiers fight ground operations as in any other form of ground combat, but they also advance and fight in sewers and blast holes through basement walls. They also have to fight an opponent that might control the floor of a building immediately above or below them, and they might move from rooftop to rooftop. City combat always consumes more time than other forms of fighting. This factor is relative, though. How slow is slow? The month-long fight for Manila was significant compared to other ground operations fought in the Pacific, but nothing compared to the eight-month-long struggle for Stalingrad or the twenty-eight-month-long siege of Leningrad.

A fifth factor in urban warfare is the presence of civilians. There are always non-combatant deaths in urban operations and their presence requires some effort at stability operations afterward, but sometimes also during the period of active combat. Civilians can be assets or liabilities when it comes to intelligence gathering, as both the Americans and Japanese would learn. The ready influence of the media is another factor. Cities by their very nature are media centers and always have resident journalists. Since urban areas are also important population, political, economic, financial, cultural, religious, trade, and transportation centers, their fate attracts the interest of reporters. A final dynamic of urban warfare is the outsized ramification of its outcomes. Location matters, and cities are always more important than undeveloped countryside, and engagements for their control have more influence than engagements in isolated areas. Each of these would be in play in Manila.

In Tokyo, the view of the Philippine city was a bit different. The defense of Manila seemed to be a rare moment of cooperation between Japan's armed services. Admiral Toyoda Soemu, commander-in-chief of the combined fleet, sent a telegram to Admiral Iwabuchi that called for the MNDF to "demonstrate superior joint operations between the navy and army under the fierce situation and almost finished preparations to counter the enemy with fighting spirit."[1]

The reality in Manila was indeed "fierce" but the "fighting spirit" of individual soldiers would not compensate for their serious shortcomings. The sailors defending Manila had no training as ground soldiers.[2] Even the soldiers of the Imperial Army in the city had little training in infantry tactics. Most were personnel from service units. There were almost no snipers. While the Japanese did use rifle fire, they were random shots and not the result of focused, deliberate target selection. They simply lacked both the skill and the equipment to engage in long-range, selective targeting. Military intelligence officers in XIV Corps observed that few rifle telescopes were recovered in Manila. One of the few exceptions was the zone of operations of the 129th Infantry Regiment, which reported that the snipers were "unusually accurate."[3]

What the Japanese had were good fortifications. Given the weapons of the 1940s, a city built with concrete, masonry, and brick conferred its defenders significant advantages in providing protection from firepower and reducing the advantages of mechanization. Many buildings had been designed to withstand earthquakes, making them resilient against even heavy US weapons. The Japanese were shrewd in selecting buildings, buttressing them with barricades outside the structure, creating sandbag barriers in doorways, windows, hallways, and rooms.[4] "Each of these buildings was a fort in itself," Captain Stephen L. Garay of the 37th Division noted after the war.[5] They also had pillboxes at key locations and had established lanes of fire.[6] The Japanese even made use of wrecked buildings. In fact, Colonel Noguchi Katsuzo told his men that it was "preferable to reuse buildings destroyed by bombing."[7] Captain Garay recalled that the Japanese resisted from "the very rubble in the streets."[8] These defensive positions produced individual citadels that often took an inordinate amount of time and firepower to overcome.

There was, however, little coordination among the defenders. While the Japanese had positions that were strong enough to hold out for days, other units offered little to no support. Even after neighboring positions were overrun, MNDF detachments could, and usually did, hold in place until they were directly targeted and destroyed.[9] These efforts earned the defenders the grudging respect of the Americans. The after-action report of the XIV Corps admitted as much: "the stubborn resistance of the garrison did credit to his truculence as a fighter, and the ruthless destruction of property was a reflection of the tenacity of his efforts."[10]

Improvisation was the basis for much of the preparations the Japanese made. Muraoka Toshisue, a probationary officer in the Army, survived the sinking of a troop transport bound for Singapore. He ended up in Manila and was assigned to a replenishment company, a position for which he had no training. Another Army officer, Second Lieutenant Murakami Kyosaku, conceded after the war that there had been little coordination between the Army and Navy units under Iwabuchi's command. Soldiers and sailors were often in units for only a few days before these formations fell under fire. Many did not even know the names of their officers.[11]

The speed of the American advance did, as many in MacArthur's headquarters had expected, catch the defenders off guard. The Japanese knew their enemy was headed toward Manila, of course, but the race between the three US divisions advanced the offensive faster than what the Japanese had thought possible. As late as February 2, the day before the Americans entered the city, the Japanese had been sending supplies and men to the mountains to the east. Given the speed of the American advance, much of those supplies were lost. Naval special forces units stationed in Obando, on the coast north of Manila, were waiting for orders to attack US ships entering Manila Bay. If that proved impossible, they were to retreat to Novaliches. The arrival of the 1st Cavalry Division eliminated that option. Realizing they could not fulfill either their primary or secondary missions, many defenders tried to retreat to the east, but US units intercepted them before they could escape. Only a few men made it to Japanese Army units outside of the city.[12]

Japanese soldiers were not well equipped, at least in comparison to US soldiers. An exception was the Nambu machine gun. Americans called them "woodpeckers" because of the way they sounded when fired. Its low velocity made a series of flat, rapid clicks as it fired. The gun made "a distinctive sound that each of us dreaded," as one US infantryman put it. Nambus were in short supply in Manila, though. In fact, the Japanese were short on almost all types of firearms. Only a few days into the battle, the defenders were starting to run out of both guns and ammunition. Private First Class Okubo Yasuhiko found that he and all the men in his infantry company were actually armed with American rifles.[13]

Reflecting the poor training of the troops, the Japanese used infantry tactics that undercut the advantages they enjoyed in fortification. In multistory buildings most of the defense was made on the ground floor. Although the upper floors would have offered high ground from which to observe the approach of the Americans and to fire on them, they were usually used mainly as a venue for retreat. "The enemy's defense was seriously impaired by his failure to coordinate centers of resistance," declared a military intelligence study conducted at XIV Corps headquarters immediately after the battle. The Japanese also failed to defend in depth. When it happened, it seemed more inadvertent than planned. This inability to coordinate led the Japanese defense to become rigid. Japanese soldiers and sailors stayed in place, firing their weapons, ignoring the maneuvering of the Americans. The result was that they became isolated and could be taken out one by one.[14]

Japanese anti-tank tactics had mixed results. Minefields were often exceptionally destructive. They could and did kill entire tanks and their crews, but they were limited by poor camouflaging. Japanese infantry also used "lunge mines" against US tanks. The mine was a steel cone at the end of a bamboo stick ranging in length from four to eight feet. The Japanese soldier was to use the mine like a pike, sticking the side of a tank. If it was placed flat against the armor plating, the six-and-a-half-pound charge had enough power to punch a hole through six inches of armor. Making contact at an angle, though, reduced the power of the mine, and in reality, most tank crews attacked by lunge mines would hear the small thunder of an explosion to their side and then a red cloud of mist would cover their vehicle.[15] In a lessons-learned report, a Japanese lieutenant noted simply: "Locally produced conical bullets with rods did not work."[16]

Night operations also ended up working against the Japanese. According to the G-2 staff of the XIV Corps: "Highly valued by the enemy but hardly worthy of the title 'counterattacks' were infiltration raids by groups normally consisting of from ten to fifteen men." Their commanders often gave them vague orders. "These infiltrators," the G-2 report added, "operating within the built-up section of the city, usually became separated or lost and were destroyed by our forces before they fulfilled their purpose."[17] The Americans usually preferred suicidal "banzai" charges. A 129th Infantry Regiment report explained why: "Seasoned troops relish the thought, after a hard day's advance, of having the enemy noisily present himself against our perimeter. It makes the next day's fighting that much easier."[18]

A surprising factor in favor of the Americans was the willingness of some defenders to surrender. The Americans took about four hundred prisoners of war during the battle. About half were from Korea and Taiwan, reflecting their limited training, the lack of discipline of units, and the poor quality of leadership. Many became prisoners after becoming lost or separated while they were on the move. A few others were wounded and usually captured by military police or guerrillas. The disposition of the guerrillas varied a great deal; they often beat and robbed their prisoners and sometimes killed them before military intelligence personnel could debrief them.[19]

The morale of the defenders was generally high in the beginning. After the first setbacks, their morale usually plunged. Many wanted to run.[20] "The gap of the weapons between ours and the enemy's is also influencing soldiers' morale," Iwabuchi reported. "In particular, I am really worried because there are many civilian employees in the navy."[21] He had good reason to be concerned.

* * *

In the south, the 11th Airborne was already fighting for Manila even if they were still on the other side of the city limits. The hard advance of the division had exhausted the paratroopers and a good number started to make simple, stupid mistakes. During the night in Las Piñas, a soldier new to the reconnaissance platoon shot a radio operator in the back. The rest of the men "scared beyond belief" dove for cover under vehicles, not knowing where the fire was coming from. After listening to the man moan for a long while, a medic reached him and sent him back to the aid station where he recovered eventually.[22]

Other lapses were more tragic. Swing was inspecting the frontlines with Colonel Irvin Schimmelpfenning. They drove right past a machine gun at the southern end of the Parañaque Bridge. Jack McGrath, a medic in the 511th Parachute Infantry, tried to wave them down, but they ignored him. Another soldier recounted that the jeep stopped and then kept going, which is possible. There might very well have been more than one roadblock. Either way, Swing and Schimmelpfenning were in a no man's land between the US and Japanese frontlines. An enemy machine gun opened up on them. The driver turned around immediately, but it was too late. Schimmelpfenning was hit. As he returned, Swing was screaming at the foot soldiers, demanding to know why they had not stopped him. The men yelled back: "Shut up, you bastard!" McGrath was incensed: "What did he think I was doing out there? Asking him the score of a baseball game?"[23]

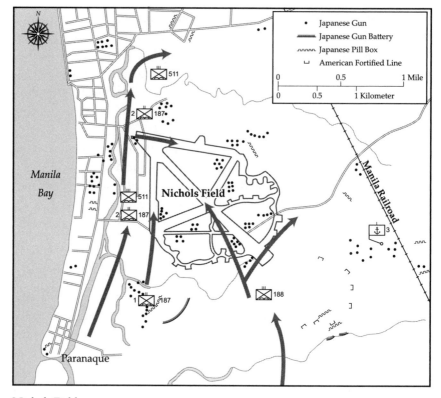

Nichols Field

McGrath and other medics rushed to attend to Schimmelpfenning, but he had died instantly. Swing was standing by just watching. "Oh, man, I could see it hurt him," McGrath recalled.[24]

Schimmelpfenning's death stunned the officers and men of the division. He was the highest-ranking US officer to die in the Battle of Manila. After the war, the 11th Airborne Division named a camp and an athletic field after him. Despite his rank, Schimmelpfenning's death was not that out of the norm. A number of other high-ranking officers had close calls. The difference between them and Schimmelpfenning seems to have been happenstance.[25]

Mines buried in the roads posed a more consistent threat. On paved roads they were fairly easy to spot. Combat engineers would mark them with flags. The best way to deal with these bombs was to avoid the roads and to stay stationary at night. Soldiers of the 511th Parachute Infantry Regiment were sitting on the side of the road in Parañaque when a M-18 tank destroyer came zigzagging up, attempting to avoid mines. It suddenly came under fire from some heavy Japanese guns, and instead of returning fire, the vehicle retreated in a straight line. This path took it over a mine made from a depth charge or an aerial bomb. The explosion turned the sky black, and the concussive force knocked soldiers backwards. "In the blackness for a split second I saw the tank upside down as high as the telephone wires," Private Deane Marks recalled. "Then, a split second of dead silence." Debris began landing, hitting many of the soldiers. When the dust from the explosion cleared, Marks saw the tank destroyer on its back.[26]

Despite the ferocity of these engagements, none of them technically occurred in the City of Manila. The 11th Airborne Division only entered the city at 5:00 a.m. on February 5 when the 511th Parachute Infantry Regiment crossed the Parañaque Bridge. Eichelberger decided that was enough to declare that the Eighth Army had officially entered Manila. As a practical matter, though, the paratroopers had already been up against the artillery of the Genko Line for over a day, a defensive line that was anchored, on the west, at Manila Bay and, on the east, at Laguna de Bay. "It was one of the toughest battles of the Luzon campaign," the division's historical report states.[27]

As the paratroopers entered Parañaque, they soon found themselves engaged in house-to house fighting. Here, the Japanese actually had more munitions than the Americans. Bombs and depth charges were rigged with trip wires to kill infantry. The Japanese had fortified this zone with twelve hundred pillboxes. They had also stripped guns from inoperable planes and sunken ships in Manila Bay. They had forty-four heavy artillery pieces, 164 anti-aircraft guns that ranged from 20 millimeters to 40 millimeters, and a high number of machine guns. "As a consequence," Captain Edwin B. Jeffress noted, "the number of automatic weapons encountered was far in excess of those to be expected from the numerical strength of the defender."[28] A joke included in an after-action report summarized the situation the division faced: "If anybody has been wondering what happened to the Japanese Navy he can stop worrying. I've found it."[29]

The 511th Parachute Infantry continued to push north along Route 1, known before the Japanese occupation as Dewy Boulevard. In 1945, a thin strip of developed urban area only a quarter-mile wide sat between the road and the coast of Manila Bay (once inside the city, the road curved to the northwest until it was a shoreline drive running right against the water). On the other side of Route 1/Dewy Boulevard was the Parañaque River and Nichols Field. The pillboxes and fortified street corners at this location made it the start of the Genko Line. "For what we lacked in heavy guns and equipment necessary to breach that line, we were forced to substitute the will and drive of the men themselves," Edward M. Flannigan, Jr. noted in the published history of the division. The sniper work of Private George Canales of Houston, Texas, offers a good example. He shot twenty-two Japanese in one day and held off a force of roughly seventy-five. His actions kept an entire squad of paratroopers from being overrun.[30]

This type of small arms fire was critical. The 511th had no large artillery. Even with the munitions that were dropped in support of the paratroopers, the Angels were going up against hardened targets and their advance was slow. It would take two days for the 511th to reach the Manila Polo Club in Pasay, another Manila suburb, a distance of about four-and-a-half miles.[31]

They were simply not trained or equipped for urban warfare. William C. Schnorr, an artillery officer in the 11th Airborne, found that being in a city required a methodical approach to securing territory.[32] Colonel Henry Burgess agreed: "Street fighting was a rude shock to us, as was the Jap mortar and artillery fire."[33] Colonel Edward H. Lahti, the executive officer of the 511th, observed, "Movement was slow and the fighting fierce."[34]

While the Japanese had the weight of firepower in their favor, the artillery was not decisive. The Japanese did not know how to use their heavy guns in a coordinated fashion. In many cases, they shot high. "They fired point blank at us," Victor M. Liptrap, a soldier in the 511th Parachute Infantry, recalled. "It would go over our heads; I don't know where it hit but it was kind of noisy." On other occasions, the time fuses on the shells were set wrong and exploded high in the air. These types of mistakes reduced the power and damage that shrapnel did to infantry. When the 1st Battalion, 511th Parachute Infantry took three 120-millimter anti-aircraft guns, they found that they were flanked by two 40-millimeter machine guns. The Japanese manning these guns had simply failed to protect the big guns with flanking fire. "They use their artillery stupidly," Swing observed. "With the five-inch naval guns they had taken from their warships and planted all around Manila they could have held out another two weeks—if they had used them properly."[35]

The 11th Airborne's problem was that its small caliber artillery tubes were not effective against the Japanese fortifications. Schnorr was on a small hill firing down on to the Japanese pillbox. "It was hitting it, but it wasn't damaging it at all. It was, apparently, a very well-constructed pillbox," he said wryly.[36]

These guns, though, were strong enough that they could devastate the Japanese out in the open. Superior Seaman Goto Tadao's battalion fell apart in two days under constant shelling. His platoon decided to retreat to the mountains in the east.[37]

The Americans kept pushing. Mines on the roads leading into Manila turned out to be one of the biggest challenges. Bonner Fellers repeated a report from a U.S. Navy lieutenant—most likely Sutton—that the coverage was denser than anything that he had seen in North Africa or Italy. A mitigating factor was that they were often designed to hinder an advance coming from the south rather than the north. Removal and neutralization of the mines was a simple but dangerous process. Combat engineer teams would advance with infantry providing covering fire. They would lay down a cloud of smoke that would obscure the vision of the Japanese defenders as the engineer teams deactivated the mines.[38]

The nights that followed belonged to the Japanese. Both the Army and Navy had trained hard in the years before the war to operate in the dark. The skills that naval personnel had acquired translated well enough to ground combat. Corporal James E. Richardson was shocked when he was spotted almost immediately on a night patrol, even though he was in a grassy area that should have absorbed the sounds he made while on the move. "The damn Japs must have been able to see in the dark," he declared.[39]

For its part, the U.S. Army had an acute reluctance to operate after dusk. Liptrap, a soldier in the 511th, was stunned while on guard duty that a Japanese infantryman came within a few feet of him. "I couldn't even hear him, but he walked by and before I could even think; here's another on right behind him and another one and there's twelve of them." Lintrap was stunned that no one else was reacting. He quickly discovered why. All the men in his unit, manning guns, were asleep.[40]

As a precaution against these types of situations, paratroopers set up trip wires that would detonate grenades. Sometimes these measures could go wrong. Believing he could hear the Japanese advancing, Private First Class Marks threw grenades randomly out into the grass field in front of him. One bounced off of a hut and exploded near him, damaging his hearing. The rest of the men in his unit thought Marks had been killed because he did not respond to them when they called out. It was not until the next morning they realized he was still alive.[41]

The Japanese tried to avoid outposts like the one Marks manned. The preferred targets of penetration units were tanks and armored cars.[42] Early in the battle the men had instructions to continue to attack random US units until they were killed. This expectation changed during the battle when Japanese commanders realized they were simply wasting manpower.[43] These men often had no real weapons. Second Class Petty Officer Sugiura Heignen was sent out on a suicide mission armed only with a bamboo spear and a hand grenade.[44] Japanese commanders at the tactical level believed they were getting good results with their approach. A field diary, recovered by the U.S. Army military intelligence at the end of February, records that at least one unit believed they had a ten-to-one kill ratio early in the battle.[45]

The Japanese had justification for this assessment. The fight in the southern reaches of the city was actually very even. The Genko Line was holding up the advance of the 11th Airborne. In Parañaque, the Japanese launched a counter-offensive. The result was desperate fighting. Herbert E. Merritt of the 511th recalled Parañaque as a place "where the rich people live," because they had to battle a group of Japanese trapped in a swimming pool. "We liberated them," he said, laughing at the memory.[46]

As the paratroopers inched forward, they began coming across signs of atrocities. Soldiers in the 511th Parachute Infantry found the bodies of eighteen Filipina student nurses at Nichols Field whom the Japanese had raped and then bayonetted.[47] Herbert E. Weiner of the 187th Glider Infantry Regiment noted that Manila was "a bitter battle."[48]

The fighting was nothing short of savage. The night of February 6, a day after the 511th crossed the city limits, the Japanese counterattacked. In the morning, Burgess, the commanding officer of the 1st Battalion, counted over a hundred dead outside his perimeter. "At times they were very stupid," he commented. "Yet they cannot be classed as being stupid."[49] After the war, Rod Serling, a veteran of the 11th Airborne, set two episodes of his television series, *The Twilight Zone*, in the Philippines of 1945. When Serling, as the on-screen narrator in "A Quality of Mercy," tells his audience that the soldiers had "dulled and tired eyes set deep in dulled and tired faces," it's clear he was speaking from experience.[50]

Medics had an exceptionally demanding job during this fighting. Japanese artillery tended to focus on aid stations and field hospitals. Bernard Coon, a medic in the same regiment as Serling, was in a field hospital in an old church when a Japanese shell scored a direct hit. He survived but was covered in white dust and the concussive effects of the detonation left him hard of hearing for several days.[51]

Medic work was also a dirty business. A captain ordered McGrath of the 511th to carry a dead man back to a field hospital. Blood from the corpse ended up all over him. "I looked like I was in a butcher's shop," he stated. "It rots in the sun. You smell like death."[52]

Collecting military intelligence put soldiers close to combat as well. Norman Kikuta, a Japanese linguist, was sitting next to another soldier when an artillery burst hit the man. He was wounded just above his heart. Kikuta had no injuries. The medics that arrived insisted that the other soldier be evacuated to a field hospital, which was hit by another shell as the stretcher team arrived, killing the soldier. "Had he remained where we were, he would've been safe," Kikuta reflected. The next day, he was at regimental headquarters when a field stove exploded. The back of his shirt caught fire. He rolled on the ground to put out the flames, narrowly avoiding a serious injury.[53]

As bad as these moments were, they were nothing compared to what combat was doing to the Filipino people. The Americans realized the damage that was taking place. Eichelberger and a few of his staff officers watched the sunset on February 5. "It looks like as though the whole city is in flames," he told his wife. "We can see and hear the various explosions." He knew he was watching Manila die. "What a shame it is," he wrote his wife in another letter. "It was something which I shall never forget."[54]

* * *

In the northeast of the city, the horsemen of the 1st Cavalry were fighting for control of the Novaliches Dam. The 7th Cavalry reached the dam on February 5 and took it quite easily. The Japanese had not rigged any demolitions. The 7th Cavalry patrolled the area for two days and took control of the Balara Water Filters on February 6, after making a "mad dash." In this situation, the Japanese had rigged the filters for demolition, but the dismounted cavalrymen took them before detonation.[55]

For the next several days, a deadly game of push and pull followed, one in which the 7th Cavalry's hold on the waterworks was tenuous. The horse soldiers would clear the area during the day; the Japanese would return at night with demolitions. The Americans were in a better position than the Japanese, but their foundation was less than secure. The entire division was facing supply issues, mainly in ammunition.[56] "Each night was like a nightmare," Richard J. Foss recalled.

With the 1st Cavalry holding strong points rather than a continuous line, the work of military police (MP) became crucial. A war correspondent found a major running one unit, looking "haggard" from his exhaustion and lack of sleep. There was a reason. The MPs often found themselves in firefights despite being in the "rear echelon." Case in point, on February 7, a platoon in northeastern Manila, where Highway 54 crosses over Diliman Creek, found itself engaged with a group of roughly ten Japanese soldiers. The MPs military police drove off the attackers, leaving three dead behind.[57]

Mobility remained a key US advantage in the campaign but getting to the dam proved difficult. The 1st Cavalry controlled a series of strong points spread out over fifty miles of road. As the rest of the division drove south, it was under fire from small groups of defenders. The Japanese often set up small roadblocks and when the truck crews dismounted, these outposts would open up with rifles and grenades. Truck drivers were a favorite target of snipers. More than a dozen in the division died in early February.[58]

The problems the Japanese were facing, though, were far worse. The diary taken off the body of a Japanese soldier at the water filters indicated that Japanese morale was "tense." The experiences of Private First Class Eudo Takeo explains why. Eudo was a medical supply clerk in charge of distribution. The Japanese Army, he explained, had adequate supplies for their needs. Eudo, though, was suffering from dysentery, so he had light sedentary duty. He was part of a six-man group tasked with standing guard at a medical supply dump. That defense quickly fell apart. He ran when he saw US tanks approaching. Alone, without food and in poor health, he did not last long. He obtained some bread from a Filipino house before the guerrillas captured him.[59]

With the 1st Cavalry in a series of fights to hold on to the waterworks, Robert B. Holland and Richard Godolphin, two of the Marines who had gone to Santo Tomás with the 1st Cavalry, left the university on February 7 to join the troopers of the 7th Cavalry and to provide Marine Corps air assets. After arriving, Holland met the regiment's chaplain, Captain Thomas E. McKnight. Sitting next to Holland's radio, the two had a long conversation that the Marine found "comforting." That evening, at midnight, the Japanese attacked with artillery and machine guns. Chaplain McKnight heard a wounded soldier crying for help and went to administer to him. This effort earned the chaplain a posthumous Silver Star.[60]

Holland, who was slightly wounded in the same attack, had spent the night refusing to get out of his foxhole to get medical attention, fearing that he would be hit by the artillery. After getting bandaged up, he went to get some morning coffee. While waiting in line, he heard about McKnight's death. Profoundly disturbed, he went and prayed where he and McKnight had talked the day before.[61]

The fight to take the dam was crucial to the larger efforts to take Manila and Luzon. As Major Kevin T. McEnery noted in a U.S. Army study of the battle: "If the Japanese had succeeded in destroying the water system, it is doubtful the Americans could have coped with the resulting epidemic of disease." The repercussions on the entire Luzon campaign would have been profound.[62]

* * *

In Manila, meanwhile, despite the fire and uncertainty, the popularity of the Americans was pervasive. Private William F. Allen of the 7th Cavalry Regiment was surprised at the welcome he and his buddies received: "When we liberated Manila I was amazed by all the help we got from the people, including little kids and old men; they would risk their lives just to help us."[63] Fernando J. Mañalac, a teenager at the time, recalled what happened when the horsemen arrived in his neighborhood. Residents began climbing the tanks, hitching rides. "More starving residents, though weak, had come out from their homes in unbridled joy and everyone was cheering wildly."[64]

The public expected freedom would bring an end to the suffering. "We thought it would be an easy victory for the Americans and that all of Manila would be liberated without much bloodshed," eighteen-year-old Elena A. Rodriquez observed.[65]

The Filipinos supported the Americans in ways large and small. One family opened their house to Lieutenant William H. Swan and two other officers, hosting a small dinner. Seeing their guests, who were "dirty bearded looking like Joe and Willie in a Bill Maulden [sic] cartoon," the family took them to different bathrooms where they could take a warm bath and a shave. Only later did Swan learn that the water had been heated outside over a fire and taken into the house in buckets.[66]

The Japanese had ruled the Philippines for three years and their reign had been abusive, even brutal. Many Filipinos had a good deal of resentment. A group of citizens saw a lone Japanese soldier on Governor Forbes Street and attacked him. After beating him savagely, a guerrilla shot and killed him with a pistol. Crowd violence targeted other Japanese individuals. Mobs also targeted Chinese merchants and other Filipinos who had collaborated with the Japanese. Some of the evidence suggests that people were using the moment to settle past differences.[67]

Rich or poor, most Manileños realized they were about to be caught in the middle of a large battle and decided to get out of the city, if they could. Some of them were pushed. South of the Pasig River, Japanese soldiers banged on doors, telling residents to evacuate. These civilians needed little convincing. They had seen *makaibo* personnel planting mines in the middle of the streets and tried to walk on the sides, carrying all the belongings they could. Many had pushcarts. Those north of the Pasig River headed north, while those still in the Japanese-controlled areas south of the river headed further south. The Americans worried that some Japanese might be hiding among the refugees. "We had to trust that the Filipinos would recognize any Japs and report their presence," one soldier admitted.[68]

For thousands of Filipinos, their concerns were far more basic. They were on their own individual odysseys just trying to survive. Mañalac, a future medical doctor in the U.S. Army, wrote a memoir of his childhood in Manila. His family refused to evacuate until it became clear the flames were coming for them. "The moving congestion could have been infiltrated by spies, saboteurs and snipers, and no one would have known," Mañalac reflected. He and his family watched US soldiers march south, and his sister offered to fill their canteens with her water. They refused. Major roads were congested, but so were narrow side streets and alley ways. The refugees, he explained, "just kept going, governed by instinct" and were "stupefied by fear and grief." They stopped only when they reached a school or park where they could rest.[69]

The search for food was a constant preoccupation. Men asked the Americans for the opportunity to work for a meal. Children were forging for scraps in garbage pits. Families were begging for rations from various Army units.[70]

The overall situation in Manila was getting worse. On February 4, civil authority in the city had effectively collapsed. Leon G. Guinto, Sr. had been the mayor of Manila since 1942. Since January, his authority had been tenuous, and he had moved from his official residence to a private home. Japanese soldiers stood guard at the house, and the phone at his house went dead. City Hall was in the hands of the Japanese, and the other main municipal building—the Second City Hall—that served the city districts north of the Pasig River was in territory that the US now controlled.[71]

The fire that engulfed Manila was proof of this collapse. There was no centralized response. Local firefighters tried to put out parts of the blaze, but Japanese riflemen fired at them.[72] Neighborhood associations did what they could, using lookouts to warn about Japanese patrols. They had good reasons for fearing the emperor's army. Some units were burning houses and killing Filipino families; sometimes as families ran from burning homes and; other times with firing squads.[73]

The fire was a major element of the battle. It was a significant cause of death in the city, but the suffering of Manila had barely begun.

10

MacArthur Returns to Manila, February 7–12

General of the Army Douglas MacArthur was in an anxious mood. He was returning to Manila on February 7. In one sense, it was something he had been trying to do for two days. In another sense, he had been trying to do it for three years. Either way, it was finally going to happen.

In northern Manila at the Balintiwak Monument, Generals William C. Chase, Oscar W. Griswold, and Robert S. Beightler were waiting for the theater commander to arrive. None of them were happy. They had more important work to do. MacArthur, on the other hand, had a different view. This moment was the culmination of years of work. Seeing Chase, he congratulated him on getting to Manila, and told him he was getting a promotion to Major General. He was also getting command of the 38th Infantry Division, which was in combat east of Subic Bay. Chase, in turn, presented the general with the Cadillac that had been recovered at Malacañan Palace. That it had taken MacArthur two days to reach Santo Tomás after American troops had first entered Manila was not particularly noteworthy. It took some elements of Chase's command two days to reach the university.[1] "He seemed to think the enemy had little force here," Griswold noted in his diary. "Was quite impatient that more rapid progress was not being made." Despite his desire for a faster pace, MacArthur was impressed with his subordinates. He had enormous respect for Griswold's leadership and command abilities. Four months later, he would recommend him for command of the Tenth U.S. Army, after its commanding general was killed on Okinawa.

Griswold wanted to implement MacArthur's plan, which was for taking Manila with little in the way of actual combat operations. "My private opinion is that the Japs will hold that part of Manila south of the Pasig River until all are killed," he noted in his diary. "Gen. MacArthur has visions of saving this beautiful city intact. He does not realize, as I do, that the skies burn red every night as they systematically sack the city."² MacArthur seemed not to notice that Manila was burning.

MacArthur's first stop on February 7 was Bilibid Prison. The general met with the civilians detainees first and they gave him an enthusiastic welcome. Then he visited with the military prisoners of war (POWs) on the other side of the complex. Many lacked the energy to join with the civilians. The recently freed POWs stood at attention as long as they could. A number murmured thanks to MacArthur: "God bless you, General" or "Thank God you're back." MacArthur was moved and even, according to witnesses, on the verge of tears.³

MacArthur then went six blocks north to Santo Tomás. There the general received another powerful reception. He arrived at the main building and shook hands with a number of internees before entering. MacArthur had an excellent memory for names and faces, but it failed him on this occasion. As had been the case with William Dunn four days earlier, many of the prisoners had to introduce themselves; starvation had made them unrecognizable.⁴ "I cannot recall, even in a life filled with emotional scenes, a more moving spectacle than my first visit to Santo Tomás camp," MacArthur stated later.⁵ Even for a man prone to grandiose statements, this was no exaggeration. One prisoner saw him wipe away tears.⁶

MacArthur walked into one of the dormitory rooms, which is where Natalie Crouter happened to live with her children. He shook her hand. "He was sincerely comprehending of my strained face which showed what all of us had suffered," she explained. "He was deeply shocked and sorry for all of us, and looked it without trying to say so. For this I was grateful."⁷ Cecily Mattocks observed that many seemed to just want to touch him. Terry Wadsworth, a fellow child prisoner, explained the importance of MacArthur's visit. "After he left there was a sense that we were truly saved."⁸

The visit hit the general emotionally, but there's no record of what lay behind it: anger at the Japanese for what they had done to his men; disgust at how they had treated non-combatants, women, and children, in particular; sadness that so many had suffered; guilt for having made operational decisions that had resulted in their incarceration; remorse, or maybe relief, that he and his family had not suffered the same fate. After the visit, MacArthur recognized the suffering of the internees in a unique way. He announced that he would award all the residents of the Santo Tomás internment camp the Overseas

Service Ribbon for the Southwest Pacific Theater.[9] After an hour at the university, MacArthur told Roger O. Egeberg, his physician, "This has been a bit too emotional for me. I want to get out and I want to go forward until I am stopped by fire."[10]

Colonel Lawrence K. White, the commanding officer of the 148th Infantry Regiment, was taking over the positions at Malacañan Palace from the 1st Cavalry Division when he heard a voice behind him ask, "White, what are you doing down here?" The colonel turned and discovered it was MacArthur. The general's greeting was an impressive example of his command for names and faces. White had briefly served on MacArthur's staff ten years earlier. The main military task facing the Americans at the moment was crossing the river, and White blurted out, "I don't see why I don't cross the river right here." MacArthur asked him if he thought he could, and White said if he had boats, he would try.

The two of them were standing on the banks of the river. No one was shooting at them. White told MacArthur that he was going to ask for the equipment. The news of his talk with McArthur traveled quickly. Everyone in the division and corps understood that they needed to support White's crossing.[11]

MacArthur wandered about the palace a bit and entered one room that had a machine gun nest with a good view of the river. The sergeant manning the position tried to stop him from coming in. He had good reason. MacArthur and his doctor looked out across the river and directly at a two-man Japanese machine gun position that was roughly 425 feet away. The Japanese spotted him and were visibly stunned. After a few moments of silence, MacArthur said it was time to leave. Just after they exited, Japanese bullets sprayed the room.[12] Later MacArthur told Egeberg that he had known that nothing would happen to them while the Japanese were trying to overcome from their shock at seeing him. He could tell when one started talking to the other that it was time to go.[13]

MacArthur's conversation with White about crossing the river had significant ramifications. At 10:15 a.m., Griswold officially gave the task to the 37th Infantry Division. White gave the mission to his 3rd Battalion under the command of Lieutenant Colonel Howard Schultz. At 3:00 p.m., the 672nd Amphibian Tractor Battalion had thirty assault boats and Landing Vehicles, Tracked (LVTs) in place and left the northern bank of the river under the cover of artillery smoke. The first wave made it across easily, but the Japanese defenders spotted the second wave while it was halfway across and delivered mortar and heavy machine-gun fire. "Hollywood could not have staged the smoke, flash and bang more dramatically," Major Charles Henne, who was Schultz's executive officer, remarked. "It was spellbinding to watch pieces of paddles and splinted chunks of boat plywood fly through the air while men paddled with shattered oars and rifles to work their boats to the far bank, seemingly oblivious to what was happening to them."[14]

The 3rd Battalion nonetheless made it to the southern bank in force and the 2nd Battalion followed quickly behind. Japanese fire concentrated on boats in the water and on the grounds of Malacañan Palace rather than the embarkation point. As a result, the regiment had a secure bridgehead by 8:00 p.m.[15]

While the men were crossing the river, the 3rd Battalion headquarters remained at the Palace, which came under Japanese artillery fire. On two separate occasions, Captain Stanley Frankel rushed out of the relative safety of the palace and pulled wounded men to aid stations. "There was no time to think about what you were doing. It was do or die."[16]

After MacArthur's visit, the former internees at Santo Tomás learned that liberation had not brought an end to the danger they faced. Since the first night the Americans arrived at Santo Tomás, people at the university could hear gunfire and shells going off in the city, although the Japanese had not targeted the compound directly. Angus Lorenzen, aged ten, ignored the sound of battle. "It was simply background noise like having a freeway running right behind your house or having an airport landing path right above your roof."[17] Everything changed on February 7. "Not long after MacArthur's visit, all hell opened up," Mattocks recalled.[18]

The Japanese began a multi-day artillery strike on Santo Tomás. On the first day, the Japanese used anti-aircraft guns and 12-centimeter incendiary shells filled with phosphorus pellets. American military intelligence officers believed the Japanese were using these shells intentionally: "These pellets appeared to penetrate the roofs of houses quite easily, quickly starting fires."[19]

The internees began rushing into the main building, believing it to be the safest spot in the compound. Wadsworth and her friends, Virginia and Leanne Blinzler, were talking to a soldier when the shells began to land. They ran into the building, but not quickly enough. While Wadsworth had no injuries, the Blinzler sisters were seriously wounded. A piece of shrapnel tore up Leanne's jaw. Virginia's arm was nearly severed. They had survived only because the soldier with whom they had been talking a few moments before had thrown himself on top of them, taking the full force of the explosion. He did not survive. The Wadsworth family spent sixteen hours hunkered down and were coated in concrete dust when it was over.[20]

Abe Zelikovsky was a child in the camp at the time. Years later he observed, "We had a regular battle going within the camp." A few moments later, he added thoughtfully, "I probably saw more of warfare than most soldiers."[21]

Three days after MacArthur's visit, the Japanese shelled the university again, using an artillery piece that they had lifted to the third floor of a building that was slightly more than two miles away. The diary of Probationary Officer Baba Masanori, the gun commander, shows that he knew he was firing at the university. He unloaded fifty to sixty shells over the course of ninety minutes without any counter-battery fire from the Americans. "I believe that the mission has been accomplished," Baba wrote. At 10:00 a.m that day, US spotter planes found the gun, and artillery fire hit the Japanese position.[22]

The Japanese had legitimate reasons for firing on the university. The 2nd Squadron, 5th Cavalry was operating out of Santo Tomás, patrolling to the south, looking for a route across the Pasig River. There was also an artillery battery stationed near the Education Building.[23] "They kept a constant barrage into the city. You could hear them, boom," Rick Lawrence, one of the recently freed internees, recalled.[24]

Being on the receiving end was quite different. "I felt certain that we would all be killed. At every strike, we hid our heads and prayed," Mattocks recalled.[25] "The shells came in at a slow rhythm, leaving time between each explosion," Lorenzen observed. He had a good idea of how long before the next shell and knew how long he had to find better shelter.[26] Charles and Emily Van Sickle decided to ride out the attack in an air raid shelter they had dug in the ground. "Night shelling was especially exhausting and nerve shattering," she recalled.[27] Caroline Bailey Pratt was a child at the time. "I remember thinking if this is freedom, I don't know if I want it."[28]

The shelling was random. Evelyn M. Witthoff agreed to help move some luggage from a room that had been damaged. She stopped to talk to a friend who was in line for dinner. The artillery fire began again, and a shell came in and hit the room she would have been in had she not been chatting.[29]

The next day, there was shock. Many people had been killed and wounded. Amelia Bradley was overwhelmed by the "wholesale death" she saw in the compound's hospital facility: "It reeked of blood and filth and dying men and women filled every conceivable square foot of it."[30] Journalist Royal

Arch Gunnison was at the hospital and found it overwhelming: "The smell of anti-septic and dead flesh made me dry retch." A nurse who had just helped performed an amputation, mistaking him for another hospital worker, handed him a severed arm and asked him to dispose of it. He nearly passed out. "Everything went green."[31]

Others tried to make sense of what had happened. "What a pity! We kept thinking as we went about our duties. After surviving starvation, and having to go like that," Tressa R. Cates recorded in her diary. She was not the only one to note the unreality of it all. Eva Anna Nixon contemplated the randomness of death. Many of her last conversations with friends were on fairly mundane matters. She found it difficult to comprehend. General Chase noted bitterly in his memoirs: "Such are the fortunes of war."[32]

As the barrages continued during the days of February 7, 8, 9, and 10, the question of who lived and who died became even more indiscriminate. The Van Sickles decided to move to the main building and the shells seemed to follow them as they made their way. "Time seemed endless," Emily Van Sickle observed. "Shellfire is truly a terrifying experience." When the shelling ended and the couple returned to their shack, they found it in ragged condition, having been peppered with shell fragments that would have killed them had they stayed.[33]

None of these views received much of an airing at theater headquarters. A report Major General Courtney Whitney, the chief civil affairs officer on the staff, sent to MacArthur noted that, overall, the internees were in good spirits. "Without exception coming to my attention they accept the continued confinement of their situation and even the casualties resulting from enemy mortar fire as but an inevitable incident to the liberation of the camp as a whole and are both philosophic [sic] and cheerful concerning the same."[34] This assessment was, at best, a simplification, but it was what Whitney figured his boss wanted to hear.

* * *

The rear areas away from the main line of resistance were quite dangerous. MacArthur's visits to Santo Tomás and Bilibid Prison underscored the fact that, on February 7, there were no well-established frontlines or rear echelons in the Battle of Manila. The Japanese threat to supply lines connecting the forward elements of the advance to the beachheads and supply depots as far back Lingayen remained active. In fact, the 40th Infantry Division was still on the offensive in the mountains west of Clark Field and Fort Stotesenburg.[35]

Organized Japanese resistance north of the Pasig had ended, but there were numerous small pockets of Japanese soldiers, who, although no longer in contact with their chain of command, were still determined to fight. Sooner or later, US soldiers had to deal with them. These efforts often took more personnel than the number of Japanese being contained, and it often posed significant threats to support units. Frank Mathias and Jimmy Mayfield discovered this danger for themselves when they decided to take a break from their duties at the 37th Division headquarters and do some sightseeing with the idea of taking a swim in Manila Bay. They were on a road that had a bend in it, and then they heard the distinctive clicks of Nambu machine guns. Only then did they realize they had walked into an active firefight. The Japanese were in a hut and apparently had not seen them approach. Nor could Mathias and Mayfield see the other Americans fighting the Japanese. Suddenly the explosions of mortar fire landed on the hut and a small squad of infantrymen rushed the building, finding three dead Japanese soldiers. Afterward, Mathias discovered that the Japanese had a clear view of them as they had rounded the bend in the road. "What in th' hell were you two guys doing out on that road?" a corporal from the infantry squad asked. The two had no good answer, and they decided quickly to return to division headquarters.[36]

Headquarters were not particularly safe areas either. Some enlisted personnel at MacArthur's headquarters slept with loaded rifles at their side. "Anyone who is truthful will say they disliked being in an area where there was a good chance of being killed," James S. Dunn, a radio operator in Krueger's headquarters, observed.[37]

The two most dangerous incidents occurred on February 7 and February 8, when the Japanese attacked the XIV Corps command post located at the Grace Park airfield in northern Manila, about a mile north of Santo Tomás. During one of these attacks—most likely the first one on February 7—Griswold was absent when the Japanese attack began. "Imagine my consternation one morning, upon returning from a visit to various fronts in the City, to find the Corps Command Post under assault by a by-passed detachment of Japanese who were attempting to capture and destroy it," he observed. The officers and men of the corps staff had taken cover, and the guard platoon was engaged in a firefight. "All work with in the Command Post ceased." That was a problem, as the general explained: "The really serious thing was that the brain and nerve centers of more than 75,000 fighting men were dead. Nothing was coming in or going out."

Griswold knew he needed to do something. As he drove up to the command post, his jeep was protected because he was in a sunken road, but he could see his men who had taken cover along the embankment looking at him. "To jump out and take cover with them was definitely not the thing to do." He was wondering to himself "what am I going to do?" He also asked, "What West Point would expect of me in this situation?"[38] He jumped out of the jeep with his rifle, and called out to the men nearby, "Let's go get the S.O.B.s." The men of his staff responded to the challenge. "Out of foxholes and other cover, the men swarmed like bees as they advanced to the attack." A twenty-minute firefight followed, before the XIV Corps staff reclaimed control of their headquarters. Within thirty minutes, operations in the command post were back to normal. "The response was heart-warming and constitutes the most thrilling experience of my entire Army career," Griswold recalled many years later.[39]

In those early days, other troops in the rear echelons often came under attack. On February 7, the 117th Engineer Battalion began trying to look for a place to build a bridge across the Pasig River. Heavy Japanese fire thwarted this effort. On February 8, the battalion returned, began building a pontoon bridge across the river, and came under mortar and rifle fire. That same day, a small Signal Corps group laying wire came under attack. The wiremen got out of their truck and took cover before returning fire. The sound of gunfire got the attention of nearby troops and, in a few moments, the Japanese found themselves outnumbered. Six of them were killed in this action. The engineers continued bridging operations until February 9. Downstream from the bridge, amphibious assault vehicles were conducting ferry operations across the river and they came under fire during this time as well.[40]

The Americans realized that they had to respond to these types of attacks or they would never take Manila. On the eastern roads leading into the city, the job fell to the 112th Cavalry. Captain Frank C. Fyke's Troop C was assigned to defend what was called the "Hot Corner." On February 10, his unit took control of the bridge, which was set amid rolling terrain. While the defenders had the high ground, the area was barren, so there was no place to hide. Fyke had his men entrenched and he sent out patrols. (Norman Mailer was not in Company C, but he went out on similar 112th Cavalry patrols at the time. "We set out, and we were scared," he admitted much later, long after he had developed a reputation as a rough-and-tough novelist.) Nothing happened the first day and night. During the second day of the fighting, Fyke spotted Japanese soldiers marching in column through positions Troop C had used the previous day to test and register the range of their guns. "This seemed almost too good to be true, for it was a real machine gunner's dream," Fyke said. There was no need to adjust their fire. They hit the Japanese force, which Fyke estimated to be an infantry company, and forced them to retreat to the north in disarray.[41]

Later that evening, the Japanese returned and launched the first of several assaults designed to retake the bridge, which would have cut the 1st Cavalry Division's supply lines. The Japanese used machine guns and mortars in the first assault, but in a second attack in the early morning hours of February 12, they used artillery, which, Fyke said, landed with "incredible accuracy." During the daylight hours, the artillery barrage continued, but it stopped when US observation planes flew overhead. After dark, the Japanese unleased a thirty-minute barrage and then launched an infantry assault, which was pushed back. During February 13, the Japanese fired harassing fire. Fyke's command was running low of ammunition, and when supplies arrived, the Japanese used their big guns again and blew up a supply truck carrying ammunition. The Japanese followed up with three separate infantry assaults during the night. "The men of my force were holding out exceedingly well considering the seemingly endless rain of artillery on our position," Fyke stated. Another attack came on February 13. Finally, on Valentine's Day, February 14, the exhausted men of his command were relieved.[42]

In addition to the "Hot Corner," combat was also taking place in the rear areas in the city. Beightler assigned the 637th Tank Destroyer Battalion and Company A, 44th Tank Battalion to the Special Security Force that was operating north of the Pasig River. The irony in this situation is that on their first day in combat the only fatality for the 44th Tank Battalion was an enlisted man in the battalion's bivouac area. He died when the rear echelon came under a mortar attack.[43]

A factor working in favor of the Americans was that they usually had the high ground. The 37th Division military intelligence observation point was located in the Great Eastern Hotel, which was a high-rise building located north of the Pasig River. The G-2 section of the division staff watched Japanese activity in a number of fortified positions and called in artillery fire on the defenders. American officers often turned themselves into targets, though. The Japanese knew the Americans were using the buildings and when too many individuals congregated on rooftops, the Japanese often began targeting these observation points. The US forces also had total air superiority, and piper cub observation planes loitered over the city looking for targets. Even the inexperienced defenders realized the danger these aircraft posed, and the Japanese stopped shooting when these planes were present.[44]

Sometimes the Japanese had the high ground, but they usually lost that advantage rapidly. The Americans had heavy machine guns which they used to deliver a thick volume of fire that forced the Japanese to take cover, reducing the benefit of holding the second and third floors, and keeping them from shooting on the streets below. The problem was that US units often went through machine gunners and assistant machine gunners quickly in combat.[45]

The mobility of US units was a powerful tool. There Americans were up against an inexperienced foe who exhausted themselves quickly because they did little maneuver work to send in support or to retreat. As combat progressed, the Japanese became "jittery," to use Gunnison's description. "They fire at anything." This lack of discipline gave away their positions as US units maneuvered against these static defenders.[46]

Tanks and tank destroyers gave the American infantrymen and the Filipino guerillas another big strength. The 637th Tank Destroyer Battalion was well-trained for doing battle against tanks but it was instead seeing its first combat targeting Japanese infiltration efforts. Despite being miscast, the gunners of the tank destroyers did impressive work. They took out a sniper shooting from the top of a building without damaging the roof. The tank destroyer battalion also hit fleeing Japanese at eight hundred yards, took out a naval gun at one thousand yards, and pulverized pill boxes in the areas.[47]

The Japanese could attest to that accuracy. The three battalions of the 117th Gyoro Unit were in Obando, a municipality on the shore of Manila Bay north of the city, were cut off after the 37th Division marched into the city. Suffering from the highly accurate US artillery fire, the Japanese decided to fight their way to the east. Guerrillas spotted them almost immediately and informed units of the 37th Division. The 145th Infantry Regiment was very soon involved in an intense firefight with these battalions.[48]

The Japanese forces had their successes, however, despite superior American firepower. The Nishihyama Battalion had actually forced elements of the 37th Division to retreat on February 7. The Japanese were proud that they had destroyed eight tanks—four from mines and four from 12-centimeter guns. The fighting on February 8 did not go as well. "The enemy destroyed our guns in one fell swoop by direct and concentrated bombardment," a supply officer who survived reported back to MNDF headquarters. In the early afternoon, they ran out of ammunition and decided to make a "rush attack," which failed.[49]

Under intense pressure by the Americans, the Japanese frequently abandoned their positions. Panic set in and the defenders frequently retreated in disarray, leaving heavy artillery pieces behind. They often made no effort to destroy them to keep them out of enemy hands.[50] The Japanese also left people behind. Lance Corporal Amaba Shigao was wounded during the retreat. After three days of hiding among the rubble, he was captured by Filipino guerrillas.[51]

Admiral Iwabuchi knew he was in trouble. His headquarters was located in the Army and Navy Club. On February 9, he realized his position was deteriorating and he decided to abandon the city and move to southeast to Fort McKinley, which gave him a position on high ground overlooking the city and which should have been more secure.[52] A major reason for this move was the advantage the Americans had over the Japanese in artillerymen and batteries. The big guns were key in overcoming Japanese defensive positions in the city. Beightler explained to a friend, "As we have progressed the fighting has grown hotter and hotter and it appears that we may not expect complete achievement of our mission until we have systematically and painfully irradicated [sic] the enemy man by man from his strong positions."[53]

There is no question that this overwhelming approach worked. The prisoner of war debriefings that military intelligence personnel conducted have a reoccurring theme: Japanese units fell apart rapidly under the heavy fire. Superior Private Tamaki Ichiro's platoon took fifty percent casualties from a mortar barrage on February 10. The results were even worse in Superior Private Inouye Zenkichi's battalion. In seven days, the seven-hundred-man force lost four hundred soldiers.[54] The key was precision. The shells were landing on positions the Japanese were holding. They had nowhere to hide—literally.[55]

While this approach worked, during early February the Sixth Army was operating with shallow reserves of ammunition. "Operations were always on a shoe string," Colonel H. D. Vogel declared. Krueger actually had to reduce the number of shells sent to units. This problem was due to shortages in theater rather than transportation issues. The reason was that, since early 1944, when the British firmly committed to the invasion of France, Europe had become the primary theater of Allied operations in fact as well as name. Eisenhower's command, not MacArthur's had the priority in both manpower and supplies.[56]

This shortage and the urban terrain influenced tactical decisions. The Americans had tanks but used them inside Manila mainly as mobile infantry rather than as artillery. This type of fighting was new for armor units. They revised their tactics, but in doing so they lost the mobility and shock power that armor offers. Tanks were also not much of a threat to defenders inside buildings. Their guns often lacked the punch needed to go through walls.[57] The minefields also posed a real threat to them because engineers often missed one or two mines.[58] "Street fighting was tough but to the liking of the boys as they aimed their big guns at windows, bunkers and pillboxes, often at close range," the privately published history of the 44th Tank Battalion notes.[59] The 754th Tank Battalion parked a company of its vehicles on the northern bank of the Pasig River and fired at targets of opportunity in the Escolta district. Officers rotated tanks every four hours, so they could replace tired crews, but kept firing continuously on the enemy.[60]

The demands of combat of this sort—continuous fire—required constant maintenance work, which normally took place behind the frontlines. Not in Manila. There were no safe, secure areas. "Keeping tanks running while in action proved to be a pretty risky job at times," Staff Sergeant Raymond F. Whitman of the 90th Ordnance Company observed. While he was working on a tank, a sniper fired at him. "It was necessary to keep right on working through and all the while I prayed that he was a bum shot or had run out of ammunition. Something must have happened to him for he didn't fire again."[61]

Although tanks gave the Americans real strength in infantry exchanges, they were adding to the destruction of the city. Griswold, as noted, knew what was happening to Manila and was angry and frustrated. He complained bitterly to a reporter from the *Chicago Daily Tribune* about the "wanton" destruction. The defenders had forced the battle on him and there was little that he could do to contain the damage.[62]

Many Manileños wanted to run from the growing devastation, but moving about in the city was dangerous, so most stayed in place. Elena A. Rodriquez found the streets empty of people as she wandered about. Father Juan Labrador noted in his diary, "We know nothing about those who are at the other side of the battlefield, and we are expecting the worst."[63]

* * *

The Tondo Peninsula, just north of the dock and port facilities in northwestern Manila, was the site of significant combat for the 37th Infantry Division from February 7–9, while the unit tried to march south. The 145th Infantry Regiment did this fighting. At 2 p.m. on February 7, the Japanese initiated an amphibious landing against the northern dock areas. The Americans used mortars and anti-tank guns to destroy all the barges before they could reach the beach. A small group of Japanese soldiers survived and made it to shore; they did not last long.[64]

The house-to-house firefights on the peninsula reflected a major characteristic of urban warfare: the compression of terrain. Intense tactical contests are often fought over control of small pieces of real estate. The Buckeye regiment forced the Japanese to the north. The climatic firefight came on February 8 at the facilities of the Philippine Manufacturing Company. The machinery, stone walls, and buildings of the factory gave the Japanese good defensive positions, and they added pillboxes and tunnels to make the facility even stronger. Lieutenant Colonel George T. Coleman, the commanding officer of the regiment's 2nd Battalion, was killed. Beightler was stunned at his loss. In a letter to an old comrade, he called Coleman "a brilliant young regular" and "one of the most promising officers I have ever met."[65]

During this fight on the Tondo Peninsula, the Japanese started turning their vengeance on the Filipinos, a feature that would come to characterize much of the Battle of Manila. Staff Sergeant Warren P. Fitch was at the Tondo Railroad station during the night. "I heard screaming, screaming, and screaming." The next day he was ordered to set up a position at a road intersection two blocks away. "Behind a corrugated sheet metal fence at that corner, there were perhaps twenty-five Filipino civilians, men, women, children, half-stripped, hands tied behind them, all bayonetted, all dead."[66]

Just south of the Tondo district, on the other side of the Pasig River, was the Walled City—Intramuros—which caught fire on February 7. "What a day of real panic and terror," Sister Concepcion Gotera explained. "Dynamite and bombs roared like thunder." Japanese soldiers rushed to put out the fire at the San Juan de Dios Hospital. That chivalry caught the nun off guard because it seemed so atypical of the Japanese treatment of the Philippines. It was only after an hour that she noticed that they were using the fire as a cover to smash the hospital in a way that facilitated its burning. "Ah! How cunningly they played their part and my . . . how we were being fooled."[67]

The soldiers in the old keep posed a real danger as the nuns of the hospital sought refuge in ruins in the Walled City. During the night of February 7–8 and throughout the following day, the Japanese rounded up foreign nationals that were patients in the hospital. Sister Concepcion noted that they were never seen again and listed them by name.[68]

By the time the 37th Infantry Division had crossed the river, the nature of the battle changed. "Not until the passage of the river was completed did the nature of the enemy defense entirely reveal itself," a military intelligence report noted. "Then it became clear that the defense was to consist, in the main, of independent centers of resistance which were well sited, well constructed, and fiercely held, but which were not coordinated in an overall plan."[69]

Japanese artillery fit into this pattern. The *makaibo* put their big guns inside buildings to protect them against a US response. They also placed their light artillery on vehicles, would fire off a few rounds, and then withdraw. "This improvisation, together with the emplacement of much artillery in buildings, was extremely effective in avoiding destruction by Blue counter-battery fire," reads a 37th Division document summarizing the battle. The defenders also had some intelligence because they continually hit command posts.

American soldiers, trained for the last two years in jungle warfare, were quickly realizing they had walked into a city fight. "Street fighting is a new technique for our men in the Pacific," Gunnison explained in his reporting.[70] The operational reports of battalions and regiments began emphasizing what was facing the soldiers, particularly heavy machine guns and grenades. By February 9, the Americans realized they had a fight on their hands.[71]

Urban warfare increases the importance of controlling infrastructure facilities. Transportation, water distribution, waste treatment, and power distribution facilities suddenly have operational and strategic importance. Manila was no different. A day after the 148th crossed the Pasig River on February 8, a company of the 129th Infantry Regiment tried to take Provisor Island, a small landmass about 400 yards by 125 yards separated from the southern bank of the river by minor estuaries. What made the island important was that it was the home of the Manila Light and Power complex. It was the biggest source of electricity for the municipality. Buildings with concrete foundations or frame structures with metal sheeting for sides and roofs covered almost every square foot of the island. The Japanese had also established sandbag barriers inside the buildings, creating a series of defensive positions within each fortification.[72]

These defenses were strong enough to drive off US soldiers. At 8:00 a.m. on February 9, the 129th tried again, advancing behind a wall of artillery fire. The first assault boat got across, but the second one was hit in the water. While most of the men survived, they had to swim to the island. After trying to enter the boiler plant and being driven back by intense Japanese fire, seventeen infantrymen found themselves pinned down behind a pile of coal. The

Japanese had positions on the southern bank of the river that could cover the entire island with machine gun and rifle fire. Two men who tried to swim back to US positions were shot and killed in the water.[73]

The remaining fifteen were cut off—they could neither attack nor retreat. Their regiment could not send any help. The machine-gun fire was so close that they had to spend the entire day in prone positions. A third man managed to swim back to his company and informed them of the situation on the island. After dark, the Japanese dispersed, which the Americans could hear. Captain George West, the company commander of the group stuck on the island, swam across the river, dragging an assault boat behind him. West was wounded but he managed to extract his men. The tactical defeat was absolute. Of the eighteen men who had landed on Provisor, seventeen were either dead, wounded, or missing.[74]

The 37th Infantry Division responded with an hour-long artillery barrage. At 2:30 a.m. on February 9, the regiment sent an entire company to take the island in six assault boats. Two made it to the island before the clouds parted and moonlight exposed the rest of the force. The Japanese sank three of the remaining four boats. A fire that broke out on the island provided enough light for the defenders to see those that had already made it ashore.

After two hours, the fires died out and the Americans charged into the boiler plant. The Americans and Japanese played a twisted version of hide and seek, and when dawn came, the soldiers from the 129th held the eastern half of the building.[75]

Iwabuchi offered a fairly accurate report to Tokyo on the progress of the battle as it stood on February 9. Observation posts on the top of the Agriculture Building had enough height over the landscape of rubble to watch US tanks and trucks to the north move into the city. His men estimated that they were up against two US divisions. Artillery fire from the Americans was intense along the riverbanks. "However, Navy units are fighting back against this enemy with all their might."[76]

The admiral's description was an accurate analysis of the fight on Provisor Island on February 10. The Americans slowly took control of the rest of the boiler house, but the Japanese controlled the rest of the island and kept the US soldiers trapped in the building with their heavy guns. The tanks, tank destroyers, mortars, and artillery of the 37th Division responded in kind, dropping all sorts of ordinance on the western end of the island, which resulted in some friendly fire deaths.[77]

The shelling continued through the night of February 10; the 129th sent more men to the island for another attack. At dawn on February 11, the Americans discovered that Japanese resistance had collapsed during the night. The island was theirs.[78]

The fight for Provisor Island was, in the end, a hollow victory. The two-day firefight had destroyed what made the island valuable in the first place. The power plant would not produce electricity for the city of Manila anytime in the near future.[79]

While the 129th was involved in the fight for Provisor, White's 148th Infantry advanced into central Manila. About three-quarters of a mile south-east of Provisor Island was the Paco Railroad station, another strategic defensive position for the Japanese. The station was in the neoclassical architecture style that characterized many of the government buildings in Manila and was at the southern end of Quirino Avenue, which, in 1945, went all the way to the Pasig River. About forty-five feet in height, the station had a commanding view of the avenue, and its marble construction offered protection against most US ordinance. The 37th Division's operational report admitted that their guns were "powerless to destroy" the Japanese positions. The 2nd Platoon, Company B, 148th Infantry Regiment made a frontal assault, which the Japanese stopped about one hundred yards from the building with "heavy and accurate" fire. A number of infantrymen moved to the left or northern end of the building. Private First Class Elbert E. Jones used his bazooka to fire twenty rounds into the building. A Japanese machine gun cut him down. While the Japanese were busy with Jones, two other first-class privates, John N. Reese and Cleto Rodriquez, were getting closer to their positions. Reese and Rodriquez had Browning automatic rifles and were carrying extra ammunition. They spent the next two-and-a-half hours firing at close range. They killed or wounded a third of the defenders in the train station and incapacitated a 20-millimeter anti-aircraft gun and a heavy machine gun. "All I knew was there was the enemy in front of me, that they were going to try to shoot, and we were going to kill or be killed," Rodriquez explained after the war.[80]

The two broke contact only after they ran out of ammunition. They had fired roughly sixteen hundred rounds at the Japanese. In the retreat back to their unit, Reese was shot and killed. Word of what they had done quickly spread through the division. Both men were awarded the Medal of Honor for their actions that day.[81]

The Japanese took a limited view of this engagement. "Our troops have fought well and defeated it," Iwabuchi reported. His men had turned back the US force attacking the station. While the Japanese still held the train station, the defenders were in a weak position, and the next day the 37th Division pushed through the Paco railroad station, quickly taking it with only light resistance.[82]

While the 37th Infantry was marching into the city and crossing the Pasig River, the 1st Cavalry was in the west hooking around in a counterclockwise direction. The 8th Cavalry advanced through the Sampaloc, Santa Mesa, and Santa Ana districts, reaching the Pasig River. A Japanese study of the battle observes: "By the end of the day, the area was virtually overwhelmed." That would have been news to the US soldiers. "The closer we got to our destination, the more intense the fighting became," Private First Class Robert R. Harrison recalled. Stopped at the Pasig River on February 9, the regiment fired on four barges that were headed west toward Manila Bay. The river blocked the regiment for less than a day. The next morning, the 672nd Amphibious Tractor Battalion ferried the cavalrymen across the waterway. The battalion, though, was exhausted. A lack of spare parts and the rapidity of the advance had kept the soldiers from doing required maintenance work. The unit was dancing on the edge of becoming combat ineffective.[83]

At this point in the battle, the Americans were starting to confront defensive positions with heavy weapons that the Japanese had worked to build and reinforce in key spots. The doctrine of the Imperial Japanese Army stated that urban warfare worked to the advantage of the defender even if they were numerically inferior. The Japanese expected that buildings of stone and concrete with basements offered facilities that could withstand heavy, direct bombardment for days, if not weeks. The road network provided easy venues for advancement and all structures worked to obscure movements from the enemy.[84]

Despite their preparation, the Japanese were not ready for what happened on February 7. Lieutenant Commander Kayashima Koichi, a staff officer in Iwabuchi's headquarters, watched in astonishment as US artillery rapidly undid all the hard work of the sailors. "We were overwhelmed by the onslaught and most of the riverbank positions were destroyed, each unit retreated to pieces, and individual fighting took place." The *toochaka* boxes—Russian-style pillboxes dug into the ground—had not had time to dry and failed quickly. There were also too many openings in the Japanese defensive lines. The defenders burned through their machine gun ammunition quickly and fired their 12-millimeter guns at too high of an angle to cover gaps in their lines. The Americans exploited the weaknesses. The lopsidedness continued on February 8: "Our troops in the Pandacan area were completely destroyed and abandoned their positions and retreated," Kayashima observed.[85]

Japanese counterattacks produced temporary success. The 1st Independent Naval Battalion carried out a night attack in Pandacan and regained control of a piece of real estate they called "Mt. Kiyomizu" after a Buddhist temple outside Kyoto. The US responded with tanks and artillery. The heavy US fire took its toll. "It was difficult for the commanding officer of the 1st Battalion to maintain control of his unit, and the situation worsened over time," Kayashima noted. The cavalrymen positioned themselves so that they broke up the internal cohesion of Japanese units. Munitions had defoliated much of the city and the destruction of many structures and the high ground. The 1st Battalion watched as the 4th Naval Battalion on its right retreated. There was no radio communication, and the two battalions were using runners to communicate with one another.[86]

Iwabuchi was fully aware of what was happening to his command. On February 10, he reported to the Southwest Fleet: "The bombardment is so accurate that we are losing our soldiers and weapons. We have no means of attack; in short, we are just the target of enemy shooting training; it is so regrettable."[87] The result was that the 1st Cavalry sliced through Japanese positions. The horsemen made contact with the 37th Infantry in the Paco district at roughly 1 p.m. on February 10.[88]

The admiral was now isolated from his command. His headquarters at Fort McKinley looked vulnerable, so he decided to move back into the city. On February 10, he and his aide, along with several guards, arrived at the Agricultural Building located at the eastern end of Luneta Park. Kayashima later speculated that the admiral was not going to command from behind. Both he and Iwabuchi believe Fort McKinley would fall to the Americans sooner than the Agricultural Building and moving kept him from being cut off from his command. This assessment about McKinley turned out to be correct.[89]

As US soldiers moved into central Manila, they began coming across even more signs of Japanese atrocities. On February 12, while patrolling, a squad of infantry came across an abandoned filling station; inside were bodies of Filipinos killed with bayonets. Private First Class Jimmie Leep noticed movement among the dead bodies. When investigating, he discovered that an eight-year-old little girl was still alive, clinging to her mother. He then discovered that the mother was still alive as well. The two were quickly evacuated to a hospital in the rear.[90]

Because cities are media-saturated, the influence of war correspondents is always a factor in urban warfare. In the case of Manila, the quality of reporting was uneven. Gene Sherman of the *Los Angeles Times* would win a Pulitzer Prize for his reporting. Homer Bigart of the *New York Herald Tribune* won two. Walter Simmons of the *Chicago Daily Tribune*, according to his colleagues, "wrote with Hemingwayesque flair." Gunnison showed professional dexterity, writing magazine and newspaper accounts while also doing radio work. Many of the reporters had lived in Manila before the war. Gunnison, Russell Brines, and Carl Mydans had been interned at Santo Tomás for a year and were there at its liberation. Mydans was part of a journalistic dynasty. His father-in-law was the director of the journalism program at Stanford University; his wife was a reporter and novelist, and one of their children would become a reporter with *The New York Times*.[91]

Yet the coverage of Manila, particularly during the crucial days in February 1945, was less than ideal. LeGrande Diller's press releases often drove much of the reporting about Manila. "Wartime coverage of outfit was zip or inaccurate," Major Henne of the 37th Infantry division reflected. "We read the crap they printed in Stateside papers and laughed. Obviously, they got their copy out of the press tent back at Sixth Army or MacArthur's headquarters."[92]

Many press accounts of the battle advance the story without any direct quotes. Julius Gassner, a lieutenant serving on the division's staff, had a view similar to Henne. "I don't remember ever seeing any journalists in our Hq area."[93] In many cases, journalists resorted to quoting other correspondents in their stories. The sloppy nature of the reporting was obvious to other war correspondents. Back in the United States, Henry W. Harris of the *Boston Daily Globe* called media coverage of the battle "confused."[94]

Reporters used theater press releases for the substance of their stories in part because some of them had been covering the campaign on Luzon and had been there since the landing on Leyte. They were generally older than the junior- and middle-grade officers doing the fighting, and did not have the physical conditioning that the soldiers had to stand up to the stress of combat. "The strain was beginning to show," Dunn admitted. The reporters were also a small lot. Few had backups or could be rotated out of the war zone without the danger of missing a story. Only the wire services and a few major media outlets like Time-Life, *The New York Times*, the *New York Herald Tribune*, the *Los Angeles Times*, the *Chicago Daily Tribune*, and the *St. Louis Post-Dispatch* had more than one reporter in the theater. There was only so much they could do with the time they had, and they cut corners where they could.[95] These limitations often showed in their articles.

Despite these professional shortcomings, journalists would get plenty more opportunities to get the story right in the fighting ahead.

11

Life Behind Japanese Lines

After a week of fighting, life in the Japanese-controlled areas of Manila was turning nightmarish. The defenders had firm control of only four of the eleven districts of Manila: Intramuros, Ermita, Malate, and Paco. All these areas were south of the Pasig River. The Japanese were well aware that the Filipinos on Luzon were welcoming the Americans enthusiastically. They resented this and they had orders—which they implemented willingly—to make the Manileños pay.

The Battle of Manila was defined by the methodical targeting of the civilian population. The Japanese historian Hayashi Hirofumi has argued, given where most of the incidents took place, that the majority of these killings were done by the Imperial Japanese Army.[1] Their orders, though, came from Rear Admiral Iwabuchi Sanji. He made the determination that there was no difference between Filipino guerrillas and civilians. "When the enemy invaded Manila, the citizens were welcoming the enemy well and disrupted all of our fighting action," he reported. "The number of citizens is estimated to be about seven hundred thousand, but on the front line north of the Pasig River between 3 and 5 February, the general public carried out the following guerrilla activities: communicate with U.S. troops before our attacks, shoot our soldiers, and report our locations to U.S. troops. As a result, our surprise attack was infeasible, and many of our troops were unable to achieve their objectives."[2]

The attitude that all Filipinos were the enemy was widespread among the Japanese defenders. Taguchi Hiroshi, a Navy aviation mechanic who became a prisoner of war, explained to U.S. Army investigators in late March: "The enlisted men in the lower ranks, believed that, since the Filipinos indicated that they were cooperative toward Americans in their attitude and had ill feeling toward the Japanese, because prices of food and other articles during the period when we occupied the Philippines went very high . . . , higher officials ordered the destruction of Manila and the Filipinos."[3]

Putting aside the morality of this type of warfare, killing everyone in Manila who was not Japanese was simply beyond the resources and abilities of the Manila Naval Defense Force. It was also catastrophically counterproductive. Military discipline and order broke down, and individual sailors in the Defense Force began plundering from civilians rather than performing their military missions. There were some deviations from this pattern, but Iwabuchi's command featured none of the traditional factors—unit pride, loyalty to comrades, strong leaders, good training—that hold military units together.

The Japanese began their battle against Filipinos by rounding up influential social and civic leaders. The Archbishop of Manila, Michael J. O'Doherty, was one of the few that avoided detention and execution. Throughout the occupation, he heard word that the Japanese were plotting to arrest him or take him into some sort of protective custody. The Japanese tried to remove him in early February, and he made it clear he would not go willingly. If they were going to take him, he would be a prisoner. That defiance worked. "As on many former occasions," the Archbishop observed after the war, "Providence kept me out of the Japanese hands."[4]

Ordered to treat all Filipinos as the enemy, Japanese soldiers saw threats everywhere. The Japanese rounded up Filipino men basically for being Filipino men. On February 5, the Japanese collected a group of six hundred and held them at St. Paul College. After several hours of no food and water, a Japanese officer brought in one bottle of beer and two boxes of cookies. He drank the beer and then threw the cookies at his hostages. Many people did not catch any. After he departed, the Japanese began throwing grenades at the crowd. They killed approximately five hundred people.[5] Many tried to escape; some succeeded when they "played dead," which underscores the limited infantry skills of the defenders.[6]

One of the bigger roundups of Filipinos took place at Fort Santiago, which is located at the northwestern tip of Intramuros. On February 7, the Japanese collected about sixteen hundred men, forced them to surrender their personal belongings, and crammed them into prison cells as they divided them into groups. The Europeans were collected in one group. Filipinos were divided into two groups. The lucky ones went back to their cells. Others were taken to the open area of the fort, lined up in a row, denounced as guerrillas, and mowed down with a machine gun. Others were bayonetted. They allowed some of the survivors—which is to say those that they did not try to kill—to leave.

The next day the Japanese decided to rid themselves of the remaining prisoners in the cells. They doused the Filipinos with gasoline and set them on fire. A U.S. Army investigation into Japanese actions inside the Walled City found that two thousand people had been killed at Fort Santiago. The actions in the fort were one of three areas in the Walled City where the Japanese conducted systematic executions. The other two were Plaza McKinley and the Santa Rosa ruins.[7]

It took little to provoke the defenders and insulting them was an exceptionally bad idea. In the late afternoon of February 7, a Japanese Army patrol pounded on the front door of the Pons family, who were Spaniards living in the Paco district of southcentral Manila. Rosario Garcia de Pons answered the door, and the Japanese patrol demanded chickens. Garcia de Pons refused and grabbed the hair of a Japanese soldier and yanked his head back and forth, screaming at him in Spanish. Her condescending behavior ended up costing her and many others their lives. The Japanese left, but they returned ninety minutes later. There were several others in the house, seeking shelter from the battle, including a pregnant woman with an eleven-month-old child. The Japanese tied the hands of these individuals behind their backs and roped them together into a line. The Japanese shot Bartolome Pons first, then his wife, and they pulled the rest of the group down. In their sloppiness, the Japanese never shot Basilio Umagap, an eighteen-year-old who worked for the Pons. With dead bodies on top of him, he did not move. He could hear the Japanese start to leave, but the child began crying. A Japanese soldier turned back and fired twice—the child stopped crying. After the Japanese left, Umagap untied himself and escaped.[8]

In addition to Japanese atrocities, American shells were also a threat to the people in the Japanese-controlled zones. In Malate, Frank Ephraim, a teenager whose Jewish family had fled Nazi Germany and found refuge in the Philippines, watched American Piper Cub airplanes moving slowly above the city. It took him a week to figure out that the planes were doing artillery observation work. Watching the planes, stuck behind Japanese lines, gave Ephraim "exhilarating feelings." The Americans were coming to liberate them.[9]

It came as a shock, then, when their liberators began shooting artillery at them. Pedro M. Picornell's family was standing near a well outside of the Remedios Hospital, which was in the Malate district of southern Manila, when a US shell exploded. Shrapnel wounded and killed several civilians. Picornell's mother, father, and infant sister were all hit. His mother came close to losing her arm. The Chinese nurse holding his sister died instantly. The survivors took the wounded to the hospital and left the dead where they lay. A series of shells followed, targeting a building. That night a friend brought Picornell part of one of the shells. "It had clear American markings on it, and it confirmed what all of us suspected and none of us wanted to believe that it was American shells that were causing the carnage at the Hospital."[10]

The Intramuros was the center of the Japanese zone, and American shells began to fall while the Daughters of Charity, an order of nuns, was celebrating Mass at the San Juan de Dios hospital. "At the solemn moment of the elevation of the Host a particularly violent explosion crashed directly overhead so that we expected the priest to be buried under the rubble. But his faith and devotion were stronger and through the perilous moments he brought the Holy Mass to conclusion," Sister Concepcion Gotera later said.[11]

The difference between survival and death was often a matter of chance. Ernest Berg was a German immigrant to the Philippines who, before the war, had operated a department store in Manila. Berg had set up a shelter in an empty lot behind his home in the Ermita district of central Manila. After the Japanese burned their house, Berg and his family built yet another shelter, using a cement wall that adjoined their home. His wife refused to move to the new location. They had already spent a great deal of effort building their first shelter and she did not want to start over. "Dad was insistent," his daughter Evelyn recalled. The family spent a lot of time and effort building the new shelter. They went to bed and were so exhausted they slept through another artillery barrage. The next morning, the Bergs got up and saw that another family had occupied their old shelter. A shell had scored a direct hit in the night. Everyone was dead. "A look of horrified realization flickered in mom's eyes. Dad never said a word."[12]

Fate was less kind to the Venturas of the Malate district. Jamie Ventura, a teenager, was sheltering near a wall with his mother, sister, and aunt. A shell exploded, causing the wall to collapse on them. All four were killed. Hans Hoeflein, Ventura's best friend, bore witness to their deaths.[13]

Hoeflein's family had many concerns themselves. The Japanese had burned down their Malate home but allowed them to leave before they set it afire. The Hoefleins and the Frieds—a young couple that had also lost their house earlier to the Japanese—went to the Remedios Hospital. Young Hoeflein, his father, and Ulrich Fried dug a shelter, expecting that there would be more shelling and that the hospital would be targeted. The shelter was a large, deep hole covered with iron security bars and a galvanized tin roof from a burned house, which they covered with the dirt from the hole. It was simple but it would protect the two families from anything other than a direct hit.[14]

Just as the three finished the work, a shell exploded; the fragments tore a hole in Fried's side. In terrible pain and convinced he was going to bleed out slowly, Fried took a razor blade and slashed his wrists. He bled out quickly.[15]

* * *

Refugees were everywhere in Manila, driven by the natural urge to get away from the fighting. Since the Japanese lines were contracting, the zones controlled by the Americans were clearly the better bet. In the Paco section of the city, south of the Pasig River, Marcial P. Lichauco, a Harvard-educated lawyer who would eventually become a Filipino ambassador to a number of European countries, wrote in his diary: "The fires and explosions from various parts of the city continue unabated." There was no water or electricity. "There is not a scrap of food available in the public markets . . . we shall be lucky if we pull through."[16]

Fleeing the fighting was one impulse. Fleeing the huge fire engulfing the city was another. As the flames neared the Red Cross Children's Home No. 1, Teresa S. Nava, who was in charge of the home, decided they needed to leave. She and others took the thirty-nine children living at the home to the Philippine General Hospital. Although only a few blocks away, the trip required several hours because they had to walk around rubble and duck during US artillery barrages. Nava led the line, carrying a child in one arm and a makeshift Red Cross flag in the other.[17]

The fact Nava was carrying both a child and a Red Cross flag would have made no difference to the Japanese. Everyone was a target. The Cojuangco family was one of the wealthier families on Luzon. Maria Corazón Cojuangco—better known as by her married name Corazón Aquino—became president of the Philippines in 1986. Her son, Benigno Aquino III, became president in 2010. In February 1945, however, the Cojuangcos were refugees, trying to survive like everyone else. José "Peping" Cojuangco was bending down to pick up some money when a Japanese shell exploded. The fragments tore into his back. Had he been standing, the metal shards would have hit him in the chest and abdomen, killing him. Another Cojuangco family member was peering over a concrete barrier when someone told him to get down. He did so just before a shell exploded, which would have killed him.[18]

In future years, Josephine Cojuangco would marry into the Reyes family. The head of that family, Nicanor Reyes, was the founder and president of Far Eastern University. During the battle, Reyes and his daughter, Lourdes, watched from the observation deck on top of his home as Japanese soldiers entered the houses of their neighbors, rounded up residents, and set fire to the buildings. Reyes told her not to worry. The Japanese were only rounding up men. When they reached the Reyes home, the soldiers went berserk, bayonetting and killing women and small children. After they finished, the Japanese set fire to the house. Reyes and his wife were still alive. Their daughter tried to drag him from the burning house with the help of a servant, but Nicanor died during that effort. His wife, Amparo, died from her wounds that evening. Their daughter Lourdes survived and was at the house when the Americans arrived on Valentine's Day. "There were no waving flags or wild cheering, nor any one for our family to greet them," she recalled.[19]

A shell crashed into the house of Elpidio Quirino, a member of the Philippine Senate. Quirino and his wife, Alicia Syquia Quirino, decided to take their five children to her mother's residence and broke into two groups. The senator and one of his sons stayed behind to collect food and valuables to take to his in-laws. Syquia Quirino took the other group to her mother's. They ducked and weaved through the rain of artillery shells until they got to the other side of the street from her parents' house. A Japanese machine gun position had been set up at an intersection. The Quirinos dashed across the street. Two of the boys made it. Their mother and sisters did not. Senator Quirino arrived at his mother-in-law's the next day. He and his son, Armando had become separated, and the younger Quirino eventually died. When Quirino arrived, some of his mother-in-law's other grandchildren had arrived. During the shelling, though, she suffered a heart attack and died.[20] After it was clear that the residence of the grandmother was no longer tenable, the group made its way to the Philippine Women's University, located to the south in Malate. They found shelter while Quirino scouted a path forward. While he was gone, artillery shells found the building in which his relatives were sheltering. Shell fragments killed one of his nephews and tore apart the head of a family servant. Her blood and brain matter covered Victoria Quirino, a future First Lady of the Philippines.[21]

For many Manileños in the Japanese controlled areas of the city, sheltering in place was often the least bad choice among a number of horrible choices. This option had its limits, though. Food and water usually ran out before the situation became safe. The need to get rid of bodily waste came into play. All these factors forced individuals to break cover.[22] Mary Barrientos, of the Paco district, managed to wait for four days before her need for water forced her to leave her shelter. She was lucky that the U.S. Army had arrived by that time. "We shouted to them and were so happy," she exclaimed.[23]

One of the more notorious incidents in a battle full of them occurred at the German Club of Manila on February 10. A social club for German nationals in Manila, it had been in existence for four decades. Very few, if any, members were Nazis, yet given that Germany was an ally of Japan, many people believed they would be safe taking refuge at this establishment. In the past, the Japanese had respected German passports and had not bothered the German residents of Manila. As a result, there were two thousand people at the club, although only five were Germans.[24]

Some of those at the club included a branch of the Rocha family. The Rochas were divided on where they should go to find shelter during the battle—Santo Tomás or the German Club. As a result, one group went to the university and another went to the club.[25] There was a large bomb shelter under the club, and many people were there when the American shelling in the area became quite heavy. When the Japanese arrived, they set fire to the club and the shelter. The refugees inside asked some of women to take their small children with them to show them that they were no threat. The Japanese responded by killing the children, and then raping and murdering the women.[26]

A second, smaller shelter was dug into the club's tennis court. Fires were started at the entrances of this shelter and the Japanese started throwing in grenades. Believing the Japanese would hold their fire if they saw that there were children in the building, the refugees sent out four boys. The Japanese mowed them down. One of them was Augusto Rodriquez. "The sight of Augusto riddled with bullets made mother break down," Elena A. Rodriquez, his sister, noted. Their mother did not last much longer. She moved toward the exit, and then had second thoughts, but by then it was too late. A Japanese grenade bounced in, detonated, and tore holes into her torso. She fell to the floor dead.[27]

Elena Rodriquez and another woman, Ines Streegan, both survived the massacre by running out of the shelter and rushing through a wall of flame a meter thick, which resulted in second- and third-degree burns. Two men went with them and all four fell into a foxhole. The Japanese were ready for escapees and shot them as they exited. They hit one of the men and he fell into the hole, dead. The Japanese bayoneted the other one over and over again. He was on top of the girls and bled over them. Rodriquez always believed that their burns and the blood convinced the soldiers they had already died. "We both played dead all the time and this saved us."[28]

The two stayed at the club for several days, unsure of where to go. During the night they heard hissing sounds, which was the release of gases from the bodies of the dead as they began to decompose in the heat and humidity.[29] In the struggle, the two women were neither emotional nor sentimental. They stumbled over the body of Henry Streegan, Ines's husband, but she had no response. They eventually managed to leave the grounds of the club.[30] Of the two thousand people who had sheltered at the German Club, only they and three others survived.[31]

The other option, of course, was evacuation, although it meant going out into the middle of an artillery duel. The Japanese were forcing many to leave their homes, either by ordering them or by shooting at them. Soldiers walked through the neighborhood where Ana Mari Calero lived, dousing houses with gasoline and setting them on fire. The Calero family was ready. They had practiced and managed to take their belongings with them as they quickly escaped.[32]

At other times, the US artillery itself forced an evacuation. The de la Vega family had to leave their house in Malate when it came under artillery fire. They left in such a hurry that they left behind the suitcase full of food they had been planning to take with them. After stopping at Philippine Christian University, Antonio de la Vega volunteered to go back for the suitcase. When he returned to the house, the suitcase was gone and he had to beg for food from neighbors.[33]

Moving about the city, and especially the zones controlled by the Japanese, was exceptionally dangerous. In addition to the artillery, the Japanese had planted obstacles in the streets. Many of the roads and sidewalks were cratered and pitted from shell explosions. Another problem was that rubble from buildings had fallen down on them. These conditions made travel not only dangerous, but slow. During the battle, the Japanese gave a group of nuns safe passage to take refugees out of the combat zone. A trip that should have taken about half an hour under normal conditions took four to six.[34]

Refugees tried to take personal belongings—clothes, food, legal documents, cash, photo albums, and jewelry—with them, and these items weighed them down. Manilieños faced difficult decisions about how to carry them. Suitcases were one answer, but they were exhausting to carry after a few hours. Families often tried to use carts but the Japanese appropriated them regularly. The broken roads often limited their utility. They were also dangerous because they obstructed the pusher's vision and made it difficult to see that there were sections of road where the Japanese had placed minefields. The three members of the Baumgarten family were fleeing the US shelling of the Masonic temple in Ermita. They were pushing their cart at a fast pace on Colorado Street when it set off a mine buried in the road. The cart and the entire family disappeared in the explosion.[35]

There was also the danger in coming across Japanese outposts and their reaction. In most cases, the defenders treated the Filipinos as the enemy, but not always. Occasionally, there were random acts of humanity. A small squad came across Carmen Guerrero Cruz and her seventeen-month-old daughter, Gemma. Cruz was seven months pregnant with her second child. The Japanese played with the toddler and then "they inexplicably let us go."[36] There might have been any number of reasons for this decision to do nothing, ranging from having no orders to kill, kill to not having the bullets. Given the racially charged nature of the Greater East Asia Co-Prosperity Sphere, it is worth noting that Cruz and her daughter looked like they could have been Japanese and these defenders could have assumed as much.

On rare occasions, individual Japanese soldiers and officers put a pause to the killing. In Ermita, a Japanese officer actually apologized to Sophy Natalie Morgin after a search of the house in which she and others were sheltering produced nothing incriminating. He explained there was a great deal of sniper fire in the area, and he was looking at all suspected vantage points.[37] As Nava's parade of children marched to the Philippine General Hospital, they came across a Japanese machine gun position. The defenders held their fire as the children moved past. Other soldiers escorted families in the area to the hospital.[38]

The Japanese soldiers and sailors usually had some type of connection with the civilians. In Malate, a Japanese unit passed the Rocha family, who were hiding behind some rubble. The soldiers saw them but marched past. One of them dropped out of formation and ran back to them. He dropped to his knee to tie his shoe, and then looked back to make sure his comrades were not watching. He pulled his crucifix out of his shirt, and said, "Me Christian." He warned them there would be an artillery barrage the next day. The Rochas took the warning to heart and took shelter.[39]

At roughly the same time, a Japanese officer and two enlisted soldiers showed up at the Brias family residence. The family were was prepared for some type of brutality. Instead, all the officer wanted was some water for him and his men. They gave them coffee. The soldiers later returned with soda crackers. A few days later, a group of Japanese soldiers showed up, forced the family outside, and lined them up to face a firing squad. As the soldiers were setting up a machine gun, an officer came up yelling "*tomodachi!*" the Japanese word for "friend." It was the officer they had given coffee. The soldiers lowered their weapons. To be safe, the officer told the family to go to the Philippine General Hospital.[40]

Sometime after the 1st Cavalry reached Santo Tomás, a small contingent of the Japanese Army arrived at the Rickards house. Carmen Rickards was related through marriage to the Bergs, after she married his nephew. She, her husband, and their daughter were staying at her parents' house during the battle. A colonel walked up to Carmen and said in English, "Hello, Nena. Remember me? I'm Kawano." Years before he had been the family chauffeur and had driven her to school. The colonel had been in Manila for some time and had never visited to avoid an embarrassing situation. On this day, he wanted to warn his old employers of the coming danger. He told them to shelter on the south side of the house. The artillery shells would come from the north. Not everyone in the family heeded the warning. Carmen's brothers, Walter and Ralph, exited their shelter to take a cigarette break. A shell hit the north side of the house, as predicted, where the brothers were smoking, mortally wounding Walter. When the Japanese torched houses in the neighborhood, gunning down families as they fled the flames, they skipped the Rickards house.[41]

The Holzers, a Jewish refugee family from Germany, decided to abandon their house as the XIV Corps and 37th Infantry Division began shelling the area around the Philippine General Hospital. They were caught out in the open by a patrol of Japanese sailors and lined up against a wall for execution. After they begged for their lives, the officer commanding the group, who spoke English, said he would not kill women and children, but demanded their wallets and flashlights.[42]

Japanese civilians also sometimes helped. At Santo Tomás, Fred Guettinger, a Swiss businessman, called on the Van Sickles. During the war, he had arranged for cash loans for work colleagues incarcerated at the university. He shared stories with the Van Sickles, as they later recalled. "The Japs didn't seem to know what there were doing anywhere," he stated. "In some parts of Manila, they actually helped civilians. In others, they killed them on sight." He told the story of a Swiss friend who was wounded and lay in the streets with a number of Filipinos. A Japanese civilian took him to his house and bandaged his wounds; he would not help the Filipinos. "Yet it was the Filipino they tried to make friends with, not the European. You just can't figure them out," Guettinger added.[43]

In a few cases, the brutality of the Japanese toward Filipinos played a role in the decision of several soldiers to surrender to the Americans. The guerrillas captured Shimida Hirachi, a Japanese civilian. He had been helping Filipino civilians in the Paco district get across the Pasig River to safety on the northern side.[44]

Speaking Japanese played a significant role in preventing Japanese soldiers from killing a Filipino boy. A large group of refugees was jammed into the garage of the Valdez Apartments in Ermita. "We were crowded like sardines," Morgin recalled. A Japanese patrol forced their way in and tried to remove a Filipino "guerrilla." Morgin spoke Japanese and told them the boy was no threat to them. The Japanese were gobsmacked. A Caucasian was speaking to them in Japanese. A bit confused, they left only to return later in the evening to remove the white woman who spoke Japanese. Morgin, expecting this move, faked a severe illness that convinced the squad that she was nearing her end. She no longer needed to be of any concern to them.[45]

* * *

The Japanese paid no attention to the non-combatant status of hospital or the diplomatic immunity of foreign consulates. This attitude is not that surprising. Medical care for the wounded was not particularly good in the Japanese zone for either the Japanese or Filipinos. The men of the MNDF were not particularly healthy when the battle started. A high percentage were infected with malaria. One captured Japanese civilian estimated that ten percent of the fighting force was incapacitated with disease.[46]

Lacking significant medical resources, the Japanese Army was soon overwhelmed by the demands of the battle. Superior Private Takahashi Tarao arrived in Manila in December 1944 as part of a medical unit. For the next two months, his unit occupied the Quezon Hospital and yet did nothing to prepare for the impending battle. Takahasi became a prisoner of war early on and told his interrogators that the unit lacked the medical supplies to meet the needs of the Manila garrison. Patients were responsible for taking care of themselves once doctors had examined them. There was also a hierarchy of rank in play. Officers got better treatment than noncommissioned officers, and enlisted personnel got very little. The Japanese had medical supplies when the battle started but they did not have military police units to stop the pilfering of bandages and medicine by individual soldiers or the civilian population.[47]

As the battle progressed, the Japanese consumed their limited medical re-sources and moved their casualties from one position to another. Case in point, Lieutenant Murakami Kyozaku, the Japanese officer who was wounded in the knee in an assault on Santo Tomás early in the battle, was carried to make-shift hospitals in the General Post Office, the Legislative Building, the Manila Hotel, and then finally the Finance Building. Those who could were expected to keep fighting. Commanders decided that the severely wounded should commit suicide.[48]

It was hardly surprising that the Japanese would not provide medical as-sistance to the Filipinos. The civilian population had to turn to their own hospitals. Almost all these facilities, though, soon became overwhelmed with patients and were the target of either Japanese atrocities or US artillery fire. The Japanese, though, were far more deliberate and vicious. During the battle, the Red Cross headquarters building in Ermita functioned as a hospital. On February 10, four Japanese sailors entered the building and began shooting and bayonetting as they entered. Patrocinio Abad, a film actress, saw them gun down a little girl and her mother. Abad was holding her ten-month-old daughter and hid behind a cabinet; one of the sailors saw her and shot her in the elbow. The sailor then walked over and began stabbing her with a bayonet. She tried to dodge and parry the thrusts but she was stabbed nine times. Her daughter was stabbed three times and died. Hearing the yelling and screaming, medical personnel entered the hallway where the Japanese were located and quickly became victims themselves. While the Japanese ransacked the building, Abad began crawling out of the building to escape the Japanese. She made it outside. Her brother Romano had been in the backyard when the shooting started and had climbed over an adobe wall separating the Red Cross property from a neighboring property, but seeing her, he went back to help. She handed him the body of her daughter and then passed out.[49]

Inside the walled city, the San Augustin church had become a makeshift hospital. Antonio O. Gisbert, a young physician, was doing most of the medical work. Jesus Azcuna, another physician, was helping, but he was a neurologist and could only do so much. "The real heroines at San Agustin were the prostitutes, they were the ones that helped," Gisbert declared. The Japanese had concentrated them in the Intramuros. Gisbert guessed that their numbers were in the hundreds. They were willing to serve as nurses. They were also quite good at scrounging. They could acquire clean linen, or whisky, which Gisbert used as anesthesia. All of which suggests that they had a way of influencing Japanese supply officers.[50]

As the Americans and Japanese engaged in a lopsided artillery duel, Filipinos in the Ermita and Malate areas of the city began looking for safe places to ride out the storm. The crowds there had begun to hear stories of Japanese atrocities. The Remedios Hospital, which was made of concrete, became a popular destination. It was assumed that everyone would respect the Red Cross insignia painted on the doors and roof. Japanese squads visited regularly, but usually to get medical attention. "Nobody was molested," recalled Picornell. He estimates that there were between eight hundred to one thousand people there as either patients or refugees. After the shooting started in earnest, the hospital only had one real doctor: Antonio "Tony" Lahorra, who had just finished medical school. A first-year medical student, Augusto "Nikolai" Felix, provided assistance, and for all practical purposes became a physician through on-the-job training during the battle. Father John Lalor also recruited a number of refugees to do volunteer work in the hospital.[51]

In a house across the street, Ephraim watched the Japanese dig foxholes and set up machine gun positions near but not on the hospital grounds. He also watched artillery explosions come closer and closer, hitting a nearby multistory apartment buildings.[52]

In their rampage to kill all non-Japanese, the defenders paid no attention to the diplomatic status or neutrality of the consulates in the city. Alberto P. Delfino was the consul of Venezuela and the Japanese kicked him and his family out of their house in Singalong. Five days later, on February 12, the Japanese entered the Spanish consulate, shooting and killing the people in the building. The Spanish had made the mistake of providing refuge to Manileños. The soldiers then set the building on fire. The next day the Japanese took the Venezuelan Counsel, his wife, and their son to an empty house where a machine gun mowed them down with roughly thirty others.

An eyewitness to Delfino's death was Umberto de Poli, an Italian national, who was standing behind the Venezuelans, but survived. The Japanese set the house on fire. Poli and ten others managed to escape the building.[53] Captured Japanese documents show that the Japanese knew the difference between various European nationalities.[54]

The brutality of these actions was overpowering, but also counterproductive. Spain, under the rule of Francisco Franco, was one of the few friends Japan still had in Europe. The attack on the consulate and the killing of so many Spanish citizens infuriated Franco's government. Spain withdrew its diplomatic protection of Japanese financial assets in Europe and demanded answers and compensation for the killings. The Japanese Foreign Ministry had no answers, so two months later, on April 12, Spain broke diplomatic relations. Franco did not stop there. He began considering declaring war against Japan. The Americans made it clear, however, that they had no interest in any Spanish assistance. Franco decided against war. He could see that the Soviet Union was preparing to enter the conflict and wanted to avoid allying himself with Communists.[55]

Another major atrocity occurred on February 12 at De La Salle College. A group of about twenty Japanese soldiers barged into the college. The chaplain of the school, Reverend Father Francis J. Cosgrave, had decided to stop holding mass at the school; it was too dangerous to hold large gatherings. That decision limited the number of victims of what came next. The soldiers ordered people to get on their knees. One of the instructors spoke Japanese and knew what was coming. He asked Cosgrave to grant absolution to the group. The soldiers began stabbing people with their bayonets. Officers slashed their victims with their swords. Dozens and dozens were killed and wounded; men, women, the young, the elderly, the healthy, and the infirm.[56]

Servillano Aquino was on the second floor with his wife of one month, her father, and her brother. His wife's brother was seriously ill, and a medical doctor, a nurse, and their father had been tending to him. The Japanese told the doctor to turn around, which he did, and they then stabbed him to death. They then ordered Aquino to turn around. He refused to cooperate in his own execution and fought back. He was stabbed twice and passed out.[57]

The Japanese ordered refugees sheltering in the cellar to come up. Ramon Cojuangco refused, even though his parents, pregnant wife, sisters, and brothers went upstairs. Reflecting their cultural expectations about authority, the Japanese never checked to see if there were any stragglers still below, and

Cojuangco listened as they stabbed and slashed his family and many others. In the evening, he went up to see what had happened. He found that his father, wife, and one of his sisters were still alive. All were severely wounded, and his father and wife died from their wounds the next day.[58]

After the killing, the Japanese sang songs outside the college, celebrating what they had done. Cosgrave was under a pile of dead bodies when he awoke. "Frequently during the afternoon, the soldiers came in to watch us and mock at our sufferings." That evening the priest pulled himself up and went from body to body, granting absolution. He then went to the chapel upstairs and passed out behind the altar. He stayed there for three days.[59]

The Japanese returned two days later and used a can of gasoline to start a fire near the door. A monk, despite serious wounds, pulled out two bottles of carbon tetrachloride and extinguished the flames. The Japanese returned to the college and set another one. This time they returned a few minutes later and saw the monk fighting the flames. Aquino heard him yell as they stabbed him with their bayonets. Then there was silence.[60]

Across the street from the College was the Campos estate. Pedro Campos, a Spanish national, had been president of the Bank of the Philippines. Given his status as a financier, the Japanese had wanted Campos to cooperate with their administration of the islands, but he died from a heart attack in February 1942. The Japanese tortured his son, Tony Campos, to death a few days before the Battle of Manila started. Tony's sister, Pilar, a leading socialite in prewar Manila, had smuggled food and medicine into Santo Tomás and the prisoner of war camps on Luzon. The Japanese barged into the mansion and shot her in the stomach and then bayoneted her. There were a number of refugees staying at the compound. The Japanese lined them up and machine gunned them. They also killed Concepcion Campos, the widow of Pedro.[61]

Pilar Campos's death has been the subject of considerable attention over the years. A few weeks later, several servants of the Campos family found Ralph Hibbs, a medical doctor in the U.S. Army, and gave him the bad news. Pilar and Hibbs had a prewar romantic relationship that they had managed to maintain somehow while he was in a POW camp. The men traveled to inform him about Pilar's death. Hibbs's second-hand account in his memoir is the best-known version of her final moments. He maintains that she lingered for three days before dying. In his book, *By Sword and Fire*, Alfonso Aluit writes that a mortally wounded Pilar in fact escaped the compound. Pilar's aunt, Maria Campos-Lopez, offered testimony at the trial of General Yamashita Tomoyuki after that war that contradicts both these accounts. Compos-Lopez escaped the slaughter at her brother's house with her children, returned the next day, and identified the bodies of her sister-in-law and niece. She found Pilar's body at the bottom of the stairs.[62] Regardless of the version one accepts, Pilar and her entire family were gone.[63]

At the nearby Assumption Convent built in the neo-Gothic style, the Japanese gathered over a hundred civilians. The Japanese told them they intended to kill them. To make their message clear, they hung a priest from a tree. In the chaos of the fighting, the Japanese got orders to evacuate and forgot to execute their hostages.[64]

The Japanese atrocities had an impact on US soldiers. "You hated them," William Tucker, a soldier in the 37th Infantry Division, told an oral history team.[65] Fifty years later, when asked what memory of Manila remained most vivid in his memory, George L. Ellis, who had been a master sergeant in an ordnance company responsible for repairing artillery guns, replied, "The brutality of Japanese against the Philippine people." Murphy Foret, a corporal in the 37th Infantry Division who would lose his leg before the war was over, said that he and others had "fought because of the methods the Japanese used on civilians and the military made us angry." He thought the Japanese were "animals" and his fury never went away. "I never changed my opinion, not because of the fighting, but because of what they made us become."[66]

Another of the major characteristics of the Battle of Manila was the use of widespread sexual violence. Early in the battle, in a systematic manner, the Taiwanese laborers that had been incorporated into the *makaibo* would visit the San Agustin Church, located in the southwestern corner of Intramuros, and divide the refugees along gender lines. They then took a number of women away to service their sexual needs. The Taiwanese soon tired of dragging the women away and simply raped them in the church in front of others.[67]

The Bayview Hotel became a rape center during the battle where the defenders could use a Filipina or a few Caucasian women to satisfy themselves sexually. Hayashi argues this behavior was primarily the work of Imperial Japanese Army units under Admiral Iwabuchi's command. The Army already had a pattern of systematically sexually exploiting the women of their subject peoples in other parts of its empire. The Philippines was no different. The rape of Manileñas continued at the Bayview continued until February 12, when the hotel caught fire.[68]

The sexual violence was widespread. Edgar Krohn, Jr., a German national living in Manila, recalled he could hear women being raped outside of his family's apartment, which was confirmed the next day when bodies were found in the street. A Japanese platoon visited the Berg family compound and separated the women from the men and the children. Evelyn Berg was thirteen years old at the time, but was told to remain. "I didn't fully understand until years later what was happening. *We were going to be raped!*" Her father, however, had a plan. A German national, he looked the part. He was tall, blond, and blue-eyed, and these types of things mattered to the Japanese. Berg invited them into his house, using his rudimentary Japanese. "A while later they came back out, smiling and laughing." He told them since they were all going to die in the battle, they might as well enjoy his Irish whisky while they could. "Dad got them snockered, and that was the end of it."[69]

Japanese military discipline was falling apart. Officers were often the glue that kept Japanese units together and fighting. If the commanding officer was killed, the men often stopped shooting and abandoned their posts. Looting became common among the soldiers. A number of Filipinos saw them steal civilian clothing, then leave behind their weapons with their uniforms.[70]

News of atrocities spread rapidly in the city after February 12, all of it traveling by word of mouth. Some of it firsthand, much of it second- and third-hand. There was shock, disbelief, and horror. But there was another reaction spreading everywhere: where were the Americans?[71]

The afternoon of February 13 found a large group of individuals in the Remidos Hospital courtyard taking a break from a long day. Father Lalor and Lahorra were sitting on the ground with their backs against the wall of the hospital when a massive artillery barrage started. Hearing the whine of an incoming shell, Picornell threw himself to the ground. "I do not know how long the barrage lasted, but it stopped as suddenly as it had started." Picornell found that he was perfectly fine with no wound. The doctor and the priest were still sitting with their backs against the wall of the building, dead. Neither had a scratch on them. The blast wave of the shell hit their bodies with such force and pressure that it sheared and fragmented organs and tissues inside their bodies. A few moments later, Picornell saw his brother Jaime under a pile of rubble. Both his legs were mangled with multiple compound fractures. His injuries were too severe to move him.[72]

Picornell and Felix conducted a quick examination of the hospital. The operating room had taken a direct hit. Felix attempted to tend to the newly wounded, but a new round of shells landed. A shell fragment hit him in the arm. The hospital now had no physician of any sort to tend to any of the wounded. When the shelling stopped, those that could still walk left the Remedios Hospital to the dead. Jaime Picornell was one of the ones staying behind, having bled to death from his wounds. "The smell was horrifying," his brother stated, "but at that point, nobody cared."[73]

* * *

The arrival of US soldiers usually translated into deliverance from the terror of the Japanese. The nature of these greetings ranged from a frenzied rapture to exhausted gratitude. Fernando J. Mañalac was reassured to see US soldiers: "The sight of a cigar-chomping, older-looking American soldier gave me an immediate reassuring feeling of familiarity, warmth and comfort, so different from any Japanese sol[d]ier. What's more, my awareness of danger suddenly disappeared." He was not alone. "People were mesmerized by the incredible reality of it all," Mañalac recalled. "I knew then that life under the Japanese was over!" Crowds assembled around individual foot soldiers and small patrols.[74]

There was some hesitation in welcoming these soldiers. Manileños knew what Americans sounded like and looked like. There had been a large US presence in the city for forty years, but the last time the U.S. Army was in Manila was in 1942, when the Japanese forced marched the defeated soldiers of the Corregidor garrison through the streets of Manila. Something had changed.[75] These men were different: they had strange accents, and some even knew Spanish, which many Filipinos still spoke.[76]

There was also a different look to these soldiers. They were bigger, particularly compared to the residents, many of whom were malnourished during the Japanese occupation. Some found their skin color confusing. Before the war, Americans had tried to minimize their exposure to the sun in an effort to stay as pale as possible, but these strangers had yellow not white skin.[77] Others noticed that their uniforms were dark green, not the khaki that characterized the prewar Army.[78] Their helmets also confused many.

Despite this confusion, the overwhelming response was joy. Blanca Calero remarked, "The American troops showered us with food, ice cream, candy, soap, and toilet articles. There was Bill Turner from New Jersey who wrote to his mother and asked her to send us clothing." Medics were often willing to provide medical assistance to treat wounded Filipinos immediately.[79] American infantrymen found Elena Rodriquez after she had spent a week surviving on the streets of Manila following the massacre at the German Club. "There was a confusion of emotions within me, but I cried mostly of happiness," she recalled. They immediately took her to an aid station. "The soldiers were very kind." They asked her many questions. She saw a man wearing the two stars of a Major General who asked about her welfare. (This was most likely Beightler.) After she had some food, the soldiers took her to the San Lazaro Hospital where she could get medical attention.[80]

Brutal as the battle had been for those in the Japanese-controlled sectors, it was still not over. More was to come.

12

Breaking the Genko Line,
February 11–13

In the middle of February there was a great deal of uncertainty in various headquarters. MacArthur and his staff were slowly coming to understand that they had a real battle on their hands. Many of his subordinates were frustrated that he was restricting their tactical and operational efforts, and they began to push back on the restrictions he placed on artillery. Despite the heavy-handedness of U.S. Army gunners—US artillery tubes would kill many civilians—the people of Manila continued to give the Americans an enthusiastic welcome. Despite the limited creativity of the artillery, foot soldiers proved capable of adapting to the new environment of city fighting. The Japanese, not so much.

The trek of Senator Elpidio Quirino and his family to US-controlled territory seems representative of the Filipino determination to survive. The Quirinos reached the west bank of the Estero de Paco, a small tributary of the Pasig River that runs north–south. The senator found a door, which he used as a raft, and five times he swam across the estero, ferrying his son, sister-in-law, nieces, and nephews to the other side. His daughter and another nephew, both teenagers, swam across on their own. On the east bank, Quirino went looking for help. His son had a leg wound, and one of his nephews was seriously wounded. "At last," he later testified, "I saw a Red Cross flag flying over the devastated and bloody area in Pandacan. My soul was simply lifted up to heaven."[1] Filipino journalist Felipe Buencamino III was accompanying the 1st Cavalry and saw him. "Senator Quirino had aged in ten days and his face had a lost expression. He was not the same man I had seen so often in the past."[2]

The Quirino odyssey was not yet over. The senator managed to acquire a vehicle and took his party to a hospital and was turned away, and then another, from which he was turned away yet again. His third try was at San Lazaro Hospital, where the senator's niece, Dr. May Quirino, was on staff. Tommy Quirino's leg wound had become gangrenous, and he was told his leg would have to be removed. He refused and asked to see his cousin. Dr. Quirino was able to save the leg.[3]

While civilians—most far less influential than Quirino—struggled to survive, MacArthur and his lieutenants where still trying to figure out where the Japanese would concentrate their forces. The fierceness of the opposition facing the 37th Division on the western side of the city suggested—at the time—that the Japanese were going to fight outside of Intramuros. It was also possible that this resistance was actually a series of outposts of a strong force waiting inside the old Spanish fort.[4]

Either way, artillery would play a key role in the next stages of the battle. While the Japanese had established their positions days before, US units were trying to figure where to put their batteries. Field artillery is more accurate when forward observers are in elevated positions. In an urban setting, that is usually the top of a building. Observers require a functioning communication network. In Manila, the US used a combination of flares, smoke grenades, two different types of radios, two types of phones, and a series of runners. Technical Sergeant William W. Owen of the 4025th Signal Group helped install and repair this network. Although he was a signal corpsman, he received small-arms training because his duties took him close to the frontlines. "There was a better way to make a living," he noted after the war.[5]

The use of artillery had divided MacArthur's staff. The purpose of the general's prohibition on using heavy weapons in the city was to minimize destruction. This injunction did not include tanks, tank destroyers, or mortars, and he was willing to allow artillery if it was direct fire; indirect fire was off limits. (Indirect fire is where the aimer cannot see the target and is usually firing at map coordinates. It can often be quite useful against road networks and keeps opponents from maneuvering, but gunners often have no idea if they are actually hitting a valuable target or not.) MacArthur's ban on the use of indirect artillery was not a popular idea among his lieutenants. Given the nature of urban terrain, artillery guns need to be close, within a few hundred yards of a target, to get a direct aim. That put artillerymen within range of machine guns and increased their losses. Krueger challenged him, and he asked that he remove his restrictions. MacArthur refused.[6]

Sutherland, despite his living dead status, insisted on removal of the restrictions, and MacArthur angrily refused. It was easy for MacArthur to ignore his chief of staff, and Sutherland knew that he would have to wait for his moment.[7] LeGrande Diller, MacArthur's public affairs officer, who now had a brigadier general's star, gave Sutherland his chance. Diller was still a soldier at heart, and he decided to use his current position to leverage the press against MacArthur and reverse the decision.

The general was genuinely horrified by what was unfolding in Manila, and seemingly unable to process it. "MacArthur was shattered by the holocaust," Lieutenant Paul P. Rogers, the headquarters typist, observed. Everything he had done to spare Manila in 1941 was being undone by his own troops, and the major coup of taking the city intact with its port facilities undamaged was falling apart in front of him. Admitting to that kind of setback was not in him. Suddenly the general and his command had a vested interest in making sure there was as little coverage of Manila—positive or negative—as possible. A press report that declared, "Manila is dying" set him off. MacArthur ordered Diller to block any usage of that phrase. He also ordered the units under his command to refrain from using artillery in the city. "That was most unlike the General, who prided himself on winning victories with minimum loss of life," Diller recalled.[8]

Artillery was an important factor in the Battle of Manila. Artillery is one of the original branches of the U.S. Army, with a lineage going back to 1775, although it was in 1917 that the "king of battle" turned into the most skilled and professional element of the Army. In an effort to develop expertise quickly after the United States had entered World War I, the Army sent many of its officers to the French artillery training schools. French expertise was grounded in experience learned painfully on the Western Front, and their lessons stuck with Americans, even in little ways, such as using the metric system for targeting.[9] Major Charles Henne, although an infantryman, admitted that "Much of our strength was in our artillery."[10]

The real issue is how significant the big guns were in the outcome of the battle. John Gordon IV, an active-duty major in the artillery, argued in a 1990 article written for *Field Artillery* magazine that the heavy guns were not that effective in Manila. The urban terrain required precision. The heavy gunners needed to put artillery shells through windows; indirect fire accounted for ninety percent of the projectiles used in the battle and was counterproductive.

Shells would bounce off buildings, creating rubble that the Japanese could use to take cover behind, and which constricted the mobility of US units.[11] They also led to heavy civilian casualties, which, after February 12, was exclusively the doing of US gunners. The Americans had destroyed all of Iwabuchi's artillery by this point.

Another Army officer offered a strikingly different take. William T. James, Jr., argues in a 1998 study on urban warfare in the twentieth century that artillery "was the application of massed fire support that proved decisive in the battle of Manila."[12] Henne had a similar view: artillery "gave us combat backbone. It was a different war when fighting without their support."[13] To Gordon, artillery was important, but it was direct fire, the ten percent of the shells that were aimed at a specific target that mattered.[14]

There were several factors that both facilitated and worked against precision. The Americans had total air superiority over Manila, allowing spotters in planes to linger over the battlefield, and the relative immobility of the Japanese allowed communication units to lay telephone wire that forward observers could use. The fact that the concrete posts that the US had built for the municipal phone network before the war had survived the occupation made it that much easier for artillery units to communicate with one another. But other factors made precision difficult. The presence of buildings restricted the trajectories for direct fire and the range of gun tubes required that artillerymen move to the forward edge of battle. A bigger problem was that the density of stones and concrete used in the construction of some buildings made them impervious to the limited shell velocity of US tubes, which required artillerymen to compensate using 105-millimeter and 155-millimeter guns in tandem to breach these structures.[15]

The role that US artillery played the Battle of Manila remains fraught with controversy. One study argues that the Japanese were responsible for sixty percent of the damage done to Manila, with the other forty percent being the work of the Americans. No hard evidence, however, is offered to support their assertion.[16]

What is clear is that artillery was destroying the Japanese defenders. By February 12, Iwabuchi probably had command of about six thousand men, roughly a fourth of what he had when the battle began a week and a half earlier. He had also lost almost all his artillery.[17]

Protests came from journalists, not due to the ban on artillery but rather because they were tired of being ignored, excluded, and manipulated. "That was one time I really did double-cross the General because I felt I had to," Diller explained. "The press was up in arms. They knew that people were dying, troops were dying for lack of support." The reporters were fed up. "And they revolted." They made it clear they would no longer use the communiques that Diller's office issued as the foundation for the dispatches they were sending home. These press releases were—at best—misleading. "Deceptive" is probably a more accurate description. After talking with a number of the journalists, Diller saw an opportunity. He appointed a three-man committee to talk with MacArthur about the artillery restrictions. After listening to the three, MacArthur, despite his vehement and emotional initial response changed course completely. His subordinates were making it clear that they were not only taking heavy losses, but at rates they could not sustain. With reporters now in the mix, he could ignore that consideration only so long. He removed all the limits on both the artillery and on the media. His public relations man was happy: "They did start using artillery, and it all worked out just exactly the way I wanted it to."[18]

The removal of restrictions on artillery was the third major event that shaped the battle for Manila. Despite their reputation as being a bunch of "yes men," the staff had pushed back against the general and gotten him to reverse himself.[19] Robert S. Beightler was happy with this decision: "From this point on, we really went to town." Beightler was advocating any means which he believed would speed up the tempo of combat and save both American and Filipino lives. After the battle ended, he reported to Krueger: "the fantastic defenses of small pockets of resistance which had been isolated required the employment of all available weapons."[20]

Some of this argument is rather weak. The infantry used indirect fire as a crutch to avoid close combat. The problem: it resulted in the deaths of thousands of civilians. Figuring the exact numbers killed in Manila is a tricky business. It seems that most casualties from artillery came from US tubes after MacArthur loosened his restrictions. The shells were indiscriminate. Evelyn Berg's family had a shelter in a field behind their house. The Japanese had burned the house a few days earlier, and they were living in the field on February 13 when there was a massive artillery barrage: "It was worse than anything we had previously experienced, an almost continuous volley of explosions, blinding flashes of light, noise, and dust throughout the night." The next day, an American shell landed in the house where members of the Cabarrus family were hiding. Jesus Cabarrus, age five, was hit in the head by shrapnel. He would have a scar and a dent for the rest of his life. His sister, Ana Maria Cabarus, age four, had both her legs severed. She bled to death in their mother's arms. Their grandmother was pinned under a beam in the house and burned to death, and their aunt's head was severed in the explosion as well. Their aunt's body, though, absorbed shrapnel and protected their cousin, Frances.[21] This randomness seems arbitrary, but it was short lived. This open range shooting lasted a week and a half, which limited the number of wounded and killed. An educated, but generous, guess is that the shelling killed no more than twelve thousand people.

With that said, those numbers are still really bad. Despite Japanese atrocities, Oscar W. Griswold and his staff anticipated that the Americans would be blamed for destroying the city. The XIV Corps report on the battle, written in July 1945, addressed this issue directly: "Long before the American troops reached the Metropolitan area, the skies were red by night and black by day by burning buildings." The destruction of buildings continued for days. "As the troops approached the Pasig they were met on every side by the sound of explosions of demolishing buildings. When the dust and smoke clear away the advancing troops saw only desolation." The report also noted that the unprovoked killing of Filipinos by the Japanese was systematic in nature. The actions of the defenders were not the work of a few depraved individuals or an isolated unit here or there. The horror the Japanese visited upon Manila was organized.[22]

On this issue, they were correct. Iwabuchi had indeed ordered this destruction—the setting of fires and routine executions—in his forty-third general order, which he had issued the day before the Americans entered Manila. "The South, Central and North forces must destroy the factories, warehouses, and other installations and material being used by naval and army forces, insofar as the combat and preparation of naval forces in Manila, and of the army forces in their vicinity will not be hindered thereby." These efforts were to be undertaken without any public announcement so as to avoid provoking any resistance. The admiral had even intended to destroy public utilities supporting everyday life in the city. "A special order will be issued concerning the demolition of the water system and electrical installations."[23]

Conflicted as they might be about what to do, MacArthur and his staff were under no illusions about Manila's fate. On February 10, Brigadier General Bonner Fellers wrote his family: "Regret that the Nips insist on destroying Manila. I suppose half is gone."[24] Fellers hinted at an assumption that was a foundation for much of the discussion. He thought that once the United States fought without reservations, US troops would end the battle quickly.

"MacA has directed we not bomb and use artillery except where no damage to buildings will result. It makes progress slow and the Nips burn anyway. In three more days they ought to be all dead in Manila." Even if MacArthur shared that assumption, he was mourning the loss of his Manila. "Mac is very depressed over the destruction," Fellers observed.[25] The general also knew that there would be strategic and diplomatic ramifications. Those should have trumped the operational imperatives on which Diller, Beightler, and Griswold were focused.

The conflicting emotions that combat produces were evident in Griswold's diary for February 10. MacArthur assigned the 11th Airborne to his corps. "Now fighting four divisions," he noted proudly. The rest of the entry shows the strain Griswold was under: "The fighting in South Manila is very bitter. Japs organize each big reinforced concrete building into a fortress, and fight to the death in the basement, on each floor, and even to the roof. This is rough. I'm getting lots of unavoidable casualties."[26]

Griswold had no good options. He was also being forced to make hard choices and to balance his manpower needs against the strategic interests of the United States. The U.S. Army needed Manila as an operational facility for invading Japan. It also needed the support of the Filipino public in the postwar era. Destroying Manila to save the lives of US soldiers might make sense to those soldiers and the commanders of tactical level units, but it might also very well work against the long-term interests of the United States. These were decisions for a theater commander, not a corps commander. MacArthur had essentially handed them off to Griswold without much warning or preparation.[27]

With the looser restrictions that MacArthur had authorized, use of artillery intensified. On February 11 at the Paco Park and Cemetery, finding the Japanese well dug in, the 148th Infantry pulled back and allowed artillery to rain down on their opponents. By nightfall, the 1st Battalion had taken half the area. The fighting continued into the night. The next morning, the Americans had control of the cemetery. However, they advanced only two to three city blocks during the day, as they were held up by machine-gun fire at several locations. Fellers, in a memo that he sent MacArthur on a daily basis, was less than impressed with their effort. "To fail to advance when the enemy is immobilized in defensive positions is super-caution."[28]

The struggle for control of the Philippine General Hospital complex that started on February 12 reflected the differences between the American and Japanese approaches to the battle. The hospital had giant red crosses painted on its roof. The hospital had large, arching windows that facilitated air circulation, which was a necessity in Manila, but which also made it easier for shell bursts to penetrate the building. On the other hand, it was made of thick concrete and could take a real beating.[29] The Japanese had fortified the complex and had a battalion defending their positions. The commander was killed during the battle, and a naval lieutenant took over. Doctor Antoino G. Sison, the hospital's director, testified at Yamashita's postwar trial in October, November, and December 1945, that the defenders were proper in their behavior and never actually entered the hospital.[30]

Although Griswold had prohibited artillery fire on the hospital complex, he removed the restriction on February 12. The compound was the southern anchor of the remaining Japanese positions in central Manila. The Japanese had picked positions that covered every approach to the hospital and had either dug heavy machine gun positions into the foundations of other buildings or had sandbagged the ground floors. Riflemen were shooting out of the windows in the upper floors of buildings in the complex. The defensive fire overlapped, making their positions quite solid and durable. The 140th Field Artillery fired 2,091 rounds into the complex, and the 82nd Chemical Mortar Battalion shot another 1,365 rounds at the enemy.[31]

* * *

Street fighting required that both combatants learn under fire. The Americans had more assets and did a much better job of adjusting to this form of warfare. The Japanese were not stupid. They recognized that US field artillery had changed the battle.

Japanese units, even within the Walled City, simply disintegrated under heavy fire and their equipment shattered. The 8th Company of the 2nd Manila Defense Battalion, an Army unit, was sent out to stop the American advance in Paco. After leaving the Walled City, machine-gun fire cut apart the unit. The Japanese became demoralized as they tried to survive the shelling. The commanding officer, First Lieutenant Yamagishi Yoshiro, decided that his formation should retreat to Fort McKinley while it still could. The artillery barrages aimed at the Intramuros destroyed an ammunition supply dump, which undercut the ability of the Japanese to hold on to the Walled City on February 22–24 when it became the focal point of the battle.[32]

While heavier firepower helped infantry on the attack, the job of clearing the streets of Manila ultimately fell to the foot soldier, and that meant urban warfare. The infantry units had to develop tactics and operational methods on their own. "Street fighting is a new technique for our men in the Pacific," Royal Arch Gunnison reported.[33]

Charging into buildings was a particularly difficult proposition. Artillery, mortars, and tanks were not useful in this type of close quarter combat. The Browning automatic rifle, on the other hand, turned out to be crucial. It allowed individual infantrymen to be mobile and to deliver a heavy volume of fire. Heavy US firepower often dazed the defenders. It was also a form of reconnaissance, which often provoked the Japanese to fire back before they had targets, giving away their positions.[34]

The Americans had tanks. "We got a tank assigned to us and that was a great life saver," John Skirvin recalled. "It could push the walls down."[35]

Tanks still had their limitations. Some of the larger Japanese mines could take them out. Joseph Holzer's tank drove over a spot and a few moments later an explosion engulfed him and his crew. A heavier vehicle behind them had detonated a depth charge that had been converted into a mine. "That's close calls, but thank God, I'm here," Holzer reflected. George Fischer of the 44th Tank Destroyer Battalion recalled driving past a vehicle from his unit after it drove over a mine. The chassis was on one side of road, the turret on other. He watched the graves registration team recover the bodies of the crew members. "These were terrible things that really happened."[36]

The urban terrain of Manila and the way the buildings were constructed gave the Japanese a resilience against much of the firepower of the U.S. Army. In his diary, a lieutenant in the 20th Harbor Survey and Construction Unit stationed in the Maloban–Navotas–Damplit area in the north of the city was confounded as to why the Shimbu Group had not come out of the hills in the east to do battle with the Americans. He knew the situation was bad, but he was also proud of the work his men had done in building fortifications. "The dugout of the [Company's Headquarters Squadron] position is so strongly built that the Base [commanding officer] and [battalion headquarters] fill up the place."[37]

The Americans looked to neutralize these advantages in several ways. One was to make the battle three dimensional. Americans would take the roof first, either moving from one rooftop to another, which was the preferred method. Other options included using fire escapes, staircases, or climbing the outside walls. Soldiers would then use grenades and rifles to take out the defenders on lower floors. Another approach was to punch through walls and basements and then use grenades or flamethrowers, doing end runs around the Japanese defenders.

Once inside a building, advancing rapidly, often in tandem, was important to keep up the tempo of the attack so that the Japanese would have little time to respond. Reinforcing these advancing soldiers was crucial in overwhelming the defensive positions the Japanese had established. Keeping them from falling back on established reserves was vital. The number of men fighting in the building had to be controlled. Squads and platoons were usually the right size to take a building. Too many personnel could create confusion.[38]

Daytime combat was one thing. The night, as always, belonged to the Japanese. If they were fighting for a building, and had not fully taken control, American infantry would retreat and place a perimeter around it during the night to prevent reinforcements from reaching the enemy garrison, with the idea of finishing the fight the next day. Frank Mendez, a dismounted horse soldier in the 8th Cavalry Regiment, 1st Cavalry Division, recalled, "In the middle of the night, sometime during the night, that's when they were getting ready to banzai, have a charge. That was one of the scariest moments. Out of the stillness of the night you'd hear that bugle blowing they were getting ready to attack."[39]

The Americans had sound reasons for avoiding fights in the dark. The terrain, including sidewalks and streets, was often broken and irregular. Shells and bullets had torn chunks of concrete and asphalt away from these areas, pitting and potholing these thoroughfares. As a result, moving in the dark was difficult and silence was next to impossible. The large number of mines in the city was a constant danger. Light and shadow often gave the advantage to the stationary soldier rather than to those on the move, who were usually silhouetted.[40]

Patrols regularly checked to see if the Japanese had reoccupied a building during the night. Many buildings by this point contained the bodies of Japanese dead, which often gave infiltrators cover. The 145th Infantry developed a simple but harsh method to avoid being tricked by riflemen pretending to be dead. "We pulled all the bodies to the walls and sat them up leaning against the wall," Tom Howard, an infantryman in the regiment, recalled. "We proceeded to shoot each one in the forehead regardless of whether they were already dead. In this way, we could immediately tell upon entering a room or a hall if any bluff was being pulled. Anything that lay in the middle of the floor was shot again, then placed against the wall." There was a logic to these ruthless tactics. "It was a grotesque, gruesome picture to see those row-by-row bodies along the walls," Howard confessed. "These were the day-by-day necessities to survive one day more."[41]

Bridges remained key points and attracted the attention of Japanese night raids. The military police of the 1st Cavalry Division became involved in a firefight in rear areas in Quezon City at 2:00 a.m. on February 11. Later that day, heavy Japanese fire forced the 117th Engineers to discontinue their repair work on a bridge over the Estero de Concordia, a tributary of the Pasig River over which division supply lines ran. That evening, Japanese infiltrators blew up a portion of the bridge. On February 12, as the 1st Cavalry was advancing counterclockwise around the city, the horsemen were slowed down when Japanese guns at Fort McKinley damaged a pontoon bridge over the eastern end of the river. Just after midnight, the Japanese followed up, floating a raft down the river that detonated next to the bridge, doing more damage. The 8th Cavalry Regiment responded using landing vehicle tanks as ferries to cross the river, but this was a slow process.[42]

The Japanese military effort in the city during this crucial second week in the battle was much like the overall strategic direction of the larger war. A US victory seemed a fairly certain outcome, but the Japanese refused to concede and could still do real damage. On February 9 and 12, Japanese artillery hit the kitchens and then the command post of the 129th Infantry Regiment's 1st Battalion.[43] "They have good casualty producing effect but ammunition has a large percentage of duds and fire is seldom massed," the authors of a study the military intelligence branch of the XIV Corps staff put together after the war noted.[44] Their counterparts in the 37th Infantry Division came to a similar conclusion.[45]

The defenders should have had done better with the assets they had. "The Jap learned how to loot and rape a large city when he moved into Nanking years ago," Gunnison observed. That expertise was missing in Manila. The room-to-room, door-to-door fighting of urban warfare is emotionally draining and requires high morale and military skill. A special study on Manila that the Japanese Ministry of Defense conducted, concluded: "In this situation, the battle in Manila was quite one-sided." There was absolutely no *esprit de corps* among the Japanese. They barely knew one another.[46]

Still, the Japanese had some advantages. One was that they had prepared zones of fire. "They had seemed like every street and alley and walkway or anything was covered by machine guns and you couldn't hardly walk without being shot," Skirvin of the 1st Cavalry Division reflected.[47]

Another was a healthy supply of hand grenades. The Japanese had built improvised hand grenades using iron pipes. Grenades were important when the fighting turned into room-to-room engagements. The Japanese had also made other grenades that could put holes in armor plating and punch holes through concrete walls.[48]

The defense of the New Police Station illustrates the power of these assets. The station blocked any movement toward the Walled City coming from the northeast. The 129th Infantry Regiment attacked the station on February 13. This attempt failed, but on the next day, the regiment had tank support. Men climbed through windows on the first floor and took control of the basement. The Japanese had abandoned their positions while taking artillery and tank fire. Infantrymen took these positions quickly before the defenders returned. A savage room-to-room fight followed. The Americans realized that they were up against a solid defense. Progress slowed and it became difficult to get to the second floor. The Japanese had blocked or destroyed the stairways. The Japanese then began punching holes in the second story floor and dropping grenades down on the Americans. The Guardsmen quickly realized they had to retreat.[49]

The 129th Regiment spent February 16 probing around the building. The unit got pushed back hard. The Japanese were effectively holding up the advance of the regiment despite the fact that the Buckeyes had howitzers, tank destroyers, and tanks supporting their advance.[50]

The secondary effects of Japanese artillery could be quite dangerous. The defenders often used incendiary shells, employing air bursts over targets that sent down fragments that could easily penetrate roofs and start fires.[51] A factor working against Japanese gunners was that they were running out of ammunition. The *makaibo* was cut off from the Japanese logistical network on Luzon and once they ran out of shells there was no resupply effort. It was also difficult for the Japanese to move shells about in Manila. Command and control among the Japanese had never been effective, and the damage that the indirect fire of US artillery was doing was taking its toll. The Japanese were basically a series of isolated islands. When the Japanese retreated, they often failed to make any effort to destroy their guns if they could not be removed.[52]

These bombardments, particularly the indirect ones, were often sudden. Fernando J. Mañalac and his family were refugees north of the Pasig River. The Japanese in the Intramuros would target the area regularly. "The shells were exploding wantonly and randomly with no set pattern, hitting the roofs of houses and the school, the streets, alleys, and grounds," he explained. "The results were ear-splitting detonations, the shattering of objects, the high-pitched twangy sound of fast-flying shrapnel and metal fragments, and the mutilation and death of the victims." After the shelling stopped, Mañalac's brother noticed that many of the buildings had metal splinters stuck in their outside walls.[53]

An incident that occurred in Paranaque before the 11th Airborne broke the Genko Line illustrates what could happen if individuals were caught out in the open. Rudy de Lara, a young medic with the guerrillas, was having dinner with the family of his old friends, Brihita and Bankoy Agustin. When a stray bullet wounded one of their pigs, they decided to kill the hog that evening and have a large feast. While de Lara and the family were cleaning the animal and preparing it for cooking, a stray Japanese shell landed on the carcass of the dead animal. The explosion stunned the group that was present. "Once they were in relative safety, de Lara examined the group to see if they were injured. A number had been wounded from flying shrapnel. Brihita had several wounds on her arms and legs, and was holding her son, who had a steel splinter lodged in his chest; de Lara tried to pull it out but burned his fingers. Brihita told him not to bother. The little boy had died. They buried him in the neighbor's backyard. "It was a very sad day," de Lara observed.[54]

It was incidents like this one that made Filipino civilians eager to share with the Americans what they knew about Japanese positions. While much of this information turned out to be vague or out of date, the intelligence on the location of minefields and artillery pieces was usually accurate and helped US units neutralize the Japanese big guns.[55]

This type of support energized the average foot soldier. Skirvin was part of the 12th Cavalry, a regiment in the 1st Cavalry Division. He remembered that his unit had to cross an open field and he expected to come under fire. "We saw Filipino civilians standing out there waiting for and cheering us on, so we didn't think we'd have too much problems." Skirvin recalled that they handed out bottles of liquor to their liberators.[56]

* * *

During this period, the battle in the south was going a bit differently for the 11th Airborne Division. The paratroopers lacked the heavy guns needed to break the Genko Line. On February 9, General Joseph Swing requested artillery support from the 1st Cavalry. General Verne Mudge was more than willing to help. What made the actions of these two generals so risky was that the 1st Cavalry would have to fire into the face of the 11th Airborne. There was a real danger of a friendly fire incident.[57] Concerned about such a development, Krueger and Griswold wanted the 11th Airborne in the XIV Corps. MacArthur agreed. Eichelberger and the Eighth Army had served their purpose. Now it was time to integrate the Angels into Griswold's command. Swing, for his part, wanted to keep pushing north.

The Manila Naval Defense Force still was waging a vicious fight to maintain control of Nichols Field, a large, flat area south of the city (later, it became Ninoy Aquino International Airport). Japanese bunkers, pillboxes, and trenches formed a series of strong points that looked south. These positions were staggered so that they were mutually supporting, although they had huge gaps. The Japanese in the rear—or north—of Nichols Field could protect the flanks of the southern positions in front of them. There were also bunkers west and north of the runways. The western positions were on both sides of the Parañaque River, which ran north–south. These positions were exceptionally strong, and combat operations to break the resistance were fierce. "This was not a bar room fight, no quarter asked for and no quarter given. The division fought with no reserve," James E. Richardson, an infantryman in the 11th Airborne, explained. During this fight Richardson was promoted to corporal. He had lied about his age when he enlisted in 1944. He was now a fifteen-year-old non-commissioned officer.[58]

At approximately 1:00 p.m. on February 10, Griswold radioed Swing: "Welcome to the XIV Corps."[59] On that same day, the division began making significant tactical advances against the Nichols Field complex. The 188th Infantry took eight hundred yards, despite making frontal assaults. The 1st Battalion of that regiment took four big Japanese guns and managed to reverse a five-inch naval gun, using it to fire on the enemy. The 187th took about three hundred yards that day as well. The Genko Line, the southern defensive line of the MNDF, was beginning to crack.[60]

On February 11, the Genko Line broke. This was the fourth crucial event in the battle leading to the eventual US victory. The 511th Infantry punched north, marching between Manila Bay on their left and the western end of the airfield on their right. As the regiment pushed north into Pansay City, word spread quickly among the residents. Gladys Savary, an American married to a Frenchman, had done much during the war to help the internees of Santo Tomás. She was excited to hear about the return of her countrymen. She ran down the street, and then stopped, terrified, before a man with yellow skin. "Are youse Americans?" he asked. It took Savary a moment to realize the soldier was not Japanese and was speaking with a Brooklyn accent.[61]

At roughly the same time, Swing made his way to the position of the 511th. Swing told Colonel Edward H. Lahti that he was putting him in command of the regiment. Later in the day, Lahti sent out a patrol that made contact with the 8th Cavalry.[62]

The linking of these two divisions resulted in the Japanese having no escape route out of Manila. Some have argued that this was a "fundamental mistake," and perhaps even the biggest blunder of the entire Philippine campaign. Now that the Japanese were trapped in Manila, so this argument goes, they had no other alternative but to fight to the end and take as much of the city with them.[63]

This maneuver was also in keeping with the U.S. Army's basic approach to fighting, and it made a great deal of operational and tactical sense. A pathway that is being used as an escape route can also be used to send in men and supplies. While many more Japanese might have escaped had the XIV Corps not cut off their route, there is a real probability that the Shimbu group would have sent men and supplies into Manila. The result: the battle would have gone on longer and become bigger than was actually the case. There is no evidence that Iwabuchi would have ordered his command to retreat, or that it would have had the ability to comply.[64]

Sparing Manila from combat was MacArthur's abiding hope, and yet he and his staff simply did not ensure the tactical and operational practices to achieve this objective. As a result, events continued to unfold on the battlefield. On February 12, the 11th Airborne attacked the Nichols Field complex again. This time they waited until after Marine Corps air units had conducted bombing strikes against the Japanese. The 188th made the main effort striking from the southeast. They marched into crossfire—from the enemy in front of them and those holding Fort McKinley, which was roughly two to three miles away.[65]

That same day, the 5th Cavalry—the unit that Griswold had wanted to have join up with the paratroopers—drove west from its position along the

Pasig River. They dashed across Nielson Field, a small airport southeast of the city, and reached Route 57, a road running on an east–west axis. There, on February 12, they made contact with the paratroopers from the 11th Airborne at approximately 10:40 a.m.[66]

One more day of fighting remained. Nichols Field fell to the 11th Airborne on February 13. The area around it was huge, though, and small bands of Japanese would either transit or attack in this area for many weeks. On patrol, Rod Serling of the 511th found himself in a situation where he was out in the open and saw a Japanese soldier taking aim at him. He had nowhere to hide and knew that he was about to die. Then a soldier behind him shot the defender first. On another patrol, a Japanese anti-aircraft gun cut through Serling's unit, killing three. He was wounded in the wrist and would spend two-and-a-half months in the hospital.[67]

During this period, MacArthur's headquarters staff continued to work on the victory parade. Staff officers plotted out the parade route. Signalmen sent radiograms to officers at different headquarters, informing them they would participate in the procession. After seven days of combat operations, reality was setting in at Hacienda Luisita. Fellers told MacArthur on February 13 that formal entry into Manila, and by implication, a victory parade, was not going to be possible for at least two more days.[68] As it became obvious that Manila was in ruins, the parade project died a quiet death.

The paratroopers certainly deserved a parade. They had done impressive work. In taking Nichols Field, the 11th Airborne had destroyed the 3rd Naval Battalion of the Defense Force.[69] Although the airport was damaged and unable to take planes, repairs to airfields and runways are relatively straightforward. The end of restrictions on artillery and the taking control of the airport was the third and fourth of seven major events in determining the final outcome of the battle. Even so, the division also had a legitimate reason to resent their recent deployment. Parachute units are trained and organized to use maneuver and surprise to take positions behind enemy lines. At the airport they were sent into the teeth of prepared positions for which they did not have the equipment. It was yet another reflection of the false assumptions that MacArthur and his staff had made about the ease of taking Manila.[70]

13

Specter of the Gun,
February 13–18

In the second half of February, the patterns established early in the battle continued. Artillery fire continued to dominate the battlefield, but with Douglas MacArthur ending his restrictions, the exchange between the big guns quickly became an uneven playing field. Troop movements and intelligence efforts were soon having a real impact. All three were related.

Pushed to the sidelines by MacArthur when the 11th Airborne became part of the XIV Corps, Robert Eichelberger watched what was unfolding in mid-February in frustration. He felt that the battle was derailing the Luzon campaign, which was necessary to invade Japan. "The fight for Manila has been a pain in the neck and a time consumer," he wrote to his wife. "The big thing is to get a fine harbor like Manila Bay where our boats will be protected."[1]

Military engineers, on the other hand, found themselves quite busy during this period. They had three different missions: digging wells to keep the city supplied with water, repairing or building new bridges, and clearing minefields. Each one was crucial. The 117th Engineer Battalion's daily report for February 13th states: "Water supply continues to be a major problem facing the engineers in Manila." Wells could—in the words of an Army report—"barely supply civilian needs." The quality of bridge construction often did nothing better than meet minimal needs. These spans often had to be limited to one-way traffic, and to certain types of vehicles. On February 14, a steel "I" beam bridge over the Estero de Concordia was strong enough to support foot, jeep, and supply truck traffic, but when a tank used the structure, it started to give way.[2]

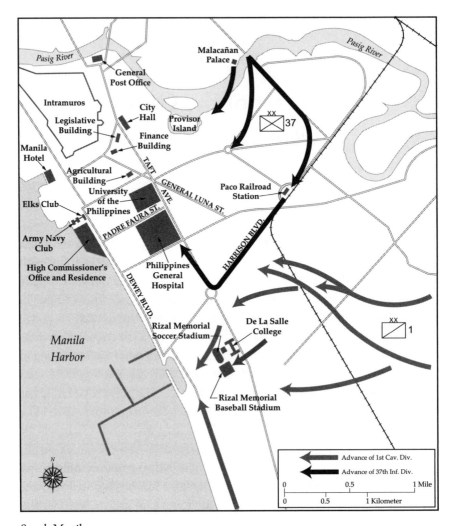

South Manila

The struggle for control of the Philippine General Hospital complex continued. On February 14, the 148th Infantry Regiment still held the same positions it had held two days earlier.[3]

A large number of refugees had headed to the hospital, expecting that the Americans would not fire on the facility. The fate of the Goicochea family shows the danger of this assumption. They were running from the fire in Malate when Pilar Chicote de Goicochea was hit by a shell fragment. Her husband, Jose

Goicochea, left his child with a family friend and carried his wife to the nearby residence of a physician. The physician said she needed a greater level of care than he could provide and told Goicochea to get to a hospital. He took his wife in his arms and left for the Philippine General Hospital. The hospital staff later found their bodies at the gate of the compound, killed by American artillery shells.[4]

Inside the hospital, the odds of survival were better but there was still danger. Luis Esteban, thirteen, was standing in a line in a courtyard to get water from a well for his family when shell fragments killed the man standing in front of him.[5] Edgar Krohn, a German teenager living in Manila, had a similar experience. When a shell exploded, he was hit in the temple, but not deeply. The man in front of him, though, took the full brunt of the explosion.[6] Conchita de Benitez was in the hospital to give birth and the shelling found her, along with her husband and nurse, in a stairwell. They changed direction and exited quickly. "A bomb fell and exploded on the stairway where we had been a few moments before," she explained. "The impact threw us to the floor but there was a cement wall protecting us so no one was hurt."[7]

The stress of being under fire was brutal. "The Americans started shelling the hospital, which filled me with despair," lamented George Parson, a Santo Tomás internee who went to the hospital for medical care. "There seemed to be no logic or reason to the nonstop bombardment." Rodolfo G. Tupas, a future editor of the *Philippine Times*, was in the hospital: "I can hear it now— the crushing, grinding, tearing sound of artillery shells exploding into a mass of concrete on the hospital grounds." Tupas found the noise the ordinance made the most unnerving. "The shells were preceded by eerie whistling sounds. Every time there was a barrage, the whole ward went into fervent prayer. I can still hear it now—the long murmur of fright." Many of the shells went long and started a fire in the residential area south of the hospital. In any case, the artillery made little difference. For the next two days, the Japanese stopped the advance of 148th Infantry Regiment in its tracks.[8]

During the middle of this contest, Krueger ordered a reorganization of fighting forces on February 15. His orders, reflecting a good deal of optimism, went into effect on February 16 and 17. Intelligence reports indicated that a Japanese force of twenty thousand men was assembling to the east of Manila, along the Antipolo–Montalban–Ipo line. Krueger realized he needed to assemble a large force to meet this threat. He assigned the 6th Infantry Division to Oscar W. Griswold's corps, and instructed Verne D. Mudge to begin preparing the 1st Cavalry Division to take offensive operations in this area. He also ordered Griswold to begin preparing for an assault on the Walled City.[9]

This effort reflected a serious problem. MacArthur and Krueger still had very different ideas as to the course of the campaign. Moving east was not a priority for MacArthur. He wanted to control Manila Bay, which would give the US use of the port facilities.[10] It also showed that Krueger was not fully aware how the battle in the city was going. While the end was in sight, there was still a lot of fight left in the Japanese garrison. An assault on Intramuros at this point could only be a planning exercise.

Reports on American artillery had reached MacArthur on February 14, two days before the Army learned of civilians in the Philippine General Hospital complex. In these reports, most of the blame fell on the 37th Infantry Division. The destruction was indeed ineffective, but what was more troubling was the fact that the division was consuming ammunition at an unsustainable rate. MacArthur sent verbal orders to Beightler on February 15, limiting the use of his cannons. Beightler would not comply, telling Griswold he would rather be removed from command. In his own words: "he expected to be out of a job pronto and possibly court-martialed for refusing to obey orders." MacArthur responded by sending General Richard Sutherland to investigate. Beightler had known Sutherland during their service on the War Department staff in Washington, DC, and expected that the chief of staff would listen to his argument. "This campaign," as he explained "is a 'toughie' and is reminiscent of what I should imagine the fighting at Stalingrad and Cassino was like. It has developed into a slow, systematic elimination of a determined enemy, building by building, ruin by ruin." Sutherland thought Beightler was correct, and he argued the division's case with the theater commander-in-chief. After listening to his chief of staff, MacArthur reversed himself.[11]

Beightler's attitude was a common one among the soldiers fighting in Manila. Ramon Echevarria saw this firsthand. He was part of a Filipino guerrilla group that was collecting detailed information on the location of Japanese defensive positions. When they made contact with the 1st Cavalry Division and shared the information, Echevarria told them they were shelling areas that were mostly residential and killing civilians. A US captain replied, "We will destroy a whole city and kill an entire population if it will save one American life." This attitude was commonplace in the 37th Division. After the battle, the 129th Infantry Regiment recommended "all buildings that are possible strong points should be reduced to rubble."[12]

On February 16, the Americans learned that there were Filipinos in the hospital compound and agreed to make efforts to restrict their heavy gun-fire. The Americans breached the two buildings in the complex but had to surrender one of them at dusk. After five days, on February 17 at 8:30 a.m., the 2nd Battalion of the 148th Regiment went back to the Science Building and attacked. The Japanese were turning back the assault wave when Technician Fourth Grade Eugene J. Callaghan took a flame thrower and charged into the building. Despite taking minor wounds to both legs, he staggered toward one of the ground floor windows that the Japanese were shooting out of, aimed the nozzle at the windows, and covered the area with liquid flame. He also attacked the doorway. His platoon followed his lead. As they entered the building, they found that Callaghan had killed twenty-eight defenders. The regiment finally made its way into the main hospital building. It was only then that they realized just how many civilians were in the complex. There were seven thousand of them.[13]

Bonner Fellers informed MacArthur of the hospital's liberation. "It was a very bloody sight." He tried to put a positive spin on the matter. "Except for a few remaining strong points, the enemy defense is spent."[14] The theater commander was about to realize in a painfully personal way that this assessment was quite wrong. To his family, Fellers was a bit more candid, "Manila is slowly crumbling." Building-to-building gun fights were killing the city. "It is a horrible thing."[15]

On February 18, the sixth day of fighting for the hospital, the 148th conducted mopping-up operations, but departed before the 5th Cavalry Regiment relieved them. The result was that Japanese survivors retook some of the smaller buildings in the complex. Beightler was angry but refused to admit his men had blundered. After the war, he got into a dispute with the official Army historian writing the volume on the liberation of Luzon for the *U.S. Army in World War II* series. Beightler called the coverage of the failed transfer "a misstatement of fact" and an "attempt to belittle the 37th Division." He had little support in this assessment. The division's historian admitted that the general was wrong, and that the hand-off did not take place until the next day.[16]

To Sergeant Peter MacFarland in the 5th Cavalry Regiment, the problem was not coordination between American forces but the dogged resistance of the defenders. An immigrant from the United Kingdom who had not yet become a US citizen, MacFarland and his men took over the nurses' dormitory from the 148th Infantry Regiment. They did a quick sweep of the building to make sure it was secure. MacFarland saw two Japanese bodies lying on the ground. "I got my M-1 and started firing at them and they started wiggling. I fired two clips of ammo and they stopped wiggling." During that sweep, he noticed that the screen to a window was missing. He did a reconnaissance by fire, using a couple rounds from his rifle. He got shots back. He and his men threw grenades into the window. One of his men had a feeling that they had not neutralized the threat. They withdrew and warned their lieutenant. Another cavalry troop that had been supporting them, set up a machine gun in a window that was opposite the open one. In the middle of the night, the crew saw Japanese soldiers exiting one by one. After waiting, the gun crew opened fire on about seven Japanese who were hiding in a nearby sweet potato patch, killing all of them.[17]

The cavalrymen—using tanks firing at point blank range—took another day before they had broken the Japanese presence in the complex. Even then, they needed to keep men behind to do mop-up operations. Norman Laub of the 5th Cavalry was part of the force holding the hospital. He and his men stopped a Japanese attempt to retake the building with rifles and grenades— for which he later received the Bronze Star. Before daylight, he and others heard singing coming from a building across the street, and then a series of small explosions. They next morning the cavalrymen found about eighty dead Japanese in a semi-circle. They had held grenades to their chests and taken their lives when they were unable to retake the hospital.[18]

The U.S. Army was responsible for a portion of the devastation visited on Manila, although how much remains a subject of intense debate. Griswold and his staff were correct about Japanese instigation and conduct, but that does not absolve the Americans of their responsibility. The official U.S. Army history of the Battle of Manila concurs, placing much of the responsibility on US artillery. MacArthur and Krueger gave Griswold no guidance, and as a result, Griswold fought the battle as he saw fit, trying to seize control of the city while minimizing losses in men and equipment. He had good reason for taking these actions. The theater was facing serious shortfalls in manpower. The artillery units in the U.S. Army were good at tearing gaping holes in Japanese positions, and the reliance on the heavy guns compensated for the shortcomings the infantry had in tactics and doctrine. Even Beightler admitted: "This fighting is new to the 37th Division."[19]

* * *

During this period, the Japanese views of the battle were quite different. Anger and resentment were waiting for Lieutenant Commander Kayashima Koichi when he arrived at General Yokoyama's headquarters on February 14 to report on the activities of the *makaibo*. The Shimbu Group's ammunition supplies had real limits, and Yokoyama's staff thought Admiral Iwabuchi was being frivolous and wasteful in his expenditure of munitions. Colonel Kobayashi Shujiro remarked, "The Navy is arrogant; neither land combat nor its reports are appropriate."[20]

Despite this bureaucratic resentment, the Army decided to try to help the Navy. On February 15, Yokoyama initiated a counterattack on the XIV Corps designed to get all Japanese troops out of Manila. General Yamashita was not happy that Admiral Iwabuchi had returned to Manila. His subordinate, Yokoyama knew he needed to act. He had done nothing as the Americans advanced on Manila. Believing the US force was both smaller than it actually was—based on an analysis of motor traffic into the city—and that the Americans were isolated, Yokoyama ordered a two-pronged attack. The northern prong was aimed at the Novaliches Dam and Route 3. The southern prong was to cross the Marikina River and move in the direction of the Balara Water Filters. The two prongs were to meet in the Grace Park area in the suburb of Caloocan, just north of the Manila city limits.[21]

Colonel Kobayashi saw no value in this operation. It would inflict no damage on the Americans and would not bolster the morale of Japanese Army units fighting on Luzon. He instead wanted to attack the areas behind US lines. Yokoyama considered this nonsense. The general knew his command was a "jumble of troops"—to use the words of one Japanese historian—and there was little chance they could perform a complicated maneuver like the one Kobayashi wanted to conduct. Yokoyama, however, failed to handle this challenge to his command authority from a lower-ranking staff officer.[22]

This dispute is important because it shows the command and control problems the Japanese had on Luzon, but it turned out to be of little operational consequence. Admiral Iwabuchi had no interest in supporting either effort. He wanted his command to achieve a glorious end. He issued an operation order on the day of the attack, instructing the entire *makaibo* to seek death in battle: "This unit will make preparations for an all-out suicide attack to annihilate the enemy to our front. On the night of the 15th each unit will carry out as many daring suicide attacks on the enemy to our front as possible." The admiral was adamant. "In the all-out suicide attack every man will attack until he achieves a glorious death. Not even one man must become a prisoner." There were no exceptions. Wounded men that could not take part would commit suicide or be forced to commit suicide.[23]

The failure of Iwabuchi's men to fight until death shows how the admiral's command of the Manila Naval Defense Force was falling apart. Communicating with subordinate units in a timely fashion had become difficult. Remaining evidence suggests that many of his men might have actually wanted to survive.[24]

The Americans operating outside and to the northeast of Manila were more than prepared. The night before the assault began, Japanese artillery fired at the 7th Cavalry. The shells fell short of the unit's position, doing no damage, but they did manage to put the Americans on alert.[25] As things turned out, the Japanese plan to attack the Americans' strengths—artillery and tanks—was poorly executed. "The enemy in front is superior to what I expected and has already been deployed," a Japanese officer reported. "We cannot get close to it." He added: "we cannot move forward and attack." Over the course of three days the Americans lost only two men, with another thirty-two wounded.[26]

The northern column had slammed into the 112th Cavalry Regimental Combat Team, a Texas National Guard unit, protecting the 1st Cavalry Division's lines of communication. Benefiting from a cadre of veteran officers, the 112th had been in position for several days and had fended off some earlier attacks. Using artillery that had already been positioned and sighted, the 112th defeated the assaults on February 15 before the Japanese really had a chance to start.[27]

The assault never raised any alarms in the XIV Corps. For many formations in the corps, it was like nothing happened at all. The 672nd Amphibious Tractor Battalion spent February 15, the first day of the attack, doing guard duty at bridges across the Pasig River and at the Novaliches Dam. The battalion's daily unit report states: "No enemy activity during period."[28]

The southern column attacked a day later, and the 7th and 8th Cavalry Regiments caught the Japanese in the open crossing of the Marikina River. Artillery cut them to pieces. The Japanese commanders were killed early, and the attacks quickly became disjointed. On February 18, the 8th Cavalry got into a firefight with a company-sized body of men that ended when a phosphorous grenade started a grass fire. The next day, the Japanese reached the pipeline south of the Novaliches Dam and attempted to destroy it, but they were stopped. The attacking units lacked decent maps and, in the dark, they walked straight into prepared US positions. "It seems that we are in the midst of the enemy," a Japanese soldier noted. Documents US military intelligence recovered later showed that elements of the Shimbu Group knew they were outnumbered and refused to attack during the day.[29]

On February 19, the southern column ended its efforts. A US intelligence study conducted after the battle noted, "The only indication of this attack was an increase in enemy infiltration attempts on the night of 15–16 February." In addition to being weak, Yokoyama's counteroffensive was poorly designed. Even if successful, a gap would have existed between the two columns in Grace Park and the defenders. The MNDF was to the south of the Pasig River and had no real ability to reach Yokoyama's men.[30]

Yokoyama sent a message to Iwabuchi instructing him to get out of Manila. He sent another message two days later, encouraging night infiltrations. Iwabuchi ignored him. He was an admiral and did not have to answer to an Army general. He was determined to pursue his own path.[31] By this point, however, Iwabuchi's ability to maneuver was gone. He was losing control. Units began fleeing Manila but as they withdrew, they lost their integrity. Men got left behind, and soon they were just a mass of small groups looking for places to hide.[32]

The Japanese units that survived Manila were the ones that left early. During the night of February 17–18, the 4th Naval Brigade and what was left of the 3rd Naval Brigade withdrew toward the mountains to the east. There they met up with Yokoyama's Shimbu Group, and about thirteen hundred men in these two formations would live to fight another day.[33]

The Japanese Army greeted these units arriving in the eastern mountains with contempt. Army officers accused the arriving unit commanders of cowardice. Their units had no orders to retreat, their casualties had been light, and they had abandoned all their heavy guns. One Army staff officer shouted at three naval officers trying to report to his headquarters: "Immediately return to fight."[34]

Other efforts were less successful. Good order and discipline were breaking down even in tactical units. The 8th Company, 2nd Manila Defense Battalion, made it to Fort McKinley on February 14, but its commanding officer had been killed in action. In seven days, the company had lost forty percent of its men. What was left of the unit decided to go to Intramuros. First Class Private Mayakawa Takeo, an alumnus of Chuo University, was captured when he became separated from his company as the formation made its way to the Walled City. He reported that his unit was well supplied and actually had to destroy ammunition that it could not carry, but admitted his comrades were poorly trained and doubted they would make it across the city. In another incident at 2:30 a.m. on February 15, the 37th Reconnaissance Troop and the 637th Tank Destroyer Battalion fired on a barge that was floating down the Pasig River. Japanese soldiers and sailors were trying to use it to get out of the city. The barge was about the size of a landing craft and it sank quickly.[35]

Despite the collapse and retreat of the Japanese defenders, atrocities in the city continued through to the end of the battle. On February 18, artillery observers in the 37th Infantry Division watched the Japanese tie a naked Filipina girl in her late teens to a telegraph pole in front of an archway of Intramuros that was in the direct line of fire of US artillery. Lieutenant John F. Robohm called off all shelling. After several hours, the Japanese released the woman, and she ran into the citadel. In Ermita, a group of Japanese entered a house where about fifty Filipinos were staying. After attempting to execute the refugees individually with handguns and grenades, they departed. They had not given up, though. They returned that evening with phosphorous grenades that set fire to the house. About forty people died in the fire.[36]

One of the reoccurring themes of many memoirs about Manila was the stench. Smells were blending together—expended munitions, burning flesh, rotting corpses. Civilians learned not to touch bodies, particularly Japanese ones, as they might be booby trapped.[37] Army engineers, though, were removing bodies floating down the Pasig River. The concern was that they might be mines intended to destroy the supporting pillars of the bridges. Army engineers put up rope and cable nets upstream of the bridges to catch the bodies before they got close enough to do any damage.[38]

* * *

In many ways, military intelligence helped win the fight for Manila. The battle was as much a conflict for information—trying to figure who was in what part of a complicated maze of a city and in what numbers—as it was an engagement of firepower and maneuver. Intelligence efforts affected combat operations and, just as was the case in the larger battle, the Americans had the advantage. Military Intelligence was one of the more cost-effective branches of the U.S. Army. There were thirty-six officers and 153 enlisted personnel doing intelligence work in the Sixth Army. The majority of the enlisted men—114—were linguists. Each division usually had a detachment of two officers and ten enlisted personnel. Most of the officers were Caucasians and the enlisted men were Japanese Americans. The overwhelming majority were volunteers. A future president of Princeton University, Lieutenant Colonel Robert F. Goheen, the assistant chief of staff for intelligence in the 1st Cavalry Division, was a graduate student when he joined the military. "As a scholar, you have to learn to take some complicated data, break them down, analyze them, come to some conclusions," he later explained. "The general utility of that showed in the Second World War. Many academic people ended up in staff positions in the various services because they had been taught to think critically and analytically, and to write."[39]

The nature of intelligence work changed significantly between Lingayen Beach and the battle for the city. Although the linguists had dictionaries, most of their work involved generating paperwork and cross-referencing translated documents and prisoner debriefings. This required office supplies like paper, ink, mimeograph machines, and file cabinets. Because the work of translating took hours and it was winter, when daylight hours were fewer, they needed blackout tents so they could put in the required time and maintain light discipline.[40]

The debriefings produced a number of surprises. There were more prisoners than expected.[41] Given the racist nature of propaganda during the war, the presence of Japanese-speaking Japanese Americans astonished many of the prisoners. "Some of them are quite surprised when they first see me," Sergeant Ereni Hirai explained to a *Los Angeles Times* reporter. "They ask me right away if I am Japanese. I tell them right away that I am American. I explain to them that America is a land of many races and nationalities." That explanation did not always work. "Sometimes they make a little trouble. But mostly they are all right when they discover they aren't going to be killed or tortured. I talk to them a bit about home and what they were doing, give them a cigarette, and put them at ease."[42]

Debriefings usually took two to three hours each and were usually one-sided conversations in which the Americans generally got the information they wanted. Yukio Kawamoto, a Japanese-language linguist in the 37th Division, noted, "Most PWs I interrogated were wounded, weak from hunger, etc. They were generally cooperative." The experiences of First Class Private Boku Eishun support Kawamoto's observation. A graduate of Keio University, Boku's unit fell apart after the officers were killed. Boku and others in his battalion tried to escape to the east, but five days without food led him to decide his best chance of survival was to surrender. He talked freely but knew little of strategic or tactical importance.[43]

Many of those the Americans captured were Formosans rather than Japanese. Few of them had a good command of Japanese and the Army linguists did not speak much Chinese. A week into the battle, the language detachment in the 37th Division hired Benjamin Wong, a Chinese civilian, to serve as an interpreter.[44]

The caliber of language skills among the Americans varied significantly. Norman Kikuta, while able to speak Japanese, did not learn to read or write in the language until after he joined the Army. Even those with excellent language skills did not know the technical military vocabulary and *kanji* characters used by the Imperial Japanese Army and Navy.[45]

Being Japanese or Japanese American in Manila created problems. Tad Ichinokuchi observed, "Even with a U.S. uniform a Japanese countenance causes many of the younger kids to shout, '*Baka, Baka*'" ("fool" or "idiot"). Kikuta faced a similar situation in southern Manila. A guerrilla band spotted him and another linguist talking to a Filipino woman who had worked for the U.S. Navy before the war. They confronted the three, thinking they had come across a Filipina collaborator and Japanese spies. "We got into some heated words but we escaped," Kikuta explained.

Despite these type of reactions—and the fact that his parents were in an internment camp in the United States—Kawamoto was undeterred. He was saving lives. "We earned our keep. Getting information which helped reduce [the loss] of American lives and shorten[ed] combat."[46] Sergeant Hirai perhaps put it best. "I consider myself American in every way," he said. "I don't know anything else."[47]

Another issue facing military intelligence teams was the safety of the prisoners. Guerrillas beat and often killed the Japanese they captured before military intelligence detachments took custody. Filipinos and Americans routinely took war trophies off the Japanese, and the prisoners resented this treatment, which often was an issue that the linguists had to confront during their debriefings. Sometimes individuals were basically kidnapped for nothing more than being Japanese.[48] Most of the times the prisoner was debriefed once, although on some occasions they had useful information and analysts wanted to talk to them again. Transporting them was a hazardous business and several were killed along the way. The fact that the stockade where the Sixth Army kept its prisoners was close to its headquarters worked to minimize some of that risk.[49]

With only one or two exceptions, most of the prisoners were low-level foot soldiers and had information of limited use. Sometimes the prisoners could tell the Americans where machine gun nests were located. Lines like "PW was a pour source of tactical information, but was very cooperative" appear in many debriefings.[50]

On occasion, the prisoners revealed more than they realized. Private First Class Okubo Yasuhiko warned the Americans that the Japanese in Manila would fight to the last man.[51] Takami Morihiko, a Japanese businessman who was born and raised in New York State, was captured on February 13, and appeared to know very little of value. His debriefer found his responses vague and suspected he might be making things up as he went along. That was not the case. When intelligence analysts combined the information he had provided with that of Shu Bu, a Formosan laborer for the Japanese Army, they suddenly had a good idea of Japanese artillery locations.

A day later, on February 14, Superior Private Inouye Zenkichi was captured. More than half of his battalion had died under the guns of US artillery during the first week of the battle. He and two dozen others decided to escape and became separated from this group. Guerrillas soon captured him. After beating him, they turned him over to the Americans. His debriefing gave the 37th Division information on the Japanese escape route out of Manila.[52] With this intelligence, the XIV Corps put artillery fire and infantry units in a position to block the Japanese retreat. As a result, Japanese formations vanished under a hail of heavy shells.[53]

That same day, Wong and others from the 173rd Language Detachment interviewed Ri Shojo, a Formosan. He gave the Americans detailed information on the location of minefields along Dewy Boulevard, which was a major north–south throughfare that ran along the shoreline, and other locations in the downtown areas. He gave specifics on the location and strength of various Japanese units still in the city. His information turned out to be accurate.[54]

Captured Japanese documents, even those on mundane matters, turned out to be quite informative. Because of documents captured and translated on February 8 and 9, Griswold had a good idea of the command structure, the names of the officers, and the manpower strength of the Manila Naval Defense Force. Accurate information on General Kobayashi's command, however, had to wait until February 11.[55]

The number of Japanese documents coming from US soldiers, Counter Intelligence Corps agents, and guerillas was overwhelming. Putting together a full picture was much like assembling a jigsaw puzzle without a guide. Individual items alone meant very little, but when put together in a bigger composite they became more informative. Pay stubs and post cards from home might not have much information that would seem all that valuable at first glance, but they often indicated what units were located on Luzon.[56]

Occasionally the analysts had reliable information but drew the wrong conclusions. Linguists were debriefing prisoners of war during the Japanese counteroffensive. Given the weakness of the effort, Americans did not know that an offensive had even happened. Their initial assessment was that the offensive was nothing more than a Japanese propaganda initiative designed to convince the defenders trapped in the city to keep fighting.[57]

Photo reconnaissance, which was a major part of intelligence in World War II, did not prove that useful in Manila. During the march on the city, the XIV Corps had requested two surveys of the road network and fortifications blocking access to the city. The Army Air Forces never flew these missions. During the battle, Griswold's headquarters requested another six reconnaissance missions. Two missions were never conducted at all, and the photos that did make it to headquarters from the other four arrived too late to be of use. The reason for the slow response time was that the photo labs were located well to the rear of the frontlines.[58] "Jointness" was a US strength, but there were clear limits.

The Japanese defenders also engaged in intelligence efforts. To conduct them, they selected soldiers who spoke English, bore some resemblance to Filipinos, were allowed to grow their hair, and had civilian clothes. Their mission was to collect information on the location of US units. These soldiers were typically sent out on missions in four-man teams.[59] Iwabuchi's headquarters distributed passwords to help these units return back to Japanese positions. They, however, had little impact on the battle.[60]

The Japanese also worked with the *makapili*, whose main assignment was to assassinate other Filipinos. As a result, they had permission to carry weapons. Admiral Iwabuchi issued orders that all men under his command were to be informed of the special status of these men. Not all Filipinos were the enemy after all.[61]

* * *

During this same period, the Japanese were collapsing in southern Manila. The 2nd Naval Battalion controlled a zone of the Pasay district that was cut off from the rest of the MNDF. This area was about three-fourths of a mile long on an east–west axis and about 450 yards going north–south. The Japanese controlled a series of strong points in this area. The Manila Yacht Club and Fort Abad, an old Spanish base, anchored access to the sea. Harrison Park lay between them, along with the Rizal Memorial Sports complex, which included a soccer/track field and a baseball stadium, which had a seating capacity of ten thousand. Both arenas were next to La Salle College. The easternmost point the Japanese controlled was Santa Escolastica College.[62]

The 1st Cavalry Division reached Manila Bay on February 12 and the 12th and 5th Cavalry Regiments spent two days eliminating small bands and patrols in this zone. During the advance, Hans Walser, a young German in his early teens, lived under constant artillery fire. "While the shells were going over us, we were still getting peppered by the shrapnel and concrete chunks from the stadiums and an occasional shell that didn't have the range." He watched the Japanese patrol his neighborhood, and on two occasions they were on the lawn of his family's compound. The Japanese in the stadium started shelling his neighborhood with mortars because they knew Americans were in the vicinity. He estimated they shot one shell for every ten that the Americans did.[63]

On February 15, the horse soldiers seized control of the eastern and western anchors of the Japanese position. On the east they took La Salle College and Santa Escolastica College, but mop-up operations would take another three days. The 5th Cavalry sliced through Harrison Park, which drove the Japanese into the two stadiums. The horse troopers breached the walls of the sports arenas but the defenders drove them back with machine gun, rifle, and mortar fire. That did not matter to Fellers. He told MacArthur, "It might require another day to reduce Harrison Park, but the enemy resistance is definitely broken."[64]

The next day, February 16, the 1st Cavalry Division punched through the baseball stadium's east wall. This opening took them into the right side of the outfield. The Japanese had placed bunkers all over the diamond, which gave them unobstructed lanes of fire as the cavalry entered the stadium. The Japanese held their fire as the Americans continued to pour in. They then opened up. Private Ernest E. Pittman charged into the outfield to retrieve a wounded comrade and was wounded in the process. General Mudge, witnessing this act, rushed in himself. As the two brought the wounded man back to a secure position, Mudge handed Pittman a Silver Star. The general— once again behaving like a platoon sergeant—then took the private's rifle and opened fire on the Japanese.[65]

In the ballpark the defense positions were strong in the left field area and under the grandstand along the third base left field foul line. The battle took the entire day, but by 4:30 p.m. it was in American hands. The fight for the soccer stadium was relatively mild in comparison, taking only until 12:30 p.m. When it was over, the Japanese had lost roughly 750 men, and their 2nd Battalion was finished as an effective fighting force.[66]

There were now clear signs that Japanese power was fading. A young Filipino stood out in the middle of San Andreas Street with a Red Cross flag. Slowly people joined him in a nearby open area and raised their hands to show they were not a threat. The Filipino boy went up to a Japanese officer, they talked, and the soldier walked away. These soldiers were going to make no effort to bother these civilians. The crowd spontaneously began walking—in a crouch—toward Malate Circle. Frank Ephraim was part of the crowd. The scenes reminded him of the "Inferno" section of Dante's epic poem. "Strewn with bloated corpses, wrecked cars, dead animals, piles of rubble, twisted metal roofing and urban debris, we could not get oriented because there was not a single landmark we recognized, and we had difficulty even detecting where a street had been in the lifeless broke landscape that was obscured by smoke and permeated by the stench of cordite and death."[67]

The cavalry then began charging through the Malate district to the north. "The Americans targeted our area with great intensity," Angelita Martinez Florio, a young Manila resident, noted. She watched a Japanese soldier shoot into a crowd of refugees and assumed that he did not shoot at her because she had spoken Japanese to him a few moments before. After the Japanese burned her house, Florio's family found refuge in the basement of a ruined building. They were safe from artillery, but they needed water. A water pump became a gathering spot, but Japanese riflemen began shooting at those trying to use it, forcing them to crawl. Her brother was wounded there—not by a Japanese bullet, but by an American shell fragment. Americans soldiers found them later and helped move them south. "What assailed our eyes as we struggled through the burned houses and blown-up streets was the carnage. There were dead people all over, including Japanese soldiers, one with his samurai sword next to him." The Red Cross took her brother to a hospital where he eventually recovered.[68]

* * *

As the Battle of Manila began to wind down, an inventory of the reckoning became the order of the day. As they advanced in areas formerly controlled by the Japanese, the Americans were finding bodies all over the area. Ramon Echeverria expected to see a lot of artillery damage as he approached the LaSalle College, his alma mater. What he saw was worse. Corpses littered the streets in small groups. Many had their hands tied behind their backs. At the college, he saw the bodies of many individuals that he had known.[69] One group of soldiers found the bodies of a Catholic priest and thirty-two nuns. Evidence showed that the nuns had been raped before the Japanese killed them. Some of the troopers began to cry.[70]

Waiting for their liberation was the Hall family, whose house was built five feet off the ground, which was a common design feature to avoid water damage from the regular flooding that visited Manila. A crowd of 150 people had gathered under their house. Many had Japanese-inflicted wounds. There were several physicians among the refugees, and they performed surgeries without anesthetics. The dead were stored in the house above since there was no need to worry about their vulnerability to shrapnel cutting through the house and its thin roof.[71]

On February 16, US soldiers made contact with this group and suggested they leave this section of Manila. A US tank destroyer blocked an intersection where a Japanese machine gun was located, giving the refugees cover as they departed.[72]

In this same area, Sergeant Clarence Fontenot was taking part in mop-up operations. Japanese sailors, as either lone riflemen or in small groups, were shooting at the patrols of the 1st Cavalry Division. These small firefights, although sometimes deadly, were hardly strong enough to block the advance of a battalion or a regiment. From one building Fontenot heard singing of what he later learned was the Japanese national anthem. "Afterwards I knew that I heard the familiar sound of how Japanese hand grenades are fused (by knocking them against a hard object). I suspected what was coming up. When they finished we heard the grenades snap." A powerful explosion followed. Then Fontenot heard it all happen again. A patrol later found the bodies of sixty-four dead Japanese.[73]

As the Americans took control of the city, Filipinos began trying to find relatives and piece together their lives. Purita Echevarria described her experience going to Malate with her mother to look for her grandparents and uncle. "It is hard to describe the shock of looking over nothingness where a city once existed. Malate was one vast open space and we could not tell one street from another. Without houses and landmarks, they all looked the same—wreckage and more wreckage. Mother and I could only stare, speechless." Where her grandparents' house had once stood was now just a field of debris. The two walked away, until US soldiers stopped them. The area was being sprayed with a disinfectant. They saw a mound of corpses and found the smell overpowering. The younger Echevarria began to grow faint. "I remember staring at the mound of bodies, wondering how many I would recognize. I had grown up in that area and knew practically all its residents."[74]

Her brother, Ramon, shared the same fears. He had joined the guerrillas and was now returning to his hometown. He had seen the destruction in Pasay, Malate, and Ermita. He was afraid his family had been slaughtered in the fighting. He went to the family residence in Singalong and was relieved to find them alive, but they looked at him blankly. It took them a minute to recognize him. He looked different. He had gained thirty pounds since joining the Army.[75]

With the battlefield contracting, Griswold gave Beightler operational control of the 1st Cavalry Brigade. This decision had nothing to do with Mudge's combat leadership, but rather a desire on Griswold's part to avoid friendly fire. This issue was a real one. Charles Henne was in a situation where the 3rd Battalion, 148th Infantry Regiment, 37th Division started coming under fire from a field artillery battalion in the 1st Cavalry Division. "The rounds bounced me high in the air, but I walked away without a scratch." They were in a vacant lot with a lot of galvanized roofing lying about on the ground. "I was more afraid of getting cut in half by a sheet of roofing than [sic] I was getting hit by a shell." Twenty men in the battalion were killed, though. "Getting hit by Jap artillery was one thing, but getting hit by your own was interminable drumfire."[76]

Even after the arrival of the Americans, the Japanese still posed a threat. Walser recalled that small bands would break into houses near the stadiums and demand food from the residents. He notes that, at the time, a company-sized force of Americans was half a block away.[77] These narrow misses were characteristic of the Battle of Manila. Combat in urban warfare is compartmentalized. Enemy forces can be close to one another and not even know there is a nearby threat. This explains why areas behind the main line of contact were often less than secure.

The American dilemma in Manila was whether to destroy a city to save it. Destruction would save American lives but do real damage to postwar relations between the United States and the Philippines. Manila was the center of gravity of the Philippine nation. What happened in the city mattered to people living in other parts of Luzon and on other islands. Had MacArthur made his intent clear to his subordinates and restricted the use of artillery, the Americans might very well have endured higher losses. But it would have saved the lives of thousands of Manileños and kept the city from being leveled. Given the atrocities committed by of the Japanese military, the Americans got a pass on their role in the destruction of the city.[78]

14

Life Behind American Lines

Even after the string of victories at the dams and water filters, Provisor Island, Paco Railway Station, the Tondo Peninsula, and the Genko Like, the battle in Manila still had many more days—even weeks—before it burned out. The experience of it was profoundly different for people in different parts of the city. For many, being in U.S. Army controlled areas seemed like this side of paradise.

Hospitals were a major reason the Americans did not suffer high losses in the battle. Only 15.3 percent of casualties in Manila became fatalities. This percentage was the lowest rate for the Luzon Campaign.[1] Hughes Seewald, an officer in the 1st Cavalry Division, called medical attention "excellent under the conditions."[2] Assessments made immediately after the battle in the summer of 1945 support this view. Hospitals performed surgeries rapidly without problems and faced no shortages of supplies.[3] "The medics should all have silver stars," Warren P. Fitch, an officer in the 37th Division, believed.[4] The injured were quickly taken to aid stations and then hospitals. "In Manila they brought Evac Hospitals up to the north bank of the Pasig River," Henne explained. "A man could be evacuated by jeep back to a hospital in 10 minutes after reaching our battalion aid station."[5] Leonard Palmero, an ambulance driver, noted that his drives were generally short.[6]

When combat started in earnest on February 4, there was an increase in admissions but medical branch units were ready. The 37th Infantry Division, for example, had five hospital units assigned to it, and a number of other medical support units. There were another five hospitals that belonged to the XIV Corps and Sixth Army. Several of the hospital units appropriated standing buildings. The 54th Evacuation Hospital had perhaps the best residence, establishing itself at the Santolan Tuberculosis Colony, a massive complex located in the Sampaloc district of eastern Manila, which had seen little fighting. The facility had large, airy rooms that were connected with spacious marble hallways. Infantry units at the front had medics to offer immediate medical attention and there were aid stations located away from the actual point of combat. These stations offered significant medical care to the civilian population, and since American casualties were relatively light during the battle, doctors and nurses had the time and resources to tend to refugees. The army even hired local physicians to help.[7]

Hospitals were not, of course, happy places. Soldiers with light wounds wrestled with going back into combat or staying behind. Martin Gonzales was one of those, but what stayed with him was the trouble of another patient. "In the next tent where I was, there was a kid got a leg blown off. He cried all night. I remember that."[8]

Some injuries required long-term recuperation and medical attention. These facilities were in areas outside of Manila, like Clark Field or even Leyte. During the Luzon campaign, the Army Air Forces flew seventeen thousand patients off the island. Technical Sergeant Richard A. Franco was the flight chief on a C-47 that was taking wounded soldiers off Luzon for more intensive medical treatment. While he was checking to see if all the wounded were strapped in properly, he saw his best friend from college. "I was almost sorry to see him because he looked so bad."[9]

Soldiers with minor wounds repeatedly showed a reluctance to seek medical treatment. "I kept going," Estanislado Reyna, a soldier in the 37th Infantry Division, explained after getting wounded in the arm from some shrapnel. Richard J. Foss remembered arguing with his commanding officer about going to the hospital because of a stomach disorder. "I must have been a little goofy saying these things," he recalled. "Here, this man was giving me a way out of this 'hell hole' and I stand here telling an officer with the authority to release me that I was all right when I was not." Julian Levin, an artilleryman in the 37th Division, received a cut to his wrist and instead of going to a medic, he had a Filipino doctor bandage his wound. Some of this hesitation might have been ego or a sense of responsibility to buddies and the unit; it also reflected the rational recognition that infirmaries were places where sickness and disease were concentrated. It was easy to get worse, not better, in a hospital.[10]

Another medical challenge during the battle, particularly for Oscar W. Griswold and his XIV Corps, was "a sharp rise in the venereal disease rate in the entire command." There were 254 cases in the month of February, or slightly more than nine a day; the vast majority were gonorrhea. This increase was mostly due to prostitution, which had not been a viable option for soldiers prior to their arrival on Luzon. The fluid nature of battle, movement of refugees, the stress of combat, and Filipina civilians turning to one of the few income-generating options available to them created the conditions for the spread and made treatment a challenge. The Army hired local physicians to trace contacts, test for the disease, and to provide treatment. Testing revealed that ninety percent of the prostitutes had syphilis, and that twenty-four percent had gonorrhea. Medical units in the Corps went through prophylactic supplies so quickly that they faced a shortage.[11]

Returning wounded personnel to units was more difficult than one might think. Soldiers suffering from what was called at the time "battle fatigue"— now called "posttraumatic stress disorder"—were not always welcomed back. They had broken during combat and officers worried that this type of reaction to the strain of fighting could be contagious. Men who were wounded and ambulatory but not ready for the rigor of field maneuvers, much less combat, were often sent to service support units like post offices. The mail service needed the extra manpower because Christmas letters and gifts were finally arriving two months late, and the volume exceeded what the current personnel could process.[12]

* * *

Capturing the mood of an entire city is a difficult thing to do, but several people tried to explain the Manila of February 1945. "A certain happiness has returned to this miserable city where life depends on food lines and army water points and few homes have escaped some tragedy," William Gray, a war correspondent for Time-Life, explained in a report back to his editorial offices in New York at the end of the month. "There is little tendency here to cry over the wreckage. The spirit is more, 'In the long run it will be a better Manila.'"[13] Brigadier General Bonner Fellers was south of the Pasig River watching civilians walk past him. "It takes all one's strength to see the refugees," he wrote to his family. A young girl, dirty and in a tattered dress holding a baby, turned to him and said, "Thank you for saving us." Fellers was moved. "How she could be grateful for anything was beyond me."[14]

Second Lieutenant Paul P. Rogers saw a different reaction. "There was no joy in our entrance. I do not remember seeing a Filipino smile during the entire duration of our stay there. A pall of death and destruction lay over the city."[15]

Carmen Guerrero Cruz, for one, agreed. She blamed the Americans for the destruction of the city and spat on the first soldier she saw.[16]

Manila might have been MacArthur's hometown, but he did not move his headquarters to the city during the battle. Until March 5, he continued to operate out of Hacienda Luisita. A roundtrip visit to Manila and back took hours and left many from his headquarters dirty and tired. "I hope," General Courtney Whitney, wrote his wife, "that it will not be long before we can move our HQ into Manila as this long ride (2 ½ hours) back and forth by jeep is a tiring ordeal in itself."[17]

One of the reasons for the slow travel was that the roads were choked with long columns of Filipino refugees, weighted down with bundles and loaded pushcarts. They had no goal, or destination. They were simply moving, wearily and numbly, away from the roar of the guns. "As we were going in, we might be said to be in a continuous stream of military material and people going about five miles an hour," Roger O. Egeberg, MacArthur's physician and aide recalled.[18]

As they sat in a massive traffic jam, Egeberg suggested to the general that he segregate road usage, giving the military primacy and restricting civilians use to off-peak periods. MacArthur looked at Egeberg for a moment with an expression "almost in disgust." He then replied, "Doc, can't you see what I see? Look at the people on both sides of this road. On the left most of them are coming out of Manila. Look at the looks on their faces. They're scared. They're freighted. They're running away from something." He added: "These people are running away from a burning Manila." On the other side of the road, people were hiking into Manila to bring food and supplies to their families. "Unless it becomes a dire emergency I certainly won't stop them from doing what their emotions and their needs dictate." It was a thoughtful assessment, the type that is not often associated with MacArthur, but it also reflected his reluctance to provide strategic direction in matters regarding Manila.[19]

Watching the refugees brought home to many the meaning of war. "I was walking in the reality of total war," William A. Owens of the 306th Counter Intelligence Corps (CIC) stated. "Around me, ahead of me, I saw what Clausewitz's total war meant—people uprooted and made destitute by battle, people terrified in the omnipresence of violent death."[20] Walter Simmons of the *Chicago Daily Tribune* reported: "Manila is a city of strange and disquieting contrasts." Battle had skipped some parts of the city entirely, while other sections were nothing more than "black ashes" and "crumpled stone."[21]

Despite the confusion, the people of Manila tended to migrate in directions away from the actual shooting, wherever it was taking place. One result, as Joquin Garcia, a pre-teen at the time, noted, was that they were able to exchange information. "The streets of Paco were full of people moving around freely. They no longer had to look over their shoulder, worried they'd meet a crazed Jap pointing a rifle with a fixed bayonet at them." The American military police and other support units in areas away from the main point of contact would share information about roads and which sections of the city to avoid.[22]

During this period, food was still a major issue. "The phantom of hunger not only hovers over the people. It holds the people captive in its claws," Father Juan Labrador stated. "The liberating troops, as they advance step by step, house by house, perform the dual function of combatants and Samaritan, gathering the survivors, assisting them with their own rations and transporting to the rearguard."[23] Normal distribution networks had broken down, and without electricity there was no cold storage of food items that perished quickly. Individual soldiers tried to give the Filipinos as much extra food as possible to keep them from rummaging through trash cans.[24] Fernando J. Mañalac stumbled upon an American artillery unit that was shelling the Walled City. They let him fire a couple of rounds, fed him lunch, and then gave him bread and cans of Spam, corned beef, and fruitcake to take back to his family. "Arriving home, it was one of our happiest moments," he remembered. "This day, the finest restaurant in Manila could never have satisfied my gastronomic grumblings as did this manna from heaven were I a connoisseur of culinary art."[25]

The Army made more systematic efforts to feed the civilian population. "Our kitchen would send food in to the civilians because they had no food, and what they would do was load a truck with food on the back end and send along a driver and a Jeep to lead us where to go, and we'd go there and the people would come up and any just pot or dish, and we'd feed them that way," Victor Kuester, a driver in the 37th Division explained.[26]

Filipinos began working to fill the void themselves and re-establish the economy at the same time. John Dos Passos found a "faint carnival air" in the city. He watched Filipinos hike into the city carrying sacks of rice with the "gleam of trade in their eyes."[27]

Facing them was the enormous challenge that most public utilities in Manila, even those in the US-controlled zones, were not functioning. The city had had a working electrical grid when the Americans had arrived on February

3, but the US failure early on to take Provisor Island intact and the Japanese systematic destruction of generators, power plants, and substations resulted in damage that was beyond the ability of the U.S. Army Corps of Engineers to replace. The problem was a shortage of spare parts and equipment, rather than expertise.[28]

Water was a major concern. The Americans lacked the equipment and man-power to repair the damage they expected the Japanese would do to the pumps and pipes supplying the city. As events developed, the Americans found less wreckage than they had expected. The danger combat posed to the system remained, though. On February 11, a Japanese infiltration team did signifi-cant damage to the Balara Filtration Plant and pipelines leading from the San Juan reservoir to Manila. Rather than do repair work, the U.S. Army Corps of Engineers figured out ways to bypass the ruined valves. This process took ten days. Until February 22, the army set up thirty water distribution points in northern Manila and drew water from the Pasig and other streams. To make the water drinkable, they used a massive amount of chlorine.[29]

Waste disposal was a problem that grew as an issue steadily as the battle progressed. The sewer system had seen little damage, but the lack of water pressure in pipes limited their use. Army units responded by burning food and human waste. Homer Bigart of the *New York Herald Tribune* saw Filipinos form bucket brigades to transfer water from wells to toilets. That solution could only do so much, and it should be no surprise then that civilians were "indiscriminately" dumping waste anywhere they could: sidewalks, gutters, streets, and backyards. By the end of February, the filth and the flies that these practices produced posed a "serious menace" to public health. After a day wandering through the city, Mañalac found himself covered in maggots and lice. He went to the Americans for help. They gave him a DDT spray bomb that took care of the infestation. "I thanked God for the U.S. Army."[30]

The lack of water also led to personal hygiene issues. Foss of the 7th Cavalry discovered that he reeked so much that it overcame manners when he arrived at a hospital for treatment: "My God, what is that awful smell?" one nurse demanded to know. "I had to admit," Foss said, "it was me. I had not changed or washed my clothing for weeks and weeks."[31]

The stench in the city was so bad it made soldiers sick even while they were in combat. "It was one place where I took a rag and put it over my nose. The flies were so thick," Robert F. Minch, a truck driver in the 756th Field Artillery Battalion, explained.[32]

The biggest waste disposal problem was burying the dead. The numbers were staggering; at this point in the battle, there were probably ten thousand unburied dead in the city. Martin Schram, a clerk in a transportation unit, was overwhelmed at what he saw: "There were so many dead people. They were in the alleys. They were lying all over the churches."[33]

Compounding this problem was that attitude of the Filipinos and Americans toward Japanese corpses. "I had never seen a dead American soldier without feeling tears. I went past the Japanese dead feeling neither curiosity nor compassion," Owens of the CIC reflected.[34] The general inclination was to treat the enemy dead as trash. While that contempt might have been satisfying emotionally, when it came to sanitation it was dangerous. Schramm recalled: "The Japanese were just—the Pasig River was just—had so many Japs in it just floating there. And you know how after a few days you got flies and maggots. And you'd go around; everything stunk."[35]

With that point made, there was often good reason to let the Japanese bodies lie where they were. Schram and a sergeant burned a Japanese body that was lying next to where they had pitched their tent. They doused the body with a five-gallon tank of gas and set it on fire. A few minutes later, Schram was tossing grenades, showing off the strength of his arm to his friends when an explosion occurred. At first, he thought he had armed one of the grenades and set it off, but he quickly figured out that the body had exploded in the fire. The Japanese soldier had planted an explosive on his himself before he died. Schram's sergeant was covered in gore and body parts and the leg of the Japanese soldier ended up in a tree.[36]

The 108th Graves Registration Platoon handled burials for the XIV Corps. In Manila, they buried 753 Americans, twenty-nine Filipinos, and only seven Japanese. The American dead were treated with respect and received the services of chaplains. The Filipinos accounted by far for most of the dead, and the 37th Division hired a full-time burial detail to handle the civilian bodies. The chief coroner and the Manila Department of Sanitation were probably the first elements of the municipal government that began to function again as they collected bodies that were out in the open.[37]

* * *

Reunions and rebuilding started almost immediately. Santo Tomás was crucial in this process. The former internees were dumb with emotion following their liberation, which mitigated to a large degree any feelings of danger they might have had about being in or near an active combat zone. "They are so happy they're in a daze," Fellers told his family.[38] The once and future university became the destination for anyone with any type of affiliation to prewar American society. "Many people formerly outside with relatives in here are coming in now," Jeanette West—an American teenager who had spent what should have been her high school years at Santo Tomás—wrote in her journal. "Oh, I could go on and on for pages and pages . . . but what's the use." Within three weeks the population of the camp had doubled.[39]

There were good reasons for people to visit the campus. It was now securely in the hands of the U.S. Army, and it had suddenly become a dependable source of food. "I am up to 120 lbs! Getting stronger and eating like a pig," Fay Cook Bailey, a prewar Manila banker, recorded in his diary. Despite the presence of the Americans, many of the internees worried about their diets, and were not happy to welcome newcomers. "We are very fearful regarding food still, and the least sign of reduction of portions has us worried," he observed. "We don't need to be, however, for the U.S. Army is feeding us now."[40]

Medical care at the university was another major consideration for people trekking to Santo Tomás. There were Red Cross aid stations to provide treatment to Filipino civilians, but many people did not make much of a distinction between the Red Cross and army medical units. A hospital was a hospital. The need was massive and intense. The numbers of civilians seeking help from the 112th Medical Battalion, a unit in the 37th Infantry Division, overwhelmed their resources. "Very few persons escaped unscathed from the southern zone," Father Juan observed. "There were countless wounded and it was almost impossible to attend to them all in spite of the fact that the doctors and nurses, both Americans and Filipinos, worked beyond their limits."[41]

Santo Tomás was also a gathering point for information. It was where people could get some type of information on the fate of family and friends. It might be second-hand and indirect, but in the chaos of battle that would do. Because the university was a relatively safe area, reunions took place there. Sometimes it was Filipino families that had been separated in the fighting, sometimes American. In several cases, soldiers had relatives in the camp. Norris Wadsworth's cousin, Tom Eddington, was in the Army and visited several times, sharing family news and giving his cousin clothing to replace his worn and tattered rags.[42]

One of the frequent visitors was Frank Hewlett of United Press. Dos Passos met him after he arrived carrying "an immense bunch of small green and purple orchids." Dos Passos knew Hewlett's back story and about his wife's internment: "He had the happiest half-crying, half-laughing look I ever saw on a man's face."[43]

One of the more awkward reunions took place between Valeria "Yay" Panlilio and her half-brother, Raymond Corpus. Panlilio, a mixed-race Filipina American journalist who had been born and raised in the United States, had moved to the Philippines after finishing her schooling. Corpus was in the Army, in the 640th Tanker Destroyer Battalion. He had grown up in the United States and, although he had two Filipino parents, he did not like the Philippines. Panlilio, on the other hand, had been a leader in the guerrilla resistance and had become a nationalist. She was visiting the camp, checking in on old friends, and learned through random chance that her half-brother was in the compound. They had not seen each other since he was twelve, but after a few moments, he began complaining about the "natives." He also had a message from their mother. It was time for her to return to the United States. He gave her five hundred pesos to pay for the trip to California. Panlilio decided to listen to her mother, brought her military career to an end, and booked passage to the United States.[44]

Along with these reunions came news of Japanese atrocities in Manila. "Horrible tales from south of the river," Bailey recorded in his diary.[45] The survivors of Santo Tomás knew something about atrocities. After liberation on February 4, the former internees began looking for a number of camp leaders that the Japanese had removed in December 1944. The former internees soon discovered that they had been executed. Their bodies were recovered and buried at the Santo Tomás cemetery.[46]

The brutality of the Japanese administration obscures the fact that the leadership of the camp had collaborated, or at least reached an accommodation, with the occupiers. Japanese control of the camp was light; at one time the facility had only eight guards. The Japanese never pushed the internees to commit treason or war crimes, but they were forced to select prisoners for deportation to other, less desirable camps, which was the same thing the Nazis had forced on civic authorities in occupied territories. The camp leadership considered itself a buffer between the Japanese and the residents, but there was real resentment aimed at them.[47]

Because the university was a gathering spot for the large group of reporters who were arriving to cover the battle, it was inevitable that news of the collaboration got out. When Dos Passos visited the camp, one former detainee came up and in a low, but bitter, voice said, "I suppose you think you are getting the truth." Not really. The Americans had jailed others without benefit of trial. "They haven't told you about the curious moral regulations by which people were not allowed to sleep with their wives." Some of the incarcerated had turned a profit off others. "No, no, they haven't told you about that. They won't either."[48]

Most correspondents were interested in combat operations rather than events behind the frontlines. "Every day more correspondents arrive to cover the Manila story," Dos Passos noted. Many of the journalists ended up living together in a house off Rizal Avenue.[49]

The quality of these reporters was a disputed issue. Major General Robert S. Beightler of the 37th Infantry Division observed that many journalists lacked the skills to relate to the savagery of the battle. "No press account can adequately describe the bitterness of the fighting."[50] Dos Passos, on the other hand, was impressed with his colleagues. They worked despite the heat and humidity of Manila and the loud, constant noise of combat. "Through it all the seasoned newspapermen work away oblivious with abstracted faces and fingers busy at the keys of their typewriters."[51]

That focus was a luxury for some. Some reporters were distracted because their employers wanted to reestablish a presence in the Philippines and insisted that their correspondents become makeshift publishers. Although these efforts reduced the time they had to cover the ongoing battle, they were done out of pride, status, and even ideology, rather than from any of the economic forces that normally drive journalism. With its shattered economy, there was no money to be made in Manila in February 1945. On February 9, the Office of War Information began printing a newspaper aimed at Filipinos, using the printing press of a Manila printer that the Army had captured. The *Chicago Daily Tribune* began publishing a Manila edition before the battle even ended. Don Starr used the printing press in the San Miguel Brewery that the beer maker had used to print the labels for its bottles. The first edition of the *Tribune* was published on February 11, during the middle of the battle, and appeared on pale blue paper; later editions were pink.[52]

A similar competition took place among the news magazines. The main New York office of Time-Life tasked Carl Mydans with responsibility of publishing a Pacific edition of *Time*. Fillmore Calhoun, an assistant managing editor for *Life*, understood that they were putting a great deal on his shoulders. He told him in the unique language of telegram and radio cables: "EYE AFRAID TOO MUCH EXTRACURRICULAR STUFF GOING BOG YOU DOWN[.]

DON'T HESITATE IF TOO MANY CHORES S[T]ART RESTRICTING
YOUR PRIMARY PICTURE REPORTING OPERATIONS[.] IF CAN
DO ALL THESE THINGS OK[A]Y. BUT ALL HANDS HERE BEEN
TOLD YOU AINT SUPERMAN JUST PART SUPERMAN.[53]

Calhoun's fears were well founded. The quality of Mydans's reporting
suffered. He had to farm out some of his writing duties to reporters from other
media organizations, paying them on an ad hoc basis. He also found it difficult
to find the materials needed to print a news magazine.[54]

He was, however, a member of the officers' mess of the general headquarters engineers. "You can be sure the GHQ Engineers will always be the first
to have a refrigerator, the first to have a shower and a dry bunk, and the best
food of any mess in the field," Major General Hugh Casey told Mydans when
he was invited to join. That was an easy sell and Mydans quickly joined the
mess. Membership had a hidden reward. Bill Grey of *Time* magazine arrived in
the middle of the battle and worked with Mydans to find a printing press and
paper stock. Neither was having much success. Mydans took Grey to the mess
after an unsuccessful hunt for the equipment.[55]

Casey could see the dejection written on their faces and asked what was
wrong. Mydans told him. Colonel Dave Chaffin replied, "You know, GHQ
Engineers not only have the first refrigerator and the first shower, but we always have the first—and usually the only presses." The engineers printed up
maps for combat units to use. He also said the engineers had extra paper and
ink. Casey asked how many copies of the magazine Mydans wanted to print
and was told one thousand; that is what Casey ordered.[56]

With this type of assistance, *Time* was in print in a few days, the first edition appearing on February 26, while the Far Eastern edition of *Newsweek* took
until late March. Within two weeks of her liberation from Sato Tomás, Bessie
Hackett Wilson got a job with Time-Life helping to distribute the new Pacific
edition of *Time* and escorting Dos Passos about the city. The intended audience of the publication was mainly the US military. Corporal Robert J. Gagyi,
a soldier from Ohio, told Mydans he found looking at *Time* magazine while in
combat a bit surreal, "Here I am reading about the battle of Manila and I'm
sitting in the middle of the God Damn thing."[57]

Filipinos appreciated the news magazines as well. A *Newsweek* reporter/
publisher found a current issue of his publication in a Manila bookstore. The
store owner was not selling the magazine. It was his only copy. He was charging
patrons to read the magazine in front of him.[58]

If nothing else, Santo Tomás was where individuals could get some well-needed recreational diversion. Commanders pulled units from combat duty because there was only so much strain men and equipment could take. Time in bivouac areas located to the north of the Pasig was often more about recovery than relaxation. Frank M. Lutze, an officer in the 37th Division, explained that their job during these periods was to "relax to get ready for the next battle."[59]

During their time off from the frontline, men focused on mundane matters like washing their clothes, sleeping, bathing, and shaving. As had been the case throughout the Southwest Pacific campaign, soldiers wrote letters home, talked with friends, got their mail, played cards, and enjoyed hot food. "After some combat experiences the boring part became enjoyable," Edwin H. Hanson, another enlisted man in the Buckeye division, recalled.[60]

More elaborate recreational activities also took place. "Church service was greatly appreciated," Pat Shovlin, of the 1st Cavalry, stated.[61] The recreation officers in various units arranged many different activities, and a showing of movies was the biggest one. Films had often been the only recreational venue for soldiers for months and months and they had sometimes watched them in situations that were less than ideal—near or in fighting zones—and by comparison Manila—at least the parts the United States occupied in mid-February 1945—were ideal. Units might see three different titles per week. Even during combat, the 37th Division began holding dances for the enlisted men; these became were quite popular because it was actually possible to bring females to these events. Each unit in the division began having weekly dances.[62] The 37th Infantry Division Band played a concert at Santo Tomás for its residents. "Some danced, some smiled, while others were still sick and dazed by it all," Frank Mathias recollected. "We sensed the need to play well here, to provide entertainment after their three harrowing years as prisoners."[63] Films began being shown in the plaza. The Army had no problems sharing films with Filipinos. Many, though, found watching cinema with the sounds of combat still rolling in the city a bit surreal.[64]

Complete relaxation was never really possible. During the third week of battle, when momentum had shifted toward the United States, the threat of Japanese stragglers and riflemen was never entirely absent in the sections of Manila behind the lines. While wandering about in the Sampaloc district—a relatively quiet region of the city—Filipino teenage Mañalac found himself in the middle of a battle between Japanese snipers and American infantrymen. He watched soldiers get shot and fall in the middle of Quezon Boulevard, Filipina nurses rushed to provide first aid. He heard a cracking metallic noise, which was the sound the bullets were making as they hit lampposts. "I felt strange that I had no lingering fear. In fact, I felt grand." As an adult, Mañalac became a medical doctor and suspected, looking back, that he had been in shock. Mañalac captured the weirdness of those later days of the Battle of Manila. "It was also strange that such a battle was taking place, under odd circumstances— no weapons heavier than Tommy guns, no tanks, no supporting infantry, no medics, no guerrillas, no visible leadership, no special tactics used, no advance or retreat, the nurses' presence, my participation without a weapon or first aid kit, GIs falling one after another while shooting at an unseen enemy whose bullets were coming from parts unknown!"[65]

Mydans had similar experiences and views. Mydans regularly visited the Ayala Building, which was on the northern bank of the carbon-colored Pasig just across from the Walled City. The bank was at the edge of the frontlines, and there were plenty of Japanese stragglers in the rubble of nearby buildings, waiting to kill before they were killed. "It was therefore not very pleasant getting to the National City Bank, for someone was more likely than not to shoot at you." Once in the building the situation was different. "Among our own troops we always felt a comforting security and would talk rather light-heartedly about the adventures we had getting there."[66]

* * *

Military intelligence and counterintelligence work was another particularly important activity taking place in rear areas. The U.S. Army was trying to do two different things at the same time. It was trying to collect information it could use against the Japanese—whether immediately, or a day later in another part of Manila, or a week later somewhere in Luzon, or in a few months when it invaded Japan. The second thing was reasserting US authority in the Philippines and collecting information about Japanese collaborators. There was no inherent conflict between these two missions, but the manpower required to do both was more than MacArthur's headquarters had allotted to the task. There were three Counterintelligence Corps (CIC) detachments in the XIV Corps and the relatively rapid advance of the 37th Infantry and the 1st Cavalry put a serious strain on these formations. In town after town, CIC agents were mainly trying to restore order, detaining only the most significant of the Japanese collaborators. Officials in many municipalities, some of them collaborators, therefore ended up staying in office. A study on intelligence activities on Luzon noted: "Conducting real investigations, however, was out of the question. There was simply not enough time, and the situation became progressively worse as the combat detachments continued their advance." Given the pace of their advance, it was difficult to keep records and they soon had to skip working in smaller towns altogether.[67]

The counterintelligence agents had to do a great deal of work outside their normal job descriptions. These tasks included obtaining local labor for engineering units, arranging hospitalization for Filipinos, finding guard units to stop looting, and establishing refugee control mechanisms.[68] Meanwhile, they did not have enough food to support the guerrillas.[69]

One of the first CIC jobs Owens did in Manila was to interview internees at Santo Tomás about the abuses they had suffered at the hands of the Japanese. After tasting some of the food that the Japanese had given the internees, Owens "wondered not that so many looked like living skeletons but that they had survived at all."[70]

In these interviews, a constant theme was the gratitude of the internees toward the people of the Philippines. Many Filipinos had brought them food, which was often the difference in surviving their incarceration. They also admired the bravery of the guerrillas. It was difficult for these expatriated Americans to believe that Filipinos had collaborated with the enemy.

These interviews were a waste of time for the agents involved, Brigadier General Elliot R. Thorpe, MacArthur's chief counterintelligence officer, noted. "They really had nothing to offer us in the way of useful information."[71]

Despite the constraints, the CIC did what it could to go after key collaborators. Since Manila was the political capital of the Philippines, there were a number of major figures. Perhaps the biggest was Emilio Aguinaldo, who had led the rebellion against the Spanish in 1898 and who, as president of the First Republic of the Philippines, fought the Americans. Owens interrogated the Filipino political legend and later admitted that the man was persuasive. "The Japanese are my friends," Aguinaldo stated. "They never betrayed me. It was only the Americans who betrayed me." He was referring to the changes in policies of the William McKinley administration about the political future of the Philippines after the Spanish–American War ended. Owens tried to dismiss this argument as ancient history.[72]

Aguinaldo turned the conversation to 1942, when the United States and the puppet leadership of the Commonwealth had abandoned the Philippines. The Japanese were friends of the Philippines. "They made us free."[73]

This statement put Owens in a bind. Aguinaldo might have a point, but he had made public statements on behalf of the Japanese, and many of his countrymen in Manila would challenge him on the idea of Japan being their friend. "I had to charge him with collaboration, but I tried to soften it," Owens later explained.[74]

In the middle of February, the issue of counterintelligence work quickly revolved around the issue of how to use the resources that were available. The bulk of CIC effort concentrated on investigating collaborators. The exchange between Aguinaldo and Owens typified this effort. It was not an assignment he wanted. "I did not know enough to do the job passably and said so. Neither did any of the five or six agents who would work with me." He did not even have a list of individuals to detain.[75]

The U.S. Army had had three years to prepare its CIC agents for the return to the Philippines and yet there was little coordination between various CIC detachments. Some were aggressive in arresting Filipinos; others were trying to use limited manpower resources carefully. There were fifty CIC agents in Manila during the first week of the battle. Quickly realizing that would not be enough, the XIV Corps doubled that number within a week.[76] Even then, they were simply inadequate to the task at hand.

As a result, the effort to collect documents on the Japanese administration of the Philippines was a hit-and-miss affair. CIC agents often arrived and discovered the Japanese had already destroyed their files. The one exception was the Japanese embassy in Manila, which the CIC could not seize due to diplomatic immunity. All they could do was seal the safes in the building and post guards.[77]

Another counterintelligence corps mission was dealing with the roughly three thousand enemy aliens in the city. German civilians were interned at the Holy Ghost College initially. Then the CIC put them in Bilibild.[78]

* * *

Fighting in an urban environment was one thing, but sustaining it was another. In this regard, important military work, crucial to the final outcome of the battle, was taking place in the rear echelons. The quartermaster and transportation units had to keep frontline soldiers supplied. The road network in most of Manila was capable of supporting the demands of the XIV Corps. The Japanese, however, had done serious damage to the bridges. That one exception was significant. Beightler, reflecting his engineer background, wrote home, "We have faced the back breaking job of bridging all the major streams because the enemy had blown existing bridges." One of the problems that engineer units faced is that they had not done the appropriate training due to a lack of equipment.[79]

These shortages made building actual bridges a difficult learn-on-the-job endeavor. This situation changed dramatically in February when the proper supplies and equipment arrived at Lingayen and were rushed south. Between February 2 and 13, the 5202nd Engineer Construction Brigade, for example, built ten bridges on the roads between Lingayen and Manila with half of that construction taking place on February 12 and 13. The after-action report of the XIV Corps notes: "When these additional bridges were installed, the flow of traffic into Manila was greatly improved."[80]

The main supply point for the troops in Manila during the entire battle was still Lingayen. Private Hanson arrived on Luzon long after the initial landings. "The entire end of the bay was covered with ships," he recalled. There were, however, no traffic jams on the beaches. "What impressed me was the constant stream of men and material to and from the various landing beaches and ships."[81]

There were two key considerations in supporting the troops in Manila during the main part of the fighting. The first was to keep the beaches at Lingayen in operation. The second was to keep the supply lines functioning. The first was easy, given the dominant position the U.S. Navy now had in the Philippines. The second was more of a challenge. "They organized a hundred truck convoys," the driver Kuester, recalled, "two 100 truck convoys to drive up to Manila, Lingayen Gulf, where our stuff was stored, bring it back, and just supply those guns. You were on 24 hours and off 24 hours on that run."[82]

Convoy work was arduous. It could take these groups about ten to twelve hours to travel the 160 miles between Lingayen and Manila. Columns of refugees on the roads slowed down traffic. The Japanese occupying the Zambales hills to the west of Highway 3 and the Sierra Madres to the east of Highway 5 were also using artillery to target the vehicles. The main way to run these gauntlets was to send trucks out in irregular patterns. This move prevented Japanese artillerymen from timing their shelling to hit the trucks. "Just like you see in a movie where the shells are falling, we went through a couple of those," Kuester explained. "So that's where I got my second Bronze Star."[83]

Isolated Japanese soldiers and riflemen posed a threat until mid-March. Even light gunfire could bring a convoy to a halt. These small efforts lacked the power to stop supply efforts, but they could slow it down and make service in the rear echelon somewhat risky.[84]

Policing was important in keeping the roads of Luzon in operation. The XIV Corps' final report notes: "Upon nearing Manila and for some time after its liberation it was necessary to establish officer control stations to reduce the excessive number of unauthorized vehicles enroute for Manila." To help achieve this mission, the Sixth Army transferred a military police battalion to the XIV Corps. By late February, the U.S. Army began recruiting Filipino civilians to serve as part of the reconstituted Manila Police District.[85]

Maintenance and upkeep put a great deal of stress on transportation efforts. A gasoline shortage confronted the XIV Corps around February 16, the middle of the second week. One solution was to pillage from Japanese tanks. There were quality issues, though. Japanese gasoline had a lower octane level. Such pilfering helped, but did not solve, the problem and fuel shortages remained an issue for the Army during the rest of the battle, and the issues was only resolved with the end of the war.[86]

Even more mundane than gasoline—but no less critical—was the need for tire replacements for trucks and jeeps. "We used to have to repair wheels, or tires, oh, about 15, 20 times a day," Joseph F. Tauchen, Jr., a truck driver, recalled. "You run over shrapnel and stuff like that, you know, and you puncture your tires."[87] The 37th Division used a car dealership as a storage warehouse and an old car garage for its transportation units. These locations offered facilities where mechanics could repair vehicles and, as one driver noted, "we had houses, more or less to sleep in."[88]

In addition to gasoline and equipment, replacement soldiers began arriving in the middle of the month, but not in the numbers MacArthur needed. The long drive into the interior of Luzon gave many of these new soldiers time to think. "I hadn't seen such beautiful country since I'd left the states and it made quite an impression," Hanson remembered. "If it hadn't been for our destination, it would have been a beautiful ride."[89] Walter Madden, another replacement, wondered "if I would make it home in one piece or at all." At the same time, he was thrilled to be participating in the liberation of the Philippines.[90]

Throughout the battle, military engineers were busy removing minefields, both in combat and in rear areas. There were barriers and fortifications on almost every street in the city. When there was no active shooting, the engineers found that they faced no real technical issues in removing the mines. They noticed patterns, though. In northern Manila, the minefields had been poorly constructed and posed little danger. Those in the south were much better and more dangerous, illustrating that the Japanese had prepared to fight an invasion coming from the south, not the north.[91]

During the Battle of Manila, the rear zones—which shifted almost day by day—were, of course, much better than conditions in the Japanese-controlled parts of the city. To many Filipinos it was an oasis that reflected the strength of US strategy, the culture of the U.S. Army, and its design of military operations. Escaping from battle allowed American soldiers to deal with the stress of combat and steel themselves for what they would face in the third and fourth weeks of the Battle of Manila.

15

Corregidor

With US units in Manila, it was inevitable that the Americans would turn their attention to the island of Corregidor. Walter Krueger initiated a two-week-long battle, which began on February 16. The fight that took place there was very different from the one taking place in the Philippine capital. In Corregidor, unlike in Manila, the Americans were outnumbered, but they also showed greater tactical creativity. The island was also a place where artillery would have limited influence.

The rationale for invading Corregidor was fairly straightforward and had a lot to do with geography. "The Rock," as Americans referred to the island, sat in the mouth of Manila Bay. Any force occupying it could undercut all the strategic advantages that came with controlling Manila. The battle for the island was the sixth major turning point in the liberation of Manila. "Corregidor controls access to and exit from Manila Bay," an Army officer noted in a postwar study of the operation. "It was nonsense to think of using Manila's port while the Japanese retained control of Corregidor and hence, Manila Bay." The Japanese understood this fact and it is reflected in the name of the formation created to hold the island: the Manila Bay Entrance Defense Force.[1]

The idea for an airborne assault on the island came from the Sixth Army staff. General Krueger presented the idea to MacArthur on February 4 and the next day the theater commander agreed to it, assigning naval units to the assault. Drawing upon his broad knowledge of military affairs, Krueger had his staff design a joint assault on the island, using air, land, and sea power.[2]

Krueger gave the task of invading Corregidor to a composite formation, consisting of the 503rd Parachute Regimental Combat Team and the 3rd Battalion, 34th Infantry Regiment, 24th Infantry Division. Commonly known as the "Rock Force," the invasion commander was Colonel George

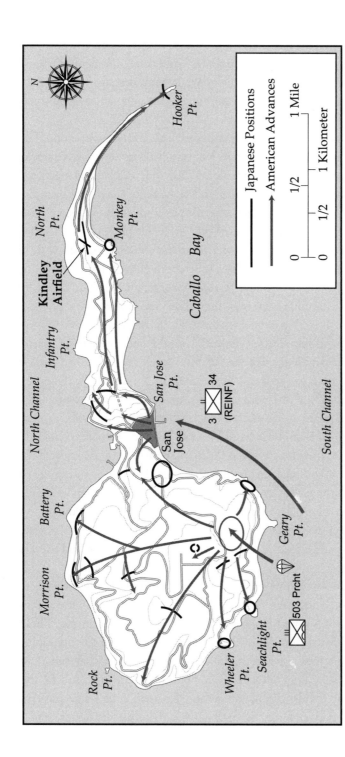

Corregidor

M. Jones. A graduate of the United States Military Academy, who was all of thirty-three years old at the time, Jones had taken command of the 503rd in 1944. *The Howitzer*, the yearbook at West Point, described him as being flexible: "George is an all-around something." That adaptability would serve him well on Corregidor.[3]

There were several significant issues with an airborne assault on the island. One of the biggest was that there was very little terrain suitable for landing. That problem was obvious to Colonel Orin "Hard Rock" Haugen, who had served on the island before the war and knew there was no good landing zone on the island. Haugen had been wounded in combat and was slowly losing his fight for his life when Jones visited him in the hospital. Jones told him about his pending jump on Corregidor. His friend's reaction stayed with him for years. "Orin was very sick but he had strength enough to look up at me and, looking very seriously into my eyes, say, 'George, they can't do that to you.'"[4]

There was sound judgment in that observation. In the best of conditions, airborne troops land in large open areas, like farms or meadows. Corregidor is shaped like a tadpole with an elevated, round western end and an eastern end that is narrow and looks like the tail. Almost all vegetation had been burned off in 1942 when the Japanese seized the island. As a result, the ground was dry and hard. On Corregidor, the best open area for a landing zone was an old airfield located at the eastern end of the island. The problem was that it was surrounded by hills. It would be easy for the Japanese to hold the high ground while firing on troops in the open. Krueger quickly rejected this idea. Other possible landing zones included the parade grounds and sports fields of Topside, located at the western end of the island. The problem with these areas was that they were narrow and small. As a result, planes would have to fly in a column rather than in a V formation. Given the small size of the landing zone, the planes would also have to circle back and drop a second and third wave of paratroopers.[5]

The Japanese themselves did not consider these fields feasible areas for paratroopers. They were close to the shattered remains of many buildings. These structures could easily become defensive fortifications. These ruins would also break up landings, acting as ground hazards that could injure men upon landing. Japanese shelling in 1942 had ripped apart all these buildings and, as a result, huge chunks of cement, steel, and tin littered the open areas, making the drop zone dangerous. Japanese guns—and also American munitions—had cratered the golf course, baseball diamonds, and parade grounds, and ripped apart trees, leaving trunks that were nothing more than wooden stakes. "The danger of being impaled on one of these tree stubs was apparent to all," Major Lawson B. Caskey, a battalion commander in the drop, observed. Krueger was aware of these drawbacks: "Although Topside was, indeed, an extremely rough area in which to make the drop, it offered us the best chance of surprising the enemy."[6]

Another concern was the limited lift capacity available to the Americans. The 317th Troop Carrier Group, the Army Air Forces unit assigned to this mission, had fifty-one planes, and, as a result, would have to fly three separate sorties over the island.[7] While the first drop might have the advantage of surprise, that would not be the case for the second and third assault waves.

A further problem was that the arsenal of democracy was starting to run short. The 503rd did not have the required equipment containers or packed parachutes to make the jump. Its parachute maintenance platoon had just joined the regiment on Mindoro, and its own equipment was still being loaded off transport ships. The solutions to these difficulties came from other elements of MacArthur's theater. Army Air Force units provided webbing and the 11th Airborne Division gave the regiment fifteen hundred packed parachutes.[8]

Intelligence on Corregidor was also mixed. The Japanese were good at cover and concealment, which led—in General Kruger's words—to some "astonishingly" bad estimates on the number of Japanese. Both MacArthur and Kruger's headquarters gave estimates of about 850 defenders on the island. Colonel Jones later said this number "was more of a 'guesstimate' than based on any bonafide information." The Japanese official history places the number of defenders between forty-five hundred and forty-nine hundred. The Americans, however, had good information on the terrain, which they drew from flights over the island, aerial reconnaissance photographs, and personnel who had been stationed on "the Rock" before the war. After a briefing with a naval officer who had been at Corregidor in 1942, Lieutenant Colonel E. M. Postlethwait, commander of the 34th Infantry Regiment, remarked, "The talk was worth an extra battalion."[9]

Moreover, the Americans had the air and naval assets to isolate the Japanese garrison on Corregidor and they pounded it without mercy in the days before the invasion. Over the course of three weeks—starting on January 23 and ending on February 16—the Fifth Air Force conducted 696 sorties and the Thirteenth Air Force conducted 316. The two Air Forces together dropped

3,128 tons of bombs.[10] These missions destroyed the torpedo boat and suicidal motorboat units, eliminating the threat that the Japanese posed to the invasion fleet.[11]

The Americans enjoyed other advantages, including junior officers, who were particularly well-trained and experienced in airborne operations. The paratroopers also had a good working relationship with the 317th Troop Carrier Group. Jones and Lieutenant Colonel John Lackey, the commanding officer of the carrier group, consulted regularly with one another, and the airmen had dropped the 503rd on previous missions. "The parachute personnel were all glad that this group, again was going to put us out over the target!" Major John Blair, a staff officer in the 3rd Battalion, declared. The 503rd Regiment showed captured Japanese films about the fall of "the rock" in 1942 that did the trick. "The urge for revenge surged in every man," 1st Lieutenant Edward Flash observed.[12]

Perhaps most in the Americans' favor was the fact that the Japanese did not consider an airborne assault feasible. Captain Itagaki Akira of the Imperial Japanese Navy took command of the Manila Bay Entrance Defense Force on December 20, 1944. He had previously been chief of staff to Admiral Iwabuchi Sanji. He had his men put mines on Kindley Field, the only place he thought possible for an airborne infantry to land, and made no other efforts to prepare against paratroopers. Krueger expected surprise to be an asset in the assault: "It seemed to me to make the drop on Topside itself, where the Japanese were not likely to expect it to be made."[13] He was, as it turned out, right.

* * *

On February 16, the 503rd Regiment began the day at 5:00 a.m. After a hot breakfast that lasted only fifteen minutes, the men began loading up on trucks that took them to the airstrips. The planes took off at 7:00 a.m. from the island of Mindoro and the one-hundred-minute flight to Corregidor was uneventful. They flew in from the southwest, giving the Japanese almost no advance notice.[14]

There were strong winds over Corregidor on February 16. In training situations, this turbulence would have cancelled the jump. With other assets already deployed, aborting the mission was simply impossible. The drop of the first sortie took slightly more than an hour after lift-off.[15]

Lieutenant Colonel John L. Erickson, the commander of the 3rd Battalion, was one of the first to jump. "Considering the location of my landing," he recalled, "the terrain and the fact that the area was covered with the jagged stumps of bomb-blasted trees, I was lucky. I had only minor bruises and scratches and was able to get on with the job." Other US commanders were less fortunate. Colonel Jones jumped after lowering the altitude, but a gust of wind caught his parachute and took him toward Manila Bay. He pulled on the risers and steered himself back toward the island but was impaled on a tree stump that took the flesh off the inside of both thighs. Captain Hudson C. Hill, a company commander in the 503rd, landed on top of a ruined three-story building in front of two Japanese pill boxes, and his parachute collapsed when he hit the top of the building. He fell to the ground floor and broke several teeth. The Japanese were sweeping the area with "intense" machine-gun fire. "The loss of the teeth was a fair exchange for possible death had I landed outside of the building," he later reflected.[16]

What Jones and his men did not know was that they were up against a far bigger Japanese force than intelligence officers estimated. The defenders outnumbered the attackers two to one.[17] "By late afternoon it was quite apparent that the G-2 estimate of the situation relative to enemy strength," Lester H. Levine observed wryly, "was more than just a little off."[18]

Elements of the intelligence failure were becoming quickly evident. Despite the massive amount of bombing and shelling, the Japanese had suffered little because they had built underground fortifications, which also helped hide their numbers. "Much of the pre-invasion bombardment had been in vain," Levine admitted. American strikes had also missed all the old US coastal artillery guns located on the island. A report conducted later found that every gun on Corregidor was in working order. The Japanese, however, had no men trained in their use.[19]

As the paratroopers landed, the airborne assault turned into a series of isolated gunfights. "If the Japanese had attacked in force at the time we were recovering from the jump," Lieutenant Donald E. Abbott, executive officer of Company E, 2nd Battalion, observed, "we could have easily been wiped out." As Levine explained in a postwar study: "Had the enemy pursued a course of relentless, coordinated attack early in the operation, instead of stubborn defense accompanied by suicidal activities, the outcome might have been different."[20]

The fighting was improvised and precarious. Private First Class Donald E. Rich shot two Japanese snipers while hanging from a tree, and Private Earl J. Williams took out another two. Not all were as fortunate as Rich and Williams.

Several were shot while still stuck in their harnesses. Father John J. Powers, the Catholic chaplain of the 503rd, was shot in the leg while coming down. "I was foolishly examining the wound instead of watching where I was going to land," he recalled. He came down on an artillery gun, broke several ribs, and suffered a concussion before landing right in front of a Japanese occupied cave. He was sitting in an exposed position with a grin on his face when his clerk rescued him. The Japanese, for some reason, held their fire. Another eight men in a similar situation were less fortunate. They were killed instantly when they landed in front of a Japanese position.[21]

Other paratroopers were severely injured in their landings. Walter Gonko could see that he was headed toward a bombed-out barracks. He blacked out when he hit the building. When he came to, he was at the bottom of the building, entangled in his chute with a broken back. Captain Probert Herb, the Protestant chaplain for the 503rd, was in no better shape. He had landed on the golf course but had broken both his legs. Herb would suffer from his injuries for the rest of his life, having to wear special corrective shoes and undergo a series of surgeries. Both men were eventually sent to medical ships for treatment.[22]

On that first day, evacuation was not realistic, though. The only real option the paratroopers had was to fight. "It should be remembered that we did not consider a man a casualty unless he was immobile as a result of a broken bone or was suffering shock as the result of wounds or injuries," Erickson explained. "Otherwise he was treated, bandaged and continued to fight."[23]

The element of surprise began to fade. The plane carrying Lieutenant Flash took fire and casualties on its first two runs over the drop zone. The second wave of paratroopers was taking more fire in the air. Men were shooting at the Japanese while floating down. One of those was Staff Sergeant Edward Gulsvich. Wounded when he landed, Japanese defenders attempted to finish him off with a bayonet charge. That was a mistake. Gulsvich had a Thompson submachine gun and proceeded to kill fourteen Japanese, before two enemy machine guns hit him with crossfire. He was posthumously awarded the Distinguished Service Cross.[24]

Paratroopers had to fight just to reach their assembly points after they landed. Flash's platoon landed on the golf course with the lieutenant landing next to the swimming pool. "As I unbuckled my parachute harness, individual Japanese riflemen started at us." As he was undoing his rigging, he saw another soldier falling to the earth. His parachute had failed to open properly and was streaming behind him. He crashed into the empty pool and was killed immediately.[25]

The casualties for the paratroopers were 10.7 percent, or 222 of the 2,065 men that jumped onto the island, which was lower than the twenty percent that Jones had expected. Most of the losses—seventy-five percent—came in the first sortie. The majority of these injuries came upon landing. Three men died due to chute malfunctions. To reduce the scattering of his unit, Jones lowered the second drop to four hundred feet. This low altitude was risky; it was just barely enough distance to allow the parachutes to open and fill before the troops hit the ground.[26]

The key to keeping the casualties low in the second assault wave, even as the Japanese responded with more firepower, was rapid adjustment in the control plane as commanders reduced the space between planes and the time between jumps. It also helped that the wind died down.[27]

The Americans had artillery that had landed in the jump, and those heavy weapons gave them extra power in the light infantry battle that was taking place. Captain Henry "Hoot" Gibson, commander of Battery B, 462nd Parachute Field Artillery Battalion, had his men disassemble a 75-millimeter-pack howitzer and put it back together in the ruins of the officers' quarters building. This effort gave them the high ground and allowed them to fire on entrenched Japanese positions, but a parachute was caught on the building and was blocking their line of fire. Private First Class John P. Prettyman, crawled out into an exposed position to try to pull it free. This effort failed and the Japanese were alerted that something was about to happen; they sprayed the position with machine-gun fire. Prettyman waited for a lull in the firing and climbed up on a balcony railing to grab the parachute. He got it off, but not before the machine-gun fire hit him in the chest. Watching him die enraged his gun crew. Gibson observed: "They poured shell after shell into that hill for about fifteen minutes when I ordered them to cease fire." Prettyman was awarded the Silver Star posthumously.[28]

Although it was quickly becoming obvious that the Americans were up against a far larger force than expected, the Japanese were also facing a serious problem, one that developed in the first few minutes of the battle. Captain Itagaki had expected an exclusively amphibious invasion. That morning, he and his staff were observing the approach of US landing craft when a group of paratroopers from Company I missed their drop zone and landed in the southeastern corner of the island. These soldiers quickly started marching toward Topside when they turned a corner and encountered Itagaki and his staff. A short gun battle resulted, and Itagaki was mortally wounded. He died that evening. At roughly the same time, another group of Colonel Erickson's soldiers seized control of the Japanese communication center on Topside. This one–two combination almost immediately eliminated the ability of the Japanese defenders to coordinate their actions. The recapture of Corregidor had started off as a series of isolated firefights and that is the way it would be fought until the very end, preventing the Japanese from using their greater superior numbers.[29]

The paratroopers quickly established a command post in one of the vacant buildings, which soon took on the appearance of a military headquarters with maps on the wall and desks arranged in order. It was, however, under small-arms fire and the fact that the paratroopers of the second sortie were landing in fields of fire constrained the ability of the Americans to return fire. Harry Akune, a Japanese American linguist, established a station there as fast as he could and began translating captured documents. One of them was a note taken from a messenger reporting the death of Itagaki and his rank, which indicated the size of the force on the island. "The message gave Colonel Jones a feel for what he was up against," Akune explained.[30]

While the airborne troops were landing on the island, soldiers from the 24th Infantry Division were landing on the southern beach, located where the tail of the island meets the round area. The first assault wave landed at 10:28 a.m. and met little resistance. "Our casualties were certainly not excessive considering the risk involved," Homer Bigart of the *New York Herald Tribune*, noted. Bigart was covering the amphibious assault from the beachhead. "But when men are killed or wounded directly beside you then the thing becomes very personal and hard to write about with any degree of dispassionate appraisal."[31]

Japanese fire, though, increased with each wave. The beach—about 125 yards long—was mined with approximately 130 anti-vehicle devices. These explosives were not particularly well-hidden, and it was easy for the infantrymen to avoid them. Not so for the tanks and trucks that landed on the beach. Within twenty minutes the Japanese had machine guns and mortars hitting the beach from the right and left flanks. Bigart and Richard G. Harris of the United Press wire service decided to stay in their shallow foxhole that they had scratched into the beach.[32]

"On my right, a doughboy suddenly raised the bloody stump of his right hand." Almost instantly, a soldier next to him fell over dead after a bullet had torn through his back and gone out his chest. "The horrible tearing power of machine-gun bullets was brought home to us for the first time." A mortar shell burst twenty feet to the left of Bigart and Harris, and fragments flew over them, hitting and killing a solider to their right.[33]

Confusion reigned over the beachhead. The Americans, to use Bigart's words, "were scattered from hell to breakfast." Mortars had taken out about half of the vehicles that had landed in the five assault waves. "The beach was too hot for any attempt at organization," Bigart observed. "The doughboys raced for cover wherever they could find it."[34]

Japanese mines were destroying vehicles but their fire was hitting relatively few US soldiers. Around 11:00 a.m., Companies L and K scrambled up to the top of Malinta Hill on their hands and knees. "We climbed like hell-bent apes," one soldier remarked. Neither company suffered casualties and Captain Frank Centenni, commanding officer of Company K, exclaimed in grateful disbelief at the top: "I'll be damned."[35]

That type of rapid advance was exactly what the Americans needed. At the end of the day, the Americans were in a fairly good situation. They held Topside and Malinta Hill, and they had cut the Japanese defending force in two. The task now was to force the enemy from their strong points scattered across the island. That evening the Japanese began counterattacking, forcing the Americans to temporarily focus on perimeter defense. There were no rear areas. Wounded men in the aid station at Topside were getting their weapons ready should the Japanese reach the building. "A silence settled over some sections of the Island, while all hell broke loose at others, as our patrols encountered the enemy," recounted Magnus L. Smith, an officer on the staff of the 503rd.[36]

* * *

The barrenness of the island surprised many Americans. "The terrain was worse than had been expected," Levine observed. The defoliation "created a sense of total desolation." Gibson, of the 462nd Field Artillery, had grown up in the Philippines due to his father's naval career and had competed in swimming contests at the pools on Corregidor. The damage and devastation stunned him.[37]

During the days that followed February 16, the paratroopers conducted patrols. The orders Colonel Jones gave to his battalion commanders were simple: "Clear the damn Nips from your area. Coordinate your operations through me or my staff." These were dangerous missions, but the training and experience of the "rock force" began to tell. The soldiers of the 503rd would slowly eliminate the Japanese defenders in one cave after another, using grenades, phosphorous grenades, mortars, naval gunfire, and artillery. At night, though, the Japanese would counterattack, and the fight would become much more vicious and—for a time—balanced. As a result, sleep became a rare commodity on the island, and added to the exhaustion and strain of battle.[38]

On February 19, three days after the landing, fortune began to favor the Americans. By that point, the 503rd had its regimental artillery located on the parade grounds at Topside and could direct fire to any part of the island. The Japanese also lacked fresh water, which degraded their health and fighting abilities in a powerful way.[39] During the night of February 19–20, however, the Japanese launched a major counteroffensive on the western part of the island. A force of roughly six hundred Japanese breached the US perimeter and overran the positions of infantry Companies D and F of the 2nd Battalion. Company F might have suffered the same fate were it not for Private Lloyd G. McCarter. A disciplinary problem, McCarter had been in the stockade for desertion when the 503rd got orders to jump on Corregidor. "I never had one moment's trouble with him when he was present for duty," Bill Calhoun, his platoon commander noted later. "He never complained and carried out his assigned duties cheerfully." That evening McCarter held his position. When his gun was disabled, he grabbed a Browning automatic rifle from a wounded comrade. When he ran out of ammunition, he got an M-1 Garand rifle until it broke right around dawn. At this point, a Japanese bullet hit him in the middle of his chest. It took until mid-morning before he could be evacuated. He remained calm during this period. "He was tough and complaint was not in his vocabulary," Calhoun observed.[40]

In the light of day, McCarter's unit found thirty-five dead Japanese in front of his position with signs that others had limped or been dragged away. Two days later, a search of the valley in front of his ditch found another three hundred dead. Staff Sergeant Chris W. Johnson stated, "I believe, if Private McCarter had not stayed in that dangerous position we would have had many more men killed and possibly lost the hill."[41] Calhoun nominated McCarter for the Medal of Honor. Lieutenant Colonel John Britten, the regimental executive officer, told him he was downgrading the recommendation to a Distinguished Service Cross. Calhoun objected. Britten told him to leave off or he would reduce it to a Silver Star. Calhoun later learned that Jones did not want a discipline problem to get the Medal of Honor. The theater awards board looked at Calhoun's nomination and realized that McCarter did indeed deserve the Medal of Honor, which President Harry S. Truman presented to him a few months later at the White House. He was the only soldier at Corregidor to receive this honor.[42]

Because of a breakdown in the radio network, Calhoun's superiors did not know about the attack until the Japanese arrived at Topside and, according to one officer, it "scared the hell out of the headquarters." Captain Robert M. "Cracker" Atkins rallied troops at the barracks, and they began shooting from the roof, although they were clad only in their underwear. The Japanese made it inside and there was hand-to-hand fighting. At dawn, the Japanese withdrew. Mopping up took hours. There were still isolated pockets of Japanese all around Topside, and Jones ordered patrols to inspect every building in the area.[43]

Although the Manila Bay Entrance Defense Force had good morale going into the battle, it was nothing more than a scrap force. As with the MNDF, most of the Japanese were sailors from the Navy or conscripts who had been civilians a few weeks earlier. The defenders were good at concealment. Major John H. Blair of the 3rd Battalion called it an example of tactical "perfection." Harold Templeman of the Red Cross called the Japanese "gophers" because of their use of caves, tunnels, and pillboxes, which made it difficult to know where the defenders were located and in what numbers. Given their shattered command and communications system, and their limited skill and training, this approach made sense but also came at a cost. The Japanese sacrificed good positions with overlapping fields of fire for disguise and camouflage. Their hiding and holding a collection of random sites meant the Americans could isolate them and take them out in small, manageable numbers without having to worry much about the danger of counterattacks.[44]

By February 20, the Japanese knew they were beaten and began trying to escape Corregidor. A large group of roughly three hundred gathered on the west side of the island. They attempted to swim to the Bataan Peninsula, which was about a mile away. Many drowned.[45]

On February 21, explosions inside Malinta Hill—seven in all—shook the island. "I thought the whole hill was going to blow, and we got no sleep that night," Captain Gibson recalled. The explosions were to have been the start of a coordinated offensive, but the Japanese lost control of the detonations, derailing their attack before it even started.[46]

* * *

Combat operations during the endgame of the battle had a similar pattern to them, with the Americans eliminating pockets of Japanese. It was grim and methodical. When they approached caves, they would use Thompson submachine guns to keep the enemy inside, while others equipped with flame throwers got in position. These incendiaries could reach deep inside, burning many alive and killing others through asphyxiation. The paratroopers then sealed up the caves, trapping an unknown number. When the hideouts were located on cliffs along the shore, the infantrymen could call upon fire from U.S. Navy PT boats and destroyers. The Americans would pull back at night and would suffer under sniper and mortar fire, which could be—and often was—deadly.[47]

On February 23, a particularly vicious fight took place to take control of Wheeler Point, a small spot on the southwestern shoreline of the island located in front of a sheer ridge that overlooked the water. The Japanese were in caves holding on to this area. Hill led E Company in the assault on these positions. Due to casualties, Hill consolidated his four platoons into two. The second platoon made contact with a Japanese-held cave. They were on both sides of the opening, firing into it, but unsure if they were scoring any hits. The Japanese fired back, and communications between the two platoons broke down when one radio operator dove for cover and broke off the antenna during the process.[48]

Stuck in a tactical situation where they were cut off and were not sure about their opponent's strength or location, a number of men peered above the geographical formations they had used for cover. First Lieutenant Roscoe Corder was next to a soldier who stood up to look at the cave entrance and was shot. Corder saw the dust fly off the back of his shirt when the bullet exited his body. "He looked me in the eye, and died," he recalled.[49] The platoon was running out of ammunition and Corder decided to retreat.[50]

On February 24, the Americans began an advance down Corregidor's tail. The Japanese resisted and that evening mortar fire hit the command post of the 1st Battalion, killing its commander, Major Robert H. Wood, and wounding or killing most of his staff. The survivors requested a response from the 462nd Parachute Field Artillery Battalion, and the gunners obliged. A barrage of 75-millimeter shells caught a detachment of Japanese out in the open, preparing for an infantry assault, killing about half of the six hundred man group, a devastating loss. The next day the 1st Battalion took roughly half of the island's "tail." The fact that there was no sniper or mortar fire the night of February 25–26 was a good indication of the toll the day had taken on the defenders.[51]

The morning of February 27 was the tenth day of the battle. The 1st Battalion was on a ridge at Monkey Point on the southern coast of the tail. The ridge overlooked Kindley Field, the air strip on Corregidor, and was directly above Radio Intercept Tunnel, a position that Major John N. Davis, the new commander of the battalion, knew was in Japanese hands. He had men guarding both entrances. At 11 a.m., Davis was watching a Sherman tank seal off caves when a massive underground explosion shook the ground. The Japanese in the tunnel had set off an explosion. Large rocks flew into the air, and one hit a US destroyer operating off the coast. The tank Davis had been watching tumbled down the ridge end over end. Only one member of the crew survived. The blast knocked Davis twenty to thirty feet back through the air. He landed, suffering no major injuries other than some coughing and sputtering. There was smoke and dust everywhere.

The ridge had simply disappeared, replaced by a hole in the ground that was 130 feet long, seventy feet wide, and thirty feet deep. "I have never seen such a sight in my life," Davis said later, "utter carnage—bodies laying everywhere, *everywhere*." Men were blown up or buried alive as coral, boulders, scrap iron, body parts, and soil rained down on them. One captain in the battalion had broken ribs and a partially crushed chest: "I was coughing blood like a Grade B movie hero!" The battalion took just under two hundred casualties, which was more than the Japanese lost in the explosion.[52]

Despite the damage done to the 1st Battalion, Jones told the 3rd Battalion to keep advancing. Erickson seized Kindley Field against light resistance, and at 4:00 p.m. the paratroopers reached East Point, the end of Corregidor's tail, only five hours after the Monkey Point explosion. They had a firefight with a small group of Japanese on Hooker Point, an islet off the tip of the island.[53]

As the Americans closed in on the tail of the island, many Japanese tried to swim to the Bataan Peninsula. Landing Craft and PT boats interdicted them. Many were armed and resisted. They became targets of opportunity for fighter aircraft and PT boats.[54]

By this point, American infantry companies were burning through ammunition at a rate twice what planners expected and, on occasion, they had to beat a tactical retreat because of shortages. The main reason was that the XIV Corps quartermaster units had not established supply points close enough to frontline combat units. More significantly, the Americans were running out of water. The heat and humidity caused men to empty their canteens in two days. The Air Force dropped containers totaling 1,250 gallons and the troops on the ground recovered most, but not all, of these chutes. Some cans of water went into the bay because of wind, and others suffered damage when they landed. The situation was finally resolved when the Navy delivered a 1,250-gallon tank that was placed on the beachhead. After the first few days, the supply situation got better, although transportation was always a problem because the Rock Force had no vehicles to support logistical efforts.[55]

As the battle progressed, public health issues became a serious matter. The decomposing bodies of the Japanese began to reek, and they became a breeding ground for disease. The heat and humidity on Corregidor only accelerated this process. After two days on Corregidor, Sergeant Thomas R. Pardue noted in his diary, "The whole place stinks." The stench of corpses—in the thousands by most estimates—was so strong that crews on destroyers operating off the island could smell the odor of the dead. The maggots covering the dead were so thick that they moved the corpses, making it look like the dead were crawling forward. The number of flies grew and grew and got into the noses, ears, and mouths of the living, and would swarm over food, making it difficult for the Americans to eat. When bulldozers arrived on the island, they dug long shallow trenches that became mass graves. Others pushed the dead over the cliffs of Topside into Manila Bay.[56]

The fly problem, though, remained. Jones told his supply officer, Captain Atkins, to fix the situation. That rather vague order gave Atkins an idea, and he contacted a supply officer he knew at XI Corps headquarters. A few hours later, an Air Force C-47 with tanks of DDT insecticide began spraying the island, even the areas still in Japanese hands. "Hot damn," Atkins exclaimed, "the flies are dropping like flies!" A second flight the next day sprayed the island again. "As improbable as it sounds, after the spraying all the flies had disappeared as if there had never been any on the island," Levine explained. Lieutenant Abbott, the executive officer of E Company, was astonished: "It was almost as if a miracle had happened."[57]

As the fly episode suggests, the force liberating Corregidor was joint in nature. The Army, Air Force, and Navy were working together. "The re-taking of 'The Rock' could not have been possible without the perfect coordination and planning of all three services," Lieutenant Flash stated. Lieutenant Colonel Postlethwait agreed, "The Corregidor operation was an example of co-ordination as it ought to be."[58]

Even after the airborne assault, the Navy continued to play a crucial support role in the battle. Some of the Navy's tasks might seem routine—US ships were firing star shells at night for illumination, resupplying the ground troops, and removing dead and wounded. The advance on the island simply would have been impossible without them. When the paratroopers moved along the rocky coast of the island, whose cliffs were heavily defended, an army officer boarded a destroyer, explained where the enemy was located, and the sailors fired point blank at the Japanese positions.[59]

The Air Force played an equally fundamental role. Even after the first day, the Air Force continued to support the advance. Fighters and bombers were dropping munitions on Japanese positions. There were so many planes that they had to circle over the target, waiting their turn. Bombers returning from missions over Luzon with unused ordinance dropped them on Corregidor.[60]

While there was an abundance of air power on Corregidor, its medical units were taxed at every point in the battle. An aide station established on the first day was "over-taxed" due to limited supplies and personnel. It took until February 18 for additional manpower to arrive. Equipment was lost in the initial drop, most of it landing in the waters of Manila Bay. Despite their non-combatant status, doctors and medics were often wounded or killed as they went forward to provide medical care. Other duties were just as dangerous. Lloyd S. Allen, a medic with the 462nd Parachute Field Artillery Battalion, dashed out of a bomb hole to recover a medical equipment canister. He got to the bundle but was shot and killed before he got back to the crater. The explosion at Monkey Point on February 26 simply overwhelmed the medical resources the Army had, and, in another example of joint operations, the Navy had corpsmen and doctors on the island within half an hour to help.[61]

The campaign to take Corregidor essentially ended on March 2, the third anniversary of the 503rd's activation. MacArthur returned to the island on that day, took a quick tour of the island before the ceremony, and, as a *New York Times* reporter observed, "the business of killing Japanese hiding out in tunnels and caves continued." Shots rang out in the distance. Despite, or perhaps because of, this lingering resistance, Rock Force held a simple flag ceremony on the desolate parade ground at Topside returning the island to US sovereignty. With a small element of his command standing in formation, many of them wearing bandages, Jones addressed MacArthur, "Sir, I present to you the Fortress Corregidor." MacArthur awarded Jones the Distinguished Service Cross. The ceremony lasted all of seven-and-a-half minutes.[62]

As with so many things associated with MacArthur and the return to the Philippines, a bit of clarification is necessary. Several hundred Japanese remained on Corregidor after March 2, and mop-up operations continued for another week. During that time, 118 Japanese were killed. A small group of about twenty held out until January 2, 1946, surrendering only after learning of the war's end.[63]

Many observers believed the ramifications of this battle were significant. In Baltimore, the editorial board of *The Sun* declared that Corregidor "opens Manila harbor and gives the rest of the campaign the character of a large mopping-up operation."[64] The authors of the U.S. Army Command & General Staff College's battle book on Corregidor—the guide for a tour of the battlefield—argue that the Japanese artillery did not have the strength to interdict US naval operations and the use of the Port of Manila. In other words, the main reason for taking the island was to avenge the humiliation of 1942.[65]

There is little doubt that there is an element of truth in that argument, but the bulk of that position is unrealistic. Was there psychological value in retaking the island? Yes, but that was not a valid enough reason for the operation. In fact, the very jointness that gave the Americans greater power in the Luzon campaign demanded the operation. The U.S. Navy would not have conducted mine clearing operations under the guns of Corregidor. It was entirely possible that the Japanese might have rushed reinforcements to the island or realized eventually the value of the cannon at their disposal. Had this happened, the Port of Manila would have been of no value at all. Psychological or pragmatic, the taking of Corregidor was a foundational requirement for the Luzon campaign to be a success. It was a crucial event in the effort to take Manila.

What the battle did show was the value of innovation. The creative adaptation that the Americans showed in attacking Corregidor stands in contrast to what was happening in Manila. While the Americans had used speed and surprise early in the Luzon campaign, those features had faded as US divisions reached the city limits. Had the Americans used airborne assault and amphibious assault in a similar fashion in the city, the battle for Manila might have turned out quite differently.

16

Battle of the Strong Points,
February 17–22

According to the press accounts of February 5, the battle had ended two weeks earlier and MacArthur's soldiers were now involved in mop-up operations. The fight was now entering its third week, making a mockery of this reporting. Most Americans believed that the battle was at the beginning of its end. Much of that fighting would be fought south of the Pasig for control of a series of strong points. Even some of the Japanese could see the end, but it was going to take a lot more combat to get the battle to its conclusion. A series of nasty engagements—fought in prominent prewar buildings—would be the fifth crucial event of the battle for Manila.

By this third week of fighting, the Japanese were relying primarily on rifle and machine-gun fire with only sporadic use of mortars, reflecting the fact that they were running out of supplies.[1] The Americans, on the other hand, realized that not all their equipment was suited for close quarter, urban conflict. Flame throwers turned out to be less useful in several situations.[2]

The fighting at this point was brutal and slow, building by building, floor by floor, even room by room. "The reduction of each building was actually a series of battles in itself," declared a Sixth Army study conducted a few months later.[3] Soldiers at the main points of contact agreed with that assessment. "Without the bazookas, it would have taken more time and lives," Sergeant Ozzie St. George stated. "The Japs held the advantage of position," he added. Solid defensive positions helped compensate for their weak infantry skills.[4]

The fight for the New Police Station illustrates these traits. The 129th Regiment spent February 17 probing around the building and took heavy fire. What hurt the regiment was that while it was trying to take the Police Station, it was also moving against the Manila Club, which was located to the north, just off Marqués de Comillas Street. The clubhouse was behind a large lawn that gave its defenders an unobstructed field of fire against any approaching force. After four days fighting to take the Police Station, Robert S. Beightler replaced the 129th with the 145th Regiment, which entered the building on February 18, but had to retreat when Japanese in neighboring buildings—like the Manila Club—hit them with small arms fire. The next day, sloppy US artillery work resulted in tree bursts that forced the regiment to retreat again. The Police Station was not taken until 2:50 p.m. on February 20.[5]

The Japanese had held in place for eight days. The men of the battalion counted one hundred dead bodies inside the building. Another fifty bodies lay outside where various units supporting the battalion had gunned down Japanese defenders as they tried to escape.[6]

Overlapping a bit with the attack on the Police Station was the 1st Cavalry's assault on the waterfront properties of Ermita. When the Americans took control of the Philippines in the late 1890s, they took over some of the best real estate to construct the High Commissioner's Residence, the Manila Hotel, the Army and Navy Club, and the Elks' Club. What made these buildings so desirable in peacetime was that they were located on the shore of Manila Bay, enjoying good views and a breeze coming off the water. In battle, these buildings, located mostly along the coast-hugging Dewy Boulevard, controlled approaches to the Port of Manila and ground transportation into and out of the city.[7] They were valuable pieces of real estate, and the Japanese were going to defended them vigorously.

These buildings were five and six stories tall, high enough to loom above the landscape of rubble that surrounded them, giving the Japanese defenders commanding views of the area. The 12th Cavalry Regiment attacked in a northerly direction at 11:00 a.m. on February 19. Under heavy machine-gun fire from the Japanese, it took the horsemen until dusk to reach the grounds and residence of the high commissioner, a distance of about a mile. The Japanese were holding a number of Filipino hostages in the residence and other buildings. Some in the Elks' Club, though, were released.[8]

The next day, the regiment attacked and took the residence, then the Army and Navy Club, and then the Elks' Club. There was less than a company of infantry holding each of these buildings, necessitating the use of military police as infantrymen. Frank S. Tenny, the commanding officer of a MP company, had his men approach the Army and Navy Club with a "pardonable amount of care." A guerilla group under the command of Arsenio Lacson (who would later become mayor of Manila) also took part in the action. "The Japanese were on the upper floors and were firing at us cowboy-style from different windows," Tenny recalled. It took two days to clear the building. When it was over, Tenny counted forty-one dead to his three wounded.[9]

By this third week, the Japanese had pulled most of their men back to Intramuros and other positions. Hostages in the Manila Hotel, some of whom had not had food or water for several days, managed to escape. "On 20 February we saw the American soldiers in front of the Army and Navy Club," Frederico Garcia, a resident of the Ermita district explained. We started to run to meet them while the snipers were shooting from behind." As a result, the seizures of these buildings were rapid, and casualties were kept quite low.[10]

The Manila Hotel came next. A high-end establishment in prewar Manila for the expatriate community and a few select Filipinos, the hotel penthouse on the fifth floor had been MacArthur's residence in the 1930s and early 1940s. He had left his personal belongings there when he departed for Corregidor in 1942. The generals of the Imperial Japanese Army had, for the most part, respected MacArthur as an officer and a gentleman by not plundering his possessions. They took an inventory of the contents and a few items disappeared during the occupation, but, by and large, the things that MacArthur had collected over his military career remained intact. These included his personal papers, a rather large library focused primarily on military history, and the Medal of Honor of Lieutenant General Arthur MacArthur.[11]

With its five floors and concrete structure, the hotel was a key strong point in the advance toward Intramuros. The 12th Cavalry, with support from the 82nd Field Artillery Battalion and a number of tanks, charged into the hotel complex on February 21. The cavalry seized the older, eastern wing of the hotel within a few hours with relatively little damage. The new wing was a different story. There was fierce room-to-room fighting, requiring a day and a half before the complex was secured.[12]

MacArthur was there, observing the fight. Just before the 1st Cavalry sent the flying column to Manila, he had received a report from the IX Corps. The unit had translated a captured Japanese document that was an inventory of his penthouse. Most of his belongings were still there. "I was anxious to rescue as much as I could of my home atop the Manila Hotel," he told reporters.[13]

From the roof garden of the Great Eastern Hotel on the northern bank of the Pasig, John Dos Passos watched the hotel burn with the other journalists. One reporter joked in a low voice, "There goes our drink at the bar."[14]

MacArthur was pinned down with a patrol from the 37th Division on Burnham Green, which was part of Luneta Park. He watched as an explosion and fire consumed the new wing, including the penthouse. "I watched, with indescribable feelings, the destruction of my fine military library, my souvenirs, my personal belongings of a lifetime. It was not a pleasant moment."[15]

Men from the 1st Cavalry Division were taking cover from the machine-gun fire coming from the hotel. "I still remember this jeep come [sic] up," Martin Gonzales, a cavalryman recalled. "And everybody looked in it and said, 'Who in the is that stupid guy driving up with a jeep?' And who walks out but General MacArthur." His presence had an immediate impact. "Everybody got up. If the old general could stand up, we could stand up too. I remember that," Gonzales added.[16]

MacArthur took a tour and could see the ruins of his personal belongings in his old residence. "Of the penthouse, nothing was left but ashes," he explained many years later. A cavalry lieutenant who had overseen the seizure of this section was happy to see the general: "Nice going, chief."

"There was nothing nice about it to me," MacArthur thought to himself. "I was tasting the last acid dregs the bitterness of a devastated and beloved home."[17]

Some have accused MacArthur of being callous, focused on the loss of a few inanimate objects while so many were dying about him. That argument needs some qualification. The general was fully aware at this point of the atrocities taking place in the city. He had seen the prisoners at Santo Tomás and Bilibid and the refugees fleeing the city. MacArthur blamed Yamashita for the slaughter on the streets and vowed to hold him personally responsible when the war ended. The destruction of Manila was symbolized by the loss of his possessions, including his father's personal papers and his library, much of it built on the foundation of his father's books. It later turned out that many of these older volumes survived the battle, as they had been stored in the hotel's basement.[18]

As the Americans closed in on the Intramuros, the Japanese continued to attack at night. Small groups were sent out on reconnaissance patrols and others were sent out on suicide missions, although it was probably difficult for the Americans to tell the difference. The men on these one-way missions were well-equipped with explosives—grenades, Molotov cocktails, and stick bombs—at this point, firearms were in short supply and only a few men had them. They were also required to wear rubber-toed shoes so they could approach their targets with a minimum of noise. Probationary Officer Baba Masanori took out a group of twenty-two on the night of February 20. Their goal was to hit the US headquarters on the south side of the Pasig. Although it was not a suicide mission, the last entry in Baba's journal was "Long Live the Emperor!" Three days later, the soldiers of the 37th Infantry Division recovered his journal off a dead Japanese body.[19]

* * *

Japanese control of Manila was rapidly shrinking to Intramuros and the northern half of Ermita, but there were isolated areas of the city still under Japanese control. One of those was the area around the Philippine General Hospital and the University of the Philippines. Both were about a third of a mile from the shore of Manila Bay. Rizal Hall, the largest building on the campus, faced south on the north side of Padre Faura Street, putting it literally across the street from the hospital. Made of reinforced concrete, Rizal Hall was a perfect stronghold for Japanese defenders. Tanks and tank destroyers shelled the building for two hours on February 20, doing little damage, but forcing the Japanese to take cover in the basement, which soon proved to be crucial. A platoon from Troop B of the 5th Cavalry attacked and entered the building at 11:30 a.m. They did not have control of the stairways and, as a result, the Japanese managed to reach the top three floors. The defenders paid a price, though. They lost the first two floors to the horse soldiers in two hours of fighting. At 5:00 p.m., the platoon reached the top floor with no loss of life.[20]

Despite their success, the commanding officer of Troop B refused to send in more replacements, fearing that the Japanese would ignite explosives and destroy the building. These concerns proved to be legitimate. Thirty minutes after they had reached the top, an explosion tore apart the center of the building. The Americans quickly withdrew.[21]

The fight for the rest of the campus followed a similar pattern. The Japanese thwarted an effort to take the Administration Building with a similar explosion. That only delayed the inevitable, and the building fell to the Americans the next day. In an article for the division alumni newsletter, Private First Class Allan MacDonald, who had fought in the regiment's other campaigns, called the engagement in the city "rough." He explained that he had lost a number of friends at the university.[22]

While the fighting was tough for individual soldiers, for the division as a whole, the operation was relatively quick. One of the reasons the capture of the university was done at a low cost and at a fairly fast pace was that the Americans had advanced warning of Japanese plans. Two prisoners of war gave detailed information on the intended use of the campus as a defensive strong point, including the location of mines and street corners that were fortified as strong points.[23]

Another reason the fight started to move quickly was that the defenders began committing suicide. Cavalrymen heard singing and speeches in Japanese throughout the night of February 22 and then explosions. In the morning, soldiers from the regiment counted the bodies of 149 soldiers. Not all defenders gave up. The last stages often required the work of flame throwers or gasoline and oil that engineers ignited to burn or suffocate the final defenders.[24]

While the 1st Cavalry Division was seizing control of the university and hospital complex, the 37th Infantry Division was turning its attention to another isolated citadel. The General Post Office was a five-story, neo-classical structure on the southern bank of the Pasig. The Post Office had Ionic columns and a rectangular Attic style with semi-circular wings at both ends that made it look like a mashup of the Jefferson and Lincoln Memorials in Washington, DC. A raised road on the south side of the building, which ran parallel to the river, provided a good natural defensive buffer. On the other side of the road was a flat, open area that had been a park in peacetime, and which offered nothing that Americans could use for concealment. The building was a major Japanese strong point, blocking any advance toward the Walled City from the north or along the river. Although only about five hundred feet from Intramuros, the Japanese made no effort to integrate it into the old Spanish fort's defensive line. They were content to let this garrison fight on its own.[25]

Artillery and tanks pounded on the building for the three days between February 19 and 21. Two platoons of Company B, 1st Battalion managed to enter the building on February 21, but the Japanese drove the Americans out with heavy machine-gun fire. The next morning the company attacked the building with greater force. A few men managed to enter through a second-floor window. With that move, the Japanese defenders cracked and retreated to the basement. At dusk, the men of the 145th raised the US flag over the Post Office. They finished off the few remaining Japanese in the basement on February 23 with flame throwers and pole charges.[26]

Concurrent with the final assault on the Post Office, the regiment also attacked City Hall. Sitting immediately to the east of the Intramuros moat that the Americans had converted into a golf course, this building was an obstacle to the seizure of the Walled City. Using point-blank fire from tank destroyers, mortars, and 155-millimeter artillery on February 22, the 3rd Battalion, 145th Infantry Regiment penetrated and secured the building before the end of the afternoon.[27]

The fight for the General Post Office was tactically more important than City Hall or the Manila Club.[28] Given that it was made from reinforced concrete, the three-day artillery barrage had done little damage. The building fell quickly, not because of the strength of firepower, but because of US mobility. It was underdefended. The MNDF's mistake was in not assigning more personnel to fight in the building.

Beightler was understandably proud of his men: "The division is performing magnificently in spite of the fact that the enemy opposition is furiously determined and bitter," he wrote to a friend. This type of combat was not what his men had faced before or were trained to expect. "This is the toughest kind of street fighting and is probably very similar to the warfare in cities of Europe. The city itself is a shambles and it would sicken your heart to see what devastation the enemy has so needlessly wrought."[29]

While infantrymen were busy driving the Japanese out of buildings, combat engineers continued to remove mines. The removal of barriers in the streets was cumbersome due to the random items the Japanese had used to barricade the streets of the city. In one instance, they planted a concrete mixer in a street. The 117th Engineer Combat Battalion did not have the equipment to remove the bigger items, so they used explosives and then filled in the resulting hole. The main threat to their efforts was Japanese small arms fire.[30]

* * *

In addition to the adjustments American soldiers were making to urban warfare, the fighting outside of Manila still affected events inside the city. In the southeast, Fort McKinley had a commanding view of the surrounding area and as long as the Japanese held this citadel, the airport was worthless. The chewed-up terrain looked like the trenches of World War I. "It was reminiscent of the old movie *All Quiet on the Western Front*," Jim Holzem recalled. "Shells were landing all around and amidst us as we advanced."[31]

For six days, the 11th Airborne and the 1st Cavalry had both advanced on the fort in a series of patrols. The area was littered with heavy machine guns, 20-millimeter guns, 5-inch naval guns, and pillboxes made of reinforced concrete. The roads were mined with 500- and 1,000-pound aerial bombs. "These mines were carelessly concealed but were an ever-present hazard to all vehicular movement," Anthony K. Gemematas of the 187th Glider Infantry Regiment remarked.[32]

As throughout the Battle of Manila, there were individual acts of valor. On a patrol near Fort McKinley on February 13, Private First Class Manuel Perez, Jr. was the lead scout for his company. He shot and killed five Japanese soldiers out in the open and then threw a series of grenades into a pillbox. There, however, was another bunker with two 50-caliber machine guns in position to stop his company's advance. Perez took a roundabout approach toward the emplacement. He encountered four Japanese along the way and killed all of them. Within twenty yards of the guns, he threw grenades into the bunker. The Japanese inside began to abandon their position, and Perez shot four before he ran out of bullets. After reloading, he hit another four. One of the fleeing defenders charged at him with a rifle fixed with a bayonet. Perez parried the blow, but his rifle fell to the ground. He picked up the Japanese soldier's weapon and shot him and two others at point-blank range. He killed three more using the rifle as a club. He then entered the bunker and used the Japanese rifle and bayonet to stab one remaining defender. All told, Perez had killed eighteen Japanese soldiers in taking the bunker.[33]

Two weeks later, Perez wrote his uncle, who was also assigned to duty in the Pacific: "They are putting me in for a medal and its not the purple heart, and you will be surprised how big it is going to be." His prediction turned out to be correct. He was awarded the Medal of Honor for his actions. He, however, never lived to receive the award. He was killed in combat a month later.[34]

At the time, though, such honors were not on the minds of most paratroopers. They were using colored smoke to mark their positions, and P-38s and dive-bombers from US carriers strafed Japanese positions. The Japanese responded with their heavy guns. The men in front of the fort dropped mortar rounds on top of the Japanese, but because they were lying prone on the ground, they were essentially firing blind.[35]

Even as the 11th Airborne neared the fort, the Japanese continued offering harsh resistance. In one instance, a Japanese sailor charged into a small patrol and threw a grenade that hit and then bounced off a sergeant's chest. The training of the Americans kicked in instantly and they all dove for cover. All of them survived when the grenade exploded, but one was wounded in a "sensitive spot."[36]

Another defender jumped up as a patrol from the 1st Cavalry approached. The Japanese sailor had a broken sword, and he charged the radio operator, who was not carrying a rifle. The man, however, had a Colt-45 pistol, and fired two rounds. The defender fell to the ground. He got up, and the radio man fired another two rounds. The Japanese man fell to the ground again, but again he got back up. This same sequence happened again. The radio operator fired, and the man got back up yet again. Many years later, Peter MacFarland, one of the troopers in this patrol, wondered if all the shots were hitting the sailor. When the defender got up a fourth time, one of the men carrying a light machine gun and standing near the radio operator stepped forward and unloaded on the man. The ordinance nearly cut his body in two.[37]

Soldiers got hurt in the advance and rank was no protection. Colonel Edward H. Lahti, the commanding officer of the 511th Parachute Infantry Regiment, was hit by a piece of shrapnel that was three inches by six inches. "Made a beautiful cut about 7 inches long just below my shoulder." After getting the wound stitched up at a field hospital, he continued to command with his arm in a sling. He stayed in the field even after he came down with a case of jaundice; the two health issues were probably related.[38]

The attack on the fort began in force on February 17. Major Henry Burgess was in command of the 1st Battalion of the 511th Parachute Regiment, and like others he thought of World War I: "The closer we got to Ft. McKinley the more artillery, ack-ack fire, small-arms fire and mortar fire from emplacements and pillboxes were encountered." He added: "At one time in the open rolling country one could see seven infantry battalions attacking on a line supported by tanks and self-propelled guns." He was worried. "The 1st Battalion of the 511th had been designated as the lead battalion in taking Fort McKinley, an assignment which was going to be expensive in troopers." The assault stopped just at the gates of the fort since it was in the area of responsibility of the 1st Cavalry Division.[39]

For the next two days, the 11th Airborne laid directed fire toward the southern end of the fort and picked off individual Japanese soldiers. The 3rd and the 4th Naval Battalions evacuated during the night of February 17–18.[40] The Japanese retreat was an admission that the paratroopers had broken their defenses. The division attacked and the 188th Paraglider Infantry Regiment entered the fort at 5 p.m. and found it empty. Although aware of this development, the 1st Cavalry was slow to react. The fort was declared secure on only February 19 when the horsemen arrived and took the northern end.[41]

That night Burgess was in no mood to worry about unit honors. He sat down and wrote a letter to his parents: "Having a battalion gives me a new slant on the war. It is a dirty, useless business; in fact, it is just a great mill for chewing fine able bodied men into bloody useless wrecks."[42]

Another key engagement was fought fifteen miles to the northeast of downtown Manila in front of the Novaliches Dam. The 8th Cavalry Regiment exchanged fire with several company-sized groups of attacking Japanese on February 18 and 19. These exchanges were lopsided, and the Japanese never posed a serious threat to the facility.[43]

* * *

After the capture of Fort McKinley, the men of the 11th Airborne spent the next few days in apartments in Parañaque. Being able to rest in modern buildings was a luxury compared to sleeping on the ground or in tents.[44]

Other soldiers still faced dangerous assignments despite the fading tempo. There was the immediate task of destroying enemy ammunition dumps at the fort. Combat engineers, in a bit of ingenious recycling, used the bombs the Japanese had used around Nichols Field as mines to detonate the supply centers at the fort.[45]

By February 20, shooting in the rear areas was a fading danger, although there were still isolated incidents of live fire. The Special Security Force that Beightler had created continued to patrol areas north of the Pasig River. Both the 82nd and 136th Field Artillery Battalions fired on boats the Japanese were using to leave the city. One sank, while the other was forced to ground on one of the islands in the river. Battalions from infantry regiments were often given guard duty of bridges because they still attracted Japanese attacks. This duty was significantly less demanding than breaching a building, but it fell far short of having a day off for recuperation.[46]

Even in the rear areas, combat still affected the duties soldiers had to perform. The men of the 672nd Amphibious Tractor Battalion spent the time doing maintenance work on their vehicles, preparing for an amphibious assault on the Walled City. They were on the Pasig at the ready to do ferry work should the Japanese destroy any of the bridges across the river.[47]

Civilians in Manila slowly tried to recover from the devastation of battle. The damage to the city was now becoming clear. The destruction in the Malate district located in the southwest corner of the city, for example, was near absolute. Marcial P. Lichauco hitched a ride into this area to retrieve family belongings from his mother's house. "The ride to Malate . . . was an experience I shall never forget," he noted in his diary. "As far as the eyes could see in every direction, nothing was visible except the remains of what had once been thousands of residential houses." His mother's house was gone, and he did not stay long. The smell of decomposing bodies was strong. He took a quick look but did not recognize any of the dead.[48]

Another problem facing Filipinos was rampant inflation. Basic commodities were going for twenty times their prewar value. One of the contributing factors to this economic situation was that transportation to and in the city had broken down. The roads were pitted or covered in rubble. The only working vehicles belonged to the U.S. Army. The soldiers were more than willing to let civilians catch rides with them, although they tended to favor women and the elderly.[49]

Despite the collapse of the road network, people began looking for family, friends, and neighbors. Silvio Escolano, a teenager, wandered up to the Echevarria house in the Singalong district. His friends Purita and Mike Echevarria welcomed him into their house. He told his story: when US shells began landing near their home, he and his family left. His mother was killed by a shell fragment and a Japanese soldier shot and killed his father. He and his brother had become separated. He had come to their house to see if they had seen him. Despite requests that he stay, he left to continue looking for his brother. He said he was staying with an uncle in Pasay. His brother, Jose Luis Escolano, was, as it turned out, in a refugee center and unhurt. The two eventually found each other.[50]

The Japanese defenders were on the brink of an abyss. Individual soldiers and sailors knew the battle had turned against them. The Manila Naval Defense Force attempted to escape on the night of February 18, but communications among the defenders were so shattered that it was not possible to coordinate the withdrawal. The experience of the 3rd Squad, 6th Platoon, 1st Mixed Company (Provisional) is a case study in the larger problems facing the Defense Force. The squad, which was about twenty men strong, consisted of a collection of Japanese individuals impressed into the Navy. Many of them were civilians and were never formally inducted into the service. The group attempted to escape on small boats from Pier 1. Their goal was to reach Malabon, a city due north of Manila, and then hike up into the mountains to the east. They landed short of their destination and the 37th Division Reconnaissance Troop quickly discovered them and engaged them in a firefight. Iwamoto Hidoichi, a civilian from Okinawa, survived but then tried to use his grenade to kill himself. He had no idea how to use the device. An American soldier stopped this rather feeble effort at suicide and took him into custody.[51]

On February 19 and 20, much larger groups of the *makaibo* tried to escape from the city. First Class Seaman Iwanaga Hisanobu was an experienced sailor. He had been on the crew of the destroyer *Naganami* and had spent a day in the water after it was sunk during the Battle of Ormoc Bay. He had little training as an infantryman, however, and it showed on the night of February 19. Iwanaga was part of a 120-man group that attempted to fight its way out of Manila. They got no further than the front of the building when a US flare caused the group to disperse. Iwanaga and two others hid in a pillbox during the night and fell asleep. Machine-gun fire woke them the next morning and, believing the situation was dire and hopeless, the three decided to commit suicide. Iwanaga tried to use a grenade to take his life, but it went off before he was ready. He surrendered to soldiers of the 1st Cavalry later in the day.[52]

On February 20, China Asakichi, another Okinawan, was part of a large group that left Pier 3 in the evening. They made it to Malabon and crossed the Malabon River, before China and several others became separated from the larger group. After two days wandering about, China and his group were captured.[53]

The work of US psychological warfare units was also having an effect on Japanese survivors. Izumida Zenzo was a thirty-nine-year-old businessman who had been impressed into the army. He surrendered toward the end of the battle after hearing surrender broadcasts blared out over loudspeakers. He did not believe in the code of *bushido* and sat down with military intelligence interrogators to freely talk about the situation facing the Japanese. Officers, he said, had begun throwing away their weapons and committing suicide as early as February 13, leaving command to those with little experience. Izumida was blunt. Junior officers were blundering idiots. There was no honor in dying for such incompetent fools. He told the Americans that many of the men in the ranks had similar views, but refused to consider surrender because they feared they would be tortured and killed. Propaganda leaflets had to address that issue.[54]

Filipinos confirmed some of what Izumida said. By this third week of the battle, the Japanese had stopped committing atrocities and were changing into civilian clothes in an attempt to smuggle themselves out of the city.[55]

Even Rear Admiral Iwabuchi Sanji knew the end was near. After returning to Manila, the admiral had set up command in the Finance Building. Yamashita was unhappy with this development. He sent a telegram to Lieutenant General Yokoyama Shizuo wanting an explanation for why the admiral had returned to the city. The implication of the message was that Yokoyama had ordered or authorized this move. At roughly the same time, Iwabuchi's headquarters sent a telegram to Yokoyama's headquarters stating that they were surrounded and were unable to leave their location. The general was unwilling to accept that answer and instructed Iwabuchi to make a strenuous effort. Communication between the two headquarters continued for several days, but nothing came of them.[56]

There was a reason. Iwabuchi was on a death ride. He was determined to take as many people with him as he could, and nothing was going to change his mind. With the close of the strong points—the fifth crucial event of the battle—that was all he could do now.

The 37th Infantry Division arrived on Luzon on January 9, 1945, in an uncontested amphibious assault on Lingayen beach. The first two weeks on Luzon were a period of easy soldiering as the Japanese made little effort to block the US advance toward Manila. (Official U.S. Army Photo)

General of the Army Douglas MacArthur, standing on a balcony of the Manila City Hall. The ruins of one of the government buildings is in the background. Manila was the closest thing that MacArthur had to a home, and he was expecting that the liberation would be an easy operation. When it proved otherwise, his large but frail ego cracked. He failed to provide any strategic guidance to his subordinates. (Official U.S. Army Photo)

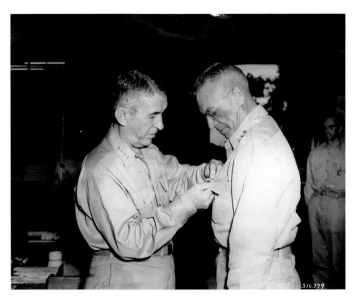

Walter Krueger (left) was the commanding general of the Sixth U.S. Army, and Oscar W. Griswold (right) was the commanding general of the XIV Infantry Corps. This photo was taken several months after the Battle of Manila ended, after both had received another general's star. Krueger is presenting Griswold an oak leaf cluster to his Distinguished Service Medal in lieu of another award. During the battle, both MacArthur and Krueger failed to give Griswold strategic direction. As a result, he made do and let operational and tactical concerns drive the fight, which posed a serious long-term threat to US strategic interests. (Official U.S. Army Photo)

Major General Robert S. Beightler, commanding general, 37th Infantry Division, was the only general from the National Guard who maintained command of his unit throughout the war, which is testimony to his professional competence. He is pictured here greeting his son, who was an officer in the 11th Airborne Division, which was also taking part in the battle for Manila. (Official U.S. Army Photo)

One of the key factors that allowed the U.S. Army to maneuver its forces quickly was clear and rapid communications. The Signal Corps began establishing radio and phone communications, which was fairly easy because the infrastructure already existed on Luzon and had not been damaged during the Japanese occupation. (Official U.S. Army Photo)

Transportation issues were major logistical problems for the Americans when they arrived on Luzon. The railroad network was still in place, but the Army lacked the rolling stock to make use of it. One solution was to put flanged wheels on jeeps, which helped a little, but not a lot. (Official U.S. Army Photo)

Major General Spencer B. Aiken (center) and Brigadier General William C. Chase (right) chat in Manila. Aiken was MacArthur's signal officer and escaped from Corregidor in 1942 with him. His signal corpsmen did an impressive job of maintaining communication between headquarters and combat units. Chase commanded the flying column that reached Manila and shortly thereafter received a promotion to major general and command of a division. (Official U.S. Army Photo)

Lieutenant General Richard Sutherland was MacArthur's chief of staff for the entire war. Their relationship soured when he put continuing an extramarital affair with a woman in Australia over his official duties. His absence had a negative impact on planning work. When he returned, his influence on the staff was basically gone, and that also had a negative impact on events concerning Manila. (Official U.S. Army Photo)

Major General Verne D. Mudge was commanding general of the 1st Cavalry Division. Mudge graduated from the University of Florida before he earned an appointment to the U.S. Military Academy. He spent his entire military career in the cavalry. He practiced leadership by example, but he tended to be reckless in this regard, often performing the job of a platoon sergeant rather than that of a two-star general. This behavior eventually resulted in a major wound that forced his retirement from the Army and created chronic health issues that cost him his life a decade later. (Official U.S. Army Photo)

The speed of the "flying column" was crucial in setting a tempo which was too fast for the Japanese to counter. The actual actions were a little less glamorous than its name suggests. Here the vehicles are fording the Angat River with tanks pulling the jeeps and trucks across. When the water reached the engines of the smaller vehicles, they would stop working. (Official U.S. Army Photo)

The 37th Infantry Division was in a race with the 1st Cavalry Division to be the first into Manila. For most of that double-pronged advance, the Guardsmen were in the lead, even though they lacked mechanization. They had a path that took them over more bridges than the horsemen, which were targets the Japanese hit to slow down the US advance. Resistance also increased just outside of the city, costing the foot soldiers the race. (Official U.S. Army Photo)

The 11th Airborne Division was one of the pioneering units in parachute infantry tactics. To goad Krueger to move faster, MacArthur authorized the Eighth Army to conduct an invasion of southern Luzon. As a result, the division did an amphibious assault and an airborne drop on Tagaytay Ridge shown in progress here to move rapidly toward Manila. The 11th Airborne's advance on the city meant that there was a three-way race into the city. (Official U.S. Army Photo)

The Japanese began burning Manila even before US soldiers reached the city. The smoke from the destruction replaced the cityscape in the view from the Paranaque Bridge south of Manila as the 11th Airborne Division approached from the south. (Official U.S. Army Photo)

The front page of the Chicago *Daily Times* shows how much of a major news story the liberation of Manila was in the United States (Library of Congress)

This editorial cartoon from *The Evening Bulletin* in Philadelphia was typical of many that appeared in newspapers across the country, giving credit exclusively to Douglas MacArthur. (Library of Congress)

The liberated internees of the Santo Tomás internment camp began celebrating their freedom immediately. A giant US flag that had clearly been kept hidden was hung in front of the main building. (Official U.S. Army Photo)

General of the Army Douglas MacArthur visited Santo Tomás on February 7. His visit to the university was a major and emotional moment for the residents. Many had known him before the war but had to introduce themselves despite MacArthur's powerful memory because starvation had changed their physical appearances. (Official U.S. Army Photo)

Soldiers of the 1st Cavalry Division work to breach the walls of the Rizal Baseball Stadium. The fight for this facility took an entire day. (Official U.S. Army Photo)

Reflecting the callousness that combat breeds, troopers of the 1st Cavalry Division march past the body of a Japanese defender in the Paco section of Manila. (Official U.S. Army Photo)

This photograph of US soldiers firing a 37-millimeter gun captures some of the nature of urban warfare. The shells created divots when they hit the asphalt of streets or the cement of sidewalks or building walls, creating clouds of dust and particles that obscured lines of sight. (Official U.S. Army Photo)

Members of a patrol from the 148th Infantry Regiment, 37th Infantry Division draw out the location of Japanese defenders by putting a helmet on a stick and exposing it around the corner of a wall. These types of playground tactics worked because of the lack of training and skill among the defenders. (Official U.S. Army Photo)

Combat support branches played crucial roles while in Manila. During the fight, military intelligence personnel took roughly four hundred prisoners of war. These prisoners often had useful tactical information. Intelligence personnel needed to debrief them quickly. Filipino guerrillas were more interested in revenge, which often created races against the clock to rescue POWs. As a result, intelligence units became an important institutional mechanism to limit the killing. (Official U.S. Army Photo)

Engineers played a crucial supporting role as the Americans liberated the city. Some units repaired bridges and others removed the thousands upon thousands of mines the Japanese had planted in Manila. The men in this photo are removing the fuse of a mine. Since the Japanese had planted these mines with little skill, removing them was not too difficult, but many times the efforts took place under fire. Artillery often used smoke shells to obscure the vision of Japanese defenders while these teams rendered this ordinance inert. (Official U.S. Army Photo)

Speed had been crucial to the US advance on Luzon, and while it slowed down, the U.S. Army still had the ability to slice through the defenders. In this photo, an infantry-tank team from the 148th Infantry Regiment, 37th Infantry Division advances against enemy fire on Taft Avenue. (Official U.S. Army Photo)

The ruins of the Great Eastern Hotel, which was on the northern bank of the Pasig River, proved to be an excellent artillery observation post for the 37th Infantry Division. The observers could call down fire with a great deal of precision. (Official U.S. Army Photo)

These dead Japanese defenders lie on the side of General Luna Street in the Walled City after making a kamikaze charge. (Official U.S. Army Photo)

The Japanese used this 5.3-inch naval gun in the defense of the Finance Building. The background of this photo makes it clear that the flat, open area around the buildings offered little place for US personnel to hide when making assaults on the government buildings. (Official U.S. Army Photo)

The U.S. Army placed artillery guns at Santo Tomás University. The open areas of the university were ideal locations for the big guns and allowed them to hit many targets in the center of the city. The problem was that these guns made the university a legitimate military target. The Japanese did indeed shell the school, and they killed or maimed many of the recently freed internees. (Official U.S. Army Photo)

Efforts to provide relief to residents of Manila began even before the fighting ended. This crowd in front of a movie theater on Rizal Avenue is waiting for a rice ration from a civil affairs unit. (Official U.S. Army Photo)

The airborne assault on Corregidor was a calculated gamble. The landing zones were small and were right in front of Japanese positions, and trees were dangerous obstacles on which a few men were impaled. (Official U.S. Army Photo)

Colonel George Jones was the commander of the US attack on Corregidor. Wounded slightly in the airborne assault, he and his men were outnumbered, but they managed to divide the Japanese defenders, neutralizing their advantage. (Official U.S. Army Photo)

An infantry tank team from the 34th Infantry Regiment advance on a Japanese defensive position. Although the Japanese had superior numbers on the island, they squandered that advantage while holding a series of isolated positions which were easy for the Americans to overwhelm. (Official U.S. Army Photo)

MacArthur attended a flag-raising ceremony at the parade grounds on Corregidor where Colonel George Jones and the men of the 503rd Parachute Infantry Regiment presented the liberated island to the general. (Official U.S. Army Photo)

17

The Attack on the Walled City, February 23–24

The battle for Manila was nearing an end, but American forces still faced a serious obstacle if they wanted to control the city. They had to do something that had never been done before: breach the walls of the Intramuros and take control of this massive fortification. The attack on the Walled City would be the seventh and final turning point of the battle.

When Miguel López de Legazpi seized control of the Philippines in 1571 in the name of King Philip II of Spain, he ordered the building of the Walled City. Located where the Pasig River meets Manila Bay, the stronghold controlled access to the north and south harbors. Although the fortress had changed hands several times in its three and half centuries, no foe had ever taken control of the citadel in combat. "The Intramuros is a formidable obstacle," Griswold noted in his diary.[1]

Americans often referred to the stronghold as "ancient" and "Medieval." These terms were wrong. The architecture actually dates from the early modern period in European history and followed the styles of sixteenth-century Europe. Its stone walls were massive. They stood twenty feet tall, they were forty feet thick at their base, and twenty feet thick at their top. The Spanish had built a moat around the fortress, although (as noted earlier) the Americans had converted it into a golf course and sunken garden. These open grounds actually served the Japanese well, giving the Americans no place to hide as they charged toward the walls.[2]

Griswold and others did not realize at the time that they had already reduced much of the citadel's military utility. The battle for the strong points the previous week—the Manila Hotel, the Post Office, the Army Navy Club—had isolated the Walled City. As the 37th Division maneuvered to attack, Stephen

L. Garay, an officer on the division staff, noted, "The fortress was practically impotent." The lack of experience in ground operations among its defenders was beginning to tell. "Consequently, the fortress itself, offered only token resistance while the division wheeled into position for the final assault." The failure to challenge this maneuver put the Japanese at a huge disadvantage when the mass and coordination of US firepower slammed down upon them.[3]

The Japanese inside the Walled City were not that impressive a force. There were two infantry battalions-worth of men, and the Japanese had whittled away at their own numbers by sending patrols out on suicidal night raids. Only about two-thirds of the men in the fortress had rifles.[4]

Even with these strengths, Griswold decided to try to avoid battle. At 1:30 p.m. on February 16, he had the following message broadcast in Japanese:

> TO THE COMMANDER OF THE JAPANESE FORCES IN INTRAMUROS:
> Your situation is hopeless—your defeat inevitable. I offer you an honorable surrender. If you decide to accept raise a large Filipino flag over the Red Cross Flag now flying and send an unarmed emissary with a white flag to our lines. This must be done shortly or I am coming in. In event you do not accept my offer I exhort you that, true to the spirit of the Bushido and the code of the Samurai, you permit all civilians to evacuate the Intramuros by the Victoria gate without delay, in order that no innocent blood be shed.[5]

Prisoners of war taken later confirmed that the Japanese received the message, yet it failed for a number of reasons. Partly this was because it used objectional terms like "surrender." The chief cause, however, was that it was an ultimatum aimed at leadership that had already decided to pursue death in combat. The note gave them no reason to turn back.[6]

Despite having the favors of fortune, Griswold could see the price combat was having on his staff and subordinates. "The strain of this battle is very noticeable on us all," he told his diary. "Very slow progress, with bitter fighting. We are constricting enemy in a smaller space day by day," the general observed.[7]

After receiving Krueger's orders to start planning an attack on the Walled City, the staff of the 37th Division began that work on February 16, which gave them a good seven days to prepare. To prevent the Japanese from moving their forces from one part of Intramuros to another, the division would attack from the north and northeast. To keep the Japanese from retreating, the 1st Cavalry Brigade would act as a blocking force on the west and southwest sides of the fort. General Beightler wanted to use firepower to destroy as much of the enemy force as possible and planned on an intense artillery barrage. He also wanted air units to bomb the citadel. Griswold agreed reluctantly. Krueger approved the request and even assigned units to the task.[8]

MacArthur rejected the idea. The benefit was not worth the cost to him. "The use of air on a part of a city occupied by a friendly and Allied population is unthinkable." The chances of accidentally hitting Filipinos were far too high. He also knew there was no real reason for this request. "It is not believed moreover that this would appreciably lower our own casualty rate although it would unquestionably hasten the conclusion of the operation."[9]

Griswold was conflicted and resentful at MacArthur's response: "I fear that the C in C's refusal to let me have bombing will result in more casualties to my men. However, I understand how he feels about bombing people—but it is being done all over the world—Poland, China, England, Germany, Italy—then why not here!" Griswold had missed the political point MacArthur had made about bombing their own allies. As a corps commander, he was thinking in operational rather than strategic terms. "War is never pretty. I am frank to say I would sacrifice civilian Philipino [sic] lives under such circumstances to save the lives of my men. I feel quite bitter about this tonight."[10]

Beightler, Griswold, and Krueger were thinking along tactical lines. In their history of the battle, the historians Richard Connaughton, John Pimlott, and Duncan Anderson argue that the US unit commanders had an aversion to taking high casualties. They focused on Beightler because he was a National Guard officer leading a Guard unit. "He would have to face hostility back home if he allowed his units to be destroyed," the three declared.[11] Beightler's own words do not support that view. He was more than willing to sacrifice lives if necessary. Nor did his staff second-guess the inevitability of casualties. His operations officer, Lieutenant Colonel Russell A. Ramsey, a Guard officer himself, rejected a proposal to use US Army Rangers in the assault, even though using a unit from outside the Ohio Guard might have reduced the casualty rates among the division.[12]

The question of using air power seems to be an example of resource overkill. Beightler was asking for everything he could get, even if the plan did not really require certain specific assets. He admitted as much to William Grey of Time-Life: He wanted "every bit of firepower I can scrape together."[13] His reasons were straight forward: "We've had it tough. I never saw such a scrap. Jungle fighting never was as tough as this."[14] As for Griswold, his support was pro forma. He had not been briefed on the plan. He would not see the details until the evening of February 22, the night before the assault.[15]

After the war, Beightler admitted the absence of airpower had not been significant. He was open about the fact that he had used his big guns to destroy the property. In his final report, he stated, "If I could have had those dive-bombers too, I might have made the big rubble into little rubble." His rationale was that the lives of his soldiers were more important than the property rights of foreigners. That argument, though, is misleading. There was no military need to make more rubble. Beightler was ignoring the wider political and economic ramifications of turning the biggest city of a nation into a giant slum, and he was ignoring the human cost.[16]

When it came to the grim accounting of lives lost, the lack of precision among the Americans in their use of heavy artillery was less significant than Japanese atrocities. The Japanese Army had started systematically killing civilians in the Walled City before the American siege. The order from the Kobayashi Group was simple and direct: Filipino guerrilla groups, which included women and children, were helping the Americans. Even public support for the guerrillas made Manileños hostile to the empire. "All people on the battle-field with the exception of Japanese military personnel, Japanese civilians, and Special Constr[uction] Units will be put to death." The diary of a Japanese soldier who served in the Walled City offers a blunt record of the massacre:

> 7 Feb 45—150 guerrillas were disposed of tonight. I personally stabbed and killed 10.
> 8 Feb 45—Guarded over 1,164 guerrillas which were newly brought in today
> 9 Feb 45—Burned 1,000 guerrillas to death tonight.
> 10 Feb 45—Guarded approx. 1,000 guerrillas.
> 13 Feb 45—Enemy tanks are lurking in the vicinity of Banzai Bridge. Our attack preparation has been completed. I am on guard duty at Guerrilla Internment Camp. While I was on duty, approx 10 guerrillas tried to escape. They were stabbed to death. At 1600 all guerrillas were burned to death.[17]

These efforts continued even after the Americans began shelling the citadel on February 18.

The Japanese were doing a lot of the killing—murdering—and were still looking to execute more "guerrillas." They were also committing sexual violence. On February 17, a group of Japanese soldiers entered the Hospital of San Juan de Dios, the largest in the Intramuros. They took the two doctors,

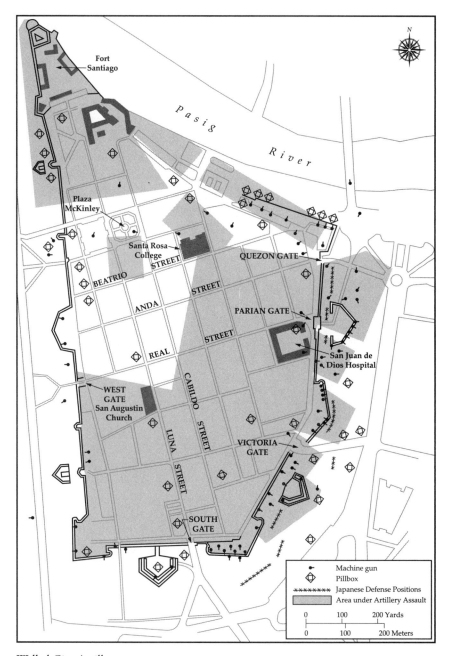

Walled City Artillery

a chemist, a dentist, and a medical assistant with them. All of them were males. They also took a female nurse. People in the hospital could hear their executions. The next day a volunteer went looking for them and found their bodies along with those of fifteen women and children the Japanese had raped before killing.[18]

The Japanese continued the slaughter, separating the men and women in the Walled City. The women were housed in the San Augustin Church. The men were housed in a warehouse across from the Santa Clara Convent. The men were marched past the church, which was last time families saw one another. The Japanese then took the men to Fort Santiago and put one group in the air raid shelters. They machine gunned another group that could not fit inside. They then dropped grenades down the air vents into the shelters. Many died slowly.[19]

Father Juan Labrador did not understand the utility of this type of killing, or even the suicidal last stand in Manila. "What are the Japanese achieving by these killings—of others and of themselves?" he wrote in his diary.[20]

Labrador made an important point. The military threat to the garrison was coming from outside the citadel, not from within. Killing civilians was a waste of their limited ammunition. The artillery units of the 37th Division spent five days firing their heavy guns against Intramuros. Expecting an attack from the landward side, the Japanese had concentrated most of their defensive positions on the east wall. As a result, most of the US ordinance fell on that wall. "Here the division used twentieth-century technology with medieval tactics, employing direct fire to expand existing gaps in the walls and to make additional openings for the infantry," John R. Walker, a historian of the artillery branch, observed.[21] Launching these projectiles began bordering on the rote for the gun crews. During the first day of the shelling, Grey, of Time-Life, found Captain Francis X. Shannon, Jr., commanding officer of an artillery company, reading while the shells whistled past. He apparently had few choices and was reading *Margery Wilson's Pocket Book of Etiquette*.[22]

As shells crashed down on them, many Japanese decided to desert the Walled City. After the 1st Company, 9th Battalion, Akatsuki Force was annihilated in the early US shelling, Takemura Shiruichi, a civilian who had been impressed into the company, decided to save himself. He and several others—a number somewhere in the mid-teens—swam out to the half-sunken hulks that littered Manila Bay. Then they simply sat on those ships, trying to figure out what to do next.[23]

The military intelligence detachments of the XIV Corps did not know about these deserters at the time, and they had more important things to do, including conducting prisoner of war debriefings and hastily translating captured documents. The Intramuros was a significant blank spot. On February 21, two days before the scheduled assault on the walls, the situation seemed to change with the capture of a prisoner of war who had deserted. Filipino guerrillas, however, killed him before language personnel had a chance to take him into custody and interrogate him.[24]

* * *

February 23 began early for the men of the 37th Infantry Division. The 129th Infantry was encamped roughly three miles away to the north, so the officers and sergeants of the 1st and 3rd Battalions had to roust their men out of their tents before dawn so they could be in their attack positions at 6:00 a.m.[25] The division staff planned for an hour-long barrage just before they crossed the Pasig River. The night before the attack, the division brought in additional artillery; there were now 120 guns and mortars ready for the final assault. The big guns were located to the east and north of walled city on the other side of the Pasig. Most of the US units were a half-mile to a mile-and-a-half away from their targets, which was a ridiculously short range. The artillery barrage began at 7:30 a.m. at a rate of one hundred shells per minute. Tanks and anti-tank guns joined in the assault a few minutes later. Donald Starr of the *Chicago Daily Tribune* observed that "the tanks buck like mules kicking as they fire their 75s." Twenty minutes after the barrage started, a column of grey-white smoke reached nearly two miles up into the air above the Intramuros.[26]

The XIV Corps, the 37th Infantry Division, and some artillery batteries were using two multi-story buildings on the northern bank of the Pasig— the Great Eastern Hotel and the Ayala Building—as observation posts. War correspondents assembled on the sixth floor of the hotel and watched as shells arced over the building and slammed into the walls of the old Spanish fort. Gene Sherman of the *Los Angeles Times* called it a "virtual press box" and compared it to covering the Rose Bowl. He was only two hundred yards away from the Walled City. In this position, they were actually in front of both the artillery gun crews and the infantry, which were several hundred yards behind them. Sherman noted a bit later, "It was a perfect grandstand seat, the most startling view of war I've ever had. You could see everything." Royal Arch Gunnison explained that the building allowed reporters to stand on one side and look down on the Japanese, and then they could walk to the other side and look down on the Americans.[27] Twenty-five minutes into the barrage, the Japanese began shooting at the building and the journalists dove for cover.[28]

The density of the bombardment was a problem for the artillerymen. Sergeant William Muller explained that he and other forward observers could no longer direct fire because of the grime in the air: "I can't see anything until the clouds of dust and smoke lift."[29] Sound was also a problem. The noise of the shells was so deafening that other spotters could not use their radios and telephones to adjust fire. They had to result to relaying commands via hand signals.[30]

The heavy guns delivered blows against the Walled City that awed many of the Americans on the north side of the river. Frank Mathias, the 37th Division bandsman, was doing duty as a machine-gun operator and was providing covering fire during the river crossing: "We stared in amazement, feeling the air shudder as the powerful shells ripped into the ancient buildings."[31] Sherman saw the concussion from shell bursts shake trees on the northern side of the river and lift birds in the air straight up.[32] Brigadier General James Lester, the commanding general of XIV corps artillery, said he had never seen artillery this condensed in either world war.[33]

To the east at Bilibald Prison, William A. Owens watched shells as they hurtled forward "like lightning bolts from the hands of an angry god." The assault soon began working against his counterintelligence work. Filipinos interviewees became less cooperative, blaming the Americans along with the Japanese for the destruction of the city.[34]

The beating those in the citadel were taking was devastating. The numbers and accuracy of US artillery impressed those on the receiving end. Noguchi Kazuo, a Japanese civilian whom the Army had given a gun, survived. He had a severe concussion and part of his skull had been crushed. In a POW debriefing he explained that the heavy and light machine guns, mortars, and anti-tank guns of his unit simply disappeared in the barrage. Superior Private Suda Kazuo figured that the artillery exchange rate was one hundred to one, and he failed to understand how the United States could afford to use that much ordinance.[35]

William Dunn of CBS was in the observation post of the XIV Corps with Griswold. "I had been impressed with the naval shore bombardments at Glouscester, Leyte, and Lingayen, but none of them could compare with the artillery barrage that struck those ancient walls," he explained. Dunn always believed that the hearing issues he suffered later in life were a side effect of the bombardment. One of the main reasons he and so many others found the artillery barrage so overpowering was its proximity.[36]

At 8:30 a.m., as planned, the shelling stopped. In that one hour, the XIV Corps had fired 11,237 rounds, or 185 tons of ordinance. That represented a fourth of the shells used during the entire Battle of Manila. Some of it was ineffective. The 105-millimeter and the 75-millimeter guns on tanks did not produce enough velocity to penetrate stone and cement, and observers actually reported seeing shells bounce off the walls and splash into the river.[37]

The artillery battalions were going through their munitions quickly, and not everything worked as planned. During the battle, Robert F. Minch, a truck driver in 756th Field Artillery Battalion, volunteered to get more ammunition. "I thought maybe I would get a good meal, because it was in the back. All the supplies and so." When he arrived at the supply dump, he found it deserted. "It was unreal, kind of unbelievable."[38]

The sudden halt was jarring to many. Within minutes, the men of the 3rd Battalion, 129th Infantry Regiment came out from where they had been hunkering down and were in boats crossing the river. In his command post, Griswold remarked, "Now there's nothing I can do but sweat. I've given them all I've got and they're under a higher command."[39]

The assault force was at its most vulnerable on the water; there was tension in the air. Mortars fired canisters of smoke to cover their advance. The division had twenty-six machine guns covering the crossing; their targets were Japanese machine gun positions, but four had orders to look for targets of opportunity. Griswold was heard muttering out loud, "God bless them! God bless them!" Dunn thought these remarks were appropriate: "You could sense the unspoken prayer behind those blessings."[40]

While the 129th was crossing the river, the 145th Infantry Regiment charged past the General Post Office and attacked the northernmost gate on the east wall of the Intramuros. It took them three minutes to cover the ground. The boats crossing the river took six. The artillery then began firing smoke canisters into the Walled City, creating a cloud in the middle of the citadel, blocking Japanese observations of the troops assaulting the walls. The artillery batteries also placed a wall of smoke in front of the Legislative and Finance Buildings, to keep them from providing fire support to the defenders inside the Intramuros. Only one Japanese machine gun fired on the advance, and it was silenced

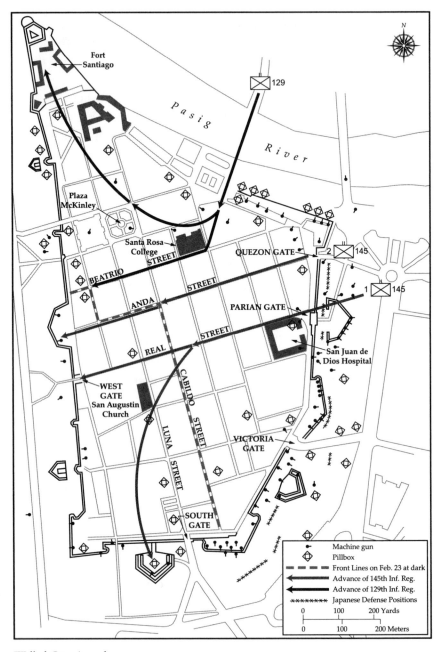

Walled City Assault

quickly. At 8:35, Company F, 2nd Battalion, 145th Infantry broke through the Quezon Gate at the northeastern corner of the fortress, becoming the first military unit in the 374-year history of the Walled City to breach its walls.[41]

Inside the complex, the two US regiments took only sporadic, isolated Japanese rifle and machine-gun fire. They met up quickly and took control of the northern tip of the citadel. Japanese resistance increased significantly as they moved deeper into the interior. A full-scale battle took place at Fort Santiago, which is located at the northwestern corner of the Intramuros. Infantry units fought floor-to-floor using bazookas, flame throwers, and got support from tanks. Even with that help, it took the rest of the day before the Americans had control of the stronghold.[42]

Maynard E. Mahan, a staff sergeant in the 129th, took cover behind some rubble and lit a cigarette. Resting, he closed his eyes until a nearby mortar explosion rained fragments down on him. He was not hurt but he realized that one shell splinter had come so close that it had ripped the cigarette out of his mouth.[43]

For the most part, though, the mortar fire was more of a threat to the Japanese. Shelling separated units, and individual Japanese sailors gave up trying to fight. Their main goal—their only goal—was to escape. Some evaded US units for several days before they were captured. Many were killed in individual incidents.[44]

The combat service-support branches began their work inside the citadel immediately. The 117th Engineer Battalion began clearing debris that was blocking the narrow roads of Intramuros. They found only one minefield inside the fortress and cleared it while under fire.[45]

During this operation, the 2nd Battalion, 129th Infantry was in reserve, guarding the regiment's encampment site several miles to the rear. What should have been easy duty instead became an example of the lack of well-established frontlines in Manila. The battalion came under fire at 10 a.m. from a group of Japanese. The attackers had mortars, wounding and killing several, but the 2nd Battalion held.[46]

Inside the walled city, the rescue of civilians began almost immediately. At 9:20 a.m., less than an hour after the walls had been broken open, Colonel John Frederick, commanding officer of the 129th, was reporting back to the division staff that he had refugees that he needed to evacuate. Many were wounded.[47] More were to come. The Japanese were holding as many as three thousand Filipinos in the San Augustine Church as prisoners. As the Americans neared the building, the Japanese decided to release their hostages. Carmen de la Vara-Minquez, one of the prisoners, believed it was a trick. "We were always prepared to meet death. We lost track of time. I could not believe that the Japanese were setting us free. I could not believe it!"[48] There was a mass confusion following this move. The Americans held their fire when they realized what the Japanese had done. The defenders, though, continued to direct machine-gun fire at their opponents. Francisco Gonzalez and ten members of his family left the church together, but a Japanese sniper—apparently acting on his own—decided to target them. "The sniper was a poor shot," Gonzales later said. "And thanks, because if he was a good one we would have all been finished."[49]

Antonio O. Gisbert was one of the few men in the group the Japanese released. A resident of the Intramuros, he was nonetheless completely lost. Familiar landmarks and buildings had been destroyed and the streets were full of rubble. He stumbled in a westerly direction until US soldiers found him and helped. Brother Jose Ma. Manjabacas, a lay Franciscan from Spain, had been hiding from the Japanese for two days, but now his resolution was broken and he decided to surrender himself. Weak and delirious from hunger and thirst, he raised his hands and approached a group of Japanese and told one of them, "Brother, I am dead of hunger and thirst." Manjabacas was delirious. The "Japanese" were actually US infantrymen, and at least one of them spoke Spanish.[50]

The Americans directed the refugees to their boats to ferry them across the river and out of the combat zone. Quartermaster units, having to take long, roundabout routes, arrived at the Parian Gate, located in the middle of the east wall to evacuate other refugees. When Sister Concepcion Gotera saw the American soldiers, she was speechless. "The feelings I felt were beyond words to utter. Heavens! Is this a dream!" She decided to kiss the hands of an American soldier. "Overwhelmed with gratitude, I pressed tightly and kissed the big strong hands of the first American soldier I met. He understood and gave a really assuring smile as a big brother would to a weak helpless sister."[51]

This type of gratitude was commonplace. Henry Keys, a British war correspondent, went into the Intramuros with the foot soldiers. A lieutenant told him to go to the St. Augustine convent if he wanted a good story. Keys approached a statue near the convent. He did not remember who the statue depicted, but realized there was a mass of dead bodies surrounding it. One belonged to a little boy; he was kneeling in a crouching position, as if he had been praying, a bullet hole at the base of his skull. There was a pile of bodies to the left, covered in ash and dust, indicating they had been killed before the artillery barrage had started. Inside the convent, he saw another officer tending to a badly wounded girl, giving her water. In another room, a soldier showed him a young woman lying on the floor covered with a blanket. The American pulled back the blanket—she had no feet. Her amputated limbs had been tied off with handkerchiefs. Keys found the scene overwhelming, and afterward would attest that he blocked much of it out. When he left the convent, he saw some stretcher bearers and asked them to get the girl without feet. They did as he requested. As they left the convent, the girl raised her head and gave the "V" for victory sign to some soldiers.[52] Keys began to sob.[53]

At midday, the Americans were coming to realize that the Walled City operation was succeeding. At noon, Griswold visited Beightler's command post. Relieved of a good deal of stress, he hugged the division commander and said, "God bless you! The 37th did it! I knew it wouldn't fail!"[54] Someone declared that the attack "was one of the most beautifully conceived and perfectly executed plans I have ever known."[55]

The refugees slowed down the advance into the Intramuros. It took six hours to remove them all. Streets within the Walled City were full of holes and littered with huge chunks of debris. Walking down them was a challenge. On the other side of the Pasig, Krueger was watching the assault with Griswold. He noted that most of the refugees were women and children, realizing that the Japanese had killed the men.[56]

* * *

When dusk on February 23 came, the Japanese still held the southwestern corner of Intramuros. The Americans were at Anda Street, which ran east–west through the Walled City and was a block from San Augustine. The XIV Corps after-action report notes: "The fighting from the lifting of artillery fire until afternoon was done by infantry with infantry weapons, inasmuch as the mines, barricades, and layers of rubble interfered with the progress of tanks until armored bulldozers and engineers had cleared paths through the city."[57]

Griswold had taken a number of calculated gambles, and they were all turning out well. In addition to breaching the walls of Intramuros, the 11th Airborne Division had conducted an operation at Los Baños, a prison camp in the Province of Laguna to the southeast of Manila, that had rescued over two thousand military and civilian prisoners. "This February 23d is the biggest day to date in XIV Corps history," he wrote in his diary.[58]

Adding to this reputation, the 5th Cavalry Regiment took full control of the University of the Philippines on that same day. Unlike other units that had engaged in room-to-room fights, the 5th Cavalry stayed in the Administrative Building after dark.[59] Accepting their defeat, the Japanese in Rizal Hall, a garrison of seventy-five, took their lives that evening.[60]

Of the two, the attack on the Walled City had weighed on him the most. "At 8:30 the Intramuros was successfully assaulted under cover of the fiercest artillery fire ever seen in the southwest Pacific area. I watched the men go through the breaches in the wall standing up. It was a great sight to see the gallant infantry of the 145th and 129th storm this strong medieval fortress manned by modern weapons. More glorious still the assault was made with very small casualties."[61]

Griswold believed this operation was almost over. "God has been good to me this day—and I am very grateful. I am sure that the battle for Manila will soon be history. It has been a great strain and responsibility."[62]

Beightler, for his part, was also happy with the operation. "Everything jibed perfectly," he declared.[63] In a letter home, he explained that it was "the perfect operation. It was tactically sound, we had the element of surprise, the artillery was perfect, and the execution of the infantry was something we all hope for but rarely get in all details."[64]

In his report on operations of the division, Beightler wrote: "We plastered the Walled City until it was a mess. It fell to us with ease we never expected."[65]

Fighting for MacArthur, though, required that soldiers be willing to forgo large amounts of public recognition, and that fact was beginning to wear on Beightler. "I'll never get much for I don't belong to the right fraternity," he groused. "I'm a National Guard officer and don't rate too high I'm afraid. But I have the satisfaction of knowing it was a job well done and was my plan entirely."[66]

While Beightler was reflecting on the battle, the Japanese were accepting that they were beaten. At 7:00 p.m. on February 23, the 3rd Battalion of the Manila Guard Unit decided to abandon the Intramuros. The plan was for the defenders to assemble at 8:00 p.m. in the southwest corner and then make their way out toward the east.[67]

The battle continued on February 24, but it was about finishing the job rather than seizing new territory. Fort Santiago was under US control, although large numbers of Japanese remained. The 3rd Battalion of the 129th Infantry spent the day fighting Japanese at the fort. Their daily G-3 report stated they killed four hundred defenders.[68]

Outside the walls of the Intramuros, the 1st Cavalry Brigade found itself busy with small groups of Japanese soldiers. On February 23, E Troop of the 5th Cavalry had been on a patrol with an accompanying tank when a Japanese machine gun in the Customs Building opened up with sputtering fire, cutting down Captain John Gregory. The rest of the patrol ran for cover. Gregory was left lying in the street in the open. Private First Class William J. Grabiarz dashed out from cover and attempted to drag his captain to safety. Taking a wound to his shoulder, he found this effort impossible. He decided instead to cover Gregory with his body and yelled directions to a tank to get in between them and the Japanese. The Japanese machine gunners hit him repeatedly before the tank blocked their fire.[69] Gregory survived. Grabiarz, nineteen years old, did not. His father accepted his Medal of Honor later that year.[70]

The fight for the Customs Building was hardly over. It took another day of "bitter floor to floor and room to room fighting" before the 12th Cavalry took the structure. With control of this facility, the troops had effectively secured the waterfront area.[71]

Now that they were in control of the Intramuros, the Americans began discovering evidence of Japanese atrocities. On that first day in the citadel, Frederick, of the 129th, found a stone building in Fort Santiago in which he saw the bodies of forty to fifty men. All of them had their hands tied behind their backs. Soldiers of the regiment found a smaller group of bodies in another building. After Fort Santiago was secured on February 24, Major Frank J. Middleberg, the regiment's intelligence officer, could smell death and took a small contingent of enlisted men looking for the source. He found the steel doors to the keep's prison cells. They had been barred from the outside and an explosion had wrenched them out of place. It took work to open them. "Men opening the doors said the stench struck them in the face as if it had physical force," Frederick noted in his report of this discovery. The bodies inside numbered in the hundreds.[72]

The destruction of the Intramuros was sobering. Two sergeants from the 145th were at the ruins of Santa Rosa College when they heard a baby crying. Digging through the debris, they found a six-month-old child in the arms of her dead mother under a staircase. The infant was rushed to an aid station, where she made a recovery.[73] George T. Folster of NBC Radio, after seeing the Walled City, called it "a wrecked place of murder."[74]

Griswold was disgusted with what he saw. On the evening of February 25, his chief of staff, Colonel Hugh M. Milton II, ordered Colonel James T. Walsh to investigate Japanese atrocities in Intramuros "to sort out fact from fancy in the many reports and rumors." Walsh's efforts were to be a supplement to another investigation under way by the XIV Corps inspector general.[75]

As far as MacArthur's headquarters was concerned, the taking of Intramuros was the end of the Battle of Manila. Press Communique Number 1055 announced: "Troops of the 37th Infantry and 1st Cavalry Divisions of the XIV Corp[s] overwhelmed the enemy's final positions in south MANILA and completed the destruction of the trapped garrison." After that LeGrande Diller and his men included no more mention of Manila in their daily press releases.[76]

This approach worked. An editorial on February 25 in *The Sun* of Baltimore declared that the city was "completely liberated." That attitude reflected the sentiment in most newsrooms and Manila disappeared as the subject of news accounts in the United States. The reporters on Luzon, for the most part, moved on to other aspects of the war.[77]

At the strategic level, this assessment had merit, but there was a problem. Taking the Walled City was the seventh turning point, giving the US control of the city and all its assets, but the battle had not ended. There were still hundreds of Japanese defenders in the government buildings. During the fight for the Intramuros, that area of the city had been a relatively inactive zone. The 1st Squadron, 5th Cavalry and small elements of the 148th Infantry Regiment had been containing the Japanese in the buildings.[78]

All of that was about to change.

18

The Fight for the Government Buildings

With the Intramuros in US hands, it appeared that reality had caught up with the press releases coming from MacArthur's headquarters. The Battle of Manila was over. That was the position of theater headquarters.[1] The problem was that the Japanese were once again not following MacArthur's script. What was left of the Manila Naval Defense Force still held the government buildings at the end of Luneta Park. These neo-classical structures were significant from a number of points of view—tactically, operationally, and even strategically. They needed to be taken.

In most parts of the city, the tempo of battle had indeed slowed down. Bridges still remained significant targets even if they were well behind the main line of contact.[2] Japanese night raids could force local retreats. The 117th Engineer Battalion was hit two nights in a row and had to cease bridge-building operations while under fire. In an inspection of Fort McKinley, George Kenney found himself in the line of fire between some Japanese holed up at the Post's Old Officers' club and Filipino guerillas.[3] Griswold noted in his diary: "Mopping up of isolated buildings and Intramuros still continuing. Army Commander here again today—and for once he was beaming."[4]

The units of the XIV Corps had ways to respond. The 37th Infantry Division did aggressive patrolling during the day, finding and fixing Japanese soldiers in place. The Intramuros was a particularly active zone for several days after its supposed liberation. In early March, the 37th Division still had snipers at work at key spots looking for Japanese stragglers.[5]

These issues were minor concerns. The Japanese main defensive perimeter had collapsed, and it was contained in the Legislative, Agricultural, and Finance Buildings at the eastern end of Luneta Park. A large rectangular area running on an east–west axis, the park comes within a few hundred yards of Manila Bay. The Finance Building was at the northeastern corner of the park, while the Agricultural Building was at its southeastern corner. They were about three hundred yards apart. Both were trapezoid-shaped with interior courtyards. The rectangular Legislative Building was located a few dozen yards to the northeast of the Finance Building, wedged in between it and the Intramuros. These buildings had been part of MacArthur's original objectives for the columns he threw at the city at the beginning of the month. All the Japanese in the building had firearms. Their supply of ammunition was limited, though, and they knew they would not be getting any more, so they conserved their shots.[6]

Renamed Rizal Park in the 1950s, the area has seen a great deal of development in the years since World War II, with many gardens, orchards, and memorials surrounding a large green space, but in 1945, it was a barren area of dirt with most of its vegetation burned off, making it impossible for the Americans to approach with any type of cover.[7] The Japanese had built trenches and tunnels connecting these buildings together. They also had the high ground, which meant that from the top floors they could fire on large expanses of the city, including the docks, which would impair US logistical and repair efforts. Griswold and Beightler's headquarters considered laying siege to the buildings, but then decided against the idea after learning from prisoners of war debriefings that the defenders had plenty of food and water. They even had beer, according to one POW.[8]

The Japanese had problems, though. Communication between and even inside these buildings was difficult. Recognizing their lack of command and control, officers in the buildings told their men to take independent action. Those orders did not necessarily translate into suicidal missions, and several groups tried to escape. Second Class Private Hayashi Toshime was in the Legislative Building when his battalion commander ordered the unit to penetrate American lines and die fighting. Hayashi had other ideas. He instead spent two days trying to evade Americans before he was captured.[9] Private First Class Okazaki Tatsumi lasted even longer, wandering the streets of Manila for several days.[10]

Active shooting had stopped in most parts of the city, but military activities continued. Engineers continued to remove obstacles from roads. They also destroyed pillboxes and other fortifications so the Japanese could not use them. The engineers managed to push the obstacles from the roads in Intramuros and within only three days had established one-way traffic. Other missions, like fixing leaking water pipes, building permanent bridges, and dismantling temporary bridges, continued to demand attention.[11]

The Japanese only complicated matters. On February 24, the daily report for the 117th Engineer Battalion states: "We find more Jap activity in the rear areas." The engineers had to do infantry work before they could do any construction. "Each morning is spent eliminating nests of enemy riflemen who had returned to our rear during the night." There was a great deal of stress to these actions. "Instead of rest and quiet anticipated they found they were spending half their time fighting and had killed more enemy there in the rest [area] than they had at the front."[12]

Japanese individuals were by now more willing to consider ending their fight. The sin of capture did not weigh as heavily on some of these individuals. Many believed because of faulty record-keeping and the slapdash nature of their incorporation into the Army and Navy, there was little chance that their names would be reported back to Japan. As a result, there would be little shame attached to surrender. The Koreans and Formosans, of course, cared little about Japanese honor and were more than willing to surrender.[13]

Some observers were beginning to contemplate the meaning of the battle. "What end did the Japanese High Command want to achieve with their plan of suicidal extermination," Father Juan Labrador asked his diary. He was attentive enough to note that the Japanese had created a situation necessitating much of the destruction of the city by Americans. "If a handful of valiant soldiers would take after Leonidas and his three hundred Spartans, that was understandable. But that hundreds of thousands or that the whole Army would be sacrificed for a national objective, only fanaticism or desperation could explain." That individual Japanese soldiers had been prevented from surrendering by their comrades and officers made the situation even more confounding. Tokyo, he figured, "wanted to drown national defeat and humiliation in blood." Their attitude seemed to be that the only redemption for defeat would be a disaster that in a way confirmed the central importance of Japan to the region. "War is hell. Men are transformed into demons converting the earth into an infernal fire."[14]

With the fighting at a low simmer, the time was right for US units to make good their losses. Replacement soldiers were arriving, but they were never enough. Even in March 1945, Europe was still the priority.[15] The replacements found that they were treated well. "I was to learn that most Infantry men try

to give the replacement the true low down as quickly and accurately as possible," Hanson recalled. The veterans played down the dangers they were going
to be facing and offered advice on how to survive combat. Lynn L. Simpson,
a sergeant in the division, recalled that the replacements were "young—
inexperienced but needed."

That was also the view of officers. "We considered replacements a gift, and
used the buddy system teaming them with an older man," Major Charles
Henne recalled. This attitude also existed toward officer replacements. Henne
noted that officer quality at this stage of the war was not as good as it had
been early on. "I found you had to help them along, just as though the[y] were
recruits." The effort was worth making. "Not all shake and bakes"—a popular term for newcomers—"were incompetent." Their presence altered the
composition of squads, platoons, and companies that had become cohesive
organizations. Scorn was also directed at them, not for being new but for being
incompetent. Those that learned quickly made those negative feelings dissipate; those that did not often never fit in or had to transfer to another unit.[16]

Those same basic patterns held in the 1st Cavalry Division. "Not a thing
wrong with them," John C. Dilks recalled of the replacements that arrived in
his field artillery unit in March. Pat Shovlin, an officer who first joined his unit
while it was still in combat, noted that he was "welcomed." The cavalrymen
had a similar program of pairing up a new soldier with a veteran and getting
him as much insight into combat as quickly as possible.[17] "They just kind of
threw us into the battle, and from our training we knew pretty much what to
do," Jim Duratz recalled.[18]

The system for getting the replacements to their units was rather haphazard,
though. It took Hanson five days in Manila before he reported to duty with
the F Company, 2nd Battalion, 148th Infantry. The fact that he was trained
as an engineer did not matter. He found others in the same situation, even
for those trained for service in combat arms branches. The army needed foot
soldiers, and he was in the infantry now—like it or not.[19]

The mopping-up of lone gunmen, the ever-present threat of attack at night,
patrolling, and the dirty work of punching through buildings covered in the
dust of masonry, stone, and concrete—along with the ever-present stench of
the dead—had a grinding effect. The 1st Cavalry's semi-official published history calls Manila "an unbelievable nightmare. By comparison, Dante's Inferno
would have seemed like a week-end at the Waldorf."[20] Foot soldiers had many
reactions to their duty in the city. Sometimes their negative reactions had a

positive boomerang effect. "Fear," Salvatore V. DeGaetano of the 1st Cavalry Division explained, "is one thing that keeps one alert + having good G.I.s left and right of you—who know the mission makes one appreciate his peers + the entire unit."[21]

A large number of soldiers and civilians turned to religion to deal with the stress. "(Yes) I prayed in our fox hole," DeGaetano observed years later.[22] There should be little surprise in that fact. If measured by regular and semi-regular church attendance, the United States was a religious nation in 1945.[23] Nonetheless, Henne, the executive officer of the 1st Battalion, 148th Infantry, thought that chaplains "were more of a hindrance than a help." He explained: "A wimp chaplain is worse than no chaplain." He appears to have been a distinct minority. "Prayer was extremely important," Frank Mathias of the 37th Division explained.[24] First Lieutenant Julius Gassner noted that religious services were well attended.[25]

Breaks from the actual shooting were necessary. For example, while a company was helping the 37th Infantry mop up in Intramuros, and another was shelling the government buildings, most of the 754th Tank Battalion spent February 28 through March 2 in inactive status, resting and repairing their vehicles.[26]

* * *

Given the dense granite, marble, and concrete construction of the three government buildings, the plan of attack was to spend two days shelling them with artillery fire at close range. The 155-millimeter howitzers of the 136th Field Artillery Battalion found positions at distances varying from 150 to 800 yards from the buildings. At those ranges, their shells could penetrate the exterior walls, although they also put artillerymen within reach of Japanese rifle and machine-gun fire.[27]

The 5th Cavalry began its assault on the Agricultural Building on the night of February 23–24. This building was the southern end of the Japanese line. At dawn, the dismounted troopers attacked and were turned back. Following this setback, the 136th Field Artillery Battalion and the 637th Tank Destroyer Battalion conducted direct fire operations against the building for the rest of the day.[28]

Despite this local victory, Rear Admiral Iwabuchi Sanji accepted that his end had come. He had apparently received messages from Kobayashi Shujiro telling him to escape. He refused. Gossip within the building was that the orders were fabricated. At dawn on February 26, Iwabuchi and several other officers committed suicide. With the Admiral's death, what little cohesion that the *makaibo* still retained vanished entirely. Military intelligence analysts inside the 37th Division noticed that hundreds of men began trying to escape from the buildings. The kill totals of various infantry units increased as well.[29]

That same day, at 9:00 a.m., the 1st Battalion, 148th Infantry Regiment attacked the Legislative Building. They got inside and the fighting was intense. The Japanese had filled the wide hallways with sandbags that turned the inside of the building into a maze. Since the sandbags did not reach all the way to the ceiling, the defenders could throw grenades over these makeshift walls. Turning corners was exceptionally dangerous. At 1:00 p.m., the battalion had control of limited portions of three floors. The Japanese held and stopped all further advances. After two hours, the battalion retreated, using smoke to cover their withdrawal. It only had two dead, but fifty-four wounded. POW interrogations later revealed that the Americans had outnumbered the defenders by three to one, or maybe even four to one.[30]

On February 27, a small group of US infantry companies tried again. Combat engineers cleared minefields around the building to facilitate the attack. Most of the 1st Battalion, though, was inactive and unable to clear the Intramuros area because of the danger that overlapping fire from the Finance and Legislative Buildings posed.[31]

After two hours, the artillery fire had turned the northern and southern wings of the Legislative Building into rubble. At 2:00 p.m., the battalion charged in again. Sergeant Cleto Rodriquez, whose actions at the Paco Railroad Station were about to result in his receiving the Medal of Honor, took his men around the rear and took out a machine-gun position. This time the unit made real progress. Rodriquez ran up the stairs to the second floor, taking out a Japanese defender before a grenade exploded. Taking a gashing wound to his face, he retreated but then rallied his platoon to charge up to the second floor. Rodriquez received the Silver Star for his efforts that day. After two hours, the Americans had control of the first floor. At 6:00 p.m., the building was under US control but dealing with the defenders in the basement would take until noon on February 28.[32]

While the 148th was attacking the Legislative Building, the 5th Cavalry again attacked the Agricultural Building. The Japanese had roughly six hundred to seven hundred men in the building at the start of the siege, most of them Navy personnel. Food supplies were plentiful, but water was not. The men were also low on ammunition.[33] The Japanese had minefields around the building, which delayed the deployment of the 136th Field Artillery Battalion's 155-millimeter guns.[34]

The first two attacks on the building failed. One of the reasons was that the Japanese were for once fighting as part of an interconnected network rather than as a series of strong points. Riflemen in the San Luis Terrace Apartments—a seven-story high-rise that was across the street and to the south of the Agricultural Building—were shooting at the troopers. This mutual support worked for a while, but on February 27, the horse soldiers turned their attention to this structure and several dwellings, clearing them of defenders. The Japanese had apparently expected such an attack, but they also expected that minefields would be enough to block an attack. They had not foreseen the effectiveness of the U.S. Army Corps of Engineers.[35]

Since a direct infantry assault on the Agricultural Building had failed, the Americans—out of tactical desperation—turned to their heavy guns. At 8:00 a.m. on February 28, several units from the XIV Corps began putting a massive, sustained barrage on the building. The Americans used 75-millimeter tanks, 76-millimeter tank destroyers, and 155-millimeter artillery guns. To avoid friendly fire incidents, units rotated firing from north and west first, then the south and east, and then back. The artillery batteries aimed only at the support structures on the first floor. After three hours, the beams and pillars gave out and the building collapsed in upon itself.[36]

As astonishing as it might sound, Japanese defenders survived and continued to fight in the ruined remains. They were in the northwest and southeast corners of the building. Since they were on opposite ends of the building, there was little the Japanese could do to support one another. The 5th Cavalry used flame throwers, bazookas, and small arms to finish off each cluster. A third group remained in the basement, and cavalrymen used burning oil and gas to finish them off.[37] Japanese resistance in this building finally ended at 2:25 p.m. on March 1.[38]

* * *

The attack on the government buildings was the work of enlisted men and junior officers. The work of generals was a bit different. To maintain the fiction that the battle was over, MacArthur decided to formally return sovereignty of the Philippines to the Commonwealth Government in a ceremony held at Malacañan Palace on February 27, the day after Iwabuchi's death.

Home of the Spanish governors of old, the palace had seen no real damage to its walls, and the wood trim and chandeliers stood in stark contrast to the rest of the city. Bonner Fellers noticed some broken glass; given conditions in the rest of the city, that damage was as nothing. Kenney observed, "It was a real oasis in the midst of desolation."[39]

MacArthur began his remarks by addressing himself to Sergio Osmeña, president of the commonwealth government in exile. "On behalf of my government, I now solemnly declare, Mr. President, the full power and responsibilities restored to the Commonwealth, whose seat is here reestablished as provided by law."[40]

Major Sam Yorty, a future mayor of Los Angeles, was standing behind the general. "I was worried at the time, because MacArthur's right hand was shaking a little bit, and I didn't know that MacArthur had palsy then, but I thought maybe he was kind of nervous, although I can't imagine him being afraid of anybody."[41] Yorty was partially right. The speech was exceptionally emotional for the general. "For me, it was a soul-wrenching moment," MacArthur later observed. The smell of the dead permeated the ceremony.[42] Being a good soldier, he tried to press on with his speech. "Your country, thus is again at liberty to pursue its destiny to an honored position in the family of free nations. Your capital city, cruelly punished though it be, has regained its rightful place—citadel of democracy in the East. Your indomitable . . . ." His voice failed him mid-sentence.[43]

The general put his hands over his face as he began to cry. "I could not go on," he later admitted. "To others it might have seemed my moment of victory and monumental personal acclaim, but to me it seemed only the culmination of physical and spiritual disaster."[44]

Osmeña responded with a speech of his own. "We mourn the destruction of our once beautiful capital city of Manila and the murder of thousands of innocent people by the Japanese vandals." He then made some bold statements. He was trying to prevent a civil war between various factions that had supported the Second Republic, the Commonwealth, and those that had opposed both. "Our independence is a settled question." The government needed the support of a united people and nation. "It would be tragic indeed if at this last state of our crucial struggle for nationhood, we should fall apart and be divided against ourselves." He announced that the reestablishment of local and national government was a top priority, but so were welfare programs to help the Filipino people and efforts to rebuild schools, roads, bridges, hospitals, banks, and the economy. In keeping with that point, the Japanese soldiers had to be punished for their "cruel and brutal" behavior. "For this reason, it is imperative that the war against him be prosecuted all over the country relentlessly and with dispatch in order that the people's agony may not be prolonged and precious human life may be salvaged."[45]

The ceremony was mainly for show. The Americans, not Filipinos, would be responsible for significant civic functions in Manila for months to come. A day earlier, Brigadier General Courtney Whitney had written his wife about a conversation he had with Osmeña: "For a time after the President's request most of the city administration will be the responsibility of my civil affairs sector—even the <u>fire department</u>."[46]

Outside of the Manila city limits, Major General Verne Mudge and the 1st Cavalry Division were continuing to advance. At Antipolo, a town east of the city, they encountered a Japanese network of caves carved into a series of ridges blocking access to the town. The division tried to use artillery and air power to seal off these openings so they could advance forward, but it was difficult for either ordinance to score a direct hit. In the end, military engineers with explosive charges and infantrymen with flame throwers had to get in close and seal off the caves. There was risk in these missions; to be effective they had to get within a few feet of Japanese positions.[47]

On February 28, Mudge was watching an attack on a cave. A Japanese solider threw a grenade that hit him in the chest. It bounced off him and then hooked on his pistol before it exploded, tearing apart his hip and abdomen. Griswold noted in his diary: "One of my best division commanders, Gen. Mudge, 1st Cavalry Division, was seriously wounded today by a hand grenade." News of the injury was front-page news back in the United States. His injuries were severe and forced his medical retirement from the U.S. Army. Complications from his wounds would eventually contribute to his death twelve years later.[48]

* * *

In Manila, the few remaining Japanese defenders—around six hundred—were in the Finance Building. While they had plenty of food, water was a different matter. A spring that the defenders had found while digging was now polluted with dirt and debris.[49] The Americans' artillery fire was not destroying the defending force, but it was having an impact. The exploding shells prevented the Japanese from moving about freely within the building. Each machine gun nest was becoming an isolated point rather than part of a cohesive defense.

Given limited mobility within the building, those who were wounded received no medical care.[50]

Morale among the defenders was low and their devotion to suicide was not strong. The large number of Formosans among them were assigned menial work—digging trenches, filling sandbags, and so forth. The Japanese did not trust them and did not let them on the upper levels of the building or allow them to carry weapons. To keep them from trying to escape, the Japanese kept them separated in small groups. Japanese officers and men, on the other hand, made a number of efforts to escape from the building. Among them was a general awareness that most of them were likely to die. The men blamed their officers for placing them in this hopeless situation. A few, however, were still committed to their duty and wanted to inflict more damage with a nighttime raid than they could in a siege.[51]

The American leaflets and broadcasts were making some of the men question their resolution. These individuals even shared their doubts with others, although remained wary of their officers. A psychological warfare broadcast on February 25 convinced Morio Shigetoshi to surrender. He slipped out of the building on the night of February 27 and troopers from G Troop, 5th Cavalry captured him the next morning. He had valuable intelligence. He provided a detailed report about the location of fortifications and gun emplacements in the Finance Building.[52]

Two of the highest-ranking men to desert were Sergeant Uchida Kensaburo and Sergeant Major Kuroda Seichi. Both did so because of broadcasts. Uchida explained that many men were considering surrender but wrestling with conflicting concerns: fear of death, worry that they would be tortured or executed after surrender, devotion to duty, and concern about the shame their families would endure back in Japan.[53] The fact that the announcement was in Japanese had a powerful impact on them. Not only could they understand what their enemy was saying, but the voice talking to them sounded Japanese. There was simply no way a Filipino or an American could speak Japanese that well. If a Japanese soldier was addressing them, that was an indicator that the Americans would take prisoners and treat them well. (The broadcast was actually made by a Japanese American soldier.)[54]

In the afternoon of March 1, after artillery had hit the building hard, a team from the 173rd Language Detachment used loudspeakers they set up across the street and spent twenty minutes broadcasting another message aimed at the soldiers and sailors holed up in the building. The Americans moved the speakers to another location and repeated the message. They gave the Japanese thirty minutes to surrender. Much to their surprise, twenty-two men walked out of the building with their hands up; eight were Formosans, two were Japanese civilians, and twelve were junior enlisted personnel in either the Army or Navy. Another five surrendered later that day. Another soldier later surrendered, waving a white flag.[55]

Second Class Private Azumida Zenzo had already left the Finance Building and was out in the open when he heard the message. He surrendered immediately. A thirty-nine-year-old lawyer who had graduated from Chuo University and been drafted into the Army because he happened to be in the Philippines, Azumida had worked for several Japanese newspapers in Tokyo before coming to Manila in the employ of a mining and shipping company. While most POW debriefings were a page to a page-and-a-half long, his was seventeen single-spaced pages. "PW [prisoner of war] is very happy to be alive and unharmed," a XIV Corps military officer noted. Given his professional background, he offered the Americans a wealth of political and strategic information about the Japanese presence in the Philippines. Some of it was nothing more than gossip, but he was particularly informative on economic and trade issues.[56]

Other surrender efforts followed. Lance Corporal Mihira Katsuji and another group of five decided to surrender. Just before they exited the building, the group began debating the wisdom of their action. Mihira had waved a white flag from a window and was no longer interested in arguing over the matter. He slipped out and surrendered himself. There was evidence that others wanted to surrender, but they were unable to do so. Some of it was due to fear about their enemy's honesty; others were killed by their own comrades.[57]

The final attack began the next day on March 2. The Americans had interrogated these prisoners about the position of defense fortifications and used that information in planning the final assault on the Finance Building. They began with a two-hour-long artillery barrage. When the shelling stopped, someone on one of the upper floors began waving a white flag. Company C of the 148th Infantry Regiment advanced warily. As it turned out, the flag was either a ploy or an isolated effort to surrender. With the company out in the open, Japanese machine gunners opened fire on the Buckeye infantrymen. The company quickly retreated and called in another two-hour artillery barrage. Companies B and C entered the building and rapidly took control of the first four floors. The fifth floor would have to wait until the next day.[58]

With the building firmly in US control, the 1st Battalion, 148th Infantry Regiment sent its flame thrower operators and engineers to search the building. They began counting the dead. The numbers told a sobering story. The soldiers found only eighty-four corpses, which, combined with the number of captured prisoners of war and those escaping, indicated that the Japanese—with what amounted roughly to four poorly trained infantry companies, or one weak battalion—had managed to absorb the efforts of two US regiments and stopped repair work on the entire port for a week. It was only when the Americans relied on their strengths, the blunt force of artillery and their plentiful supply of shells, that they managed to neutralize the Japanese threat.[59]

Griswold was appalled at what had happened. He blamed MacArthur for what had been required of him and poured his frustration out into his diary: "All organized resistance in Manila has ended. Again Gen. MacArthur had announced its capture several days ahead of the actual event. The man is publicity crazy." He believed MacArthur had made actually fighting the war more difficult. "When soldiers are dying and being wounded, it doesn't make for their morale to know that the thing they are doing has been officially announced as finished days ago. The one weakness of a really great man—publicity!" Griswold kept these feelings to himself. He never wrote a memoir nor is there any evidence that he ever went public with his views, giving interviews with reporters or even doing an oral history with a historian.[60]

Even officers in the Japanese Army were shocked at the battle. The repulsion was not so much at the defeat, that outcome was fairly clear, or even the human damage done to the civilian population—the Japanese Army had never had any reservations about killing foreign civilians—rather it was anger at Yamashita for pursuing a strategy that ceded central Luzon to the Americans and, with it, Manila. A Japanese officer on Mindanao noted that the loss of Manila combined with the bombing of Tokyo and the Battle of Iwo Jima made it clear that the war had turned on Japan. "I feel uneasy lest these things keep up from now on."[61]

War correspondents were about the only group that could make problems for MacArthur and there was no inclination among any of them to challenge his conduct of the battle. There were many reasons for this—some personal and some professional. As William Dunn explains in his memoirs, many of the reporters were physically exhausted. Few were operating as part of a team and the stress of staying on top of such a huge story had taken its toll. Tiring of the general's publicity management, many had moved to Nimitz's theater to cover the invasion of Okinawa. Iwo Jima was the story of the moment. It had become a far bloodier battle than Manila. It also helped that the Marine Corps and Navy were far less manipulative of news coverage than MacArthur.[62]

On March 3, from his command post in Grace Park, Griswold sent a teletype message to Walter Krueger, announcing the end of organized enemy resistance in Manila.[63] What MacArthur thought could have been done in a day had taken a month. For all his military experience and expertise, he should have known better. Toward the end of the Cold War, a study the U.S. Army commissioned on urban warfare noted as much: "What the city does consume in almost every case is <u>time</u>."[64]

What soon become clear to the Americans—as they sat in the rubble that had once been a city—was that the battle they had fought had made their victory a poisoned one.

19

On the Edge of Forever

When the shooting stopped, the U.S. Army had to turn its attention to converting the operational victory in Manila into strategic advantage. This effort turned out to be extremely challenging. Some of the difficulty Americans faced in stabilizing the city was due to how they had chosen to fight. Much more of the onus, however, was on the Japanese defenders. The city that the Americans now controlled was a shambles. Many found the destruction visited upon Manila difficult to comprehend. Senator Millard Tydings of Maryland led an investigation for the Senate after the war that found that 32,192 buildings had been destroyed in the battle. The losses in the city amounted to hundreds of millions of dollars.[1]

Those numbers only go so far in documenting the misery. In the middle of March, during a visit to the city, Father Juan Labrador wrote: "My mind was filled with deeply engraved squadron of gloomy silhouettes, sketches of apocalyptic visions, and the chanting of Jeremiac lamentations." He turned to literature to bear witness to the suffering. "Neither Poe with his raven, nor Dumas with his dungeons nor Blasco Ibañez with his horsemen, could capture in words this immense picture of desolation." He was not sure any media or genre could represent in full the scale of destruction. "For one who had not seen this, it is impossible to believe or imagine it. And even if believed and imagined, it could not be reproduced."[2]

Douglas MacArthur, while driving through the remains of the city with Fellers, offered an American perspective on the loss. The best moments of his career, he explained, had been in the Philippines. Important turning points—his first overseas service, the death of his mother, the birth of his son, key promotions—had all been in Manila. Now he mourned. "The Manila I knew is gone and my work here is finished."[3]

Many soldiers echoed these feelings. Eichelberger visited the city a number of times after the battle ended. "It is all just graveyard," he wrote to his wife. "Manila in effect has ceased to exist." He looked for their old house and only found the walls and gate around the compound remaining. "I cannot tell you how sad all this made me feel."[4]

Even common foot infantrymen struggled with the enormity of it all. "I was with a water supply unit," Master Sergeant Francis D. Donahue of the 177th Engineer Construction Battalion observed, "and we had a terrific problem at Manila. It'll take years to build that city up again."[5] Private First Class Keron E. Horan noted that "Even just cleaning up the streets will take a good while."[6]

Labrador, for his part, offered a Spanish perspective. "I entered the walled city, with a holy fear and a revolting feeling, thinking about the victims and the henchmen." He looked upon what remained, knowing what had been lost. "This was the abomination of desolation of the holy city. The lordly ancestral mansion of families belonging to the noblest lineage in the Philippines, the Colleges, convents and churches of three centuries of history, the hospitals and government edifices founded by the first Captains General were nothing more than mounds of dust being blown by the winds—the dust of centuries."[7]

While the old empire was gone, the young republic was simply not ready for its new obligations. During the planning for the invasion of Luzon and the capture of Manila, the working assumption among Krueger's and MacArthur's staffs was that the existing municipal government would continue to run the city. Once US regiments seized control of the northern neighborhoods and urban districts, once combat moved south across the Pasig River, once the bodies began piling up, it became obvious there was no one in a position of authority to administer the city; provide water, food, and electricity; or regulate any type of economy. The only organization with the resources to perform these tasks in any meaningful way was the United States Army.[8]

Civil affairs were never a high priority in either MacArthur's or Krueger's headquarters. The lack of preparation for running the city showed the limits of a planning process that had focused on easy tactical and operational issues. Until January 26, the staff of the Sixth Army had believed that MacArthur's headquarters would be responsible for the city. Krueger delayed for a week in deciding that the XIV Corps would have the duty. He did not inform Oscar W. Griswold of his new responsibilities until February 3, the day the battle began. Civil affairs units, as a result, had only forty-eight hours of notice about their new assignments.[9] The after-action report for the corps uses controlled but blunt language in describing the situation these units faced: "The relief problems were greater, by far, than had been anticipated."[10]

What was required to run a city was starting to dawn on U.S. Army officers. On February 9, Krueger, as Eddleman noted in an interview after the war, "took the whole 37th Infantry Division and put them on guard duty in Manila." Eddleman then repeated himself for effect, "The whole damn division." Giles H. Kidd, an officer in the division, noted that the problems of civic administration were immense. Roughly 350,000 people, or about a third of the city's population, needed some form of "direct relief." Krueger called this duty "onerous."[11]

While the battle was ongoing, the division had had a number of duties that were unique to a city that was a battleground. First, the division had to protect both civilians and the military in the rear areas. There was a stunning amount of unexploded ordinance in the city—most of it Japanese. The 117th Engineers continued to remove these explosives and pile them in small dumps in open fields and parks, where they then detonated them in controlled explosions. There were, however, several occasions when the shells, bombs, and mines went off on their own.[12]

The issue of Japanese stragglers in the city was another serious problem. Most of these men had become separated from their units. There were still some small groups of two and three that were trying to perform infiltration missions. Around this time, Henry J. Brien, a sergeant in the 40th Infantry Division, was in a replacement center in Manila awaiting transport home. "The snipers shot at us in the chow line. We forgot about chow and took cover plenty quick as we had nothing to shoot back at 'em with."[13]

The vast majority of the Japanese, however, were trying to escape to the foothills of the Sierra Madre mountains to the east of the city, where they could connect again with other Japanese units. A small, but statistically significant, number of Japanese soldiers managed to make it to the Sierra Madres mountains. It is hard to give much precision because many of these survivors died in later battles on Luzon. The U.S. Army official history estimates that it was twenty-five percent. The historian Hayashi Yoshifumi, using demobilization records of the Imperial Japanese Navy, argues that about ten percent of the *makaibo* were alive at the end of the war. Both numbers might be correct since many that escaped did not survive the war. What needs to be stressed, though, is that most of those who made it to the mountains did so in units that escaped early in mid-February and maintained some cohesiveness.[14]

The odds were against both the individual stragglers and those in small groups that were still in Manila. Private First Class Okazaki Tatsumi was an exception to this trend. When his commanding officer told his unit to take independent action, he and three others interpreted that to mean escape rather than to make a futile suicide assault. It took a week, but the four managed to get out of the city. On March 1, they ran into a guerrilla band. Okazaki survived but the other three died in the gun battle that followed. In the mountains, Okazaki twice came across large Japanese Army units. He was done with the war, and so he simply watched his countrymen trudge on by. The day after seeing the second group, he turned himself into the 99th Field Artillery Battalion. Not wanting to be tagged as a coward who had failed to do his duty, he told the military intelligence detachment that interrogated him that he was an orphan from Formosa. The Americans did not buy his story. There were too many logical contradictions in his account, and he spoke with a Hiroshima accent. Confronted with these facts, he quickly confessed his true identity.[15]

Many other individual stragglers tried to hide. They often had no plans beyond avoiding the shame of surrender. There were a lot of places in the devastated city to disappear. The problems with vanishing, though, were significant. Sooner or later, individuals would need food and water, which would force them to come out of hiding. Manila was a foreign city in which the population was hostile and would quickly report their presence to guerillas or some nearby US unit. Second Lieutenant Murakami Kyozaku and his adjutant hid in the basement of the Legislative Building for five days after it had fallen. The two then tried to escape. With Murakami's damaged knee from the attack on Santo Tomás not having healed, they only reached Rizal Stadium before they were captured.[16]

A significant number of Japanese, particularly those who were sailors, swam out to the hulks that littered Manila Bay. During the battle, these half-sunk ships offered a decent place to hide. Tanks did use them as target practice on occasion, but distance and metal plating offered the isolated soldiers and sailors decent protection. The problem was, again, the lack of food and fresh water. Many of the Japanese stragglers quickly realized this and most were spotted and killed while trying to leave the ships. Takemura Shiruichi was a civilian employed by the Army. He and ten comrades had survived the shelling at Intramuros, and then made for the hulks. They spent a week onboard before the food and water situation forced them to leave. Takemura and two others became separated from the main group. Guerrillas found them as they were trying to cross the Pasig River south of Taytay. A firefight resulted in Takemura's capture and the death of his two companions.[17]

Those that still had firearms shot at U.S. Army engineers and U.S. Navy construction battalions trying to repair the city. Military intelligence and psychological warfare personnel tried to convince these holdouts to turn themselves in. Very few chose that option. As a result, the 37th Division sent small units to board the ships and kill the Japanese. Two days of ship boardings finished off the remainder. Some ships, though, had to be cleared as many as ten times. Those that managed to escape detection ended up dying slowly from dehydration in Manila Bay.[18]

As a result of the straggler situation, U.S. Army personnel stationed in the city had to carry firearms on their persons. This requirement lasted until March 17.[19] Other safety precautions continued for several more months. Bilibid Prison was converted into a hospital. When Colonel Hugh Milton, chief of staff of the XIV Corps, visited in May, he found it locked with armed soldiers on guard duty. He discovered why when his visit came to an end. He had to wait while a small patrol was engaged in a firefight immediately outside the compound. Two Japanese soldiers ended up getting killed.[20]

Manila was quite dangerous for Japanese Americans. The headquarters of the Allied Translator and Interpreter Section moved to Manila after the battle to prepare for the invasion of Japan. Sutherland assigned them the facilities at the Santa Ana racetrack. The facility was well suited for the 3,500-person unit. It was intact, had plenty of space for tent housing, and was easy to isolate and guard. Despite these facts, a large crowd gathered to watch the translation personnel arrive. The ATIS commanding officer, Colonel Sidney F. Mashbir, had a lengthy exchange with the Filipino major in command of the Philippine battalion guarding the facility. The major explained that the people wanted to see the Japanese prisoners. Mashbir, realizing the confusion, explained that these individuals were not Japanese but Americans of Japanese descent.[21]

* * *

Another major consideration was the intention of the U.S. Army to use the city as a staging area to invade Japan itself. After the battle, the Army began rebuilding Manila so that it could be a military base for future operations. Construction projects began even before the shooting stopped. "From Manila north for a hundred miles were vast piles of arms, ammunition, and equipment spaced to allow for possible bomb damage," Brigadier General Elliot R.

Thorpe recalled. "Near where I was billeted in Quezon City was a field of several acres covered solidly with new tanks and armored vehicles."[22]

The biggest issue in preparing Manila for the rest of the war was its dock and port facilities. MacArthur had always stressed the moral and political reasons for liberating Manila, but control of the city would also give the United States significant transportation resources. As American forces drove through the Pacific, the logistical demands they faced grew. There was no other city on the western side of the Pacific that could substitute for Manila. MacArthur's staff had understood this reason for taking the city; however, it was never communicated to the soldiers on the frontlines nor to the field-grade officers that commanded the battalions, brigades, regiments, and batteries that had fought in the city. Senator Tydings, in his report to the Senate, found that ninety percent of the port area had been destroyed. The cold irony was that while the US artillery's use of indirect fire might have destroyed the Manila Naval Defense Force, it had also helped serve Japan's strategic interests.[23]

That fact became obvious quite quickly. Much of Manila had simply disappeared. Engineers were astonished at what they saw—or what they did not see. "It is almost impossible to comprehend the destruction done to these cities until you see them," a student wrote back to the dean of engineering at New Mexico A&M University. Many buildings were made of reinforced concrete to withstand earthquakes, and many had turned to powder in the heat and flames. "The steel is just a twisted mass."[24]

Brigadier General Henry Hutchins, commanding general of the 4th Engineer Special Brigade, understood the strategic problem facing the United States. The port facilities were unable to support the logistical needs of the Army, or even just of Manila. He found an area that he turned into an artificial beach that could accommodate landing craft, trucks, and track mounted cranes—all of which could supply the city.[25]

Real repair work on the harbor, however, had to wait until the arrival of Commodore William A. Sullivan. An expert on salvage, Sullivan had led the efforts to repair several docks in Europe. As he slowly made his way across the Pacific, he came to realize the effort in the Philippines was going to be much more difficult than anything he had faced before. Many of the problems he was going to address were self-inflicted. The U.S. Navy had no officers in the Pacific with training in port salvage operations. Staff officers began reassigning navy salvage personnel to other duties rather than let them sit idle for a few days until they could be shipped to MacArthur's theater. It took Sullivan months to get those sailors and chiefs assigned back to his command and in a number of cases they never arrived back at all. He also lacked the resources he had enjoyed in Europe, ranging from specialized machines to trained civilian personnel.[26]

Sullivan arrived on Luzon in the middle of February. A jeep and ambulance were waiting for him. "Travel in the vicinity was very risky," Sullivan observed. "Both the ambulance and the jeep had bullet holes from sniper's bullets, made that very morning."[27]

In a sign of Sullivan's importance, he quickly ended up at Hacienda Luisitana, meeting with MacArthur himself. The general wanted to know about his orders. Sullivan was in a bind because he had to answer to a naval superior even though he was operating in an Army theater. He explained his situation to MacArthur and told him that his main goal was to rebuild the harbor and port as quickly as possible; he wanted to use Filipino and American civilian labor in that effort. MacArthur, who had spent the first half of his career in the Corps of Engineers, understood and agreed with Sullivan's assessment. He thought Sullivan's idea of using Filipino labor was sound but warned him that he would find that the American specialists who had survived the internment camps in terrible physical shape. None of them would be of use to him. Sullivan tried nonetheless and found MacArthur's assessment to be entirely accurate. As the meeting ended, the general promised Sullivan the complete cooperation of his command. "It was splendid—I mean, the cooperation from the Army couldn't have been better," he declared. He was also impressed with MacArthur: "He was far better than any of the commanding generals I ran across in Europe. Oh, there's no comparison!"[28]

Sullivan attempted to begin salvage operations on the harbor areas north of the Pasig River even before the storming of the Intramuros or the seizure of the government buildings. He only succeeded in getting a bulldozer operator shot and turning his men into naval infantry. He realized that salvage operations would have to wait until the shooting stopped. Even his efforts to inspect the waterfront led him to accidentally wander into an active combat zone. He eventually got an airplane to give him a view of the city and harbor. "It was a mess."[29]

There were over two hundred boats and ships in the Pasig alone. There were another two hundred in the north harbor area and another two hundred in the south. After a trip to Leyte, where he learned he was losing his men because of bureaucratic issues, he returned to Luzon. Arriving after dark, he reported to MacArthur's headquarters and had a meeting with the general. Dressed in his

night robe, MacArthur sat and listened to Sullivan. The general was not surprised about losing the salvage men, but he said the Army would support him.
"What do you really need," he asked.

Sullivan replied that he required men with some experience in diving. He
would have to have all sorts of equipment. Within twenty-four hours, Army
personnel began arriving at Sullivan's headquarters. The numbers were not
huge, but they all had done some diving before in civilian life. They were in
no way replacements for the men that Sullivan had lost, but they would do for
the time being.[30]

With each day, salvage operations moved forward slowly. "The Japanese
did a perfect job here in blocking the entrance," the commodore admitted.
"The man who directed this job knew what he was doing."[31] The Japanese had
sunken a number of hulks together that made it impossible for the divers to access them individually, and they were positioned so that they blocked access to
the piers and slips. Wind patterns caused swells in the water at these spots that
made it difficult for the divers to stand on the floor of the bay for more than
a few hours. The men doing this work soon began to suffer from skin diseases
due to the water, which soon became another factor complicating the salvage
effort. Even when they could work, the mud often reduced the visibility to
almost nothing. The ships were also riddled with holes that made it exceptionally difficult to raise them. Gear and trained men began arriving, but work
slowed again when a dredge detonated a bomb that ripped the machine apart.
"I lived every minute of this job and was a bundle of nerves when I stepped
ashore," the commodore confessed.[32] Creative work at patching tears in the
hulls and actually turning ships 180 degrees so that they could be transported
upside down to a ship graveyard where they would be out of the way allowed
Sullivan and his men to make progress.[33]

Despite the commodore's hard work, Manila's port was always behind.
Although it began taking ships in mid-March—to a great deal of media
attention—that was more of a publicity stunt than anything else.[34] In July, the
last full month of the war, ships often had to wait ten days in Manila Bay before they could offload their cargo.[35]

Manila, though, was a prized assignment. "Stevedoring is a fair paying job,
but I just happened to be in the wrong union," Corporal Joseph Timpano
of the 612th Port Battalion joked. "I was out there 29 months and of all the
places I hit I think Manila was the best because it was halfway civilized."[36]
The Army established the General Engineer District, Philippine Islands, a

month-and-a-half after the battle ended. It was originally a command of only 450 officers and men, but it grew quickly into an organization of 140,000. Much of their job consisted of clearing streets of rubble, getting the electrical system back in operation, repairing bridges, and building buildings for the army. For weeks, the men in this command found body parts littering the city. It took them until the end of the year to get the electrical system for the entire city back in working order. Until then, individual units used portable diesel generators for their immediate needs.[37]

While Sullivan and his men tried to salvage the docks, the Quartermaster Corps began turning Manila into the biggest Army supply depot in the Southwest Pacific Theater. The U.S. Army was well supplied in certain items. There were, however, real shortages that supply officers never rectified during the war for low-priority items. These included replacement parts for typewriters, sewing machines, ovens, washers and dryers, refrigerators, and shoe repair machinery. Cannibalization was one answer, and another was to hire Filipinas to wash uniforms.[38]

Other parts of the Army, though, were ready. On February 27—during the fight for the government buildings—Major General Spencer B. Akin had his signal equipment in ships in Manila Bay. Two weeks later, when the docks could handle the heavy radio equipment, the Army offloaded the communications gear and power generators. In less than forty-eight hours, Akin had his transmitters working and was in contact with the United States and Australia. One of the biggest users of this new communications center were the journalists on Luzon.[39]

Despite the civil administration work, more combat was required to keep the city functioning. The Ipo Dam to the east of the city provided a third of the municipality's water. The Wawa Dam was not connected to the city's water system, but it could provide up to fifteen percent of the municipality's requirements if needed. The Japanese controlled both these structures. MacArthur and Krueger thought the city needed both dams. Operations to seize territory to the east of the city began in late February, even before the seizure of the Intramuros. After a month of combat operations, however, neither dam was under US control. The reason was that the manpower shortage in the Pacific theater was beginning to take its toll. Many of the infantry companies in the divisions marching east were down to sixty percent of their normal table of organization. While this fighting was taking place, a water shortage was starting in the city. On April 19, fearing a massive public health crisis,

MacArthur ordered Krueger to take the dams immediately. The Sixth Army commander had learned that Wawa did not supply Manila. He sent a telegram and asked if MacArthur wanted him to take Ipo. The staff at general headquarters studied the situation and MacArthur informed Krueger that Ipo was the preferred target.[40]

The job of taking the dam went to Major General Leonard "Red" Wing's 43rd Infantry Division. Wing, a National Guard officer like Beightler, maneuvered his unit to advance rapidly and take the dam. He was aware of the situation facing Manila, that the rainy season was approaching, and that storms would complicate ground operations. Charging over hill tops, the division made steady progress. On May 13, regiments in the division had captured the hills overlooking the dam.[41]

When the rains started, they slowed the advance, just as Wing had feared. Despite this development, the Americans had superiority in firepower. On May 16, US artillery battered the Japanese defenders with two massive barrages. The next day, Army Air Forces planes dropped bombs and shattered the Japanese opposition. Wing's unit was at the dam, but it took another eleven days of slow ground operations in the rain before the dam was securely under US control.[42]

A number of other issues muddied the lines between being a military or a civic responsibility. Caring for the sick and wounded was one. Field hospital facilities normally serve a military function, but given the political context of the liberation, US medical personnel could not turn away Filipinos. In her memoir of the battle, Evelyn Berg wrote that soldiers saw that her sister and mother were wounded and sent them to the hospital. The physician on duty attempted to refuse service. That was an untenable argument with her angry father, and he got them to reverse themselves.[43] "The U.S. Army was everywhere," Joaquin Garcia, a Filipino civilian, recalled. Soldiers set up medical aid stations at various locations to help. Corporal Alfred J. Vaccacio of the 112th Medical Battalion, 37th Infantry Division was overwhelmed at the gratitude of Filipinos, "They just idealized us."[44]

The civilian demands, though, nearly broke the U.S. Army hospital system. By March some of the facilities were filled beyond capacity. The arrival of the 49th General Hospital, a full-service facility designed to provide complex, definitive care in the areas of trauma and disease, brought the crisis to an end. The Army established the facility at the Manila Jockey Club and actually put beds in the grandstands.[45]

Even after combat operations moved away from the city, Manila remained a significant medical center for the U.S. Army. Soldiers were suffering from a variety of health problems, be it the strain that the stress of combat creates or the climate of Luzon. One needed to look no further for an example than Oscar Griswold. The XIV Corps commander was hospitalized in May with an infection. When he and his chief of staff, Hugh Milton, received promotions that summer, they posed for a photo that shows them looking like exhausted, gaunt, old men.[46]

Plundering and ransacking was another issue in the city. "The civilians found their capacity to steal and loot practically without ceiling," Stanley Frankel observed in the 37th Division's published unit history. The prominent Filipino historian, Teodor Agoncillo, who lived through the battle, came to a similar conclusion: "The looting was 'democratic,' for the participants belonged to all classes."[47] In this environment, the military police had to guard against the pilfering of US supplies for months. Joe A. Racklley, a radioman in the 145th Infantry Regiment, was infuriated with the actions of the Filipinos. "They would steal you blind, you couldn't get nothing. Everything cost you."[48]

The disposal of the dead was another concern, which would grow and change as time went on. Given the heat and humidity of Manila, the timely disposition of dead bodies was imperative. In some situations, decomposition would actually begin within an hour. During active combat operations, the mortuary services focused on US soldiers. Americans, though, made up a small proportion of the dead in the city—less than one percent. Concerns about public health moved to the forefront during the occupation, and the U.S. Army had to do something about the estimated twenty thousand to thirty thousand dead Filipinos and twenty thousand Japanese. Carmen Del Gallego told her nephew, the historian John A. Del Gallego, that there were dead bodies in the streets for a month.[49]

The stench of death permeated the city. "The rotten-sweet odor of death hung over the city like a fog," Mathias, of the 37th Division, recalled. It reached six miles out and grew stronger the closer one got to the city. There were few ways to combat it. People drove fast, hoping the wind would help alleviate the smell. Some soldiers wore gas masks.[50]

The odor was demoralizing. Paul P. Rogers hated staying in Manila: "There was an overpowering stench of death and decay. It pervaded the air, and there was no escape." During the first meal of MacArthur's headquarters' mess in the city, the officers and men of the general's staff gathered under a large canvas tent while large black flies covered the tables and attacked the food.

"Everyone knew where and how they had grown so large. "We had brought death to the city, and perhaps we deserved to eat it." Afterward, Rogers tended to eat canned rations. "This was not Manila. It was simply hell."[51]

Policing was a final concern that had only grown in importance after the fighting was over. It was an issue that was close to a normal municipal function, but the military police and Counter Intelligence Corps were often involved in matters. The MPs were controlling traffic, guarding prisoners, and protecting supply dumps. Guarding bridges was something they did on occasion, but that was now generally the responsibility of combat units. It was not easy work. "By the middle of March, Manila was a traffic cop's nightmare," Frankel noted. The reason—there were too many unauthorized vehicles visiting the city. Very little was due to Filipino action because fuel still limited their ability to use automobiles. The military police also established a forensic science laboratory in Manila in March, recruiting Constable Thomas Martin Batty of the Queensland Police Department in Queensland, Australia to run the facility. A year later, Batty called Manila the most crime-ridden city in the world due to a massive number of murders. He did not explain the reasons for the homicides, but theft was rampant for months following the battle, and it would also appear that others were settling personal and political grievances stemming from the occupation.[52]

The Counter Intelligence Corps operated out of Bilibid Prison for a time, until it became a hospital. Its mission was to collect information on collaborators for criminal prosecution. "I tried to help the CIC officers to determine which Americans had cooperated with the Japanese, but we found casting the first stone very difficult," U. Alexis Johnson, a career foreign service officer who had been sent to Manila to open a consulate, reflected. Deciding who had aided and abetted the Japanese became a politically charged issue in the Philippines for decades, lasting well into the twenty-first century. "Sorting out villains, heroes, and those who had alternately been both was beyond our powers," Johnson confessed. The CIC still tried, and had 1,216 persons—mostly Filipino—incarcerated at the end of March. A study the Sixth Army's military intelligence section conducted after the war admitted the Counter Intelligence Corps was "woefully ill-prepared."[53] In the end, the CIC focused on easy objectives. Of the six thousand people they investigated, half were members of the *makapili*, and Philippine Courts held that membership in the organization was, in and of itself, a crime.[54]

* * *

With the battle over, the people of Manila tried to get on with the business of living. That was no easy thing. The battle had created thousands upon thousands of refugees in and out of the city. Outside the city, long columns of people were hiking out of the city looking for some place to stay. Others walked back into the city with food for their families.[55]

After Ermita was liberated, Purita Echevarria de Gonzalez and her mother went looking for her aunt and cousins. They found them in a refugee center in San Miguel. One cousin had died, and they had carried his body with them until a Japanese patrol separated the women from the men. Her aunt placed her son's body on the porch column of a house that was catching fire, so he would be cremated. The Japanese took Gonzalez's aunt and four cousins to the Bayview Hotel. At the refugee center, the five were in shock. "My beautiful and normally boisterous cousins appeared haggard and lifeless. None of them seemed to have anything to say." Only after a while did they talk about their brother's death. None of them said a word about being raped at the hotel. Her aunt sat "silent and impassive" with a "dazed expression" and had no response when her sister embraced her. "Tia Paquita, in her mid-forties, never uttered a word and would remain a passive ghost of her former self for the rest of her life."[56]

The mood in the city among the Filipinos varied a great deal. Brigadier General Carlos P. Romulo went from one extreme to another. The prewar publisher and editor of the *Philippines Herald*, he had not been back to Manila since the Japanese had taken control. He found his mother alive and well in her home, but he had no idea about the fate of his wife and children. He recognized many of the dead in the streets. At Elpidio Quirino's home, he saw the dead and learned about the fate of his friend. (Quirino became president of the Philippines after the war and appointed Romulo as his foreign minister.) Romulo went to his home, which was nothing more than burned timber. As he approached the remains, the stink of death stopped him cold. With some unstated relief, he saw the decomposing corpse of his next-door neighbor, but not his family. (His wife and children survived the war and they reunited later.)[57]

Gene Sherman of the *Los Angeles Times* was an eyewitness to the suffering of the city, and he wrote a series of essays about Manila for his "Pacific Echoes" column. "An afternoon in Manila now is a frightful, gloomy afternoon," he observed. "You catch the ugly tenor of war and a great sense of frustration and depression grips you." Sherman's commentaries tell us more about his emotional state than Manila. He looked at a church service as "a bleak and grim pageant of misery."[58] While his editorializing is open to question, it was a strong counter to earlier reporting and MacArthur's suggestion that all was well in Manila.

Many turned to religion in reaction to the traumas they had suffered. "Religious fervor has intensified," Labrador observed. "The piety, firmness and simplicity of the Catholic American soldiers are a living example. The devotion and frequency with which they receive the Sacraments cannot but impress both their non-Catholic comrades-in-arms as well as the Filipinos who are non-Catholic in practice."[59]

There was also a revival in religious practices among the Jewish population of the city. Passover came three weeks after the battle ended. The San Lazaro Racetrack, three-quarters of a mile north of Santo Tomás, was the site of Seder. The bleachers were full of four thousand to five thousand people. Frank Ephraim called the size of the event "staggering." The American servicemen, many of them still in dirty fatigues from fighting to the east, were surprised at the number of Jews in the Philippines. Their generosity was no less than that of their Christian comrades. "They gave us all their C-rations and K-rations, their cigarettes, and the ubiquitous small bars of Hershey 'tropics proof' chocolate," Ephraim recalled.[60] The numbers grew and on Rosh Hoshana and Yom Kippur services had to be held in Rizal Stadium because it had more seating.[61]

Hunger was everywhere. Restoring food distribution networks was a fundamental requirement if there was to be any type of recovery in the city. The Philippine Civil Affairs Units—unprepared though they were—played a crucial role in keeping starvation at bay. Filipinos sought work with the U.S. Army because the Army would pay with either cash (that could purchase food) or in foodstuffs. Filipinos also learned when and where US units fed their men and lined up around the dining facilities, hoping the Americans would share, which they often did.[62]

There were limits to the resources of the U.S. Army, though. Refrigeration was scarce, so fresh meat, fruit, and vegetables were difficult to keep for more than a few hours. When Filipinos demanded payment in kind, the Americans often had to refuse. The result was a series of small strikes.[63]

Sherman reported that Filipinos were surviving with small forms of commerce even with a currency that was less than secure. Despite that, the lack of food was important. "There may not be starvation here in the backwash of war, but there certainly is hunger," Sherman stated.[64] He was not the only journalist to report on the food problem. George E. Jones of *The New York Times* investigated the issue as well. "Yesterday we handled 5,700 evacuees," Major John S. Carlisle, the commanding officer of a civil affairs unit working south of the Pasig River, told Jones. "We had to feed them and treat their wounds and see that they were canalized into the proper evacuation route." His unit was running a kitchen, serving rice and corned beef. His men went back into the ruins to look for the wounded. "It will be a hell of a while before we get Manila straightened out."[65]

Individual soldiers were also moved by the hunger. "There was a line of Filipino kids, with tin cans waiting for us to come out, and we would dump our food into their tin cans, and as soon as they got it filled, they'd run and take it home, and that kind of poverty really affected me," Milton Berkes, a signal corpsman, remembered.[66]

The occupation of Manila created a huge deficit in the logistical resources of the U.S. Army. Yet there was a positive outcome to this drain on manpower and material. "If not for the limitless generosity of the US Army, we all would have died of hunger," Labrador observed. "They fed those who did not have anything to eat nor the means to obtain it. They fed and clothed those who had lost everything. Those that they employed, they paid with a good wage."[67]

In another sign that the city was recovering, more and more newspapers began appearing, and soon economic forces came into play. *The New York Times* had a Manila edition in April. Many prewar Filipino publishers started their own printing operations and, by May, there were thirty newspapers in the city. Many of them were only two or four pages long. Due to local demand, most of the wire services had a presence in the city before the battle ended. At the same time, the newspaper that the Office of War Information was supporting stopped printing because local publishers complained about government subsidization of the news media.[68]

Even after the battle, LeGrande Diller and his staff worked to minimize reporting on the damage done to Manila. They directed reporters toward topics like the establishment of civil order in the city and the relief supplies the U.S. Army was offering, explaining that the Filipinos were amply fed. Press releases focused on the fact that the Americans began using the port facilities on March 1.[69]

It was clear to many in and out of the military that the press had failed to offer an accurate account of the battle. Coverage was, in and of itself, a reward to the fighting men. Soldiers were doing dangerous, difficult work and the risks they were running deserved recognition. General Beightler made that point directly: "There is no doubt about it, the 37th Division achieved nation wide recognition for its part in the Philippines campaign. I am heartily glad because for two and one half years my officers and men have been working and sweating and some of them dying in the the stinking South Pacific jungles of anonymity. This is the first campaign, of the three in which we have participated, where our presence was revealed officially and quickly."[70]

There were other reasons for media attention. Many in the United States had friends and family in the Philippines (both civilians and military) and were eager to learn about their status. With a breakdown in postal service between the two countries during the war, Americans in the United States had little information. Specifics and details were in high demand. Often the first news that Americans had that their friends and family were alive was when newsreels, radio reports, and newspaper articles mentioned individuals. In an ironic twist, one of the people working to keep this friends-of-the-Philippines community informed was Harriet "Hat" Diller, the wife of MacArthur's public affairs officer. She was producing a newsletter for the Philippines expatriate community that she was printing and mailing at her own expense. Her main sources of information were news stories that her husband was often constraining in the theater.[71]

After they returned to the United States, several reporters had to explain—at least to their colleagues—how and why they had gotten the story so wrong. A month after the battle ended, Gordon Walker of *The Christian Science Monitor* offered an account in the paper with the page one headline: "Now the Story of Manila Can Be Told." Walker placed blame for the failure to report the truth on MacArthur's headquarters. Censorship restrictions had resulted in piecemeal reporting of events which prevented journalists from presenting the story in its full context. He also added that the premature announcement of Manila's seizure "rendered anticlimactical the three weeks of intensive fighting which followed." He argued that while the bravery of American fighting men was always deserving of respect, what made the Battle of Manila stand out was the suffering of the Filipino people. He then spent the rest of a fairly lengthy article documenting the devastation that had been visited upon the city. Royal Arch Gunnison took two almost contradictory approaches. In newspaper articles, he blamed military censors for the misleading early reports. On the other hand, in a long article for *Collier's* magazine, he argued that his early reporting had been correct at the time it was made. It was only when the

Japanese quickly turned to wanton destruction for its own sake that the story changed.[72]

Another story that the contemporary news gathering failed to cover was the impact the battle had on the culture of the Philippines. Manila was not only the political center of the Philippine nation, but it was also the heart and soul of its arts and literature. The battle altered intellectual trends in the nation in profound ways. Combat devastated many physical resources beyond just buildings. The holdings of the National Museum and the National Library were destroyed. Some historical records survived, but mainly in smaller collections. Two big exceptions were the National Archives and the archives of the archdiocese of Manila. The University of the Philippines lost its entire library during the fighting, a loss that would set back the educational missions of the university for decades. Most of the buildings on the campus took physical damage, but that was much easier to recover from.[73]

Large numbers of Filipino writers died during the battle. The historian Jose Ma. Bonifacio M. Escoda argues that February 1945 was a dramatic turning point in Filipino prose, turning it from a Spanish-centric nation to one where English was the dominant language. This argument is a bit exaggerated. Spanish had held out for several decades after the Americans took control of the archipelago, but the nation had been trending toward English even before the war started. English-language newspapers had bigger circulations than those printed in Spanish. During the war, these trends accelerated. At the start of 1945, the Philippines seemed to have another decade or two in front of it as a bilingual nation before English won out. The battle sped up the future. The fight destroyed the resources of Spanish-language publishers, and it killed many readers and writers. Before the end of the 1940s, Spanish was surviving in schools as a second language and mainly because of a congressional mandate.[74]

Not only did the battle accelerate the decline of Spanish, but it created a new category of memoirs that would dominate Filipino writing for years to come. Many cities have an immense amount of literature—fiction and nonfiction—written about them, be it Sir Arthur Conan Doyle writing about London in his *Sherlock Holmes* short stories and novels, or Raymond Chandler's novels set in Los Angeles. Manila is no different. What is unique is that nonfiction seems to have dominated over fiction in offering works that express affection and familiarity with the city. Narratives about the People's Power Revolution of 1986 have become a major topic, but stories about Manila's war years still dominate.[75]

Like many of those other metropolitan areas, Manila was an international city and another issue that the American government had to face was determining the nationality of its residents. This task was simply beyond the expertise of Army officers and Johnson, of the State Department, was pressed into duty after a casual and random conversation with a colonel while in line for food at Santo Tomás.[76]

This process started before the battle had even ended. "Manila's devastation was immense," Johnson observed. With many legal records destroyed, Johnson had to improvise. He created a one-page questionnaire that he used to determine nationality. After an individual signed it, the document served as both a ticket and visa for military transit back to their homeland. "Deciding the nationality of the original Santo Tomás internees was not too complicated," Johnson observed. The issue became much more involved as people showed up with foreign wives and children. "Often I just improvised and hoped for the best."[77]

* * *

The American soldiers who found themselves in Manila after the shooting had stopped appreciated what they had. "Manila is by far about the best place short of Tokyo or Shanghai to be stationed in the Pacific," a veteran of the struggle on the undeveloped islands of the South Pacific wrote a former college professor. "It is certainly not half so bad as New Guinea."[78]

After suffering months of privation, the GIs appreciated little things. "Most of the time the work was hard and dull but once in a while we had a movie to break up the routine," Lloyd Tolson of the 236th Port Company remarked.[79] In Manila, the supply of different titles was much better than it had been in other elements of MacArthur's command. Soldiers could watch a different Hollywood film every night. "I think every movie I saw outside the USA was shown outdoors," Edwin E. Hanson, a foot soldier in the 37th Infantry Division, reflected. "Sometimes rain would shut it down, but not often." These open-air showings allowed Filipinos, who had been deprived of American films for three years, to attend in massive numbers.[80]

The soldiers found they could simply hire Filipinos to wash their laundry, shine their shoes, and do kitchen and janitorial assignments. There were also experienced barbers in Manila, and soldiers discovered they could actually get decent haircuts.[81]

Manila also offered the opportunity for soldiers to reconnect with family and friends. The army cleaned up the General Post Office and converted it into a Red Cross center. Soldiers could grab coffee and doughnuts, or they could take advantage of a reading room with a number of magazines and books. There was also a huge bulletin board where individuals could leave notes for others who might be traveling through the city.[82]

Mail began arriving in droves. Norman Mailer got a letter from his wife and held it for five minutes before opening it. "I can't tell you how I loved that note though," he told her. According to Sergeant William K. Nelms, Jr., who had been in the U.S. Postal Service before the war, the Army Postal Service in Manila was well run. Others serving there would have agreed. Letters arrived slightly more than seven days after they had been mailed, rather than weeks or months later as had been the case earlier in the war. Postal delivery in the Pacific was actually faster than it was in Europe.[83]

The converse of receiving mail was sending letters back to the United States. Writing became another recreational activity. The Red Cross center at the General Post Office provided writing paper for soldiers to write home.[84]

Mailer wrote to his wife a great deal during this period. He was bored. "We're bivouaced in a very nice area where we sit on our butts all day." Even in Manila there were significant supply shortages. "It's never been easier," he told her. "You have no conception of how unessential things like toilet bowls and napkins and bath tubs and mattresses are once you've done without them for a little while." He admitted, though, that things were much rougher for Filipinos. "A really frightful inflation exists; eggs are 15 cents apiece, a small watermelon is 2 dollars."[85]

Sport was another recreation. The 37th Division organized leagues for volleyball, basketball, and softball. The after-action report for the unit's special service officer noted that units in the division were more enthusiastic about athletic events than they had been before entering combat.[86] On July 4, a crowd of forty-four thousand gathered in Rizal Stadium despite a strong rain to watch a football game between a team representing the 11th Airborne Division and another playing for the U.S. Navy. Both teams featured players from a number of major colleges and universities. "As we peered through the downpour, it appeared that twenty-two big mud balls were shoving one another about," a paratrooper recalled. The game ended in a scoreless tie.[87]

Officers had opportunities not open to enlisted men and non-commissioned officers. Members of the Army and Navy Club began making immediate efforts to rebuild the institution. Given its membership, it was easy for the club to obtain building supplies that military officials had deemed surplus. The club reopened on December 2 for the broadcast of the Army–Navy football game. The two service academies were ranked first and second in the polls and were playing for the national championship of college football. The Army won, 32–13.[88]

Manila offered other venues for recreation in manners both positive and negative. Soldiers had their first opportunity in several years to drink alcohol on a wide scale. "Most men did not drink, but would binge when on the loose," Major Charles Henne of the 148th Infantry Regiment observed. Much of the alcohol available was homemade and of dubious quality and sanitation. The Army had a billboard at the Bonafacio Monument listing the number of deaths from liquor. Unlike other locals, in the Pacific theater there was a great deal of perfectly acceptable liquor in Manila. The only trick was in obtaining it. Success in this endeavor usually required rank, money, and connections among the civilian population.[89] The popular idea, though, of alcohol-starved soldiers building stills to drink booze of dubious quality that film and television have pushed needs serious qualification. Many men, no matter how long it had been since they had a drink, knew better. "I don't know who made it or how, but when I saw the dirt and mosquitos floating around in the bottom of the bottle, I decided against it," Hanson explained. "Besides, it tasted like raw turpentine."[90] With that said, there were a few men that were desperate. "We had alcoholics that would drink anything (shaving lotion, anti-freeze, vanilla extract), anything with alcohol," Henne stated. When they learned that the needles of compasses on Japanese ships floated in alcohol, several made their ways to the hulks in the harbor to drain these devices. Others mixed alcohol from Japanese motors into their drinks. None of these were particularly safe.[91]

The Army eventually resolved this situation when it established an enlisted men's club in the Walled City. This facility had ice and beer, but it took some time to get the facility up and running. Since the men in the 37th Division had already left the city for more fighting on Luzon, most of the soldiers using the facility were from service and support units.[92]

Gambling continued to be an easy way to while away free time. "We had one payday," one enlisted man recalled, "and for a few days most of the money in the company changed hands via poker, but I was still green so I sent my money home."[93]

Prostitution was a growth industry in Manila. According to memoirs from a number of soldiers, they believed that most of the women selling themselves were "mostly unprofessionals," meaning they had just recently turned to prostitution out of desperation and were not particularly experienced sexually.[94]

Housing was a serious issue for civilians and soldiers of all ranks. "Every usable building has been taken over by the Army," Sergeant Joseph Pino of the 978th Signal Service Company observed.[95] The demand increased after MacArthur brought his headquarters to the city. Acceptable facilities were quite rare and the Army appropriated buildings despite having significant damage. An officer's barracks was established in the Admiral Hotel. Commodore Sullivan had a room with a huge hole in the wall that looked down to the ground below. The opening was big enough for him to stand in. Even though he had a suite, his furniture was a cot, un-upholstered chairs, and two wooden crates that the commodore used as a desk and a chair.[96]

MacArthur made Sullivan the official host for Robert Sherwood, the Pulitzer Prize–winning playwright who was also a speechwriter for President Roosevelt, when he visited the island. The writer stayed with Sullivan in one of the bedrooms in his hotel suite that he had not used. As Sullivan showed his guests the accommodations, they noticed a leg sticking out of the bathroom. Inside were two bloated bodies of Japanese riflemen who had been shooting from the window of the bathroom when they were killed. Sherwood became sick. After having the bodies removed—through the gaping hole in the wall—Sullivan decided to use a bottle of scotch that he had handy. "It was after 5 o'clock so I suggested that Sherwood and I have a drink before we left for dinner. I thought he needed a big one."[97]

Sullivan later moved to a tent city next to the Manila Hotel that he had established for his command. "As long as I had a cot, mosquito net, and shelter for the night, I was quite satisfied."[98]

* * *

The trauma Manila had endured took a long time to dissipate. A year after the battle, Carmen Guerrero Cruz went out on a date with a U.S. Army lieutenant. He took her to a restaurant in a building that her cousin had once owned. She was in Ermita, where she had been born and raised. She had not recognized the area at first. She turned and looked across the street, where her old home had been located. It was now a U.S. Army storage facility. "What is it?" her date asked, "it's just a lumberyard."

Guerrero Cruz turned away. "I did not feel like taking him into my confidence." She went into the eatery. "I did not tell him that I was looking for a town called Ermita." The massive change the battle had inflicted on the city was a reminder that her own scars had not healed. "I needed a drink badly."[99]

Conclusion

The Battle of Manila is not one of the better remembered engagements of World War II, but its legacies—both positive and negative—indicate it deserves more attention. The US victory was the product of seven factors: intelligence work, joint operations, skilled leadership, adaptability, firepower, maneuver, and an incompetent opponent. Six of these seven factors were the work of the Americans fighting for the city. There were seven major turning points in the battle and six of them were the result of US initiative.

The US soldiers fighting in Manila did an impressive job. Their training, equipment, leadership, and experience in combat gave them enormous advantages over their opponents, but they adapted rapidly to the new type of warfare. Commanders rotated units out of combat on a regular basis to limit battle fatigue and managed to keep engagements that could have turned into uncoordinated low-level fights moving in a coherent direction. Casualties were low for the US forces, even though they were fighting in an environment in which they had no specialized training or experience. The efforts of military intelligence units and the ethical treatment of Filipinos contributed to the American understanding of the battle that the Japanese had no chance of equaling. Manila never made the kind of demands on manpower other urban warfare had done. The Americans got better at fighting in a city as time went on, such as seeing the battle space as three-dimensional and using armored vehicles.

The measure of a battle—any battle—is the effects of its outcome and here the story of Manila becomes more complicated. Some battles matter more than others. Far more than any other type of engagement, urban battles can alter the course of wars, the stability of states, and the structure of societies. Manila was a US victory that worked against the interests of the United States. In the end, though, this engagement had less of an effect on its war than, for example, the fall of Richmond in 1865 or Paris in 1871 had on their wars. This limited impact was because the war ended before the full ramifications of this "poisoned victory" became clear.

The depravity of the Japanese atrocities in Manila has no justification, but their defense of the city followed a hard military logic. The harbor facilities were shattered and unusable. Had the war continued longer than it did, the effects of this destruction would have become more obvious; it would have taken the U.S. Navy months and months to repair the harbor, and, even then, it would not have met the crucial requirements for a port of the kind that the United States needed as a supply point for the invasion of Japan. All those facilities had vanished in the battle. The vast majority of this destruction was the work of the Japanese, but a healthy percentage was the work of the Americans. The Japanese had actually gotten the U.S. Army to do its work for them.

Instead of being a strategic asset in the march toward Tokyo, Manila was a liability. The battle had destroyed most of the civic administration and social services that normally exist in any municipality. The demands for medical care, food, sanitation, civil engineering, and law enforcement had to be met quickly. The only agency even remotely capable of making the effort at the time was the United States Army. Men and material that might have been used fighting the Japanese ended up in Manila. Even then, the demands were so huge that the Army could never make good on its obligations. Manila started to become the drain on manpower that Stalingrad had been for the Germans, and Berlin for the Soviets.

Another factor to think through is what happened to the people of Manila in 1945. Maybe as much as ten percent of the population—an estimated one hundred thousand people—died during the battle. As shocking and profoundly tragic as that figure is, it is worth considering what happened to the other ninety percent. They were essentially refugees. Few buildings survived the battle. Combat had de-housed the Manileños. Given that the population of Luzon in 1945 was eight million, that meant that more than ten percent of the population of the biggest island in the Philippines had become displaced. It was a logistical nightmare.

The battle had a huge impact on the Philippines. The fight in the city guaranteed that the Philippines would stay in the US orbit for decades to come. There might have been legitimate reason to question US actions and behaviors because of the way it fought in Manila, but the harshness of Japanese occupation followed by the brutality of the battle gave the Americans a free pass. The United States would be the architect of the regional order in the Pacific and the Philippines would support that effort. There were many in the

Philippines who questioned the orientation of their nation toward the United States, but the battle silenced them.

The Battle of Manila also altered Filipino society because it was an urban battle in the political capital and cultural heart of the Philippine nation. The month-long engagement decimated the nation. Spanish Manila had survived the departure of the Spaniards for five decades, but it died in the war. The war also devastated the country's future. Politicians who had cooperated with the Japanese during the occupation had been discredited but the battle killed off many of those who would have replaced them.

* * *

As appalling as those considerations are, the Japanese could have done even more damage. General Yamashita's plan was to fight as long as possible in Luzon to keep the Americans away from Japan. In a real sense, he was successful in this effort. The Fourteenth Area Army was still offering active resistance in northeastern Luzon against the Sixth U.S. Army when the war ended in August 1945. The rapid advance American soldiers made after landing on Luzon had created a number of gaps between the various subordinate units of the Sixth U.S. Army. Walter Krueger worried that the Japanese might exploit these openings. Douglas MacArthur believed that speed and maneuver were the best measures to neutralize this danger.

Krueger's worries were not misplaced entirely. Five years later in Korea, the Chinese Peoples' Liberation Army, with far fewer resources than the Japanese had on Luzon, exploited the gaps between formations of the Eighth U.S. Army and forced American soldiers into the longest retreat in their service's history. This development, however, lay in the (near) future. At the time, Krueger worried about putting his command between two Japanese formations. He saw Yamashita and his field army as a hammer and Iwabuchi and the Manila Naval Defense Force as an anvil. That the Japanese failed to exploit this opportunity illuminates the intra-service hostility that plagued their war effort.

Still, the battle was devastating, and there is an understandable desire to apportion blame for the physical destruction of Manila and the deaths of one hundred thousand people. The Americans contributed to this horrific outcome. However, the main responsibility lies with Iwabuchi and the Naval Defense Force. The defenders fought with tenacity and resolution—which deserves a certain amount of respect—but those characteristics pale in comparison to the atrocities they visited on the people of Manila. The real issue is: why?

The answer to this question lies in the character of Iwabuchi and his command. The MNDF was a hodge-podge of individuals with little cohesion and no training in ground warfare. The only tactics they had were to point the weapon at the enemy and keep firing until they ran out of ammunition or died. That primitive approach required resolve—which the Japanese had—but the Japanese were poorly led. The atrocities, the instructions to kill all non-Japanese persons in Manila, diverted them from their main task of resisting the US advance.

Many students of this battle blame the Americans. Surely the Americans could have adopted another operational approach or used a different set of tactics to minimize the damage. The problem with this argument is that it requires individuals to accept that there was no real difference between the Americans and the Japanese. The Japanese chose to make Manila a battle ground, to engage in systematic rape and mass murder, and to set fire to the city. The Americans pulled short when they had good information that civilians were in live fire zones and offered food and medical help to refugees. It was to the Americans, not the Japanese, that Filipinos flocked for protection. The Japanese were ultimately responsible for visiting the whirlwind of death upon Manila.

A second problem with these contentions is that they involve a good deal of hindsight. Robert S. Beightler was simply doing what his command position required: trying to meet his mission while suffering as few losses as possible. Oscar W. Griswold, as corps commander, also did his job, leading his tactical formation in impressive fashion. He realized that fighting in Manila with a huge civilian population was different than advancing through the central plans of Luzon and requested strategic direction.

In this responsibility, both Krueger and MacArthur failed Griswold. Krueger's only input was that the XIV Corps secure the municipal water supply. This was a major issue. Without water for drinking and sanitation, a public health crisis of astronomical proportions could have easily occurred that would have made the fatalities of battle look puny in comparison. Griswold, however, was otherwise left to his own devices and had to develop his own plans. The ones he came up with were impressive in the technical delivery of firepower and maneuver, but they did not serve the larger interests of the United States. No one was more aware of this situation than Griswold, and he resented his lot.

The individual most responsible for this situation was MacArthur. Manila shows him at his best and worst. He had used surprise, speed, and maneuver to deliver firepower against the Japanese in key locations. At first, the march on Manila only confirmed the efficacy of this approach. When the Army landed at Lingayen Gulf, it caught the Japanese flatfooted; they had prepared for an attack from the south. Krueger's caution in his march south was understandable—his assessment came from an analysis of the evidence—but his conclusions were wrong. MacArthur's view appears to have been the product of intuition, feelings, and wishful thinking. MacArthur's guess work began to fall apart when American soldiers reached Manila. As the theater commander, it was his responsibility to develop strategy and communicate those plans to his subordinates in ways that allowed them to design military operations to support his intent.

Planning documents show that MacArthur saw Manila as the heart and soul of Luzon. In this regard, he was correct. He believed that the center of gravity of the city was Malacañan Palace and the government buildings at the east end of Luneta Park. While targeting the detention camp at the University of Santo Tomás was understandable, it did nothing to alter the course of the battle. He, however, failed to include the docks as objectives. When the Japanese thwarted the initial US efforts to liberate Manila at minimal costs, it was incumbent on MacArthur to adapt and adjust the efforts of command, which he never did.

The general cared about the fate of Manila. A number of firsthand accounts make that point. The city was the closest thing he had to a permanent home in his nomadic military life. MacArthur had left most of his worldly belongings in Manila in 1942. The loss of these items and the destruction of his hometown clearly hurt him in a personal way.

Many people accuse the general of having an oversized ego. Criticizing a general—in any army at any time—for having an ego is like criticizing them for breathing. What one can say about MacArthur's ego is that it was also exceptionally brittle. Facing profound personal losses, he froze.

While MacArthur might not have been at his best in the Battle of Manila, he had few good options. Once Iwabuchi decided to fight inside Manila, the die was cast. Arguments that MacArthur should have kept the XIV Corps from encircling the city to allow the Japanese a path for retreat have little merit. Had MacArthur, Krueger, and Griswold left a door open, it appears far more likely that the Japanese would have used it to send in reinforcements rather than as a venue for evacuation.

There was talk in MacArthur's headquarters of bypassing Manila, but that option only seems viable in hindsight. Manila was always the objective. Had

MacArthur passed it by, it would have demoralized the 250,000 Filipinos fighting under him and would have failed to achieve one of the major goals of the Luzon campaign. It would have also left a million people to continued and brutal Japanese occupation.

Would a larger but lighter force have gotten better results? Krueger's concerns about Yamashita's Fourteenth Area Army kept Griswold from committing the bulk of his corps to the fight to retake Manila. More men and units might have overwhelmed the Japanese more quickly, but MacArthur would have been forced to prohibit their use of artillery. Cannons and mortars killed Filipinos and destroyed buildings—there is no debate on that question—but reduced American casualties. In essence, MacArthur would have needed to say that taking Manila intact and limiting the deaths of Filipinos was worth more American lives. That argument would have put anyone in a difficult situation, even one with the forceful personality of Douglas MacArthur.

The evidence indicates that the best option might indeed have been greater speed and more maneuver. The Japanese feared an airborne assault or an amphibious assault directly against the city. In order to prod Krueger, MacArthur played Robert Eichelberger against him. Eichelberger, the commanding general of the Eighth Army, did the very things the Japanese feared. The problem was the unit he assigned to this assault—the 11th Airborne Division—was too small to have the impact that he and MacArthur desired. These assessments, though, are all speculative.

* * *

The job of history is to explain what happened. Why is the Manila story worth re-telling? This battle tells us a great deal about what shapes the use of military force, an issue that absorbs the attention of many. One view holds that values are important. Another view—tracing its origins back to Thucydides— argues that the use of military force has a logic all its own. Both views have merit. There is evidence for both in this story, but in the end, rational decision-making drove more of what happened in Manila. Moral, ideological, and cultural values were in play but they proved secondary to power. The Japanese defenders did what they did because they were poorly equipped, trained, and led; the Americans won because they were better in all three categories. Despite these lopsided considerations, the outcome of the battle was a poisoned one because war is an interactive and dynamic event in which no one controls all the inputs, and some are more important than others.

Acknowledgments

Many people think that writing is a solitary undertaking. They are wrong. I had enormous help along the way. It is now time to acknowledge and thank them for their assistance.

In 2011, Timothy Bent, an editor at Oxford University Press, contacted me and asked me if I would be interested in writing a book on the Battle of Manila. I had been recommended by some people, and he was calling to gauge my interest. I always think about future products and often thought about doing a straight, out-and-out battle history. It would have been something different for me. Despite what people may think, I was not trained as a military historian. I am a specialist in US diplomatic history, often focusing on the strategic level, where it easily blends with military history. While in graduate school, I had been a teaching assistant for the courses that the University of Southern California offered in US military history and the US Civil War. Long story made short, military history was not an entirely alien field to me, and I agreed to take on this project. I always figured that the two biggest problems in writing a history at the operational level for a World War II battle would be getting quality maps and source material from the other side. As things turned out, those two things were the most difficult items for me to get for this book. Cartography has suffered enormously with the rise of digital technology. Software programs have made it easier to make lower quality maps that look acceptable on a computer screen but lack the resolution needed for the printed page. Toshi Yoshihara, my friend and colleague in the strategy departments at both the U.S. Air War College and the U.S. Naval War College, helped by putting me in touch with Chris Robinson, who drew the maps that appear in this study. There was a fair amount of back and forth as Chris and I nailed down the maps. Some of this work made me see the battle differently and I went back and changed some of what I had written. It was a good exercise.

Japanese documents were another problem for two different reasons. First, my Japanese language skills are less than ideal. Second, there is very little in Japanese on the Battle of Manila. No memoirs, no articles, no documents. This dearth of material is easy to understand. Given the level of atrocities that took place, it is not a battle that many in Japan want to remember. There are very few publications in Japanese on Manila. You can probably count the number using your fingers. The *Senshi Sosho*—the official Japanese history of the war—is the most important, and it has two volumes that are relevant to Manila: one for the Army and another for the Navy. Calling these publications "histories" is a bit misleading. Most of them are collections of documents followed by some more documents with a sentence or two connecting them together. My Japanese was just good enough that I could figure out which sections of the volumes were important to me. I then asked my student, Captain Tanaka Masaomi of the Japanese Maritime Self Defense Force (*kaijōjieitai*), if he could help. He looked at it and translated it instantly. He ended up translating about forty pages for me, and he noted that the older style was not that accessible even to Japanese individuals. Toshi Yoshihara proved helpful here again, clarifying some of these passages. Another publication that was almost as important as the *Senshi Sosho* was an official study that the Japanese Ministry of Defense commissioned in the early 1980s on urban warfare. This publication, *Manira Boeisen*, used the Battle of Manila as a case study on issues involved in fighting in a city. Since this study still has an officially limited circulation and the Japanese are sticklers for following rules and protocols, it is probably best that I not publicly thank the people who helped me acquire and translate this report. All I can do is say: *domo arigato*.

One of the advantages of teaching in the professional military education system is that you have many colleagues you can turn to for detailed information about military matters. Lieutenant Colonel Fredrick Black, U.S. Army, and Lieutenant Colonel Jon O'Gorman, U.S. Marine Corps, explained artillery. Phil Haun, the Dean of Academics at the Naval War College, arranged for me to get the first sabbatical of my academic career to do the writing for this book. I have watched many people get release time, sabbaticals, and fellowships and then end up with nothing to show for all that support. I was determined to do better. Unfortunately for me, I spent the spring semester of 2020 teaching elementary school to two children who did not really want to learn from their dad as the nation locked down in the face of the COVID-19 pandemic. I did, however, manage to get the first draft of the book written before I returned to my teaching duties at the War College and that would not have happened otherwise. The Naval War College Foundation also provided the funding for a trip to Manila, where I conducted research in the archives but also took tours of the city and key battlefields.

Jason Parker of the history department at Texas A&M University played a supporting role. I needed to get research done at A&M but simply did not have time to visit College Station. Jason put me in touch with Tristan Osteria, a graduate student in the A&M history program. He did research for me in their archives. He even gave me advice for my research trip to Manila. Osteria has since finished his PhD and is, as of this writing, an assistant professor at the University of Santo Tomás.

In 1999, I was a Fellow of the West Point Summer Seminar in Military History, which was a program that West Point ran, off and on, for several decades. In 1999, the purpose of the seminar had changed from training faculty to teach the military history course required of Reserve Officers' Training Corps (ROTC) programs to one designed to develop expertise in military history. Mark Danley, then a PhD candidate at Kansas State and now a librarian at West Point, was part of the seminar. During my work on this project, he has helped me immensely. While I was in Manila, he emailed me copies of documents that I had left in the United States, which helped in the historical research I was doing and allowed me to start writing while I was in Manila. He also helped me with citations, answered questions about military historiography, and put me in touch with Captain James A. Villanueva, a professor in the history department, who had just finished a PhD in history at The Ohio State University on the guerrilla movement in the Philippines. Villanueva shared documents that he was using to teach his courses at West Point. These helped a great deal.

Others helped in many different ways. My cousin David E. Thompson II, a retired U.S. Army colonel and a veteran of the two Iraq wars, and I had a good conversation about leadership and command during the time I was in the writing stage of this book, which I found informative. Mike Creswell of Florida State University and Sal Mercagliano of Campbell University were both members of the summer seminar. They both did research for me, pulling material from archives that were local to them. Mike also read portions of the manuscript. Mitch Lerner of the history department at Ohio State University and Craig Symonds, a naval historian who taught for years at the U.S. Naval Academy and was a colleague for time while he was here at the War College, both read an early draft and gave me profoundly good advice. Randy Papadopoulos, another member of the 1999 Summer Seminar, answered questions for me about military historiography, and then called and told me that Rod Serling, best known as the creator and on-screen host of the television series, *The Twilight Zone,* was a veteran of the 11th Airborne Division. Biographies of the writer/actor make it clear his World War II service had been a fundamental, life-altering experience, and he set one episode in the Manila of 1945, which eventually was incorporated into this study. I would not have known about these biographies or the episode if not for Randy. Seth Paridon of the National World War II Museum in New Orleans, Louisiana, provided several oral histories that proved useful.

During the research phase of this book, I had a chance to visit my uncle, Colonel David E. Thompson, U.S. Army (retired), just before he died. A combat veteran of Vietnam, where he led a brigade and did things that are still remembered in the Army Aviation and Special Forces communities, we discussed the work I was doing on the book. In the last communication I had from him, he wrote (with minor corrections):

> If your current research at the Div./brigade levels has revealed some of the human elements that influence the outcomes of tactical operations (making time-sensitive decisions with incomplete knowledge of the actual situation on the ground, or a commander's resolution of conflicting information/intelligence inputs in order to promote mission accomplishments), I believe you will be on to presenting your readers with a fresh perspective on the [way] the US used to fight our wars.

That email helped shape my research questions.

During my travels to various archives, my aunt, Peggy Thompson, and Kirk Steffensen, a friend from undergraduate days, gave me place to stay. During the revision stage, my wife cut short a trip to California and returned to Rhode Island so she could care for our kids while I finished makings changes and met deadlines.

This book is dedicated to seven professors who made a significant difference in my professional development. At the University of Texas at Austin, I was fortunate to take a course on the US Civil War and Reconstruction that George B. Forgie taught. A few weeks earlier, Forgie had appeared on the ABC television network news program *Nightline*, talking about the craft of teaching at the college level. The course was difficult. I earned a B, but it was massively rewarding. I still have the books and notes. It also convinced me to change my major to history. A year later, I took the second half of the US diplomatic history survey from Robert A. Divine. The course started off interesting and then got electric. It was 1988 and the Cold War was still ongoing. Divine offered historical explanations for current events—I was enthralled and had to have more. That course convinced me to earn a PhD in US diplomatic history. I took two more classes from Divine including a research course that produced my first academic article, which later became a chapter in my dissertation/first book. Much later, after I had finished graduate school and was a professor in my own right, he gave a guest lecture for a course I taught on the Korean War.

I took a number of graduate-level courses at the University of Texas after I earned my BA. The first graduate course I took was on world economic history, taught by Walt W. Rostow. The class met in the Conference Room at the Lyndon Baines Johnson Presidential Library, with an entire wall covered in a photo of a meeting of Johnson's cabinet. Rostow walked into the room and started telling stories about every individual in the photograph. I remember that Ramsey Clark, the 66th Attorney General of the United States, was in the photograph and Rostow made some comment about him being a real left-winger. Rostow also made note of the aides sitting against the wall and said whatever was discussed in the meeting was probably leaked to the media because of their presence. Another thing I remember from that moment is that he said the people in the cabinet were so diverse that the only thing they could chat about in down moments was the weather.

What I learned over the course of the semester was that "Walt"—we never called him that to his face, he was always "Dr. Rostow"—was a charming, upbeat individual, who cared about his students and name-dropped like crazy. He had one session of the seminar meet at his house for dinner, and during an informal session was talking about how a friend of his who was director of the Central Intelligence Agency had arranged for him to do some research on leadership styles. He spent some time talking about how he had seen an academic administrator use the same approach to leadership as Stalin. What stuck with everyone was not the leadership style, but rather his friend. After he left to chat with another group, someone said, "That was Alan Dulles."

Rostow's course was insanely difficult. I say that, some thirty years later, having taken many other courses and taught some as well. After counting up all the readings I was doing that semester, I realized I was reading a book a day and about half of that was due to Rostow's course, which is to say he was assigning about three and a half books a week. During that semester, we would take a break in the middle of the three-hour seminar, and at first it was ten minutes, and during the course of the semester it grew to fifteen minutes, which eventually became twenty and then thirty. Everyone was tired.

In addition to our heavy reading load, we had to write a research paper and take a final exam. My research paper on the economics of German naval expansion in the 1890s became the first conference paper I ever presented. I remember after finishing the paper—or at least thinking I was finished—taking a break and sitting down to watch *Nightline*. This was December 1989, and it was the day the Berlin Wall came down. As I sat in front of the television, watching Ted Koppel interview his guest, I kept thinking that guy Koppel is talking to someone who looks like Walt. During the course, Walt sat at the end of the conference table, and I sat immediately to his left. I knew his left profile far better than the frontal view the television camera was giving. A few minutes later a caption at the bottom of the screen identified Koppel's guest and it was indeed Walt Rostow. I figured this was a message that I should keep working on the paper, so I got up and went back to the computer. I "survived" that course. After doing that, I knew I could do the rest of grad school. No problem.

Glen Cope was my Sunday School teacher during my high school years. She also happened to be the associate dean of the Lyndon Johnson School of Public Affairs and the president of the Society for Public Administration. I stopped into her office to say hello when I was a grad student, and we ended up having a conversation that was profoundly important in shaping my career. It basically amounted to what will impress a search committee: a scholar without a plan or one with plans that have some detail without being overly rigid. Glen told me I needed to have a second project before I finished my first project. Even though my first "second project" remains unfinished—I have six thousand photocopies of documents I copied for a biography of General William C. Westmoreland sitting in my attic—that advice stuck. This book is my seventh, and I have two more manuscripts sitting on computer hard drives, waiting to go.

After leaving Texas, I went to the University of Kentucky, where I wrote my MA thesis under the direction of George C. Herring, Jr. After a poor start, I worked hard and eventually turned in a thesis, leading Herring to say he had never had a student improve as much in one year as me.

I wish Cope and Herring had lived to see this project finished. Events developed otherwise, but both knew about this dedication, and for that I am grateful. They and Divine, Rostow, and my uncle are missed.

While in Lexington, I took the readings seminar that David E. Hamilton offered. The heavy emphasis on historiography was important and helped me develop a skill at getting to the author's central argument, boiling down a book of several hundred pages into one sentence. I believe that is a real strength of mine as a historian. That skill became useful in writing historiographical essays. I even used his syllabus as a model for the ones I have designed for graduate courses. That readings seminar might have been the single most important class I took during my graduate school days.

At the University of Southern California, I wrote my dissertation under the direction of Roger Dingman. I could not have asked for a better dissertation advisor. His demanding standards produced a good historian. Over the years, I have been amazed at how much influence he had on me. When people questioned my work, I could always tell myself that I might be capable of making those type of mistakes, but Dingman would never have let anything that bad get past him. He was also good about supporting my overall development as a scholar. He made sure I was his teaching assistant the first semester I arrived in Los Angeles, and he made myself and his other assistant, John Reed, deliver lectures as part of the course. As a result, he was able to write strong letters of recommendation attesting to both our scholarship and teaching.

What follows would be nowhere near as good as what I would have produced without such assistance. If there are any defects in this text, it is despite the assistance my family, friends, and colleagues rendered.

I have also managed to use my time productively, writing often on trips when I have time to spare on planes, or in hotel rooms after a day of research in the archives. I have written parts of this book in many different places. My personal motto might be: Have laptop. Will travel.

NEΣ
Spring 2024

Pasay, Metro Manila, Philippines
Nagoya, Japan
Saratoga Springs, New York
Portsmouth, Rhode Island
Middletown, Rhode Island
Tiverton, Rhode Island
Newport, Rhode Island
Fort Worth, Texas
Detroit, Michigan

A Note on Sources

A few words are in order about the sources that are the foundation of this study. Studying a battle presents considerable challenges. These conflicts involve thousands upon thousands of people. There were roughly forty thousand Americans involved in the battle, about twenty thousand Japanese, and a million Filipinos caught between them. How can anyone capture the experiences of that many people? An added complication is that many died during or shortly after the battle. What of their voices? Choosing which voices to use shapes the narrative.

I decided to provide a variety of perspectives. That turned out to be easier in theory than in practice. Most of the senior US commanders—Douglas MacArthur, Walter Krueger, Robert Eichelberger, Oscar W. Griswold, Joseph Swing, and Robert S. Beightler—left behind personal paper collections that have been stored in archives across the country. General William C. Chase wrote memoirs in retirement, as did MacArthur, Krueger, and Eichelberger. All of these helped document their roles in the battle.

After examining those top-level records, research started to become more of a challenge. The U.S. National Archives proved exceptionally useful, but there were limits to the records that remained. The 1st Cavalry Division and the 37th Infantry Division had records that were impressive and exceptionally well-organized. Not, alas, the 11th Airborne. The unit records for that division were destroyed in a fire during the occupation of Japan. There were ways to compensate for the loss of these documents. A good deal of daily reports survived in the files of other units because they issued duplicate copies. The daily reports of the divisions and their sub-units made for fascinating reading. Some of them were quite dry, but some officers made genuine, creative efforts to record as much information as possible. Taken as a whole, they did an excellent job of recording the use of military power during the battle.

The perspective of enlisted men, and middle-grade and junior officers was much tougher to capture. I expected the World War II Army Service Experiences Questionnaires stored at the U.S. Army Heritage and Education Center in Carlisle, Pennsylvania, to be a gold mine of personal information. Other historians have mined this collection to great profit, winning Pulitzers and endowed chairs. The collection turned out not to have much from veterans of the divisions that fought in Manila. I also expected oral histories to be helpful. Again, the results were rather disappointing. No institution has an overwhelming number. I also discovered there was no central publication or database listing oral histories held at various archives, museums, and historical societies. The advent of internet search engines helped find lone interviews here and there. Finding these items might have been impossible had I been writing this study in the mid-1990s, which is when I wrote my first book. I hoped the alumni newsletters of the various units might contain a number of war stories. Some did, but much of those newsletters contained updates on what veterans had been up to since they left the service.

Much to my surprise, I discovered that a number of state historical archives had collections related to the war. In the 1990s, the State of Tennessee began a questionnaire program similar to the one at Carlisle in an effort to record the experiences of residents of the Volunteer State. There are roughly seventy-five hundred filled out forms in Record Group 237 of the Tennessee State Library and Archives. My research assistant, Elizabeth Lambert, and I spent a day going through these items, culling those that had served in Luzon from those that had been in North Africa, Italy, Northwestern Europe, or other parts of the Pacific. We found about fifty forms, but most of them were quite meager in their responses, usually summarizing their experiences in a few words or—maybe—a full sentence. The state of Connecticut published a series of pamphlets immediately after the war—*Connecticut Men of the U.S. Army*—which gave brief, paragraph-length summaries of returning veterans' experiences. Although short, these profiles had direct quotes, which often added color.

Developing the Filipino side of this triangular story was more of a challenge than I had expected. Libraries and archives vanished in the inferno of the battle, and years passed before they were rebuilt. Many Manileños (Filipino residents of the city) and Manilaners (foreign residents of the city) left behind memoirs of their World War II experiences with almost all containing emotionally charged chapters on the battle. The Filipinas Heritage Library at the Ayala Museum in Makati has been collecting firsthand accounts. Many of these documents have been quite useful in developing this history. Many discuss friends and family members who did not survive, but the physical destruction of the city, and along with it its archives, has put real limits on the ability of a historian to give them voice.

The Japanese side was even more difficult to capture, even though I read and speak some Japanese. Although it is the general perception that the Manila Naval Defense Force stood and fought to the last man, that is not true. A small number made it back to Japan after the war, although the veterans did not write memoirs of this engagement. I found part of the solution to this problem in the files of US military intelligence units. About four hundred members of the MNDF surrendered during the battle, and prisoner of war debriefings were conducted within hours, giving US commanders an idea of what was happening on the "other side of the hill." Intelligence analysis also cobbled these reports together, which told an interesting story of how the Americans won the spy war in Manila. The POW debriefings were also of interest to historians seven decades later, wanting to answer more esoteric questions related to the morale and motivation of the defenders. Another source of information on the Japanese side of the battle were the documents that US infantryman recovered off the bodies of dead Japanese. Diaries, letters, training documents, and orders all added more information that allowed for a partial reconstruction of the story of the defenders.

The use of the *Senshi Sosho*—the official Japanese history of the war—was also crucial in evoking the Japanese perspective. Written using an older version of Japanese that was confounding, the account of the two relevant volumes offered was of profound importance. Others wishing to write on Manila should make use of these histories.

The history that emerges from all these documents is one that is trilateral in nature, even if it is best described as a scalene triangle (the sides and angles are not equal). This account looks at all three levels of war—tactical, operational, and strategic—but probably spends more text at the operational level. Ultimately, what makes some battles more significant than others is their effect. This book tries to offer something new in describing the impact of this battle, while also keeping a focus on what happened.

Notes

INTRODUCTION

1. "President Leads World-Wide Tribute to One of Nation's Great Heroes," *The Washington Post Times-Herald*, April 6, 1964.
2. Jack Raymond, "M'Arthur is Dead; Led Allied Force in Japan's Defeat," *The New York Times*, April 6, 2018.
3. William Moore, "M'Arthur Eulogized in Halls of Congress," *Chicago Tribune*, April 7, 1964.
4. "President Leads World-Wide Tribute."
5. "President Leads World-Wide Tribute"; Italics of the ship's name added by the author. Jean M. White, "Throngs at Crossroads Salute General's Funeral Train," *The Washington Post Times-Herald*, April 9, 1964; William Anderson, "Johnson, Nation Pay Homage to M'Arthur," *Chicago Tribune*, April 9, 1964.
6. Edward T. Folliard, "100,000 Pay Homage to MacArthur," *The Washington Post Times-Herald*, April 9, 1964; "Silent Thousands Line Route of Procession," *The Washington Post Times-Herald*, April 9, 1964; Phil Casey, "Salute at Plane Marks Last MacArthur Flight," *The Washington Post Times-Herald*, April 10, 1964
7. "Body of MacArthur is Flown to Norfolk, Va. For Last Rites," *The New York Times*, April 10, 1964; Ben A. Franklin, "M'Arthur Rites in Norfolk Today: World Dignitaries to Attend—Thousands Visit Coffin," *The New York Times*, April 11, 1964; Sterling Seagrave, "MacArthur Bier Saluted In Norfolk: Thousands View 6-Mile Procession to His Memorial," *The Washington Post Times-Herald*, April 11, 1964.
8. "Body of MacArthur is Flown to Norfolk."
9. The most detailed of MacArthur biographies is D. Clayton James, *The Years of MacArthur*, vol. 2, *1941–1945* (Boston: Houghton Mifflin, 1975). Other accounts include William Manchester, *American Caesar: Douglas MacArthur, 1880–1964* (Boston: Little, Brown, & Co, 1978); Carol Morris Petillo, *Douglas MacArthur: The Philippine Years* (Bloomington: Indiana University Press, 1981); Michael Schaller, *Douglas MacArthur: The Far Eastern General* (New York: Oxford University Press, 1989); Geoffrey Perret, *Old Soldiers Never Die: The Life of Douglas MacArthur* (New York: Random House, 1996); Jack Gallaway, *The Odd Couple: Blamey and MacArthur at War* (St. Lucia, Queensland, Australia: University of Queensland Press, 2000); Richard B. Frank, *MacArthur: A Biography* (New York: Palgrave Macmillan, 2009); Mark Perry, *The Most Dangerous Man in America: The Making of Douglas MacArthur* (New York: Basic Books, 2014).

10. John G. Norris, "MacArthur One of Great U.S. Soldiers," *The Washington Post Times-Herald*, April 6, 1964.

11. "That MacArthur Interview—Why?" *Los Angeles Times*, April 10, 1964; "Verdicts on Korea," *The Wall Street Journal*, April 14, 1964.

12. This work hopes to address two broad historiographies. The first and the most obvious is the military history of World War II, which, in the Pacific, is like an ice cream sandwich. It is hard and well developed at both the beginning and the end, while soft in the middle. Ronald H. Spector agrees with only half of this in his general history of the Pacific. He contends that the atomic bombs have "inspired a mountain of writing so immense as to dwarf the total literature devoted to all other aspects of the conflict." Ronald H. Spector, *Eagle Against the Sun: The American War with Japan* (New York: The Free Press, 1984), xiii. Either way, Manila is an understudied topic.

General accounts are few in number compared to the European theater. Akira Iriye, *Power and Culture: The Japanese–American War, 1941–1945* (Cambridge: Harvard University Press, 1981) is a well-written book that stays at the policy and strategic levels. Spector's *Eagle Against the Sun* is a military history, but one that does a good job of discussing the activities of each branch of the armed forces. Dan van der Vat provides an account that focuses solely on the naval aspect of the conflict in *The Pacific Campaign: The US-Japanese Naval War 1941–45* (New York: Simon and Schuster, 1991). John Dower argues that the main factor driving the conflict between the United States and Japan was the racial attitudes of the two belligerents in *War Without Mercy: Race and Power in the Pacific War* (New York: Pantheon Books, 1986). At first glance, Manila would seem to be a perfect example of Dower's thesis. The atrocities the Japanese committed during this battle against a people that they viewed as inferior would certainly seem to support his position. The thing is, passion and hatred are nothing new in war. It has and will always be a driving factor in all conflicts, but a close and detailed examination shows that the atrocities in Manila were due more to poor training and weak leadership than racial driven hate.

Books on ground combat in the Pacific theater are produced less frequently than those about the European theater. Eric Bergerud's account of ground operations in the South Pacific was a major historiographical event in that it was the first major study on the topic—beyond official and unit histories—that gave the U.S. Army its due: Eric Bergerud, *Touched With Fire: The Land Warfare in the South Pacific* (New York: Viking, 1996). For another account, see Harry A. Gailey, *MacArthur's Victory: The War in New Guinea, 1943–1944* (New York: Ballantine Books, 2004). While MacArthur and his staff made avoidable mistakes, Stephen R. Taaffe gives the general a good deal of credit for the allied victories in New Guinea in his book, *MacArthur's Jungle War: The 1944 New Guinea Campaign* (Lawrence: University Press of Kansas, 1998). James P. Duffy's book on the Philippine campaign is a light, easy read that is vague on a central argument, but Duffy does put the responsibility for the disaster that befell Manila squarely on the shoulders of Rear Admiral Iwabuchi Sanji: James P. Duffy, *Return to Victory: MacArthur's Epic Liberation of the Philippines* (New York: Hachette Books, 2021).

The limited studies about Manila then are in keeping with publishing trends that favor Europe over the Pacific and the tendency for historians of the war against Japan to focus on the Navy and Marine Corps over the Army. A major exception to these trends is John C. McManus, *Fire and Fortitude: The U.S. Army in the Pacific War, 1941–1943* (New York: Dutton Caliber, 2019). This book is the first of a proposed trilogy and is in position to have a major impact on the literature.

An important book that has turned much of the previous literature on its head is Waldo Heinrichs and Marc Gallicchio, *Implacable Foes: War in the Pacific, 1944–1945* (New York: Oxford University Press, 2017). Heinrichs and Gallicchio argue that the United States was not fighting in the Pacific from a position of plenty, but rather was at or near its culmination point—a concept that the nineteenth-century military theorist General-Major Carl von Clausewitz developed. This book confirms the findings of Heinrichs and Gallicchio and pushes them further.

A second historiography this work contributes to is the growing field of intelligence history. Early works on intelligence efforts in the Pacific focused on code breaking: W. J. Holmes, *Double Edged Secrets: U.S. Naval Intelligence in the Pacific During World War II* (Annapolis: Naval Institute Press, 1979); Ronald Lewin, *The American Magic: Codes, Ciphers, and the Defeat of Japan* (New York: Farrar Straus Giroux, 1982); Edwin T. Layton, *And I Was There: Pearl Harbor and Midway Breaking Secrets* (New York: Morrow, 1985); Edward J. Drea, *MacArthur's Ultra: Codebreaking and the War against Japan, 1942– 1945* (Lawrence: University Press of Kansas, 1992); John Prados, *Combined Fleet Decoded: The Secret History of American Intelligence and the Japanese Navy in World War II* (New York: Random House, 1995). In more recent years, Roger Dingman, Allison B. Gilmore, and Douglas Ford have focused on translations and analysis efforts. See Allison B. Gilmore, *You Can't Fight Tanks with Bayonets: Psychological Warfare against the Japanese in the Southwest Pacific* (Lincoln: University of Nebraska Press, 1998). Ford argues the US Army did a good deal of analysis on the Japanese Army and its approach toward combat: Douglas Ford, "US Assessments of Japanese Ground Warfare Tactics and the Army's Campaigns in the Pacific Theaters, 1943–1945: Lessons Learned and Methods Applied," *War in History* 16, no. 3 (2009): 323–358. Dingman, in particular, takes on Dower directly, showing that the intelligence branches of the US military were mechanisms that worked against killing: Roger Dingman, *Deciphering the Rising Sun: Navy and Marine Corps Codebreakers, Translators and Interpreters in the Pacific War* (Annapolis: Naval Institute Press, 2009). The interrogation teams needed living prisoners to get information from.

13. There are five books on the battle for Manila. The first book is Lawrence
    Cortesi's study. This book is more novel than a historical monograph. Cortesi
    exceeds his sources and quotes without documentation, leaving his readers with
    the impression that he has manufactured many of his facts: Lawrence Cortesi,
    The Battle for Manila (New York: Kensington Publishers, 1984).
        The other four books all stress the suffering of the Filipino public during the
    battle. Alfonso Aluit offers an extensive urban history of Manila before 1945. His
    account of military operations is solid, based primarily on the official U.S. Army
    history, but explaining military operations is not his primary task: Alfonso Aluit,
    *By Sword and Fire: The Destruction of Manila in World War II, 3 February–
    3 March 1945* (Manila: National Commission for Culture and Arts, 1994). In
    1993, Richard Connaughton, John Pimlott, and Duncan Anderson, a team of
    British and Australian historians, produced a short synthesis of official histories
    and memoirs that contends that the Americans pursued a strategy designed to
    avoid US casualties, even if they increased the numbers among the Filipinos:
    Richard Connaughton, John Pimlott, and Duncan Anderson, *The Battle of
    Manila* (Novato, CA: Presidio Press, 1995), 123, 142–143, 163, 175, 195. Jose
    Ma. Bonifacio M. Escoda's book is far more episodic than Aluit's, and it suffers
    from a number of production issues: Jose Ma. Bonifacio M. Escoda, *Warsaw
    of Asia: The Rape of Manila* (Quezon City, Philippines: Giraffe Books, 2000).
    James M. Scott, *Rampage: MacArthur, Yamashita, and the Battle of Manila*
    (New York: W.W. Norton, 2018) advances a thesis that the battle was a monu-
    mental ego clash between two generals. Although it is a well-written account that
    is based on impressive research, the book really does not support this position,
    but focuses primarily on the suffering of the Filipino people. While Scott has a
    much larger audience than any of these other books, he offers no real explana-
    tion for Japanese actions, or how the battle fit into the larger course of events in
    World War II.
        The rescue of the civilian internees at the University of Santo Tomás has
    dominated the literature with a surplus of memoirs from the prisoners. There are
    also several accounts from the soldiers that participated in the "flying column"
    and the rescue of the prisoners. A number of journalists were part of the "flying
    column" and others were held captive at the university. As a result, they wrote
    numerous firsthand accounts of the liberation of the prisoners in the form of
    books, newspaper stories, and magazine articles, and many will be cited in the
    pages to come. Frances B. Cogan wrote a scholarly study of American civilians
    who were prisoners of the Japanese, and this account includes a chapter on
    the arrival of the 1st Cavalry at Santo Tomás: Frances B. Cogan, *Captured:
    The Internment of American Civilians in the Philippines, 1941–1945* (Athens:
    University of Georgia Press, 2000).
        There are many differing views on the importance of the battle. Major William
    T. James, Jr., "From Siege to Surgical: The Evolution of Urban Combat from
    World War II to the Present and its Effect on Current Doctrine" (Master of

Military Art and Science: U.S. Army Command & General Staff College, 1998) calls Manila "the key to Luzon, and Luzon was the key to the entire Philippine archipelago" (James, "From Siege to Surgical," 15). Connaughton, Pimlott, and Anderson disagree. They do not believe that Manila was the center of gravity of the Philippines in 1945, which was the idea that shaped MacArthur's thinking, along with his personal obsession with the city. They do, however, believe that the city was an important transportation hub because of its port facilities and airfields, which made it vital to take the city (Connaughton, Pimlott, and Anderson, *The Battle of Manila*, 179–180, 205). They are correct in their first assessment, but wrong in the second because of the damage the city took during the engagement. John Kennedy Ohl, the biographer of General Robert S. Beightler, argues that the city had no military value: John Kennedy Ohl, *Minuteman: The Military Career of General Robert S. Beightler* (Boulder, CO: Lynne Rienner Publishers, 2001), 195.

A number of observers believe the battle was all about MacArthur and his large ego. Mark Leigh offers his readers a well-written and informative article, Mark Leigh, "Liberation and Death in Manila," *Military Illustrated* (June 2002), 48–55, and sees little value in the battle, stating that the battle took place for "emotional reasons." Norman Mailer, the Pulitzer Prize–winning novelist, was on Luzon in 1945 as an infantryman and he saw little significance to the fight. "Our victory in the great city means no more symbolically than Harvard beating Yale to avenge a humiliating defeat of the previous season," he wrote his wife (Mailer to Mailer, March 6, 1945, Folder 517.5, Box 517, Papers of Norman Mailer, Harry Ransom Center, University of Texas, Austin, TX). The problem with these types of arguments is that they ignore the logic of power that drove the planning of this battle.

What is different about this study? It offers a different account of MacArthur and Yamashita. Neither general figured significantly in the battle. MacArthur fades away once the shooting starts as his large but fragile ego cracks during the battle. The Japanese general barely figures into this story at all. The Japanese individual most responsible for the course of the battle was Rear Admiral Iwabuchi Sanji. This book documents the suffering of the Filipino people—to do otherwise would be misleading—but it will also focus on the military course of events in an effort to analyze the strategic effects of the Battle of Manila.

It is also worth noting that this book is also the result of a wider research foundation than what is found in previous accounts. The narrative and findings of this book are the product of research in official U.S. Army unit records at the US National Archives, but also MacArthur's papers at the MacArthur Memorial and the papers of many of his subordinate commanders, including Walter Krueger, Oscar W. Griswold, and Beightler. Numerous memoirs and oral histories from archives across the country also found their way into the footnotes. Americans were not the only ones at this battle and the Japanese and Filipino perspectives are also present, based on prisoner of war (POW) debriefs, captured documents, memoirs, and official histories. It is the first work in English on the battle to use Japanese-language sources.

Manila has been the subject of several documentary television productions, which have probably had more impact than all the previously mentioned books put together. On October 9, 1955, the CBS television network aired the *You Are There* program. "The Rescue of the American Prisoners from Santo Tomás" episode, which was narrated by the highly respected newsman Walter Cronkite, focused on the arrival of the 1st Cavalry at the detention center (Internet Movie Database, https://www.imdb.com/title/tto751953/?ref_=ttfc_fc_tt). Four years later, the ABC television network aired the "Battle of Manila" episode of *The Big Picture*. In the 1950s and 1960s, the U.S. Army Signal Corps produced this show as an effort to inform the public of the Army's achievements. The Manila episode is quite superficial as history, offering little more than the basic facts with no analysis of the engagement (https://youtube.com/watch?v=SYVRtsE95u8). In 2007, the Japanese Broadcasting Corporation, better known as NHK, telecast *Remembering the Battle of Manila*, which aired on The History Channel in both the United States and the Philippines. A number of veterans were interviewed and none of them admitted to taking part in the atrocities that took part in the city. In fact, the documentary downplayed the atrocities that took place, arguing that Japanese actions were in response to unprovoked guerrilla attacks, and blaming MacArthur and U.S. Army artillery for the destruction of Manila.

To be blunt, those arguments are absurd. To be sure, many Filipino civilians died as the result of actions the U.S. Army. To argue otherwise is impossible, but the Japanese defenders, often without provocation, killed many civilians in quite cruel fashion. The documentation is extensive and irrefutable. The U.S. Army tried to fight a battle with power and speed to limit the destruction. Japan, on the other hand, intentionally visited pain upon the city. Benito J. Legarda, Jr., a Harvard economics PhD, writer, and journalist, has made this point over and over and over again in his columns in the *Philippines Free Press*, which he collected and published as a book: Benito J. Legarda, Jr., *Occupation: The Later Years* (Manila: Vibal Publishing House, 2007), 179–180, 204–205.

CHAPTER 1

1. Perret, *Old Soldiers Never Die*, 37–39, 44–45.
2. Perret, *Old Soldiers Never Die*, 70–73; James, *Years of MacArthur*, vol. 1, 118–125.
3. Perret, *Old Soldiers Never Die*, 92–95, 108–110; James, *Years of MacArthur*, vol. 1, 217–223, 238–239.
4. James, *Years of MacArthur*, vol. 1, 263–265.
5. Perret, *Old Soldiers Never Die*, 125–127, 136–137.
6. Perret, *Old Soldiers Never Die*, 125–127, 136–139; James, *Years of MacArthur*, vol. 1, 322–324.

7. Perret, *Old Soldiers Never Die*, 154–161; James, *Years of MacArthur*, vol. 1, 343–344, 358, 402–404.

8. Mark Perry, *The Most Dangerous Man in America: The Making of Douglas MacArthur* (New York: Basic Books, 2015), 15–18, 57–62, 273–280, 355–356.

9. Perret, *Old Soldiers Never Die*, 192–193; James, *Years of MacArthur*, vol. 1, 494–495, 554–555; "Jean MacArthur, General's Widow Dies at 101," *The New York Times*, January 24, 2000.

10. James, *The Years of MacArthur*, vol. 2, 1–15, 100–103, 130–132; Perret, *Old Soldiers Never Die*, 226–229, 248–252, 272–273; Spector, *Eagle Against the Sun*, 107–119; Perry, *The Most Dangerous Man in America*, 59, 143–153.

11. Kenney to McCarthy, August 23, 1976, Folder 7, Box 2, Papers of Frank McCarthy, George C. Marshall Research Library, Virginia Military Institute, Lexington, VA; Christopher Thorne, *Allies of a Kind: The United States, Britain, and the War against Japan, 1941–1945* (New York: Oxford University Press, 1978), 370. On the bonus army incident, see Jerome Tuccille, *The War Against the Vets: The World War I Bonus Army During the Great Depression* (Lincoln: University of Nebraska Press, 2018), 117–122. For the non-salute, see Michael D. Pearlman, *Truman and MacArthur: Policy, Politics, and the Hunger for Honor and Renown* (Bloomington: Indiana University Press, 2008), 113. For a small sampling of historians that have stressed the general's personality, ego, and inflated sense of worth, see John Dower, *Embracing Defeat: Japan in the Wake of World War II* (New York: W.W. Norton, 1998); Michael Schaller, *Douglas MacArthur: The Far Eastern General* (New York: Oxford University Press, 1989); Laura Belmonte, "Anglo-American Relations and the Dismissal of MacArthur," *Diplomatic History* 19, no. 4 (Fall 1995): 641–667; Peter Lowe, "An Ally and a Recalcitrant General: Great Britain, Douglas MacArthur and the Korean War, 1950–1," *English Historical Review* 105, no. 416 (July 1990): 624–653; Samuel F. Wells, *Fearing the Worst: How Korea Transformed the Cold* (New York: Columbia University Press, 2020), 145–147, 153–158, 176–177. On Peck's views, see Jeanne Miller, "How a Liberal Came to Love MacArthur," *San Francisco Examiner*, July 5, 1977.

12. Spector, *Eagle Against the Sun*, 142–145; van der Vat, *The Pacific Campaign*, 147–148; James, *Years of MacArthur*, vol. 2, 122–123.

13. Carl von Clausewitz, *On War*, ed. and trans. Michael Howard and Peter Paret (Princeton: Princeton University Press, 1976), 618–623.

14. Nicholas Evan Sarantakes, *Allies Against the Rising Sun: The United States, the British Nations, and the Defeat of Imperial Japan* (Lawrence: University Press of Kansas, 2009); Perry, *The Most Dangerous Man in America*, 1801–1810; James, *The Years of MacArthur*, vol. 2, 211–219; Williamson Murray and Allan R. Millett, *A War to be Won: Fighting the Second World War* (Cambridge: Harvard University Press, 2000), 199–200.

15. Craig Symonds, *Nimitz at War: Command Leadership from Pearl Harbor to Tokyo Bay* (New York: Oxford University Press, 2022).

16. Unmarked correction to spelling error in the transcript. George H. Decker, Oral History, part two (November 9, 1972), 36, Senior Officer Debriefing Program, U.S. Army Heritage and Education Center, Carlisle Barracks, PA.

17. James S. Powell, "Learning Under Fire: Military Units in the Crucible of Combat: A Monograph," *School of Advanced Military Studies Monographs* (U.S. Army Command & General Staff College, 2006), 11.

18. James, *Years of MacArthur*, vol. 2, 349–353, 464–465; Spector, *Eagle Against the Sun*, 142–147.

19. George H. Decker, Oral History, part two (November 9, 1972), p. 36, Senior Officer Debriefing Program, U.S. Army Heritage and Education Center, Carlisle Barracks, PA.

20. George H. Decker, Oral History, part two (November 9, 1972), p. 36, Senior Officer Debriefing Program, U.S. Army Heritage and Education Center, Carlisle Barracks, PA.

21. Perry, *The Most Dangerous Man in America*, 159–160.

22. James, *The Years of MacArthur*, vol. 2, 229; Murray and Millett, *A War to be Won*, 199–200.

23. Perry, *The Most Dangerous Man in America*, 354–355.

24. Thomas E. Griffith, Jr., *MacArthur's Airman: General George C. Kenney and the War in the Southwest Pacific* (Lawrence: University Press of Kansas, 1998), 92–96.

25. James, *Years of MacArthur*, vol. 2, 464–465; Spector, *Eagle Against the Sun*, 227–229, 232–233, 242–247, 282–287, 291–294, 417–442.

26. Ian W. Toll, *Twilight of the Gods: War in the Western Pacific, 1944–1945* (New York: W.W. Norton & Company, 2020), 50–56.

27. The author conducted this exercise using The True Size website (http://www.thet ruesize.com), which allows the user to superimpose foreign nations and US states on top of one another to get an idea of the relative size of different pieces of geography. Toll, *Twilight of the Gods*, 55–56; "Agenda POA-CBI-SWPA Conference on Mike I and Future Operations," [no date] Annexes I and II to Agenda with Inclosures A, B, and C to Annex II and Annex III with Inclosure B and C to Annex III, Folder 5, Box 25, Papers of Richard Sutherland, Record Group 30, MacArthur Memorial, Norfolk, VA; George B. Eaton, *From Teaching to Practice: General Walter Krueger and the Development of Joint Operations, 1921–1945* (Newport, RI: Center for Naval Warfare Studies, U.S. Naval War College, 1994), 105–106; "Invasion of Japan," *New York Herald Tribune*, February 18, 1945.

28. Toll, *Twilight of the Gods*, 74–75.

29. James Kelly Morningstar, *War and Resistance in the Philippines, 1942–1945* (Annapolis: Naval Institute Press, 2021).

30. Robert Ross Smith, *United States Army in World War II: The War in the Pacific: Triumph in the Philippines* (Washington, DC: U.S. Government Printing Office, 1963), 240; Kevin T. McEnery, *The XIV Corps Battle for Manila, February 1945* (Stamford, UK: Verdun Press, 2015), 42, 44; Laurel quote in N. Roxas Statement, Appendix N to Emil Krause, R. Graham Bosworth, and James T.

Walsh, Report of Investigation of Atrocities Committed by Japanese Imperial Forces in Intramuros (Walled City) Manila, PI. During February 1945, April 9, 1945, Folder Japanese Atrocities, Box 4, Papers of Oscar Griswold, Academy Library, U.S. Military Academy, West Point, NY.

31. Mark C. Bender, *Watershed at Leavenworth: Dwight D. Eisenhower and the Command and General Staff College* (Fort Leavenworth, KS: Combat Studies Institute, 1990), 40.

32. George H. Decker, Oral History, part one (November 3, 1972), 32, Senior Officer Debriefing Program, U.S. Army Heritage and Education Center, Carlisle Barracks, PA.

33. McEnery, *The XIV Corps Battle for Manila*, 19, 27, 36, 37; Powell, "Learning Under Fire," 16–17; Ford, "US Assessments of Japanese Ground Warfare Tactics," 340.

34. Frank F. Mathias, 37th Infantry Division, World War II Army Service Experiences Questionnaire, U.S. Army Heritage and Education Center, Carlisle Barracks, PA.

35. Floyd N. Birdwell, Folder 4, Box 4, World War II Veteran Surveys, Record Group 237, Tennessee State Library & Archives, Nashville, TN.

36. Murphy Foret, 37th Infantry Division, World War II Army Service Experiences Questionnaire, U.S. Army Heritage and Education Center, Carlisle Barracks, PA.

37. Horrace W. Craddock, Folder 1, Box 10, World War II Veteran Surveys, Record Group 237, Tennessee State Library & Archives, Nashville, TN.

38. Johnston S. Harrison, Folder 8, Box 17, World War II Veteran Surveys, Record Group 237, Tennessee State Library & Archives, Nashville, TN.

39. Salvatore V. DeGaetano, 1st Cavalry Division, World War II Army Service Experiences Questionnaire, US Army Heritage and Education Center, Carlisle Barracks, PA.

40. Frank F. Mathias, 37th Infantry Division, World War II Army Service Experiences Questionnaire, U.S. Army Heritage and Education Center, Carlisle Barracks, PA.

41. Willard H. Higdon, Folder 2, Box 19, World War II Veteran Surveys, Record Group 237, Tennessee State Library & Archives, Nashville, TN.

42. Charles A. Henne, 37th Infantry Division, World War II Army Service Experiences Questionnaire, U.S. Army Heritage and Education Center, Carlisle Barracks, PA.

43. Warren F. Fitch, 37th Infantry Division, World War II Army Service Experiences Questionnaire, U.S. Army Heritage and Education Center, Carlisle Barracks, PA.

44. Murphy Foret, 37th Infantry Division, World War II Army Service Experiences Questionnaire, U.S. Army Heritage and Education Center, Carlisle Barracks, PA.

45. Frank M. Lutze, 37th Infantry Division, World War II Army Service Experiences Questionnaire, U.S. Army Heritage and Education Center, Carlisle Barracks, PA.

46. Charles A. Henne, 37th Infantry Division, World War II Army Service Experiences Questionnaire, U.S. Army Heritage and Education Center, Carlisle Barracks, PA.

47. Rex H. Gaskins, Folder 1, Box 15, World War II Veteran Surveys, Record Group 237, Tennessee State Library & Archives, Nashville, TN.

48. Charles A. Henne, 37th Infantry Division, World War II Army Service Experiences Questionnaire, U.S. Army Heritage and Education Center, Carlisle Barracks, PA.

49. Hughes Seewald, 1st Cavalry Division, World War II Army Service Experiences Questionnaire, U.S. Army Heritage and Education Center, Carlisle Barracks, PA.

50. Frank F. Mathias, 37th Infantry Division, World War II Army Service Experiences Questionnaire, U.S. Army Heritage and Education Center, Carlisle Barracks, PA; John Wyman, Oral History, no date, 1, Veterans History Project, American Folklife Center, Library of Congress, Washington, DC.

51. Julius Gassner, 37th Infantry Division, World War II Army Service Experiences Questionnaire, U.S. Army Heritage and Education Center, Carlisle Barracks, PA.

52. Floyd E. Todd, 37th Infantry Division, World War II Army Service Experiences Questionnaire, U.S. Army Heritage and Education Center, Carlisle Barracks, PA.

53. Emanuel F. Jensen, Folder 2, Box 21 and Wilson M. Pennington, Folder 6, Box 30, World War II Veteran Surveys, Record Group 237, Tennessee State Library & Archives, Nashville, TN.

54. Bruce Palmer, Oral History by U.S. Military History Institute (December 5, 1975), 343, U.S. Army Heritage and Education Center, Carlisle Barracks, PA. Quote from Gassner, 37th Infantry Division, World War II Army Service Experiences Questionnaire, U.S. Army Heritage and Education Center, Carlisle Barracks, PA. On saving money because there was nowhere to spend it, see the following World War II Veteran Surveys from individuals that were in Manila housed Record Group 237 at the Tennessee State Library & Archives, Nashville, TN: Earl Passmore, Folder 1, Box 30; Robert L. Boyd, Folder 1, Box 5; Charlie Quill Samples, Folder 1, Box 34; Edward William King, Folder 4, Box 22; William Kennedy Nelms, Jr., Folder 6, Box 28; and Wilson M. Pennington, Folder 6, Box 30. On the same topic, see the following World War II Army Service Experiences Questionnaires housed at the U.S. Army Heritage and Education Center: Cletus J. Schwaf, Frank F. Mathias, Frank M. Lutze, and Yukio Kawamoto.

55. The quote on reading is from Daniel Jackson Sears, 37th Infantry Division, World War II Army Service Experiences Questionnaire, U.S. Army Heritage and Education Center, Carlisle Barracks, PA. On volleyball, the World War II Veteran Surveys in Record Group 237, Tennessee State Library & Archives, see L. D. Brandon, Folder 4, Box 5. On the same topic, see the questionnaires of Daniel Jackson Sears and Robert G. Knauss, World (both of the 37th Infantry Division), 37th Infantry Division, War II Army Service Experiences Questionnaire, U.S. Army Heritage and Education Center, Carlisle Barracks, PA.

56. Kevin C. Holzimmer, "Joint Operations in the Southwest Pacific, 1943–1945," *Joint Forces Quarterly* 38 (3rd quarter 2005): 102–106; George H. Decker, Oral History, part two (November 9, 1972), 37, Senior Officer Debriefing Program, U.S. Army Heritage and Education Center, Carlisle Barracks, PA; Willie M.

Gilbert, 37th Division, World War II Army Service Experiences Questionnaire, U.S. Army Heritage and Education Center, Carlisle Barracks, PA.

57. Smith, *United States Army in World War II*, 250.

58. McEnery, *The XIV Corps Battle for Manila*, 25, 28; James S. Powell argues it was divisions that had the resources to learn lessons and transmit them to lower levels. Smaller units did not and could not perform these missions: Powell, "Learning Under Fire," 5, 8–9, 53–59. In a historiographical sense, learning under fire has been a new area of exploration in the history of the U.S. Army, but most of these studies have focused on the fight in Europe: John S. Brown, *Draftee Division: The 88th Infantry Division in World War II* (Lexington: University Press of Kentucky, 1986); Michael D. Doubler, *Closing With the Enemy: How GIs Fought the War in Europe, 1944–1945* (Lawrence: University Press of Kansas, 1994); Peter R. Mansoor, *The GI Offensive in Europe: The Triumph of American Infantry Divisions, 1941–1945* (Lawrence: University Press of Kansas, 1999). This study will offer some insights into this discussion, but it is not the main focus of this study. It will, of course, be significantly different from the Brown, Doubler, and Mansoor books in that it looks at events in the Pacific rather than those in Europe.

59. "Old Soldier," *Time* (January 29, 1945), 29–30; Walter Krueger, "Policy," December 5, 1925, Folder 19, Box 7, Student Papers Collection, Record Group 13, Naval Historical Collection, U.S. Naval War College, Newport, RI.

60. Harry Mayo, "Krueger Heads 6th Army Drive on Luzon Beach," *The Cincinnati Post*, January 10, 1945; Nixson Denton, "First Interview with Krueger: Denton Paints Pen Picture of Cincinnati's 3-Star General," *The Cincinnati Times-Star*, December 13, 1944; Gordon Walker, "General Krueger: Mystery Man of Pacific," *The Christian Science Monitor*, June 9, 1945; Felix R. McKnight, "General With a GI's Heart: That's Walter Krueger, USA," *The Dallas Morning News*, June 10, 1945.

61. George H. Decker, Oral History, part one (November 3, 1972), 19, Senior Officer Debriefing Program, U.S. Army Heritage and Education Center, Carlisle, PA.

62. Walter Krueger, "Responsibilities in a Joint Command," April 18, 1947, Folder 73, Box 12, Papers of Walter Krueger, Academy Library, U.S. Military Academy.

63. George H. Decker, Oral History, part one (November 3, 1972), 31, Senior Officer Debriefing Program, U.S. Army Heritage and Education Center, Carlisle, PA.

64. Bruce Palmer, Oral History by U.S. Military History Institute (December 5, 1975), 326.

65. Kevin C. Holzimmer, *General Walter Krueger: Unsung Hero* (Lawrence: University Press of Kansas, 2007), 16; Stephen R. Taaffe, *Marshall and His Generals: U.S. Army Commanders in World War II* (Lawrence: University Press of Kansas, 2011), 224–225, 229–231; "Old Soldier," *Time* (January 29, 1945), 30; Joseph M. Swing, Oral History by D. Clayton James, August 26, 1971, 22, MacArthur Memorial, Norfolk, VA; February 9, 1945 entry, Diary of Oscar

W. Griswold, Box 1, Papers of Oscar W. Griswold, U.S. Army Heritage and Education Center, Carlisle, PA.

66. George H. Decker, Oral History (November 3, 1972), 6; Roger O. Egeberg, Oral History by D. Clayton James, June 30, 1971, 24 and 29, Box 2, Record Group 49, MacArthur Memorial, Norfolk, VA; Walter Krueger, "Additional Comments on the Leyte Campaign: In re the Exercise of Command," attached to Krueger to Ward, September 12, 1951, Folder Orders and Misc. Papers 1927–1966, Box 1, Papers of Walter Krueger, Academy Library, U.S. Military Academy; Taaffe, *Marshall and His Generals*, 321; Frank L. Kluckhorn, "Master of Amphibious Warfare," *The New York Times Magazine,* December 31, 1944, 11.

67. Holzimmer, *General Walter Krueger: Unsung Hero,* 94–95, 125–126, 204, 216–218; Carlo D'Este, *Eisenhower: A Soldier's Life* (New York: Henry Hold and Company, 2002), 270; John H. McDonald, Jr., "General Walter Krueger: A Case Study in Operational Command: A Monograph" (Fort Leavenworth, KS: School of Advanced Military Studies, U.S. Army Command & General Staff College, 1988–1989), 20–21; Walter Krueger, "Command Responsibilities in a Joint Operation," April 18, 1947, Folder 73, Box 12, Papers of Walter Krueger, Academy Library, U.S. Military Academy.

68. Kluckhorn, "Master of Amphibious Warfare," 32.

69. Paul P. Rogers, *The Bitter Years: MacArthur and Sutherland* (Westport, CT: Praeger, 1990), 224.

70. C. D. Eddleman, "The Lingayen Operation," 15, February 4, 1946, Folder Lingayen Operation, Box 1, Papers of Clyde Eddleman, U.S. Army History and Heritage Command, Carlisle Barracks, PA.

71. Bonner F. Fellers, Oral History by D. Clayton James, June 26, 1971, 8, Box 2, Record Group 49, MacArthur Memorial, Norfolk, VA.

72. Bonner F. Fellers Oral History by D. Clayton James, June 26, 1971, 8, Box 2, Record Group 49, MacArthur Memorial, Norfolk, VA.

73. Michael E. Bigelow, "Intelligence in the Philippines," *Military Intelligence Professional Bulletin* 21, no. 2 (April–June 1995): 36–40.

74. Bigelow, "Intelligence in the Philippines," 36–40.

75. Bigelow, "Intelligence in the Philippines," 36–40.

76. Bigelow, "Intelligence in the Philippines," 36–40.

77. Bigelow, "Intelligence in the Philippines," 36–40.

78. Bigelow, "Intelligence in the Philippines," 36–40.

79. Bigelow, "Intelligence in the Philippines," 36–40.

80. Rogers, *The Bitter Years,* 240.

81. Rogers, *The Bitter Years,* 240.

82. Rogers, *The Bitter Years,* 240.

83. Rogers, *The Bitter Years,* 240.

84. Sixth U.S. Army, "Report of the Luzon Campaign 9 January 1945–30 June 1945," vol. 1, 10, Skelton Combined Arms Research Library, Fort Leavenworth, KS.

85. Walter Krueger, "The Luzon Campaign of 1945," April 6, 1945, Folder 73, Box 12, Papers of Walter Krueger, Academy Library, U.S. Military Academy, West Point, NY.

86. Rogers, *The Bitter Years*, 222–224.

87. Walter Krueger, "Command Responsibilities in a Joint Operation," April 18, 1947, and Walter Krueger, "The Luzon Campaign of 1945," April 6, 1945, Folder 73, Box 12, Papers of Walter Krueger, U.S. Military Academy, West Point, NY; General Headquarters, Southwest Pacific Area, "Staff Study Operations: MIKE ONE," 4, 12, 16, Folder 7, Box 1, Record Group 30, Papers of Richard Sutherland, MacArthur Memorial, Norfolk, VA; Sixth U.S. Army, "Report of the Luzon Campaign 9 January 1945–30 June 1945," vol. 1, 1.

88. McEnery, *The XIV Corps Battle for Manila*, 48–49.

89. C. D. Eddleman, "The Lingayen Operation," 3, February 4, 1946, Folder Lingayen Operation, Box 1, Papers of Clyde Eddleman, U.S. Army History and Heritage Command, Carlisle Barracks, PA.

90. Eddleman, "The Lingayen Operation," 5, February 4, 1946, Folder Lingayen Operation, Box 1, Papers of Clyde Eddleman, U.S. Army History and Heritage Command, Carlisle Barracks, PA.

91. Eddleman, "The Lingayen Operation," 5, February 4, 1946, Folder Lingayen Operation, Box 1, Papers of Clyde Eddleman, U.S. Army History and Heritage Command, Carlisle Barracks, PA.

92. Morningstar, *War and Resistance in the Philippines*, 235–237; Giles H. Kidd, "The Operations of the 37th Infantry Division in the Crossing of the Pasig River and Closing to the Walls of Intramuros, Manila, 7–9 February 1945 (Luzon Campaign)," 20, Advanced Infantry Officers Course, 1949–1950, Staff Department, The Infantry School, Fort Benning, GA.

93. McEnery, *The XIV Corps Battle for Manila*, 106, 128; R. D. McLaurin, Paul A. Jureidini, David S. McDonald, and Kurt J. Sellers, *Modern Experience in City Combat* (Aberdeen Proving Ground, MD: Abbott Associates, Inc., Human Engineering Laboratory, 1987), 18.

CHAPTER 2

1. Summary of Interrogation of General Yamashita and Other Responsible Command and Staff Officers, no date, Folder Summary-Interrogation of General Yamashita, Box 8640, Records of the 37th Infantry Division, World War II Operational Records, Records of Adjutant General's Staff, Record Group 407, U.S. National Archives, College Park, MD; Nishimura Toshio statement, December 16, 17, 1948, document number 50553, in U.S. Army, Far Eastern Command, Military Intelligence Section, "Statements of Japanese Officials on World War II (English Translations)" (Washington, DC: U.S. Army Center of Military History).

2. Yamashita quote in Arima Kaoru statement, December 1, 1949, document number 53438, and Shujiro Kobayashi statement, December 1, 1949, document number 56423, in "Statements of Japanese Officials on World War II."
3. Smith, *Triumph in the Philippines*, 245; Aluit, *By Fire and Sword*, 147–149.
4. Noboru Kojima, *Manira Kaigun Rikusentai* [Manila Naval Defense Force] (Tokyo: Shinchosha, 1969), 28–29, 46.
5. Arima Kaoru statement, December 27, 1949, document number 53438; Asano Kenichiro statement, February 20, 1950, document number 55830, in "Statements of Japanese Officials on World War."
6. Kayashima Koichi statement, December 10, 1949, document number 56696, in "Statements of Japanese Officials on World War II."
7. Shujiro Kobayashi statement, December 1, 1949, document number 56423; Asano Kenichiro statement, February 20, 1950, document number 55830, in "Statements of Japanese Officials on World War II."
8. Asano Kenichiro statement, February 20, 1950, document number 55830, in "Statements of Japanese Officials on World War II."
9. McEnery, *The XIV Corps Battle for Manila*, 56–59. Between January 9 and July 1, 1945, the military intelligence units of the divisions, corpses in the Sixth Army, as well as the Sixth Army itself translated 14,651 documents, captured 7,297 prisoners of war, and interviewed 3,421: Sixth U.S. Army, "Enemy on Luzon: An Intelligence Summary," December 1, 1945, 133–136, Skelton Combined Arms Research Library, Fort Leavenworth, KS; Shujiro Kobayashi statement, December 1, 1949, document number 56423, in "Statements of Japanese Officials on World War II."
10. "Manila Defense Unit Operations Order A Number 25," January 10, 1945, XIV Corps Advanced Echelon Translation Number 60, document number 26 T 60, in *Wartime Translations of Seized Japanese Documents: Allied Translator and Interpreter Section Reports, 1942–46* (Bethesda, MD: Congressional Information Service, 1988).
11. "Directions Concerning Combat by Shimbu Group in Manila and Vicinity," January 16, 1945, XIV Corps Advanced Echelon Translation Number 56, document number 26 T 56, in *Wartime Translations of Seized Japanese Documents*.
12. Manila Defense Unit Staff Instructions Number 2, January 2, 1945, XIV Corps Advanced Echelon Translation Number 60, document number 26 T 60, in *Wartime Translations of Seized Japanese Documents*.
13. Asano Kenichiro statement, February 20, 1950, document number 55830; Shujiro Kobayashi statement, December 1, 1949, document number 56423; Kayashima Koichi statement, December 10, 1949, document number 56696, in "Statements of Japanese Officials on World War II"; Smith, *Triumph in the Philippines*, 242; Prisoner of War Preliminary Interrogation Report: Izumida Zenzo, March 13, 1945, in XIV Corps Advanced Echelon Interrogation Report Number 63, document number 26 IR 63, in *Wartime Translations of Seized Japanese Documents*; Prisoner of War Interrogation Report: 37-15:

Okubo Yasuhiko, February 6, 1945; Preliminary Prisoner of War Interrogation Report 37-48: Iwamoto Hidoichi, February 21, 1945; Preliminary Prisoner of War Interrogation Report 37-55: Suda Kazuo, February 24, 1945; Preliminary Prisoner of War Interrogation Report 37-63: Akitake Noriichi, February 27, 1945, Folder 337-2 A/A Rpt—Annex 2 Int—Appendix A(3), Box 8617, Records of the 37th Infantry Division, World War II Operational Records, Records of the Adjutant General's Staff, Record Group 407, U.S. National Archives, College Park, MD.

14. Prisoner of War Preliminary Interrogation Report: Izumida Zenzo, March 13, 1945, in XIV Corps Advanced Echelon Interrogation Report Number 63, document number 26 IR 63, in *Wartime Translations of Seized Japanese Documents*; Smith, *Triumph in the Philippines*, 242; Preliminary Prisoner of War Interrogation Report 37-48: Iwamoto Hidoichi, February 21, 1945; Preliminary Prisoner of War Interrogation Report 37-55: Suda Kazuo, February 24, 1945; Preliminary Prisoner of War Interrogation Report 37-63: Akitake Noriichi, February 27, 1945, Folder 337-2 A/A Rpt—Annex 2 Int—Appendix A(3), Box 8617, Records of the 37th Infantry Division, World War II Operational Records, Records of the Adjutant General's Staff, Record Group 407, U.S. National Archives, College Park, MD; Manila Naval Defense Force Operations Order Number 39, February 2, 1945, in General Headquarters Bulletin 1875, document number 10 B 1875, in *Wartime Translations of Seized Japanese Documents*; Connaughton, Pimlott, and Anderson, *The Battle for Manila*, 180; Toru Maehara, *Manira Boeisen: Nihongun no Toshi no Tatakai* [The Defense in the Battle of Manila: The Urban Warfare of the Japanese Army] (Tokyo: Boei Nenshujo, 1982), 254.

15. Smith, *Triumph in the Philippines*, 246–247; John B. Lukens, "Description of Typical Japanese Installations for Defense of a Street Intersection in South Manila," March 28, 1945, Folder 337-0.5, Box 8606, Records of the 37th Infantry Division, World War II Operational Records, Records of Adjutant General's Staff, Record Group 407, U.S. National Archives, College Park, MD.

16. Ma. Felisa A. Syjuco, *The Kempei Tai in the Philippines, 1941–1945* (Quezon City, The Philippines: New Day Publishers, 1988), 48, 50–52.

17. Smith, *Triumph in the Philippines*, 246.

18. Manila Naval Defense Force Operation Order Number 40, February 2, 1945, XIV Corps Advanced Echelon Translation Number 54, document number 26 T 54, in *Wartime Translations of Seized Japanese Documents*; Ford, "US Assessments of Japanese Ground Warfare Tactics," 329, 334; Connaughton, Pimlott, and Anderson, *The Battle for Manila*, 74.

19. Assistant Chief of Staff (G-2), Headquarters, Sixth Army, "Japanese Defense of Cities as Exemplified by the Battle for Manila: A Report by XIV Corps," 2, Folder 31, Box 3, Papers of Walter Krueger, Cushing Library, Texas A&M University, College Station, TX; Manila Naval Defense Order Number 1, December 22, 1944, in XIV Corps Advanced Echelon Translation Number 61, 26 T 61; Regulations Regarding Combat Command of the Northern (Noguchi)

Force, January 23, 1945, in XIV Corps Advanced Echelon Translation Number 54, 26 T 54; Manila Defense Force Operation Order Number 65, December 19, 1945, Manila Defense Force Operation Order Number 74, December 21, 1945, Manila Defense Force Operation Order Number 111, December 29, 1945, Manila Defense Force Operation Order Number 117, December 28, 1945, in XIV Corps Advanced Echelon Translation Number 79, document number 26 T 79, in *Wartime Translations of Seized Japanese Documents*.

20. Charts of Organization and Disposition of Naval Landing Party, [January 31, 1945] in XIV Corps Advanced Echelon Translation Number 74, document number 26 T 74; Manila Defense Force Op Order No. 65, December 14, 1944; Manila Defense Force Op Order No. 74, December 21, 1944; Manila Defense Force Op Order No. 95, December 24, 1944; Manila Defense Force Op Order No. 117, December 28, 1944, in XIV Corps Advanced Echelon Translation Number 79, document number 26 T 79, in *Wartime Translations of Seized Japanese Documents*.

21. Prisoner of War Preliminary Interrogation Report: Izumida Zenzo, March 13, 1945, in XIV Corps Advanced Echelon Interrogation Report Number 63, document number 26 IR 63 and Prisoner of War Preliminary Interrogation Report: Saito Yoshio, February 24, 1945, in Sixth Army Advanced Echelon Interrogation Report Number 381, document number 21 IR 381, in *Wartime Translations of Seized Japanese Documents*; Prisoner of War Interrogation Report: 37-15: Okubo Yasuhiko, February 6, 1945; Prisoner of War Interrogation Report: 37-64, February 28, 1945 and Prisoner of War Interrogation Report: 37-74, March 7, 1945, Folder 337-2 A/A—Annex 2 Int—Appendix A (3), Box 8617, Records of the 37th Infantry Division, World War II Operational Records, Records of the Adjutant General's Staff, Record Group 407, U.S. National Archives College Park, MD; Smith, *Triumph in the Philippines*, 242; Shujiro Kobayashi statement, December 1, 1949, document number 56423, in "Statements of Japanese Officials on World War II"; Manila Naval Defense Force Operations Order Number 39, February 2, 1945, in General Headquarters Bulletin Number 1875, document number 10 B 1875, in *Wartime Translations of Seized Japanese Documents*; Connaughton, Pimlott, and Anderson, *The Battle for Manila*, 180.

22. Maehara, *Manira Boeisen*, 254.

23. George K. Sitzler, Lynn L. Simpson, and Daniel J. Sears, 37th Infantry Division, World War II Army Service Experiences Questionnaires, U.S. Army Heritage and Education Center, Carlisle Barracks, PA; Regulations Regarding Combat Command of the Northern (Noguchi) Force, January 23, 1945, document number 26 T 54, in *Wartime Translations of Seized Japanese Documents*; Frank Mendez, Oral History (April 23, 2005), 10, Oral History Collection, Record Group 32, MacArthur Memorial, Norfolk, VA; Assistant Chief of Staff (G-2), Headquarters, Sixth Army, "Japanese Defense of Cities as Exemplified by the Battle for Manila: A Report by XIV Corps," 1, Folder 31, Box 3, Papers of Walter Krueger, Cushing Library, Texas A&M University, College Station, TX.

24. Shujiro Kobayashi statement, December 1, 1949, document number 56423, in "Statements of Japanese Officials on World War II."

25. "City and Town Defense," *Intelligence Bulletin* 12, no. 111 (August 1945): 28; Manila Naval Defense Force Order Number 43, February 3, 1945, in General Headquarters Bulletin Number 1875, document number 10 B 1875, in *Wartime Translations of Seized Japanese Documents*; Assistant Chief of Staff (G-2), Headquarters, Sixth Army, "Japanese Defense of Cities as Exemplified by the Battle for Manila: A Report by XIV Corps," 1, Folder 31, Box 3, Papers of Walter Krueger, Cushing Library, Texas A&M University, College Station, TX; Maehara, *Manira Boeisen*, 254.

26. Escoda, *Warsaw of Asia*, 10; Smith, *Triumph in the Philippines*, 240; McEnery, *The XIV Corps Battle for Manila*, 42, 44.

27. Smith, *Triumph in the Philippines*, 240; Fellers to Fellers, January 28, 1945, Folder 1, Box 2, Papers of Bonner Fellers, Record Group 44A, MacArthur Memorial, Norfolk, VA.

28. McLaurin et al., *Modern Experiences in City Combat*, 18; Unsent draft of MacArthur to Field Marshal Count Terauchi [Hisaichi], [no date], Folder 2, Box 6, Papers of Richard Sutherland, Record Group 30, MacArthur Memorial, Norfolk, VA; Connaughton, Pimlott, and Anderson, *The Battle for Manila*, 185–186.

29. Fellers to Wilson, December 11, 1945, Folder 15, Box 5, Series I, Papers of Bonner Fellers, Record Group 44A, MacArthur Memorial, Norfolk, VA.

30. Angelito L. Santos, Joan Orendain, Helen N. Mendoza, Bernard L. M. Karganilla, and Renato Constantino, ed., *Under Japanese Rule: Memories and Reflections* (Makati City, Philippines: The Manila Daily Shimbun, 2012), 133.

31. She is best known as Carmen Guerrero Nakpil, which reflected her name following her second marriage. At the time, she used the name of her first husband and was known as Carmen Guerrero Cruz, which is how she is referred to later in the text. Carmen Guerrero Nakpil, *Myself, Elsewhere* (San Juan, Philippines: Nakpil Publishing, 2006), 180–181.

32. Connaughton, Pimlott, and Anderson, *The Battle for Manila*, 54, 71; Guerrero Nakpil, *Myself, Elsewhere*, 180–181; Smith, *Triumph in the Philippines*, 239; Francis K. Danquah, "Reports on Philippine Industrial Crops in World War II from Japan's English Language Press," *Agricultural History* 79, no. 1 (Winter 2005): 74–96; Daniel F. Doeppers, *Feeding Manila in Peace and War, 1850–1945* (Madison: University of Wisconsin Press, 2016), 324–325; Syjuco, *The Kempei Tai in the Philippines*, 57.

33. Jeremy A. Yellen, *The Greater East Asia Co-Prosperity Sphere: When Total Empire Met Total War* (Ithaca, NY: Cornell University Press, 2019), 116–118, 156, 163, 181, 185, 187.

34. Yellen, *The Greater East Asia Co-Prosperity Sphere*, 116–118, 156, 163, 181, 185, 187.

35. Yellen, *The Greater East Asia Co-Prosperity Sphere*, 116–118, 156, 163, 181, 185, 187.

36. Yellen, *The Greater East Asia Co-Prosperity Sphere*, 116–118, 156, 163, 181, 185, 187.

37. Yellen, *The Greater East Asia Co-Prosperity Sphere*, 116–118, 156, 163, 181, 185, 187.

38. Manifesto No. 1, July 4, 1943, in Ricardo Trota Jose, ed., *World War II and the Japanese Occupation* (Quezon City: University of the Philippines Press, 2006), 254–259; James A. Villanueva, "Awaiting the Allies' Return: The Guerrilla Resistance Against the Japanese in the Philippines during World War II" (PhD diss., Ohio State University, 2019), 17.

39. Terami-Wada Motoe, "The Filipino Volunteer Armies," in *The Philippines Under Japan: Occupation Policy and Reaction*, ed. Ikehata Setsuho and Ricardo Trota Jose (Manila: Atendeo de Manila University Press, 1999), 80–82; David Joel Steinberg, *Philippine Collaboration in World War II* (Ann Arbor: University of Michigan Press, 1967), 106–107; Santos to Garcia, March 16, 1944, in Jose, ed., *World War II and the Japanese Occupation*, 196–200; Connaughton, Pimlott, and Anderson, *The Battle for Manila*, 70; XIV Corps, "After Action Report: XIV Corps: M-1 Operation," July 29, 1945, 255–256, Folder 32, Box 3, Papers of Walter Krueger, Cushing Library, Texas A&M University, College Station, TX.

40. Danquah, "Reports on Philippine Industrial Crops," 74–96.

41. Prisoner of War Preliminary Interrogation Report 37-19: Marioka Sakae, February 8, 1945, Folder 337-2/2.13 A/A Rpt—Annex #2—Intelligence Appendix A 173d Language Detachment Appendix (3) Interrogations, Box 8640, Records of the 37th Infantry Division, World War II Operational Records, Records of the Adjutant General's Staff, U.S. National Archives, College Park, MD.

42. Villanueva, "Awaiting the Allies' Return," 27, 98, 139, 142; Morningstar, *War and Resistance*, 249–250.

CHAPTER 3

1. Entry for January 9, 1945, in 1st Battalion, 129th Infantry Regiment, 37th Infantry Division Journal, Folder 337 INF 129, 7-0.7 Unit Journal, Box 8733, Records of the 37th Infantry Division, World War II Operational Records, Records of the Adjutant General's Staff, Record Group 407, U.S. National Archives, College Park, MD.

2. Krueger to Ward, September 12, 1951, Folder Orders & Misc. Papers, Box 1, Walter Krueger, "Command Responsibilities in a Joint Operation," April 18, 1947, Folder 73, Box 12, Papers of Walter Krueger, Academy Library, U.S. Military Academy, West Point, NY; George B. Eaton, "From Teaching to Practice: General Walter Krueger and the Development of Joint Operations, 1921–1945" (U.S. Naval War College, Newport, RI, 1994), 106–110; Holzimmer, "Joint Operations in the Southwest Pacific," 102, 103.

3. Holzimmer, "Joint Operations in the Southwest Pacific," 105–106.

4. Sixth U.S. Army, "Report of the Luzon Campaign 9 January 1945–30 June 1945," 14–15, Skelton Combined Arms Research Library, Fort Leavenworth, KS; General Headquarters, Southwest Pacific Area, "Staff Study Operations: MIKE ONE," 2, Folder 7, Box 1, Record Group 30, Papers of Richard Sutherland, MacArthur Memorial, Norfolk, VA.

5. "Bill Chickering Dies in Action," *Life* (January 22, 1945), 32; Headquarters 37th Infantry Division, Report After Action: Luzon Campaign 1 November 44–30 June 45, Part VI, G-1 Section, 3, Folder G-1 A/A Rpt Luzon Campaign, Box 8609, Records of the 37th Infantry Division, World War II Operational Records, Records of the Adjutant General's Staff, Record Group 407, U.S. National Archives, College Park, MD.

6. "Elko Native, Retired Army General Dies," *Reno Evening Gazette*, October 2, 1959; "Oscar Griswold, Retired General," *The New York Times*, October 7, 1959; Nicholas Evan Sarantakes, ed., *Seven Stars: The Okinawa Battle Diaries of Simon Bolivar Buckner, Jr., and Joseph Stilwell* (College Station: Texas A&M University Press, 2004), 87.

7. McEnery, *The XIV Corps Battle for Manila*, 62–73; Villanueva, "Field Artillery and Flying Columns," 139, fn. 9. Underlining in the original: January 8, 1945 entry, Diary of Oscar W. Griswold, Box 1, Papers of Oscar W. Griswold, U.S. Army Heritage and Education Center, Carlisle, PA.

8. "Bill Chickering Dies in Action," 32; Richard Humble, *Fraser of North Cape: The Life of Admiral of the Fleet Lord Fraser [1888–1981]* (London: Routledge & Kegan Paul, 1983), 254–257; Headquarters 37th Infantry Division, "Report After Action: Luzon Campaign 1 Nov 44–30 June 45," Part VI, G-1 Section, 3, Folder G-1 A/A Rpt Luzon Campaign, Box 8609, Records of the 37th Infantry Division, World War II Operational Records, Records of the Adjutant General's Staff, Record Group 407, U.S. National Archives, College Park, MD.

9. "Bill Chickering Dies in Action," 32; James M. Scott, "Terror & Triumph at Lingayen Gulf," *Naval History Magazine* (October 2018): 36–41; Mydans to Chickering, February 28, 1945, Folder War in the Pacific: Bill Chickering, Box 117, Papers of Carl and Shelly Mydans, Beinecke Library, Yale University, New Haven, CT.

10. Carl Mydans, *More Than Meets the Eye* (New York: Harper & Brothers, 1959), 183.

11. January 8, 1945 entry, Diary of Oscar W. Griswold, Box 1, Papers of Oscar W. Griswold, U.S. Army Heritage and Education Center, Carlisle, PA.

12. January 8, 1945 entry, Diary of Oscar W. Griswold, Box 1, Papers of Oscar W. Griswold, U.S. Army Heritage and Education Center, Carlisle, PA.

13. Walter Krueger, "Command Responsibilities in a Joint Operation," April 18, 1947, Folder 73, Box 12, Papers of Walter Krueger, Academy Library, U.S. Military Academy, West Point, NY.

14. Walter Krueger, "The Luzon Campaign of 1945," April 6, 1954, Folder 73, Box 12, Papers of Walter Krueger, Academy Library, U.S. Military Academy, West Point, NY.

15. Hori Rizo Statement, July 14, 1949, document number 49604, in "Statements of Japanese Officials on World War II"; Headquarters 37th Infantry Division, "Summary of Interrogation of General Yamashita and Other Responsible Commanders and Staff Officers," no date, 3–4, Folder 337-2.13 Summary Interrogation of Gen. Yamashita, Box 8640, Records of the 37th Infantry Division, World War II Operational Records, Records of the Adjutant General's Staff, Record Group 407, U.S. National Archives, College Park, MD.

16. Hori Rizo Statement, July 14, 1949, document number 49604, in "Statements of Japanese Officials on World War II"; Headquarters 37th Infantry Division, "Summary of Interrogation of General Yamashita and Other Responsible Commanders and Staff Officers," no date, 3–4, Folder 337-2.13 Summary Interrogation of Gen. Yamashita, Box 8640, Records of the 37th Infantry Division, World War II Operational Records, Records of the Adjutant General's Staff, Record Group 407, U.S. National Archives, College Park, MD.

17. Operation Order, 23rd Reconnaissance Regiment, January 1, 1945, Translation Number L 37D4, Folder 337-2 A/A Rpt—Annex 2 Int—Appendix A(3), Box 8616, Records of the 37th Infantry Division, World War II Operational Records, Records of the Adjutant General's Staff, Record Group 407, U.S. National Archives, College Park, MD.

18. Sixth United States Army, "Report of the Luzon Campaign 9 January 1945–30 June 1945," 15, Skelton Combined Arms Research Library, Fort Leavenworth, KS; Walter Krueger, "Command Responsibilities in a Joint Operation," April 18, 1947, Folder 73, Box 12, Papers of Walter Krueger, Academy Library, U.S. Military Academy, West Point, NY; Walter Krueger, "Luzon Campaign of 1945," April 6, 1954, Folder 73, Box 12, Papers of Walter Krueger, Academy Library, U.S. Military Academy, West Point, NY.

19. January 10, 1945 entry, Diary of Oscar W. Griswold, Box 1, Papers of Oscar W. Griswold, U.S. Army Heritage and Education Center, Carlisle, PA.

20. Smith, *Triumph in the Philippines*, 64–65; Sixth U.S. Army, "Report of the Luzon Campaign 9 January 1945–30 June 1945," 16, Skelton Combined Arms Research Library, Fort Leavenworth, KS; XIV Corps, "After Action Report: XIV Corps: M-1 Operation," July 29, 1945, 245, Folder 32, Box 3, Papers of Walter Krueger, Cushing Library, Texas A&M University, College Station, TX.

21. Gerald Astor, *Crisis in the Pacific: The Battles for the Philippine Islands by the Men Who Fought Them* (New York: Dell Publishing, 1996), 469, 477.

22. Astor, *Crisis in the Pacific*, 471.

23. Astor, *Crisis in the Pacific*, 478; Ray E. Hale, Oral History (September 29, 2007), 7, Veterans History Project, American Folklife Center, Library of Congress, Washington, DC.

24. Ozzie Smith, "Return to Luzon," *Yank* (February 16, 1945), 4–5.

25. C. D. Eddleman, "The Lingayen Operation," 15, February 4, 1946, Folder Lingayen Operation, Box 1, Papers of Clyde Eddleman, U.S. Army Heritage and Education Center, Carlisle, PA; Astor, *Crisis in the Pacific*, 478.

26. Attachment to Robert H. Kiser, Army Service Experiences Questionnaire, 37th Infantry Division, World War II, Veteran Surveys, U.S. Army Heritage and Education Center, Carlisle, PA; 37th Cavalry Reconnaissance Troop, Mechanized, "Troop History for Period 8 January to 3 February, 1945, September 1, 1945," Folder 337-Cav D.1, Box 8710, Records of the 37th Infantry Division, World War II Operational Records, Records of the Adjutant General's Staff, Record Group 407, U.S. National Archives, College Park, MD; Yukio Kawamoto, 37th Infantry Division, World War II Army Service Experiences Questionnaire, U.S. Army Heritage and Education Center, Carlisle, PA.

27. January 14, 1945 entry, in Juan Labrador, *A Diary of the Japanese Occupation: December 7, 1941–May 7, 1945* (Manila: Santo Tomás University Press, 1989), 257.

28. Smith, *Triumph in the Philippines*, 68.

29. William J. Dunn, *Pacific Microphone* (College Station: Texas A&M University Press, 1988), 274.

30. James E. Caudle, Oral History, in Lynn L. Sims, ed., *"They Have Seen the Elephant": Veterans Reembraces from World War II for the 40th Anniversary of V-E Day* (Fort Lee, VA: US Army Logistics Center, 1985), 1–2.

31. January 9, 1945 entry, Diary of Oscar W. Griswold, Box 1, Papers of Oscar W. Griswold, U.S. Army Heritage and Education Center, Carlisle, PA; C. D. Eddleman, "The Lingayen Operation," 15, February 4, 1946, Folder Lingayen Operation, Box 1, Papers of Clyde Eddleman, US Army Heritage and Education Center, Carlisle, PA.

32. Astor, *Crisis in the Pacific*, 472–473.

33. Nagata Takeji, "Escape," trans. Ernst Kazuko (Unknown Publisher, 1970), 7, U.S. Army Heritage and Education Center, Carlisle, PA.

34. Rogers, *Bitter Years*, 229; "U.S. Force Drives on into Luzon," *The Cincinnati Post*, January 10, 1945.

35. Fellers to Fellers, January 9, 1945, Folder 1, Box 2, Papers of Bonner Fellers, Record Group 44A, MacArthur Memorial, Norfolk, VA.

36. Fellers to Fellers, January 16, 1945, Folder 1, Box 2, Bonner Fellers, Record Group 44A, MacArthur Memorial, Norfolk, VA.

37. February 4, 1945 entry, in Labrador, *A Diary of the Japanese Occupation*, 266.

38. Radio Report Transcript 17, January 16, 1945, Folder 47, Box 3, Papers of William J. Dunn, Record Group 52, MacArthur Memorial, Norfolk, VA.

39. XIV Corps, "After Action Report: XIV Corps: M-1 Operation," July 29, 1945, vol. III, "Administration," 117, Folder 32, Box 3, Papers of Walter Krueger, Cushing Library, Texas A&M University, College Station, TX; William J. Dunn, Radio Transcript 29, January 30, 1945, Folder 47, Box 3, Papers of William J. Dunn, Record Group 52, MacArthur Memorial, Norfolk, VA; Walter Krueger, "The Commander's Appreciation of Logistics," January 3, 1955, Folder 73, Box 12, Papers of Walter Krueger, Academy Library, U.S. Military Academy, West Point, NY; Francis K. Danquah, "Reports on Philippine Industrial Crops in

World War II from Japan's English Language Press," *Agricultural History* 79, no. 1 (Winter 2005): 74–96; George Raynor Thompson and Dixie R. Harris, *United States Army in World War II: The Technical Services: The Signal Corps: The Outcome (Mid-1943 Through 1945)* (Washington, DC: U.S. Government Printing Office, 1966), 258, 262, 282–283.

40. Smith, *Triumph in the Philippines*, 41; H. D. Vogel, "Logistical Support of the Lingayen Operation," February 4, 1946, Folder February 4, 1946, Box 25, Papers of Walter Krueger, Academy Library, U.S. Military Academy, West Point, NY.

41. Frank F. Mathias, *G.I. Jive: An Army Bandsman in World War II* (Lexington: University Press of Kentucky, 1982), 112.

42. Sixth U.S. Army, "Report of the Luzon Campaign 9 January 1945–30 June 1945," 64, Skelton Combined Arms Research Library, Fort Leavenworth, KS; H. D. Vogel, "Logistical Support of the Lingayen Operation," February 4, 1946, Folder February 4, 1946, Box 25; Walter Krueger, "The Commander's Appreciation of Logistics," January 3, 1955, Folder 73, Box 12, Papers of Walter Krueger, Academy Library, U.S. Military Academy, West Point, NY.

43. H. D. Vogel, "Logistical Support of the Lingayen Operation," February 4, 1946, Folder February 4, 1946, Box 25, Papers of Walter Krueger, Academy Library, U.S. Military Academy, West Point, NY; C. D. Eddleman, "The Lingayen Operation," 15, February 4, 1946, Folder Lingayen Operation, Box 1, Papers of Clyde Eddleman, U.S Army Heritage and Education Center, Carlisle, PA; Sixth U.S. Army, "Report of the Luzon Campaign 9 January 1945–30 June 1945," 19, Skelton Combined Arms Research Library, Fort Leavenworth, KS.

44. January 10, 1945 entry, Diary of Oscar W. Griswold, Box 1, Papers of Oscar W. Griswold, U.S. Army Heritage and Education Center, Carlisle, PA.

45. Walter Krueger, *From Down Under to Nippon: The Story of Sixth Army in World War II* (Washington, DC: Combat Forces Press, 1953), 225; Walter Krueger, "The Luzon Campaign of 1945," April 6, 1954, Folder 73, Box 12, Papers of Walter Krueger, Academy Library, U.S. Military Academy, West Point, NY; H. D. Vogel, "Logistical Support of the Lingayen Operation," February 4, 1946, Folder February 4, 1946, Box 25, Papers of Walter Krueger, Academy Library, U.S. Military Academy, West Point, NY.

46. Walter Krueger, "The Commander's Appreciation of Logistics," January 3, 1955, Folder 73, Box 12, Papers of Walter Krueger, Academy Library, U.S. Military Academy, West Point, NY.

47. Konuma Harno, document number 52018, in "Statements of Japanese Officials on World War II."

48. Konuma Harno, document number 52018, in "Statements of Japanese Officials on World War II"; Kobayashi Group Order, Manila Defense Op Order 45, February 2, 1945, Item 1, in XIV Corps Advanced Echelon Translation 75, document number 26 T 75, in *Wartime Translations of Seized Japanese Documents*.

49. Iwano Masataka and Aoshima Ryoichiro, "Japanese Monograph Number 7: Philippine Operations Record, Phase III, January–February 1945" (October

1946), 38–39, 51–52, U.S. Army Heritage and Education Center, Carlisle, PA; Estimate of the Enemy Situation, November 22, 1944, Folder 4, Box 22, Records of Headquarters, U.S. Army Forces Pacific Area, Record Group 4, MacArthur Memorial, Norfolk, VA; Bigelow, "Intelligence in the Philippines," 36–40.

CHAPTER 4

1. Rogers, *Bitter Years*, 231–232.
2. Rogers, *Bitter Years*, 235.
3. Rogers, *Bitter Years*, 238.
4. Rogers, *Bitter Years*, 243, 245.
5. "A History of the 129th Infantry," Folder 337-INF (129)0.1 History–129th Inf Regt, Box 8730, Record of the 37th Infantry Division, World War II Operational Records, Record of the Adjutant General's Staff, Record Group 407, U.S. National Archives, College Park, MD.
6. Lee Van Atta, "Krueger Carries Ball on M'Arthur's Winning Team," *San Antonio Light*, February 11, 1945.
7. George C. Kenney, *General Kenney Reports: A Personal History of the Pacific War* (New York: Duell, Sloan and Pearce, 1949), 512; Konuma Haruo Statement, February 19, 1949, document number 52018, in "Statements of Japanese Officials on World War II."
8. Rogers, *Bitter Years*, 242; William J. Dunn, *Pacific Microphone* (College Station: Texas A&M University Press, 1988), 279.
9. Holzimmer, *General Walter Krueger*, 224; Walter Krueger, "The Luzon Campaign of 1945," April 6, 1954, Folder 73, Box 12, Papers of Walter Krueger, Academy Library, U.S. Military Academy, West Point, NY.
10. Holzimmer, *General Walter Krueger*, 224–225; Taafe, *Marshall and His Generals*, 221.
11. Holzimmer, *General Walter Krueger*, 216; Clyde D. Eddleman, Oral History (February 11, 1975), 32, Senior Officers Debriefing Program, U.S. Army Heritage and Education Center, Carlisle, PA.
12. George H. Decker, Oral History (November 3, 1972), 20, Senior Officer Debriefing Program, U.S. Army Heritage and Education Center, Carlisle, PA.
13. January 14, 1945 entry, Diary of O. W. Griswold, Box 1, Papers of Oscar W. Griswold, U.S. Army Heritage and Education Center, Carlisle, PA.
14. Taafe, *Marshall and His Generals*, 223.
15. John Dos Passos, *Tour of Duty* (Boston: Houghton Mifflin Company, 1946), 161–166; Joseph P. McCallus, *The MacArthur Highway and Other Relics of American Empire in the Philippines* (Washington, DC: Potomac Books, 2010), 166–167.
16. Taafe, *Marshall and His Generals*, 225.
17. January 23, 1945 entry, Diary of Robert Eichelberger, Folder 1945–1946, Box 1, Papers of Robert L. Eichelberger, Rubenstein Rare Book and Manuscript Library, Duke University, Durham, NC.

18. C. D. Eddleman, "The Lingayen Operation," February 4, 1946, Folder Lingayen Operation, Box 1, Papers of Clyde Eddleman, U.S. Army Heritage and Education Center, Carlisle, PA; Isaac Hoppenstein, "The Operation of the 187th Glider Infantry Regiment, (11th Airborne Division) in the Landing at Nasugbu, Luzon, Philippine Islands 31 January–3 February 1945 (The Luzon Campaign) (Personal Experiences of a Regimental Supply Officer)," 8–9, Advanced Infantry Officers Course, 1947–1948, Academic Department, The Infantry School, Fort Benning, GA; Nishimura Toshio statement, December 16, 17, 1948, document number 50553, in "Statements of Japanese Officials on World War II."

19. Walter Krueger, "The Luzon Campaign of 1945," April 6, 1954, Folder 73, Box 12, Papers of Walter Krueger, Academy Library, U.S. Military Academy, West Point, NY.

20. Walter Krueger, "The Luzon Campaign of 1945," April 6, 1954, Folder 73, Box 12, Papers of Walter Krueger, Academy Library, U.S. Military Academy, West Point, NY.

21. January 19–20, 1945 entry, Diary of O. W. Griswold, Box 1, Papers of Oscar W. Griswold, U.S. Army Heritage and Education Center, Carlisle, PA.

22. Rogers, *Bitter Years*, 248.

23. McEnery, *The XIV Corps Battle for Manila*, 116.

24. Roger O. Egeberg, Oral History (June 30, 1971), 24–25, D. Clayton James Collection, Record Group 49, MacArthur Memorial, Norfolk, VA.

25. Summary of Interrogation of General Yamashita and Other Responsible Command and Staff Officers, no date, Folder Summary-Interrogation of General Yamashita, Box 8640, Records of the 37th Infantry Division, World War II Operational Records, Records of Adjutant General's Staff, Record Group 407, U.S. National Archives, College Park, MD.

26. "Elko Native, Retired Army General Dies," *Reno Evening Gazette*, October 2, 1959; Griswold to Davidson, June 17, 1958, Folder unmarked, Box 2, Papers of Oscar Griswold, Academy Library, U.S. Military Academy, West Point, NY.

27. Griswold to Davidson, June 17, 1958, Folder unmarked, Box 2, Papers of Oscar Griswold, Academy Library, U.S. Military Academy, West Point, NY.

28. Griswold to Davidson, June 17, 1958, Folder unmarked, Box 2, Papers of Oscar Griswold, Academy Library, U.S. Military Academy, West Point, NY.

29. Griswold to Davidson, June 17, 1958, Folder unmarked, Box 2, Papers of Oscar Griswold, Academy Library, U.S. Military Academy, West Point, NY.

30. Bruce Palmer, Oral History (December 5, 1975), 331, Senior Officer Debriefing Program, U.S. Army Heritage and Education Center, Carlisle, PA.

31. Estanislado Reyna, Oral History (February 2, 2002) transcription by the author, VOCES: The US Latino and Latina Oral History Project, Benson Latin American Collection, University of Texas, Austin, TX; Griswold to Davidson, June 17, 1958, Unmarked Folder, Box 2, Papers of Oscar Griswold, Academy Library, U.S. Military Academy, West Point, NY; Mathias, *G.I. Jive*, 86; XIV Corps, "After Action XIV Corps Report M-1 Operation," July 29, 1945, vol.

II, "Administration," 143–147, Folder 32, Box 3, Papers of Walter Krueger, Cushing Library, Texas A&M University, College Station, TX; John McLeod, "The Heavyweight," *Yank* (September 21, 1945), 3–4; Robert Beightler, "Major General Robert S. Beightler's Report on the Activities of the 37th Infantry Division, 1940-1945," Folder MS593/1/7, Box 1, Papers of Robert S. Beightler, Ohio Historical Society, Columbus, OH.

32. Griswold to Davidson, June 17, 1958, Unmarked Folder, Box 2, Papers of Oscar Griswold, Academy Library, U.S. Military Academy, West Point, NY; Headquarters 37th Infantry Division, Report After Action: Luzon Campaign 1 Nov 44–30 June 45, Part VI, G-1 Section, 4, Folder G-1 A/A Rpt Luzon Campaign, Box 8609, Records of the 37th Infantry Division, World War II Operational Records, Records of the Adjutant General's Staff, Record Group 407, U.S. National Archives, College Park, MD.

33. John Kennedy Ohl, *Minuteman: The Military Career of General Robert S. Beightler* (Boulder, CO: Lynne Rienner Publishers, 2001), 2–5, 35, 45–46, 50–51, 54, 57, 61; "Major General Robert Sprauge Beightler, Commanding 37th (Ohio) Infantry Division," no date, Folder 337-1.19 Biographical Sketches, Box 8609, Records of the 37th Infantry Division, World War II Operational Records, Records of the Adjutant General's Staff, Record Group 407, U.S. National Archives, College Park, MD.

34. John R. Walker, *Bracketing the Enemy: Forward Observers in World War II* (Norman: University of Oklahoma Press, 2013), 87–89, 93.

35. "Major General Robert Sprauge Beightler, Commanding 37th (Ohio) Infantry Division," no date, and "Major General Robert Sprauge Beightler, Commanding 37th (Ohio) Infantry Division," October 16, 1945, Folder 337-1.19 Biographical Sketches, Box 8609, Records of the 37th Infantry Division, World War II Operational Records, Records of the Adjutant General's Staff, Record Group 407, U.S. National Archives, College Park, MD.

36. James Hanrahan, "Soldier, Manager, Leader: An Interview with Former CIA Executive Director Lawrence K. 'Red' White," *Studies in Intelligence* 43, no. 3 (Winter 1999–2000): 31.

37. Ohl, *Minuteman*, 99; Headquarters 37th Infantry Division, Report After Action: Luzon Campaign 1 Nov 44–30 June 45, Part VI, G-1 Section, 4, Folder G-1 A/A Rpt Luzon Campaign, Box 8609, Records of the 37th Infantry Division, World War II Operational Records, Records of the Adjutant General's Staff, Record Group 407, U.S. National Archives, College Park, MD.

38. Delmore Evans (November 20, 2010), 1, Veterans History Project, American Folklife Center, Library of Congress, Washington, DC.

39. Mathias, *G.I. Jive*, 115.

40. John Carney, Oral History (May 22, 2015), transcription by author, New York State Military Museum, Saratoga Springs, NY.

41. January 12–13, 1945, entry, Diary of O. W. Griswold, Box 1, Papers of Oscar W. Griswold, U.S. Army Heritage and Education Center, Carlisle, PA.

42. Julius S. Gassner Army Service Experiences Questionnaire, 37th Infantry Division, World War II Army Service Experiences Questionnaire, U.S. Army Heritage and Education Center, Carlisle, PA.

43. James E. Caudle, Oral History, in Sims, ed., *"They Have Seen the Elephant."*

44. Radio Transcript, January 22, 1945, Folder 47, Box 3, Papers of William Dunn, Record Group 52, MacArthur Memorial, Norfolk, VA. The friendliness of the Filipino people is a consistent theme in the surveys of veterans of the Luzon campaign that the State of Tennessee conducted. See Robert L. Boyd, Folder 1, Box 5; William O. Batts, Jr., Folder 5, Box 3; Garland Bennett, Jr., Folder 1, Box 4; Norman Kingsley Bentley, Folder 1, Box 4; William Wells Berry, Folder 2, Box 4; Eugene M. Cole, Folder 1, Box 9; Horace Warren Craddock, Folder 1, Box 10; James S. Dunn, Folder 5, Box 12; James H. Grant, Folder 4, Box 16; George Lawrence Ellis, Folder 1, Box 13; Johnston Shull Harrison, Folder 8, Box 17; Emanuel F. Jensen, Folder 1, Box 21; William C. Keaton, Folder 7, Box 21; Clyde M. King, Folder 4, Box 22; Edward William King, Folder 4, Box 22; Walter I. Madden, Folder 6, Box 24; Robert Wood Moore, Folder 4, Box 27; Clay William Morton, Folder 6, Box 27; W. K. Nelms, Folder 6, Box 28; William W. Owen, Folder 5, Box 29; Mahlon R. Peden, Folder 5, Box 30; Dorsey Robbins, Folder 1, Box 33; John Frederick Scarbrough, Jr., Folder 4, Box 34, World War II Veteran Surveys, Record Group 237, Tennessee State Library & Archives, Nashville, TN.

45. Mathias, *G.I. Jive*, 116; Labrador, *Diary of the Japanese Occupation*, 260–261.

46. Journal of the 1st Battalion, 129th Infantry Regiment, January 11 and 16, 1945, Folder 337-INF (129) 7-0.7-Unit Journal, Box 8733, Records of the 37th Infantry Division, World War II Operational Records, Records of the Adjutant General's Staff, Record Group 407, U.S. National Archives, College Park, MD.

47. Astor, *Crisis in the Pacific*, 486.

48. Giles H. Kidd, "The Operations of the 37th Infantry Division in the Crossing of the Pasig River and Closing to the Walls of Intramuros, Manila 7–9 February 1945 (Luzon Campaign)," 8, 21, Advanced Infantry Officers Course Number 1, 1949–1950, Infantry School, Fort Benning, GA.

49. Headquarters XIV Corps, "After Action Report: XIV Corps: M-1 Operation," July 29, 1945, vol. II, "Administration," 133, Folder 32, Box 3, Papers of Walter Krueger, Cushing Library, Texas A&M University, College Station, TX.

50. Yuk-wai Yung Li, *The Huaqiao Warriors: Chinese Resistance Movement in the Philippines, 1942–1945* (Hong Kong: Hong Kong University Press, 1995), 75–152; Antonio S. Tan, *The Chinese in the Philippines During the Japanese Occupation* (Quezon City: University of Philippines Press, 1981), 81–93; Jay D. Vanderpool, Oral History (1983), 122, Senior Officer Debriefing Program, U.S. Army Heritage and Education Center, Carlisle, PA.

51. Rudy de Lara with Bob Fancher, *Boy Guerrilla: The World War II Metro Manila Serenader* (Mandaluyong City, Philippines: National Book Store, 2002), 75.

52. Taruc statement in Jose, ed., *World War II and the Japanese Occupation*, 296–297; Jay D. Vanderpool, Oral History (1983), 122, Senior Officer Debriefing Programs, U.S. Military History Institute, U.S. Army Heritage and Education Center, Carlisle, PA.

53. Jay D. Vanderpool, Oral History (1983), 122, Senior Officer Debriefing Program, U.S. Military History Institute, U.S. Army Heritage and Education Center, Carlisle, PA.

54. Jay D. Vanderpool, Oral History (1983), 122, Senior Officer Debriefing Program, U.S. Military History Institute, U.S. Army Heritage and Education Center, Carlisle, PA.

55. Dos Passos, *Tour of Duty*, 198.

56. William A. Owen, *Eye-Deep in Hell: A Memoir of the Liberation of the Philippines, 1944–45* (Dallas: Southern Methodist University Press, 1989), 84–85, 87; Elliott R. Thorpe, *East Wind, Rain: The Intimate Account of an Intelligence Officer in the Pacific, 1939–49* (Boston: Gambit, 1969), 168; Escoda, *Warsaw*, 65–67; Astor, *Crisis in the Pacific*, 489–492, 503, 508–509; Frank Kelly, "U.S. Disarming 'Communistic' Filipino Band," *New York Herald Tribune*, March 12, 1945; Frank M. Lutze, 37th Infantry Division, Murphy Foret, 37th Infantry Division and Charles A. Henne, 37th Infantry Division, World War II Army Service Experiences Questionnaire, U.S. Army Heritage and Education Center, Carlisle, PA; Jay D. Vanderpool, Oral History (1983), 122, Senior Officer Debriefing Program, U.S. Military History Institute, U.S. Army Heritage and Education Center, Carlisle, PA; January 28, 1945, entry, Diary of O. W. Griswold, Box 1, Papers of Oscar W. Griswold; "The Battle History of the 3rd Battalion, 148th Infantry, Second Luzon P.I. Campaign 11 November 44–15 August 1945" (Buckeye, Arizona), 8, U.S. Army Heritage and Education Center, Carlisle, PA.

57. Robert H. Kiser, 37th Infantry Division, and Salvatore V. DeGaetano, 1st Cavalry Division, World War II Army Service Experiences Questionnaire, U.S. Army Heritage and Education Center, Carlisle, PA; C. D. Eddleman, "The Lingayen Operation," February 4, 1946, 5, Folder: Lingayen Operation, Box 1, Papers of Clyde Eddleman, U.S. Army History and Heritage Command, Carlisle Barracks, PA.

58. The point about the Filipinos is stated in both the 129th's lessons learned report and the division's after action report: Headquarters, 129th Infantry, Lessons Learned in the Luzon Campaign with Recommendations and Comments: 1 November 1944 to 30 June 1945, Section VII, Folder 337-INF (129) 0.3, Box 8732 and After Action Report: Operations of the 37th Infantry Division on Bougainville, BSI, and Luzon, 21 Nov 44 to 30 June 45, Part IV: Annex 2 Intelligence, 3, Folder 337-2-A/A/Rpt-Intelligence Narrative, Box 8617, Record of the 37th Infantry Division, World War II Operational Records, Record of the Adjutant General's Staff, Record Group 407, U.S. National Archives, College Park, MD.

59. Labrador, *Diary of the Japanese Occupation*, 262–263.

60. XIV Corps Advanced Echelon Prisoner of War Preliminary Interrogation Report Number 34: Miyakawa Takeo, February 19, 1945, document 26 IR 34, in *Wartime Translations of Seized Japanese Documents*.

61. Preliminary Interrogation of Prisoner of War: Private First Class Nakazono Wakaichi, February 17, 1945, Folder 901-2.13 PW Interrogation Reports—Luzon Operation—1st Cavalry Division, Box 427, Records of the 1st Cavalry Division, World War II Operational Records, Record of the Adjutant Staff, Record Group 407, U.S. National Archives, College Park, MD.

62. Charles A. Henne, 37th Infantry Division, World War II Army Service Experiences Questionnaire, U.S. Army Heritage and Education Center, Carlisle, PA.

63. Mathias, *G.I. Jive*, 113; "The Battle History of the 3rd Battalion, 148th Infantry, Second Luzon P.I. Campaign 11 November 44–15 August 1945" (Buckeye, Arizona), 6–7.

64. Attachment to Robert H. Kiser Army Service Experiences Questionnaire, 37th Infantry Division, World War II Army Service Experiences Questionnaire, U.S. Army Heritage and Education Center, Carlisle, PA.

65. Spelling errors corrected without indication. Mahlon R. Peden Survey, Folder 5, Box 30, World War II Veteran Surveys, Record Group 237, Tennessee State Library & Archives, Nashville, TN.

66. Radio Transcript, January 19, 1945, and Radio Transcript, January 24, 1945, Folder 47, Box 3, Papers of William Dunn, Record Group 52, MacArthur Memorial, Norfolk, VA.

67. January 24–25, 1945, entry, Diary of O. W. Griswold, Box 1, Papers of Oscar W. Griswold, U.S. Army Heritage and Education Center, Carlisle, PA; McEnery, *The XIV Corps Battle for Manila, February 1945*, 69.

68. C. D. Eddleman, "The Lingayen Operation," February 4, 1946, Folder: Lingayen Operation, Box 1, Papers of Clyde Eddleman, U.S. Army Heritage and Education Center, Carlisle, PA.

69. January 26, 1945, entry, Diary of O. W. Griswold, Box 1, Papers of Oscar W. Griswold, U.S. Army Heritage and Education Center, Carlisle, PA.

70. Giles H. Kidd, "The Operations of the 37th Infantry Division in the Crossing of the Pasig River and Closing to the Walls of Intramuros, Manila 7–9 February 1945 (Luzon Campaign)," 19, Advanced Infantry Officers Course Number 1, 1949–1950, Infantry School, Fort Benning, GA.

71. XIV Corps, "After Action Report: XIV Corps: M-1 Report," July 29, 1945, vol. II, 134, Folder 32, Box 3, Papers of Walter Krueger, Cushing Library, Texas A&M University, College Station, TX.

72. John R. Walker, *Bracketing the Enemy: Forward Observers in World War II* (Norman: University of Oklahoma Press, 2013), 90–91.

73. George E. Jones, "Big Air Base Taken" M'Arthur's Men Make Important Stride on Luzon: Fort Stotsenburg Also Seized—MacArthur 43 Miles From Manila," *The New York Times*, January 26, 1945.

74. Emphasis in the original. January 26, 1945, entry, Diary of O. W. Griswold, Box 1, Papers of Oscar W. Griswold, U.S. Army Heritage and Education Center, Carlisle, PA.

75. "A History of the 129th Infantry," Folder 337-INF (129)0.1 History—129th Inf Regt, Box 8730, Record of the 37th Infantry Division, World War II Operational Records, Record of the Adjutant General's Staff, Record Group 407, U.S. National Archives, College Park, MD; James Villanueva, "Field Artillery and Flying Columns: Combined Arms Maneuver in the Advance on and Seizure of Manila, 1945," in Peter J. Schifferle, *Bringing Order to Chaos: Historical Case Studies of Combined Arms Maneuver in Large Scale Combat Operations* (Fort Leavenworth, KS: Army University Press, 2018), 128.

76. Translation L37D7: 99th Airfield Battalion Op Order #12, January 24, 1945, Folder 337-2-A/A/Rpt-Annex 2 Int—Appendix G-2, Box 8616, Record of the 37th Infantry Division, World War II Operational Records, Records of the Adjutant General's Staff, Record Group 407, U.S. National Archives, College Park, MD; "A History of the 129th Infantry," Folder 337-INF (129)0.1 History—129th Inf Regt, Box 8730, Record of the 37th Infantry Division, World War II Operational Records, Record of the Adjutant General's Staff, Record Group 407, U.S. National Archives, College Park, MD; Entry for January 29, 1945, in "637th Tank Destroyer Battalion After Action Report, Luzon Campaign," Combined Arms Research Library, Fort Leavenworth, KS.

77. Villanueva, "Field Artillery and Flying Columns," 128.

78. Ohl, *Minuteman*, 164.

79. Sasaki to Company, [undated], Translation Number L37D10 (Section 31), January 29, 1945, "After Action Report: Operations of the 37th Infantry Division on Bougainville, BSI, and Luzon, 21 Nov 44 to 30 June 45, Part IV: Annex 2 Intelligence: Appendix A 173D Language Detachment, Appendix (2) Translations, Folder 337-2-A/A/Rpt-Annex 2 Int—Appendix G-2, Box 8616, Record of the 37th Infantry Division, World War II Operational Records, Records of the Adjutant General's Staff, Record Group 407, U.S. National Archives, College Park, MD.

80. January 30, 1945, entry, Diary of O. W. Griswold, Box 1, Papers of Oscar W. Griswold, US Army Heritage and Education Center, Carlisle, PA; *40th Infantry Division The Years of World War II: 7 December 1941–7 April 1946* (Baton Rouge, LA: Army & Navy Publishing Company, 1947), 111–113.

81. Ohl, *Minuteman*, 164–166; Smith, *Triumph in the Philippines*, 185–187; *40th Infantry Division The Years of World War II*, 111–113. The 754th Tank Battalion had companies sitting as corps reserve in Manila, but others fighting in the hills against the Japanese well into mid-February: Headquarters, 754th Tank Battalion, "Battle of Luzon 9 January–30 June '45," Combined Arms Research Library, Fort Leavenworth, KS; XIV Corps, After Action Report: XIV Corps: M-1 Operation," July 29, 1945, vol. II, 134, Folder 32, Box 3, Papers of Walter Krueger, Cushing Library, Texas A&M University, College Station, TX.

82. January 28, 1945, entry, Diary of O. W. Griswold, Box 1, Papers of Oscar W. Griswold, U.S. Army Heritage and Education Center, Carlisle, PA.

83. January 31, 1945, entry, Diary of O. W. Griswold, Box 1, Papers of Oscar W. Griswold, U.S. Army Heritage and Education Center, Carlisle, PA.

84. Rogers, *Bitter Years*, 251.

85. Kobayashi Group Order, Manila Defense Op Order 45, February 2, 1945, XIV Corps Advanced Echelon Translation Number 75, document number 26 T 75, in *Wartime Translations of Seized Japanese Documents.*

86. Joseph D. Harrington, *Yankee Samurai (The Secret Role of Nisei in America's Pacific Victory)* (Detroit: Pettigrew Enterprises, 1979), 259; Austin Bach, Annex 2: Intelligence: Appendix 4 173D Language Detachment, 37th Infantry Division, Report After Action, July 25, 1945, Folder 337-2—A/A/Rpt Annex #2—Appendix A—Language Det, Box 8617, Records of the 37th Infantry Division, World War II Operational Records, Records of the Adjutant General's Staff, U.S. National Archives, College Park, MD.

87. Kenney, *General Kenney Reports*, 513–514.

88. "The Battle History of the 3rd Battalion, 148th Infantry, Second Luzon P.I. Campaign 11 November 44–15 August 1945" (Buckeye, Arizona), 8.

89. "A History of the 129th Infantry," Folder 337-INF (129)0.1 History – 129th Inf Regt, Box 8730, Record of the 37th Infantry Division, World War II Operational Records, Record of the Adjutant General's Staff, Record Group 407, U.S. National Archives, College Park, MD. Minor punctuation changes made without notice to Norman Mailer quote in Glenn T. Johnson, ed., *We Aint No Heroes: The 112th Cavalry in World War II* (Denton, TX: Privately Published, 2005), 263.

CHAPTER 5

1. "General Mudge Addresses Reunion," *Saber News*, October 1953, 1.

2. William A. Richardson, 1st Cavalry Division, World War II Army Service Experiences Questionnaire, U.S. Army Heritage and Education Center, Carlisle, PA.

3. Alexander M. Bielakowski, *From Horses to Horsepower: The Mechanization and Demise of the US Cavalry, 1916–1920* (Stroud, England: Fonthill Media, 2019), 159.

4. George F. Hofmann, *Through Mobility We Conquer: The Mechanization of US Cavalry* (Lexington: The University Press of Kentucky, 2006), 275; Billy Frank Brumley, Folder 2, Box 6, World War II Veteran Surveys, Record Group 237, Tennessee State Library and Archives, Nashville, TN; Allen MacDonald, "My Life in the 1ˢᵗ Cavalry Division," *Saber*, January/February 2013, 21.

5. "The Cavalry Rides Again," *Saber News* (April 1952), 8; "Horses Among the Boondocks Again," *Saber News* (July 1952), 2; John K. Herr, "Remount the 1st Cavalry Division," *Saber News*, January 1954, 4; "Biographical Sketch of Major General Verne D. Mudge," Folder 901-0, Box 13283, Records of the 1st Cavalry Division, World War II Operational Records, Records of the Adjutant General's Staff, Record Group 407, U.S National Archives, College Park, MD.

6. Bertram C. Wright, *The 1st Cavalry Division in World War II* (Tokyo: Toppan Printing Company, 1947), 125; Clyde D. Eddleman, Oral History (February 11, 1975), 31, Senior Officers Debriefing Program, U.S. Army Heritage and Education Center, Carlisle, PA.

7. William C. Chase, *Front Line General: The Commands of Wm. C. Chase: An Autobiography* (Houston, TX: Pacesetter Press, 1975), 78; Wright, *The 1st Cavalry Division in World War II*, 125.

8. Walter Krueger, "Command Responsibilities in a Joint Operation," and Walter Krueger, "The Luzon Campaign of 1945," April 6, 1954, Folder 73, Box 12, Papers of Walter Krueger, Academy Library, U.S. Military Academy, West Point, NY; C. D. Eddleman, "The Lingayen Operation," February 4, 1946, Folder Lingayen Operation, Box 1, Papers of Clyde Eddleman, U.S. Army Heritage and Education Center, Carlisle, PA; Rogers, *Bitter Years*, 249.

9. Wright, *The 1st Cavalry Division in World War II*, 126.

10. Ohl, *Minuteman*, 167.

11. Wright, *The 1st Cavalry Division in World War II*, 126.

12. Wright, *The 1st Cavalry Division in World War II*, 126–127.

13. Wright, *The 1st Cavalry Division in World War II*, 127; Robert B. Holland, *The Rescue of Santo Tomás Manila WWII—The Flying Column: 100 Miles to Freedom* (Puducah, KT: Turner Publishing Company, 2003), 39.

14. "Battle Diary of the 1st Cavalry Division," Folder 901-0, Box 13283, Records of the 1st Cavalry Division, World War II Operational Records, Records of the Adjutant General's Staff, Record Group 407, U.S. National Archives, College Park, MD.

15. Dunn, *Pacific Microphone*, 290.

16. Ohl, *Minuteman*, 167.

17. LeGrande Diller, Oral History by D. Clayton James (May 31, 1977), 5, Box 5, Record Group 49, MacArthur Memorial, Norfolk, VA.

18. Lewis Sebring, Jr., "The MacArthur Circus" manuscript first draft, 154, Reel 7, Frame 185, Papers of Lewis Sebring, Jr., Wisconsin Historical Society, Madison, WI; Russell Brines Oral History by D. Clayton James (June 18, 1977), 28, Box 5, Record Group 49, MacArthur Memorial, Norfolk, VA.

19. LeGrande Diller, Oral History by D. Clayton James (May 31, 1977), 3, Box 5, Record Group 49, MacArthur Memorial, Norfolk, VA.

20. Dunn, *Pacific Microphone*, 152–154.

21. Dunn, *Pacific Microphone*, 283–288.

22. Dunn, *Pacific Microphone*, 283–288.

23. Dunn, *Pacific Microphone*, 283–288.

24. Dunn, *Pacific Microphone*, 283–288.

25. Dunn, *Pacific Microphone*, 289, 296; McManus, *Fire and Fortitude*, 126; J. Y. Smith, "Frank Hewlett, Reporter for Utah Paper," *The Washington Post*, July 9, 1983.

26. "Department of Defense Office of Public Information Press Branch: Major General William Curtis Chase," June 1955, Folder William Chase, Box 22, World War II Collection, 1st Cavalry Division Museum, Fort Hood, TX.

27. Peter MacFarlane, Oral History: Interview A (January 19, 2011), 23, Oral History Collection, Record Group 32, MacArthur Memorial, Norfolk, VA.

28. Chase, *Front Line General*, 82; Wright, *The 1st Cavalry Division in World War II*, 126.

29. Frank Mendez, Oral History (April 23, 2005), 10–12, Oral History Collection, Record Group 32, MacArthur Memorial, Norfolk, VA.

30. Chase, *Front Line General*, 83; Dunn, *Pacific Microphone*, 290–292; Radio Transcript #32, February 2, 1945, Folder 12, Box 3, Papers of William J. Dunn, Record Group 52, MacArthur Memorial, Norfolk, VA.

31. Chase, *Front Line General*, 83; Mydans, *More Than Meets the Eye*, 186; Dunn, *Pacific Microphone*, 290–292; Radio Transcript #32, February 2, 1945, Folder 12, Box 3, Papers of William J. Dunn, Record Group 52, MacArthur Memorial, Norfolk, VA.

32. Radio Transcript #32, February 2, 1945, Folder 12, Box 3, Papers of William J. Dunn, Record Group 52, MacArthur Memorial, Norfolk, VA.

33. Dunn, *Pacific Microphone*, 292–293; Holland, *The Rescue of Santo Tomás*, 44; William F. Daugherty, "Flying Columns," *Armor*, March–April 1967, 19–23; Sixth U.S. Army, "Report of the Luzon Campaign 9 January 1945–30 June 1945," vol. I, 32–33, Skelton Combined Arms Research Library, Fort Leavenworth, KS.

34. Attachment to Robert H. Kiser Army World War II Army Service Experiences Questionnaire, 37th Infantry Division, World War II Army Service Experiences Questionnaire, U.S. Army Heritage and Education Center, Carlisle Barracks, PA.

35. Statement of Konuma Harue, February 19, 1949, document number 52018, in "Statements of Japanese Officials on World War II."

36. Wright, *The 1st Cavalry Division in World War II*, 126.

37. Wright, *The 1st Cavalry Division in World War II*, 126.

38. Prisoner of War Preliminary Interrogation Report 1CD-9644J: Kitamura Takeshi, February 1, 1945, Folder 901-2.13, Box 427, Records of the 1st Cavalry Division, Record Group 407, U.S. National Archives, College Park, MD.

39. Chase, *Front Line General*, 83; Wright, *The 1st Cavalry Division in World War II*, 126.

40. Marci Andrews Wahlquist, ed., *Beyond the Bend: The Journey of Normand Laub from World War II to Peace of Mind* (North Salt Lake, UT: Sheridan Publishing, 2006), 152–153; Fred Hampson, "Brewery Called High Point in One Group's Manila Dash," *The Sun* (Baltimore, MD), February 5, 1945; Ralph C. McGraw, "We Were First in Manila," *Cavalry Journal* 54, no. 4 (July–August 1945): 2–5; Radio Transcript #33, February 4, 1945, Folder 12, Box 3, Papers of William Dunn, Record Group 52, MacArthur Memorial, Norfolk, VA.

41. George Fischer, "The Flying Column Writing Project," May 21, 2010, Folder 4, Box 89, Record Group 15, MacArthur Memorial, Norfolk, VA.

42. Chase, *Front Line General*, 85.

43. Edgar F. Raines, Jr., *Eyes of Artillery: The Origins of Modern U.S. Army Aviation in World War II* (Washington, DC.: U.S. Government Printing Office, 2000), 261.

44. Holland, *The Rescue of Santo Tomás*, 47.

45. George Fischer, "The Flying Column Writing Project," May 21, 2010, Folder 4, Box 89, Record Group 15, MacArthur Memorial, Norfolk, VA; William F. Daugherty, "Flying Columns," *Armor*, March–April 1967, 19–23.

46. Ralph C. McGraw, "We Were First in Manila," 3–4; Astor, *Crisis in the Pacific*, 495.

47. Holland, *The Rescue of Santo Tomás*, 47–49; Hampson, "Brewery Called High Point"; William H. Swan, "Recollection of Luzon, 1945 U.S. 1st Cavalry" Folder 3, Box 59, Papers of William H. Swan, Record Group 59, MacArthur Memorial, Norfolk, VA; Astor, *Crisis in the Pacific*, 513; Chase, *Front Line General*, 84; Radio Transcript #32, February 2, 1945, Folder 12, Box 3, Papers of William J. Dunn, Record Group 52, MacArthur Memorial, Norfolk, VA.

48. Boyd filled out two veteran surveys and gives very different descriptions of his reaction to combat, which shows that the reactions are diverse. He was both scared and professional. There is no contradiction to say both of these descriptions are accurate. Robert L. Boyd, Folder 1, Box 5, and Jackson T. Jones, Folder 5, Box 21, World War II Veteran Surveys, Record Group 237, Tennessee State Library and Archives, Nashville, TN.

49. Dorsey Robbins Survey, Folder 1, Box 21, World War II Veteran Surveys, Record Group 237, Tennessee State Library and Archives, Nashville, TN.

50. Carlos P. Romulo, *I See the Philippines Rise* (Garden City, NY: Doubleday & Company, 1946), 222, 227–216.

51. Pacita Pestaño-Jacinto, *Living with the Enemy: A Diary of the Japanese Occupation* (Pasig City, Philippines: Anvil Publishing, 1999), 283.

52. Homer Bigart, "Two Divisions Stage Race for Gates of Manila," *New York Herald Tribune*, February 4, 1945.

53. Dunn, *Pacific Microphone*, 295.

54. Report After Action (Provost Marshal Section), July 20, 1945, included in 37th Infantry Division, "Report After Action," July 25, 1945, Folder 337-0.3 A/A Rpts, Box 8604, Records of the 37th Infantry Division, Records of the Adjutant General's Office, Record Group 407, U.S. National Archives, College Park, MD.

55. Mudge, G-3 Operations Report, January 31–February 1, 1945, Folder 901-3.1 G-3 Opns Rpt—(Periodic)—1st Cavalry Division, Box 13305, Records of the 1st Cavalry Division, World War II Operational Records, Record of the Adjutant General's Staff, Record Group 407, U.S. National Archives, College Park, MD.

56. Wahlquist, ed., *Beyond the Bend*, 152–153.

57. Richard J. Foss, "How It Was" manuscript memoir, 226, Veterans History Project, American Folklife Center, Library of Congress.

58. Sixth U.S. Army, "Report of the Luzon Campaign 9 January 1945–30 June 1945," vol. IV, "The Engineer," 107–108, Skelton Combined Arms Research Library, Fort Leavenworth, KS; Bigart, "Two Divisions Stage Race"; Kidd, "Operations of the 37th Infantry Division in the Crossing of the Pasig River," 18; *Japanese Defense of Cities*, 8.

59. Sixth U.S. Army, "Report of the Luzon Campaign 9 January 1945–30 June 1945," vol. IV, "The Engineer," 107–108, Skelton Combined Arms Research Library, Fort Leavenworth, KS; Bigart, "Two Divisions Stage Race"; Kidd, "Operations of the 37th Infantry Division in the Crossing of the Pasig River," 18; *Japanese Defense of Cities*, 8.

60. Ohl, *Minuteman*, 166; 37th Cavalry Reconnaissance Troop, Mechanized, "Troop History for period 8 January 1945 to 3 February 1945," September 1, 1945, 26 and 30, Folder 337-CAV 0.1, Box 8710, Records of the 37th Infantry Division, World War II Operational Records, Records of the Adjutant General's Staff, Record Group 407, U.S. National Archives, College Park, MD.

61. 37th Cavalry Reconnaissance Troop, Mechanized, "Troop History for period 8 January 1945 to 3 February 1945," September 1, 1945, 16 and 29, Folder 337-CAV 0.1, Box 8710, Records of the 37th Infantry Division, World War II Operational Records, Records of the Adjutant General's Staff, Record Group 407, U.S. National Archives, College Park, MD.

62. Wright, *The 1st Cavalry Division in World War II*, 128.

63. Dunn, *Pacific Microphone*, 295; Radio Transcript, February 2, 1945, Folder 12, Box 3, Papers of William Dunn, Record Group 52, MacArthur Memorial, Norfolk, VA.

64. Holland, *Rescue of Santo Tomás*, 47; Wright, *The 1st Cavalry Division in World War II*, 127.

65. Diary of John "Jack" Titcomb included in Holland, *The Rescue of Santo Tomás*, 151; Lewis B. Sebring, Jr., "First into Manila," *New York Herald Tribune*, February 6, 1945.

66. Ohl, *Minuteman*, 166.

67. February 2, 1945 entry, Diary of Oscar W. Griswold, Box 1, Papers of Oscar W. Griswold, U.S. Army Heritage and Education Center, Carlisle, PA.

68. Krueger, *From Down Under to Nippon*, 244; Thompson and Harris, *The Signal Corps: The Outcome*, 285.

69. 37th Cavalry Reconnaissance Troop, Mechanized, "Troop History for period 8 January 1945 to 3 February 1945," September 1, 1945, 30, Folder 337-CAV 0.1, Box 8710, Records of the 37th Infantry Division, World War II Operational Records, Records of the Adjutant General's Staff, Record Group 407, U.S. National Archives, College Park, MD; February 2, 1945 entry, Diary of Oscar W. Griswold, Box 1, Papers of Oscar W. Griswold, U.S. Army Heritage and Education Center, Carlisle, PA; Owen, *Eye-Deep in Hell*, 83.

70. Bruce Palmer, Oral History (December 5, 1975), 345, Senior Officer Debriefing Program, U.S. Army Heritage and Education Center, Carlisle, PA.

71. Report After Action (Headquarters Commandant), July 20, 1945, included in 37th Infantry Division, "Report After Action," July 25, 1945, Folder 337-0.3 A/A Rpts, Box 8604, Records of the 37th Infantry Division, Records of the Adjutant General's Office, Record Group 407, U.S. National Archives, College Park, MD.

72. 37th Cavalry Reconnaissance Troop, Mechanized, "Troop History for period 8 January 1945 to 3 February 1945," September 1, 1945, 29 and 30, Folder 337-CAV 0.1, Box 8710, Records of the 37th Infantry Division, World War II Operational Records, Records of the Adjutant General's Staff, Record Group 407, U.S. National Archives, College Park, MD.

73. Robert Beightler, "Major General Robert S. Beightler's Report on the Activities of the 37th Infantry Division, 1940–1945," Folder MS593/1/7, Box 1, Papers of Robert S. Beightler, Ohio Historical Society, Columbus, OH. The finding of the beer is also documented in files of the 37th Infantry Division: "A History of the 129th Infantry Regiment," Folder 337-INF (129) 0.1, Box 8730, Records of the 37th Infantry Division, World War II Operational Records, Records of the Adjutant General's Staff, Record Group 407, U.S. National Archives, College Park, MD. Robert Minch, Oral History (March 29, 2007), 11, Wisconsin Veterans Museum, Madison, WI; Ray Smith, Oral History (August 18, 2017), 37, Nimitz Education and Research Center, National Museum of the Pacific War, Fredericksburg, TX; Stanley Frankel, "'B' Stands for Beer," *The 37th Division Veterans' News* (no date), included in Edwin E. Hanson, "My Military History," 37th Infantry Division, World War II Army Service Experiences Questionnaire, U. S. Army History and Heritage Command, Carlisle, PA; Hampson, "Brewery Called High Point"; Dick Hanley, "Hike to Manila," *Yank* (March 9, 1945), 5; "A History of the 129th Infantry Regiment," Folder 337-INF (129) 0.1, Box 8730, Records of the 37th Infantry Division, World War II Operational Records, Records of the Adjutant General's Staff, Record Group 407, U.S. National Archives, College Park, MD.

74. Clyma, ed., *Connecticut Men of the US Army: Connecticut Veterans Commemorative Booklet* 8, no. 15 (October 25, 1945): 6.

75. William Harvey, Oral History (no date), Oshkosh Public Museum, Oshkosh, WI.

76. Robert Beightler, "Major General Robert S. Beightler's Report on the Activities of the 37th Infantry Division, 1940–1945"; Folder MS593/1/7, Box 1, Papers of Robert S. Beightler, Ohio Historical Society, Columbus, OH. The finding of the beer is also documented in files of the 37th Infantry Division: "A History of the 129th Infantry Regiment," Folder 337-INF (129) 0.1, Box 8730, Records of the 37th Infantry Division, World War II Operational Records, Records of the Adjutant General's Staff, Record Group 407, U.S. National Archives, College Park, MD. Robert Minch, Oral History (March 29, 2007), 11, Wisconsin Veterans Museum, Madison, WI; Ray Smith, Oral History (August 18, 2017),

37, Nimitz Education and Research Center, National Museum of the Pacific War, Fredericksburg, TX; Stanley Frankel, "'B' Stands for Beer," *The 37th Division Veterans' News* (no date), included in Edwin E. Hanson, "My Military History," 37th Infantry Division, World War II Army Service Experiences Questionnaire, U. S. Army History and Heritage Command, Carlisle, PA; Hampson, "Brewery Called High Point"; Hanley, "Hike to Manila," 5; "A History of the 129th Infantry Regiment," Folder 337-INF (129) o.1, Box 8730, Records of the 37th Infantry Division, World War II Operational Records, Records of the Adjutant General's Staff, Record Group 407, U.S. National Archives, College Park, MD.

77. Robert Beightler, "Major General Robert S. Beightler's Report on the Activities of the 37th Infantry Division, 1940–1945," Folder MS593/1/7, Box 1, Papers of Robert S. Beightler, Ohio Historical Society, Columbus, OH.

78. James Hanrahan, "Soldier, Manager, Leader: An Interview with Former CIA Executive Director Lawrence K. 'Red' White," *Studies in Intelligence* 43, no. 3 (Winter 1999–2000): 29–41.

79. Dunn, *Pacific Microphone*, 296.

80. Dunn, *Pacific Microphone*, 297.

81. Dunn, *Pacific Microphone*, 297.

82. Madeline Ullom essay, and February 7, 1945 entry in diary of John "Jack" Titcomb, in Holland, *The Rescue of Santo Tomás*, 139, 152.

83. Dunn, *Pacific Microphone*, 297–298; "Ex-Salon Gets Year in Counterfeiting," *The Tuscaloosa News*, November 3, 1964; Wright, *The 1st Cavalry Division in World War II*, 128; "XIV Operations on Luzon," no date, loose in box, Box 1A, Papers of Oscar Griswold, U.S. Military Academy, West Point, NY.

84. Walter Hines, *Aggies of the Pacific War: New Mexico A&M and the War with Japan* (Las Cruces, NM: Yucca Tree Press, 1999), 116.

85. Smith, *Triumph in the Pacific*, 219.

86. February 6 entry in Titcomb diary, printed in Holland, *Rescue of Santo Tomás*, 151.

87. Charles W. Boggs, Jr. *Marine Aviation in the Philippines* (Washington, DC: U.S. Government Printing Office, 1951), 79.

88. Frankel, *The 37th Infantry Division in World War II*, 243–254; Ohl, *Minuteman*, 169–170; Bigart, "Two Divisions Stage Race"; Mudge, G-3 Operations Report, February 2–3, 1945, Folder 901-3.1 G-3 Opns Rpt—(Periodic)—1st Cavalry Division, Box 13305, Records of the 1st Cavalry Division, World War II Operational Records, Record of the Adjutant General's Staff, Record Group 407, U.S. National Archives, College Park, MD.

89. Frankel, *The 37th Infantry Division in World War II*, 243–254; Ohl, *Minuteman*, 169–170; Mudge, G-3 Operations Report, February 2–3, 1945, Folder 901-3.1 G-3 Opns Rpt—(Periodic)—1st Cavalry Division, Box 13305, Records of the 1st Cavalry Division; 3rd Base Operation Order #43, Captured on February 11, 1945 by 145th Infantry Regiment, Folder 337-2, Box 8616, Records of the 37th

Infantry Division, World War II Operational Records, Records of the Adjutant General's Staff, Record Group 407, U.S. National Archives, College Park, MD.

90. Ohl, *Minuteman*, 169–170; Mudge, G-3 Operations Report, February 2–3, 1945, Folder 901-3.1 G-3 Opns Rpt—(Periodic)—1st Cavalry Division, Box 13305, Records of the 1st Cavalry Division, World War II Operational Records, Records of the Adjutant General's Staff, Record Group 407, U.S. National Archives, College Park, MD.

91. "XIV Operations on Luzon," no date, loose in the box, Box 1A, Papers of Oscar Griswold, U.S. Military Academy, West Point, NY.

92. "A History of the 129th Infantry Regiment," Folder 337-INF (129) 0.1, Box 8730, Records of the 37th Infantry Division, World War II Operational Records, Records of the Adjutant General's Staff, Record Group, 407, U.S. National Archives, College Park, MD.

CHAPTER 6

1. Paul Chwialkowski, *In Caesar's Shadow: The Life of General Robert Eichelberger* (Westport, CT: Greenwood Press, 1993), 32; John F. Shortal, *Forged by Fire: General Robert L. Eichelberger and the Pacific War* (Columbia: University of South Carolina Press, 1987), 1, 3, 17, 19.

2. Shortal, *Forged by Fire*, 46–48: Chwialkowski, *In Caesar's Shadow*, 25, 27–28; Howard M. Norton, "Champion 'Jap Outsmarter,' Army Says of Eichelberger," *The Sun* (Baltimore, MD), February 6, 1945.

3. Chwialkowski, *In Caesar's Shadow*, 53.

4. Shortal, *Forged by Fire*, 95.

5. Chwialkowski, *In Caesar's Shadow*, 114.

6. Chwialkowski, *In Caesar's Shadow*, 115.

7. "Story Behind Famed Patch," *Voice of the Angels*, March 15, 1975; Joseph Swing, Oral History (June 21, 1971), 1–2, Butler Library Oral History Archives, Columbia University, New York, NY.

8. Major "Ripcord" Walker, "LTG Joseph M. Swing and the 11th Airborne Division," *Voice of the Angels*, March 15, 1985, 24; Graduate Class of 1945, "General Swing," *Voice of the Angels*, March 15, 1985, 35; "News Briefs," *Voice of the Angels*, March 15, 1974; James Scudder, "1,000 Veterans Pay Emotional Tribute to Late Commander," *Arkansas Gazette*, July 21, 1985.

9. Philip Schweitzer, Oral History (October 23, 2007), transcription by author, National World War II Museum, New Orleans, LA.

10. Foster Arnett, Oral History (July 7, 2000), 45, Center for the Study of War and Society, University of Tennessee, Knoxville, TN; Dick Hoyt, "Recollections of General Joe Swing," *Voice of the Angels*, January 15, 1985, 31; Lyman "Tex" Black, Oral History (September 19, 2001 and November 21, 2005), Veterans History Project, American Folklife Center, Library of Congress, Washington, DC. This oral history was conducted by oral history program at the Park Tudor

School, a private school in Indianapolis. The Tudor Park School oral histories are available on the Indiana Memory website. The oral history is also at the Library of Congress and is cited at the Library because it is more likely the more durable location.

11. Swing to March, December 24, 1944, and Swing to March, December 30, 1945, in Dale F. Yee, ed., *Dear General: World War II Letters, 1944–1945 From: Major General Joseph M. Swing To: General Peyton C. March* (Palo Alto, CA: 11th Airborne Association, 1987), 13, 14, 15.

12. Swing to March, December 30, 1944, in Yee, ed., *Dear General*, 15.

13. Swing to March, January 25, 1945, in Yee, ed., *Dear General*, 17.

14. Robert L. Eichelberger, *Our Jungle Road to Tokyo* (New York: Viking, 1950),188.

15. Chwialkowski, *In Caesar's Shadow*, 116–117; January 27, 1945 entry, Diary of Robert Eichelberger, Folder 1945–1946, Box 1, Papers of Robert L. Eichelberger, Rubenstein Rare Book and Manuscript Library, Duke University, Durham, NC.

16. Swing to March, January 25, 1945, in Yee, ed., *Dear General*, 17.

17. Hoppenstein, "The Operation of the 187th Glider Infantry Regiment," 17–18.

18. Different documents give the time as 8:15 a.m. and 8:30 a.m. The most contemporary list it as 8:15 a.m. Headquarters 11th Airborne Division, G-3 Periodic Report, January 3–February 1, 1945, Folder 311-0.3 11th Airborne Division Operations Reports Luzon, and "11th Airborne Division History," February 1943–May 1945, Folder 311-0.1 History 11th Airborne Division, 11th Airborne Division Operations Reports Luzon, Box 6545, Records of the 11th Airborne Division, World War II Operational Records, Records of the Adjutant General's Office, Record Group 407, U.S. National Archives, College Park, MD; Hoppenstein, "The Operation of the 187th Glider Infantry Regiment," 18.

19. Hoppenstein, "The Operation of the 187th Glider Infantry Regiment," 19.

20. January 31, 1945 entry, Diary of Robert Eichelberger, Folder 1945–1946, Box 1, Papers of Robert L. Eichelberger, Rubenstein Rare Book and Manuscript Library, Duke University, Durham, NC; Hoppenstein, "The Operation of the 187th Glider Infantry Regiment," 31, 33; Flanagan, *The Rakkasans*, 77; Joseph M. Swing, "Historical Narrative Operation Mike Six (Referred to in Some Places as Operation 'Shoestring')," Folder 311-0.3 11th Airborne Division Operations Reports Luzon, Box 6545, Records of the 11th Airborne Division, World War II Operational Records, Records of the Adjutant General's Office, Record Group 407, U.S. National Archives, College Park, MD.

21. Hoppenstein, "The Operation of the 187th Glider Infantry Regiment," 17–19.

22. Eichelberger to Eichelberger, February 1, 1945, in Jay Luvaas, ed., *Dear Miss Em: General Eichelberger's War in the Pacific, 1942–1945* (Westport, CT: Greenwood Press, 1981), 207; Swing to March, January 25, 1945, in Yee, ed., *Dear General*, 17.

23. Toi Hannosuke, 11th Sea Raiding Base Operation Order A Number 12, 111th Fishing Battalion Order, January 31, 1945; Toi Hannosuke, 11th Sea Raiding Base Operation Order A Number 13, 111th Fishing Battalion Order, February

1, 1945, XIV Corps Advanced Echelon Translation Number 97, document number 26 T 97; Iwabuchi Mitsuji, Manila Naval Defense Force Operation Order Number 38, February 1, 1945, XIV Corps Advanced Echelon Translation Number 56, document number 26 T 56, in *Wartime Translations of Seized Japanese Documents.*

24. Eichelberger, *Our Jungle Road*, 189–190, 193; Shortal, *Forged by Fire*, 109–110; Eichelberger to Eichelberger, February 12, 1945, in Luvaas, ed., *Dear Miss Em,* 215; Swing to March, January 25, 1945, in Yee, ed., *Dear General*, 17.

25. Flanagan, *The Rakkasans*, 77–78.

26. Eichelberger, *Our Jungle Road*, 191.

27. Flanagan, *The Rakkasans*, 79–80; Hoppenstein, "The Operation of the 187th Glider Infantry Regiment," 25–26; Joseph M. Swing, "Historical Narrative Operation Mike Six (Referred to in Some Places as Operation 'Shoestring')," Folder 311-0.3 11th Airborne Division Operations Reports Luzon, Box 6545, Records of the 11th Airborne Division, World War II Operational Records, Records of the Adjutant General's Office, Record Group 407, U.S. National Archives, College Park, MD.

28. Joseph Swing, "Report After Action with the Enemy Operation Mike VI, Luzon Campaign," January 24, 1946, loose in the box, Box 3, Papers of Oscar Griswold, Academy Library, U.S. Military Academy, West Point, NY; Headquarters 11th Airborne Division, G-3 Periodic Report, January 1–February 2, 1945, Folder 311-0.3 11th Airborne Division Operations Reports Luzon, Box 6545, Records of the 11th Airborne Division, World War II Operational Records, Records of the Adjutant General's Office, Record Group 407, U.S. National Archives, College Park, MD.

29. Philip Schweitzer, Oral History (October 23, 2007), transcription by author, National World War II Museum, New Orleans, LA.

30. Swindler to Burgess, May 12, 1988, Folder Correspondence with ex-members of the 11th Airborne Division Sch-Swing, Box 3, Papers of Edward M. Flanagan, Jr., U.S. Army Heritage and Education Center, Carlisle, PA.

31. Flanagan, *The Rakkasans*, 82–83; Joseph Swing, "Report After Action with the Enemy Operation Mike VI, Luzon Campaign," January 24, 1946, loose in the box, Box 3, Papers of Oscar Griswold, Academy Library, U.S. Military Academy, West Point, NY.

32. Hoppenstein, "The Operation of the 187th Glider Infantry Regiment," 21.

33. "11th Airborne Division History," February 1943–May 1945, Folder 311-0.1 History 11th Airborne Division, 11th Airborne Division Operations Reports Luzon, Box 6545, Records of the 11th Airborne Division, World War II Operational Records, Records of the Adjutant General's Office, Record Group 407, U.S. National Archives, College Park, MD.

34. Deane Marks, "The Day the Tank Blew Up," Folder Correspondence with ex-members of the 11th Airborne Division Mar-McC, Box 3. Papers of Edward M. Flanagan, Jr., U.S. Army Heritage and Education Center, Carlisle, PA.

35. Shortal, *Forged by Fire*, 110–111; Edward H. Lahti, *Memoirs of an Angel* (Privately Published, 1994), 69.

36. Henry A. Burgess, *Looking Back* (Missoula, MO: Pictorial History Publishing Company, 1993), 100.

37. Steve M. Hegedus, Oral History (January 14, 2003), 9, Veterans History Project, American Folklife Center, Library of Congress, Washington, DC.

38. Richard C. Bergholz, "Yank Paratroopers Land Behind Luzon Japanese," *Los Angeles Times*, February 5, 1945.

39. Edwin B. Jeffress, "Operations of the 2nd Battalion, 511th Parachute Infantry (11th Airborne Division) in the Battle for Southern Manila, 3–10 February (Luzon Campaign) (Personal Experiences of a Battalion Intelligence Officer)," 13, Advanced Infantry Officers Course, Academic Department, The Infantry School, 1948–1949.

40. Jim Holzem, "Jim Holzem's Story," *Voice of the Angels*, June 15, 1982, 10.

41. Larry Davis, "Eleventh Airborne Drive Manila, 1945," *Voices of the Angels*, January 15, 1984, 24.

42. Frank Smith, "How Sky Army Took Ridge on Manila Bay," *Daily Times* (Chicago, IL), February 4, 1945; Holzem, "Jim Holzem's Story," 10; Gene Eric Salecker, *Blossoming Silk Against the Rising Sun: US and Japanese Paratroopers at War in the Pacific in World War II* (Mechanicsburg: Stackpole Books, 2010), 241.

43. Victor M. Liptrap, Oral History (February 25, 2005), 26, Nimitz Education and Research Center, National Museum of the Pacific War, Fredericksburg, TX.

44. Earl Winsor, Oral History (May 19, 2007), Veterans History Project, American Folklife Center, Library of Congress, Washington, DC; Victor M. Liptrap, Oral History (February 25, 2005), 26, Nimitz Education and Research Center, National Museum of the Pacific War, Fredericksburg, TX; February 3, 1945 entry, Diary of Robert Eichelberger, Folder 1945–1946, Box 1, Papers of Robert L. Eichelberger, Rubenstein Rare Book and Manuscript Library, Duke University, Durham, NC.

45. Joseph Swing, "Report After Action with the Enemy Operation Mike VI, Luzon Campaign," January 24, 1946, loose in the box, Box 3, Papers of Oscar Griswold, Academy Library, U.S. Military Academy, West Point, NY; Salecker, *Blossoming Silk Against the Rising Sun*, 244.

46. Eichelberger, *Our Jungle Road*, 196.

47. Flanagan, *The Rakkasans*, 86–89.

48. Terry H. Santos, "Recon Platoon Slighted?" *Voices of the Angels*, March 15, 1990.

49. Astor, *Crisis in the Pacific*, 521.

50. James E. Richardson, *Under Age Angel* (Amherst, WI: Palmer Publications, 1995), 95–96.

51. Shortal, *Forged by Fire*, 110–111; February 4, 1945 entry, Diary of Robert Eichelberger, Folder 1945–1946, Box 1, Papers of Robert L. Eichelberger, Rubenstein Rare Book and Manuscript Library, Duke University, Durham, NC.

52. Theolbald Kobus statement, in Clyma, ed., *Connecticut Men of the US Army: Connecticut Veterans Commemorative Booklet* 9, no. 20 (January 12, 1946): 8–9; Joseph M. Swing, Oral History by D. Clayton James (August 26, 1971), 13; Edward M. Flanagan, Jr., *The Angels: A History of the 11th Airborne Division, 1943–1946* (Washington, DC: Infantry Journal Press, 1948), 80.

53. Eichelberger to Eichelberger, February 2, 1945, and Eichelberger to Eichelberger, February 3, 1945, in Luvaas, ed., *Dear Miss Em*, 208–209.

54. January 31, February 4, and February 6, 1945 entry, Diary of Robert Eichelberger, Folder 1945–1946, Box 1, Papers of Robert L. Eichelberger, Rubenstein Rare Book and Manuscript Library, Duke University, Durham, NC.

55. Joseph M. Swing, Oral History (August 26, 1971), 18, D. Clayton James Collection, Record Group 49, MacArthur Memorial, Norfolk, VA; John C. McManus, *Island Infernos: The U.S. Army's Pacific Odyssey, 1944* (New York: Caliber, 2021), 542–543.

56. Burgess, *Looking Back*, 101; Serling was actually describing a road march on Leyte, but the section quoted describes the situation of paratroopers as the advance on the ground and works for Luzon as well: Jerry Davis, Ed Lahti, John Ringler, Lee E. Walker, and Foster Arnett, *511th Parachute Infantry Regiment* (Paducah, KT: Turner Publishing Company, 1997), 29; Eichelberger to Eichelberger, February 2, 1945, in Luvaas, ed., *Dear Miss Em*, 208; Headquarters 11th Airborne Division, G-3 Periodic Report, February 2–3, 1945, Folder 311-0.3 11th Airborne Division Operations Reports Luzon, Box 6545, Records of the 11th Airborne Division, World War II Operational Records, Records of the Adjutant General's Office, Record Group 407, U.S. National Archives, College Park, MD.

57. Joseph M. Swing, Oral History (August 26, 1971), 16, D. Clayton James Collection, Record Group 49, MacArthur Memorial, Norfolk, VA.

58. Joseph Swing, "Report After Action with the Enemy Operation Mike VI, Luzon Campaign," January 24, 1946, loose in the box, Box 3, Papers of Oscar Griswold, Academy Library, U.S. Military Academy, West Point, NY.

59. Hoppenstein, "The Operation of the 187th Glider Infantry Regiment," 33; Banning Repplier, "This Barringer Grad Is 'Making Good,'" undated, unidentified newspaper clipping in Yee, ed., *Dear General*, 47.

60. Flannagan, *The Angels*, 79–80; Swindler to Burgess, May 12, 1988, Folder Correspondence with ex-members of the 11th Airborne Division Sch-Swing, Box 3, Papers of Edward M. Flanagan, Jr., U.S. Army Heritage and Education Center, Carlisle, PA; Headquarters 11th Airborne Division, G-3 Periodic Report, February 3–4, 1945, Folder 311-0.3 11th Airborne Division Operations Reports Luzon, Box 6545, Records of the 11th Airborne Division, World War II Operational Records, Records of the Adjutant General's Office, Record Group 407, U.S. National Archives, College Park, MD.

61. Jeffress, "Operations of the 2nd Battalion, 511th Parachute Infantry," 21–23.

62. "11th Airborne Division History," February 1943–May 1945, Folder 311-0.1 History 11th Airborne Division, 11th Airborne Division Operations Reports Luzon, Box 6545, Records of the 11th Airborne Division, World War II Operational Records, Records of the Adjutant General's Office, Record Group 407, U.S. National Archives, College Park, MD; Houston Jolley, "Recollections," *Voice of the Angels*, April 15, 1991, 6; Holzem, "Jim Holzem's Story," 10, 12; Francisco Quesada, "Guerrillas & 11th A/B Division Nasugbu to Manila," *Voice of the Angels*, March 15, 1981, 8; Flanagan, *The Angels*, 80; Steve M. Hegedus, Oral History (January 14, 2003), 10, Veterans History Project, American Folklife Center, Library of Congress, Washington, DC; Deane Marks, "The Day the Tank Blew Up," Folder Correspondence with ex-members of the 11th Airborne Division Mar-McC, Box 3. Papers of Edward M. Flanagan, Jr., U.S. Army Heritage and Education Center, Carlisle, PA.

63. Holzem, "Jim Holzem's Story," 12.

64. February 4, 1945 entry, Diary of Robert Eichelberger, Folder 1945–1946, Box 1, Papers of Robert L. Eichelberger, Rubenstein Rare Book and Manuscript Library, Duke University, Durham, NC.

65. Joseph M. Swing, Oral History by D. Clayton James (August 26, 1971), 16, D. Clayton James Collection, Record Group 49, MacArthur Memorial, Norfolk, VA.

66. Eichelberter to Eichelberger, January 31, 1945, in Luvass, ed., *Dear Miss Em*, 207; Hoppenstein, "The Operation of the 187th Glider Infantry Regiment," 22–24, 32–34, 37; John Wyman, Oral History, no date, 1, Veterans History Project, American Folklife Center, Library of Congress, Washington, DC.

67. Deane Marks, "The Day the Tank Blew Up," Folder Correspondence with ex-members of the 11th Airborne Division Mar-McC, Box 3. Papers of Edward M. Flanagan, Jr., U.S. Army Heritage and Education Center, Carlisle, PA.

68. Flagagan, The Angels, 80–83.

69. Gene Sherman, "Pacific Echoes," *Los Angeles Times*, February 28, 1945; Shortal, *Forged by Fire*, 113; Matthew H. Faith, "Intrepidity, Iron Will, and Intellect: General Robert L. Eichelberger and Military Genius," MA thesis, U.S. Army Command & General Staff College, 2004, 84–85; Joseph M. Swing, Oral History by D. Clayton James (August 26, 1971), 18, D. Clayton James Collection, Record Group 49, MacArthur Memorial, Norfolk, VA; Eichelberger, *Our Jungle Road*, 195. Eichelberger repeatedly expressed his pride in the work of the 11th Airborne Division in letters to Swing: Eichelberger to Swing, February 11, 11945, and Eichelberger to Swing, March 19, 1945, and Eichelberger to Swing, June 22, 1945, Folder Correspondence with Eichelberger, Box 1, Papers of Joseph M. Swing, Academy Library, U.S. Military Academy, West Point, NY.

70. "11th Airborne Division History," February 1943–May 1945, Folder 311-0.1 History 11th Airborne Division, 11th Airborne Division Operations Reports Luzon, Box 6545, Records of the 11th Airborne Division, World War II Operational Records, Records of the Adjutant General's Office, Record

Group 407, U.S. National Archives, College Park, MD; Fidel V. Ramos, Speech Transcript of "Tagaytay's Proud Moment," February 3, 1995, Folder 3, Box 59, Papers of William H. Swan, Record Group 59, MacArthur Memorial, Norfolk, VA.

CHAPTER 7

1. Sixth U.S. Army, "Report of the Luzon Campaign 9 January–30 June 1945," vol. I, 34, Skelton Combined Arms Research Library, Fort Leavenworth, KS.
2. Sarah Kovner, *Prisoners of the Empire: Inside Japanese POW Camps* (Cambridge: Harvard University Press, 2020), 86; Tressa Cates, *The Drainpipe Diary* (New York: Vantage Press, 1957), 240–245.
3. Cates, *Drainpipe Diary*, 241; Terry Wadsworth Warne, *Terry: The Inspiring Story of a Little Girl's Survival as a POW During WWII* (Denver: Outskirts Press, 2013), 213; Robin Prising, *Manila, Goodbye* (Boston: Houghton Mifflin, 1975), 179; Emily Van Sickle, *The Iron Gates of Santo Tomás: The Firsthand Account of an American Couple Interned by the Japanese in Manila, 1942–1945* (Chicago: Academy Chicago Publishers, 1992), 306.
4. Caroline Bailey Pratt, ed., *Only a Matter of Days: The World War II Prison Camp Diary of Fay Cook Bailey* (Bennington, VT: Merriam Press, 2001), 89; Frank Carry, *Letters from an Internment Camp: Davao and Manila* (Ashland, OR: Independent Printing Company, 1993), 120.
5. Herman E. Strong, *A Ringside Seat to War* (New York: Vantage Press, 1965), 84; Cates, *Drainpipe Diary*, 240; Carry, *Letters from an Internment Camp*, 119.
6. Evelyn M. Witthoff and Geraldine V. Chappell, *Three Years' Internment in Santo Tomás* (Kansas City: Beacon Hill Press, 1945), 48–49, 53.
7. Lewis B. Sebring, Jr., "First into Manila: 'Wainwright Division,' the 1st Cavalry, Lives Up to Its Tradition," *New York Herald Tribune*, February 6, 1945.
8. George Fischer, "The Flying Column Writing Project" (May 25, 2010), 1–3, Folder 4, Box 89, Material Donated by the General Public, Record Group 15, MacArthur Memorial, Norfolk, VA.
9. George Fischer, Oral History, (May 21, 2010), 31, Oral History Collection, Record Group 32, MacArthur Memorial, Norfolk, VA.
10. Cates, *Drainpipe Diary*, 240–245.
11. Wright, *The 1st Cavalry Division in World War II*, 125; Van Sickle, *Iron Gates of Santo Tomás*, 313; Frances B. Cogan, *Captured: The Internment of American Civilians in the Philippines, 1941–1945* (Athens: University of Georgia Press, 2000), 269; Rick Lawrence, Oral History (no date), 15, Oral History Collection, Record Group 32, MacArthur Memorial, Norfolk, VA.
12. Hal D. Steward, "Front Line Correspondents," *Army Information Digest* 2, no. 2 (February 1947): 45.
13. Aluit, *By Sword and Fire*, 163–164.
14. Aluit, *By Sword and Fire*, 163–164.

15. Chase, *Front Line General*, 87.

16. Mydans, *More Than Meets the Eye*, 188.

17. Dunn, *Pacific Microphone*, 299–300; Holland, *Rescue of Santo Tomás*, 54; Bruce E. Johansen, *So Far from Home: Manila's Santo Tomás Internment Camp, 1942–1945* (Omaha, NE: PBI Press, 1996), 141.

18. Smith, *Triumph in the Philippines*, 251; Holland, *Rescue of Santo Tomás*, 54; Escoda, *Warsaw of Asia*, 130–131; a photo of Conner shows him with his wounded leg: Rupert Wilkinson, *Surviving a Japanese Internment Camp: Life and Liberation at Santo Tomás, Manila in World War II* (Jefferson, NC: McFarland & Company, 2014), 158.

19. Carry, *Letters from an Internment Camp*, 122.

20. Doug Luyendyck, Oral History (no date), 17, Oral History Collection, Record Group 32, MacArthur Memorial, Norfolk, VA.

21. Amelia Mary Bradley, "Internment in the University of Santo Tomás," 120, Papers of Amelia Mary Bradley, Academy Library, U.S. Military Academy, West Point, NY.

22. Johansen, *So Far from Home*, 142.

23. Wayne Warner, "The 1945 Rescues in Manila: A/G Missionaries Included in Dramatic Military Liberation," *Assemblies of God Heritage* 24, no. 4 (Winter 2004–2005), 9.

24. Sixth U.S. Army, "Report of the Luzon Campaign 9 January–30 June 1945," vol. I, 34, Skelton Combined Arms Research Library, Fort Leavenworth, KS.

25. Bailey Pratt, ed., *Only a Matter of Days*, 90; Radio Transcript, February 4, 1945, Folder 12, Box 3, Papers of William Dunn, Record Group 52, MacArthur Memorial, Norfolk, VA.

26. Rick Lawrence, Oral History (no date), 17, Oral History Collection, Record Group 32, MacArthur Memorial, Norfolk, VA.

27. Johansen, *So Far from Home*, 143.

28. Witthoff and Chappell, *Three Years' Internment*, 55.

29. Strong, *A Ringside Seat*, 87.

30. William Rowan, *On the Spring Tide: A Special Kind of Courage* (Greensboro, NC: Cenografix, 1998), 51; Aluit, *By Sword and Fire*, 162.

31. Prising, *Manila, Goodbye*, 183; Warne, *Terry*, 221.

32. Van Sickle, *Iron Gates of Santo Tomás*, 316.

33. Eva Anna Nixon, "*Delayed, Manila*" (Canton, OH: Friends Foreign Missionary Society, 1981), 84; Strong, *A Ringside Seat*, 89.

34. Angus M. Lorenzen, *A Lovely Little War: Life in a Japanese Prions Camp Through the Eyes of a Child* (New York: History Publishing Company, 2008), 142; Frank Mendez, Oral History (April 23, 2005), 12, 15, Oral History Collection, Record Group 32, MacArthur Memorial, Norfolk, VA.

35. Crytser to Norton and Norton, no date, World War II Collection, 1st Cavalry Division Museum, Fort Hood, TX; Sam E. Harris, Oral History (September 29,

2002), 6–7, Nimitz Education and Research Center, National Museum of the Pacific War, Fredericksburg, TX.

36. Strong, *A Ringside Seat*, 87.

37. Ullom essay, in Holland, *Rescue of Santo Tomás*, 139; Walter M. Macdougall, *Angel of Bataan: The Life of a World War II Army Nurse in the War Zone and at Home* (Camden, ME: Down East Books, 2015), 123.

38. Escoda, *Warsaw of Asia*, 134, 205.

39. Hal D. Steward, "Front Line Correspondents," *Army Information Digest* 2, no. 2 (February 1947): 45; Emily Van Sickle, "How Far the Dawn," manuscript, 358, Papers of Emily Van Sickle, Academy Library, U.S. Military Academy, West Point, NY; Ray Moseley, *Reporting War: How Foreign Correspondents Risked Capture, Torture and Death to Cover World War II* (New Haven: Yale University Press, 2017), 332.

40. Dunn, *Pacific Microphone*, 300.

41. Dunn, *Pacific Microphone*, 301.

42. Frank Hewlett, "Finds Wife Safe After 3 Years at Santo Tomás," *New York Herald Tribune*, February 6, 1945; Moseley, *Reporting War*, 332

43. Rita G. Palmer, as told to Ada N. Hayes, "Three Years in a Prison Camp," *Hampton Union & Rockingham County Gazette*, May 10, 1945, http://www.hampton.lib.nh.us/hampton/biog/ritapalmer/3yearsinaprisoncamp.htm. This news story from 1945 is reproduced on the website of the Lane Memorial Library of Hampton, New Hampshire, which has an extensive local history collection that it has digitized, including multiple stories about Palmer. While the original citation is more durable, the website is more accessible and is the way the story was originally accessed and is included in the bibliography accordingly.

44. Ohl, *Minuteman*, 171; Wright, *The 1st Cavalry Division in World War II*, 132; Mathias, *G.I. Jive*, 129.

45. Aluit, *By Sword and Fire*, 165; Smith, *Triumph in the Philippines*, 252; William H. Swan, "Recollection of Luzon, 1945 U.S. 1st Cavalry," Folder 3, Box 59, Papers of William H. Swan, Record Group 59, MacArthur Memorial, Norfolk, VA.

46. Wright, *The 1st Cavalry Division in World War II*, 130; William H. Swan, "Recollection of Luzon, 1945 U.S. 1st Cavalry," Folder 3, Box 59, Papers of William H. Swan, Record Group 59, MacArthur Memorial, Norfolk, VA.

47. XIV Corps Operations on Luzon, 133, loose in the box, Box 1A, Papers of Oscar Griswold, Academy Library, U.S. Military Academy, West Point, NY; Chase, *Front Line General*, 86, 89; Sixth U.S. Army, "Report of the Luzon Campaign 9 January–30 June 1945," vol. I, 34, and vol. IV, "The Engineer," 118, Skelton Combined Arms Research Library, Fort Leavenworth, KS.

48. Elizabeth "Bim" Meyer, *Teenage Diary: Santo Tomás Internment Camp* (Claremont, CA: The Paige Press, 2005), 218.

49. George Fischer, "The Flying Column Writing Project," 1–3; Van Sickle, *Iron Gates of Santo Tomás*, 316–317.

50. Margaret Gillooly, Oral History (March 18, 1995), 85, Oral History Collection, Willis Library, University of North Texas, Denton, TX; Peter Wygle essay, in Holland, *Rescue of Santo Tomás*, 123; Hecht, "Santo Tomás Liberation," *Beyond the Wire Bay Area Civilian Ex-Prisoners of War* newsletter, 6, no. 3 (September 2013): 4, Filipinas Heritage Library, Ayala Museum, Makati, Metro Manila, Philippines.

51. Robert Yelton Robb, "Nightmare in Santo Tomás," *Collier's*, February 5, 1949, 64.

52. Wilkinson, *Surviving a Japanese Internment Camp*, 151; Preliminary Interrogation of Enemy Alien: Hirose Toshio, February 7, 1945, Folder 901–2.13 PW Interrogation Reports—Luzon Opn—1st Cav Div, Box 427, Records of the 1st Cavalry Division, World War II Operational Records, Records of the Adjutant General's Staff, Record Group 407, U.S. National Archives, College Park, MD.

53. Van Sickle, *Iron Gates of Santo Tomás*, 314–315; Rick Lawrence, Oral History (no date), 17, Oral History Collection, Record Group 32, MacArthur Memorial, Norfolk, VA; Wilkinson, *Surviving a Japanese Internment Camp*, 151.

54. Chase, *Front Line General*, 89; Frank Hewlett, "61 Armed Japs Quit Santo Tomás Unhurt, Price for 241 Hostages," *The Atlanta Constitution*, February 6, 1945; Carry, *Letters from an Internment Camp*, 123–124; Harrington, *Yankee Samurai*, 263; Wilkinson, *Surviving a Japanese Internment Camp*, 153–155.

55. Holland, *Rescue of Santo Tomás*, 57; Hewlett, "61 Armed Japs Quit Santo Tomás Unhurt"; Carry, *Letters from an Internment Camp*, 123–124; Harrington, *Yankee Samurai*, 263; Wilkinson, *Surviving a Japanese Internment Camp*, 153–155; Wright, *The 1st Cavalry Division in World War II*, 132; George Fischer, Oral History (May 21, 2010), second part, 1, Record Group 32, MacArthur Memorial, Norfolk, VA; Preliminary Interrogation of Enemy Alien: Hirose Toshio, February 7, 1945, Folder 901–2.13 PW Interrogation Reports—Luzon Opn—1st Cav Div, Box 427, Records of the 1st Cavalry Division, World War II Operational Records, Records of the Adjutant General's Staff, Record Group 407, U.S. National Archives, College Park, MD.

56. XIV Corps Advanced Echelon Prisoner of War Joint Interrogation Report Number 64: Murakami Kyozaku, March 19, 1945, document number 26 IR 64, in *Wartime Translations of Seized Japanese Documents*.

57. The photo is in Bailey Pratt, ed., *Only a Matter of Days*, 90.

58. Aluit, *By Sword and Fire*, 175–176; Escoda, *Warsaw of Asia*, 154; Lorenzen, *A Lovely Little War*, 149; Connaughton, Pimlott, and Anderson, *Battle for Manila*, 94–95; Mydans, *More Than Meets the Eye*, 195–196.

59. XIV Corps Operations on Luzon, 131, loose in the box, Box 1A, Papers of Oscar Griswold, Academy Library, U.S. Military Academy, West Point, NY.

60. Wayne Warner, "The 1945 Rescues in Manila: A/G Missionaries Included in Dramatic Military Liberation," *Assemblies of God Heritage* 24, no. 4 (Winter 2004–2005): 10.

61. Hecht, "Santo Tomás Liberation," *Beyond the Wire Bay Area Civilian Ex-Prisoners of War* newsletter, 6, no. 3 (September 2013): 4, Filipinas Heritage Library, Ayala Museum, Makati, Metro Manila, Philippines.

62. Radio Transcript, February 4, 1945, Folder 12, Box 3, Papers of William J. Dunn, Record Group 52, MacArthur Memorial, Norfolk, VA.

63. Lorenzen, *A Lovely Little War*, 145.

64. Cates, *Drainpipe Diary*, 249.

65. William H. Swan, "Recollection of Luzon, 1945 U.S. 1st Cavalry" Folder 3, Box 59, Papers of William H. Swan, Record Group 59, MacArthur Memorial, Norfolk, VA.

66. Van Sickle, *Iron Gates of Santo Tomás*, 326–327; Aluit, *By Sword and Fire*, 226; Carry, *Letters from an Internment Camp*, 126.

67. Carry, *Letters from an Internment Camp*, 127.

68. Amelia Mary Bradley, "Internment in the University of Santo Tomás," 124–125, Papers of Amelia Mary Bradley, Academy Library, U.S. Military Academy, West Point, NY.

69. XIV Corps, "Japanese Defense of Cities as Exemplified by the Battle for Manila" (July 1, 1945), 4, Folder 31, Box 3, Papers of Walter Krueger, Cushing Library, Texas A&M University, College Station, TX; Aluit, *By Sword and Fire*, 170–171; Smith, *Triumph in the Philippines*, 252–254; Emily Van Sickle, "How Far the Dawn" manuscript, 365, Papers of Emily Van Sickle, Academy Library, U.S. Military Academy, West Point, NY.

70. XIV Corps, "Japanese Defense of Cities as Exemplified by the Battle for Manila" (July 1, 1945), 4, Folder 31, Box 3, Papers of Walter Krueger, Cushing Library, Texas A&M University, College Station, TX; Aluit, *By Sword and Fire*, 170–171; Smith, *Triumph in the Philippines*, 252–254; Emily Van Sickle, "How Far the Dawn" manuscript, 365, Papers of Emily Van Sickle, Academy Library, U.S. Military Academy, West Point, NY.

71. Arthur Veysey, "Gen. Beightler Leads Buckeye Boys Into City," *Chicago Daily Tribune*, February 5, 1945; Hanley, "Hike to Manila," 5; Royal Arch Gunnison, "Reporter Enters Manila With Battling Troops," *The Boston Daily Globe*, February 5, 1945; Frankel, *The 37th Infantry Division in World War II*, 253.

72. Hanley, "Hike to Manila," 5.

73. "A History of the 129th Infantry Regiment," Folder 337-INF (129) 0.1, Box 8730, Records of the 37th Infantry Division, World War II Operational Records, Records of the Adjutant General's Staff, Record Group 407, U.S. National Archives, College Park, MD.

74. Hanley, "Hike to Manila," 5.

75. Dunn, *Pacific Microphone*, 306.

76. Dunn, *Pacific Microphone*, 306.

77. Beightler to Mudge, February 26, 1957, Folder 2, Box 1, Papers of Robert S. Beightler, Ohio Historical Society, Columbus, OH.

78. Beightler to the Editor of *Newsweek* magazine, February 26, 1957, Folder 2, Box 1, Papers of Robert S. Beightler, Ohio Historical Society, Columbus, OH.

79. Bigart, "Two Divisions Stage Race."

80. Ohl, *Minuteman*, 172.

81. "Manila Day 1948 Program," Folder 13, Box 2, World War II Collection, 1st Cavalry Division Museum, Ft. Hood, TX; Cartoon, *Saber News*, January–February 1953, 3; "Chapter 1 Meets on Manila Day," *Saber News*, April 1959, 4; "Manila Day Dinner," *Saber*, March–April 1977, 4; Mark Wohlfeld, "B Troop 7th Probes," *Saber*, January–February 1978, 3.

82. Headquarters, XIV Corps, "After Action Report: XIV Corps: M-1 Operation," July 29, 1945, part II, "Administration," 28, Folder 32, Box 3, Papers of Walter Krueger, Cushing Library, Texas A&M University, College Station, TX.

83. Journal entries, February 3–4, 1945, 637th Tank Destroyer Battalion After Action Report: Luzon Campaign 22 November 44 to 30 June 45, Combined Arms Research Library, Fort Leavenworth, KS.

84. Aluit, By *Sword and Fire*, 164.

CHAPTER 8

1. "U.S. Forces Capture Half of Manila, Big Prison Camp in Surprise Thrust," *The Washington Post*, February 5, 1945; "Yanks Drive to Mop Up Manila," *The Evening Star* (Washington, DC), February 5, 1945; "Americans in Manila, Seize Prison Camp," *The New York Times*, February 5, 1945; "Pocket Japs Below Manila Yanks Mop Up Northern Half of Blazing City," *New York World-Telegram*, February 5, 1945; "U.S. Troops Enter Manila," *Los Angeles Times*, February 5, 1945; "U.S. Flag Over Manila: 3000 More Americans Are Liberated," *The Boston Daily Globe*, February 5, 1945; "Eyewitness: How Yanks Slogged Way Into Manila," *The Christian Science Monitor*, February 5, 1945; "U.S. Army in Manila! Free 3,000 Internees After Battle for Prison," *Chicago Daily Tribune*, February 5, 1945; "Manila Captives HAIL YANKS," *Chicago Daily News*, February 5, 1945; "Manila Prison Terror Told," *Chicago Herald American*, February 5, 1945; "MacArthur's Men Capture North Manila, Liberate 3,700 Captives," *The Fresno Bee*, February 5, 1945; "Yanks Mop Up Japs in Manila; Tank Smashes Prison Gates," *Oakland Tribune*, February 5, 1945; "Yanks Reach Mania's Heart; Nippons Destroy City Docks," *The Bend Bulletin* (Bend, OR), February 5, 1945; "U.S. Troops Reach Heart of Manila," *Arizona Republic*, February 5, 1945; "Avenging American Forces Enter Philippine Capital," *The El Paso Times*, February 5, 1945; "U.S. First Cavalry Reaches Heart of Manila," *The Austin American*, February 5, 1945; "U.S. Troops Seize Northern Half of Manila: Release 3,000 Civilians Interned by Enemy," *The Daily Oklahoman* (Oklahoma City, OK), February 5, 1945; "Yanks Hold Half of Manila, Closing In on Rest, 3700 Internees Freed From Jap Prison Camp," *St. Louis Post-Dispatch*, February 5, 1945; "M'Arthur's Men Enter Manila," *The Des Moines Register*,

February 5, 1945; "Americans Seize Half of Manila, Release 3,700 Internees," *Green Bay Press-Gazette*, February 5, 1945; "North Half of Manila in American Hands," *The Milwaukee Journal*, February 5, 1945; "Yanks Drive Into Manila," *The Philadelphia Inquirer*, February 5, 1945; "Americans Press Fight Inside Manila after Liberating Half of Capital," *The Evening Bulletin* (Philadelphia, PA), February 5, 1945; "Yanks Seize Half of Manila," *Akron Beacon Journal*, February 5, 1945; "MacArthur's Troops Drive to Heart of Manila; Release 3,000 Internees 37th Division Presses for Knockout; Bridge Blast Delays General," *Cleveland Plain Dealer*, February 5, 1945; "Yanks in Half of Manila, Push On," *The Cleveland Press*, February 5, 1945; "Yanks Capture Half of Manila Tank Rips Gate to Free Internees 1st and 37th Drive To Heart of City," *Toledo Blade*, February 5, 1945; "U.S. Troops Drive to Center of Manila; Free Thousands At Concentration Camp," *The Courier-Journal* (Louisville, KY), February 5, 1945; "Manila Taken by Yanks; 3,000 Captives Released," *The Nashville Tennessean*, February 5, 1945; "Americans Drive Into Manila, Capture Capitol and Airfield," *The Cincinnati Enquirer*, February 5, 1945; "Yanks Take Manila," *The Detroit Free Press*, February 5, 1945; "U.S. Flag Over Manila; Sky Troops Clinch Fall," *The Detroit News*, February 5, 1945; "Manila Resistance Weak; Yanks Press for Mop-Up," *Miami Daily News*, February 5, 1945; "All Manila Won: M'Arthur," *Chicago Daily Tribune*, February 6, 1945; "Manila Freed! Big Jap Prison Camp Seized; First Story from Inside City," *The Chicago Sun*, February 5, 1945; "'On to Tokyo!'"—Macarthur: All of Manila Falls—1350 More Liberated," *The Boston Daily Globe*, February 6, 1945; "Manila Falls, 1,350 Freed From Second Prison," *The New York Times*, February 6, 1945.

2. "Yank Tanks Mass to Storm Manila," *San Francisco Examiner*, February 5, 1945; "M'Arthur's Men in Heart of Manila," *Daily News* (New York, New York), February 5, 1945; "MacArthur Liberates Internees at Manila," *The Kokomo Tribune*, February 5, 1945.

3. "The Complete Story How Yanks Won Manila, 3,700 Prisoners Describe Rescue," *Daily Times* (Chicago, IL), February 5, 1945.

4. Chase, *Front Line General*, 94; Walter Simmons, "M'Arthur's Censors Help to Speed News of Fall of Manila," *Chicago Daily Tribune*, February 8, 1945.

5. Russell Brines, "Church Bells Hail Arrival of Yanks in Manila Suburbs," *San Francisco Examiner*, February 5, 1945.

6. "Battle of the Pacific: Victory! Mabuhay!" *Time*, February 12, 1945, 19.

7. There was no Manila headline in *The Wall Street Journal*, February 5, 1945 nor in *The Evening Sun* (Baltimore, MD), February 5, 1945.

8. "Asia's Torch of Freedom at Manila," *The Chicago Sun*, February 6, 1945; "Manila," *San Francisco Chronicle*, February 6, 1945; "Teamwork Frees Manila," *Chicago Daily News*, February 5, 1945; "The Liberation of Manila," *Rocky Mountain News* (Denver, CO), February 5, 1945; "A Great Victory," *Medford Mail Tribune* (Medford, OR), February 5, 1945; "A Majestic Saga of Men, of Ships and of Planes," *The Seattle Daily Times*, February 5, 1945; "The Liberation

of Manila," *Seattle Post-Intelligencer*, February 5, 1945; "Back in Manila!" *The St. Louis Times and Star*, February 5, 1945; "Dawn Over Manila," *St. Louis Post-Dispatch*, February 5, 1945; "We Return to Manila," *The Milwaukee Journal*, February 5, 1945; "Manila Retaken," *The Herald-Press* (Saint Joseph, MI), February 5, 1945; "Stars and Stripes Over Manila," *The Muncie Star* (Muncie, IN), February 5, 1945; "Old Glory Over Manila Again," *The Indianapolis Star*, February 5, 1945; "Manila Is Ours!" *The Detroit News*, February 5, 1945; "Stars and Stripes Over Manila," *Cleveland Plain Dealer*, February 5, 1945; "Manila and After," *The Cleveland Press*, February 5, 1945; "Capture of Manila," *Toledo Blade*, February 6, 1945; "Manila and After," *Akron Beacon Journal*, February 5, 1945; "Stars and Stripes Over Manila," *Mansfield News-Journal* (Mansfield, OH), February 5, 1945; "Manila," *Dayton Daily News*, February 5, 1945; "Manila," *Miami Daily News*, February 5, 1945; "Jap Fears of Blockade," *The Greenville News* (Greenville, SC), February 5, 1945; "MacArthur Returns to Manila," *The Sun* (Baltimore, MD), February 5, 1945; "MacArthur in Manila," *Warren Times-Mirror* (Warren, PA), February 5, 1945; "Manila and After," *The Pittsburgh Press*, February 5, 1945; "After Manila and Berlin," *The Wilkes-Barre Record* (Wilkes-Barre, PA), February 5, 1945; "Manila and Honor Restored," *Wilkes-Barre Times Leader Evening News* (Wilkes-Barre, PA), February 5, 1945; "Back in Manila," *The Evening Bulletin* (Philadelphia, PA), February 5, 1945; "Stars and Stripes Over Manila," *Binghamton Press* (Binghamton, NY), February 5, 1945; "And Now Manila!" *The Ithaca Journal* (Ithaca, NY), February 5, 1945; "MacArthur Back in Manila," *Middletown Times Herald* (Middletown, NY), February 5, 1945; "MacArthur in Manila," *The Sun* (New York, NY), February 5, 1945; "Manila," *New York Post*, February 5, 1945; "U.S. Flag Over Manila," *The Boston Daily Globe*, February 5, 1945; "Manila Regained," and "Notes on Manila," *The Evening Sun* (Baltimore, MD), February 5, 1945; "Manila Liberated," *The Providence Journal*, February 5, 1945; "Manila Liberated," *The Evening Bulletin* (Providence, RI), February 5, 1945; "Back to Manila," *The Evening Star* (Washington, DC), February 5, 1945; "Victory at Manila," *Honolulu Star-Bulletin*, February 6, 1945; "'Man the Battle Stations!,'" *San Francisco Examiner*, February 6, 1945; "Capture of Manila," *The San Bernardino County Daily Sun* (San Bernardino, CA), February 6, 1945; "Our Manila Victor Is a Catastrophe to Japanese," *The Fresno Bee*, February 6, 1945; "Keeps Promise," *The Bakersfield Californian*, February 6, 1945; "Philippine Drama Reaches Climax," *Arizona Republic* (Phoenix, AZ), February 6, 1945; "Back in Manila," *Albuquerque Journal*, February 6, 1945; "What is Japanese New Philippine Strategy?," *Minneapolis Morning Tribune*, February 6, 1945; "Old Glory Over Manila," *The State Journal* (Lansing, MI), February 6, 1945; "Manila," *The Detroit Free Press*, February 6, 1945; "Americans Back in Manila," *The Dayton Herald* (Dayton, OH), February 6, 1945; "They Did Return," *The Cincinnati Enquirer*, February 6, 1945; "In Manila," *The Evening News* (Harrisburg, PA), February 6, 1945; "Manila: Epic of Faith and Courage," *The Philadelphia Inquirer*, February

6, 1945; "The Enemy We Face," *The Pittsburgh Press*, February 6, 1945; "The Meaning of Manila," *The New York Times*, February 6, 1945; "Back in Manila," *The Burlington Free Press* (Burlington, VT), February 6, 1945; "Manila Freed Lifts American Hearts," *The Courier-Journal* (Louisville, KY), February 6, 1945; "Mistress of the Seas," *The Nashville Tennessean*, February 6, 1945; "Christmas in Manila," *The Montgomery Advertiser* (Montgomery, AL), February 6, 1945; "They're Laughing Today in Manila," *The Atlanta Constitution*, February 6, 1945; "Manila Ours; Tokyo Next," *Tampa Morning Tribune*, February 6, 1945; "Manila Free," *The Honolulu Advertiser*, February 7, 1945.

9. "Manila Regained," *Alton Evening Telegraph* (Alton, IL), February 5, 1945; "The Capture of Manila," *Pittsburgh Post-Gazette*, February 5, 1945; "One Great Day Points to Another," *The Tampa Daily Times*, February 5, 1945; "He Kept His Promise," *Los Angeles Times*, February 5, 1945; "Brilliant Campaign," *The Washington Post*, February 6, 1945; Lewis B. Sebring, Jr., "Manila Entry Ends Chief Phase of Campaign in the Philippines," *New York Herald Tribune*, February 5, 1945.

10. "Intercepted Letters," *Akron Beacon Journal*, February 5, 1945; "The Manila Victory," *The El Paso Times*, February 6, 1945; "The 1st U.S. Cavalry Division," *The Honolulu Advertiser*, February 7, 1945.

11. "A Humiliating Delay," *The Arizona Daily Star* (Tucson, AZ), February 6, 1945.

12. Beightler to Baxter, February 22, 1945, Folder 2, Box 1, Papers of Robert Beightler, Ohio Historical Society, Columbus, OH.

13. Smith, *Triumph in the Philippines*, 259.

14. Manila Naval Defense Force to Higher Headquarters, February 6, 1945, Masao, *Senshi Sosho*, vol. 54, 507.

15. Fellers to Dorothy, Nancy Jane, and Mother, February 3, 1945, Folder 1, Box 2, Papers of Bonner Fellers, Record Group 44a, MacArthur Memorial, Norfolk, VA; Holland, *Rescue of Santo Tomás*, 52–53; February 4, 1945 entry, Diary of Lieutenant General O. W. Griswold, Box 1, Papers of Oscar W. Griswold, U.S. Army Heritage and Education Center, Carlisle, PA; Rogers, *Bitter Years*, 261.

16. Rogers, *Bitter Years*, 242, 255.

17. Titcomb diary in Holland, *Rescue of Santo Tomás*, 151.

18. Michael E. Bigelow, "Intelligence in the Philippines," *Military Intelligence Professional Bulletin* 21, no. 2 (April–June 1995): 36–40; XIV Corps, "Japanese Defense of Cities as Exemplified by the Battle for Manila" (July 1, 1945), 19, Folder 31, Box 3, Papers of Walter Krueger, Cushing Library, Texas A&M University, College Station, TX.

19. Michael E. Bigelow, "Intelligence in the Philippines," 36–40; XIV Corps, "Japanese Defense of Cities as Exemplified by the Battle for Manila" (July 1, 1945), 19, Folder 31, Box 3, Papers of Walter Krueger, Cushing Library, Texas A&M University, College Station, TX.

20. Bigelow, "Intelligence in the Philippines," 36–40; Rogers, *Bitter Years*, 260.

21. Smith, *Triumph in the Philippines*, 250.

22. Holzimmer, *General Walter Krueger*, 225.

23. Sixth U.S. Army, "Report of the Luzon Campaign 9 January 1945–30 June 1945," vol. I, 37.

24. Patterson essay, in Carol Adele Kelly, ed., *Voices of My Comrades: America's Reserve Officers Remember World War II* (New York: Fordham University Pres, 2007), 411. This book is a compilation of essays that veterans wrote in the early 1990s for *The Officer*, the magazine of the Reserve Officer Association.

25. Hanley, "Hike to Manila," 5; "Cheers Greet Americans on Manila Entry," *New York Herald Tribune*, February 5, 1945.

26. Patterson essay, in Kelly, ed., *Voices of My Comrades*, 411.

27. XIV Corps Advanced Echelon Prisoner of War Preliminary Interrogation Report Number 20: Kuwahata Yoshikazu, February 11, 1945, document number 26 IR 20 and XIV Corps Advanced Echelon Prisoner of War Preliminary Interrogation Report Number 34: Miyakawa Takeo, February 19, 1945, document 26 IR 34, in *Wartime Translations of Seized Japanese Documents*. Other prisoners from a number of different formations reported on the high morale of their units: Sixth Army Advanced Echelon Prisoner of War Preliminary Interrogation Report Number 420: Izumida Zenzo, April 7, document number 21 IR 420; Sixth Army Advanced Echelon Prisoner of War Preliminary Interrogation Report Number 377: Tatsumi Kenji, February 23, 1945, document number 21 IR 377; XIV Corps Advanced Echelon Prisoner of War Preliminary Interrogation Report Number 54: Kikuike Shuzo, March 6, 1945, document number 26 IR 54, in *Wartime Translations of Seized Japanese Documents*.

28. 1st Lieutenant John E. Winn, "Troop History for Period 8 January to 3 February 1945," September 1, 1945, Folder 337-Cav-0.1, Box 8710, Records of the 37th Infantry Divisions, World War II Operational Records, Records of the Adjutant General's Staff, Record Group 407, U.S. National Archives, College Park, MD. Despite its title, this report includes information for events after February 3, 1945.

29. 129th Infantry Regiment, Lessons Learned in the Luzon Campaign, Section VII, Folder 337-INF (129) 0.3, Box 8733, Records of the 37th Infantry Division, World War II Operational Records, Records of the Adjutant General's Staff, Record Group 407, U.S. National Archives, College Park, MD.

30. Aluit, *By Sword and Fire*, 170–171; Joseph E. DuPont, Jr. Oral History (May 11, 2001), 43–44, Williams Center for Oral History, Louisiana State University, Baton Rouge, LA; Charles Brown, *Bars from Bilibid Prison* (San Antonio, TX: The Naylor Company, 1947), 120; R. Renton Hind, *Spirits Unbroken: The Story of Three Years in a Civilian Internment Camp, under the Japanese at Baguio and at Old Bilibid Prison in the Philippines from December, 1941, to February, 1945* (San Francisco: John Howell, 1946), 264–265; James V. Thompson, Oral History (December 10 and 17, 1990, and April 24, 1991), 92–93, Oral History Center, Bancroft Library, University of California, Berkeley, Berkeley, CA.

31. Warner, "The 1945 Rescues in Manila: A/G Missionaires Included in Dramatic Military Liberation," 13; Smith, *Triumph in the Philippines*, 253–254; James V. Thompson, Oral History (December 10 and 17, 1990, and April 24, 1991), 90, Oral History Center, Bancroft Library, University of California, Berkeley, Berkeley, CA; Cogan, *Captured*, 280–283; Foret to Downer, September 25, 1997, attached to Murphy Foret, 37th Infantry Division, World War II Army Service Experiences Questionnaire, U.S. Army Heritage and Education Center, Carlisle, PA.

32. Charles A. Henne, Frank F. Mathias, and Robert G. Knauss, 37th Infantry Division, World War II Army Service Experiences Questionnaire, U.S. Army Heritage and Education Center, Carlisle, PA.

33. Homer Bigart, "The Road Back: 800 Americans Leave Bilibid," *New York Herald Tribune*, February 15, 1945; Frank F. Mathias, 37th Infantry Division, World War II Army Service Experiences Questionnaire, U.S. Army Heritage and Education Center, Carlisle, PA; James V. Thompson, Oral History (December 10 and 17, 1990, and April 24, 1991), 93, Oral History Center, Bancroft Library, University of California, Berkeley, Berkeley, CA.

34. Cogan, *Captured*, 280–283.

35. Hines, *Aggies of the Pacific War*, 118; Walter G. Hines and Martha Shipman Andrews, *Hugh Meglone Milton: A Life Beyond Duty* (Los Ranchos, NM: Rio Grande Books, 2015), 41.

36. Smith, *Triumph in the Philippines*, 255; Juergen Goldhagen, ed., *Manila Memories: Four Boys Remember Their Lives Before, During and After the Japanese Occupation* (Exeter, England: Searsman Books, 2008), 92.

37. Ohl, *Minuteman*, 178; Mathias, *G.I. Jive*, 136; Robert S. Beightler, Major General Robert S. Beightler's Report of the Activities of the 37th Infantry Division, 1940–1945, Folder 7, Box 1, Ohio Historical Society, Columbus, OH.

38. Dos Passos, *Tour of Duty*, 149; Owen, *Eye Deep in Hell*, 89–91. The physical description of the building is based on photographs the author found on the internet of the brewery as it was in 1945.

39. Juergen Goldhagen essay, in Goldhagen, ed., *Manila Memories*, 96.

40. Witthoff and Chappell, Three Years Internment, 56-57; Nixon, "Delayed, Manila," 86; William H. Swann, "Recollections of Luzon, 1945 U.S. 1st Cavalry," Folder 3, Box 59, Papers of William Swann, Record Group 59, MacArthur Memorial, Norfolk, VA; Jose Espino, "A Suburban View of the Liberation of Manila," Personal Narrative File: Jose Espino, Manila Memorare 1945 Collection, Filipinas Heritage Library, Ayala Museum, Makati, Metro Manila, Philippines.

41. Chase, *Front Line General*, 94; "Describes Burning City," *Chicago Daily Tribune*, February 7, 1945.

42. Estanislado Reyna, Oral History (February 2, 2002) transcription by the author, VOCES: The U.S. Latino and Latina Oral History Project, Benson Latin American Collection, University of Texas, Austin, TX.

43. Item 12, Unnamed Japanese soldier's diary, February 5, 1945, XIV Corps Advanced Echelon Translation Number 26, document number 26 T 74, in *Wartime Translations of Seized Japanese Documents*.

44. Manila Naval Defense Force to Higher Headquarters, Feburary 6, 1945, Masao, *Senshi Sosho*, vol. 54, 507.

45. Ohl, *Minuteman*, 178; Robert S. Beightler, "Major General Robert S. Beightler's Repont of the Activities of the 37th Infantry Division," 1940–1945, Folder 7, Box 1, Ohio Historical Society, Columbus, OH.

46. Frankel, *The 37th Infantry Division*, 254.

47. Russell Brines, Oral History by D. Clayton James (June 18, 1977), 29–30, Box 5, Record Group 49, MacArthur Memorial, Norfolk, VA.

48. Dunn, *Pacific Microphone*, 309.

49. "How MacArthur Won in Pacific Told by Veysey," *Chicago Daily Tribune*, February 21, 1945.

50. Cogan, *Captured*, 283; Hind, *Spirits Unbroken*, 269–270; Frankel, *The 37th Infantry Division*, 254–255; James V. Thompson, Oral History (December 10 and 17, 1990, and April 24, 1991), 94, Oral History Center, Bancroft Library, University of California, Berkeley, Berkeley, CA.

51. James V. Thompson, Oral History (December 10 and 17, 1990, and April 24, 1991), 94, Oral History Center, Bancroft Library, University of California, Berkeley, Berkeley, CA.

52. Dos Passos, *Tour of Duty*, 148–149.

53. February 6, 1945 entry, Diary of Lieutenant General O. W. Griswold, Box 1, Papers of Oscar W. Griswold, U.S. Army History and Heritage Command, Carlisle, PA; XIV Corps, "After Action Report: XIV Corps: M-1 Operation," July 29, 1945, vol. II, "Administration," 49, Folder 32, Box 3, Papers of Walter Krueger, Cushing Library, Texas A&M University, College Station, TX.

54. Tessie Dumana, ed., *The German Club—Manila, 1906–1986* (Manila: German Club, 1986), 61–62.

55. Dumana, ed., *The German Club—Manila*, 61–62.

56. Frankel, *The 37th Infantry Division*, 256–257.

57. Frankel, *The 37th Infantry Division*, 256; author transcription of Vogel and Henne, in "In Their Own Words: MOH Recipient 2nd Lt. Robert M. Viale," http://www.youtube.com/watch?v=S2xN8SW8Cal. This video was made and posted online by Sergeant First Class Josh Mann, Ohio Army National Guard historian. Astor, *Crisis in the Pacific*, 535; "Hero's Widow Gets Medal of Honor," *Capital Journal* (Salem, OR), November 13, 1945.

58. Dos Passos, *Tour of Duty*, 161–166; Joseph P. McCallus, *The MacArthur Highway and Other Relics of American Empire in the Philippines* (Washington, DC: Potomac Books, 2010), 166–167.

59. Dos Passos, *Tour of Duty*, 170–171.

60. Dunn, *Pacific Microphone*, 307–308.

61. Eichelberger to Echelberger, February 14 and 18, 1945, in Luvaas, ed., *Dear Miss Em*, 216, 218.

62. Chase, *Front Line General*, 95.
63. McEnery, *The XIV Corps Battle for Manila, February 1945*, 50, 60–61.

CHAPTER 9

1. Toyoda to Manila Naval Defense Force, Feburary 5, 1945, Masao, *Senshi Sosho*, vol. 54, 504.
2. Prisoner of War Preliminary Interrogation Report: Goto Tadao, February 23, 1945, Folder 901-2.13 PW Interrogation Rpts., Box 427, Records of the 1st Cavalry Division, World War II Operational Records, Records of the Adjutant General's Staff, Record Group 407, U.S. National Archives, College Park, MD.
3. Prisoner of War Preliminary Interrogation Report: Oshiro Koichi, February 16, 1945, Folder 901-2.13 PW Interrogation Rpts., Box 427, Records of the 1st Cavalry Division, World War II Operational Records, Records of the Adjutant General's Staff, Record Group 407, U.S. National Archives, College Park, MD; Prisoner of War Preliminary Interrogation Report 37-60: Hayashi Toshime, February 27, 1945, Folder 337-2 A/A Rpt—Annex 2 Int—Annex A(3), Box 8617; Prisoner of War Preliminary Interrogation Report 37-39: Tanaka Toshio, February 16, 1945, Folder 337-2 A/A Rpt—Annex 2 Int—Appendix A(3), Box 8616, Records of the 37th Infantry Division, World War II Operational Records, Records of the Adjutant General's Staff, Record Group 407, U.S. National Archives, College Park, MD; XIV Corps, "Japanese Defense of Cities as Exemplified by the Battle for Manila" (July 1, 1945), 3, 10, Folder 31, Box 3, Papers of Walter Krueger, Cushing Library, Texas A&M University, College Station, TX.
4. XIV Corps, "Japanese Defense of Cities as Exemplified by the Battle for Manila" (July 1, 1945), 4–5, Folder 31, Box 3, Papers of Walter Krueger, Cushing Library, Texas A&M University, College Station, TX.
5. He was a captain during the battle; a major when he wrote the report. Stephen L. Garay, "The Breach of Intramuros" (May 1, 1948), Advanced Officers Class 1, The Armored School, Fort Knox, KY.
6. XIV Corps, "Japanese Defense of Cities as Exemplified by the Battle for Manila" (July 1, 1945), 4–5, Folder 31, Box 3, Papers of Walter Krueger, Cushing Library, Texas A&M University, College Station, TX.
7. XIV Corps, "Japanese Defense of Cities as Exemplified by the Battle for Manila" (July 1, 1945), 3, Folder 31, Box 3, Papers of Walter Krueger, Cushing Library, Texas A&M University, College Station, TX.
8. Stephen L. Garay, "The Breach of Intramuros" (May 1, 1948), Advanced Officers Class 1, The Armored School, Fort Knox, KY.
9. XIV Corps, "Japanese Defense of Cities as Exemplified by the Battle for Manila" (July 1, 1945), 9, Folder 31, Box 3, Papers of Walter Krueger, Cushing Library, Texas A&M University, College Station, TX.
10. XIV Corps, "After Action Report: XIV Corps: M-1 Operation," July 29, 1945, Folder 32, Box 3, Papers of Walter Krueger, Cushing Library, Texas A&M University, College Station, TX .

11. Prisoner of War Preliminary Interrogation Report: Oshiro Koichi, February 16, 1945 and Muraoka Toshisue, February 16, 1945, Folder 901-2.13 PW Interrogation Rpts., Box 427, Records of the 1st Cavalry Division, World War II Operational Records, Records of the Adjutant General's Staff, Record Group 407, U.S. National Archives, College Park, MD; Prisoner of War Preliminary Interrogation Report 37-60: Hayashi Toshime, February 27, 1945, Folder 337-2 A/A Rpt—Annex 2 Int—Annex A(3), Box 8617; Prisoner of War Preliminary Interrogation Report 37-39: Tanaka Toshio, February 16, 1945, Folder 337-2 A/A Rpt—Annex 2 Int—Appendix A(3), Box 8616, Records of the 37th Infantry Division, World War II Operational Records, Records of the Adjutant General's Staff, Record Group 407, U.S. National Archives, College Park, MD; Prisoner of War Joint Interrogation Report: Murakami Kyozaku, March 19, 1945, document number 26 IR 64, in *Wartime Translations of Seized Japanese Documents*; XIV Corps, "Japanese Defense of Cities as Exemplified by the Battle for Manila" (July 1, 1945), 3, 10, Folder 31, Box 3, Papers of Walter Krueger, Cushing Library, Texas A&M University, College Station, TX.

12. Hashimoto Hiroshi statement, March 18, 1949, document number 52362, in "Statements of Japanese Officials on World War II"; "Japanese Monograph No. 8: Philippines Operations Records, Phase III, Dec. 1944–Aug. 1945" (October 1946), 7–11, U.S. Army History and Heritage Command, Carlisle, PA.

13. Edwin E. Hanson, 37th Infantry Division; and Salvatore V. DeGaetano, 1st Cavalry Division, World War II Army Service Experiences Questionnaires, U.S. Army Heritage and Education Center, Carlisle, PA; Prisoner of War Preliminary Interrogation Report 37-15: Okubo Yasuhiko, February 6, 1945, Folder 337-2 A/A Rpt—Annex 2 Int—Appendix A(3), Box 8616, Records of the 37th Infantry Division, World War II Operational Records, Records of the Adjutant General's Staff, Record Group 407, U.S. National Archives, College Park, MD.

14. XIV Corps, "Japanese Defense of Cities as Exemplified by the Battle for Manila" (July 1, 1945), 14, Folder 31, Box 3, Papers of Walter Krueger, Cushing Library, Texas A&M University, College Station, TX; 129th Infantry Regiment, Lessons Learned in the Luzon Campaign, Section VII, Folder 337-INF (129) 0.3, Box 8733, Records of the 37th Infantry Division, World War II Operational Records, Records of the Adjutant General's Staff, Record Group 407, U.S. National Archives, College Park, MD.

15. "New Weapons for Jap Tank Hunters," *Intelligence Bulletin*, III, no. 7 (March 1945): 64–66; 129th Infantry Regiment, Lessons Learned in the Luzon Campaign, Section VII, Folder 337-INF (129) 0.3, Box 8733, Records of the 37th Infantry Division, World War II Operational Records, Records of the Adjutant General's Staff, Record Group 407, U.S. National Archives, College Park, MD.

16. Masao, *Senshi Sosho*, vol. 54, 506.

17. XIV Corps, "Japanese Defense of Cities as Exemplified by the Battle for Manila" (July 1, 1945), 15, Folder 31, Box 3, Papers of Walter Krueger, Cushing Library, Texas A&M University, College Station, TX.

18. 129th Infantry Regiment, Lessons Learned in the Luzon Campaign, Section VII, Folder 337-INF (129) o.3, Box 8733, Records of the 37th Infantry Division, World War II Operational Records, Records of the Adjutant General's Staff, Record Group 407, U.S. National Archives, College Park, MD.

19. Prisoner of War Preliminary Interrogation Report: Koshoe Bok, February 13, 1945, Folder 901-2.13 PW Interrogation Rpts., Box 427, Records of the 1st Cavalry Division Files; and Prisoner of War Preliminary Interrogation Report 37-14: Tatsumi Kenji, February 6, 1945; Prisoner of War Preliminary Interrogation Report 37-16: Okubo Yasuhiko, February 6, 1945; Prisoner of War Preliminary Interrogation Report 37-15: Okubo Yasuhiko, February 6, 1945; Prisoner of War Preliminary Interrogation Report 37-17: Arai Seiji, February 7, 1945; Prisoner of War Preliminary Interrogation Report 37-20: Domoto Hideaki, February 8, 1945; Prisoner of War Preliminary Interrogation Report 37-21: Sho Meitatsu, February 9, 1945; Prisoner of War Preliminary Interrogation Report 37-23: Hanatani Yu, February 10, 1945; Prisoner of War Preliminary Interrogation Report 37-30: Saito Kichiya, February 13, 1945; and Prisoner of War Preliminary Interrogation Report 37-31: Takami Morihiko, February 14, 1945, Folder 337-2 A/A Rpt—Annex 2 Int-Appendix A(3), Box 8616, Records of the 37th Infantry Division, World War II Operational Records, Records of the Adjutant General's Staff, Record Group 407, U.S. National Archives, College Park, MD.

20. Prisoner of War Preliminary Interrogation Report: Goto Tadao, February 23, 1945, Yano Tadashi, February 16, 1945 and Suganoma Kunihiko, February 12, 1945, Folder 901-2.13 PW Interrogation Rpts., Box 427, Records of the 1st Cavalry Division; Prisoner of War Preliminary Interrogation Report 37-40: Tanji Genzo, February 17, 1945, Report: 37-64, February 28, 1945 and Prisoner of War Interrogation Report: 37-74, March 7, 1945, Folder 337-2 A/A—Annex 2 Int—Appendix A (3), Box 8617, Records of the 37th Infantry Division, World War II Operational Records, Records of the Adjutant General's Staff, Record Group 407, U.S. National Archives College Park, MD.

21. Iwabuchi to Southwest Fleet, Feburary 10, 1945, Masao, *Senshi Sosho*, vol. 54, 511.

22. Houston Jolley, "Recollections," *Voice of the Angels*, April 15, 1991, 6.

23. O'Donnell, *Into the Rising Sun*, 186; Holzem, "Jim Holzem's Story," 12.

24. O'Donnell, *Into the Rising Sun*, 186.

25. The near misses of a number of officers is a major theme in Walter Simmons, "New Invaders of Luzon Start Manila March," *Chicago Tribune*, February 3, 1945; "11th ABN DVN Boxing Team, Sept. 1948 Camp Schimmelfenning, Sedai," *Voice of the Angels*, December 1, 1975, 1.

26. Deane Marks, "The Day the Tank Blew Up," Folder Correspondence with ex-members of the 11th Airborne Division Mar-McC, Box3. Papers of Edward M. Flanagan, Jr., U.S. Army History and Heritage Command, Carlisle, PA.

27. Even then the Eighth Army was not actually in the City of Manila. It was in the City of Parañaque, a suburb of Manila. Today Parañaque is part of Metro Manila. One soldier had crossed the bridge at midnight, but heavy Japanese gunfire drove

him back. Flanagan, *The Angels*, 83; Jeffress, "Operations of the 2nd Battalion, 511th Parachute Infantry," 6–7.

28. Even then the Eighth Army was not actually in the City of Manila. It was in the City of Parañaque, a suburb of Manila. Today Parañaque is part of Metro Manila. Jeffress, "Operations of the 2nd Battalion, 511th Parachute Infantry," 6–7.

29. "History of the 11th Airborne Division," 20, Folder 311-0.1 History, Box 6545, Records of the 11th Airborne Division, World War II Operational Records, Records of the Adjutant General's Staff, Record Group 407, U.S. National Archives, College Park, MD.

30. Flanagan, *The Angels*, 83, 85.

31. Smith, *Triumph in the Philippines*, 267; Flanagan, *The Angels*, 83–85.

32. William C. Schnoor, Oral History (August 28, 2003), Rutgers Oral History Archive, Rutgers University, New Brunswick, NJ.

33. Burgess to Burgess and Burgess, February 19, 1945, in Burgess, *Looking Back*, 101.

34. Lahti, *Memoirs of an Angel*, 72.

35. Victor M. Liptrap, Oral history (February 25, 2005), 29, Nimitz Education and Research Center, National Museum of the Pacific War, The National Museum of the Pacific War, Fredericksburg, TX; Burgess to Burgess and Burgess, February 19, 1945, in Burgess, *Looking Back*, 101; Banning Replier, "This Barringer Grad Is 'Making Good,'" undated, unidentified news article included in Yee, ed., *Dear General*, 47.

36. William C. Schnoor, Oral History (August 28, 2003), Rutgers Oral History Archive, Rutgers University, New Brunswick, NJ.

37. Prisoner of War Preliminary Interrogation Report: Goto Tadao, February 23, 1945, Folder 901-2.13 PW Interrogation Rpts., Box 427, Records of the 1st Cavalry Division Files, World War II Operational Records, Records of the Adjutant General's Staff, Record Group 407, U.S. National Archives, College Park, MD.

38. Fellers to Commander in Chief, February 9, 1945, Folder 26, Box 5, Papers of Bonner Fellers, Record Group 44a, MacArthur Memorial, Norfolk, Virginia; "A Preliminary Report on Jap Demolitions in Manila," *Intelligence Bulletin* III, no. 9 (May 1945): 26–29; "City and Town Defense," *Intelligence Bulletin* III, no. 12 (August 1945): 39–41.

39. Richardson, *Under Age Angel*, 97.

40. Victor M. Liptrap, Oral History (February 25, 2005), 28, Nimitz Education and Research Center, National Museum of the Pacific War, The National Museum of the Pacific War, Fredericksburg, TX.

41. Richardson, *Under Age Angel*, 97; Victor M. Liptrap, Oral History (February 25, 2005), 28, Nimitz Education and Research Center, National Museum of the Pacific War, The National Museum of the Pacific War, Fredericksburg, TX; Deane Marks, "The Day the Tank Blew Up," Folder Correspondence with

ex-members of the 11th Airborne Division Mar-McC, Box 3. Papers of Edward M. Flanagan, Jr., U.S. Army History and Heritage Command, Carlisle, PA.

42. Prisoner of War Preliminary Interrogation Report 37-23: Hanatani Yu, February 9, 1945; Prisoner of War Interrogation Report 37-65: Ota Akira, February 27, 1945, Folder 337-2 A/A Rpt Annex 2 Int—Appendix A(3) 173rd Language Detachment, Box 8617, Records of the 37th Infantry Division, World War II Operational Records, Records of the Adjutant General's Staff, Record Group 407, U.S. National Archives College Park, MD; XIV Corps Advanced Echelon Prisoner of War Joint Interrogation Report Number 64: Murakami Kyozaku, March 19, 1945, document number 26 IR 64, in *Wartime Translations of Seized Japanese Documents*; XIV Corps Advanced Echelon Prisoner of War Joint Interrogation Report Number 27: Hanatani Ieamu, February 13, 1945, document number 26 IR 27, in *Wartime Translations of Seized Japanese Documents*.

43. XIV Corps Advanced Echelon Prisoner of War Preliminary Interrogation Report Number 51: Uchida Kensaburo, March 4, 1945, document number 26 IR 51, in *Wartime Translations of Seized Japanese Documents*.

44. XIV Corps Advanced Echelon Prisoner of War Preliminary Interrogation Report Number 38: Sugiura Heignen, February 22, 1945, document number 26 IR 38, in *Wartime Translations of Seized Japanese Documents*. This incident was hardly an isolated one. Seaman First Class Ito Shunji reported that his platoon was armed only with hand grenades and spears: Prisoner of War Preliminary Interrogation Report: Ito Shunji, February 16, 1945, Folder 901-2.13 PW Interrogation Rpts., Box 427, Records of the 1st Cavalry Division, World War II Operational Records, Records of the Adjutant General's Staff, Record Group 407, U.S. National Archives, College Park, MD.

45. February 8, 1945 entry in Bound Field Diary, Item 1, XIV Corps Advanced Echelon Translation Number 74, document number 26 T 74, in *Wartime Translations of Seized Japanese Documents*.

46. Herbert E. Merritt, Oral History (June 17, 2005), 20, Nimitz Education and Research Center, National Museum of the Pacific War, The National Museum of the Pacific War, Fredericksburg, TX.

47. Willis R. Phillips, Folder 8, Box 30, World War II Veteran Surveys, Record Group 237, Tennessee State Archives, Nashville, TN.

48. Herbert E. Weiner, Oral History (June 8, 1993), 3, The Association for Diplomatic Studies and Training Foreign Affairs Oral History Project, Lauinger Library, Georgetown University, Washington, DC.

49. Burgess to Burgess and Burgess, February 19, 1945, in Burgess, *Looking Back*, 101.

50. Rod Serling, "A Quality of Mercy," script number seventy-two, May 23, 1961, Folder 10, Box 66, Papers of Rod Serling, Wisconsin Historical Society, Madison, WI. The other episode of The Twilight Zone set in the Philippines was "The Purple Testament."

51. McGrath and Coon statements in O'Donnell, *Into the Rising Sun*, 185–187.

52. McGrath and Coon statements in O'Donnell, *Into the Rising Sun*, 187–188.
53. Norman Kikuta, Oral History, no date, Center for Oral History, University of Hawaii at Manoa, Honolulu, Hawaii.
54. Eichelberger to Echelberger, February 5 and 6, 1945, in Luvaas, ed., *Dear Miss Em*, 211–212.
55. Smith, *Triumph in the Philippines*, 256–257; XIV Corps Operations on Luzon, 152, loose in box, Box 1A, Papers of Oscar W. Griswold, Academy Library, U.S. Military Academy, West Point, NY; Headquarters, 1st Cavalry Division, G-3 Operations Report, February 4–5 and 5–6, 1945, Folder 901-3.1 G-3 Opns Repts, Box 13301, Records of the 1st Cavalry Division, World War II Operational Records, Records of the Adjutant General's Staff, Record Group 407, U.S. National Archives, College Park, MD; Luther Adams (December 12, 2008), Veterans History Project, American Folklife Center, Library of Congress, Washington, DC.
56. Fellers, Memorandum for the Commander-in-Chief (MacArthur), February 13, Folder 26, Box 5, Papers of Bonner Fellers, Record Group 44A, MacArthur Memorial, Norfolk, VA.
57. Dos Passos, *Tour of Duty*, 147; Headquarters, 1st Cavalry Division, G-3 Operations Report, February 6–7, 1945, Folder 901-3.1 G-3 Opns Repts, Box 13301, Records of the 1st Cavalry Division, World War II Operational Records, Records of the Adjutant General's Staff, Record Group 407, U.S. National Archives, College Park, MD.
58. Wright, *The 1st Cavalry Division in World War II*, 133; Headquarters, 1st Cavalry Division, G-3 Operations Report, February 4–5, 1945, Folder 901-3.1 G-3 Opns Repts, Box 13301, Records of the 1st Cavalry Division, World War II Operational Records, Records of the Adjutant General's Staff, Record Group 407, U.S. National Archives, College Park, MD.
59. Prisoner of War Preliminary Interrogation Report Number 22: Eudo Takeo, February 11, 1945, 26 IR 22, in *Wartime Translations of Seized Japanese Documents*; Batch 1CD245, Item 1, February 13, 1945, unnamed Japanese soldier's diary, Folder 901-2.9 Translation of Captured Enemy Documents, Box 13301, Records of the 1st Cavalry Division, World War II Operational Records, Records of the Adjutant General's Staff, Record Group 407, U.S. National Archives, College Park, MD.
60. Holland, *Rescue of Santo Tomás*, 64–66.
61. Holland, *Rescue of Santo Tomás*, 64–66.
62. McEnery, *The XIV Corps Battle for Manila, February 1945*, 109; Connaughton, Pimlott, and Anderson dismiss the importance of the dam (*The Battle of Manila*, 193). They are wrong. They fail to take into account that the Luzon campaign was producing massive amounts of non-battle casualties. Without proper sanitary resources, Manila would have been a public health disease cluster that would have spread several diseases to Americans regardless of how rigorous the soldiers were in their sanitation habits. Smith, *Triumph in the Philippines*, 652.

63. William H. Swan, "Recollection of Luzon, 1945 U.S. 1st Cavalry," Folder 3, Box 59, Papers of William H. Swan, Record Group 59, MacArthur Memorial, Norfolk, VA; William F. Allen statement in Clyma, ed., *Connecticut Men of the United States Army: Connecticut Veterans Commemorative Booklet* 9, no. 1 (December 9, 1945): 3.
64. Escoda, *Warsaw of Asia*, 160.
65. Elena A. Rodriquez, "My 16-Day Tragic Diary," Folder 7, Box 78, Material Donated by the General Public, Record Group 15, MacArthur Memorial, Norfolk, VA.
66. William H. Swan, "Recollections of Luzon," 6–7, Folder 3, Box 59, Papers of William H. Swan, Record Group 59, MacArthur Memorial, Norfolk, VA.
67. Escoda, *Warsaw of Asia*, 153; Fernando J. Mañalac, *Manila: Memories of World War II* (Quezon City, The Philippines: Girafee Books, 1995), 133–139.
68. Elena A. Rodriquez, "My 16-Day Tragic Diary," Folder 7, Box 78, Material Donated by the General Public, Record Group 15, MacArthur Memorial, Norfolk, VA; Astor, *Crisis in the Pacific*, 532–533.
69. Mañalac, *Manila*, 133–139.
70. Elena A. Rodriquez, "My 16-Day Tragic Diary," Folder 7, Box 78, Material Donated by the General Public, Record Group 15, MacArthur Memorial, Norfolk, VA; Astor, *Crisis in the Pacific*, 532–533.
71. Aluit, *By Sword and Fire*, 151.
72. Arthur Veysey, "Civilians Flee Manila as Fire Sweeps Homes," *Chicago Daily Tribune*, February 8, 1945.
73. Ana Mari S. Calero, *Three Continents* (Manila: De La Salle University Press, 2001), 38; Purita Echevarria de Gonzalez, *Manila: A Memoir of Love & Loss* (Maryborough, Australia: Hale & Iremonger, 2000), 177–178.

CHAPTER 10

1. Chase, *Front Line General*, 95–96.
2. February 7, 1945 entry, Diary of Lieutenant General O. W. Griswold, Box 1, Papers of Oscar W. Griswold, U.S. Army Heritage and Education Center, Carlisle, PA; Sarantakes, ed., *Seven Stars*, 87.
3. Hines, *Aggies of the Pacific War*, 119.
4. Fellers to Fellers, February 10, 1945, Folder 1, Box 2, Papers of Bonner Fellers, Record Group 44A, MacArthur Memorial, Norfolk, VA.
5. Aluit, *By Fire and Sword*, 194.
6. Nixon, *Delayed, Manila*, 87.
7. Aluit, *By Fire and Sword*, 195.
8. Cecily Mattocks Marshall, *Happy Life Blues: A Memoir of Survival* (Clinton, MA: Angus MacGregor Books, 2007), 174; Warne, *Terry*, 233.
9. Press Release, February 25, 1945, Folder; 4, Box 49, Records of U.S. Army Pacific Area, Record Group 4, MacArthur Memorial, Norfolk, VA.

10. Rogers, *Bitter Years*, 262; Roger O. Egeberg, *The General: MacArthur and the Man He Called "Doc"* (New York: Hippocrene Books, 1983), 139.

11. Hanrahan, "Soldier, Manager, Leader," 29–41.

12. Rogers, *Bitter Years*, 262.

13. Rogers, *Bitter Years*, 262.

14. Frankel, *The 37th Infantry Division*, 269–271; Smith, *Triumph in the Philippines*, 258–260; Connaughton, Pimlott, and Anderson, *The Battle of Manila*, 109.

15. Charles A. Henne, 37th Infantry Division, World War II Army Service Questionnaire, U.S. Army Heritage and Education Center, Carlisle Barracks, PA.

16. "Spotlight on Stanley Frankel," *37th Division Veterans News* 56, no. 4 (August 1986): 10; White to Beightler, Subject: Award of Legion of Merit, April 4, 1945, Folder 6, Box 1, Papers of Stanley Frankel, McCormick Library, Northwestern University, Evanston, IL.

17. Lorenzen, *A Lovely Little War*, 156.

18. Marshall, *Happy Life Blues*, 175.

19. Annex #2 to G-2 Daily Report #46, "Memorandum; Japanese 10th Year Type, 12 cm High Angle Gun," [no date], Folder 337-0.5, Box 8606, Records of the 37th Infantry Division, World War II Operational Records, Records of the Adjutant General's Staff, Record Group 407, U.S. National Archives, College Park, MD.

20. Warne, *Terry*, 234–236.

21. Abe Zelikovsky, Oral History (December 3, 1979), transcription by the author, Special Collections Library, University of Washington, Seattle, WA.

22. Diary of Probationary Officer Baba Masanori, February 10, 1945, in XIV Corps, "Japanese Defense of Cities as Exemplified by the Battle for Manila" (July 1, 1945), 12, Folder 31, Box 3, Papers of Walter Krueger, Cushing Library, Texas A&M University, College Station, TX.

23. Wright, *The 1st Cavalry Division in World War II*, 133; Lorenzen, *A Lovely Little War*, 154.

24. Rick Lawrence, Oral History, no date, 18, Oral History Collection, Record Group 32, MacArthur Memorial, Norfolk, VA.

25. Marshall, *Happy Life Blues*, 176.

26. Lorenzen, *A Lovely Little War*, 162.

27. Van Sickle, *Iron Gates of Santo Tomás*, 321–322.

28. Caroline Bailey Pratt, Oral History (no date), 58, Oral History Collection, Record Group 32, MacArthur Memorial, Norfolk, VA.

29. Witthoff and Chappell, *Three Years' Internment*, 59.

30. Amelia Mary Bradley, "Internment in the University of Santo Tomas, 1942–1945," 128, Papers of Amelia Mary Bradley, Academy Library, U.S. Military Academy, West Point, NY.

31. Royal Arch Gunnison, "Jap Shelling of Civilians at Santo Tomás Described," *Baltimore Sun*, March 7, 1945.

32. Cates, *Drainpipe Diary*, 250; Nixon, *Delayed, Manila*, 87–89; Chase, *Front Line General*, 97.

33. Van Sickle, *Iron Gates of Santo Tomás*, 324–325.

34. Whitney to C-in-C (MacArthur), "Report on Conditions at Santo Tomás Internment Camp," February 11, 1945, Folder 2, Box 4, Record Group 16, MacArthur Memorial, Norfolk, VA.

35. Smith, *Triumph in the Philippines*, 118–134, 187–208.

36. Mathias, *G.I. Jive*, 141–143; McEnery, *The XIV Corps Battle for Manila*, 83.

37. James S. Dunn, Folder 5, Box 2; Norman K. Bentley, Folder 1, Box 4, World War II Veteran Surveys, Record Group 237, Tennessee State Library and Archives, Nashville, TN.

38. In his diary, Griswold states he was inspecting units on February 7. He might have easily been doing that on February 8 as well. February 7 and 8, 1945 entry, Diary of Lieutenant General O. W. Griswold, Box 1, Papers of Oscar W. Griswold, U.S. Army Heritage and Education Center, Carlisle, PA; Griswold to Davidson, June 17, 1958, Unmarked Folder, Box 2, Papers of Oscar W. Griswold, Academy Library, U.S. Military Academy, West Point, NY.

39. Griswold to Davidson, June 17, 1958, Unmarked Folder, Box 2, Papers of Oscar W. Griswold, Academy Library, U.S. Military Academy, West Point, NY.

40. 117th Engineer Battalion unit report, February 9, 1945, Folder 337-3.3 G-3 JNL Reports vol. 10, Box 8674, Records of the 37th Infantry Division, World War II Operational Records, Records of the Adjutant General's Staff, Record Group 407, U.S. National Archives, College Park, MD; Sixth U.S. Army, "Report of the Luzon Campaign," vol. IV, "The Engineer," 118, Skelton Combined Arms Research Library, Fort Leavenworth, KS.

41. Frank C. Fyke Historical Monograph, May 27, 1946, Folder Personal Account, Frank C. Fyke, Subject Files, Texas Military Forces Museum, Austin, TX; Johnson, ed., We Aint No Heroes, 258.

42. Frank C. Fyke Historical Monograph, May 27, 1946, Folder Personal Account Frank C. Fyke, Subject Files, Texas Military Forces Museum, Austin, TX.

43. 754th Tank Battalion, "Battle of Luzon: 754th Tank Battalion, 9 Jan–30 March '45," February 9, 1945 entry; 637th Tank Destroyer Battalion, "After Action Report: 637th T. D. Bn: Luzon Campaign, 22 Nov. 44 thru 30 June 45," January 26, 1945, 9, 26, Combined Arms Research Library, Ft. Leavenworth, KS.

44. Royal Arch Gunnison, "The Burning of Manila," *Collier's* (April 7, 1945), 21; Report After Action: Intelligence Narrative, [no date], 8, Folder 337-2 A/ A Reports Intelligence Narrative, Box 8617, Records of the 37th Infantry Division, World War II Operational Records, Records of the Adjutant General's Staff, Record Group 407, U.S. National Archives, College Park, MD; February 10, 1945 entry, Diary of Baba Masanori in XIV Corps Advanced Echelon Translation Number 78, document number 26 T 78, in *Wartime Translations of Seized Japanese Documents*.

45. 129th Infantry, "Lessons Learned in the Luzon Campaign," Folder [no date], 337-INF (129) 0.3, Box 8733, Records of the 37th Infantry Division, World War II Operational Records, Records of the Adjutant General's Staff, Record Group 407, U.S. National Archives, College Park, MD.

46. Gunnison, "The Burning of Manila," 44.

47. 754th Tank Battalion, "Battle of Luzon: 754th Tank Battalion, 9 Jan–30 March '45," February 9, 1945 entry; 637th Tank Destroyer Battalion, "After Action Report: 637th T. D. Bn: Luzon Campaign, 22 Nov. 44 thru 30 June 45," January 26, 1945, 9, 26, Combined Arms Research Library, Fort Leavenworth, KS.

48. Preliminary Interrogation of Prisoner of War: Amaba Shigao, February 14, 1945; Prisoner of War Preliminary Interrogation Report: Izumida Zenzo, March 13, 1945, in XIV Corps Advanced Echelon Interrogation Report Number 28, document 26 IR 28, in *Wartime Translations of Seized Japanese Documents*; 117th Engineer Battalion unit report, February 9, 1945; 37th Infantry Division G-3 Report, February 11, 1945, Folder 337-3.3 G-3 JNL Reports vol. 10, Box 8674, Records of the 37th Infantry Division, World War II Operational Records, Records of the Adjutant General's Staff, Record Group 407, U.S. National Archives, College Park, MD.

49. Masao, *Senshi Sosho*, vol. 54, 506.

50. Preliminary Interrogation of Prisoner of War 1CD-17508-J: Iwazu Masato, February 10, 1945, Folder 901-2.13: PW Interrogation Reports, Box 427, Records of the 1st Cavalry Division, World War II Operational Records, Records of the Adjutant General's Staff, Record Group 407, U.S. National Archives, College Park, MD.

51. Preliminary Interrogation of Prisoner of War: Amaba Shigao, February 14, 1945; Prisoner of War Preliminary Interrogation Report: Izumida Zenzo, March 13, 1945, in XIV Corps Advanced Echelon Interrogation Report Number 28, document 26 IR 28, in *Wartime Translations of Seized Japanese Documents*; 117th Engineer Battalion unit report, February 9, 1945; 37th Infantry Division G-3 Report, February 11, 1945, Folder 337-3.3 G-3 JNL Reports vol. 10, Box 8674, Records of the 37th Infantry Division, World War II Operational Records, Records of the Adjutant General's Staff, Record Group 407, U.S. National Archives, College Park, MD.

52. Smith, *Triumph in the Philippines*, 245, 271.

53. Beightler to Brown, February 10, 1945, Folder 2, Box 1, Papers of Robert S. Beightler, Ohio Historical Society, Columbus, OH.

54. Prisoner of War Preliminary Interrogation Report 37-25: Himura Fukuzo, February 11, 1945, Folder 337-2 A/A Rpt—Annex 2 Int—Appendix A(3), Box 8616; Prisoner of War Preliminary Interrogation Report 37-33: Inouye Zenkichi, February 15, 1945; Prisoner of War Preliminary Interrogation Report 37-25: Tamaki Ichiro, February 11, 1945, Folder 337-2 A/A—Annex 2 Int—Appendix A (3), Box 8617, Records of the 37th Infantry Division; Preliminary Interrogation of Prisoner of War: 1CD 17511-J: Oshiro Koichi, February 15,

1945, Folder 901-2.13, Box 427, Records of the 1st Cavalry Division, World War II Operational Records, Records of the Adjutant General's Staff, Record Group 407, U.S. National Archives, College Park, MD.

55. G-3 Periodic Report, February 10, 1945, Folder 337-3.3, Box 8675, Records of the 37th Infantry Division, World War II Operational Records, Records of the Adjutant General's Staff, Record Group 407, U.S. National Archives, College Park, MD.

56. Heinrichs and Gallicchio, 16, 321–325; McEnery, *The XIV Corps Battle for Manila*, 113; H. D. Vogel, "Logistical Support of the Lingayen Operation," February 4, 1946, Folder February 4, 1946, Box 25, and Walter Krueger, "The Commander's Appreciation of Logistics," January 3, 1955, Folder 73, Box 12, Papers of Walter Krueger, U.S. Military Academy, West Point, NY.

57. Preliminary Interrogation of Prisoner of War 1CD-17551-J: Yano Tadashi, February 23, 1945, Folder 901-2.13, Box 427, Records of the 1st Cavalry Division, World War II Operational Records, Records of the Adjutant General's Staff, Record Group 407, U.S. National Archives, College Park, MD; Phase VI: The Battle of Manila, February 10, 1945 daily diary entry, 754th Tank Battalion, "Battle of Luzon: 754th Tank Battalion 9 Jan–30 June '45, Combined Arms Research Library, Fort Leavenworth, KS; John Gordon IV, "Battle in the Streets—Manila 1945," *Field Artillery*, August 1990, 28–29.

58. Phase VI: The Battle of Manila, February 7, 1945 daily diary entry, 754th Tank Battalion, "Battle of Luzon: 754th Tank Battalion 9 Jan–30 June '45, Combined Arms Research Library, Fort Leavenworth, KS.

59. "44th Tank Battalion: Tank Tracks—Tennessee to Tokyo," 35, Folder 4, Box 69, Material Donated by the General Public, Record Group 15, MacArthur Memorial, Norfolk, VA.

60. Preliminary Interrogation of Prisoner of War 1CD-17551-J: Yano Tadashi, February 23, 1945, Folder 901-2.13, Box 427, Records of the 1st Cavalry Division, World War II Operational Records, Records of the Adjutant General's Staff, Record Group 407, U.S. National Archives, College Park, MD; Phase VI: The Battle of Manila, February 10, 1945 daily diary entry, 754th Tank Battalion, "Battle of Luzon: 754th Tank Battalion 9 Jan–30 June '45, Combined Arms Research Library, Fort Leavenworth, KS; Gordon, "Battle in the Streets," 28–29.

61. Raymond F. Whitman, quoted in Clyma, ed., *Connecticut Men of the U.S. Army: Connecticut Veterans Commemorative Booklet* 8, no. 16 (December 3, 1945): 12.

62. "M'Arthur Men Push on Under Jap Shellfire," *Chicago Daily Tribune*, February 10, 1945.

63. Labrador, *Diary of the Japanese Occupation*, 267; Elena A. Rodriques, "My 16-Day Tragic Diary," 11–12, Folder 7, Box 78, Material Donated by the General Public, Record Group 15, MacArthur Memorial, Norfolk, VA.

64. Frankel, *The 37th Infantry Division*, 261.

65. Frankel, *The 37th Infantry Division*, 266; Beightler to Baxter, February 22, 1945, Folder 2, Box 1, Papers of Robert S. Beightler, Ohio Historical Society, Columbus, OH.

66. In his statement, Fitch states that the incident happened in March, but unit records and official histories make it clear it was February, and it was most likely the night of February 7. Warren P. Fitch, 37th Infantry Division, World War II Army Service Experiences Questionnaire, Army History and Heritage Command, Carlisle Barracks, PA.

67. Exhibit D-5: Written Statement of Sister Concepcion Gotera March 2, 1945, in James T. Walsh, "Report of Investigation of Atrocities Committed by Japanese Imperial Forces in Intramuros (Walled City) Manila, P.I. During February 1945," Folder 3, Box 15, Papers of James T. Walsh, Record Group 15, MacArthur Memorial, Norfolk, VA.

68. Exhibit D-5: Written Statement of Sister Concepcion Gotera March 2, 1945, in James T. Walsh, "Report of Investigation of Atrocities Committed by Japanese Imperial Forces in Intramuros (Walled City) Manila, P.I. During February 1945," Folder 3, Box 15, Papers of James T. Walsh, Record Group 15, MacArthur Memorial, Norfolk, VA.

69. XIV Corps, "Japanese Defense of Cities as Exemplified by the Battle for Manila" (July 1, 1945), 14, Folder 31, Box 3, Papers of Walter Krueger, Cushing Library, Texas A&M University, College Station, TX.

70. Gunnison, "The Burning of Manila," 21.

71. XIV Corps G-3 Operations Report, February 10, 1945, Folder 337-3.3 37th Inf. Div. G-3 Jnl, Box 8675, Records of the 37th Infantry Division, World War II Operational Records, Records of the Adjutant General's Staff, Record Group 407, U.S. National Archives, College Park, MD.

72. Smith, *Triumph in the Philippines*, 260–261; "A History of the 129th Infantry Regiment," Folder 337-INF (129) 0.1, Box 8730, Records of the 37th Infantry Division, World War II Operational Records, Records of the Adjutant General's Staff, Record Group 407, U.S. National Archives, College Park, MD.

73. Frankel, *The 37th Infantry Division in World War II*, 272–273; Smith, *Triumph in the Philippines*, 260–261; G-3 Periodic Report, February 9, 1945, Folder 337-3.3, Box 8675, Records of the 37th Infantry Division, World War II Operational Records, Records of the Adjutant General's Staff, Record Group 407, U.S. National Archives, College Park, MD.

74. Gunnison, "The Burning of Manila," 44; Frankel, *The 37th Infantry Division in World War II*, 273; Donald Starr, "Captain Swims Pasig River to Save Wounded," *Chicago Daily Tribune*, February 14, 1945; Smith, *Triumph in the Philippines*, 261; "A History of the 129th Infantry Regiment," Folder 337-INF (129) 0.1, Box 8730, Records of the 37th Infantry Division, World War II Operational Records, Records of the Adjutant General's Staff, Record Group 407, U.S. National Archives, College Park, MD.

75. Smith, *Triumph in the Philippines*, 263.

76. Maehara, *Manira Boeisen*, 175.

77. Smith, *Triumph in the Philippines*, 263

78. Smith, *Triumph in the Philippines*, 263; G-3 Periodic Report, February 11, 1945, Folder 337-3.3, Box 8674, Records of the 37th Infantry Division, World War II Operational Records, Records of the Adjutant General's Staff, Record Group 407, U.S. National Archives, College Park, MD.

79. Smith, *Triumph in the Philippines*, 263.

80. Cleto L. Rodriquez, Oral History (June 12, 1976), 20–21, Institute of Oral History, University of Texas at El Paso, El Paso, TX; Frankel, *The 37th Infantry Division*, 274; G-3 Periodic Report, 37th Infantry Division, February 8–9, 1945, Folder 337.3.3 G-3 Jnl. File, Box 8674, 37th Infantry Division Files, Records of the Adjutant General's Office, Record Group 407, U.S. National Archives, College Park, MD.

81. Frankel, *The 37th Infantry Division*, 274–276; Mathias, *G.I. Jive*, 141; Connaughton, Pimlott, and Anderson state that both men died in the attack on the railroad station, but this is in error. After a brief stint in the U.S. Air Force, Rodriquez retired from the U.S. Army as a Master Sergeant (*The Battle of Manila*, 112); Cleto L. Rodriquez, Oral History (June 12, 1976), 1, Institute of Oral History, University of Texas at El Paso, El Paso, TX.

82. Frankel, *The 37th Infantry Division*, 274–276; Mathias, *G.I. Jive*, 141; Maehara, *Manira Boeisen*, 178.

83. Kelsey Miller, "Manila Remembered 75 Years Later: Former Trooper Shares Personal Experience of Santo Tomás Liberation," March 2, 2020, https://www.army.mil/article/233320/manila_remembered_75_years_later_former_trooper_shares_personal_experrience_of_santo_tomas_liberation; Maehara, *Manira Boeisen*, 170; XIV Corps G-3 Operations Report, February 9, 1945; 672nd Amphibious Tractor Battalion Unit Report, February 19, 1945; XIV Corps G-3 Operations Report, February 10, 1945, Folder 337-3.3 37th Inf. Div. G-3 Jnl, Box 8675, Records of the 37th Infantry Division, World War II Operational Records, Records of the Adjutant General's Staff, Record Group 407, U.S. National Archives, College Park, MD.

84. Maehara, *Manira Boeisen*, 179.

85. Maehara, *Manira Boeisen*, 163, 165, 172.

86. Maehara, *Manira Boeisen*, 165.

87. Iwabuchi to Southwest Fleet, Feburary 10, 1945, Masao, *Senshi Sosho*, vol. 54, 511.

88. XIV Corps G-3 Operations Report, February 9, 1945; 672nd Amphibious Tractor Battalion Unit Report, February 19, 1945; XIV Corps G-3 Operations Report, February 10, 1945, Folder 337-3.3 37th Inf. Div. G-3 Jnl, Box 8675, Records of the 37th Infantry Division, World War II Operational Records, Records of the Adjutant General's Staff, Record Group 407, U.S. National Archives, College Park, MD.

89. Maehara, *Manira Boeisen*, 192.

90. Frankel, *The 37th Infantry Division*, 275–276.

91. Trevor Jensen, "Walter Simmons, 1908–2006: Editor and War Reporter," *Chicago Tribune*, December 1, 2006; Dunn, *Pacific Microphone*, 289; Carolyn Coggins, "What Goes on Backstage in the Literary Pageant," *The Atlanta Constitution*, February 18, 1945; "Gene Sherman, Former Times Writer and Pulitzer Prize Winner, Dies," *Los Angeles Times*, March 6, 1969; Richard Severo, "Homer Bigart, Acclaimed Reporter, Dies," *The New York Times*, April 17, 1991; Claudia Luther, "Carl Mydans, 97; Noted Life Magazine War Photographer," *Los Angeles Times*, August 18, 2004.

92. Charles Arthur Henne, 37th Infantry Division, World War II Army Service Experiences Questionnaires, U.S. Army Heritage and Education Center, Carlisle, PA.

93. Dunn, *Pacific Microphone*, 289; Coggins, "What Goes on Backstage in the Literary Pageant"; Julius Stephen Gassner, 37th Infantry Division, World War II Army Service Experiences Questionnaires, U.S. Army Heritage and Education Center, Carlisle, PA.

94. Henry W. Harris, "The Strategic Slant," *The Boston Daily Globe*, February 7, 1945.

95. Dunn, *Pacific Microphone*, 315.

CHAPTER 11

1. Hayashi Hirofumi, "Shiryo Shokai: Nihongun no Meirei Denpo ni Miru Manira-sen," [Introduction of Documents: The Battle of Manila as Seen in Japanese Force Orders and Telegrams] *Shizen, Ninghen, Shakai* 48 (2010): 69–95.

2. Manila Naval Defense Force to Higher Headquarters, February 6, 1945, in Masao, *Senshi Sosho*, vol. 54, 507.

3. Exhibit B-72: Testimony of Taguchi Hiroshi, March 30, 1945, 122, in James T. Walsh, "Report of Atrocities Committed by Japanese Imperial Forces Intramuros (Walled City) Manila P.I. During February, 1945," Folder 3, Box 15, Papers of James T. Walsh, Record Group 15, MacArthur Memorial, Norfolk, VA.

4. Exhibit B-36: Testimony of the Archbishop of Manila (Michael J. O'Doherty), 59, in James T. Walsh, "Report of Atrocities Committed by Japanese Imperial Forces Intramuros (Walled City) Manila P.I. During February, 1945," 1, 3, 5, Folder 3, Box 15, Papers of James T. Walsh, Record Group 15, MacArthur Memorial, Norfolk, VA.

5. Exhibit B-47: Testimony of Ceriaco Ruiz, March 5, 1945, in James T. Walsh, "Report of Atrocities Committed by Japanese Imperial Forces Intramuros (Walled City) Manila P.I. During February, 1945," Folder 3, Box 15, Papers of James T. Walsh, Record Group 15, MacArthur Memorial, Norfolk, VA.

6. Aluit, *By Sword and Fire*, 198–199, 234–236, 306; Exhibit B-15: Testimony of Jose Cabenero, February 28, 1945; Exhibit B-17: Testimony of Ricardo Macale,

February 28, 1945; Exhibit B-18: Testimony of William D. Tigertt, February 28, 1945; Exhibit: B-19: Testimony of Godofredo Rivera, February 28, 1945; Exhibit B-21: Testimony of Emiliana Gonzaga, March 2, 1945; Exhibit B-24: Testimony of Aquilino Rivera, March 4, 1945; Exhibit B-28: Testimony of Asuncion Marvas, March 2, 1945; Exhibit B-50: Testimony of Sy Suan, March 6, 1945; Exhibit B-56: Testimony of Wang Chi Chen, March 6, 1945; and Exhibit B-62: Testimony of Jose Cristabal, March 7, 1945, 24, 27, 28, 29, 35, 38, 43, 85, 94, 104, in James T. Walsh, "Report of Atrocities Committed by Japanese Imperial Forces Intramuros (Walled City) Manila P.I. During February, 1945," Folder 3, Box 15, Papers of James T. Walsh, Record Group 15, MacArthur Memorial, Norfolk, VA.

7. Aluit, *By Sword and Fire*, 185–186, 197, 203–204, 206; Exhibit B-5: Alejandro Dagami Affidavit, February 26, 1945; Exhibit C-7: Maria Rosa Agcaoili Affidavit, March 7, 1945; Exhibit C-8: Statement of Unidentified 20-year Old Spanish Girl, no date, and Main Report, in James T. Walsh, "Report of Atrocities Committed by Japanese Imperial Forces Intramuros (Walled City) Manila P.I. During February, 1945," 1, 3, 5, in James T. Walsh, "Report of Atrocities Committed by Japanese Imperial Forces Intramuros (Walled City) Manila P.I. During February, 1945," Folder 3, Box 15, Papers of James T. Walsh, Record Group 15, MacArthur Memorial, Norfolk, VA.

8. Aluit, By Sword and Fire, 198–199.

9. Pedro M. Picornell, *The Remedios Hospital, 1942–1945: A Saga of Malate* (Manila: De La Salle University Press, 1995), 43; Frank Ephraim, *Escape to Manila: From Nazi Tyranny to Japanese Terror* (Urbana: University of Illinois Press, 2003), 144.

10. Picornell, *The Remedios Hospital*, 43; Ephraim, *Escape to Manila*, 144.

11. Aluit, *By Sword and Fire*, 189.

12. Evelyn Berg Empie and Stephen H. Mette, *A Child in the Midst of Battle: One Family's Struggle for Survival in War-torn Manila* (Rolling Hills Estates, CA: Satori Press, 2001), 126.

13. Hans Hoeflien narrative, in Goldhagen, ed., *Manila Memories*, 100–101.

14. Hans Hoeflien narrative, in Goldhagen, ed., *Manila Memories*, 100–101.

15. Hans Hoeflien narrative, in Goldhagen, ed., *Manila Memories*, 100–101.

16. Aluit, *By Sword and Fire*, 188.

17. Aluit, *By Sword and Fire*, 264–265.

18. Marisse Reyes McMurray, *Tide of Time* (Makati City: Philippines: Jose Cojuangco & Sons, 1996), 192.

19. Nick Joaquin, *Mr. F.E.U.: The Cultural Hero That Was Nicanor Reyes* (Manila: Far Eastern University Press, 1995), 163–171; Lourdes R. Montinola, *Breaking the Silence* (Quezon City, Philippines: University of the Philippines Press, 1996), 97–101.

20. Aluit, *By Sword and Fire*, 217–218, 240, 270.

21. Aluit, *By Sword and Fire*, 276–277.

22. Gonzalez, *Manila*, 185; Hans Walser narrative, in Goldhagen, ed., *Manila Memories*, 104; Mañalac, *Manila*, 122.

23. Exhibit B-8: Testimony of Marry Barrientos, February 28, 1945, 11, in James T. Walsh, "Report of Atrocities Committed by Japanese Imperial Forces Intramuros (Walled City) Manila P.I. During February, 1945," Folder 3, Box 15, Papers of James T. Walsh, Record Group 15, MacArthur Memorial, Norfolk, VA.

24. Dumana, ed., *The German Club—Manila*, 57, 59, 60; Edgar Krohn, Jr., "The Way It Was," *Philippine Free Press*, February 21, 2008, 23.

25. Berg Empie and Mette, *A Child in the Midst of Battle*, 108–112.

26. Aluit, *By Sword and Fire*, 238–240.

27. Elena A. Rodriques, "My 16-Day Tragic Diary," 11–12, Folder 7, Box 78, Material Donated by the General Public, Record Group 15, MacArthur Memorial, Norfolk, VA.

28. Elena A. Rodriques, "My 16-Day Tragic Diary," 11–12, Folder 7, Box 78, Material Donated by the General Public, Record Group 15, MacArthur Memorial, Norfolk, VA.

29. Elena A. Rodriques, "My 16-Day Tragic Diary," 11–12, Folder 7, Box 78, Material Donated by the General Public, Record Group 15, MacArthur Memorial, Norfolk, VA.

30. Elena A. Rodriques, "My 16-Day Tragic Diary," 11–12, Folder 7, Box 78, Material Donated by the General Public, Record Group 15, MacArthur Memorial, Norfolk, VA.

31. Dumana, ed. *The German Club—Manila*, 60.

32. Reyes McMurray, *Tide of Time*, 191; Escoda, *Warsaw of Asia*, 205; Calero, *Three Continents*, 58–59.

33. Escoda, *Warsaw of Asia*, 245–246.

34. Aluit, *By Sword and Fire*, 198; Elena A. Rodriques, "My 16-Day Tragic Diary," 11–12, Folder 7, Box 78, Material Donated by the General Public, Record Group 15, MacArthur Memorial, Norfolk, VA.

35. Hans Hoeflien narrative, in Goldhagen, ed., *Manila Memories*, 114; Ephraim, *Escape to Manila*, 156–157.

36. Guerrero Nakpil, *Myself, Elsewhere*, 184.

37. Aluit, *By Sword and Fire*, 208.

38. Aluit, *By Sword and Fire*, 265.

39. Berg Empie and Mette, *A Child in the Midst of Battle*, 108–109.

40. Gonzalez, *Manila*, 216–217.

41. Berg Empie and Mette, *A Child in the Midst of Battle*, 141–144.

42. Ephraim, *Escape to Manila*, 157.

43. Van Sickle, *Iron Gates of Santo Tomás*, 337.

44. The interrogation reports of Masua Toyoki (a soldier of Japanese and Korean ancestry who took his mother's name when he joined the army), Sho Maitatsu, Ryu Bikusei, Oshiro Taro (a Japanese soldier with a Filipina wife and five children), Shim Sang Wook; Ri Shoju; and Koshoe Bok show that none of them

enjoyed the Japanese treatment of non-Japanese individuals. For more, see the individual debriefings—Preliminary Prisoner of War Interrogation Report 37-1: Masuda Toyoki, January 10, 1945; Preliminary Prisoner of War Interrogation Report 37-21: Sho Maitatsu, February 9, 1945; Preliminary Prisoner of War Interrogation Report 37-22: Ryu Bikusei, February 9, 1945; Preliminary Prisoner of War Interrogation Report 37-27: Oshiro Taro, February 11, 1945; Preliminary Prisoner of War Interrogation Report 37-37: Shim Sang Wook, February 16, 1945; Interrogation Report 37-38: Ri Shoju; Preliminary Prisoner of War Interrogation Report 37-32: Shimida Hirachi, February 14, 1945, Folder 337-2 A/A—Annex 2 Int—Appendix A (3), Box 8617, Records of the 37th Infantry Division; and Preliminary Interrogation of Enemy Alien EA5899: Koshoe Bok, February 13, 1945, Folder 901-2.13 (12093), Box 427, Records of the 1st Cavalry Division, World War II Operational Records, Records of the Adjutant General's Staff, Record Group 407, U.S. National Archives, College Park, MD.

45. Aluit, *By Sword and Fire*, 268.
46. Preliminary Interrogation of Enemy Alien EA5924: Morita Kunizo, February 15, 1945, Folder 901-2.13 (12093), Box 427, Records of the 1st Cavalry Division, World War II Operational Records, Records of the Adjutant General's Staff, Record Group 407, U.S. National Archives, College Park, MD.
47. Memorandum: Medical Technical Intelligence, March 15, 1945, Folder 337-2, Box 8617, Records of the 37th Infantry Division; Preliminary Interrogation of Prisoner of War: 1CD-17505-J: Takahashi Tarao, February 10, 1945, Folder 901-2.13 (12093), Box 427, Records of the 1st Cavalry Division, World War II Operational Records, Records of the Adjutant General's Staff, Record Group 407, U.S. National Archives, College Park, MD.
48. Prisoner of War Joint Interrogation Report: Murakami Kyozaku, March 19, 1945, 26 IR 64, in XIV Corps Advanced Echelon Interrogation Report Number 64; Prisoner of War Preliminary Interrogation Report: Uchida Kensaburo, March 4, 1945, in XIV Corps Advanced Echelon Interrogation Report Number 51, document number 26 IR 51, in *Wartime Translations of Seized Japanese Documents*; Prisoner of War Interrogation Report: 37-64, February 28, 1945, Folder 337-2 A/A—Annex 2 Int—Appendix A (3), Box 8617, Records of the 37th Infantry Division, World War II Operational Records, Records of the Adjutant General's Staff, Record Group 407, U.S. National Archives College Park, MD.
49. Aluit, *By Sword and Fire*, 257–259.
50. Aluit, *By Sword and Fire*, 345.
51. Picornell, *The Remedios Hospital*, 39–41, 55.
52. Ephraim, *Escape to Manila*, 145–146.
53. Aluit, *By Sword and Fire*, 201, 296–297.
54. 2nd Platoon Commander to 6th Company Commander, no date in Translation Number L37024, February 19, 1945, Folder 337-2 Appendix A(2) Translations, Box 8616, Records of the 37th Infantry Division, World War II Operational

Records, Records of the Adjutant General's Staff, Record Group 407, U.S. National Archives, College Park, MD.

55. Wayne H. Bowen, *Spain during World War II* (Columbia: University of Missouri Press, 2006), 57–59.

56. Aluit, *By Sword and Fire*, 278–282.

57. Aluit, *By Sword and Fire*, 281–282.

58. Reyes McMurray, *Tide of Time*, 193–195.

59. Aluit, *By Sword and Fire*, 285; Exhibit B-38: Testimony of Father Francis J. Cosgrave, March 7, 1945, 70, in James T. Walsh, "Report of Atrocities Committed by Japanese Imperial Forces Intramuros (Walled City) Manila P.I. During February, 1945," Folder 3, Box 15, Papers of James T. Walsh, Record Group 15, MacArthur Memorial, Norfolk, VA.

60. Aluit, *By Sword and Fire*, 308.

61. Aluit, *By Sword and Fire*, 295; Ralph Emerson Hibbs, *Tell MacArthur to Wait* (New York: Carlton Press, 1988), 231–235.

62. Aluit, *By Sword and Fire*, 295; Hibbs, *Tell MacArthur to Wait*, 231–235; Maria Campos-Lopez testimony in *United States vs. Yamashita* trial transcript (October 31, 1945) vols. 1–10, 369-371, Military Legal Resources, Library of Congress, https://www.loc.gov//rr/frd/Military_Law/Yamashita_trial.html.

63. Exhibit B-48: Testimony of Florencia Lao Vita Cruz, March 5, 1945; Exhibit B-54: Testimony of Ernesta Augustin, March 6, 1945; and Exhibit B-65: Testimony of Eustacio Barros, March 3, 1945, 83, 92, 112, in James T. Walsh, "Report of Atrocities Committed by Japanese Imperial Forces Intramuros (Walled City) Manila P.I. During February, 1945," Folder 3, Box 15, Papers of James T. Walsh, Record Group 15, MacArthur Memorial, Norfolk, VA.

64. Hilario L. Ziaicita, "Our Imprisonment During the Battle of Manila," Manila Memorare 1945 Collection, Filipinas Heritage Library, Ayala Museum, Makati, Metro Manila, Philippines.

65. William Tucker, Oral History (May 13, 2002), transcription by author, Nunn Center for Oral History, University of Kentucky, Lexington, KY.

66. George L. Ellis World War II Veteran Survey, Folder 1, Box 13, Record Group 237, Tennessee State Library and Archives, Nashville, Tennessee; Murphy Foret, 37th Infantry Division, World War II Army Service Experiences Questionnaire, U.S. Army Heritage and Education Center, Carlisle, PA.

67. Exhibit C-7: Maria Rosa Agcaoili Affidavit, March 7, 1945, Exhibit C-8: Statement of Unidentified 20-year Old Spanish Girl, no date and Main Report, in James T. Walsh, "Report of Atrocities Committed by Japanese Imperial Forces Intramuros (Walled City) Manila P.I. During February, 1945," 1, 3, 5, Folder 3, Box 15, Papers of James T. Walsh, Record Group 15, MacArthur Memorial, Norfolk, VA.

68. Escoda, *Warsaw of Asia*, 222; Aluit, *By Sword and Fire*, 229–232, 276; Hayashi Hirofumi, "Manira-sen to Beibyo Hoteru Jiken" [The Battle of Manila and the Bayview Hotel Incident] *Shizen, Ningen, Shakai* 52 (January 2012): 49–83.

69. Berg Empie and Mette, *A Child in the Midst of Battle*, 121; Krohn, Jr., "The Way It Was," 22.

70. Exhibit B-2: Testimony of Genoveva Pozon Lopez Jaena Pasig Rizal, February 25, 1945; Exhibit B-40: Testimony of Eugene Donstoff, March 5, 1945, in James T. Walsh, "Report of Atrocities Committed by Japanese Imperial Forces Intramuros (Walled City) Manila P.I. During February, 1945," Folder 3, Box 15, Papers of James T. Walsh, Record Group 15, MacArthur Memorial, Norfolk, VA; Smith, *Triumph in the Philippines*, 275.

71. Escoda, *Warsaw of Asia*, 168, 273; Gonzalez, *Manila*, 186–187.

72. Picornell, *The Remedios Hospital*, 44–48.

73. Picornell, *The Remedios Hospital*, 44–48.

74. Mañalac, *Manila*, 127, 129. For the wide range of reactions described here, see Picornell, *The Remedios Hospital*, 47; Berg Empie and Mette, *A Child in the Midst of Battle*, 138.

75. McManus, *Fire and Fortitude*, 245–247.

76. Rafiel Fierro, Oral History (October 23, 2003), VOCES: The U.S. Latino and Latina Oral History Project, Benson Latin American Collection, University of Texas, Austin, TX; Berg Empie and Mette, *A Child in the Midst of Battle*, 129; Calero, *Three Continents*, 81.

77. Gonzalez, *Manila*, 189; Berg Empie and Mette, *A Child in the Midst of Battle*, 129; Ephraim, *Escape to Manila*, 159; Hans Walser narrative, in Goldhagen, ed., *Manila Memories*, 111.

78. Gonzalez, *Manila*, 188; Mañalac, *Manila*, 127; Ephraim, *Escape to Manila*, 158, 163; Hans Hoeflein narrative, in Goldhagen, ed., *Manila Memories*, 101.

79. Calero, *Three Continents*, 63, 81; Ephraim, *Escape to Manila*, 159.

80. Elena A. Rodriques, "My 16-Day Tragic Diary," 11–12, Folder 7, Box 78, Material Donated by the General Public, Record Group 15, MacArthur Memorial, Norfolk, VA.

CHAPTER 12

1. Aluit, *By Sword and Fire*, 299–300.

2. Aluit, *By Sword and Fire*, 299–300.

3. Aluit, *By Sword and Fire*, 300–301.

4. XIV Corps, "After Action Report: XIV Corps: M-1 Operation," July 29, 1945, 98, Folder 32, Box 3, Papers of Walter Krueger, Cushing Library, Texas A&M University, College Station, TX.

5. William W. Owen World War II Veterans Survey, Folder 5, Box 29, Record Group 237, Tennessee State Library and Archives, Nashville, TN; 145th Infantry Regiment, "Combat in Manila," 4 attached to Beightler to Commanding General, Sixth Army, April 5, 1945, Folder 337-0.5 Rpt.w/5 annexes, Box 8606, Records of the 37th Infantry Division, World War II Operational Records, Records of the Adjutant General's Staff, Record Group 407, U.S. National Archives, College Park, MD.

6. Rogers, *Bitter Years*, 263.

7. Rogers, *Bitter Years*, 263.

8. LeGrande Diller, Oral History (May 31, 1977), 39–40, D. Clayton James Collection, Record Group 49, MacArthur Memorial, Norfolk, VA; Rogers, *The Bitter Years*, 263.

9. Russell Weigley, *Eisenhower's Lieutenants: The Campaign of France and Germany, 1944–1945* (Bloomington: Indiana University Press, 1981), 27–28, 127–128; Scott R. McMeen, "Field Artillery Doctrine Development, 1917–1945," Master's thesis, U.S. Army Command & General Staff College, 1991.

10. Charles A. Henne, 37th Infantry Division, World War II Army Service Experiences Questionnaire, U.S. Army Heritage and Education Center, Carlisle, PA.

11. Gordon, "Battle in the Streets," 24–29.

12. William T. James, Jr., "From Siege to Surgical: The Evolution of Urban Combat from World War II to the Present and its Effect on Current Doctrine," Masters Thesis, U.S. Army Command & Staff College, 1998, 15.

13. Charles A. Henne, 37th Infantry Division, World War II Army Service Experiences Questionnaire, U.S. Army Heritage and Education Center, Carlisle, PA.

14. Gordon, "Battle in the Streets," 24–29.

15. Gordon, "Battle in the Streets," 24–29; D. W. Eddy, "Manila and the Capitulation," *Signals* 1, no. 5 (May–June 1947): 42–47.

16. Connaughton, Pimlott, and Anderson, *Battle for Manila*, 123.

17. Smith, *Triumph in the Philippines*, 274–275.

18. LeGrande Diller, Oral History (May 31, 1977), 39–40, D. Clayton James Collection, Record Group 49, MacArthur Memorial, Norfolk, VA; Rogers, *The Bitter Years*, 263; Smith, *Triumph in the Pacific*, 263–264; Diller Memo for Paul P. Rogers, no date, Folder 4, Box 1, Papers of Paul P. Rogers, Record Group 46, MacArthur Memorial, Norfolk, VA.

19. LeGrande Diller, Oral History (May 31, 1977), 40, D. Clayton James Collection, Record Group 49, MacArthur Memorial, Norfolk, VA.

20. Ohl, *Minuteman*, 182–185; Beightler to Commanding General, Sixth Army, April 5, 1945, 3, Folder 337-0.5 Rpt.w/5 annexes, Box 8606, Records of the 37th Infantry Division, World War II Operational Records, Records of the Adjutant General's Staff, Record Group 407, U.S. National Archives, College Park, MD.

21. Ford, "US Assessments of Japanese Ground Warfare Tactics," 340; Berg Empie and Mette, *A Child in the Midst of Battle*, 127; Ines Cabaruss, "A Tale of One City: Memoirs From World War Two Manila: A New Understanding of Loss," unpublished manuscript (May 6, 2000), Manila Memorare 1945 Collection, Filipinas Heritage Library, Ayala Museum, Makati, Metro Manila, Philippines.

22. "XIV Corps Operations on Luzon," 139–141, loose in the box, Box 1A, Papers of Oscar Griswold, Academy Library, U.S. Military Academy, West Point, NY. This document uses slightly different language than the version of the Corps report that was circulated with the Army, and it appears to be an early draft.

23. "XIV Corps Operations on Luzon," 139–141, loose in the box, Box 1A, Papers of Oscar Griswold, Academy Library, U.S. Military Academy, West Point, New York. This document uses slightly different language than the version of the Corps report that was circulated within the Army.

24. Fellers, Memorandum for the Commander-in-Chief, February 10, 1945, Folder 1, Box 2, Papers of Bonner Fellers, Record Group 44A, MacArthur Memorial, Norfolk, VA.

25. Fellers, Memorandum for the Commander-in-Chief, February 10, 1945, Folder 1, Box 2, Papers of Bonner Fellers, Record Group 44A, MacArthur Memorial, Norfolk, VA.

26. February 10, 1945 entry, Diary of Oscar W. Griswold, Box 1, Papers of Oscar W. Griswold, U.S. Army History and Heritage Command, Carlisle Barracks, PA.

27. McEnery, *The XIV Corps Battle for Manila*, 102; XIV Corps, "After Action Report: XIV Corps: M-1 Operation," July 29, 1945, 111, Folder 32, Box 3, Papers of Walter Krueger, Cushing Library, Texas A&M University, College Station, TX.

28. Fellers, Memorandum for the Commander-in-Chief, February 14, 1945, Folder 26, Box 5, Papers of Bonner Fellers, Record Group 44A, MacArthur Memorial, Norfolk, VA.

29. Smith, *Triumph in the Philippines*, 285–286; Aluit, *By Sword and Fire*, 249.

30. Smith, *Triumph in the Philippines*, 285–286; Connaughton, Pimlott, and Anderson, *Battle for Manila*, 148; Prisoner of War Preliminary Interrogation Report 37-40: Tanji Genzo, February 17, 1945, Folder 337-2 A/A—Annex 2 Int—Appendix A (3), Box 8617, Records of the 37th Infantry Division, World War II Operational Records, Records of the Adjutant General's Staff, Record Group 407, U.S. National Archives, College Park, MD.

31. Smith, *Triumph in the Philippines*, 285–288.

32. Prisoner of War Preliminary Interrogation Report: Miyakawa Takeo, February 19, 1945, in XIV Corps Advanced Echelon Interrogation Report Number 34, document number 26 IR 34, in *Wartime Translations of Seized Japanese Documents*; Prisoner of War Interrogation Report 37-25: Himura Fukuzo, February 21, 1945; Prisoner of War Interrogation Report 37-44: Kato Soichi, February 19, 1945, Folder 337-2 a/a Rpt—Annex 2, Int—Appendix A (3) 173d Language Det, Box 8616, Records of the 37th Infantry Division; Preliminary Interrogation of Prisoner of War: 1CD 17551-J: Tano Tadashi, February 23, 1945, Folder 901-2.13, Box 27, Records of the 1st Cavalry Division, World War II Operational Records, Records of the Adjutant General's Staff, Record Group 407, U.S. National Archives, College Park, MD; Prisoner of War Preliminary Interrogation Report: Saito Yoshio, February 24, 1945, in Sixth Army Advanced Echelon Interrogation Report Number 381, document number 21 IR 381, in *Wartime Translations of Seized Japanese Documents*.

33. Gunnison, "The Burning of Manila," 21, 40, 44.

34. XIV Corps, "Japanese Defense of Cities as Exemplified by the Battle for Manila" (July 1, 1945), 21, 23, Folder 31, Box 3, Papers of Walter Krueger, Cushing Library, Texas A&M University, College Station, TX; Headquarters, 129th Infantry Regiment, "Lessons Learned in the Luzon Campaign With Recommendations and Comments," 2, 8, November 1, 19—June 30, 1945, Folder 337-INF (129) 0.3, Box 8733; 145th Infantry Regiment, "Combat in Manila," 4 attached to Beightler to Commanding General, Sixth Army, April 5, 1945, Folder 337-0.5 Pt./5 annexes, Box 8606, Records of the 37th Infantry Division, World War II Operational Records, Records of the Adjutant General's Staff, Record Group 407, U.S. National Archives, College Park, MD.

35. XIV Corps, "Japanese Defense of Cities as Exemplified by the Battle for Manila" (July 1, 1945), 21, Folder 31, Box 3, Papers of Walter Krueger, Cushing Library, Texas A&M University, College Station, TX; John Skirvin, Oral History (April 3, 2003), 13, Nimitz Education and Research Center, National Museum of the Pacific War, National Museum of the Pacific War, Fredericksburg, TX.

36. Joseph Holzer, Oral History (August 5, 2008), 30, Rutgers Oral History Archive, Rutgers University, New Brunswick, NJ; George Fischer, Oral History (May 21, 2010), second part, 5, MacArthur Memorial, Norfolk, VA.

37. Diary of 1st Lieutenant Hori [no personal name given], February 7, 11, 1945, Item 4, in ADVATIS Bulletin 438, document number 50 B 438, in *Wartime Translations of Seized Japanese Documents*.

38. XIV Corps, "Japanese Defense of Cities as Exemplified by the Battle for Manila" (July 1, 1945), 21, Folder 31, Box 3, Papers of Walter Krueger, Cushing Library, Texas A&M University, College Station, TX; Gunnison, "The Burning of Manila," 21, 40, 44.

39. Frank Mendez, Oral History (April 23, 2005), 22–23, Record Group 32, MacArthur Memorial, Norfolk, VA; Beightler to Commanding General, Sixth Army, April 5, 1945, 8, Folder 337-0.5 Rpt.w/5 annexes, Box 8606, Records of the 37th Infantry Division, World War II Operational Records, Records of the Adjutant General's Staff, Record Group 407, US National Archives, College Park, MD.

40. XIV Corps, "Japanese Defense of Cities as Exemplified by the Battle for Manila" (July 1, 1945), 24, 26, Folder 31, Box 3, Papers of Walter Krueger, Cushing Library, Texas A&M University, College Station, TX; Dunn, *Pacific Microphone*, 310.

41. Astor, *Crisis in the Pacific*, 536.

42. 1st Cavalry Operations Report, February 11, 1945, and 117th Engineer (C) Battalion Report, February 12, 1945, Folder 337-3.3 G-3 JNL File Vol. 10, Box 8674, Records of the 37th Infantry Division, World War II Operational Records, Records of the Adjutant General's Staff, Record Group 407, U.S. National Archives, College Park, MD.

43. Operations Journal of the 1st Battalion, 129th Infantry Regiment, February 9 and 12, 1945 entries, Folder 337-INF (129) 0.3, Box 8733, Records of the 37th Infantry Division, World War II Operational Records, Records of the

Adjutant General's Staff, Record Group 407, U.S. National Archives, College Park, MD.

44. Headquarters, 129th Infantry Regiment, "Lessons Learned in the Luzon Campaign with Recommendations and Comments," 8, November 1, 19–June 30, 1945, Folder 337-INF (129) 7-0.7, Box 8733, Records of the 37th Infantry Division, Record Group 407, U.S. National Archives, College Park, MD.

45. G-2 Section, "Japanese Weapons used in the Defense of Manila" attached to Beightler to Commanding General, Sixth Army, April 5, 1945, Folder 337-0.5 Rpt.w/5 annexes, Box 8606, Records of the 37th Infantry Division, World War II Operational Records, Records of the Adjutant General's Staff, Record Group 407, U.S. National Archives, College Park, MD.

46. Gunnison, "The Burning of Manila," 21, 40, 44; Maehara, *Manira Boeisen*, 179–180.

47. John Skirvin, Oral History (April 3, 2003), 13, Nimitz Education and Research Center, National Museum of the Pacific War, National Museum of the Pacific War, Fredericksburg, TX.

48. XIV Corps G-3 Operations Report, February 10, 1945, Folder 337-3.3 37th Inf. Div. G-3 Jnl, Box 8675, Records of the 37th Infantry Division, World War II Operational Records, Records of the Adjutant General's Staff, Record Group 407, U.S. National Archives, College Park, MD.

49. Smith, *Triumph in the Philippines*, 282.

50. 37th Infantry Division, "Report After Action," September 10, 1945, 71, Folder 4, Box 4, Papers of Robert Krueger, Cushing Library, Texas A&M University, College Station, TX; Frankel, *37th Infantry Division in World War II*, 279–282; Smith, *Triumph in the Philippines*, 283; S-3 Periodic Reports, 145th Infantry, February 19 and 20, 1945, Folder 337-3.3 G-3 JNL File Vol. 12, Box 8675; "A History of the 129th Infantry Regiment," September 15, 1945, Folder 337-INF (129) 0.1, Box 8730, Records of the 37th Infantry Division, Records of the 37th Infantry Division, Record World War II Operational Records, Records of the Adjutant General's Staff, Group 407, U.S. National Archives, College Park, MD.

51. Annex 2 of G-2 Section, "Japanese Weapons Used in the Defense of Manila" attached to Beightler to Commanding General, Sixth Army, April 5, 1945, Folder 337-0.5 Rpt.w/5 annexes, Box 8606, Records of the 37th Infantry Division, World War II Operational Records, Records of the Adjutant General's Staff, Record Group 407, U.S. National Archives, College Park, MD.

52. Preliminary Interrogation of Prisoner of War: 1CD 17508-J: Iwazu Masato, February 10, 1945, Folder 901-2.13, Box 27, Records of the 1st Cavalry Division, World War II Operational Records, Records of the Adjutant General's Staff, Record Group 407, U.S. National Archives, College Park, MD.

53. Mañalac, *Manila*, 144.

54. Lara, *Boy Guerrilla*, 67–68.

55. Beightler to Commanding General, Sixth Army, April 5, 1945, 3, Folder 337-0.5 Rpt.w/5 annexes, Box 8606, Records of the 37th Infantry Division, World War II Operational Records, Records of the Adjutant General's Staff, Record Group 407, U.S. National Archives, College Park, MD.

56. John Skirvin, Oral History (April 3, 2003), 13–14, Nimitz Education and Research Center, National Museum of the Pacific War, National Museum of the Pacific War, Fredericksburg, TX.

57. XIV Corps, "After Action Report: XIV Corps: M-1 Operation," July 29, 1945, 92, Folder 32, Box 3, Papers of Walter Krueger, Cushing Library, Texas A&M University, College Station, TX.

58. Richardson, *Under Age Angel*, 96.

59. Smith, *Triumph in the Pacific*, 268.

60. XIV Corps, "After Action Report: XIV Corps: M-1 Operation," July 29, 1945, 93, Folder 32, Box 3, Papers of Walter Krueger, Cushing Library, Texas A&M University, College Station, TX.

61. Aluit, *By Fire and Sword*, 264.

62. Lahti, *Memoirs of an Angel*, 73; Smith, *Triumph in the Pacific*, 268–269; Wright, *The 1st Cavalry Division in World War II*, 135.

63. Connaughton, Pimlott, and Anderson, *Battle of Manila*, 142–143.

64. Maehara, *Manira Boeisen*, 190.

65. XIV Corps, "After Action Report: XIV Corps: M-1 Operation," July 29, 1945, 94, Folder 32, Box 3, Papers of Walter Krueger, Cushing Library, Texas A&M University, College Station, TX.

66. Smith, *Triumph in the Pacific*, 269.

67. XIV Corps, "After Action Report: XIV Corps: M-1 Operation," July 29, 1945, 94, Folder 32, Box 3, Papers of Walter Krueger, Cushing Library, Texas A&M University, College Station, TX; Gordon F. Sander, *Serling: The Rise and Twilight of Television's Last Angry Man* (New York: Dutton, 1992), 50.

68. Bonner Fellers, Memorandum for the Commander-in-Chief, February 13, 1945, Folder 26, Box 5, Papers of Bonner Fellers, Record Group 44A, MacArthur Memorial, Norfolk, VA.

69. Smith, *Triumph in the Pacific*, 269.

70. McEnery, *The XIV Corps Battle for Manila*, 102; XIV Corps, "After Action Report: XIV Corps: M-1 Operation," July 29, 1945, 110, Folder 32, Box 3, Papers of Walter Krueger, Cushing Library, Texas A&M University, College Station, TX.

CHAPTER 13

1. Eichelberger to Eichelberger, February 15, 1945, in Luvaas, ed., *Dear Ms. Em*, 217.

2. 117th Engineer Battalion Report, February 13, 1945, and 117th Engineer Battalion Report, February 14, 1945, Folder 337-3.3, Box 8674, Records of the 37th Infantry Division, World War II Operational Records, Records of the Adjutant General's Staff, Record Group 407, U.S. National Archives, College Park, MD.

3. Smith, *Triumph in the Philippines*, 285–288.

4. Smith, *Triumph in the Philippines*, 285–286; Aluit, *By Sword and Fire*, 249.

5. Connaughton, Pimlott, and Anderson, *Battle for Manila*, 149; Smith, *Triumph in the Philippines*, 287–288; Aluit, *By Sword and Fire*, 308.

6. Edgar Krohn, Jr. "The Way It Was (Conclusion)," *Philippines Free Press*, March 1, 2008, 28–30, 34.

7. Conchita L. Benitez Statement, April 6, 1994, Folder Personal Narrative: Benitez, Cochita, Manila Memorare 1945 Collection, Filipinas Heritage Library, Ayala Museum, Makati, Metro Manila, Philippines.

8. Gonzalez, *Manila*, 213; Connaughton, Pimlott, and Anderson, *Battle for Manila*, 149; Smith, *Triumph in the Philippines*, 287–288; Aluit, *By Sword and Fire*, 308.

9. Sixth US Army, "Report of the Luzon Campaign 9 January 1945–30 June 1945," vol. I, 39, Skelton Combined Arms Research Library, Fort Leavenworth, KS.

10. MacArthur to Commanding General, Sixth Army, February 5, 1945, in Sixth US Army, "Report of the Luzon Campaign 9 January 1945–30 June 1945," vol. I, 113, Skelton Combined Arms Research Library, Fort Leavenworth, KS.

11. Ohl, *Minuteman*, 184; Beightler to Hard, February 14, 1945, Folder 2, Box 1, Papers of Robert S. Beightler, Ohio Historical Society, Columbus, OH.

12. Headquarters, 129th Infantry, Lessons Learned in the Luzon Campaign with Recommendations and Comments," Folder 337-INF (129) 0.3, Box 8733, Records of the 37th Infantry Division, World War II Operational Records, Records of the Adjutant General's Staff, Record Group 407, U.S. National Archives, College Park, MD; Gonzalez, *Manila*, 191.

13. Aluit, *By Sword and Fire*, 319–321; Connaughton, Pimlott, and Anderson, *Battle for Manila*, 144–148; Smith, *Triumph in the Philippines*, 187.

14. Memorandum for the Commander-in-Chief, February 17, 1945, Folder 26, Box 5, Papers of Bonner Fellers, Record Group 44A, MacArthur Memorial, Norfolk, VA.

15. Fellers to Dearest Girls, February 16, 1945, Folder 1, Box 2, Papers of Bonner Fellers, Record Group 44A, MacArthur Memorial, Norfolk, VA.

16. Smith, *Triumph in the Philippines*, 287–288; Frankel, *The 37th Division in World War II*, 283.

17. Peter MacFarland, Oral History: Interview C (January 19, 2011), 5–6, Record Group 32, MacArthur Memorial, Norfolk, VA.

18. Wahlquist, ed., *Beyond the Bend*, 165.

19. Beightler to Hard, February 14, 1945, Folder 2, Box 1, Papers of Robert S. Beightler, Ohio Historical Society, Columbus, OH.

20. Maehara, *Manira Boeisen*, 173.

21. Smith, *Triumph in the Philippines*, 272; Shujiro Kobayashi Statement, December 1, 1949, document number 52266, in "Statements of Japanese Officials on World War II"; Maehara, *Manira Boeisen*, 164, 191–192.

22. Maehara, *Manira Boeisen*, 191–192.

23. Central Force Operation Order Number 4, February 15, 1945, in XIV Corps, "Japanese Defense of Cities as Exemplified by the Battle for Manila" (July 1, 1945), 15, Folder 31, Box 3, Papers of Walter Krueger, Cushing Library, Texas A&M University, College Station, TX.

24. XIV Corps, "Japanese Defense of Cities as Exemplified by the Battle for Manila" (July 1, 1945), 15, Folder 31, Box 3, Papers of Walter Krueger, Cushing Library, Texas A&M University, College Station, TX.

25. G-3 Operations Report, 1st Cavalry Division, February 15, 1945, Folder 337-3.3, Box 8675, Records of the 37th Infantry Division, World War II Operational Records, Records of the Adjutant General's Staff, Record Group 407, U.S. National Archives, College Park, MD.

26. Maehara, *Manira Boeisen*, 211.

27. Powell, "Learning Under Fire," 27–34; Smith, *Triumph in the Philippines*, 272–273; 1st Attack Unit Order, February 15, 1945, Item 1 and unknown S-2 to unknown G-2, February 15, 1945, Item 2, Batch 1CD 282, Folder 901-2.9 (48692), Box 13301, Records of the 1st Cavalry Division, World War II Operational Records, Records of the Adjutant General's Staff, Record Group 407, U.S. National Archives, College Park, MD.

28. 672nd Amphibious Tractor Battalion Unit Report, February 15, 1945, Folder 337-3.3, Box 8675, Records of the 37th Infantry Division, World War II Operational Records, Records of the Adjutant General's Staff, Record Group 407, U.S. National Archives, College Park, MD.

29. Smith, *Triumph in the Philippines*, 272; Unidentified message book sheet, February 15 and 17, 1945, Item 1, Batch 1CD 284, Folder 901-2.9 (48692), Box 13301, Records of the 1st Cavalry Division; G-3 Operations Reports, XIV Corps, February 16 and 19, 1945, Folder 337-3.3, Box 8675, Records of the 37th Infantry Division, World War II Operational Records, Records of the Adjutant General's Staff, Record Group 407, U.S. National Archives, College Park, MD; Hashimoto Hiroshi Statement, March 18, 1949, document number 52362, in "Statements of Japanese Officials on World War II." The testimony of a Lance Corporal Tsukahara Masujiro documents that once Japanese commanders died, cohesion among the defenders quickly fell apart: Prisoner of War Preliminary Interrogation Report 37-35: Tsukahara Masujiro, February 15, 1945, Folder 337-2 A/A—Annex 2 Int—Appendix A (3), Box 8617, Records of the 37th Infantry Division, World War II Operational Records, Records of the Adjutant General's Staff, Record Group 407, U.S. National Archives, College Park, MD.

30. XIV Corps, "Japanese Defense of Cities as Exemplified by the Battle for Manila" (July 1, 1945), 15, Folder 31, Box 3, Papers of Walter Krueger, Cushing Library, Texas A&M University, College Station, TX.

31. Smith, *Triumph in the Philippines*, 273.

32. 637th Tank Destroyer Battalion Daily Report, February 15, 1945, Folder 337-3.3 G-3 Journal vol. 11, Box 8675; Prisoner of War Preliminary Interrogation Report 37-28: Kitano Tatsumi, February 12, 1945; Prisoner of War Preliminary

Interrogation Report 37-35: Tsukahara Masujiro, February 15, 1945; Prisoner of War Preliminary Interrogation Report 37-41: Kiyoyama Hideo, February 18, 1945; Prisoner of War Preliminary Interrogation Report 37-42: Matsumoto Koichi, February 18, 1945; Prisoner of War Preliminary Interrogation Report 37-43: Boku Eishun, February 19, 1945; Prisoner of War Preliminary Interrogation Report 37-44: Kato Shoichi, February 19, 1945; and Prisoner of War Preliminary Interrogation Report 37-51: Tanaka Konichi, February 24, 1945, Folder 337-2 A/A—Annex 2 Int—Appendix A (3), Box 8617, Records of the 37th Infantry Division; Preliminary Interrogation of Enemy Alien EA5899: Koshoe Bok; Preliminary Interrogation of Prisoner of War 1CD 17509-J: Suganon Kunihiko, February 12, 1945; and Preliminary Interrogation of Prisoner of War 1CD 17541-J: Ito Shunji, Folder 901-2.13 (12093), Box 427, Records of the 1st Cavalry Division, World War II Operational Records, Records of the Adjutant General's Staff, Record Group 407, U.S. National Archives, College Park, MD; Prisoner of War Preliminary Interrogation Report: Miyakawa Takeo, February 19, 1945, in XIV Corps Advanced Echelon Interrogation Report Number 34, document number 26 IR 34, in *Wartime Translations of Seized Japanese Documents*.

33. Prisoner of War Preliminary Interrogation Report 37-28: Kitano Tatsumi, February 12, 1945; Prisoner of War Preliminary Interrogation Report 37-35: Tsukahara Masujiro, February 15, 1945; Prisoner of War Preliminary Interrogation Report 37-44: Kato Shoichi, February 19, 1945; Prisoner of War Preliminary Interrogation Report 37-51: Tanaka Konichi, February 24, 1945, Folder 337-2 A/A—Annex 2 Int—Appendix A (3), Box 8617, Records of the 37th Infantry Division, World War II Operational Records, Records of the Adjutant General's Staff, Record Group 407, U.S. National Archives, College Park, MD.

34. Maehara, *Manira Boeisen*, 172.

35. XIV Corps Advanced Echelon Prisoner of War Preliminary Interrogation Report Number 34: Miyakawa Takeo, February 19, 1945, document 26 IR 34, in *Wartime Translations of Seized Japanese Documents*; 37th Cavalry Reconnaissance Troop Mechanized Report, February 15, 1945 and 637th Tank Destroyer Battalion G-3 Periodic Report, February 15, 1945, Folder 337-3.3 G-3 JNL File Vol. 11, Box 8675, Records of the 37th Infantry Division, World War II Operational Records, Records of the Adjutant General's Staff, Record Group 407, U.S. National Archives, College Park, MD.

36. Frank Kelly, "Japanese Tie Girl in Line of American Fire," *New York Herald Tribune*, February 18, 1945; Testimony of Joseph Maldonado, February 27, 1945, James T. Walsh, "Report of Investigation of Atrocities Committed by Japanese Imperial Forces," Exhibit B-7, 9, Folder Japanese Atrocities, Box 4, Papers of Oscar Griswold, Academy Library, U.S. Military Academy, West Point, NY.

37. Berg Empie and Mette, *A Child in the Midst of Battle*, 128, 133; Hans Walser narrative, in Goldhagen, ed., *Manila Memories*, 115.

38. 117th Engineer Battalion Daily Report, February 16, 1945, Folder 337-3.3, Box 8675, Records of the 37th Infantry Division, World War II Operational Records, Records of the Adjutant General's Staff, Record Group 407, U.S. National Archives, College Park, MD; Donald Starr, "Pontoon Spans on Pasig Built by Illinoisans," *Chicago Daily Tribune*, February 16, 1945.

39. Sixth U.S. Army, "Enemy on Luzon: An Intelligence Summary," December 1, 1945, 132, Skelton Combined Arms Research Library, Fort Leavenworth, KS; Robert F. Goheen Oral History, December 15, 1988, 14, Association for Diplomatic Studies and Training Foreign Affairs Oral History Project, Lauinger Library, Georgetown University, Washington, DC.

40. Austin W. Bach, "37th Infantry Division Report After Action, Annex 2 Intelligence—Appendix A 173d Language Detachment," 10, 13, Folder 337-2—A/A/Rpt Annex 2 Appendix A 173d Language Detachment, Box 8617, Records of the 37th Infantry Division, World War II Operational Records, Records of the Adjutant General's Staff, Record Group 407, U.S. National Archives, College Park, MD.

41. Ibid

42. Sherman "Pacific Echoes," Los Angeles Times, March 5, 1945.

43. Yukio Kawamoto and Julius Gassner World War II Army Service Experiences Questionnaires, 37th Infantry Division, U.S. Army Heritage and Education Center, Carlisle, PA; Preliminary Interrogation Report 37-43: Boku Eishun, February 18, 1945, Folder 337-2 A/A—Annex 2 Int—Appendix A (3), Box 8617; Austin W. Bach, "37th Infantry Division Report After Action, Annex 2 Intelligence—Appendix A 173d Language Detachment," 5, Folder 337-2—A/A/Rpt Annex 2 Appendix A 173d Language Detachment, Box 8617, Records of the 37th Infantry Division, World War II Operational Records, Records of the Adjutant General's Staff, Record Group 407, U.S. National Archives, College Park, MD.

44. Austin W. Bach, "37th Infantry Division Report After Action, Annex 2 Intelligence—Appendix A 173d Language Detachment," 14, Folder 337-2—A/A/Rpt Annex 2 Appendix A 173d Language Detachment, Box 8617, Records of the 37th Infantry Division, World War II Operational Records, Records of the Adjutant General's Staff, Record Group 407, U.S. National Archives, College Park, MD.

45. Norman Kikuta, Oral History, [no date] Center for Oral History, University of Hawaii at Maoa.

46. Yukio Kawamoto World War II Army Service Experiences Questionnaire, 37th Infantry Division, US Army Heritage and Education Center, Carlisle, PA; Lyn Crost, *Honor by Fire: Japanese Americans at War in Europe and the Pacific* (Novato, CA: Presidio, 1994), 216; Norman Kikuta, Oral History, [no date] Center for Oral History, University of Hawaii at Maoa.

47. Sherman, "Pacific Echoes," Los Angeles Times, March 5, 1945.

48. Yukio Kawamoto, 37th Infantry Division, World War II Army Service Experiences Questionnaire, U.S. Army Heritage and Education Center, Carlisle, PA; Escoda, *Warsaw of Asia*, 302–303; Prisoner of War Preliminary Interrogation Report 37-9: Unnamed individual, January 29, 1945; Prisoner of War Preliminary Interrogation Report 37-18: Makihara Shizuo, February 8, 1945; Prisoner of War Preliminary Interrogation Report 37-21: Sho Maitatsu, February 9, 1945; Prisoner of War Preliminary Interrogation Report 37-33: Inouye Zenkichi, February 15, 1945; Prisoner of War Preliminary Interrogation Report 37-45:Aike Hideo, February 20, 1945; Prisoner of War Preliminary Interrogation Report 37-49: Watanabe Minoru, February 22, 1945, Folder 337-2 A/A—Annex 2 Int—Appendix A (3), Box 8617, Records of the 37th Infantry Division, World War II Operational Records, Records of the Adjutant General's Staff, Record Group 407, U.S. National Archives, College Park, MD; Prisoner of War Preliminary Interrogation Report: Hanada Toshio, February 12, 1945, in XIV Corps Advanced Echelon Interrogation Report Number 23, document number 26 IR 23, in *Wartime Translations of Seized Japanese Documents*.

49. Sixth U.S. Army, "Enemy on Luzon: An Intelligence Summary," December 1, 1945, 132, Skelton Combined Arms Research Library, Fort Leavenworth, KS.

50. Norman Kikuta, Oral History, [no date] Center for Oral History, University of Hawaii at Maoa. For typical debriefings of prisoners with limited information, look at: Prisoner of War Preliminary Interrogation Report 37-10: Yamasaki Tomoji, January 30, 1945 and Prisoner of War Preliminary Interrogation Report 37-44: Kato Shoichi, February 19. 1945, Folder 337-2 A/A—Annex 2 Int—Appendix A (3), Box 8617, Records of the 37th Infantry Division, World War II Operational Records, Records of the Adjutant General's Staff, Record Group 407, U.S. National Archives, College Park, MD.

51. Prisoner of War Preliminary Interrogation Report 37-15: Okubo Yasuhiko, February 6, 1945, Folder 337-2 A/A—Annex 2 Int—Appendix A (3), Box 8617, Records of the 37th Infantry Division, World War II Operational Records, Records of the Adjutant General's Staff, Record Group 407, U.S. National Archives, College Park, MD.

52. Prisoner of War Preliminary Interrogation Report 37-26: Shu Bu, February 11, 1945; Prisoner of War Preliminary Interrogation Report 37-31: Takami Merihiko, February 14, 1945; Prisoner of War Preliminary Interrogation Report 37-33: Inouye Zenkichi, February 15, 1945, Folder 337-2 A/A Rpt—Annex 2 Int—Annex A(3), 37th Infantry Division Report After Action, Annex 2 Appendix A 173d Language Detachment, 19–20, Folder 337-2, Box 8617, Records of the 37th Infantry Division, World War II Operational Records, Records of the Adjutant General's Staff, Record Group 407, U.S. National Archives, College Park, MD.

53. Prisoner of War Preliminary Interrogation Report 37-42: Matsumoto Koichi, February 18, 1945; Prisoner of War Preliminary Interrogation Report 37-43: Boku Eishun, February 19, 1945; Prisoner of War Preliminary Interrogation

Report 37-44: Kato Shoichi, February 19, 1945, Folder 337-2 A/A—Annex 2 Int—Appendix A (3), Box 8617, Records of the 37th Infantry Division, World War II Operational Records, Records of the Adjutant General's Staff, Record Group 407, U.S. National Archives, College Park, MD.

54. 37th Infantry Division Report After Action, Annex 2 Appendix A 173d Language Detachment, 20, Folder 337-2, Box 8617, Records of the 37th Infantry Division, World War II Operational Records, Records of the Adjutant General's Staff, Record Group 407, U.S. National Archives, College Park, MD.

55. XIV Corps, "After Action Report: XIV Corps: M-1 Operation," July 29, 1945, 240, Folder 32, Box 3, Papers of Walter Krueger, Cushing Library, Texas A&M University, College Station, TX.

56. 37th Infantry Division Report After Action, Annex 2 Appendix A 173d Language Detachment, 21–22, Folder 337-2, Box 8617, Records of the 37th Infantry Division, World War II Operational Records, Records of the Adjutant General's Staff, Record Group 407, U.S. National Archives, College Park, MD.

57. 37th Infantry Division Report After Action, Annex 2 Appendix A 173d Language Detachment, 19–20, Folder 337-2, Box 8617, Records of the 37th Infantry Division, World War II Operational Records, Records of the Adjutant General's Staff, Record Group 407, U.S. National Archives, College Park, MD.

58. XIV Corps, "After Action Report: XIV Corps: M-1 Operation," July 29, 1945, 246–247, Folder 32, Box 3, Papers of Walter Krueger, Cushing Library, Texas A&M University, College Station, TX.

59. Ogawa Sautami to All Company Commanders and Platoon Leaders, 4th Battalion Daily Order Number 2, January 28, 1945 Item 7, in XIV Corps Advanced Echelon Translation 69, document number 26 T 69, in *Wartime Translations of Seized Japanese Documents*; Organizational Chart of Special Attack Unit, February 13, 1945, Item 3, Batch 1CD 282, Folder 901-2.9 (48692), Box 13301, Records of the 1st Cavalry Division, World War II Operational Records, Records of the Adjutant General's Staff, Record Group 407, U.S. National Archives, College Park, MD.

60. Iwabuchi Mitsuji, Manila Naval Defense Force Operation Order Number 40, February 2, 1945, in General Headquarters Bulletin Number 1875, document number 10 B 1875, in *Wartime Translations of Seized Japanese Documents*.

61. Manila Naval Defense Force HQ to Each Unit under the command of the above HQ, February 4, 1945, in General Headquarters Bulletin Number 1875, document number 10 B 1875, in *Wartime Translations of Seized Japanese Documents*.

62. Smith, *Triumph in the Philippines*, 276.

63. Smith, *Triumph in the Philippines*, 277–278.

64. Smith, *Triumph in the Philippines*, 277–278; Fellers to MacArthur, February 15, 1945, Folder 26, Box 5, Papers of Bonner Fellers, Record Group 44A, MacArthur Memorial, Norfolk, VA.

65. Wright, *The 1st Cavalry in World War II*, 138–139; George Fisher, Oral History (May 21, 2010), third part, 7, Oral History Collection, Record Group 32, MacArthur Memorial, Norfolk, VA.

66. Smith, *Triumph in the Philippines*, 278–279; G-3 Operations Report, 1st Cavalry Division, February 15–16, 1945, Folder 901-3.1 (7559), Box 13305, Records of the 1st Cavalry Division, World War II Operational Records, Records of the Adjutant General's Staff, Record Group 407, U.S. National Archives, College Park, MD.

67. Smith, *Triumph in the Philippines*, 277–278; Ephraim, *Escape to Manila*, 162–163.

68. Angelita Martinez Florio, "Hell in Malate," *Philippine Free Press*, February 10, 2007, 28–30; Angelita Martinez Florio, "Hell in Malate (Conclusion)," *Philippine Free Press*, February 17, 2007, 17–18.

69. Gonzalez, *Manila*, 193–194; Hans Walser narrative, in Goldhagen, ed., *Manila Memories*, 109–113.

70. Escoda, *Warsaw of Asia*, 258.

71. Roderick Hall, "The Battle for Manila: A Personal Memory," *Bulletin of the American Historical Collection* 34, no. 3 (July–September 2006): 26–27.

72. Hall, "The Battle for Manila," 27.

73. Escoda, *Warsaw of Asia*, 259.

74. Gonzalez, *Manila*, 196–198.

75. Gonzalez, *Manila*, 199–201.

76. Wright, *The 1st Cavalry Division in World War II*, 139; Charles A. Henne, 37th Infantry Division, World War II Army Service Experiences Questionnaire, U.S. Army Heritage and Education Center, Carlisle, PA.

77. Hans Walser narrative, in Goldhagen, ed., *Manila Memories*, 114.

78. Smith, *Triumph in the Philippines*, 264.

CHAPTER 14

1. Tabulation by the author based on numbers provided in Appendix H, Smith, *Triumph in the Philippines*, 692.

2. Hughes Seewald, 1st Cavalry Division, World War II Army Services Experiences Questionnaire, U.S. Army Heritage and Education Center, Carlisle, PA.

3. 129th Infantry Regiment, Lessons Learned in the Luzon Campaign, Folder 337-INF (129) 0.3, Box 8733, Records of the 37th Infantry Division, World War II Operational Records, Records of the Adjutant General's Staff, Record Group 407, U.S. National Archives, College Park, MD; Headquarters XIV Corps, "After Action Report: XIV Corps: M-1 Operation," July 29, 1945, part II, 132–133, Folder 32, Box 3, Papers of Walter Krueger, Cushing Library, Texas A&M University, College Station, TX.

4. Warren P. Fitch, 37th Infantry Division, World War II Army Services Experiences Questionnaire, U.S. Army Heritage and Education Center, Carlisle, PA.

5. Charles A. Henne, 37th Infantry Division, World War II Army Services Experiences Questionnaire, U.S. Army Heritage and Education Center, Carlisle, PA.

6. Leonard Palmero, Oral History (October 11, 1980), 11, Oral History Collection, Maag Library, Youngstown State University, Youngstown, OH.

7. 37th Infantry Division, "Report After Action: Operations of the 37th Infantry Division," 208–209, Folder 4, Box 4, Papers of Walter Krueger, Cushing Library, Texas A&M University, College Station, TX; Mary Ellen Condon-Rall and Albert E. Cowdrey, *United States Army in World War II: The Technical Services: The Medical Department: Medical Services in the War Against Japan* (Washington, DC: U.S. Government Printing Office, 1998), 337–338.

8. Martin Gonzales, Oral History (November 21, 2011), 67, Nimitz Education and Research Center, National Museum of the Pacific War, Fredericksburg, TX.

9. Clyma, ed., *Connecticut Men of the United States Army* 9, no. 15 (January 5, 1946): 6; "The Commander's Appreciation of Logistics," January 3, 1955, Folder 73, Box 12, Papers of Walter Krueger, Academy Library, U.S. Military Academy, West Point, NY.

10. Transcription by the author of Estanislado Reyna, Oral History (February 2, 2002), VOCES: The U.S. Latino and Latina Oral History Project, Benson Latin American Collection, University of Texas, Austin, TX; Richard J. Foss, "How It Was" manuscript memoir, 270, Veterans History Project, American Folklife Center, Library of Congress; Julian Levin, Oral History (June 5, 2002), Rutgers Oral History Archive, Rutgers University, New Brunswick, NJ.

11. XIV Corps, "After Action Report: XIV Corps: M-1 Operation," July 29, 1945, part II, 134–136, Folder 32, Box 3, Papers of Walter Krueger, Cushing Library, Texas A&M University, College Station, TX.

12. 37th Infantry Division, "Report After Action: Operations of the 37th Infantry Division," 234, 237, 272–273, Folder 4, Box 4, Papers of Walter Krueger, Cushing Library, Texas A&M University, College Station, TX.

13. Gray to Hulburd, February 25, 1945, Folder 1945 Feb. 25, Box 254, Dispatches from *Time* Magazine Correspondents: First Series, Houghton Library, Papers of Roy E. Larsen, Harvard University, Cambridge, MA.

14. Fellers to Dorothy and Nancy Jane, February 14, 1945, Folder 17, Box 1, Papers of Bonner Fellers, Record Group 44A, MacArthur Memorial, Norfolk, VA.

15. Rogers, *Bitter Years*, 265.

16. Guerrero Nakpil, *Myself, Elsewhere*, 186.

17. Whitney to Whitney, February 21, 1945, Folder 7, Box 10, Papers of Courtney Whitney, Record Group 16, MacArthur Memorial, Norfolk, VA.

18. Roger Egeberg, Oral History (June 30, 1971), 4, D. Clayton James Collection, Record Group 49, MacArthur Memorial, Norfolk, VA.

19. Egeberg, *The General*, 133–134; Roger Egeberg, Oral History (June 30, 1971), 5, D. Clayton James Collection, Record Group 49, MacArthur Memorial, Norfolk, VA; Walter Simmons, "Peace and Quiet, Horror of War—Manila Is Both," *Chicago Daily Tribune*, February 16, 1945.

20. Owen, *Eye-Deep in Hell*, 92.
21. Simmons, "Peace And Quiet, Horror of War."
22. Joquin Garcia, *It Took Four Years for the Rising Sun to Set (1941–1945)* (Manila: De La Salle University Press, 2001), 157.
23. February 18, 1945 entry, in Labarador, *Diary of the Japanese Occupation*, 270.
24. George Fischer, Oral History (May 21, 2010), second interview, 10, Oral History Collection, Record Group 32, MacArthur Memorial, Norfolk, VA.
25. Mañalac, *Manila*, 158.
26. Victor Kuester, Oral History (May 23, 2007), 9–10, Wisconsin Veterans Museum, Madison, WI.
27. Dos Passos, *Tour of Duty*, 191–192.
28. Sixth U.S. Army, "Report of the Luzon Campaign, 9 January 1945–30 June 1945," vol. IV, 134, Skelton Combined Arms Research Library, Fort Leavenworth, KS; Smith, *Triumph in the Philippines*, 251.
29. XIV Corps, "After Action Report: XIV Corps: M-1 Operation," July 29, 1945, part II, 135, Folder 32, Box 3, Papers of Walter Krueger, Cushing Library, Texas A&M University, College Station, TX; Headquarters, Sixth U.S. Army, "Report of the Luzon Campaign, 9 January 1945–30 June 1945," vol. IV, 134, Skelton Combined Arms Research Library, Fort Leavenworth, KS.
30. Homer Bigart, "Center of Manila Lies in Ruins, Water Rationed, Snipers a Peril," *New York Herald Tribune*, February 8, 1945; XIV Corps, "After Action Report: XIV Corps: M-1 Operation," July 29, 1945, part II, 135, Folder 32, Box 3, Papers of Walter Krueger, Cushing Library, Texas A&M University, College Station, TX; Mañalac, *Manila*, 166; Sixth U.S. Army, "Report of the Luzon Campaign, 9 January 1945–30 June 1945," vol. IV, 134, Skelton Combined Arms Research Library, Fort Leavenworth, KS.
31. Richard J. Foss, "How It Was" manuscript memoir, 273, Veterans History Project, American Folklife Center, Library of Congress.
32. Robert F. Minch, Oral History (March 29, 2007), 12, Wisconsin Veterans Museum, Madison, WI.
33. Martin Schram, Oral History (May 7, 2005), 5, Wisconsin Veterans Museum, Madison, WI.
34. Owen, *Eye-Deep in Hell*, 96.
35. Martin Schram, Oral History (May 7, 2005), 5, Wisconsin Veterans Museum, Madison, Wisconsin.
36. Martin Schram, Oral History (May 7, 2005), 5, Wisconsin Veterans Museum, Madison, Wisconsin.
37. XIV Corps, "After Action Report: XIV Corps: M-1 Operation," July 29, 1945, part II, 109, 135, Folder 32, Box 3, Papers of Walter Krueger, Cushing Library, Texas A&M University, College Station, TX; 37th Infantry Division, "Report After Action," Part VI, G-1 Section, 5, 13, Folder 337-0.3, Box 8604, Records of the 37th Infantry Division, World War II Operational Records, Records of the Adjutant General's Staff, Record Group 407, U.S. National Archives, College Park, MD.

38. Fellers to Girls, February 14, 1945, Folder 17, Box 1, Papers of Bonner Fellers, Record Group 44A, MacArthur Memorial, Norfolk, VA.
39. Van Sickle, *Iron Gates of Santo Tomás*, 331; Rowan, *On the Spring Tide*, 54.
40. Bailey Pratt, ed., *Only a Matter of Days*, 91–93.
41. Prising, *Manila, Goodbye*, 194; Frankel, *The 37th Infantry Division in World War II*, 277; February 18, 1945 entry, in Labarador, *Diary of the Japanese Occupation*, 270.
42. Warne, *Terry*, 253–254.
43. Dos Passos, *Tour of Duty*, 200.
44. Yay Panlilio, *The Crucible: An Autobiography by Colonel Yay, Filipina America Guerrilla*, edited by Denise Cruz (New Brunswick, NJ: Rutgers University Press, 2010), 299–300; Theresa Kaminski, *Angels of the Underground: The American Women Who Resisted the Japanese in the Philippines in World War II* (New York: Oxford University Press, 2016), 390–391, 400.
45. Bailey Pratt, ed., *Only a Matter of Days*, 91–93.
46. Warne, *Terry*, 250; James Mace Ward, "Legitimate Collaboration: The Administration of Sato Tomas Internment Camp and Its Histories, 1942–1943," *Pacific Historical Review* 77, no. 2 (May 2008): 159–201; Cogan, *Captured*, 197.
47. Dos Passos, *Tour of Duty*, 206–207; Ward, "Legitimate Collaboration," 159–201; Cogan, *Captured*, 197.
48. Dos Passos, *Tour of Duty*, 206–207; Ward, "Legitimate Collaboration," 159–201; Cogan, *Captured*, 197.
49. Dos Passos, *Tour of Duty*, 192.
50. Beightler to Fillman, February 22, 1945, Folder 3, Box 1, Papers of Robert S. Beightler, Ohio Historical Society, Columbus, OH.
51. Dos Passos, *Tour of Duty*, 193.
52. Earl M. Hoff, "A Free Press for Manila" manuscript, 6–7, Folder Flashbacks From My War Files on the Philippines, Box 117 and February 13, 1945 entry, Diary of Carl Mydans, Folder Notebook 10, Box 179, Papers of Carl and Shelly Mydans, Beinecke Library, Yale University, New Haven, CT.
53. Calhoun to Mydans, February 3, 1945, in February 7, 1945 entry, Diary of Carl Mydans, Folder Notebook 10, Box 179, Papers of Carl and Shelly Mydans, Beinecke Library, Yale University, New Haven, CT.
54. Mydans to Elson, May 25, 1970, Folder Flashbacks From My War Files on the Philippines, Box 117, and February 21, 1945 entry, Diary of Carl Mydans, Folder Notebook 10, Box 179, Papers of Carl and Shelly Mydans, Beinecke Library, Yale University, New Haven, CT.
55. Mydans to Elson, May 25, 1970, Folder Flashbacks From My War Files on the Philippines, Box 117, and February 21, 1945 entry, Diary of Carl Mydans, Folder Notebook 10, Box 179, Papers of Carl and Shelly Mydans, Beinecke Library, Yale University, New Haven, CT.

56. Mydans to Elson, May 25, 1970, Folder Flashbacks From My War Files on the Philippines, Box 117, and February 21, 1945 entry, Diary of Carl Mydans, Folder Notebook 10, Box 179, Papers of Carl and Shelly Mydans, Beinecke Library, Yale University, New Haven, CT.

57. Bessie Hackett Wilson, *Memories of the Philippines* (Fullerton, CA: Pacific Rim Books, 1989), 17; Mydans to Elson, May 25, 1970, Folder Flashbacks From My War Files on the Philippines, Box 117, and February 21, 1945 entry, Diary of Carl Mydans, Folder Notebook 10, Box 179, Papers of Carl and Shelly Mydans, Beinecke Library, Yale University, New Haven, CT.

58. Wilson, *Memories of the Philippines*, 17; Mydans to Elson, May 25, 1970 and Mydans to Elson, May 26, 1970, Folder Flashbacks From My War Files on the Philippines, Box 117, and February 21, 1945 entry, Diary of Carl Mydans, Folder Notebook 10, Box 179, Papers of Carl and Shelly Mydans, Beinecke Library, Yale University, New Haven, CT.

59. Frank M. Lutze, 37th Infantry Division, World War II Army Services Experiences Questionnaire, U.S. Army Heritage and Education Center, Carlisle, PA.

60. Floyd E. Todd, Robert H. Kiser, Daniel J. Sears, Cletus J. Schwab, and Edwin H. Hanson, 37th Infantry Division, World War II Army Services Experiences Questionnaires and Pat Shovlin, 1st Cavalry Division, World War II Army Services Experiences Questionnaire, U.S. Army Heritage and Education Center, Carlisle, PA.

61. Pat Shovlin, 1st Cavalry Division, World War II Army Services Experiences Questionnaire, U.S. Army Heritage and Education Center, Carlisle, PA.

62. Amel L. Cox, Report After Action: Office of the Special Service Officer, July 25, 1945, Folder 337-0.3 A/A Rpts, Box 8604, Records of the 37th Infantry Division, Records of the Adjutant General's Office, Record Group 407, U.S. National Archives, College Park, MD.

63. Mathias, *G.I. Jive*, 157.

64. Mañalac, *Manila*, 149; Warne, *Terry*, 250.

65. Mañalac, *Manila*, 151–152.

66. Mydans, *More than Meets the Eye*, 202.

67. Sixth U.S. Army, "Enemy on Luzon: An Intelligence Summary," December 1, 1945, 71–73, Skelton Combined Arms Research Library, Fort Leavenworth, KS.

68. Sixth U.S. Army, "Enemy on Luzon: An Intelligence Summary," December 1, 1945, 73, Skelton Combined Arms Research Library, Fort Leavenworth, KS.

69. Sixth U.S. Army, "Enemy on Luzon: An Intelligence Summary," December 1, 1945, 74, Skelton Combined Arms Research Library, Fort Leavenworth, KS.

70. Owen, *Eye-Deep in Hell*, 99.

71. Owen, *Eye-Deep in Hell*, 99; Eliot R. Thorpe, *East Wind, Rain: The Intimate Account of an Intelligence Officer in the Pacific, 1939–1949* (Boston: Gambit Incorporated, 1969), 169.

72. Owen, *Eye-Deep in Hell*, 102–103.

73. Owen, *Eye-Deep in Hell*, 102–103.

74. Owen, *Eye-Deep in Hell*, 102–103.

75. Owen, *Eye-Deep in Hell*, 104–105; Sixth U.S. Army, "Enemy on Luzon: An Intelligence Summary," December 1, 1945, 76–77, Skelton Combined Arms Research Library, Fort Leavenworth, KS.

76. Owen, *Eye-Deep in Hell*, 104–105; Sixth U.S. Army, "Enemy on Luzon: An Intelligence Summary," December 1, 1945, 75–77, Skelton Combined Arms Research Library, Fort Leavenworth, KS.

77. XIV Corps, "After Action Report: XIV Corps: M-1 Operation," July 29, 1945, part I, 253, Folder 32, Box 3, Papers of Walter Krueger, Cushing Library, Texas A&M University, College Station, TX.

78. Ephraim, *Escape to Manila*, 164; Dumana, ed., *The German Club—Manila*, 65.

79. Beightler to Brown, February 10, 1945, Folder 2, Box 1, Papers of Robert Beightler, Ohio Historical Society, Columbus, OH.

80. Sixth U.S. Army, "Report of the Luzon Campaign, 9 January 1945–30 June 1945," vol. IV, 143–144, Skelton Combined Arms Research Library, Fort Leavenworth, KS.

81. Edwin H. Hanson, 37th Infantry Division, World War II Army Services Experiences Questionnaire, U.S. Army Heritage and Education Center, Carlisle, PA.

82. Victor Kuester, Oral History (May 23, 2007), 9–10, Wisconsin Veterans Museum, Madison, WI.

83. Victor Kuester, Oral History (May 23, 2007), 9–10, Wisconsin Veterans Museum, Madison, WI.

84. Wright, *The 1st Cavalry Division in World War II*, 134–135.

85. XIV Corps, "After Action Report: XIV Corps: M-1 Operation," July 29, 1945, part II, 5, Folder 32, Box 3, Papers of Walter Krueger, Cushing Library, Texas A&M University, College Station, TX.

86. XIV Corps, "After Action Report: XIV Corps: M-1 Operation," July 29, 1945, part II, 110–111, Folder 32, Box 3, Papers of Walter Krueger, Cushing Library, Texas A&M University, College Station, TX.

87. Joseph F. Tauchen, Jr., Oral History (March 6, 1997), 15, Wisconsin Veterans Museum, Madison, WI.

88. Joseph F. Tauchen, Jr., Oral History (March 6, 1997), 15, Wisconsin Veterans Museum, Madison, WI; Change No. 1 to Adm O No. 18, February 23, 1945, Folder 337-3.3, Box 8675, Records of the 37th Infantry Division, World War II Operational Records, Records of the Adjutant General's Staff, Record Group 407, U.S. National Archives, College Park, MD.

89. Edwin H. Hanson, 37th Infantry Division, World War II Army Services Experiences Questionnaire, U.S. Army Heritage and Education Center, Carlisle, PA; Heinrichs and Gallicchio, *Implacable Foes*, 321–323.

90. Walter I. Madden World War II Veteran Survey, Folder 6, Box 24, Record Group 237, Tennessee State Library and Archives, Nashville, TN.

91. XIV Corps, "Japanese Defense of Cities as Exemplified by the Battle for Manila" (July 1, 1945), 14, 24, Folder 31, Box 3, Papers of Walter Krueger, Cushing Library, Texas A&M University, College Station, TX.

CHAPTER 15

1. Edwin H. Felsher, Jr., "The Seizure of Corregidor—February 1945: Role of Airborne Forces in Joint Operations," 7 (May 1973), Folder 4, Box 6, Papers of Edward M. Flanagan, Jr., U.S. Army Heritage and Education Center, Carlisle, PA; James H. Belote and William M. Belote, *Corregidor: The Saga of a Fortress* (New York: Harper and Row, 1967), 198.
2. Edward L. Jenkins, "The Corregidor Operation," *Military Review* 26, no. 1 (April 1946): 59.
3. E. M. Flanagan, Jr., *Corregidor: The Rock Force Assault, 1945* (Novato, CA: Presidio Press, 1994), 155–159; Belote and Belote, *Corregidor*, 214; Don Abbott, "The Warden: George Madison Jones," The 503D P.R.C.T. Heritage Battalion Online, https://503prct.org/abbott/warden/warden_01.html. The 503D P.R.C.T. Heritage Battalion Online is one of a series of interrelated websites that veterans of the regiment created to commemorate their unit and their experiences on Corregidor. The quality of these websites is particularly good. The utility of their many articles, essays documents, and photographs varies, but there are some impressive finds. The contemporary documents, diaries, and letters from 1945 that alumni of the regiment have contributed are quite useful. Other items, such as obituaries and correspondence from subsequent years, have less utility to a historian of World War II.
4. Parentheses in the Flannagan book removed in this construction of the quote. Flannagan, *Corregidor*, 174.
5. Donald A. Crawford, "Operations of 503D Parachute Regiment Combat Team in Capture of Corregidor Island, 16 February–2 March 1945 (Northern Philippines Campaign) (Personal Experience of Regimental Assistant S-1)," 20, Advanced Infantry Officers Course, 1948–1949, Academic Department, The Infantry School, Fort Benning, GA.
6. Krueger, *From Down Under to Nippon*, 265; Flanagan, *Corregidor*, 169–170; Lawson B. Caskey, "The Operations of the 503d Parachute Infantry Regiment Combat Team in the Recapture of Corregidor Island, 16 February–8 March 1945 (Luzon Campaign) (Personal Observations of a Parachute Battalion Commander)," 7, Advanced Infantry Officers Course, 1948–1949, Academic Department, The Infantry School, Fort Benning, GA; Edward T. Flash, "The Operations of the 2D Battalion, 503d Parachute Infantry Regiment Combat Team in the Recapture of Corregidor Island, 16 February–23 February 1945 (Luzon Campaign) (Personal Observations of a Parachute Rifle Platoon Leader)," 7, Advanced Infantry Officers Course, 1949–1950, Academic Department, The Infantry School, Fort Benning, GA.
7. Caskey, "Operations of the 503d Parachute Infantry Regiment Combat Team," 9.
8. Lester H. Levine, "The Operations of the 503d Parachute Infantry Regiment in the Attack on Corregidor Island, 16 February–2 March 1945 (Luzon Campaign) (Personal Experience of a Regimental Adjutant)," 15–17, Advanced Infantry

Officers Course, 1947–1948, Academic Department, The Infantry School, Fort Benning, GA.

9. Flannagan, *Corregidor*, 104; Walter Krueger, "The Luzon Campaign of 1945," Folder 73, Box 12, Academy Library, Papers of Walter Kruger, U.S. Military Academy, West Point, NY; Flash, "The Operations of the 2D Battalion, 503d Parachute Infantry Regiment Combat Team," 7; Caskey, "Operations of the 503d Parachute Infantry Regiment Combat Team," 9; Magnus L. Smith, "Operations of the 'Rock Force' (603D RCT Reinforced) in the Recapture of Corregidor Island, 16 February–8 March 1946 (Luzon Campaign) (Personal Experience of an Assistant Regimental Operations Officer)," 8, Advanced Infantry Officers Course, 1949–1950, Staff Department, The Infantry School, Fort Benning, GA; E. M. Postlethwait, "Corregidor Coordination," *Infantry Journal*, August 1945, 16; Matsuki, *Senshi Sosho*, vol. 60, 269.

10. Jenkins, "The Corregidor Operation," 60.

11. Matsuki, *Senshi Sosho*, vol. 60, 269.

12. John H. Blair, "Operations of the 3D Battalion, 503d Parachute Infantry Regiment in the Landing on Corregidor, P.I., 16 February–2 March 1945 (Luzon Campaign) (Personal Experiences of a Battalion Staff Officer)," 9, Advanced Infantry Officers Course, 1949–1950, Academic Department, The Infantry School, Fort Benning, GA; Levine, "Operations of the 503d Parachute Infantry Regiment," 20; Flash, "The Operations of the 2D Battalion, 503d Parachute Infantry Regiment Combat Team," 8, 10; Caskey, "Operations of the 503d Parachute Infantry Regiment Combat Team," 14.

13. Caskey, "Operations of the 503d Parachute Infantry Regiment Combat Team," 11; Flanagan, *Corregidor*, 169.

14. Crawford, "Operations of 503D Parachute Regiment Combat Team," 27–28; Blair, "Operations of the 3D Battalion, 503d Parachute Infantry Regiment," 14; Laurence S. Browne, "Airborne Operation on Corregidor," 7–8, 20, April 10, 1948, Advance Officers Course #1, The Armor School, Fort Knox, KY.

15. Crawford, "Operations of 503D Parachute Regiment Combat Team," 27; William B. Breuer, *Retaking the Philippines: America's Return to Corregidor and Bataan, October 1944–March 1945* (New York: St. Martin's Press, 1986), 198.

16. Belote and Belote, *Corregidor*, 214–215; Flanagan, *Corregidor*, 205; Breuer, *Retaking the Philippines*, 198; Hudson C. Hill, "The Operations of Company 'E', 503d Parachute Regiment at Wheeler Point, Island of Corregidor, Philippine Islands 23 February, 1945 (Luzon Campaign) (Personal Experience of a Company Commander)," 6, Advanced Infantry Officers Course, 1947–1948, Academic Department, The Infantry School, Fort Benning, GA.

17. Matsuki, *Senshi Sosho*, vol. 60, 269.

18. Levine, "Operations of the 503d Parachute Infantry Regiment," 30, 33, 58, 65.

19. Levine, "Operations of the 503d Parachute Infantry Regiment," 33–34; Headquarters, 14th Antiaircraft Command, "Report on War Damage to the

Harbor Defenses of Manila and Subic Bays," October 6, 1945, U.S. Army Heritage and Education Center, Carlisle, PA.

20. Belote and Belote, *Corregidor*, 215; Flannagan, *Corregidor*, 219; Levine, "Operations of the 503d Parachute Infantry Regiment," 64; Prisoner of War Preliminary Interrogation Report: Kusama Kazuo, March 19, 1945, in Sixth Army Advanced Echelon Interrogation Report Number 392, document number 21 IR 392, in *Wartime Translations of Seized Japanese Documents*; Flash, "The Operations of the 2D Battalion, 503d Parachute Infantry Regiment Combat Team," 22; Harold Templeman, *The Return to Corregidor* (New York: Strand Press, 1945), 10.

21. Belote and Belote, *Corregidor*, 215, 217–219; Flannagan, *Corregidor*, 219; Breuer, *Retaking the Philippines*, 196; Hill, "The Operations of Company 'E', 503d Parachute Regiment," 6.

22. Breuer, *Retaking the Philippines*, 193–195; Flannagan, *Corregidor*, 197.

23. Belote and Belote, *Corregidor*, 216.

24. Caskey, "Operations of the 503d Parachute Infantry Regiment Combat Team," 17; Flannagan, *Corregidor*, 207–208, 220.

25. Flannagan, *Corregidor*, 208; Breuer, *Retaking the Philippines*, 208.

26. Crawford, "Operations of 503D Parachute Regiment Combat Team," 27; Breuer, *Retaking the Philippines*, 196–198; Belote and Belote, *Corregidor*, 217–219; Blair, "Operations of the 3D Battalion, 503d Parachute Infantry Regiment," 16; Caskey, "Operations of the 503d Parachute Infantry Regiment Combat Team," 18; Levine, "Operations of the 503d Parachute Infantry Regiment," 40; Edwin H. Felsher, Jr., "The Seizure of Corregidor—February 1945: Role of Airborne Forces in Joint Operations," 7 (May 1973), Folder 4, Box 6, Papers of Edward M. Flannagan, Jr., U.S. Army Heritage and Education Center, Carlisle, PA.

27. Belote and Belote, *Corregidor*, 217–219; Breuer, *Retaking the Philippines*, 196; Hill, "The Operations of Company 'E', 503d Parachute Regiment," 6; Blair, "Operations of the 3D Battalion, 503d Parachute Infantry Regiment," 16; Caskey, "Operations of the 503d Parachute Infantry Regiment Combat Team," 18; Levine, "Operations of the 503d Parachute Infantry Regiment," 40; Edwin H. Felsher, Jr., "The Seizure of Corregidor—February 1945: Role of Airborne Forces in Joint Operations," 7 (May 1973), Folder 4, Box 6, Papers of Edward M. Flannagan, Jr., U.S. Army Heritage and Education Center, Carlisle, PA.

28. Belote and Belote, *Corregidor*, 221.

29. Flannagan, *Corregidor*, 205–206; Matsuki, *Senshi Sosho*, vol. 60, 271.

30. Other writers on the battle for Corregidor attribute the information to Prisoner of War debriefs, but as the only linguist involved in the Rock force, Akune's recollections should be given greater credit. Smith, "Operations of the 'Rock Force,'" 22 and 25; Harrington, *Yankee Samurai*, 264; O'Donnell, *Into the Rising Sun*, 200. Writers attributing the intelligence to prisoner of war debriefs, include Flannagan, *Corregidor*, 268; Breuer, *Retaking the Philippines*, 241.

31. Homer Bigart, "Landing on Corregidor, February 1945: Corregidor Invaders Battle Way Ashore in Hail of Enemy Bullets: Reporter With Them Tells How Machine Guns Raked Up Landing Craft and Men Fought Up Beaches to Make Contact with Paratroopers," in *Forward Positions: The War Correspondence of Homer Bigart*, ed. Betsy Wade (Fayetteville: University of Arkansas Press, 1992), 60.

32. Bigart, "Landing on Corregidor, February 1945," 60; Belote and Belote, *Corregidor*, 124.

33. Bigart, "Landing on Corregidor, February 1945," 60–61.

34. Bigart, "Landing on Corregidor, February 1945," 61.

35. Flannagan, *Corregidor*, 214; Belote and Belote, *Corregidor*, 225.

36. Smith, "Operations of the 'Rock Force,'" 27.

37. Levine, "Operations of the 503d Parachute Infantry Regiment," 33; Flanagan, *Corregidor*, 216.

38. Belote and Belote, *Corregidor*, 231; Caskey, "Operations of the 503d Parachute Infantry Regiment Combat Team," 24; Hill, "The Operations of Company 'E', 503d Parachute Regiment," 18.

39. Crawford, "Operations of 503D Parachute Regiment Combat Team," 33; Flannagan, *Corregidor*, 254; Belote and Belote, *Corregidor*, 235.

40. Bill Calhoun, "The Best Warrior I Ever Knew," The 503D P.R.C.T. Heritage Battalion Online, https://503prct.org/moh/mccarter_calhoun.html; Belote and Belote, *Corregidor*, 237

41. Calhoun, "Best Warrior"; Belote and Belote, *Corregidor*, 237.

42. Calhoun, "Best Warrior"; Belote and Belote, *Corregidor*, 237.

43. Calhoun, "Best Warrior"; Belote and Belote, *Corregidor*, 237–238.

44. Levine, "Operations of the 503d Parachute Infantry Regiment," 64; Prisoner of War Preliminary Interrogation Report: Kusama Kazuo, March 19, 1945, in Sixth Army Advanced Echelon Interrogation Report Number 392, document number 21 IR 392, in *Wartime Translations of Seized Japanese Documents*; Flash, "The Operations of the 2D Battalion, 503d Parachute Infantry Regiment Combat Team," 22; Harold Templeman, *The Return to Corregidor* (New York: Strand Press, 1945), 10.

45. Mastsuki, *Senshi Sosho*, vol. 60, 271.

46. Flannagan, *Corregidor*, 288; Belote and Belote, *Corregidor*, 240; Breuer, *Retaking the Philippines*, 239–240; Matsuki, *Senshi Sosho*, vol. 60, 271.

47. Belote and Belote, *Corregidor*, 238–243; Flannagan, *Corregidor*, 237–238, 247–248; Hill, "The Operations of Company 'E', 503d Parachute Regiment," 39

48. The best-known account of the action on that day is the paper that Hudson Hill wrote while a student at the Infantry School. Writers on the battle have used this account and spread his version of events. Several officers that served under Hill have challenged his version of events: William T. Calhoun and Paul F. Whitman, "The Lost Road," http://corregidor.org/BEA503/features/lostroad. html. The account here is based on the Calhoun/Whitman article. While Hill wrote his account two years afterwards, it is far more colorful and dramatic than

the Calhoun/Whitman article. At first glance, the Calhoun and Whitman article seems suspect. It was written five decades after the battle for Corregidor and memories fade over time. Calhoun and Whitman also used emotional words and assertions, and challenged many accounts as false if they did not line up with their memories. With those points made, there are far more strengths to their account than weaknesses. They consulted others, offered details, and admitted when they did have all the facts. Their account is less colorful than Hill's but is also far more plausible and realistic.

49. Calhoun and Whitman, "The Lost Road," http://corregidor.org/BEA503/featu res/lostroad.html.

50. Calhoun and Whitman, "The Lost Road," http://corregidor.org/BEA503/featu res/lostroad.html. One of the few points of agreements between the Hill and the Calhoun/Whitman account is that Brown died from his wounds, and that Jando and Ball's bodies were never recovered.

51. Belote and Belote, *Corregidor*, 244–246; Flannagan, *Corregidor*, 298.

52. Belote and Belote, *Corregidor*, 244–246.

53. Belote and Belote, *Corregidor*, 246

54. Caskey, "Operations of the 503d Parachute Infantry Regiment Combat Team," 29.

55. Hill, "The Operations of Company 'E', 503d Parachute Regiment," 24, 36–37; XIV Corps, "After Action Report: XIV Corps: M-1 Operation," July 29, 1945, part II, "Administration," 97, Folder 32, Box 3, Papers of Walter Krueger, Cushing Library, Texas A&M University, College Station, TX; Flannagan, *Corregidor*, 254, 259; Smith, "Operations of the 'Rock Force,'" 30–31, 33; Flash, "The Operations of the 2D Battalion, 503d Parachute Infantry Regiment Combat Team," 9, 25.

56. February 18, 1945 entry, in Thomas R. Pardue, "'A' Co. Diary," James Pardue and Paul Whitman, eds. https://www.corregidor.org/BEA503/journals/A_co_diary.html; Levine, "Operations of the 503d Parachute Infantry Regiment," 58; Breuer, *Retaking the Philippines*, 227–228; Flannagan, *Corregidor*, 302.

57. February 18, 1945 entry, in Thomas R. Pardue, "'A' Co. Diary," James Pardue and Paul Whitman, eds. https://www.corregidor.org/BEA503/journals/A_co_diary.html; Levine, "Operations of the 503d Parachute Infantry Regiment," 58; Breuer, *Retaking the Philippines*, 227–228; Flannagan, *Corregidor*, 302.

58. Flash, "The Operations of the 2D Battalion, 503d Parachute Infantry Regiment Combat Team," 25; Postlethwait, "Corregidor Coordination," 16.

59. Hill, "The Operations of Company 'E', 503d Parachute Regiment," 19; Flash, "The Operations of the 2D Battalion, 503d Parachute Infantry Regiment Combat Team," 23; Caskey, "Operations of the 503d Parachute Infantry Regiment Combat Team," 26–27; Levine, "Operations of the 503d Parachute Infantry Regiment," 62.

60. Levine, "Operations of the 503d Parachute Infantry Regiment," 62; Caskey, "Operations of the 503d Parachute Infantry Regiment Combat Team," 26–27.

61. Flannagan, *Corregidor*, 298.

62. Harold Templeman, *The Return to Corregidor*, 24–26; Flannagan, *Corregidor*, 310; George E. Jones, "M'Arthur Raises Corregidor Flag," *The New York Times*, March 3, 1945.

63. Levine, "Operations of the 503d Parachute Infantry Regiment," 58; Flannagan, *Corregidor*, 310–311; "20 Japanese Out of Cave Surrender on Corregidor," *The New York Times*, January 2, 1946.

64. Homer Bigart, "Corregidor's Seizure Opens Up Manila Bay," *New York Herald Tribune*, February 18, 1945; Homer Bigart, "Corregidor's Garrison of 6,000 Destroyed With U.S. Loss 675," *New York Herald Tribune*, March 1, 1945; "The Philippine Liberation and the White Man in Asia," *The Sun* (Baltimore, MD), February 20, 1945; Smith, "Operations of the 'Rock Force,'" 4.

65. James E. Bush, William M. Cochrane, John R. Gingrich, David F. Gross, Craig D. Hackett, and Douglas P. Schultz, "Corregidor—1945," 7–10, Staff Ride Battlebook, 1983, Combat Studies Institute, Combined Arms Research Library, Fort Leavenworth, KS.

CHAPTER 16

1. Report of the 129th Infantry, [no date], Folder 337-INF (129) 0.3 Section III: Intelligence Report, Box 8732, Records of the 37th Infantry Division, World War II Operational Records, Records of the Adjutant General's Staff, Record Group 407, U.S. National Archives, College Park, MD.

2. "Technical Intelligence Team #3 Activity Report, 19 February 1945 to 6 March 1945," March 6, 1945, Folder 337-2, Box 8617, Records of the 37th Infantry Division, World War II Operational Records, Records of the Adjutant General's Staff, Record Group 407, U.S. National Archives, College Park, MD.

3. XIV Corps, "Japanese Defense of Cities as Exemplified by the Battle for Manila" (July 1, 1945), 22, Folder 31, Box 3, Papers of Walter Krueger, Cushing Library, Texas A&M University, College Station, TX.

4. Aluit, *By Fire and Sword*, 5–336.

5. 37th Infantry Division, "Report After Action," September 10, 1945, 71, Folder 4, Box 4, Papers of Robert Krueger, Cushing Library, Texas A&M University, College Station, TX; Frankel, *37th Infantry Division in World War II*, 279–282; Smith, *Triumph in the Philippines*, 283; S-3 Periodic Reports, 145th Infantry, February 19 and 20, 1945, Folder 337-3.3 G-3 JNL File Vol. 12, Box 8675, Box 8675; "A History of the 129th Infantry Regiment," September 15, 1945, Folder 337-INF (129) 0.1, Box 8730, Records of the 37th Infantry Division, Records of the 37th Infantry Division, Record World War II Operational Records, Records of the Adjutant General's Staff, Group 407, U.S. National Archives, College Park, MD.

6. 37th Infantry Division, "Report After Action," September 10, 1945, 71, Folder 4, Box 4, Papers of Robert Krueger, Cushing Library, Texas A&M University, College Station, TX; Frankel, *37th Infantry Division in World War II*, 279–282; Smith, *Triumph in the Philippines*, 283; S-3 Periodic Reports, 145th Infantry,

February 19 and 20, 1945, Folder 337-3.3 G-3 JNL File Vol. 12, Box 8675, Box 8675; "A History of the 129th Infantry Regiment," September 15, 1945, Folder 337-INF (129) 0.1, Box 8730, Records of the 37th Infantry Division, Records of the 37th Infantry Division, Record World War II Operational Records, Records of the Adjutant General's Staff, Group 407, U.S. National Archives, College Park, MD.

7. Smith, *Triumph in the Philippines*, 279–280.

8. Escoda, *Warsaw of Asia*, 278; Exhibit B-60: Testimony of Frederico Garcia, March 8, 1945, 103, in James T. Walsh, "Report of Atrocities Committed by Japanese Imperial Forces Intramuros (Walled City) Manila P.I. During February, 1945," Folder 3, Box 15, Papers of James T. Walsh, Record Group 15, MacArthur Memorial, Norfolk, VA; Smith, *Triumph in the Philippines*, 279–280.

9. Lewis E. Gleeck, Jr. *Over Seventy-Five Years of Philippine-American History (The Army and Navy Club of Manila)* (Manila: Carmello & Bauermann, 1976), 47.

10. Escoda, *Warsaw of Asia*, 278; Exhibit B-60: Testimony of Frederico Garcia, March 8, 1945, 103, in James T. Walsh, "Report of Atrocities Committed by Japanese Imperial Forces Intramuros (Walled City) Manila P.I. During February, 1945," Folder 3, Box 15, Papers of James T. Walsh, Record Group 15, MacArthur Memorial, Norfolk, VA; Smith, *Triumph in the Philippines*, 279–280.

11. "Inventory of General Douglas MacArthur's and Manila Hotel's Properties in the Presidential Suite" no date, Folder 1, Box 5, Records of Headquarters, Southwest Pacific Area, Record Group 5, MacArthur Memorial, Norfolk, VA.

12. Smith, *Triumph in the Philippines*, 280.

13. Douglas MacArthur, *Reminiscences* (New York; McGraw-Hill, 1964), 247; Swift to MacArthur, January 31, 1945 and "Inventory of General Douglas MacArthur's and Manila Hotel's Properties in the Presidential Suite," no date, Folder 1, Box 5, Records of Headquarters, Southwest Pacific Area, Record Group 5, MacArthur Memorial, Norfolk, VA.

14. Dos Passos, *Tour of Duty*, 194–195.

15. MacArthur, *Reminiscences*, 247.

16. Martin Gonzales, Oral History (November 21, 2011), 68–69, Nimitz Education and Research Center, National Museum of the Pacific War, Fredericksburg, TX.

17. MacArthur, *Reminiscences*, 247.

18. Based on personal observations of the author of the Arthur and Douglas MacArthur book collection housed at the MacArthur Memorial, Norfolk, VA. Kenneth Ray Young, *The General's General: The Life and Times of Arthur MacArthur* (Boulder, CO: Westview Press, 1994), xv

19. Translation of Japanese Field Order, February 17, 1945, Translation Number L378D22, February 19, 1945 and Translation of Captured Platoon Leader's Order, February 17, Translation Number L378D23, February 19, 1945, Folder 337-2 A/A Rpt Annex 2 Int—Appendix A(2) 173rd Language Detachment, Box 8616, Records of the 37th Infantry Division, World War II Operational Records, Records of the Adjutant General's Staff, Record Group 407, U.S.

National Archives, College Park, MD; Baba to Commanding Officer, February 20, 1945, in *Message Book of Probationary Officer Baba Masanori* in XIV Corps Advanced Echelon Translation Number 78, document number 26 T 78, in *Wartime Translations of Seized Japanese Documents*.

20. Smith, *Triumph in the Philippines*, 288–289.

21. Smith, *Triumph in the Philippines*, 288–289.

22. Smith, *Triumph in the Philippines*, 288–289; Allan MacDonald, "My Life in the 1st Cavalry Division," *Saber* (January/February 2013), 21–22; 1st Cavalry Division S-3 Periodic Report, February 22, 1945, Folder 337-3.3 G-3 JNL File Vol. 12, Box 8675, Records of the 37th Infantry Division, World War II Operational Records, Records of the Adjutant General's Staff, Record Group 407, U.S. National Archives, College Park, MD.

23. 37th Infantry After Action Report: Annex 2: Appendix A p. 19, Folder 337-2, Box 8617, Records of the 37th Infantry Division, World War II Operational Records, Records of the Adjutant General's Staff, Record Group 407, U.S. National Archives, College Park, MD.

24. Smith, *Triumph in the Philippines*, 288–289; 1st Cavalry Brigade G-2 to 1st Cavalry Brigade G-3, February 23, 1945, Folder 337-3.3 G-3 JNL File Vol. 12, Box 8675, Records of the 37th Infantry Division, World War II Operational Records, Records of the Adjutant General's Staff, Record Group 407, U.S. National Archives, College Park, MD.

25. Frankel, *37th Infantry Division in World War II*, 286–287; Smith, *Triumph in the Philippines*, 285.

26. Frankel, *37th Infantry Division in World War II*, 286–287; Smith, *Triumph in the Philippines*, 285; XIV Corps, "After Action Report: XIV Corps: M-1 Operation," July 29, 1945, 113–114, Folder 32, Box 3, Papers of Walter Krueger, Cushing Library, Texas A&M University, College Station, TX.

27. XIV G-3 Operations Report, February 22, 1945, Folder 337-3.3 G-3 JNL File Vol. 12, Box 8675, Records of the 37th Infantry Division, World War II Operational Records, Records of the Adjutant General's Staff, Record Group 407, U.S. National Archives, College Park, MD.

28. Connaughton, Pimlott, and Anderson, *Battle for Manila*, 157.

29. Beightler to Kirk, February 21, 1945, Folder 2, Box 1, Papers of Robert Beightler, Ohio Historical Society, Columbus, OH.

30. 117th Engineer Combat Battalion Unit Report, February 18, 19, and 22, 1945, Folder 337-3.3 G-3 JNL File Vol. 12, Box 8675, Records of the 37th Infantry Division, World War II Operational Records, Records of the Adjutant General's Staff, Record Group 407, U.S. National Archives, College Park, MD.

31. Holzem, "Jim Holzem's Story," 13.

32. Anthony K. Gemematas, "Headquarters Second Battalion: Nasugbu to Manila," *Voice of the Angels*, August 15, 1984, 12–13, 17.

33. Smith, *Triumph in the Philippines*, 274: Angela Perez Miller, "Manuel Perez, Jr." (March 2004), VOCES Oral History Center, University of Texas, Austin, TX, http://www.voces.moody.utexas.edu/collections/stories/manuel-perez-jr.

34. Smith, *Triumph in the Philippines*, 274: Angela Perez Miller, "Manuel Perez, Jr." (March 2004), VOCES Oral History Center, University of Texas, Austin, TX http://www.voces.moody.utexas.edu/collections/stories/manuel-perez-jr.

35. Holzem, "Jim Holzem's Story," 13.

36. D. J. McSweeny, "C-127 Engrs," Voice of the Angels (June 15, 1982), 16–17.

37. Peter MacFarland, Oral History (January 19, 2011), second part, 21, Oral History Collection, Record Group 32, MacArthur Memorial, Norfolk, VA.

38. Lahti, Memoirs of an Angel, 75.

39. E. M. Flanagan, Jr., *The Rakkasans: The Combat History of the 187th Airborne Infantry* (Novato, CA: Presidio Press, 1997), 99–100.

40. Smith, *Triumph in the Philippines*, 274; Wright, *The 1st Cavalry in World War II*, 136.

41. Swing to March, February 21, 1945, in Yee, ed., *Dear General*, 18; 1st Cavalry Division G-3 Operations Report, February 18, 1945; XIV Corps G-3 Operations Reports, February 18 and 19, 1945, Folder 337-3.3, Box 8675, Records of the 37th Infantry Division, World War II Operational Records, Records of the Adjutant General's Staff, Record Group 407, U.S. National Archives, College Park, MD.

42. Henry A. Burgess, *Looking Back* (Missoula, MT: Pictorial History Publishing Company, 1993), 100.

43. XIV Corps G-3 Operations Report, February 19, 1945, Folder 337-3.3 G-3 JNL File Vol. 12, Box 8675, Records of the 37th Infantry Division, World War II Operational Records, Records of the Adjutant General's Staff, Record Group 407, U.S. National Archives, College Park, MD.

44. D. J. McSweeny, "C-127 Engrs," Voice of the Angels (June 15, 1982), 16–17; 1st Cavalry Division G-3 Operations Report, February 20, 1945, Folder 901-3.1, Box 13305, Records of the 1st Cavalry Division, World War II Operational Records, Records of the Adjutant General's Staff, Record Group 407, U.S. National Archives, College Park, MD.

45. Swindler to Burgess, May 12, 1988, Folder 4, Box 6, Papers of Edward M. Flanagan, U.S. Army Heritage and Education Center, Carlise Barracks, PA.

46. 672nd Amphibious Tractor Battalion Unit Report, February 18, 1945; 37th Infantry Division Artillery S-3 Report, February 20, 1945; 37th Infantry Division G-3 Periodic Report, February 20, 1945, Folder 337-3.3 37th Inf Div G-3 JNL File Vol. 11, Box 8675, Records of the 37th Infantry Division, World War II Operational Records, Records of the Adjutant General's Staff, Record Group 407, U.S. National Archives, College Park, MD.

47. 672nd Amphibious Tractor Battalion Unit Report, February 18, 1945; 37th Infantry Division Artillery S-3 Report, February 20, 1945; 37th Infantry Division G-3 Periodic Report, February 20, 1945, Folder 337-3.3 37th Inf Div G-3 JNL File Vol. 11, Box 8675, Records of the 37th Infantry Division, World

War II Operational Records, Records of the Adjutant General's Staff, Record Group 407, U.S. National Archives, College Park, MD.

48. Escoda, *Warsaw of Asia*, 283–284.

49. Escoda, *Warsaw of Asia*, 284.

50. Gonzalez, *Manila*, 199–200.

51. Kayashima Koichi Statement, December 10, 1949, Document Number 56696, in "Statements of Japanese Officials on World War II"; Prisoner of War Interrogation Report 37-48: Iwamoto Hidoichi, Folder 337-2 A/A Rpt—Annex 2 Int—Appendix A(3), Box 8617, Records of the 37th Infantry Division, World War II Operational Records, Records of the Adjutant General's Staff, Record Group 407, U.S. National Archives, College Park, MD.

52. Prisoner of War Interrogation Report 37-47: Iwanaga Hisanobu, February 20, 1945, Folder 337-2 A/A Rpt—Annex 2 Int—Appendix A(3), Box 8617, Records of the 37th Infantry Division, World War II Operational Records, Records of the Adjutant General's Staff, Record Group 407, U.S. National Archives, College Park, MD.

53. 1st Cavalry Division G-3 Operations Report, February 21, 1945, Folder 901-3.1, Box 13305, Records of the 1st Cavalry Division, World War II Operational Records, Records of the Adjutant General's Staff, Record Group 407, U.S. National Archives, College Park, MD; Kayashima Koichi Statement, December 10, 1949, Document Number 56696, in "Statements of Japanese Officials on World War II"; Interrogation Report 37-56: China Asakichi, February 26, 1945, Folder 337-2 A/A Rpt—Annex 2 Int—Appendix A(3), Box 8617, Records of the 37th Infantry Division, World War II Operational Records, Records of the Adjutant General's Staff, Record Group 407, U.S. National Archives, College Park, MD.

54. Prisoner of War Preliminary Interrogation Report: Izumida Zenzo, March 13, 1945, in XIV Corps Advanced Echelon Interrogation Report Number 63, document number 26 IR 63, in *Wartime Translations of Seized Japanese Documents*.

55. Exhibit B-40: Eugene Donstoff Affidavit, March 5, 1945, in James T. Walsh, "Report of Atrocities Committed by Japanese Imperial Forces Intramuros (Walled City) Manila P.I. During February, 1945," 74, Folder 3, Box 15, Papers of James T. Walsh, Record Group 15, MacArthur Memorial, Norfolk, VA.

56. Shujiro Kobayashi Statement, December 1, 1949, Document Number 564523, in "Statements of Japanese Officials on World War II."

CHAPTER 17

1. February 18–22, 1945 entry, Diary of Oscar W. Griswold, Box 1, Papers of Oscar W. Griswold, U.S. Army Heritage and Education Center, Carlisle Barracks, PA.

2. Stanley Karnow, *In Our Image: America's Empire in the Philippines* (New York: Random House, 1989), 30–77.

3. Martha Pollak, *Cities at War in Early Modern Europe* (New York: Cambridge University Press, 2010), 1–8; Stephen L. Garay, "The Breach of the Intramuros" (May 1, 1948), 17, 19, Advanced Officers Class Number 1, General Instruction Department, The Armored School, Fort Knox, KY.

4. Prisoner of War Interrogation Report 37-52: Hashi Mitsuo and Toka Toshimatsu, February 24, 1945; Prisoner of War Interrogation Report 37-54: Fujikawa Masami, February 25, 1945, Folder 337-2 a/a Rpt—Annex 2, Int—Appendix a (3) 173d Language Det, Box 8616, Records of the 37th Infantry Division, World War II Operational Records, Records of the Adjutant General's Staff, Record Group 407, U.S. National Archives, College Park, MD.

5. XIV Corps, "After Action Report: XIV Corps: M-1 Operation," July 29, 1945, 114–115, 249, Folder 32, Box 3, Papers of Walter Krueger, Cushing Library, Texas A&M University, College Station, TX.

6. XIV Corps, "After Action Report: XIV Corps: M-1 Operation," July 29, 1945, 114–115, 249, Folder 32, Box 3, Papers of Walter Krueger, Cushing Library, Texas A&M University, College Station, TX.

7. February 18–22, 1945 entry, Diary of Oscar W. Griswold, Box 1, Papers of Oscar W. Griswold, U.S. Army Heritage and Education Center, Carlisle, PA.

8. Ohl, *Minuteman*, 188–189; Smith, *Triumph in the Philippines*, 291.

9. Ohl, *Minuteman*, 189–190.

10. February 11–17, 1945 entry, Diary of Oscar W. Griswold, Box 1, Papers of Oscar W. Griswold, U.S. Army Heritage and Education Center, Carlisle, PA.

11. Connaughton, Pimlott, and Anderson, *Battle for Manila*, 163, 195.

12. Beightler to Drugan, February 23, 1945, Folder 2, Box 1, Papers of Robert Beightler, Ohio Historical Society, Columbus, OH; Richard Wilcox Ramsey, *On Law & Country: The Biography and Speeches of Russell Archibald Ramsey* (Boston: Branden Publishing, 1993), 41.

13. Gray to Hulburd, February 24, 1945, Folder 1945 Feb. 21, Box 252, Dispatches from *Time* Magazine Correspondents: First Series, Papers of Roy E. Larsen, Houghton Library, Harvard University, Cambridge, MA.

14. Gray to Hulburd, February 24, 1945, Folder 1945 Feb. 21, Box 252, Dispatches from *Time* Magazine Correspondents: First Series, Papers of Roy E. Larsen, Houghton Library, Harvard University, Cambridge, MA.

15. Smith, *Triumph in the Philippines*, 291, n.1.

16. "Major General Robert S. Beightler's Report on the Activities of the 37th Infantry Division, 1940–1945," 8, Folder 2, Box 1, Papers of Robert Beightler, Ohio Historical Society, Columbus, OH.

17. Exhibit A-2a: Kobayashi Group Order, February 13, 1945 and Exhibit A-2a: Notebook-diary, recovered on February 28, 1945, in James T. Walsh, "Report of Investigation of Atrocities Committed by Japanese Imperial Forces in Intramuros (Walled City) Manila, P.I. During February 1945," Folder 3, Box 15, Papers of James T. Walsh, Record Group 15, MacArthur Memorial, Norfolk, VA.

18. Exhibit D-4: Written Statement of Sister Teresa Vilatela March 9, 1945, in James T. Walsh, "Report of Investigation of Atrocities Committed by Japanese Imperial Forces in Intramuros (Walled City) Manila, P.I. During February 1945," Folder 3, Box 15, Papers of James T. Walsh, Record Group 15, MacArthur Memorial, Norfolk, VA.

19. Escoda, *Warsaw of Asia*, 273–276.

20. February 21, 1945 diary entry, in Labrador, *Diary of the Japanese Occupation*, 275.

21. Walker, *Bracketing the Enemy*, 96.

22. Gray to Hulburd, February 19, 1945, Folder 1945 Feb. 19, Box 252, Dispatches from *Time* Magazine Correspondents: First Series, Papers of Roy E. Larsen, Houghton Library, Harvard University, Cambridge, MA.

23. Prisoner of War Interrogation Report 37-52: Hashi Mitsuo and Toka Toshimatsu, February 24, 1945; and Prisoner of War Interrogation Report 37-54: Fujikawa Masami, February 25, 1945, Folder 337-2 a/a Rpt—Annex 2, Int—Appendix a (3) 173d Language Det, Box 8616, Records of the 37th Infantry Division; Preliminary Interrogation of Prisoner of War: Takemura Shiruichi, March 10, 1945, Folder 901-2.I3 PW Interrogation Reports—Luzon Opn—1st Cav Div, Box 427, Records of the 1st Cavalry Division, World War II Operational Records, Records of the Adjutant General's Staff, Record Group 407, U.S. National Archives, College Park, MA, MD.

24. Report After Action: 173d Language Detachment, 20, Folder 337-2-AA Rpt— Intelligence Narrative Part IV, Box 8617, Records of the 37th Infantry Division, World War II Operational Records, Records of the Adjutant General's Staff, Record Group 407, U.S. National Archives College Park, MD.

25. G-3 Periodic Report, February 23, 1945, Folder 337-3.3 G-3 JNL, Vol. 11 No 2668-2923, Box 8675, Records of the 37th Infantry Division, World War II Operational Records, Records of the Adjutant General's Staff, Record Group 407, U.S. National Archives College Park, MD.

26. Donald Starr, "Tells Hour by Hour Story of Manila Battle," *Chicago Daily Tribune*, February 25, 1945; Frank Kelly, "Manila Battle Over as Infantry Kills Last of Foe in Intramuros," *New York Herald Tribune*, February 25, 1945; Ohl, *Minuteman*, 191.

27. Nelson H. Randall, "The Battle of Manila," *The Field Artillery Journal* (August 1945): 451–456; Gene Sherman, "'Times' Writer Depicts Blasting of Walled City," *Los Angeles Times*, February 22, 1945; Sherman, "Pacific Echoes," Los Angeles Times, March 3, 1945; Gunnison, "The Burning of Manila," 21, 40, 44.

28. Starr, "Tells Hour by Hour Story of Manila Battle."

29. Starr, "Tells Hour by Hour Story of Manila Battle."

30. Walker, *Bracketing the Enemy*, 97.

31. Mathias, *G.I. Jive*, 147.

32. Sherman, "'Times' Writer Depicts Blasting of Walled City."

33. Kelly, "Manila Battle Over as Infantry Kills Last of Foe in Intramuros"; Randall, "The Battle of Manila," 451–456.

34. Owens, *Eye-Deep in Hell*, 122.

35. Prisoner of War Interrogation Report 37-50: Noguchi Kazuo, February 24, 1945, and Prisoner of War Interrogation 37-55: Suda Kazuo February 24, 1945, Folder 337-2 a/a Rpt—Annex 2, Int—Appendix a (3) 173d Language Det, Box 8616, Records of the 37th Infantry Division, World War II Operational Records, Records of the Adjutant General's Staff, Record Group 407, U.S. National Archives, College Park, MD.

36. Dunn, *Pacific Microphone*, 313.

37. Randall, "The Battle of Manila," 451–456; Gordon, "Battle in the Streets," 28; Kelly, "Manila Battle Over as Infantry Kills Last of Foe in Intramuros"; Gray to Hulburd, February 21, 1945, Folder 1945 Feb. 21, Box 252, Dispatches from *Time* Magazine Correspondents: First Series, Papers of Roy E. Larsen, Houghton Library, Harvard University, Cambridge, MA.

38. Robert F. Minch, Oral History (March 29, 2007), 14, Wisconsin Veterans Museum, Madison, WI.

39. Starr, "Tells Hour by Hour Story of Manila Battle"; Dunn, *Pacific Microphone*, 313–314; Kelly, "Manila Battle Over as Infantry Kills Last of Foe in Intramuros."

40. Dunn, *Pacific Microphone*, 314; XIV Corps, "After Action Report: XIV Corps: M-1 Operation," July 29, 1945, 121, Folder 32, Box 3, Papers of Walter Krueger, Cushing Library, Texas A&M University, College Station, TX; Frankel, *The 37th Infantry Division in World War II*, 288.

41. XIV Corps, "After Action Report: XIV Corps: M-1 Operation," July 29, 1945, 121–122, Folder 32, Box 3, Papers of Walter Krueger, Cushing Library, Texas A&M University, College Station, TX; Garay, "The Breach of the Intramuros," 12; G-3 Periodic Report, February 23, 1945, Folder 337-3.3 G-3 JNL, Vol. 11 No 2668-2923, Box 8675, Records of the 37th Infantry Division, World War II Operational Records, Records of the Adjutant General's Staff, Record Group 407, U.S. National Archives College Park, MD.

42. G-3 Periodic Report, 129th Infantry Regiment, February 23, 1945, Folder 337-3.3 G-3 JNL, Vol. 11 No 2668-2923, Box 8675, Records of the 37th Infantry Division, World War II Operational Records, Records of the Adjutant General's Staff, Record Group 407, U.S. National Archives College Park, Maryland; XIV Corps, "After Action Report: XIV Corps: M-1 Operation," July 29, 1945, 122–123, Folder 32, Box 3, Papers of Walter Krueger, Cushing Library, Texas A&M University, College Station, TX.

43. Frankel, *The 37th Infantry Division in World War II*, 291.

44. Prisoner of War Interrogation Report 37-59: Ko Shiu, February 24, 1945; Prisoner of War Interrogation Report 37-53: Mataoka Takashi, February 24, 1945; and Prisoner of War Interrogation Report 37-50: Noguchi Kazuo, February 24, 1945, Folder 337-2 a/a Rpt—Annex 2, Int—Appendix a (3) 173d Language Det, Box 8616, Records of the 37th Infantry Division, World War II Operational Records, Records of the Adjutant General's Staff, Record Group 407, U.S. National Archives, College Park, MD.

45. 117th Engineer Battalion Unit Report, February 24, 1945, Folder 337-3.3 G-3 JNL, Vol. 11 No 2668-2923, Box 8675, Records of the 37th Infantry Division, World War II Operational Records, Records of the Adjutant General's Staff, Record Group 407, US National Archives College Park, Maryland.

46. G-3 Periodic Report, February 23, 1945, Folder 337-3.3 G-3 JNL, Vol. 11 No 2668-2923, Box 8675, Records of the 37th Infantry Division, World War II Operational Records, Records of the Adjutant General's Staff, Record Group 407, U.S. National Archives College Park, MD.

47. G-3 Journal, February 23, 1945, Folder 337-3.3 G-3 JNL, Vol. 11 No 2668-2923, Box 8675, Records of the 37th Infantry Division, World War II Operational Records, Records of the Adjutant General's Staff, Record Group 407, U.S. National Archives College Park, MD.

48. XIV Corps, "After Action Report: XIV Corps: M-1 Operation," July 29, 1945, 123–124, Folder 32, Box 3, Papers of Walter Krueger, Cushing Library, Texas A&M University, College Station, TX; Escoda, *Warsaw of Asia*, 294.

49. XIV Corps, "After Action Report: XIV Corps: M-1 Operation," July 29, 1945, 123–124, Folder 32, Box 3, Papers of Walter Krueger, Cushing Library, Texas A&M University, College Station, TX; Escoda, *Warsaw of Asia*, 295.

50. Aluit, *By Sword and Fire*, 359.

51. Aluit, *By Sword and Fire*, 359–360; Frankel, *The 37th Infantry Division in World War II*, 291; Exhibit D-5: Testimony of Sister Concepcion Gotera taken by Col. James T. Walsh, March 2, 1945, in James T. Walsh, "Report of Investigation of Atrocities Committed by Japanese Imperial Forces in Intramuros (Walled City) Manila, P.I. During February 1945," Folder 3, Box 15, Papers of James T. Walsh, Record Group 15, MacArthur Memorial, Norfolk, VA.

52. Aluit, *By Sword and Fire*, 361–362.

53. Aluit, *By Sword and Fire*, 361–362.

54. Ohl, *Minuteman*, 192.

55. Frankel, *The 37th Infantry Division in World War II*, 289.

56. XIV Corps, "After Action Report: XIV Corps: M-1 Operation," July 29, 1945, 125, Folder 32, Box 3, Papers of Walter Krueger, Cushing Library, Texas A&M University, College Station, TX; Frankel, *The 37th Infantry Division in World War II*, 291; Krueger, *From Down Under to Nippon*, 250–251.

57. XIV Corps, "After Action Report: XIV Corps: M-1 Operation," July 29, 1945, 125, Folder 32, Box 3, Papers of Walter Krueger, Cushing Library, Texas A&M University, College Station, TX; Frankel, *The 37th Infantry Division in World War II*, 291.

58. February 23, 1945 entry, Diary of Oscar W. Griswold, Box 1, Papers of Oscar W. Griswold, U.S. Army Heritage and Education Center, Carlisle, PA; Bruce Henderson, *Rescue at Los Baños: The Most Daring Prison Camp Raid of World War II* (New York: William Morrow, 2015).

59. Smith, *Triumph in the Philippines*, 288–289; 1st Cavalry Division S-3 Periodic Report, February 22, 1945, Folder 337-3.3 G-3 JNL File Vol. 12, Box 8675, Records of the 37th Infantry Division, World War II Operational Records,

Records of the Adjutant General's Staff, Record Group 407, U.S. National Archives, College Park, MD.

60. Smith, *Triumph in the Philippines*, 288–289; 1st Cavalry Brigade G-2 to 1st Cavalry Brigade G-3, February 23, 1945, Folder 337-3.3 G-3 JNL File Vol. 12, Box 8675, Records of the 37th Infantry Division, World War II Operational Records, Records of the Adjutant General's Staff, Record Group 407, U.S. National Archives, College Park, MD.

61. February 23, 1945 entry, Diary of Oscar W. Griswold, Box 1, Papers of Oscar W. Griswold, U.S. Army Heritage and Education Center, Carlisle, PA.

62. February 23, 1945 entry, Diary of Oscar W. Griswold, Box 1, Papers of Oscar W. Griswold, U.S. Army Heritage and Education Center, Carlisle, PA.

63. Ohl, *Minuteman*, 193.

64. Ohl, *Minuteman*, 193.

65. Ohl, *Minuteman*, 193.

66. Ohl, *Minuteman*, 193.

67. Preliminary Interrogation of Prisoner of War: Takemura Shiruichi, March 10, 1945, Folder 901–2.I3 PW Interrogation Reports—Luzon Opn—1st Cav Div, Box 427, Records of the 1st Cavalry Division, World War II Operational Records, Records of the Adjutant General's Staff, Record Group 407, U.S. National Archives, College Park, MD.

68. G-3 Periodic Report, February 25, 1945, Folder 337-3.3 G-3 JNL, Vol. 11 No 2668-2923, Box 8675, Records of the 37th Infantry Division, World War II Operational Records, Records of the Adjutant General's Staff, Record Group 407, U.S. National Archives College Park, MD.

69. Wright, *The 1st Cavalry Division in World War II*, 140.

70. Wright, *The 1st Cavalry Division in World War II*, 140.

71. Wright, The 1st Cavalry Division in World War II, 140–142.

72. Exhibit B-4: Incl. 1: John Fredrick, "Report of Atrocities at Fort Santiago, Intramuros, City of Manila, March 1, 1945; Incl. 2: Affidavit of John D. Fredrick, March 1, 1945, in James T. Walsh, "Report of Investigation of Atrocities Committed by Japanese Imperial Forces in Intramuros (Walled City) Manila, P.I. During February 1945," Folder 3, Box 15, Papers of James T. Walsh, Record Group 15, MacArthur Memorial, Norfolk, VA.

73. Frankel, *The 37th Infantry Division in World War II*, 292.

74. "Americans Rip Through Walls of Intramuros," *New York Herald Tribune*, February 24, 1945.

75. Exhibit A-1: Introduction, 1, in James T. Walsh, "Report of Investigation of Atrocities Committed by Japanese Imperial Forces in Intramuros (Walled City) Manila, P.I. During February 1945," Folder 3, Box 15, Papers of James T. Walsh, Record Group 15, MacArthur Memorial, Norfolk, VA.

76. Communique 1055, February 25, 1945, Folder 3, Box 48, Records of Headquarters, U.S. Army Pacific Area, Record Group 4, MacArthur Memorial, Norfolk, VA.

77. Communique 1055, February 25, 1945, Folder 3, Box 48, Records of Headquarters, U.S. Army Pacific Area, Record Group 4, MacArthur Memorial, Norfolk, VA. "Manila Foe Annihilated," *The Sun* (Baltimore, Maryland), February 25, 1945.

78. Smith, *Triumph in the Philippines*, 302.

CHAPTER 18

1. Sixth U.S. Army, "Report of the Luzon Campaign 9 January 1945–30 June 1945," vol. I, 40, Skelton Combined Arms Research Library, Fort Leavenworth, KS.

2. 37th Cavalry Reconnaissance Troop Mechanized, February 23, 1945; 117th Engineer Battalion Unit Report, February 23 and 24, 1945, Folder 337-3.3 37th INF DIV G-3 JNL Files, Box 8676, Records of the 37th Infantry Division, Record Group 407, U.S. National Archives College Park, MD.

3. "A History of the 129th Infantry," Folder 337-INF (129)0.1, Box 8730; XIV Corps G-3 Report, February 25, 1945, and 1st Cavalry Division G-3 Report, February 28, 1945 and 37th Infantry Division G-3 Report, February 26, 1945; 37th Cavalry Reconnaissance Troop Mechanized, February 23, 1945; 117th Engineer Battalion Unit Report, February 23 and 24, 1945, Folder 337-3.3 37th INF DIV G-3 JNL Files Vol. 12, Box 8675; XIV Corps G-3 Report, February 26, 27 and 28, 1945 and 37th Infantry Division G-3 Report, March 3, 1945, Folder 337-3.3 37th INF DIV G-3 JNL Files Vol. 13, Box 8676, Records of the 37th Infantry Division, World War II Operational Records, Records of the Adjutant General's Staff, Record Group 407, U.S. National Archives College Park, MD; George C. Kenney, *General Kenney Reports: A Personal History of the Pacific War* (New York: Duell, Sloan and Pearce, 1949), 524–525.

4. February 24, 1945 entry, Diary of Oscar W. Griswold, Box 1, Papers of Oscar W. Griswold, U.S. Army Heritage and Education Center, Carlisle Barracks, PA.

5. Prisoner of War Interrogation Report 37-53: Nataoka Takoshi, February 24, 1945, Folder 337-2 A/A Rpt Annex 2 Int—Appendix A(3) 173rd Language Detachment, Box 8617; XIV Corps G-3 Report, February 25, 1945; 37th Infantry Division G-3 Report, February 27, 1945; 1st Cavalry Division G-3 Report, February 26, 1945; S-3 Periodic Report 1st Cavalry Brigade, March 1, 1945; 1st Cavalry Division G-3 Report, February 28 and March 1, 1945, Folder 337-3.3 37th INF DIV G-3 JNL Files, Box 8676, Records of the 37th Infantry Division, World War II Operational Records, Records of the Adjutant General's Staff, Record Group 407, U.S. National Archives College Park, MD; Gray to Hulburd, March 1, 1945, Folder 1945 Mar. 1, Box 255, Dispatches from *Time* Magazine Correspondents: First Series, Papers of Roy E. Larsen, Houghton Library, Harvard University, Cambridge, MA.

6. On March 1, 1945, the military intelligence specialists produced one document reporting on their interrogations of twenty-two prisoners that surrendered. Rather than list the names of all twenty-two, this citation refers to the interrogation report number for all twenty-two. Prisoner of War Interrogation Report

37-68, March 1, 1945, Folder 337-2 A/A Rpt—Annex 2 Int—Annex A(3), Box 8617, Records of the 37th Infantry Division, World War II Operational Records, Records of the Adjutant General's Staff, Record Group 407, U.S. National Archives College Park, MD, and Prisoner of War Interrogation Report 37-65: Morio Shigetoshi, February 28, 1945, Folder 337-2 A/A Rpt Annex 2 Int—Appendix A(3) 173rd Language Detachment, Box 8617, Records of the 37th Infantry Division, World War II Operational Records, Records of the Adjutant General's Staff, Record Group 407, U.S. National Archives College Park, MD; Prisoner of War Joint Preliminary Interrogation Report: Kichiei Minoru, March 18, 1945, in XIV Corps Advanced Echelon Interrogation Report Number 61, document number 26 IR 61, in *Wartime Translations of Seized Japanese Documents.*

7. XIV Corps, "After Action Report: XIV Corps: M-1 Operation," July 29, 1945, 129–130, Folder 32, Box 3, Papers of Walter Krueger, Cushing Library, Texas A&M University, College Station, TX.

8. Smith, *Triumph in the Philippines*, 301–302; Prisoner of War Preliminary Interrogation Report: Izumida Zenzo, March 13, 1945, in XIV Corps Advanced Echelon Interrogation Report Number 63, document number 26 IR 63, *Wartime Translations of Seized Japanese Documents.*

9. Prisoner of War Preliminary Interrogation Report 37-60: Hayashi Toshime, February 27, 1945, Folder 337-2 A/A Rpt—Annex 2 Int—Annex A(3), Box 8617, Records of the 37th Infantry Division, World War II Operational Records, Records of the Adjutant General's Staff, Record Group 407, U.S. National Archives College Park, MD.

10. Preliminary Interrogation of Prisoner of War 1CD-17556J: Okazaki Tatsumi, March 5, 1945, Folder 901-2.13 PW Intelligence Reports, Box 427, Records of the 1st Cavalry Division, Records of the Adjutant General's Office, Record Group 407, U.S. National Archives, College Park, MD.

11. 117th Engineer Battalion Unit Report, February 26 and 27, 1945, Folder 337-3.3 37th INF DIV G-3 JNL Files Vol. 13, Box 8676, Records of the 37th Infantry Division, Records of the Adjutant General's Office, Record Group 407, U.S. National Archives, College Park, MD.

12. 117th Engineer Battalion Unit Report, February 24, 1945, Folder 337-3.3 37th INF DIV G-3 JNL Files Vol. 12, Box 8675, Records of the 37th Infantry Division, Records of the Adjutant General's Office, Record Group 407, U.S. National Archives, College Park, MD.

13. Prisoner of War Preliminary Interrogation Report: Izumida Zenzo, March 13, 1945, in XIV Corps Advanced Echelon Interrogation Report Number 63, document number 26 IR 63, in *Wartime Translations of Seized Japanese Documents.*

14. Labrador, *A Diary of the Japanese Occupation*, 279–280.

15. Heinrichs and Gallicchio, *Implacable Foes*, 257, 314, 321–325.

16. Edwin E. Hanson, "My Military History," 46–47, 37th Infantry Division, World War II Army Service Experiences Questionnaire, U.S. Army History and

Heritage Command, Carlisle, PA. The questionnaires of many other soldiers support this assessment: George K. Sitzler, Cletus J. Schwab, Charles A. Henne, Floyd E. Todd, and Lynn L. Simpson, Army Service Experiences Questionnaires, 37th Infantry Division, World War II Army Service Experiences Questionnaires, U.S. Army Heritage and Education Center, Carlisle, PA. Sitzler's comments are something of an outlier. He noted that resentment of replacements continued on into the postwar years at unit reunions.

17. John C. Dilks, Pat Shovlin, and Salvatore V. DeGaetano, 1st Cavalry Division Collection, World War II Army Service Experiences Questionnaires, U.S. Army Heritage and Education Center, Carlisle, PA.

18. Brian Lockman, *World War II Reflections: An Oral History of Pennsylvania's Veterans* (Mechanicsburg, PA: Stackpole Books, 2009), 119.

19. Edwin E. Hanson, "My Military History," 46–47, 37th Infantry Division, World War II Army Service Experiences Questionnaire, U.S. Army History and Heritage Command, Carlisle, PA.

20. Wright, *The 1st Cavalry Division in World War II*, 139.

21. Salvatore V. DeGaetano, 1st Cavalry Division, World War II Army Service Experiences Questionnaire, U.S. Army Heritage and Education Center, Carlisle, PA.

22. Salvatore V. DeGaetano, 1st Cavalry Division, World War II Army Service Experiences Questionnaire, U.S. Army Heritage and Education Center, Carlisle, PA.

23. James T. Patterson, *Grand Expectations: The United States, 1945–1974* (New York: Oxford University Press, 1996), 17.

24. For other veterans surveys that discuss religion, see Lynn L. Simpson and Floyd E. Todd, 37th Infantry Division, World War II Army Service Experiences Questionnaires, Pat Shovlin, 1st Cavalry Division Collection, World War II Army Service Experiences Questionnaire, U.S. Army Heritage and Education Center, Carlisle, PA; Emanuel F. Jensen Word War II Veteran Survey, Folder 1, Box 21, Record Group 237, Tennessee State Archives, Nashville, TN.

25. Charles A. Henne, Julius Gassner, and Frank F. Mathias, 37th Infantry Division, World War II Army Service Experiences Questionnaires, U.S. Army Heritage and Education Center, Carlisle, PA.

26. February 28, March 1, and March 2 unit diary entries, Headquarters, 754th Tank Battalion, "Battle of Luzon: 754th Tank Battalion," Ike Skelton Combined Arms Research Library, Ft. Leavenworth, KS.

27. Smith, *Triumph in the Philippines*, 303.

28. XIV Corps, "After Action Report: XIV Corps: M-1 Operation," July 29, 1945, 130, Folder 32, Box 3, Papers of Walter Krueger, Cushing Library, Texas A&M University, College Station, TX.

29. Matsuki, *Senshi Sosho*, vol. 60, 272; Connaughton, Pimlott, and Anderson, *Battle for Manila*, 171; Prisoner of War Interrogation Report 37-62: Nishioka Hanichi, February 27, 1945, Folder 337-2 A/A—Annex 2 Int—Appendix A

(3), Box 8617, Records of the 37th Infantry Division, World War II Operational Records, Records of the Adjutant General's Staff, Record Group 407, U.S. National Archives College Park, MD; S-3 Periodic Report 1st Cavalry Brigade, February 27, 1945 and S-3 Periodic Report, 145th Infantry, February 26 and 27, 1945; G-3 Report, 37th Infantry Division, February 28, 195, Folder 337-3.3 37th INF DIV G-3 JNL Files, Box 8676, Records of the 37th Infantry Division, World War II Operational Records, Records of the Adjutant General's Staff, Record Group 407, U.S. National Archives College Park, MD; Intelligence Narrative, Box 8617, Records of the 37th Infantry Division, World War II Operational Records, Records of the Adjutant General's Staff, Record Group 407, U.S. National Archives College Park, MD; Prisoner of War Interrogation Report: 37-64, February 28, 1945, Folder 337-2 A/A—Annex 2 Int—Appendix A (3), Box 8617, Records of the 37th Infantry Division, World War II Operational Records, Records of the Adjutant General's Staff, Record Group 407, U.S. National Archives College Park, MD; Prisoner of War Preliminary Interrogation Report: Izumida Zenzo, March 13, 1945, in XIV Corps Advanced Echelon Interrogation Report Number 63, document number 26 IR 63, in *Wartime Translations of Seized Japanese Documents*.

30. Prisoner of War Preliminary Interrogation Report 37-60: Hayashi Toshime, February 27, 1945, and Prisoner of War Interrogation Report 37-63: Akitake Moriichi, February 27, 1945, Folder 337-2 A/A Rpt—Annex 2 Int—Annex A(3), Box 8617, and 37th Infantry Division G-3 Report, February 26 and 27, 1945, Folder 337-3.3 37th INF DIV G-3 JNL Files, Box 8676, Records of the 37th Infantry Division, World War II Operational Records, Records of the Adjutant General's Staff, Record Group 407 U.S. National Archives College Park, MD.

31. 117th Engineer Battalion Unit Report, February 28, 1945; 37th Infantry Division G-3 Report, February 26 and 27, 1945, Folder 337-3.3 37th INF DIV G-3 JNL Files, Box 8676, Records of the 37th Infantry Division, World War II Operational Records, Records of the Adjutant General's Staff, Record Group 407, U.S. National Archives College Park, MD.

32. Smith, *Triumph in the Philippines*, 304; Frankel, *The 37th Infantry Division in World War II*, 294.

33. Prisoner of War Interrogation Report 37-62: Nishioka Hanichi, February 27, 1945, Folder 337-2 A/A—Annex 2 Int—Appendix A (3), Box 8617, Records of the 37th Infantry Division, World War II Operational Records, Records of the Adjutant General's Staff, Record Group 407, U.S. National Archives College Park, MD; Prisoner of War Preliminary Interrogation Report Number 63, document 26 IR 63, Izumida Zenzo, March 13, 1945, in *Wartime Translations of Seized Japanese Documents*.

34. S-2 Periodic Report, 1st Cavalry Brigade, February 24, 1945, Folder 337-3.3 G-3 JNL File Vol. 12, Box 8675, Records of the 37th Infantry Division, World War

II Operational Records, Records of the Adjutant General's Staff, Record Group 407 U.S. National Archives College Park, MD.

35. Smith, *Triumph in the Philippines*, 304–305; S-3 Periodic Report, March 1, 1945, Folder 337-3.3 37th INF DIV G-3 JNL Files Vol. 13, Box 8676, Records of the 37th Infantry Division, World War II Operational Records, Records of the Adjutant General's Staff, Record Group 407, U.S. National Archives College Park, MD.

36. Smith, *Triumph in the Philippines*, 304–305.

37. Smith, *Triumph in the Philippines*, 306.

38. McEnery, *The XIV Corps Battle for Manila*, 102; XIV Corps, "After Action Report: XIV Corps: M-1 Operation," July 29, 1945, 130, Folder 32, Box 3, Papers of Walter Krueger, Cushing Library, Texas A&M University, College Station, TX.

39. Fellers to Fellers, February 1945, Folder 17, Box 1, Papers of Bonner Fellers, Record Group 44A, MacArthur Memorial, Norfolk, VA; Kenney, *General Kenney Reports*, 525.

40. Aluit, *By Sword and Fire*, 367.

41. Samuel Yorty, Oral History (August 15–October 3, 1985), 73, Oral History Program, University of California Los Angeles, Los Angeles, CA.

42. Aluit, *By Sword and Fire*, 367.

43. Aluit, *By Sword and Fire*, 367–368.

44. Aluit, *By Sword and Fire*, 367–368.

45. Osmeña Speech, February 27, 1945, in Jose, ed. *World War II and the Japanese Occupation*, 307–310.

46. Emphasis in the original. Whitney to Whitney, February 26, 1945, Folder 7, Box 10, Papers of Courtney Whitney, Record Group 16, MacArthur Memorial, Norfolk, VA.

47. Wright, *The 1st Cavalry Division in World War II*, 141.

48. February 28, 1945 entry, Diary of Oscar W. Griswold, Box 1, Papers of Oscar W. Griswold, U.S. Army Heritage and Education Center, Carlisle Barracks, PA; Wright, *The 1st Cavalry Division in World War II*, 141; Stevens to Winzeler, July 17, 1972, Folder MG Vernon D. Mudge, Box 22, World War II Collection, 1st Cavalry Division Museum, Fort Hood, TX.

49. Prisoner of War Interrogation Report 37-57: Yap Yon Yok, February 26, 1945; and Prisoner of War Interrogation Report 37-65: Ota Akira, February 27, 1945, Folder 337-2 A/A Rpt Annex 2 Int—Appendix A(3) 173rd Language Detachment, Box 8617, Records of the 37th Infantry Division, World War II Operational Records, Records of the Adjutant General's Staff, Record Group 407, U.S. National Archives College Park, MD.

50. Prisoner of War Interrogation Report 37-68, March 1, 1945, Folder 337-2 A/A Rpt—Annex 2 Int—Annex A(3), Box 8617, Records of the 37th Infantry Division, World War II Operational Records, Records of the Adjutant General's Staff, Record Group 407, U.S. National Archives College Park, MD, and

Prisoner of War Interrogation Report 37-65: Morio Shigetoshi, February 28, 1945, Folder 337-2 A/A Rpt Annex 2 Int—Appendix A(3) 173rd Language Detachment, Box 8617, Records of the 37th Infantry Division, World War II Operational Records, Records of the Adjutant General's Staff, Record Group 407, U.S. National Archives College Park, MD.

51. Prisoner of War Interrogation Report 37-57: Yap Yon Yok, February 26, 1945; and Prisoner of War Interrogation Report 37-65: Ota Akira, February 27, 1945, Folder 337-2 A/A Rpt Annex 2 Int—Appendix A(3) 173rd Language Detachment, Box 8617, Records of the 37th Infantry Division, World War II Operational Records, Records of the Adjutant General's Staff, Record Group 407, U.S. National Archives College Park, MD; Prisoner of War Preliminary Interrogation Report: Uchida Kensaburo, March 4, 1945, in XIV Corps Advanced Echelon Interrogation Report Number 51, document number 26 IR 51; Prisoner of War Preliminary Interrogation Report: Kichiei Minoru, Nakamura Hideo and Mihara Katsuji, March 18, 1945, in XIV Corps Advanced Echelon Interrogation Report Number 61, document number 26 IR 61, in *Wartime Translations of Seized Japanese Documents*.

52. Prisoner of War Interrogation Report 37-57: Yap Yon Yok, February 26, 1945 and Prisoner of War Interrogation Report 37-65: Morio Shigetoshi, February 28, 1945, Folder 337-2 A/A Rpt Annex 2 Int—Appendix A(3) 173rd Language Detachment, Box 8617, Records of the 37th Infantry Division, World War II Operational Records, Records of the Adjutant General's Staff, Record Group 407, U.S. National Archives College Park, MD.

53. Prisoner of War Preliminary Interrogation Report: Uchida Kensaburo, March 4, 1945, in XIV Corps Advanced Echelon Interrogation Report Number 51, document number 26 IR 51, in *Wartime Translations of Seized Japanese Documents*.

54. Prisoner of War Preliminary Interrogation Report: Kichiei Minoru, Nakamura Hideo and Mihara Katsuji, March 18, 1945, in XIV Corps Advanced Echelon Interrogation Report Number 61, document number 26 IR 61, in *Wartime Translations of Seized Japanese Documents*.

55. Prisoner of War Interrogation Report 37-69: Hihihara Katsuji, March 3, 1945; Prisoner of War Interrogation Report 37-68, March 1, 1945, Folder 337-2 A/A Rpt—Annex 2 Int—Annex A(3), Box 8617, Records of the 37th Infantry Division, World War II Operational Records, Records of the Adjutant General's Staff, Record Group 407, U.S. National Archives College Park, MD; Prisoner of War Joint Preliminary Interrogation Report: Kichiei Minoru, March 18, 1945, in XIV Corps Advanced Echelon Interrogation Report Number 61, document number 26 IR 61, in *Wartime Translations of Seized Japanese Documents*; Report After Action, 1 November 1944–30 June 1945, Annex 2 Intelligence Appendix A 173rd Language Detachment, 23, Folder 337-3.3, Box 8617, Records of the 37th Infantry Division, World War II Operational Records, Records of the Adjutant General's Staff, Record Group 407, U.S. National Archives College Park, MD; Prisoner of War Interrogation Report Murakami Kyozaku, March 19,

1945, in XIV Corps Advanced Echelon Interrogation Report Number 64, document number 26 IR 64, in *Wartime Translations of Seized Japanese Documents*; 37th Infantry Division G-3 Report, March 2, 1945, Folder 337-3.3 37th INF DIV G-3 JNL Files Vol. 13, Box 8676, Records of the 37th Infantry Division, World War II Operational Records, Records of the Adjutant General's Staff, Record Group 407, U.S. National Archives College Park, MD.

56. Prisoner of War Preliminary Interrogation Report: Izumida Zenzo, March 13, 1945, in XIV Corps Advanced Echelon Interrogation Report Number 63, document number 26 IR 63, in *Wartime Translations of Seized Japanese Documents*.

57. Prisoner of War Interrogation Report 37-69: Hihihara Katsuji, March 3, 1945; Prisoner of War Interrogation Report 37-68, March 1, 1945, Folder 337-2 A/A Rpt—Annex 2 Int—Annex A(3), Box 8617, Records of the 37th Infantry Division, World War II Operational Records, Records of the Adjutant General's Staff, Record Group 407, U.S. National Archives College Park, MD; Prisoner of War Joint Preliminary Interrogation Report: Kichiei Minoru, March 18, 1945, in XIV Corps Advanced Echelon Interrogation Report Number 61, document number 26 IR 61, in *Wartime Translations of Seized Japanese Documents*; Report After Action, 1 November 1944–30 June 1945, Annex 2 Intelligence Appendix A 173rd Language Detachment, 23, Folder 337-3.3, Box 8617, Records of the 37th Infantry Division, World War II Operational Records, Records of the Adjutant General's Staff, Record Group 407, U.S. National Archives College Park, MD; Prisoner of War Interrogation Report Murakami Kyozaku, March 19, 1945, in XIV Corps Advanced Echelon Interrogation Report Number 64, document number 26 IR 64, in *Wartime Translations of Seized Japanese Documents*; 37th Infantry Division G-3 Report, March 2, 1945, Folder 337-3.3 37th INF DIV G-3 JNL Files Vol. 13, Box 8676, Records of the 37th Infantry Division, World War II Operational Records, Records of the Adjutant General's Staff, Record Group 407, U.S. National Archives College Park, MD.

58. XIV Corps G-3 Operations Report, March 2, 1945, Folder 337-3.3, Box 8676, Records of the 37th Infantry Division, World War II Operational Records, Records of the Adjutant General's Staff, Record Group 407, U.S. National Archives College Park, MD.

59. G-3 Periodic Report, March 2–3, 1945, Folder 337-3.3, Box 8676, Records of the 37th Infantry Division, World War II Operational Records, Records of the Adjutant General's Staff, Record Group 407, U.S. National Archives College Park, MD.

60. March 3, 1945 entry, Diary of Oscar W. Griswold, Papers of Oscar W. Griswold, U.S. Army Heritage and Education Center, Carlisle, PA.

61. This quotation is from a diary without a name that was recovered in Manila: Diary entry: March 6, 1945, Batch 9073, Item 1, in General Headquarters Bulletin Number 1986, document number 10 B 1986, in *Wartime Translations of Seized Japanese Documents*.

62. Dunn, *Pacific Microphone*, 315; McEnery, *The XIV Corps Battle for Manila*, 126.

63. Frankel, *The 37th Infantry Division in World War II*, 295.

64. McLaurin, Jureidini, and McDonald, "Modern Experience in City Combat" (Aberdeen Proving Ground, MD: U.S. Army Human Engineering Laboratory, 1987), 35; XIV Corps, "After Action Report: XIV Corps: M-1 Operation," July 29, 1945, 135, Folder 32, Box 3, Papers of Walter Krueger, Cushing Library, Texas A&M University, College Station, TX.

CHAPTER 19

1. Millard Tydings, *Providing for the Rehabilitation of the Philippine Islands Report*, Report 755, US Senate, 79th Congress, 1st Session (Washington, DC: U.S. Government Printing Office, 1945).

2. March 17, 1945 diary entry, in Labrador, *Diary of the Japanese Occupation*, 283.

3. "On Riding Home with the C-in-C," May 2, 1945, Folder 7, Box 1, Papers of Bonner Fellers, Record Group 44A, MacArthur Memorial, Norfolk, VA.

4. Eichelberger to Eichelberger, March 4, 24, 1945, in Luvaas, ed., *Dear Miss Em*, 229–231, 236.

5. Clyma, ed., *Connecticut Men of the U.S. Army* 7, no. 14 (October 23, 1945): 3.

6. Clyma, ed., *Connecticut Men of the U.S. Army* 7, no. 11 (October 16, 1945): 6–7.

7. March 17, 1945 diary entry, in Labrador, *Diary of the Japanese Occupation*, 285.

8. "Special Plan for Philippine Civil Administration and Relief," Folder 4, Box 27, Papers of Richard Sutherland, Record Group 30, MacArthur Memorial, Norfolk, VA.

9. McEnery, *The XIV Corps Battle for Manila*, 72, 108–109.

10. XIV Corps, "After Action Report: XIV Corps: M-1 Operation," July 29, 1945, part II, "Administration," 2, Folder 32, Box 3, Papers of Walter Krueger, Cushing Library, Texas A&M University, College Station, TX; Sixth U.S. Army, "Report of the Luzon Campaign 9 January 1945–30 June 1945," vol. IV, "The Engineer," 124, Skelton Combined Arms Research Library, Fort Leavenworth, KS.

11. Clyde D. Eddleman, Oral History (February 11, 1975), 34, Senior Officers Debriefing Program, U.S. Army Heritage and Education Center, Carlisle, PA. Frankel, *The 37th Infantry Division in World War II*, 297; Kidd, "Operations of the 37th Infantry Division," 22; Kevin C. M. Benson, "Manila, 1945: City Fight in the Pacific," in *City Fights: Selected Histories of Urban Combat from World War II to Vietnam*, ed. John Antal and Bradely Gericke (New York: Ballantine Books, 2003), 244.

12. Frankel, *The 37th Infantry Division in World War II*, 299.

13. Clyma, ed., *Connecticut Men of the U.S. Army: Connecticut Veterans Commemorative Booklet* 7, no. 3 (September 18, 1945): 3.

14. Smith, *Triumph in the Philippines*, 306–307; Hayashi Yoshifumi, "Shiryo Shokai: Nihongun no Meirei Denpo ni Miru Manira-sen," [Introduction of Documents: The Battle of Manila as Seen in Japanese Force Orders and Telegrams] *Shizen, Ninghen, Shakai* 48 (2010): 69–95.

15. Preliminary Interrogation of Prisoner of War 1CD-17556J: Okazaki Tatsumi, March 5, 1945, Folder 901-2.13 PW Intelligence Reports, Box 427, Records of the 1st Cavalry Division, Records of the Adjutant General's Office, Record Group 407, U.S. National Archives, College Park, MD.

16. Prisoner of War Interrogation Report Murakami Kyozaku, March 19, 1945, in XIV Corps Advanced Echelon Interrogation Report Number 64, document number 26 IR 64, in *Wartime Translations of Seized Japanese Documents*.

17. Preliminary Interrogation of Prisoner of War 1CD-17560J: Takemura Shiruichi, March 10, 1945, Folder 901-2.13 PW Intelligence Reports, Box 427, Records of the 1st Cavalry Division, Records of the Adjutant General's Office, Record Group 407, US National Archives, College Park, MD.

18. Frankel, *The 37th Infantry Division in World War II*, 300; Yukio Kawamoto, 37th Infantry Division, World War II Army Service Experiences Questionnaire, U.S. Army Heritage and Education Center, Carlisle, PA; William A. Sullivan, Oral History, Interview Number 21 (December 22, 1965), 1651, Columbia University, New York, NY.

19. Frankel, *The 37th Infantry Division in World War II*, 302.

20. Hines and Andrews, *Hugh Meglone Milton*, 47.

21. Sidney F. Mashbir, *I Was an American Spy* (New York: Vantage Press, 1953), 256.

22. Thorpe, *East Wind, Rain*, 179.

23. Millard Tydings, *Providing for the Rehabilitation of the Philippine Islands Report*; "Agenda POA-CBI-SWPA Conference on Mike I and Future Operations," [no date] Annexes I and II to Agenda with Inclosures A, B, and C to Annex II and Annex III with Inclosure B and C to Annex III, Folder 5, Box 25, Papers of Richard Sutherland, Record Group 30, MacArthur Memorial, Norfolk, VA.

24. Pino to Jett, August 15, 1945, in Martha Shipman Andrews, ed., *The Whole Damned World: New Mexico Aggies at War: 1941–1945—World War II Correspondence of Dean Daniel B. Jett* (Las Cruces: New Mexico State University Libraries/Rio Grande Books, 2009), 226.

25. Louis C. Resenstein, Oral History, in Kelly, ed., *Voices of my Comrades*, 408.

26. William A. Sullivan, Oral History, Interview Number 21 (December 22, 1965), 1638–1639, 1645, 1664–1665, 1676, Columbia University, New York, NY.

27. William A. Sullivan, Oral History, Interview Number 21 (December 22, 1965), 1642, Columbia University, New York, NY.

28. William A. Sullivan, Oral History, Interview Number 21 (December 22, 1965), 1642–1646, 1656–1657, 1719, Columbia University, New York, NY.

29. William A. Sullivan, Oral History, Interview Number 21 (December 22, 1965), 1649, 1657–1659, 1663, Columbia University, New York, NY.

30. William A. Sullivan, Oral History, Interview Number 21 (December 22, 1965), 1668–1670, Columbia University, New York, NY.

31. William A. Sullivan, Oral History, Interview Number 21 (December 22, 1965), 1701, Columbia University, New York, NY.

32. William A. Sullivan, Oral History, Interview Number 21 (December 22, 1965), 1701, Columbia University, New York, NY.

33. William A. Sullivan, Oral History, Interview Number 21 (December 22, 1965), 1676–1677, 1681–1691, 1694, Columbia University, New York, NY.

34. Communique 1059, March 1, 1945, Folder 3, Box 48, Record Group 4, MacArthur Memorial, Norfolk, VA; George E. Jones, "First U.S. Freighter Enters Manila Harbor Amid Sniping: First Supply Ship in Manila Harbor: Hungry Mouths and Eager Hands in Manila," *The New York Times*, March 1, 1945; Homer Bigart, "PT Boats Enter Manila Harbor Unchallenged," *New York Herald Tribune*, February 21, 1945.

35. Heinrichs and Gallicchio, *Implacable Foes*, 307–308.

36. Clyma, ed., *Connecticut Men of the United States Army: Connecticut Veterans Commemorative Booklet* 9, no. 4 (December 13, 1945): 12.

37. Forward, Walter Tabary, Jr., Ralph L. Bryant, and Harold G. Martin statements in "GENED History: General Engineer District APO 75 Manila, Philippine Islands, 1945–1946: The Mission and the Men" (1998), 19, 23–24, 29–30. Lewis K Ambrose statement in "GENED History: General Engineer District APO 75 Manila, Philippine Islands, 1945–1946," Addendum I, "The Mission and the Men (Continued)" (1998), 15–18, U.S. Army Heritage and Education Center, Carlisle, PA. These documents appear to have been produced on a desktop computer and bound at a local print shop. It was a retirement project for a number of veterans of this unit and includes many biographical sketches that alumni of the unit provided.

38. Alvin P. Staufer, *United States Army in World War II: The Technical Services: The Quartermaster Corps: Operations in the War Against Japan* (Washington, DC: U.S. Government Printing Office, 1956), 91, 211–212, 235.

39. Thompson and Harris, *The Signal Corps: The Outcome*, 283–284.

40. The numbers on water usage come from Smith, *Triumph in the Philippines*, 367. Heinrichs and Gallicchio, *Implacable Foes*, 310–314 is cited on the condition of ground combat.

41. Smith, *Triumph in the Philippines*, 404–412.

42. Heinrichs and Gallicchio, *Implacable Foes*, 316–317.

43. Empie and Mette, *A Child in the Midst of Battle*, 136–137; XIV Corps, "After Action Report: XIV Corps: M-1 Operation," July 29, 1945, part II, 129–130, Folder 32, Box 3, Papers of Walter Krueger, Cushing Library, Texas A&M University, College Station, TX.

44. Garcia, *It Took Four Years for the Rising Sun to Set*, 157; Alfred J. Vaccacio, Oral History (July 3, 2002), transcription by the author, National Guard Militia Museum of New Jersey, Sea Girt, NJ.

45. Mary-Ellen Condon-Rall and Albert E. Cowdrey, *United States Army in World War II: The Technical Services: The Medical Department: Medical Services in the War Against Japan* (Washington, DC: U.S. Government Printing Office, 1998), 338–339; Garcia, *It Took Four Years for the Rising Sun to Set*, 157.

46. Hines and Andrews, *Hugh Meglone Milton*, 47, 49.

47. Frankel, *The 37th Infantry Division in World War II*, 298; Doeppers, *Feeding Manila*, 330.

48. Em. J. Ghianni World War II Veteran Survey, Folder 4, Box 15, Record Group 237, Tennessee State Library and Archives, Nashville, TN; Joe A. Rackley, Oral History (April 29, 2002), 25, Nimitz Education and Research Center, National Museum of the Pacific War, The National Museum of the Pacific War, Fredericksburg, TX.

49. John A. Del Gallego, *The Liberation of Manila: 28 Days of Carnage, February– March 1945* (Jefferson, NC: McFarland & Company, 2020), 11. The number of one hundred thousand comes from Robert Ross Smith in *Triumph in the Philippines*, 307. This book is a volume in the U.S. Army's official history of World War. Given the authority of this series, many scholars have repeated it, even though Smith offers no documentation for this claim. A careful read of this volume shows that Smith admitted his numbers were, at best, educated guesses. In fact, Richard B. Meixsel, a professor of history at George Mason University, in a detailed study on this figure published on the Corregidor. org website, shows that the original figure in the first draft of the manuscript was five thousand. (Meixsel even includes a digital photograph of the original manuscript.) Beightler argued with Smith that the figure could not have been more than ten thousand. The U.S. Army accused Yamashita of allowing his soldiers to kill sixty thousand people throughout the Philippines Islands, not just Luzon or Manila. Before the publication of *Triumph in the Philippines* the numbers often used for Manila included three thousand, but also thirty thousand. Meixsel casts serious doubt on the number, showing that thirty-five hundred people would have had to die per day to reach one hundred thousand. Since the last week was the siege of the government buildings, this number would have been 4,761, which means the Japanese were killing Americans and Filipinos on a five-to-one basis. The MNDF never approached that type of military efficiency. Even one-to-one seems beyond their abilities. With that point made, it is worth noting that killing unarmed people is a much easier task than doing combat with a competent opponent, and Filipinos died because of factors other than the Japanese. The fire was one. Comparing the deaths in Manila to those in the Chicago Fire of 1871, and the fire that followed the San Francisco earthquake of 1906, suggests a number in the low thousands. Artillery was another source of Filipino deaths. Could US and Japanese artillery be responsible for something around one hundred thousand dead? That seems unlikely. Once MacArthur removed restrictions more Filipinos died, but artillery would have had to kill more than eight thousand per day during the week and a half before the battle became a siege of the government buildings. One thousand per day seems generous but far more realistic. Comparing that number to the amount of ordinance available suggests that the United States simply lacked the munitions necessary to kill that many people. Japanese atrocities were not

an efficient way to kill large numbers and it seems unlikely that these numbers exceeded a ratio of one-half a Filipino killed for every Japanese that died. Taken together, all these "educated guesses" suggest something between twenty thousand to thirty thousand, and even then that range seems generous. Regardless of these calculations, all these numbers represented a serious public health issue, and given the need to quickly dispose of human remains, there is little likelihood of ever obtaining a dependable estimate. As a result, it is better to think not of the human loss, but of the impact the battle had on the living. R. B. Meixsel, "Did 100,000 Civilians Die in the Battle of Manila in 1945?—Robert Ross Smith's Triumph in the Philippines and the Story of a Number," *Corregidor.org*, https://corregidor.org/refdoc/Reference_Reading/Meixsel/DID-100,000-CIVILIANS-DIE-IN-THE-BATTLE-OF-MANILA-IN-1945-/index.html.

50. Mathias, *G.I. Jive*, 149; Lara and Fancher, *Boy Guerrilla*, 73–74; Mañalac, *Manila*, 155; Juergen Goldhagen essay, in Goldhagen, ed., *Manila Memories*, 124; Witthof and Chappell, *Three Years' Internment*, 61; Warne, *Terry*, 256.

51. Rogers, *Bitter Years*, 265.

52. Frankel, *The 37th Infantry Division in World War II*, 301; XIV Corps, "After Action Report: XIV Corps: M-1 Operation," July 29, 1945, part II, "Administration," 3, Folder 32, Box 3, Papers of Walter Krueger, Cushing Library, Texas A&M University, College Station, TX; Francis K. Danquah, "Reports on Philippine Industrial Crops in World War II from Japan's English Language Press," *Agricultural History* 79, no. 1 (Winter 2005): 74-96; Patrick V. Garland and David B. Flohr, "Forensic Sciences in the Pacific Theater of War," *Military Police* (Spring 2019), 36-40.

53. U. Alexis Johnson, with Jef Olivarius McAllister, *The Right Hand of Power* (Englewood Cliffs, NJ: Prentice-Hall, 1984), 72; "Counter Intelligence Corps History and Mission in World War II" (Counter Intelligence Corps School Fort Holabird Baltimore, Maryland), 81; Sixth U.S. Army, "Enemy on Luzon: An Intelligence Summary," December 1, 1945, 77, Skelton Combined Arms Research Library, Fort Leavenworth, KS.

54. David Joel Steinberg, *Philippine Collaboration in World War II* (Ann Arbor: University of Michigan Press, 1967), 200, n. 23.

55. Sherman, "Pacific Echoes," Los Angeles Times, March 1, 1945.

56. Gonzalez, *Manila*, 203–204, 215–216.

57. Carlos P. Romulo, *I See the Philippines Rise* (Garden City, NY: Doubleday & Company, 1946), 222, 227–228.

58. Sherman, "Pacific Echoes," Los Angeles Times, March 1, 2, 4 and 7, 1945.

59. March 17, 1945 diary entry, in Labrador, *Diary of the Japanese Occupation*, 290. Even Sherman's reporting that found many people in church oblivious to their pain worked against his commentary. For an example, see Sherman, "Pacific Echoes," Los Angeles Times, March 4, 1945.

60. Ephraim, *Escape to Manila*, 169–170.

61. Sam Kraus, Oral History (January 28, 2002), 19–23, Florida State University, Tallahassee, FL.

62. Staufer, *Quartermaster Corps: Operations in the War Against Japan*, 318.

63. Staufer, *Quartermaster Corps: Operations in the War Against Japan*, 318.

64. Sherman, "Pacific Echoes," Los Angeles Times, March 2, 1945.

65. George E. Jones, "Manila Hospitals Also Waging a War," *The New York Times*, February 23, 1945.

66. Milton Berkes, Oral History (October 11, 2007), 8, Oral History Project, Pennsylvania House of Representatives Archives, Harrisburg, PA.

67. March 17, 1945 diary entry, in Labrador, *Diary of the Japanese Occupation*, 287.

68. Earl M. Hoff, "A Free Press for Manila," manuscript, 9–13, Folder Flashbacks From My War Files on the Philippines, Box 117, Papers of Carl and Shelly Mydans, Beinecke Library, Yale University, New Haven, CT.

69. Communique 1059, March 1, 1945, Folder 3, Box 48, Record Group 4, MacArthur Memorial, Norfolk, VA; Jones, "First U.S. Freighter Enters Manila Harbor Amid Sniping"; Bigart, "PT Boats Enter Manila Harbor Unchallenged."

70. Beightler to Kirk, February 21, 1945, Folder 3, Box 1, Papers of Robert S. Beightler, Ohio Historical Society, Columbus, OH.

71. Warne, *Terry*, 140–141; "Parents See Son's Picture in Movies," *The Amherst News-Times* (Amherst, OH), October 11, 1945; Marie Grimes and Hat Diller, eds. *Philippine Postscripts* (March 1945) and (April 1945), Folder G, Box 2, Papers of Edmund J. Lilly, Jr., Ike Skelton Combined Arms Research Library, U.S. Army Command and General Staff College, Fort Leavenworth, KS.

72. Gordon Walker, "Now the Story of Manila Can Be Told: Battle of Manila an Epic of American Heroism," *Christian Science Monitor*, March 28, 1945; Gunnison, "The Burning of Manila," 21, 40, 44; Royal Arch Gunnison, "Jap Shelling of Civilians at Santo Tomás Described," *The Sun* (Baltimore, MD), March 7, 1945.

73. Escoda, *Warsaw of Asia*, 292, 307, 325, 331; Aluit, *By Sword and Fire*, 407–409.

74. Escoda, *Warsaw of Asia*, 325; Florentino Rodao, "Spanish Language in the Philippines: 1900–1940," *Philippine Studies* 45, no. 1 (First Quarter 1997): 94–107.

75. Cristina Patoja Hidalgo, "Metro Manila: City in Search of a Myth," *Philippine Studies* 50, no. 3 (Third Quarter, 1997): 303–326.

76. U. Alexis Johnson, Oral History (June 19, 1975), 4–5, Harry S. Truman Presidential Library, Independence, MO.

77. U. Alexis Johnson, *The Right Hand of Power*, 71–72.

78. Ball to Jett, October 24, 1945, in Andrews, ed., *The Whole Damned World*, 235.

79. Clyma, ed., *Connecticut Men of the United States Army* 9, no. 17 (): 12.

80. Edwin E. Hanson, "My Military History," 46, 37th Infantry Division, World War II Army Service Experiences Questionnaire, U.S. Army History and Heritage Command, Carlisle, PA; Frankel, *The 37th Infantry Division in World War II*, 299.

81. Sherman, "Pacific Echoes," Los Angeles Times, March 8, 1945, Herbert Yudenfriend, *Dear Everybody...: Adventures of a Teenage Soldier* (Bloomington, Indiana: Xlibris, 2009), 99–100.

82. Earl L. Urish, *The Education of Private Urish: An Infantry Replacement in World War II: Army Serial # 36 909 179 Military Occupation Specialty 604-Light Machine Gunner* (Green Valley, IL: U&U Publications, 2000), 130–131.

83. Mailer to Mailer, February 28, 1945, Folder 517.5, Box 517, Papers of Norman Mailer, Ransom Center, University of Texas, Austin, TX; Mathias, *G.I. Jive*, 156; Urish, *The Education of Private Urish*, 130–131; William K. Nelms, Jr. World War II Veteran Survey, Folder 6, Box 28, Record Group 237, Tennessee State Library and Archives, Nashville, TN; Bruce Palmer, Oral History (December 5, 1975), 343, Senior Officer Debriefing Program, U.S. Army Heritage and Education Center, Carlisle, PA; John D. Millet, *United States Army in World War II: The Army Service Forces: The Organization and Role of the Army Service Forces* (Washington, DC: U.S. Government Printing Office, 1954), 108.

84. Mailer to Mailer, February 28, 1945, Folder 517.5, Box 517, Papers of Norman Mailer, Ransom Center, University of Texas, Austin, TX; Mathias, *G.I. Jive*, 156; Urish, *The Education of Private Urish*, 130–131; William K. Nelms, Jr., World War II Veteran Survey, Folder 6, Box 28, Record Group 237, Tennessee State Library and Archives, Nashville, TN; Bruce Palmer, Oral History (December 5, 1975), 343, Senior Officer Debriefing Program, U.S. Army Heritage and Education Center, Carlisle, PA. Millet, *United States Army in World War II*, 108.

85. Adjusted for inflation that would be $2.35 and $31.33 in 2001. Mailer to Mailer, March 2, 3, and 6, 1945, Folder 517.5, Box 517, Papers of Norman Mailer, Ransom Center, University of Texas, Austin, TX.

86. Amel L. Cox, Report After Action: Office of the Special Service Officer, July 25, 1945, Folder 337-0.3 A/A Rpts, Box 8604, Records of the 37th Infantry Division, Records of the Adjutant General's Office, Record Group 407, U.S. National Archives, College Park, MD.

87. Urish, *The Education of Private Urish*, 139; "40,000 See Army Navy Deadlock," *511th Prop Blast*, July 7, 1945, vol. 1, no. 6, reprinted in *Voice of the Angels*, December 1, 1975, 3.

88. Gleeck, *Over Seventy-Five Years*, 47–49.

89. Mathias, *G.I. Jive*, 155, 157; Lynn L. Simpson, 37 Infantry Division, World War II Army Service Experiences Questionnaire, U.S. Army Heritage and Education Center, Carlisle, PA; Charles A. Henne, 37 Infantry Division World War II Army Service Experiences Questionnaire, U.S. Army Heritage and Education Center, Carlisle, PA.

90. Edwin E. Hanson, "My Military History," 44, 37th Infantry Division, World War II Army Service Experiences Questionnaire, U.S. Army History and Heritage Command, Carlisle, PA.

91. Mathias, *G.I. Jive*, 155, 157; Lynn L. Simpson, 37 Infantry Division, World War II Army Service Experiences Questionnaire, U.S. Army Heritage and Education

Center, Carlisle, PA; Charles A. Henne, 37 Infantry Division World War II Army Service Experiences Questionnaire, U.S. Army Heritage and Education Center, Carlisle, PA.

92. Harold G. Martin statement, in GENED History: General Engineer District APO 75 Manila, *Philippine Islands, 1945–1946: The Mission and the Men* (1998), 29–30. This document appears to have been produced on a desktop computer and bound at a local print shop. It was a retirement project for a number of veterans of this unit and many biographical sketches that alumni of the unit provided.

93. Edwin E. Hanson, "My Military History," 46–47, 37th Infantry Division, World War II Army Service Experiences Questionnaire, U.S. Army History and Heritage Command, Carlisle, PA.

94. Edwin E. Hanson, "My Military History," 44, 37th Infantry Division, World War II Army Service Experiences Questionnaire, U.S. Army History and Heritage Command, Carlisle, PA.

95. Pino to Jett, August 15, 1945, in Andrews, ed., *The Whole Damned World*, 226.

96. William A. Sullivan, Oral History, Interview Number 21 (December 22, 1965), 1671, 1708, Columbia University, New York, NY.

97. William A. Sullivan, Oral History, Interview Number 21 (December 22, 1965), 1672–1673, Columbia University, New York, NY.

98. William A. Sullivan, Oral History, Interview Number 21 (December 22, 1965), 1671, 1708, Columbia University, New York, NY.

99. Guerrero Nakpil, *Myself, Elsewhere*, 191.

Bibliography

ARCHIVES

Ayala Museum   Makati, Metro Manila, Philippines
    Filipinas Heritage Library
      Beyond the Wire Newsletter Collection
      Manila Memorare 1945 Collection

Duke University   Durham, North Carolina
    Rubenstein Rare Book and Manuscript Library
      Papers of Robert Eichelberger

1st Cavalry Division Museum   Ft. Hood, Texas
    Saber Newsletter Collection
    World War II Collection

Harvard University   Cambridge, Massachusetts
    Houghton Library
      Papers of Roy E. Larsen

MacArthur Memorial   Norfolk, Virginia
    Record Group 4:   Records of Headquarters, U.S. Army Pacific Area
    Record Group 15:   Material Donated by the General Public
                        Papers of James T. Walsh
    Record Group 16:   Papers of Courtney Whitney
    Record Group 30:   Papers of Richard Sutherland
    Record Group 44A: Papers of Bonner Fellers
    Record Group 46:   Papers of Paul P. Rogers
    Record Group 52:   Papers of William J. Dunn
    Record Group 59:   Papers of William H. Swan

Northwestern University   Evanston, Illinois
    McCormick Library
      Papers of Stanley Frankel

Ohio Historical Society   Columbus, Ohio
    Papers of Robert S. Beightler

Tennessee State Library & Archives   Nashville, Tennessee
    Record Group 237:   World War II Veteran Surveys

Texas A&M University   College Station, Texas
    Cushing Memorial Library
      Papers of Walter Krueger

Texas Military Forces Museum　　　　　　　　　　　Austin, Texas
　Subject Files

U.S. Army Heritage and Education Center　　　　　Carlisle, Pennsylvania
　Papers of Clyde Eddleman
　Papers of Edward M. Flanagan, Jr.
　Papers of Oscar Griswold
　World War II Army Service Experiences Questionnaires
　Voice of the Angels Newsletter Collection

U.S. Military Academy　　　　　　　　　　　　West Point, New York
　Academy Library
　　　Papers of Amelia Mary Bradley
　　　Papers of Oscar Griswold
　　　Papers of Walter Krueger
　　　Papers of Joe Swing
　　　Papers of Emily Van Sickle

U.S. National Archives　　　　　　　　　　College Park, Maryland
　Record Group 407: Records of Adjutant General's Staff
　　World War II Operational Records
　　　Records of the 1st Cavalry Division
　　　Records of the 11th Airborne Division
　　　Records of the 37th Infantry Division

U.S. Naval War College　　　　　　　　　Newport, Rhode Island
　Naval Historical Collection
　　Record Group 13: Student Papers Collection

University of Texas at Austin　　　　　　　　　　Austin, Texas
　Harry Ransom Center
　　Papers of Norman Mailer

Virginia Military Institute　　　　　　　　　Lexington, Virginia
　Marshall Research Library
　　Papers of Frank McCarthy (*MacArthur* Collection)

Wisconsin Historical Society　　　　　　　Madison, Wisconsin
　Papers of Lewis Sebring, Jr.
　Papers of Rod Serling

Yale University　　　　　　　　　　New Haven, Connecticut
　Beinecke Library
　　Papers of Carl and Shelly Mydans

ORAL HISTORIES

University of California, Berkeley　　　　　　Berkeley, California
　Bancroft Library Oral History Center
　　James V. Thompson

University of California, Los Angeles   Los Angeles, California
 Oral History Program
  Sam Yorty

Columbia University   New York, New York
 Butler Library Oral History Archives
  Joseph Swing
  William A. Sullivan

Library of Congress   Washington, DC
 American Folklife Center
  Veterans History Project
   Luther Adams   Steve M. Hegedus
   Lyman Tex Black   Edward P. Kysar
   Delmore Evans   James Loveall
   Richard Foss   Morris J. Weiner
   Ray E. Hale   Earl Windsor
   Lynn E. Hall   John Wyman

Florida State University   Tallahassee, Florida
 Special Collections and Archives
 Reichelt Oral History Collection
 Sam Kraus

Georgetown University   Washington, DC
 Lauinger Library
 Association for Diplomatic Studies and
 Training Foreign Affairs Oral History Project
  Robert F. Goheen
  Herbert E. Weiner

University of Hawaii at Manoa   Honolulu, Hawaii
 Center for Oral History
  Norman Kikuta

University of Kentucky   Lexington, Kentucky
 Nunn Center for Oral History
  William Tucker

Louisiana State University   Baton Rouge, Louisiana
 Williams Center for Oral History
  Joseph E. DuPont, Jr.

MacArthur Memorial   Norfolk, Virginia
 Record Group 32: Oral History Collection
  George Fischer   Peter MacFarlane
  Rick Lawrence   Frank Mendez
  Doug Luyendyck   Caroline Bailey Pratt

Record Group 49: D. Clayton James Collection
    Russell Brines
    LeGrande Diller   Bonner F. Fellers
    Roger O. Egeberg   Joseph M. Swing

National Guard Militia Museum of New Jersey   Sea Girt, New Jersey
    Alfred J. Vaccacio

National Museum of the Pacific War   Fredericksburg, Texas
    Nimitz Education and Research Center
        Cesar Forezan   Herbert E. Merritt
        Martin Gonzales   Joe A. Rackley
        Sam E. Harris   John Skirvin
        Victor M. Liptrap   Ray Smith

National World War II Museum   New Orleans, Louisiana
    Philip Schweitzer

New York State Military Museum   Saratoga Springs, New York
    John Carney

University of North Texas   Denton, Texas
    Willis Library
        Oral History Collection
            Margaret Gillooly
            Ernest L. Kelly, Jr.

Oshkosh Public Museum   Oshkosh, Wisconsin
    William Harvey

Pennsylvania House of Representatives   Harrisburg, Pennsylvania
    House Archives Oral History Project
        Milton Berkes

Rutgers University   New Brunswick, New Jersey
    Rutgers Oral History Archive
        Joseph Holzer
        Julian Levin
        William C. Schnoor

University of Tennessee   Knoxville, Tennessee
    Center for the Study of War and Society
        Foster Arnett

University of Texas   Austin, Texas
    Voces Oral History Center
        Rafael Fierro
        Manuel Perez, Jr.
        Estanislado Reyna

University of Texas at El Paso   El Paso, Texas
   Institute of Oral History
      Cleto L. Rodriquez

Harry S. Truman Presidential Library   Independence, Missouri
   U. Alexis Johnson

U.S. Army Heritage and Education Center   Carlisle, Pennsylvania
   Senior Officer Debriefing Program
      George H. Decker
      Bruce Palmer
      Jay D. Vanderpool

University of Washington   Seattle, Washington
   Special Collections Library
      Abe Zelikovsky

Wisconsin Veterans Museum   Madison, Wisconsin
   Research Center
      Victor Kuester   V. G. Rowley
      Carl H. Mapps   Martin Schram
      Robert Minch   Joseph F. Tauchen, Jr.

Youngstown State University   Youngstown, Ohio
   Maag Library
      Oral History Collection
         Leonard Palmero

NEWSPAPERS AND MAGAZINES

Akron Beacon Journal

Arizona Republic

Arkansas Gazette

The Atlanta Constitution

The Austin American

The Bend Bulletin (Bend, Oregon)

The Boston Boston Globe

Brooklyn Eagle

Chicago Daily News

Chicago Herald American

The Chicago Sun

Chicago Daily Tribune

The Christian Science Monitor

The Cincinnati Enquirer

The Cincinnati Post

The Cincinnati Times-Star

Cleveland Plain Dealer

The Cleveland Press

The Courier-Journal (Louisville, Kentucky)

Daily News (New York, New York)

The Daily Oklahoman (Oklahoma City, Oklahoma)

Daily Times (Chicago, Illinois)

The Dallas Morning News

The Denver Post

The Des Moines Register

The Detroit Free Press

The Detroit News

The El Paso Times

The Evening Bulletin (Philadelphia, Pennsylvania)

The Evening Star (Washington, DC)

Fort Worth Star-Telegram

The Evening Sun (Baltimore, Maryland)
The Fresno Bee
Green Bay Press-Gazette
The Kokomo Tribune
Life
Los Angeles Times
Malaya (Manila, Philippines)
Miami Daily News
The Milwaukee Journal
Milwaukee Sentinel
The Nashville Tennessean
New York Herald Tribune
The New York Times
The New York Times Magazine
New York World-Telegram

Oakland Tribune
The Philadelphia Inquirer
Reno Evening Gazette
San Antonio Light
San Francisco Examiner
The Seattle Daily Times
Seattle Post-Intelligencer
St. Louis Post-Dispatch
The Sun (Baltimore, Maryland)
The Sun (New York, New York)
Time
Toledo Blade
The Wall Street Journal
The Washington Post
Yank

UNPUBLISHED DOCUMENTS

McLaurin, R. D., Paul A. Jureidini, David S. McDonald, and Kurt J. Sellers. *Modern Experiences in City Combat.* Aberdeen Proving Ground, MD: U.S. Army Human Engineering Laboratory, 1987.

Tydings, Millard. *Providing for the Rehabilitation of the Philippine Islands Report.* Report 755, U.S. Senate, 79th Congress, 1st Session. Washington, DC: U.S. Government Printing Office, 1945.

GOVERNMENT DOCUMENTS

Connecticut State Library, Hartford, Connecticut

Carleton B. Clyma, ed., *Connecticut Men of the U.S. Army: Connecticut Veterans Commemorative Booklet* vol. 7, no. 3. September 18, 1945.

Carleton B. Clyma, ed., *Connecticut Men of the U.S. Army: Connecticut Veterans Commemorative Booklet* vol. 7, no. 11. October 16, 1945.

Carleton B. Clyma, ed., *Connecticut Men of the U.S. Army: Connecticut Veterans Commemorative Booklet* vol. 7, no. 14. October 23, 1945.

Carleton B. Clyma, ed., *Connecticut Men of the U.S. Army: Connecticut Veterans Commemorative Booklet* vol. 8, no. 15. October 25, 1945.

Carleton B. Clyma, ed., *Connecticut Men of the U.S. Army: Connecticut Veterans Commemorative Booklet* vol. 8, no. 16. December 3, 1945.

Carleton B. Clyma, ed., *Connecticut Men of the United States Army: Connecticut Veterans Commemorative Booklet* vol. 9, no. 1. December 9, 1945.

Carleton B. Clyma, ed., *Connecticut Men of the United States Army: Connecticut Veterans Commemorative Booklet* vol. 9, no. 4. December 13, 1945.

Carleton B. Clyma, ed., *Connecticut Men of the United States Army: Connecticut Veterans Commemorative Booklet* vol. 9, no. 15. January 5, 1946.

Carleton B. Clyma, ed., *Connecticut Men of the United States Army: Connecticut Veterans Commemorative Booklet* vol. 9, no. 17. January 7, 1946.

Carleton B. Clyma, ed., *Connecticut Men of the U.S. Army: Connecticut Veterans Commemorative Booklet* vol. 9, no. 20. January 12, 1946.

JAPANESE DOCUMENTS

U.S. Army Heritage and Education Center, Carlisle, Pennsylvania

Allied Forces, Southwest Pacific Area. *Wartime Translations of Seized Japanese Documents: Allied Translator and Interpreter Section Reports, 1942–46.* Bethesda, MD: Congressional Information Service, 1988.

Iwano, Masataka, and Aoshima Ryoichiro. "Japanese Monograph Number 7: Philippine Operations Record, Phase III, January – February 1945." October 1946.

Iwano, Masataka, and Aoshima Ryoichiro. "Japanese Monograph No. 8: Philippines Operations Records, Phase III, Dec. 1944 – Aug. 1945." October 1946.

Nagata, Takeji. "*Escape.*" Translated by Ernst Kazuko. Unknown Publisher, 1970.

MILITARY DOCUMENTS

U.S. Army Heritage and Education Center, Carlisle, Pennsylvania

"The Battle History of the 3rd Battalion, 148th Infantry, Second Luzon P.I. Campaign 11 November 44–15 August 1945." Buckeye, AZ, no date.

"GENED History: General Engineer District APO 75 Manila, Philippine Islands, 1945–1946: The Mission and the Men." 1998.

"GENED History: General Engineer District APO 75 Manila, Philippine Islands, 1945–1946." Addendum I, "The Mission and the Men (Continued)." 1998.

U.S. Army, Far Eastern Command, Military Intelligence Section. *Statements of Japanese Officials on World War II (English Translations).* Washington, DC: U.S. Army Center of Military History.

Skelton Combined Arms Research Library, Fort Leavenworth, Kansas

Bush, James E., William M. Cochrane, John R. Gingrich, David F. Gross, Craig D. Hackett, and Douglas P. Schultz. *Corregidor—1945, Staff Ride Battlebook.* Fort Leavenworth, KS: Combat Studies Institute, Combined Arms Research Library, 1983.

Counter Intelligence Corps School. "Counter Intelligence Corps History and Mission in World War II." Fort Holabird Baltimore, MD: Counter Intelligence Corps School.

Sims, Lynn L., ed., *"They Have Seen the Elephant": Veterans Rembrances from World War II for the 40th Anniversary of V-E Day* (Fort Lee, VA: U.S. Army Logistics Center, 1985).

Sixth U.S. Army. "Enemy on Luzon: An Intelligence Summary." December 1, 1945.

Sixth U.S. Army. "Report of the Luzon Campaign 9 January 1945–30 June 1945." July 29, 1945.

XIV Corps. "After Action Report: XIV Corps: M-1 Operation." July 29, 1945.

XIV Corps. "Japanese Defense of Cities as Exemplified by the Battle of Manila." Headquarters: Sixth U.S. Army, July 1, 1945.

637th Tank Destroyer Battalion. "637th Tank Destroyer Battalion After Action Report." Luzon Campaign."

754th Tank Battalion. "Battle of Luzon 9 January–30 June '45."

DISSERTATIONS/STUDENT PAPERS/THESES

Blair, John H. "Operations of the 3D Battalion, 503d Parachute Infantry Regiment in the Landing on Corregidor, PI, 16 February–2 March 1945 (Luzon Campaign) (Personal Experiences of a Battalion Staff Officer)." Advanced Infantry Officers Course, Academic Department, The Infantry School, 1949–1950.

Boynton, Frank R. "Power Projection Operations and Urban Combat: An Avoidable Combination?" School of Advanced Military Studies Monograph. U.S. Army Command & General Staff College, 1995.

Campbell, James L. "Task Organizing for Urban Combat." Master's thesis, U.S. Army Command & General Staff College, 1978.

Caskey, Lawson B. "The Operations of the 503d Parachute Infantry Regiment Combat Team in the Recapture of Corregidor Island, 16 February–8 March 1945 (Luzon Campaign) (Personal Observations of a Parachute Battalion Commander)." Advanced Infantry Officers Course, Academic Department, The Infantry School, 1948–1949.

Crawford, Donald A. "Operations of 503D Parachute Regiment Combat Team in Capture of Corregidor Island, 16 February–2 March 1945 (Northern Philippines Campaign) (Personal Experience of Regimental Assistant S-1)." Advanced Infantry Officers Course, Academic Department, The Infantry School, 1948–1949.

Eaton, George B. "From Teaching to Practice: General Walter Krueger and the Development of Joint Operations, 1921–1945." Center for Naval Warfare Studies: U.S. Naval War College, 1994.

Faith, Matthew H. "Intrepidity, Iron Will, and Intellect: General Robert L. Eichelberger and Military Genius." Master's thesis, U.S. Army Command & General Staff College, 2004.

Flash, Edward T. "The Operations of the 2D Battalion, 503d Parachute Infantry Regiment Combat Team in the Recapture of Corregidor Island, 16 February–23 February 1945 (Luzon Campaign) (Personal Observations of a Parachute Rifle Platoon Leader)." Advanced Infantry Officers Course, Academic Department, The Infantry School, 1949–1950.

Garay, Stephen L. "The Breach of Intramuros." Advanced Officers Class 1, The Armored School (May 1, 1948).

Hill, Hudson C. "The Operations of Company 'E', 503d Parachute Regiment at Wheeler Point, Island of Corregidor, Philippine Islands 23 February, 1945

(Luzon Campaign) (Personal Experience of a Company Commander)." Advanced Infantry Officers Course, Academic Department, The Infantry School, 1947–1948.

Hoppenstein, Isaac. "The Operation of the 187th Glider Infantry Regiment (11th Airborne Division) in the Landing at Nasugbu, Luzon, Philippine Islands 31 January–3 February 1945 (The Luzon Campaign) (Personal Experiences of a Regimental Supply Officer)." Advanced Infantry Officers Course, Academic Department, The Infantry School, 1947–1948.

James, William T., Jr., "From Siege to Surgical: The Evolution of Urban Combat from World War II to the Present and its Effect on Current Doctrine." Master's thesis, U.S. Army Command & General Staff College, 1998.

Jeffress, Edwin B. "Operations of the 2nd Battalion, 511th Parachute Infantry (11th Airborne Division) in the Battle for Southern Manila, 3–10 February (Luzon Campaign) (Personal Experiences of a Battalion Intelligence Officer)." Advanced Infantry Officers Course, Academic Department, The Infantry School, 1948–1949.

Kidd, Giles H. "The Operations of the 37th Infantry Division in the Crossing of the Pasig River and Closing to the Walls of Intramuros, Manila, 7–9 February 1945 (Luzon Campaign)." Advanced Infantry Officers Course, Staff Department, The Infantry School, 1949–1950.

Levine, Lester H. "The Operations of the 503d Parachute Infantry Regiment in the Attack on Corregidor Island, 16 February–2 March 1945 (Luzon Campaign) (Personal Experience of a Regimental Adjutant)." Advanced Infantry Officers Course, Academic Department, The Infantry School, 1947–1948.

McDonald, John H., Jr. "General Walter Krueger A Case Study in Operational Command: A Monograph." School of Advanced Military Studies Monograph. U.S. Army Command & General Staff College, 1988–1989.

McEnery, Kevin T. "The XIV Corps Battle for Manila, February 1945." Master's thesis, U.S. Army Command & General Staff College, 1993.

McMeen, Scott R. "Field Artillery Doctrine Development, 1917–1945." Master's thesis, U.S. Army Command & General Staff College, 1991.

Powell, James S. "Learning Under Fire: Military Units in the Crucible of Combat: A Monograph." School of Advanced Military Studies Monograph. U.S. Army Command & General Staff College, 2006.

Preysler, Charles A. "Going Down Town: The Need for Precision MOUT—A Monograph." School of Advanced Military Studies Monograph. U.S. Army Command & General Staff College, 1994.

Smith, Magnus L. "Operations of the 'Rock Force' (603D RCT Reinforced) in the Recapture of Corregidor Island, 16 February–8 March 1946 (Luzon Campaign) (Personal Experience of an Assistant Regimental Operations Officer)." Advanced Infantry Officers Course, Staff Department, The Infantry School, 1949–1950.

Steckel, Glenn A. "The Role of Field Artillery in the Siege on Intramuros, Manila, P.I." The Armored School, May 7, 1948.
Villanueva, James A. "Awaiting the Allies' Return: The Guerrilla Resistance Against the Japanese in the Philippines during World War II." PhD diss., The Ohio State University, 2019.

WEBSITES

The 503D P.R.C.T. Heritage Battalion Online
Abbott, Don. "The Warden: George Madison Jones." https://503prct.org/abbott/warden/warden_01.html.
Calhoun, Bill. "The Best Warrior I Ever Knew," *The 503D P.R.C.T. Heritage Battalion Online*. https://503prct.org/moh/mccarter_calhoun.html.
Calhoun, William T., and Paul F. Whitman. "The Lost Road." http://corregidor.org/BEA503/features/lostroad.html.

Corregidor.com
Meixsel, R. B. "Did 100,000 Civilians Die in the Battle of Manila In 1945? Robert Ross Smith's Triumph in the Philippines and the Story of a Number." https://corregidor.org/refdoc/Reference_Reading/Meixsel/DID-100,000-CIVILIANS-DIE-IN-THE-BATTLE-OF-MANILA-IN-1945-/index.html.
Pardue, James and Paul Whitman, eds. "'A' Company Diary." https://www.corregidor.org/BEA503/journals/A_co_diary.html.

Internet Movie Database
You Are There. Episode: "The Rescue of the Americans Prisoners from Santo Tomás." https://www.imdb.com/title/tt0751953/?ref_=ttfc_fc_tt.

Lane Memorial Library, Hampton, New Hampshire
Palmer, Rita. "Three Years in a Prison Camp." May 10, 1945. https://history.lanememoriallibrary.org/hampton/biog/ritapalmer/3yearsinaprisoncamp.htm.

Library of Congress
"*United States of America vs. Tomoyuki Yamashita*. Record of Trial." *Military Legal Resources*. https://www.loc.gov//rr/frd/Military_Law/Yamashita_trial.html.

U.S. Army
Miller, Kelsey. "Manila Remembered 75 Years Later: Former Trooper Shares Personal Experience of Santo Tomás Liberation." March 2, 2020. https://www.army.mil/article/233320/manila_remembered_75_years_later_former_trooper_shares_personal_experrience_of_santo_tomas_liberation.

YouTube
"Battle of Manila—The Big Picture." https://youtube.com/watch?v=SYVRtsE95u8.
"In Their Own Words: MOH Recipient 2nd Lt. Robert M. Viale." http://www.youtube.com/watch?v=S2xN8SW8Cal.

OFFICIAL HISTORIES

Boggs, Charles W., Jr. *Marine Aviation in the Philippines*. Washington, DC: U.S. Government Printing Office, 1951.

Condon-Rall, Mary Ellen, and Albert E. Cowdrey. *United States Army in World War II: The Technical Services: The Medical Department: Medical Services in the War Against Japan*. Washington, DC: U.S. Government Printing Office, 1998.

Maehara, Toru. *Manira Boeisen: Nihongun no Toshi no Tatakai* [The Defense in the Battle of Manila: The Urban Warfare of the Japanese Army]. Tokyo: Boei Nenshujo, 1982.

Masao, Sasaki. *Senshi Sosho* [War History Series], vol. 54, *Nansei homen kaigun sakusen; dainidan sakusen iko* [Southwest Area Naval Operations; Second Stage and Later]. Tokyo: Asagumo Shinbunsha, 1972.

Matsuki, Hidemitsu. *Senshi Sosho* [War History Series], vol. 60, *Shogo Rikugun Sakusen*, part 2, *Ruson kessen* [Sho-Go Ground Operations, part 2, The Battle of Luzon]. Tokyo: Asagumo Shinbunsha, 1972.

Millet, John D. *United States Army in World War II: The Army Service Forces: The Organization and Roll of the Army Service Forces*. Washington, DC: U.S. Government Printing Office, 1954.

Raines, Edgar F., Jr. *Eyes of Artillery: The Origins of Modern U.S. Army Aviation in World War II*. Washington, DC: U.S. Government Printing Office, 2000.

Smith, Robert Ross. *United States Army in World War II: The War in the Pacific: Triumph in the Philippines*. Washington, DC: U.S. Government Printing Office, 1963.

Staufer, Alvin P. *United States Army in World War II: The Technical Services: The Quartermaster Corps: Operations in the War Against Japan*. Washington, DC: U.S. Government Printing Office, 1956.

Thompson, George Raynor, and Dixie R. Harris. *United States Army in World War II: The Technical Services: The Signal Corps: The Outcome (Mid-1943 Through 1945)*. Washington, DC: U.S. Government Printing Office, 1966.

BOOKS

Aluit, Alfonso. *By Sword and Fire: The Destruction of Manila in World War II, 3 February–3 March 1945*. Manila: National Commission for Culture and Arts, 1994.

Andrews, Martha Shipman, ed. *The Whole Damned World: New Mexico Aggies at War: 1941–1945—World War II Correspondence of Dean Daniel B. Jett*. Las Cruces: New Mexico State University Libraries/Rio Grande Books, 2009.

Astor, Gerald. *Crisis in the Pacific: The Battles for the Philippine Islands by the Men who Fought Them*. New York: Dell Publishing, 1996.

Belote, James, and William M. Belote. *Corregidor: The Saga of a Fortress*. New York: Harper and Row, 1967.

Bender, Mark C. *Watershed at Leavenworth: Dwight D. Eisenhower and the Command and General Staff College*. Fort Leavenworth, KS: Combat Studies Institute, 1990.

Bergerud, Eric. *Touched With Fire: The Land Warfare in the South Pacific*. New York: Viking, 1996.

Bielakowski, Alexander M. *From Horses to Horsepower: The Mechanization and Demise of the U.S. Cavalry, 1916–1920*. Stroud, England: Fonthill Media, 2019.

Bowen, Wayne H. *Spain during World War II*. Columbia: University of Missouri Press, 2006.

Breuer, William B. *Retaking the Philippines: America's Return to Corregidor and Bataan, October 1944–March 1945*. New York: St. Martin's Press, 1986.

Brown, Charles. *Bars from Bilibid Prison*. San Antonio, TX: The Naylor Company, 1947.

Brown, John S. *Draftee Division: The 88th Infantry Division in World War II*. Lexington: University Press of Kentucky, 1986.

Builder, Carl H. *The Masks of War: American Military Styles in Strategy and Analysis*. Baltimore: Johns Hopkins University Press, 1989.

Burgess, Henry A. *Looking Back*. Missoula, MT: Pictorial History Publishing Company, 1993.

Calero, Ana Mari S. *Three Continents*. Manila: De La Salle University Press, 2001.

Carry, Frank. *Letters from an Internment Camp: Davao and Manila*. Ashland, OR: Independent Printing Company, 1993.

Cates, Tressa. *The Drainpipe Diary*. New York: Vantage Press, 1957.

Chase, William C. *Front Line General: The Commands of Wm. C. Chase: An Autobiography*. Houston, TX: Pacesetter Press, 1975.

Chwialkowski, Paul. *In Caesar's Shadow: The Life of General Robert Eichelberger*. Westport, CT: Greenwood Press, 1993.

Clausewitz, Carl von. *On War*. Edited and translated by Michael Howard and Peter Paret. Princeton: Princeton University Press, 1976.

Cogan, Frances B. *Captured: The Internment of American Civilians in the Philippines, 1941–1945*. Athens: University of Georgia Press, 2000.

Connaughton, Richard, John Pimlott, and Duncan Anderson. *The Battle of Manila*. Novato, CA: Presidio Press, 1995.

Cortesi, Lawrence. *The Battle for Manila*. New York: Kensington Publishers, 1984.

Crost, Lyn. *Honor by Fire: Japanese Americans at War in Europe and the Pacific*. Novato, CA: Presidio, 1994.

Davis, Jerry, Ed Lahti, John Ringler, Lee E. Walker, and Foster Arnett. *511th Parachute Infantry Regiment*. Paducah, KY: Turner Publishing Company, 1997.

Del Gallego, John A. *The Liberation of Manila: 28 Days of Carnage, February–March 1945*. Jefferson, NC: McFarland & Company, 2020.

D'Este, Carlo. *Eisenhower: A Soldier's Life*. New York: Henry Holt & Company, 2002.

DiMarco, Louis A. *Concrete Hell: Urban Warfare from Stalingrad to Iraq*. Oxford: Osprey 2012.

Dingman, Roger. *Deciphering the Rising Sun: Navy and Marine Corps Codebreakers, Translators and Interpreters in the Pacific War*. Annapolis: Naval Institute Press, 2009.

Doeppers, Daniel F. *Feeding Manila in Peace and War, 1850–1945*. Madison: University of Wisconsin Press, 2016.

Dos Passos, John. *Tour of Duty*. Boston: Houghton Mifflin, 1946.

Doubler, Michael D. *Closing with the Enemy: How GIs Fought the War in Europe, 1944–1945*. Lawrence: University Press of Kansas, 1994.

Dower, John W. *War Without Mercy: Race and Power in the Pacific War*. New York: Pantheon Books, 1986.

Drea, Edward J. *MacArthur's Ultra: Codebreaking and the War against Japan, 1942–1945*. Lawrence: University Press of Kansas, 1992.

Duffy, James P. *Return to Victory: MacArthur's Epic Liberation of the Philippines*. New York: Hachette Books, 2021.

Dumana, Tessie, ed. *The German Club—Manila, 1906–1986*. Manila: German Club, 1986.

Dunn, William J. *Pacific Microphone*. College Station: Texas A&M University Press, 1988.

Eichelberger, Robert L. *Our Jungle Road to Tokyo*. New York: Viking, 1950.

Egeberg, Roger O. *The General: MacArthur and the Man He Called 'Doc'*. New York: Hippocrene Books, 1983.

Empie, Evelyn Berg, and Stephen H. Mette. *A Child in the Midst of Battle: One Family's Struggle for Survival in War-torn Manila*. Rolling Hills Estates, CA: Satori Press, 2001.

Ephraim, Frank. *Escape to Manila: From Nazi Tyranny to Japanese Terror*. Urbana: University of Illinois Press, 2003.

Escoda, Jose Ma. Bonifacio M. *Warsaw of Asia: The Rape of Manila*. Quezon City, Philippines: Giraffe Books, 2000.

Flanagan, Edward M., Jr. *The Angels: A History of the 11th Airborne Division, 1943–1946*. Washington, DC: Infantry Journal Press, 1948.

Flanagan, E. M., Jr. *Corregidor: The Rock Force Assault, 1945*. Novato, CA: Presidio Press, 1994.

Flanagan, E. M., Jr. *The Rakkasans: The Combat History of the 187th Airborne Infantry*. Novato, CA: Presidio Press, 1997.

40th Infantry Division. *The Years of World War II: 7 December 1941–7 April 1946*. Baton Rouge, LA: Army & Navy Publishing Company, 1947.

Frank, Richard B. *MacArthur: A Biography*. New York: Palgrave Macmillan, 2009.

Frankel, Stanley A. *The 37th Infantry Division in World War II*. Washington, DC: Infantry Journal Press, 1948.

Gailey, Harry A. *MacArthur's Victory: The War in New Guinea, 1943–1944*. New York: Ballantine Books, 2004.

Gallaway, Jack. *The Odd Couple: Blamey and MacArthur at War*. St. Lucia, Queensland, Australia: University of Queensland Press, 2000.

Garcia, Joquin. *It Took Four Years for the Rising Sun to Set (1941–1945)*. Manila: De La Salle University Press, 2001.

Gilmore, Allison B. *You Can't Fight Tanks with Bayonets: Psychological Warfare against the Japanese in the Southwest Pacific*. Lincoln: University of Nebraska Press, 1998.

Gleeck, Lewis E., Jr. *Over Seventy-Five Years of Philippine–American History (The Army and Navy Club of Manila)*. Manila: Carmello & Bauermann, 1976.

Goldhagen, Juergen, ed., *Manila Memories: Four Boys Remember their Lives Before, During and After the Japanese Occupation*. Exeter, England: Searsman Books, 2008.

Gonzalez, Purita Echevarria de. *Manila: A Memoir of Love & Loss*. Maryborough, Australia: Hale & Iremonger, 2000.

Harrington, Joseph D. *Yankee Samurai (The Secret Role of Nisei in America's Pacific Victory)*. Detroit: Pettigrew Enterprises, 1979.

Heinrichs, Waldo, and Marc Gallicchio. *Implacable Foes: War in the Pacific, 1944–1945*. New York: Oxford University Press, 2017.

Henderson, Bruce. *Rescue at Los Baños: The Most Daring Prison Camp Raid of World War II*. New York: William Morrow, 2015.

Hibbs, Ralph Emerson. *Tell MacArthur to Wait*. New York: Carlton Press, 1988.

Hills, Alice. *Future War in Cities: Rethinking a Liberal Dilemma*. New York: Frank Cass, 2004.

Hind, R. Renton. *Spirits Unbroken: The Story of Three Years in a Civilian Internment Camp, under the Japanese at Baguio and at Old Bilibid Prison in the Philippines from December, 1941, to February, 1945*. San Francisco: John Howell, 1946.

Hines, Walter. *Aggies of the Pacific War: New Mexico A&M and the War with Japan*. Las Cruces, NM: Yucca Tree Press, 1999.

Hines, Walter G., and Martha Shipman Andrews. *Hugh Meglone Milton: A Life Beyond Duty*. Los Ranchos, NM: Rio Grande Books, 2015.

Hofmann, George F. *Through Mobility We Conquer: The Mechanization of U.S. Cavalry*. Lexington: University Press of Kentucky, 2006.

Holland, Robert B. *The Rescue of Santo Tomás Manila WWII—The Flying Column: 100 Miles to Freedom*. Puducah, KY: Turner Publishing Company, 2003.

Holmes, W. J. *Double Edged Secrets: U.S. Naval Intelligence in the Pacific During World War II*. Annapolis: Naval Institute Press, 1979.

Holzimmer, Kevin C. *General Walter Krueger: Unsung Hero of the Pacific War*. Lawrence: University Press of Kansas, 2007.

Humble, Richard. *Fraser of North Cape: The Life of Admiral of the Fleet Lord Fraser [1888–1981]*. London: Routledge & Kegan Paul, 1983.

Iriye, Akira. *Power and Culture: The Japanese–American War, 1941–1945*. Cambridge, MA: Harvard University Press, 1981.

James, D. Clayton. *The Years of MacArthur*, vol. 1, *1880–1941*. Boston: Houghton Mifflin, 1970.

James, D. Clayton. *The Years of MacArthur*, vol. 2, *1941–1945*. Boston: Houghton Mifflin, 1975.

Joaquin, Nick. *Mr. F.E.U.: The Cultural Hero That Was Nicanor Reyes*. Manila: Far Eastern University Press, 1995.

Johansen, Bruce E. *So Far from Home: Manila's Santo Tomás Internment Camp, 1942–1945* Omaha, NE: PBI Press, 1996.

Johnson, Glenn T., ed. *We Aint No Heroes: The 112th Cavalry in World War II*. Denton, TX: Privately Published, 2005.

Johnson, U. Alexis, with Jef Olivarius McAllister. *The Right Hand of Power*. Englewood Cliffs, NJ: Prentice-Hall, 1984.

Jose, Ricardo Trota, ed. *World War II and the Japanese Occupation*. Quezon City: University of the Philippines Press, 2006.

Karnow, Stanley. *In Our Image: America's Empire in the Philippines*. New York: Random House, 1989.

Keegan, John. *The Face of Battle*. New York: Vintage Books, 1973.

Kelly, Carol Adele, ed., *Voices of My Comrades: America's Reserve Officers Remember World War II*. New York: Fordham University Press, 2007.

Kenney, George C. *General Kenney Reports: A Personal History of the Pacific War*. New York: Duell, Sloan and Pearce, 1949.

Kojima, Noboru. *Manira Kaigun Rikusentai* [Manila Naval Defense Force]. Tokyo: Shinchosha, 1969.

Kovner, Sarah. *Prisoners of the Empire: Inside Japanese POW Camps*. Cambridge, MA: Harvard University Press, 2020.

Krueger, Walter. *From Down Under to Nippon: The Story of the Sixth Army in World War II*. Washington, DC: Combat Forces Press, 1953.

Labrador, Juan. *A Diary of the Japanese Occupation: December 7, 1941–May 7, 1945*. Manila: Santo Tomás University Press, 1989.

Lahti, Edward H. *Memoirs of an Angel*. Herndon, VA: Privately Published, 1994.

Lara, Rudy de, with Bob Fancher. *Boy Guerrilla: The World War II Metro Manila Serenader*. Mandaluyong City, Philippines: National Book Store, 2002.

Layton, Edwin T. *And I Was There: Pearl Harbor and Midway Breaking Secrets*. New York: Morrow: 1985.

Legarda, Benito J., Jr. *Occupation: The Later Years*. Manila: Vibal Publishing House, 2007.

Li, Yuk-wai Yung. *The Huaqiao Warriors: Chinese Resistance Movement in the Philippines, 1942–1945*. Hong Kong: Hong Kong University Press, 1995.

Lockman, Brian. *World War II Reflections: An Oral History of Pennsylvania's Veterans*. Mechanicsburg, PA: Stackpole Books, 2009.

Lorenzen, Angus M. *A Lovely Little War: Life in a Japanese Prions Camp Through the Eyes of a Child*. New York: History Publishing Company, 2008.

Luvaas, Jay, ed., *Dear Miss Em: General Eichelberger's War in the Pacific, 1942–1945*. Westport, CT: Greenwood Press, 1981.

MacArthur, Douglas. *Reminiscences*. New York: McGraw-Hill, 1964.

Macdougall, Walter M. *Angel of Bataan: The Life of a World War II Army Nurse in the War Zone and at Home*. Camden, ME: Down East Books, 2015.

Mañalac, Fernando J. *Manila: Memories of World War II*. Quezon City, Philippines: Giraffe Books, 1995.

Manchester, William. *American Caesar: Douglas MacArthur, 1880–1964*. Boston: Little, Brown, & Co, 1978.

Mansoor, Peter R. *The GI Offensive in Europe: The Triumph of American Infantry Divisions, 1941–1945*. Lawrence: University Press of Kansas, 1999.

Marshall, Cecily Mattocks. *Happy Life Blues: A Memoir of Survival*. Clinton, MA: Angus MacGregor Books, 2007.

Mashbir, Sidney F. *I Was an American Spy*. New York: Vantage Press, 1953.

Masuda, Hiroshi. *MacArthur in Asia: The General and His Staff in the Philippines, Japan, and Korea*. Translated by Reiko Yamamoto. Ithaca, NY: Cornell University Press, 2012.

Mathias, Frank F. *G.I. Jive: An Army Bandsman in World War II*. Lexington: University Press of Kentucky, 2000.

McCallus, Joseph P. *The MacArthur Highway and Other Relics of American Empire in the Philippines*. Washington, DC: Potomac Books, 2010.

McManus, John C. *Fire and Fortitude: The U.S. Army in the Pacific War, 1941–1943*. New York: Dutton Caliber, 2019.

McMurray, Marisse Reyes. *Tide of Time*. Makati City: Philippines: Jose Cojuangco & Sons, 1996.

Meyer, Elizabeth "Bim". *Teenage Diary: Santo Tomás Internment Camp*. Claremont, CA: Paige Press, 2005.

Montinola, Lourdes R. *Breaking the Silence*. Quezon City, Philippines: University of the Philippines Press, 1996.

Morningstar, James Kelly. *War and Resistance in the Philippines, 1942–1945*. Annapolis: Naval Institute Press, 2021.

Moseley, Ray. *Reporting War: How Foreign Correspondents Risked Capture, Torture and Death to Cover World War II*. New Haven: Yale University Press, 2017.

Murray, Williamson, and Allan R. Millett. *A War to be Won: Fighting the Second World War* Cambridge, MA: Harvard University Press, 2000.

Nakpil, Carmen Guerrero. *Myself, Elsewhere*. San Juan, Philippines: Nakpil Publishing, 2006.

Nixon, Eva Anna. *"Delayed, Manila."* Canton, OH: Friends Foreign Missionary Society, 1981.

O'Donnell, Patrick K. *Into the Rising Sun: In Their Own Words, World War II's Pacific Veterans Reveal the Heart of Combat*. New York: The Free Press, 2002.

Ohl, John Kennedy. *Minuteman: The Military Career of General Robert S. Beightler*. Boulder, CO: Lynne Rienner Publishers, 2001.

Owen, William A. *Eye-Deep in Hell: A Memoir of the Liberation of the Philippines, 1944–45*. Dallas: Southern Methodist University Press, 1989.

Panlilio, Yay. *The Crucible: An Autobiography by Colonel Yay, Filipina America Guerrilla*. Edited by Denise Cruz. New Brunswick, NJ: Rutgers University Press, 2010.

Patterson, James T. *Grand Expectations: The United States, 1945–1974.* New York: Oxford University Press, 1996.

Perret, Geoffrey. *Old Soldiers Never Die: The Life of Douglas MacArthur.* New York: Random House, 1996.

Perry, Mark. *The Most Dangerous Man in America: The Making of Douglas MacArthur.* New York: Basic Books, 2014.

Pestaño-Jacinto, Pacita. *Living with the Enemy: A Diary of the Japanese Occupation.* Pasig City, Philippines: Anvil Publishing, 1999.

Petillo, Carol Morris. *Douglas MacArthur: The Philippine Years.* Bloomington: Indiana University Press, 1981.

Picornell, Pedro M. *The Remedios Hospital, 1942–1945: A Saga of Malate.* Manila: De La Salle University Press, 1995.

Pollak, Martha. *Cities at War in Early Modern Europe.* New York: Cambridge University Press, 2010.

Prados, John. *Combined Fleet Decoded: The Secret History of American Intelligence and the Japanese Navy in World War II.* New York: Random House, 1995.

Pratt, Caroline Bailey, ed., *Only a Matter of Days: The World War II Prison Camp Diary of Fay Cook Bailey.* Bennington, VT: Merriam Press, 2001.

Prising, Robin. *Manila, Goodbye.* Boston: Houghton Mifflin, 1975.

Ramsey, Richard Wilcox. *On Law & Country: The Biography and Speeches of Russell Archibald Ramsey.* Boston: Branden Publishing, 1993.

Rhodes, Weldon E. *Flying MacArthur to Victory.* College Station: Texas A&M University Press, 1987.

Richardson, James E. *Under Age Angel.* Amherst, WI: Palmer Publications, 1995.

Rogers, Paul P. *The Bitter Years: MacArthur and Sutherland.* Westport, CT, Praeger, 1990.

Romulo, Carlos P. *I See the Philippines Rise.* Garden City, NY: Doubleday & Company, 1946.

Rowan, William. *On the Spring Tide: A Special Kind of Courage.* Greensboro, NC: Cenografix, 1998.

Salecker, Gene Eric. *Blossoming Silk Against the Rising Sun: U.S. and Japanese Paratroopers at War in the Pacific in World War II.* Mechanicsburg, PA: Stackpole Books, 2010.

Sander, Gordon F. *Serling: The Rise and Twilight of Television's Last Angry Man.* New York: Dutton, 1992.

Santos, Angelito L., Joan Orendain, Helen N. Mendoza, Bernard L. M. Karganilla, and Renato Constantino, eds. *Under Japanese Rule: Memories and Reflections.* Makati City, Philippines: The Manila Daily Shimbun, 2012.

Sarantakes, Nicholas Evan. *Allies against the Rising Sun: The United States, the British Nations, and the Defeat of Imperial Japan.* Lawrence: University Press of Kansas, 2009.

Sarantakes, Nicholas Evan, ed. *Seven Stars: The Okinawa Battle Diaries of Simon Bolivar Buckner, Jr., and Joseph Stilwell.* College Station: Texas A&M University Press, 2004.

Schaller, Michael. *Douglas MacArthur: The Far Eastern General*. New York: Oxford University Press, 1989.

Scott, James M. *Rampage: MacArthur, Yamashita, and the Battle of Manila*. New York: W.W. Norton, 2018.

Shortal, John F. *Forged by Fire: General Robert L. Eichelberger and the Pacific War*. Columbia: University of South Carolina Press, 1987.

Spector, Ronald H. *Eagle Against the Sun: The American War with Japan*. New York: The Free Press, 1984.

Steinberg, David Joel. *Philippine Collaboration in World War II*. Ann Arbor: University of Michigan Press, 1967.

Strong, Herman E. *A Ringside Seat to War*. New York: Vantage Press, 1965.

Syjuco, Ma. Felisa A. *The Kempei Tai in the Philippines, 1941–1945*. Quezon City, Philippines: New Day Publishers, 1988.

Taaffe, Stephen R. *MacArthur's Jungle War: The 1944 New Guinea Campaign*. Lawrence: University Press of Kansas, 1998.

Taaffe, Stephen R. *Marshall and His Generals: U.S. Army Commanders in World War II*. Lawrence: University Press of Kansas, 2011.

Tan, Antonio S. *The Chinese in the Philippines During the Japanese Occupation*. Quezon City, Philippines: University of Philippines Press, 1981.

Templeman, Harold. *The Return to Corregidor*. New York: Strand Press, 1945.

Thorpe, Elliot R. *East Wind, Rain: The Intimate Account of an Intelligence Officer in the Pacific, 1939–1949*. Boston: Gambit Incorporated, 1969.

Toll, Ian W. *Twilight of the Gods: War in the Western Pacific, 1944–1945*. New York: W.W. Norton & Company, 2020.

Urish, Earl L. *The Education of Private Urish: An Infantry Replacement in World War II: Army Serial # 36 909 179 Military Occupation Specialty 604-Light Machine Gunner*. Green Valley, IL: U&U Publications, 2000.

Van Sickle, Emily. *The Iron Gates of Santo Tomás: The Firsthand Account of an American Couple Interned by the Japanese in Manila, 1942–1945*. Chicago: Academy Chicago Publishers, 1992.

Vat, Dan van der. *The Pacific Campaign: The US–Japanese Naval War 1941–45*. New York: Simon and Schuster, 1991.

Wade, Betsy, ed. *Forward Positions: The War Correspondence of Homer Bigart*. Fayetteville: University of Arkansas Press, 1992.

Wahlman, Alec. *Storming the City: U.S. Military Performance in Urban Warfare from World War II to Vietnam*. Denton: University of North Texas Press, 2015.

Wahlquist, Marci Andrews, ed. *Beyond the Bend: The Journey of Normand Laub from World War II to Peace of Mind*. North Salt Lake, UT: Sheridan Publishing, 2006.

Walker, John R. *Bracketing the Enemy: Forward Observers in World War II*. Norman: University of Oklahoma Press, 2013.

Warne, Terry Wadsworth. *Terry: The Inspiring Story of a Little Girl's Survival as a POW During WWII*. Denver: Outskirts Press, 2013.

Weigley, Russell. *The American Way of War: A History of United States Military Strategy and Power*. New York: Macmillan, 1973.

Weigley, Russell. *Eisenhower's Lieutenants: The Campaign of France and Germany, 1944–1945*. Bloomington: Indiana University Press, 1981.

Wilkinson, Rupert. *Surviving a Japanese Internment Camp: Life and Liberation at Santo Tomás, Manila in World War II*. Jefferson, NC: McFarland & Company, 2014.

Witthoff, Evelyn M., and Geraldine V. Chappell. *Three Years' Internment in Santo Tomás* Kansas City, MO: Beacon Hill Press, 1945.

Wright, Bertram C. *The 1st Cavalry Division in World War II*. Tokyo: Toppan Printing Company, 1947.

Yee, Dale F., ed. *Dear General: World War II Letters, 1944–1945 From: Major General Joseph M. Swing To: General Peyton C. March*. Palo Alto, CA: 11th Airborne Association, 1987.

Yellen, Jeremy A. *The Greater East Asia Co-Prosperity Sphere: When Total Empire Met Total War*. Ithaca, NY: Cornell University Press, 2019.

Young, Kenneth Ray. *The General's General: The Life and Times of Arthur MacArthur*. Boulder, CO: Westview Press, 1994.

Yudenfriend, Herbert. *Dear Everybody . . . : Adventures of a Teenage Soldier*. Bloomington, IN: Xlibris, 2009.

ARTICLES

"A Preliminary Report on Jap Demolitions in Manila." *Intelligence Bulletin* III, no. 9 (May 1945): 26–29.

Beall, Jonathan A. "The United States Army and Urban Combat in the Nineteenth Century." *War in History* 16, no. 2 (2009): 157–188.

Benson, Kevin C. M. "Manila, 1945: City Fight in the Pacific." In *City Fights: Selected Histories of Urban Combat from World War II to Vietnam*, edited by John Antal and Bradley Gericke, 230–250. New York: Ballantine, 2003.

Betz, David, and Hugo Stanford-Tuck. "The City Is Neutral: On Urban Warfare in the 21st Century." *Texas National Security Review* 2, no. 4 (August 2019): 60–87.

Bigelow, Michael E. "Intelligence in the Philippines." *Military Intelligence Professional Bulletin* 21, no. 2 (April–June 1995): 36–40.

Bracken, Paul. "Urban Sprawl and NATO Defense." *Military Review* 61, no. 10 (October 1977): 32–39.

"City and Town Defense." *Intelligence Bulletin* 12, no. 111 (August 1945): 28.

Danquah, Francis K. "Reports on Philippine Industrial Crops in World War II from Japan's English Language Press." *Agricultural History* 79, no. 1 (Winter 2005): 74–96.

Daugherty, William F. "Flying Columns." *Armor* 76, no. 2 (March–April 1967): 19–23.

Dioguardi, Ralph. "Roll Out the Barrel . . . The Tanks Are Coming." *Weapons and Warfare Quarterly*, no. 20 (1983).

Eddy, D. W. "Manila and the Capitulation." *Signals* 1, no. 5 (May–June 1947): 42–47.

Florio, Angelita Martinez. "Hell in Malate." *Philippine Free Press*, February 10, 2007, 28–30.

Florio, Angelita Martinez. "Hell in Malate (Conclusion)." *Philippine Free Press*, February 17, 2007, 17–18.

Ford, Douglas. "US Assessments of Japanese Ground Warfare Tactics and the Army's Campaigns in the Pacific Theaters, 1943–1945: Lessons Learned and Methods Applied." *War in History* 16, no. 3 (2009): 323–358.

Garland, Patrick V., and David B. Flohr. "Forensic Sciences in the Pacific Theater of War." *Military Police* (Spring 2019): 36–40.

Gunnison, Royal Arch. "The Burning of Manila." *Collier's*, April 7, 1945, 21, 40, 44.

Gordon, John, IV, "Battle in the Streets—Manila 1945." *Field Artillery* (August 1990): 24–29.

Hall, Roderick. "The Battle for Manila: A Personal Memory." *Bulletin of the American Historical Collection* 34, no. 3 (July–September 2006): 26–27.

Hanrahan, James. "Soldier, Manager, Leader: An Interview with Former CIA Executive Director Lawrence K. 'Red' White." *Studies in Intelligence* 43, no. 3 (Winter 1999–2000): 29–41.

Hayashi, Hirofumi. "Manira-sen to Beibyo Hoteru Jiken." [The Battle of Manila and the Bayview Hotel Incident]. *Shizen, Ningen, Shakai* 52 (January 2012): 49–83.

Hayashi, Hirofumi. "Shiryo Shokai: Nihongun no Meirei Denpo ni Miru Manira-sen." [Introduction of Documents: The Battle of Manila as Seen in Japanese Force Orders and Telegrams]. *Shizen, Ninghen, Shakai* 48 (2010): 69–95.

Hidalgo, Cristina Patoja. "Metro Manila: City in Search of a Myth." *Philippine Studies* 50, no. 3 (Third Quarter 1997): 303–326.

Holzimmer, Kevin C. "Joint Operations in the Southwest Pacific, 1943–1945." *Joint Forces Quarterly* no. 38 (3rd quarter 2005): 102–106.

Hubner, Thomas M. "The Battle of Manila." In *Block By Block: The Challenge of Urban Operations*, edited by William G. Robertson and Lawrence A. Yates, 91–120. Fort Leavenworth: U.S. Army Command & General Staff College Press, 2003.

Jenkins, Edward L. "The Corregidor Operation." *Military Review* 26, no. 1 (April 1946): 59–60.

Krohn, Edgar, Jr. "The Way It Was." *Philippine Free Press*, February 21, 2008, 23.

Krohn, Edgar, Jr. "The Way It Was (Conclusion)." *Philippines Free Press*, March 1, 2008, 28–30, 34.

Leigh, Mark. "Liberation and Death in Manila." *Military Illustrated*, June 2002, 48–55.

McGraw, Ralph C. "We Were First in Manila." *The Cavalry Journal* 54, no. 4 (July–August 1945): 2–5.

Motoe, Terami-Wada. "The Filipino Volunteer Armies." In *The Philippines Under Japan: Occupation Policy and Reaction*, edited by Ikehata Setsuho and Ricardo Trota Jose, 80–82. Manila: Atendeo de Manila University Press, 1999.

"New Weapons for Jap Tank Hunters." *Intelligence Bulletin* III, no. 7 (March 1945): 64–66.

Postlethwait, E. M. "Corregidor Coordination." *Infantry Journal* (August 1945): 16.

Randall, Nelson H. "The Battle of Manila." *The Field Artillery Journal* (August 1945): 451–456.

Robb, Robert Yelton. "Nightmare in Santo Tomás." *Collier's*, February 5, 1949, 34, 64–67.

Rodao, Florentino. "Spanish Language in the Philippines: 1900–1940." *Philippine Studies* 45, no. 1 (First Quarter 1997): 94–107.

Scott, James M. "Terror & Triumph at Lingayen Gulf." *Naval History* (October 2018): 36–41.

Steward, Hal D. "Front Line Correspondents." *Army Information Digest* 2, no. 2 (February 1947): 45.

Villanueva, James. "Field Artillery and Flying Columns: Combined Arms Maneuver in the Advance on and Seizure of Manila, 1945." In *Bringing Order to Chaos: Historical Case Studies of Combined Arms Maneuver in Large Scale Combat Operations*, edited by Peter J. Schifferle, 127–144. Fort Leavenworth, KS: Army University Press, 2018.

Ward, James Mace. "Legitimate Collaboration: The Administration of Santo Tomás Internment Camp and Its Histories, 1942–1943." *Pacific Historical Review* 77, no. 2 (May 2008): 159–201.

Warner, Wayne. "The 1945 Rescues in Manila: A/G Missionaries Included in Dramatic Military Liberation." *Assemblies of God Heritage* 24, no. 4 (Winter 2004–2005): 9–10, 13.

Index